Russian Literature and Its Demons

Studies in Slavic Literature, Culture and Society

General Editor: Thomas Epstein, Visiting Scholar at
Brown University

Volume 1
Vladimir Odoevsky and Romantic Poetics: Collected Essays.
Neil Cornwell

Volume 2
Women and Russian Culture: Projections and Self-Perceptions.
Edited by Rosalind Marsh

Volume 3
Russian Postmodernism: New Perspectives on Post-Soviet Literature.
Mikhail Epstein, Alexander Genis, and Slobodanka Vladiv-Glover

Volume 4
Sight and Sound Entwined: Studies of the New Russian Poetry.
Gerald Janecek

Volume 5
Cold Fusion: Aspects of the German Cultural Presence in Russia.
Gennady Barabtarlo

Volume 6
Russian Literature and Its Demons.
Edited by Pamela Davidson

Volume 7
Voices from the Void: The Genres of Liudmila Petrushevskia.
Sally Dalton-Brown

RUSSIAN LITERATURE AND ITS DEMONS

Edited by Pamela Davidson

Berghahn Books
New York • Oxford

First published in 2000 by **Berghahn Books**

www.berghahnbooks.com

Editorial matter and selection © 2000 Pamela Davidson
The copyright of each contribution remains the property of the
individual author concerned.

Library of Congress Cataloging-in-Publication Data
Russian literature and its demons / edited by Pamela Davidson.
     p. cm. -- (Studies in Slavic literature, culture, and society ;
     v. 6)
Includes bibliographical references and index.
ISBN 1-57181-758-1 (alk. paper)
     1. Russian literature--History and criticism.   2. Demonology in
literature.   3. Devil in literature.   I. Davidson, Pamela.
II. Series.

PG2987.D45 R87 2000
891.709'37--dc21

                                                           99-045400

British Library Cataloguing in Publication Data
A catalogue for this book is available from the British Library.

Printed in the United Kingdom on acid-free paper.

ISBN 1-57181-758-1 (hardback)

CONTENTS

LIST OF ILLUSTRATIONS

Above: I.V. Simakov, "The Devils," 1904. Zinc engraving.
Illustration to A.S. Pushkin's poem "The Devils."
From A.S. Pushkin, *Polnoe sobranie sochinenii*, ed. P.N. Krasnov
(St. Petersburg: T-vo M.O. Vol'f, 1904).

Illustrations are reproduced by kind courtesy of the individuals,
museums, and publishers listed above. Every effort has been made
to contact the relevant sources for permissions.

NOTES ON CONTRIBUTORS

Michael Basker is Senior Lecturer in Russian at the University of Bristol, England. His main publications are on Nikolai Gumilev and Anna Akhmatova. He is the co-editor of Nikolai Gumilev, *Neizdannoe i nesobrannoe* (Paris: YMCA-Press, 1986), and is collaborating with the Russian Academy of Sciences (Pushkinskii Dom) as one of the editors of N. Gumilev's *Complete Works* (*Polnoe sobranie sochinenii*) in ten volumes, currently in progress (Moscow: Voskresen'e, 1998–). He is the author of *Rannii Gumilev: Stanovlenie poeta-akmeista* (St. Petersburg: Russkii Khristianskii gumanitarnyi institut, forthcoming).

Philip Cavendish is Lecturer in Russian at the School of Slavonic and East European Studies, University College London. He is the author of articles on Pushkin and of *Mining for Jewels in the Russian Language: Evgenii Zamiatin and the Literary Stylization of Rus'* (London: Modern Humanities Research Association, forthcoming).

Pamela Davidson is Senior Lecturer in Russian at the School of Slavonic and East European Studies, University College London. In 1997 she was awarded a two-year British Academy Research Readership to study the relationship between religion and culture in the Russian literary tradition. Her publications include *The Poetic Imagination of Viacheslav Ivanov: A Russian Symbolist's Perception of Dante* (Cambridge: Cambridge University Press, 1989), *Viacheslav Ivanov: A Reference Guide* (New York: G.K. Hall, 1996), and an edited anthology of poems dedicated to Akhmatova, *Posviashchaetsia Akhmatovoi* (Tenafly, N.J.: Hermitage Publishers, 1991).

Liza Dimbleby is a painter. She completed her PhD thesis on "Rozanov and the Word" at the School of Slavonic and East European Studies, University of London, in 1996, and is currently preparing further publications on Rozanov.

Simon Franklin is a Fellow of Clare College and Reader in Slavonic Studies at the University of Cambridge, England. His research interests are in Russian and Slavonic cultural history and Early Russia and Byzantium. Recent publications include *Sermons and Rhetoric of Kievan Rus* (Cambridge, Mass.: Harvard University Press, 1991) and, with Jonathan Shepard, *The Emergence of Rus, 750–1200* (London and New York: Longman, 1996).

Julian Graffy is Senior Lecturer in Russian at the School of Slavonic and East European Studies, University College London. He is the editor, with Geoffrey A. Hosking, of *Culture and the Media in the USSR Today* (London: Macmillan, 1989), and, with Ian Christie, of *Protazanov and the Continuity of Russian Cinema* (London: BFI/NFT, 1993). He has also published a number of articles on Russian literature and Russian cinema, and is currently preparing a reception history of Gogol's story "The Overcoat" (London: Bristol Classical Press, forthcoming).

W.J. Leatherbarrow is Professor of Russian at the University of Sheffield, England. His publications include *Fedor Dostoevsky* (Boston: Twayne Publishers, 1981), *A Documentary History of Russian Thought* (Ann Arbor: Ardis, 1987), *Fedor Dostoevsky: A Reference Guide* (Boston: G.K. Hall, 1990), *Dostoevsky: The Brothers Karamazov* (Cambridge: Cambridge University Press, 1992), *Dostoevskii and Britain* (Oxford: Berg, 1995), and *Dostoevsky's 'The Devils': A Critical Companion* (Evanston, Ill.: Northwestern University Press, 1999). He is currently editing *The Cambridge Companion to Dostoevsky*.

Rosalind Marsh is Professor of Russian Studies and former Director of the Centre of Women's Studies at the University of Bath, England. In 1997 she became President of the British Association for Slavonic and East European Studies. She is the author of *Soviet Fiction since Stalin: Science, Politics and Literature* (London: Croom Helm, 1986), *Images of Dictatorship: Portraits of Stalin in Literature* (London: Routledge, 1989), and *History and Literature in Contemporary Russia* (Basingstoke: Macmillan, 1995). She is the editor of *Gender and Russian Literature: New Perspectives*, of *Women in Russia and Ukraine* (both published at Cambridge: Cambridge University Press, 1996), and of *Women and Russian Culture: Projections and Self-Perceptions* (New York and Oxford: Berghahn Books, 1998).

Kevin Platt is Associate Professor of Russian at Pomona College, Claremont, U.S.A. He is the author of *History in a Grotesque Key: Russian Literature and the Idea of Revolution* (Stanford: Stanford University Press, 1997) and of a number of articles on Russian literature and interpretations of history. He is currently working on a book-length study of Russian notions of political authority as they are communicated in representations of Ivan the Terrible and Peter the Great.

Avril Pyman is Emeritus Reader in Russian Literature at the University of Durham, England, and a Fellow of the British Academy. Her publications include *The Life of Aleksandr Blok* (Oxford: Oxford University Press, 1979-80), *Aleksandr Blok. The Twelve* (Durham: University of Durham, 1989), and *A History of Russian Symbolism* (Cambridge: Cambridge University Press, 1994). As well as numerous articles on Silver Age culture, thought, and literature, she has also published several editions and translations of works of Russian literature.

Robert Reid is Reader in Russian Studies at Keele University, England. His publications include *Problems of Russian Romanticism* (Aldershot, Hants.: Gower, 1986), *Pushkin's "Mozart and Salieri": Themes, Character, Sociology* (Amsterdam: Rodopi, 1995), and *Lermontov: "A Hero of Our Time"* (London: Bristol Classical Press, 1997). He is co-editor of the journal *Essays in Poetics* and is currently completing a critical study, *Mikhail Lermontov: From Russia to the Caucasus* (New York and Oxford: Berghahn Books, forthcoming).

Adam Weiner is Assistant Professor at the Russian Department of Wellesley College, near Boston, U.S.A. He is the author of *By Authors Possessed: The Demonic Novel in Russia* (Evanston, Ill.: Northwestern University Press, 1998) and has published essays on Fedor Dostoevsky, symbolist poetry, Joseph Brodsky, and Vasilii Aksenov. He is currently researching Russian and Soviet poetry of the 1920s and 1930s.

Faith Wigzell is Reader in Russian at the School of Slavonic and East European Studies, University College London. She is the author of *Reading Russian Fortunes: Gender, Print Culture and Divination in Russia from 1765* (Cambridge: Cambridge University Press, 1998) and, under the name Faith C.M. Kitch, of *The Literary Style of Epifanij Premudryj: "Pletenije sloves"* (Munich: Otto Sagner, 1976), as well as of articles on Russian literature and folklore. She is the editor of *Russian Writers on Russian Writers* (Oxford and Providence: Berg, 1994) and, with Jane Grayson, of *Nikolay Gogol. Text and Context* (Basingstoke: Macmillan, 1989).

PREFACE

A few words on the origins of this volume may be of interest to the curious. Each year, the Department of Russian at the School of Slavonic and East European Studies of the University of London organizes a series of seminars devoted to a particular topic. For some time I had been harbouring an interest in Russian literary demonism, and my suggestion of this subject as the theme for our next series was met with enthusiastic support by my colleagues. A preliminary outline of the project was drawn up and several specialists were invited to prepare contributions, both broadly contextual and more specific. Some of these papers were first aired during the seminar series which took place in 1996–97, giving rise to much lively debate. As drafts of the written essays arrived, they were circulated among all the contributors. The aim was to produce a multi-faceted study, which on the one hand would not be limited by the imposition of any single point of view or approach, but on the other hand would be compiled and written with an awareness of the wider picture and of links with other contributions. This process of mutual collaboration was further refined during the various stages of detailed editing which the essays passed through.

Once the project was under way, it became apparent that demonism, as a field of academic enquiry, is alive and burgeoning, and has become a focus of widespread interest in recent years.[1] I hope that this collection will provide a stimulating impetus to further reflection on this intriguing strand of the Russian cultural tradition.

It remains for me to express my profound gratitude to the British Academy, which, by generously awarding me a Research Readership (1997–99) for a study of the relationship between religion and culture in the Russian literary tradition, made it possible for me to devote considerable time to this volume. I would also like to thank the School of Slavonic and East European Studies and Berghahn Books for their support of the project, and, last but by no means least, my loyal contributors for their hard work and patience with my editorial interventions.

Pamela Davidson
School of Slavonic and East European Studies
University of London   *October 1998*

Notes

1.   A few examples of recent publications are given below. Adam Weiner's study, *By Authors Possessed: The Demonic Novel in Russia* (Evanston, Ill.: Northwestern University Press, 1998), traces the development of the demonic novel through works by Gogol, Dostoevsky, Bely, and Nabokov. A.E. Makhov, comp., *Sad demonov: Slovar' infernal'noi mifologii Srednevekov'ia i Vozrozhdeniia* (Moscow: Intrada, 1998), represents the first Russian attempt to produce a broad reference work on the Christian myth of the devil and demons. It complements the very useful earlier work by T.A. Novichkova, *Russkii demonologicheskii slovar'* (St. Petersburg: Peterburgskii pisatel', 1995). An aspect of seventeenth-century demonology is explored in A.V. Pigin, *Iz istorii russkoi demonologii XVII veka: Povest' o besnovatoi zhene Solomonii. Issledovanie i teksty* (St. Petersburg: Izdatel'stvo "Dmitrii Bulanin," 1998). Mikhail Iampol'skii, *Demon i labirint (Diagrammy, deformatsii, mimesis)* (Moscow: Novoe literaturnoe obozrenie, 1996), discusses literary treatments of the body in the work of various nineteenth-century writers, including Gogol and Dostoevsky. S.L. Slobodniuk, *'D'iavoly' 'Serebrianogo' veka (Drevnii gnostitsizm i russkaia literatura 1880-1930 gg.)* (St. Petersburg: Aleteiia, 1998), carries the theme forward into the early twentieth century, covering writers such as Merezhkovsky, Briusov, Bal'mont, Sologub, Gumilev, Blok, and Zamiatin; the author's analysis of the evolution of the idea of world evil in Russian literature leads him to the conclusion that the Silver Age created an anti-Christian trend in literature, related to the ideas of the early Gnostics. Most recently, a new contribution to the field has been made by the study *Vostochnaia demonologiia: Ot narodnykh verovanii k literature* (Moscow: Nasledie, 1999).

RUSSIAN LITERATURE AND ITS DEMONS: INTRODUCTORY ESSAY

Pamela Davidson

> All Russian literature is, to a certain degree, a struggle with the
> temptation of demonism, an attempt to undress Lermontov's Demon
>
> Merezhkovsky[1]

One of the most memorable dreams in Russian literature occurs in Goncharov's novel *Oblomov* (1859). The slumbering hero recalls in detail the fantastic tales his nanny would tell him: after describing evil robbers, sleeping beauties, cities and people turned to stone, "at last she would turn to our demonology, to corpses, monsters and werewolves."[2] There is something curiously captivating about the rhythm of this sentence; in particular, the phrase "at last she would turn to our demonology" suggests that this topic was not only the long-awaited climax of the story-telling session, but was also regarded as quintessentially (and somehow comfortingly) Russian.

It would be rash, however, to draw any conclusions from Oblomov's dream about actual demonic beliefs in the Russian folk imagination: the demonic beings described form the subject of a story within a story, recollected through the prism of a dream, and have become creatures of the *literary* imagination (although, as the narrator stresses, this in no way diminishes their very considerable power).[3] This may serve to signal a warning: it is not the purpose of this volume to trace the manifold representations of Russian demonology as a system of beliefs (although this aspect will inevitably be touched upon, particularly in the two opening essays on the devil in Orthodox tradition and Russian folklore). The intention is rather to investigate some of the forms which this body of beliefs assumes when transposed into a literary context. How did the devils and demons of Orthodox and folk tradition make the transition into literature? What forms or guises did they assume to survive in their new habitat? What was their impact on literature, both in terms of thematic concerns and formal technique?

Pushkin himself, albeit somewhat tongue-in-cheek, broached this very question. In a poem of 1827 he commented that in olden times a simple folk phrase of ritual exorcism, opening with a double "amen," would suffice to despatch any unwelcome Satanic spirit or vision. By contrast:

> ... В наши дни
> Гораздо менее бесов и привидений;
> Бог велает, куда девалися они.[4]
>
> [... In our days
> There are far fewer devils and visions;
> God knows where they have got to.]

And yet, as the poem continues to imply, demons were still at large in Pushkin's day, even if less outwardly manifest. The poet describes how his heart is captivated by the eyes, voice, and features of the charming lady to whom his verses are addressed. This new form of demonic possession is evidently more powerful than the earlier, undisguised varieties, as it successfully resists the poet's attempts at exorcism by ritual phrase.

The light-hearted tone of the poem masks its more serious import. The demons of Orthodox and folk belief may seem to have disappeared, but in fact they have merely been internalized. Whereas previously they were objectified as absolute, external forces, they are now absorbed into the individual's subjective and relative perception; indeed, the very fact of their assimilation makes them more invasive and less easily dispelled. This observation remains true even when Pushkin appears to be dealing with "real" devils, as in his well-known poem "The Devils" (Besy, 1830); a close examination of this text reveals the central role of the narrator's subjective consciousness in conjuring up the vision of demonic forces.[5]

This tendency to make demons immanent, to locate them in the here and now of individual perception, is not just a result of their displacement into literature; it is also, significantly, a distinguishing feature of their representation in both Orthodox and folk tradition. In his contribution to this volume Simon Franklin comments that "neither in Byzantium nor in Russia was there much emphasis on a towering figure of Satan in splendour;" likewise, Faith Wigzell, in her essay on the Russian folk devil, underlines the pervasive, ubiquitous nature of the *nechistaia sila* (unclean force), manifested through numerous spirits which inhabit a disconcertingly wide variety of natural and man-made locations. As a result, Russian writers in search of a powerful literary image of Satan with strong theological backing were often obliged to turn to other traditions, most notably to Catholicism or Protestantism (Dante's vision of Hell and Milton's portrayal of Satan were both widely influential). For example, Pushkin's most impressive depiction of Satan as the "cursed ruler" (prokliatomu vladyke), to whom the devils of hell bring Judas for torment, turns out to be a foreign import: a free rendering of an Italian sonnet, made via a French translation, with the addition of Dantesque motifs.[6] More surprisingly, given its specifically Russian frame of reference, Solzhenitsyn's *The First Circle* (*V kruge pervom*, 1968, revised version 1978) draws on Dante's description of Satan for its portrayal of Stalin.[7] The same relative lack of a grand-scale Devil in the Russian tradition may explain the magnetic attraction exerted upon Russian writers by the impressive demonic figures of European Romanticism: Byron's Cain, Vigny's Eloa, Goethe's Mephistopheles.

Russian writers therefore found themselves on the receiving end of several distinct traditions: an ingrained native preference for the shabby, immanent, and pervasive devil over the grand Devil in his majesty; a strong Western European theological tradition (often transmitted through its reflection in literary works), stressing the power and majesty of the Devil as a single figure; seductive literary images of the Demon as a figure of Western European Romanticism. All these different strands combined in various ways to produce the hybrid phenomenon of Russian literary demonism. Indeed, a particular difficulty involved in studying this complex phenomenon derives from its eclectic nature: disentangling native sources from foreign influences is not always an easy task, particularly given the innate Russian tendency to "Russify" Western sources. When Zhukovsky informed A.I. Turgenev that he had almost finished a long work with the devil as chief protagonist, he was referring to his ballad "Gromoboi" (written in 1810, first published in 1811), whose eponymous hero sells his soul to the devil and subsequently repents.[8] The work is set in medieval Rus and saturated with local colour, but on closer inspection what appears to be a Romantic retelling of an old Russian legend in fact turns out to be a reworking of an eighteenth-century German novel based on a medieval Catholic legend. Zhukovsky has clearly substituted old Russian names for the original German ones and changed the details of the background setting in order to impart a national Russian flavour to this account of man's relations with the devil. Although Russian writers were able in this way to build a distinctively Russian tradition of literary demonism, many of the ingredients which they drew on were foreign.

The awareness that literary demonism was a highly eclectic phenomenon, to a large extent shaped by non-literary sources, and the desire to provide material for an exploration of these links, has determined the structure of this volume and its division into two parts. The first part, "Traditions and Contexts," considers some of the main formative approaches and traditions: Orthodoxy, folklore, historiography, and the view of art itself as demonic. Although these opening essays include some discussion of individual works of literature to illustrate their argument, they are primarily intended as broad introductions to the contexts in which the subsequent literary manifestations of demonism are rooted and best understood. By contrast, the ten essays which make up part II, "Literary Demons," are closely based on particular periods, authors, and texts, and seek to relate these to the background contexts previously explored. They testify to the pervasive presence of the demonic in Russian literature and to the many different forms in which this obsession manifested itself. The authors examined fall into distinct clusters, reflecting the periods when the cult of demonism was at its height in Russian literature: in poetry, this centres on Romanticism (Pushkin and Lermontov) and turn-of-the century modernism (particularly the symbolists and the acmeists); in prose, it leads to Gogol and Dostoevsky, to thinkers such as Vladimir Solov'ev and Vasilii Rozanov, and to a range of twentieth-century writers for whom the literary demonism of their predecessors acquired a tragic new resonance in the light of historical developments. Special attention has been devoted to works which have not previously been investigated from the point of view of their treatment of the demonic. A few well-known works of the Russian demonic tradition, such as Dostoevsky's *The Brothers Karamazov* (*Brat'ia Karamazovy*, 1879–80), Sologub's *The Petty Demon* (*Melkii bes*, 1907), or Bulgakov's *The Master and Margarita* (*Master i Margarita*, 1928–40), although discussed in different parts of the volume, have not been included as the subjects of individual essays, since an extensive critical literature on their approaches to the demonic already exists.[9]

The volume opens with a wide-ranging study of the impact of Orthodox tradition on literary demonism. Simon Franklin chooses to focus on hagiography as the main medieval narrative genre which also had a particular influence on subsequent literature. His examples emphasize a feature which one might have thought to be more characteristic of later literary demonism than of medieval narrative: the ambiguity of the devil, inherent in his many deceptive appearances (good masked as evil as well as the reverse). The detailed analysis of Gogol's quasi-hagiographical tale "Christmas Eve" (Noch' pered rozhdestvom, 1832) reveals some of the salient areas of overlap and difference between medieval narrative and literary text. Franklin concludes with the paradoxical observation that perhaps the most important element of the literary legacy of Orthodox demonology was the gap created by the devil's *absence*, leading writers to invent or borrow surrogate demons or to create a new aesthetic.

Notwithstanding the difficulty of disentangling Orthodox belief from folk tradition (each absorbed and adapted features of the other), the next contribution by Faith Wigzell addresses the broad topic of the Russian folk devil in his multifarious guises and highlights elements that distinguish him from his Orthodox counterpart. A major difference concerns the moral dimension of the demonic: whereas in Christianity the devil is the very embodiment of sinful temptation, in folkloric tradition the unclean force is not necessarily evil, although it is always dangerous. Attention is also drawn to the respect bordering on worship accorded to the unclean force in order to placate it. It is possible that these two aspects – the lesser role played by morality and the respectful, utilitarian approach to the demonic – may have influenced the literary cult of demonism as a springboard to a poetics of transcendence and redemption. Although Wigzell is wary of assuming links between folklore and literature, recognizing that the main source of literary demonism lies in European Romanticism, she argues that some facets of folk belief may have underlain the pull of demonism for Russian writers. The association between the sorcerer, tapping the unclean force in charms, and the poet, casting spells with words, provides one example. This link was recognized by Blok, who, in his essay "The Poetry of Charms and Incantations" (Poeziia zagovorov i zaklinanii, 1906), paid particular attention to the invocation of demonic forces in folk literature, and asserted that the charms and incantations of folk belief are the primitive source from which true poetry draws its strength and to which it should return[10] – a claim which the experiments of writers such as Sergei Gorodetsky and Aleksei Remizov would certainly substantiate.

The various approaches to the demonic which emerge from the confluent traditions of Orthodoxy and folk belief were from an early date applied by Russians to the understanding of their own historical process. Indeed, given the traditional preoccupation of Russian writers with history, this developing area of awareness served as one of the main channels through which Orthodox and folk attitudes to the demonic passed into literature. In his contribution to this volume Kevin Platt shows how the demonization of Russian rulers – at times anathematized as personifications of Satan or the Antichrist – resulted from their traditional elevation to the status of earthly god. The hermeneutic quandary presented by a ruler who deviates from the sacral notion of authority as divinely sanctioned was already tackled in late medieval writings and later generated a rich variety of conflicting historiographic and literary interpretations. Focusing on two particularly controversial tsars – Ivan the Terrible and Peter the Great – Platt singles out for attention a number of works which, in his view, through their exploitation of this interpretive dilemma, are among the most talented and suggestive; these include Pushkin's *The Bronze Horseman* (*Mednyi vsadnik*, 1833) and part two of Eizenshtein's film *Ivan the Terrible* (*Ivan Groznyi*, 1946).

Part I of the volume concludes with an analysis of the way in which the understanding of the demonic shaped by the traditions of Orthodoxy, folklore, and historiography infiltrated the perception of art itself. Pamela Davidson sets out some of the broad contexts for the view of art as demonic, dwelling on biblical attitudes (illustrated through reference to the prototype of the artist and his creation, Bezalel and the Tabernacle) and classical models (Apollo, Dionysus, and Orpheus). She then examines the particular historical circumstances which coloured the reception of these traditions in Russia and led to a marked emphasis on the demonic properties of art. The debate over correct attitudes to secular culture, although not yet a major issue in Kievan Rus, gathered momentum in the sixteenth and seventeenth centuries and was considerably intensified as a result of Peter's reforms. The new culture which subsequently developed was a curious hybrid: to a large extent divorced from the Church, it carried the burden of displaced religious aspirations and thus provided an optimum climate in which a preoccupation with the demonic could flourish.

Part II marks the transition from shaping traditions and contexts to the study of particular texts and authors. It opens with an investigation of the way in which the view of art as demonic outlined in the previous essay took root and developed in the Russian literary tradition. Focusing on the treatment of the muse and the Demon in the work of three key authors – Pushkin, Lermontov, and Blok – Pamela Davidson illustrates the progression of the view of art as demonic from nineteenth-century Romanticism into early twentieth-century modernism. She argues that Pushkin laid the foundation for this view by introducing two different types of Demon in his verse: the benign Demon, closely associated with the sacred madness of poetic inspiration and the muse, and the destructive Demon of negation and doubt. Although a clear distinction between these two figures was maintained in Pushkin's work, it subsequently became blurred. This was largely due to Lermontov, who, by endowing the Demon of negation with a powerful new dimension of verbal artistry and enchantment, released his creative potential and paved the way for the association between the Demons of inspiration and corruption – an association later more fully developed by Blok, in whose verse the muse and the Demon merge into a single force for spiritual perdition.

The next essay returns to Lermontov's *The Demon*, this time from a philosophical perspective. After addressing the problem of the hero's identity, Robert Reid analyses the treatment of aesthetics and ethics in *The Demon*. He finds that both areas are problematized by the demonic nature of the protagonist, and that as a result a range of Romantic ideological issues is estranged. Awareness of the complexity of this problem intensifies in the course of the nineteenth century; indeed, as is argued, Lermontov's fundamental contribution to the development of the demonic tradition in Russian literature was largely a consequence of the very "fuzziness" of his demonic creature. Reid also points out that an essential stage in the process of secularizing demonism was marked by the later equation between Lermontov's two heroes – the supernatural Demon and the human Pechorin.

Although Gogol's Petersburg tales were published together for the first time in the same year as fragments of Lermontov's *The Demon* originally appeared (1842), their approach to the demonic could hardly be more different. Lermontov's demonism is on a grand scale, related to his Romantic maximalism; Gogol's approach, by contrast, although it clearly also derives from frustrated aspirations to transcendence, marks a return to the shabbier, immanent demons of the native Orthodox and folk traditions. Julian Graffy singles out a particular aspect of Gogol's treatment of the demonic in the Petersburg tales, showing how it is imbricated in the very nature of the city. Through a wide range of detailed examples he reveals how the demonic forces latent in Petersburg distort spatial and temporal coordinates, attack its inhabitants, undermine traditional expressions of heavenly perfection such as art and women, and lead to a total dismantling and final fragmentation of logical sense. His argument that Gogol's achievement was "to blend the folkloric consciousness of the devil that informed his earlier writings with a modern sensibility that finds the demonic expressed through elements of the illogical and of existential alienation" points to the importance of Gogol's role as an innovator. The Petersburg tales initiated an important new strand in Russian literary demonism, which later became particularly prominent in the work of the modernists: a concern with the pervasive, invisible demon of the modern urban environment was combined with the development of new literary techniques for conveying the dislocation of coherent meaning.

Both Gogol and Lermontov exerted a considerable influence on one of the central works of the Russian demonic tradition, published some thirty years later: Dostoevsky's *The Devils (Besy,* 1872). In his essay on this novel, W.J. Leatherbarrow links these sources to two distinct strands inherent in the novel's treatment of the demonic: the comic, grotesque strand, which he relates to Bakhtin's category of the carnivalesque, and its apocalyptic, redemptive dimension. The novel's first epigraph, taken from Pushkin's "The Devils" (1830), anticipates the carnival strand, associated with the revolutionary activities of Petr Verkhovensky and his circle, whose Gogolian antics degenerate into a grotesque farce, unable to sustain the serious import of the novel. As Leatherbarrow demonstrates, in his depiction of this devils' vaudeville Dostoevsky draws on the carnival traditions of folklore, the Russian puppet theatre, and the cultural-historical phenomenon of role-play and imposture. The second epigraph, Saint Luke's parable of the Gadarene swine, anticipates the apocalyptic theme of regeneration, which is superimposed on the carnival strand of the novel; through a blend of Christian tradition with Romantic motifs and echoes of Lermontov's Demon, the tragic figure of Stavrogin is lent a redemptive dimension.

Leatherbarrow's analysis of *The Devils* draws together several strands of the Russian demonic tradition explored in this volume: it relates the novel's treatment of the demonic to native Orthodox and folk traditions and to literary sources such as Lermontov and Gogol, and it explores the way in which existing historical and literary approaches to the nature of demonic power are used to construct a new vision of Russia's spiritual mission. Although Lermontov and Gogol had already introduced the metaphysical and historical aspects of the demonic character as a social type into Russian literature, Dostoevsky took this process one stage further by integrating the sociopolitical dimension of demonism into a broader Christian vision of its redemptive role within the scheme of Russia's religious destiny.

The seriousness of Dostoevsky's preoccupation with demonism as a social and spiritual reality perhaps precluded too great an engagement with the possibility that the medium of his message – the art of writing – might itself be demonically tainted. The most extreme example in Russian literature of a writer whose literary output was almost entirely motivated and became increasingly dominated by this awareness was Vasilii Rozanov, a mysterious and controversial figure, whose paradoxical ideas on the sacred potential and yet demonic danger of the word form the subject of Liza Dimbleby's contribution. Rozanov never tired of inveighing against the printed word and literary forms of expression, despite the fact that this was the only medium of expression available to him. His concern about the demonic temptations surrounding print and publication prompted the development of his "manuscript" genre, where intimate thoughts, private family documents and conversations are set in print for publication alongside reflections on the pernicious influence of journals and the printing press. The same attitudes determined his approach to other writers. While championing Lermontov as a true prophet of a sacred verbal tradition, rooted in an understanding of the physical nature of the word, he demonized Vladimir Solov'ev and Merezhkovsky for their loss of a sense of sacred reality in everyday life, evident in their empty, "bloodless" words. In his late writing he directed his attack at Gogol, who is portrayed as the supreme Devil of Russian literature, the originator of the nihilist and satirical tendencies that would destroy Russian life. Rozanov's examination of other writers was clearly a way to further his own self-questioning, since he felt the conflicts, the demonic temptations with which verbal activity was fraught, most acutely in himself and yet was unable to resolve them. His awareness of the demonic properties of art became a central driving-force in his work, stimulating his own experiments in the area of stylistic innovation and leading him to categorize other writers as devils or prophets, while himself aspiring to the role of prophet.

Avril Pyman's essay on the mythopoetic world model in the art of Lermontov, Vrubel, and Blok introduces two new perspectives of particular value to this collection. Firstly, it considers the evolution of the image of the Demon from Lermontov's Romantic individualism to the *mifotvorchestvo* (mythopoeia) of Vrubel and Blok within the context of the mythopoetic world model, as elaborated by Toporov; this approach reinstates the image of the Demon as an archetypal, primitive force and avoids the pitfalls of either completely identifying him with Christian tradition or totally disassociating him from it. Secondly, it demonstrates that the tradition of literary demonism did not develop in isolation from the other arts. As well as dwelling on the role of Rubinshtein's opera of 1875, Pyman shows how Vrubel's visual images of the Demon served as a stepping-stone between Lermontov and Blok by acting as a catalyst to the symbolist revival of faith in the mythic dimension of Lermontov's Demon.

The translation of text into myth noted by Pyman served to bridge the gap between Romanticism and modernism. A further aspect of this transition is reflected in the trend away from religion towards myth, a shift of emphasis which allowed demonism to shed its ethical dimension and facilitated its transformation from a moral category into a purely metaphysical or aesthetic one; from being viewed as an impediment to spiritual growth it became a means to self-transcendence, defined in relation to the artist's own goals rather than in terms of any absolute values. This attitude is well illustrated by Blok's statement, written at the beginning of the century: "there is no difference – whether one struggles with the devil or with God, they are equal and alike."[11] While Blok's words may relate to either the metaphysical or the aesthetic aspects of the artist's search for self-transcendence, the following lines from Bal'mont give clear prominence to the aesthetic dimension:

> Я люблю тебя, дьявол, я люблю тебя, Бог,
> Одному – мои стоны, и другому – мой вздох,
> Одному – мои крики, а другому – мечты,
> Но вы оба велики, вы восторг Красоты.[12]

> [I love you, devil, I love you, God,
> To one – my groans, and to the other – my sigh,
> To one – my cries, and to the other – dreams,
> But you are both great, you are Beauty's delight.]

The shift of focus from moral absolute to a personal aesthetic led to the unprecedented peak in the cult of demonism which manifested itself at the turn of the century in the work of the symbolists. This area has already been explored in this volume in relation to poetry in the essays of Pamela Davidson and Avril Pyman; its further ramifications in the area of symbolist prose form the subject of the next contribution by Adam Weiner. Through a detailed analysis of three representative works – Merezhkovsky's trilogy *Christ and Antichrist (Khristos i Antikhrist,* 1895–1904), Briusov's *The Fiery Angel (Ognennyi angel,* 1908), and Sologub's *The Created Legend (Tvorimaia legenda,* 1914) – Weiner demonstrates that symbolist fiction in its chronological development reveals not only a progressive demonization of the authorial personae (protagonists, narrator, and implied author), but also an increasingly disorientating use of narrative point of view. This points towards the infiltration of the theme of demonic possession into the very form, manner, and style of its literary expression – an area which prose (following the example of Gogol) could develop more successfully than lyric verse, given its greater freedom in the use of multiple, shifting points of view. It would be interesting to speculate on which came first: was the loss of ethical absolutes a cause or an indirect consequence of the fragmented viewpoint of the modernist aesthetic which gradually took hold in Russia? Whatever the case, these twin aspects of the legacy of symbolist demonism (the obsession with the theme and its impact on literary technique) had a strong influence on the work of later writers in ways which will be discussed below.

Before taking leave of symbolism, however, we should perhaps note one further point. A considerable amount of space in this volume has been devoted to the symbolist cult of the demonic, not just because it was such a prominent feature of Silver Age culture, but also because of its "organizing" role in establishing a self-conscious tradition of literary demonism in Russia. The symbolists stood at a crossroads between their twentieth-century successors and an earlier chain of nineteenth-century writers (principally Lermontov, Gogol, and Dostoevsky), who, while dealing with demonic themes, did not regard themselves as the bearers of any clearly defined "demonic" tradition. Taking their lead from Vladimir Solov'ev's late essay of 1899 on Lermontov,[13] the symbolists were the first to construct a "genealogy" of demonic writers, thus establishing the existence of such a tradition, defining their own place within it, and to a large extent determining the perspective of future generations. By advancing a new reading of the past, they created a platform for themselves and a foundation for subsequent developments.

Two different aspects of the symbolists' catalytic role are illustrated by the next pair of contributions. The first aspect relates to the symbolist transformation of the demonic from a moral category into a metaphysical or aesthetic one. This could prompt two different types of reaction: it could either win adherents by casting its spell over like-minded disciples, or it could provoke a "corrective" response, a desire to overcome or exorcize the legacy of symbolist demonism by reinstating its moral dimension. Both responses and their intriguing interaction are evident in Michael Basker's exploration of the demonic in the work of two leading acmeists: Nikolai Gumilev, a true child of symbolism and the most persistent acmeist demonist, and Anna Akhmatova, who sought to overcome aspects of the symbolist legacy of demonism in her own poetry and through her reading of Gumilev. Although the anti-demonic went hand in hand with the anti-symbolist in Gumilev's formulation of an acmeist aesthetic, his exorcism of former demons was never complete. This unresolved aspect of his literary output had a profound influence on Akhmatova and underlies an important strand of her most demonic creation, *Poem Without a Hero* (*Poema bez geroia*, 1940–62). This work is demonic both in its chosen theme (the representation of turn-of-the-century Petersburg) and in its self-avowed literary genesis and formal strategies. Basker argues that Gumilev, commonly identified as the "absent hero" of the *Poem*, and thus, implicitly, as an antipode to the demonic, is in fact demonically associated or "doubled" with each of the poem's major negative prototypes. Akhmatova's particular reading of Gumilev's "creative path" and of certain key texts by him suggests that this apparent paradox finds its resolution in terms of a conscious, morally exacting self-transformation. Her "absent hero" is specifically one who attempts, at immense personal cost, to "overcome demonism." Just as for Gumilev, however, Akhmatova's exorcism of demons in practice remains incomplete. Not only certain demonic imagery of the early Gumilev, but also the sense that she was, biographically, the chief demon behind his texts, returns to haunt some of her late poetry.

Another aspect of the legacy of symbolist demonism noted above was the impact that it had on techniques of literary narration. Later writers may no longer have been obsessed with the moral, metaphysical, or even aesthetic dimensions of demonism, but many of them retained a strong interest in the formal innovations which this preoccupation had engendered: the literary techniques developed for portraying an unstable world of shifting appearances, and the very notion of writing as inherently ambiguous or indecipherable, infected by the demonic reality which it seeks to express. Philip Cavendish's discussion of Zamiatin's miracle tales (chudesa) stresses the playful rather than serious intent in their blasphemous subversion of the conventions of hagiography. His detailed analysis of "The Miracle of Ash Wednesday" (O chude, proisshedshem v Pepel'nuiu Sredu, 1926) uncovers a further significant development in the author's demonic strategy: the tale presents a disturbing enigma and riddle, tainted by the devil of absurdity and nonsense, which effectively resists all attempts at a coherent or logical interpretation. As Cavendish argues, this may well have been a reaction to the increasing seriousness of Soviet literature in the 1920s.

Gratuitous playfulness in literary demonism was, however, largely eroded by the advent of Stalinism, which introduced a tragic new dimension into the understanding of the demonic. For most writers of this era the preoccupation with demonism, which had earlier been purely literary or abstractly metaphysical, was now firmly grounded in historical reality. Rosalind Marsh's discussion of literary representations of Stalin and Stalinism takes up some of the issues raised by Kevin Platt in his analysis of Russian attitudes to sacral authority. Not surprisingly, the same process identified by Platt – the translation of idolization into demonization – occurs in literary responses to the quasi-religious cult of Stalin. Although these exhibit a considerable variety of style and genre, ranging from realism through fantasy and allegory to carnivalesque comedy, they do not, as a general rule, reflect the same degree of inherent ambiguity as some of the representations of Ivan the Terrible or Peter the Great discussed by Platt. Unlike his predecessors, whenever he is not being eulogized as the object of cultic veneration, Stalin is generally portrayed as wholly evil and demonic. A certain degree of ambiguity is, however, retained in the value attributed to the historical process of which he formed a part. As Marsh points out, the extreme demonization of Stalin, together with the redemptive, purgatorial value sometimes assigned to the evil and suffering which he inflicted on Russian society, could in certain instances, by appearing to absolve the Russian people of their guilt and complicity, lead to yet another myth of Russia's positive historical development.

Although this volume does not aim to be comprehensive or exhaustive, the range of its contents, outlined above, should nevertheless give some indication of the wide variety of ways in which the Russian interest in the demonic has manifested itself in literary tradition. At first glance this variety may appear bewilderingly heterogeneous, but on closer inspection it can be seen to harbour a number of key themes, which recur throughout the collection and suggest the possibility of drawing some preliminary conclusions. The first most striking point is the fact that the preoccupation with the demonic in Russian literature invariably has its roots in the aspiration to transcendence, and is at its most prominent when this aspiration is most fully developed. This can be seen in the religious sphere in hagiographical texts (the greater the saint, the stronger the demons which beset him), in the historical sphere (the sacralization of rulers leads to their demonization), and in the literary sphere (art is regarded as demonic precisely because it is burdened with the functions of sacred prophecy). In other words, as demonstrated in diverse ways in the essays of part I, demonic concerns tend to proliferate when the impulse towards sacralization is frustrated. The same root cause informs the appearance of demonic themes in the literary works discussed in part II. For example, as Julian Graffy shows, it is because Gogol first dreams of Petersburg as a "paradisaical place" that he later comes to invest it with demonic attributes.

One should add that two interrelated types of demonism can result from this cycle, one dynamic, the other static and inert. The first continues the dynamic of frustrated aspirations to transcendence and represents a sort of Luciferian fall from grace, which can, however, be regarded as a possible springboard to redemption. The second type embodies the stagnation which follows the exhaustion engendered by the failure of the original impulse towards the sacred. The close link between both types is well captured by the critic Dmitrii Pisarev in his characterization of the painful struggle taking place in the hero of Turgenev's novel *Fathers and Children* (*Ottsy i deti*, 1862): Bazarov is described as torn between "hatred and love, a merciless, steely and cold, spasmodically smiling, demonic scepticism, and a hot, melancholy, sometimes happy and rejoicing romantic striving into the distance."[14]

Both these extremes can be traced back to Lermontov's Demon, whose combination of frustrated idealism and cosmic, existential boredom made him a rich source model for later demonic heroes. Lermontov's subsequent satiric dismissal of his early Demon as a "mad, passionate, childish delirium" (bezumnyi, strastnyi, detskii bred) and attempted introduction of a new breed of demonic hero ("But this devil is of a quite other kind" [No etot chort sovsem inogo sorta]) in his unfinished *Fairy-tale for Children* (*Skazka dlia detei*, 1840) suggests the beginning of a shift of emphasis away from the Romantic strand of demonism towards its more negative, stagnant extreme,[15] such as that described in Gogol's Petersburg tales. For a later, unadulterated expression of this inert variety of demonism, entirely stripped of its potentially redemptive dimension, one would need to turn to Sologub's novel *The Petty Demon*, or, in poetry, to some of Blok's later cycles, such as "The Dances of Death" (Pliaski smerti, 1912–14) or "The Life of a Friend of Mine" (Zhizn' moego priiatelia, 1913–15), with their frozen images of shadowy dream and living death.[16]

It is important, however, to emphasize that this state of stagnation, although it may appear to be a complete dead end, can in fact turn out to be productive. This paradoxical ambivalence originates in the religious sphere. Many Christian mystics, including the fourth-century monk Evagrius, whose writings entered the Russian tradition through translations of the *Philokalia* (published in a Slavonic translation in 1793, and in Russian from 1877), interpreted the Psalmist's "destruction, that doth waste at noon-day openly" (Ps. 91.6) as the "demon of noontide" who instils the dangerous state of *acedia* or spiritual aridity. Evagrius gives special prominence to this sin, commenting that the "demon of despondency," while generally "more grievous than all others," can nevertheless, if conquered, lead to a "peaceful state" of "ineffable joy." *Acedia* is therefore in a sense almost a precondition to achieving celestial bliss.[17] The embracing of nothingness was subsequently cultivated by a number of spiritual seekers as a *via negativa* to prepare the soul for mystic receptivity. In similar fashion, the state of ennui, a modern secularized form of *acedia*, although usually linked with artistic sterility, was regarded by many as conducive to creativity.[18] It has been demonstrated, for example, that Albrecht Dürer's engraving *Melencolia I* (1514) is a representation of Artist's Melancholy, "frustrated because she cannot attain her goal," and, although herself sterile, "the source of another's artistic endeavour." The potential fertility of sterility is also reflected in Goethe's well-known description of boredom as the "mother of the Muses."[19] Among leading modern exponents of the aesthetics of ennui, one thinks in the first instance of Baudelaire, the poet of spleen *par excellence*, or, in the Russian tradition, of Blok, who significantly identified his own states of apathetic depression and emotional aridity with the very "demon of dejection" (demon pechali) described by Evagrius in the *Philokalia*, and yet insisted that this particular demon was "essential to the artist."[20] This association finds an echo in the close link between depression and creativity experienced by artists suffering from manic depression.[21]

It would seem therefore that, whichever type of literary demonism is encountered (whether dynamic or stagnant), one is dealing with an extremely fluid and constantly self-renewing cycle, in which the apparent antipodes of the demonic and the sacred keep translating themselves into their opposites. One of the most European of Russians, Viacheslav Ivanov, identified this very tendency to merge antithetic categories as an endemic trait of the Russian national character. In an early fragment entitled "The Jews and the Russians" (Evrei i russkie, 1888) he wrote of the "inability to distinguish between the clean and the unclean," which makes the fate of certain non-Jewish nations "a series of wanderings along muddled paths, a series of passions and falls." In his view this characteristic is manifest in its purest form among the Slav peoples, who exhibit a particularly strong syncretic sense of the unity inherent in diversity. As a result, "a Russian sees the link between good and evil more clearly than anyone else and is therefore usually sinful when righteous and righteous when sinful."[22] Many years later, in conversation with one of his students in post-Revolutionary Baku, Ivanov made a comment which casts some light on why this might be the case: "the Russian people ... is either God-bearing (Bogonosets) (Christopher) or Satan-bearing (satanonosets), but it is not self-bearing (sebianosets), as are the German, the Frenchman, the Greek, the Englishman."[23] It may well be that the flexible attitude to opposite extremes, which Ivanov had earlier identified as a specifically Russian trait, is related to the tendency to define national identity in terms of abstract absolutes, which, once juxtaposed, can more easily be interchanged. This idea, expressed intuitively by Ivanov in his usual aphoristic style, finds further support in the more recent academic work of Lotman and Uspensky on the defining role of binary models in the dynamics of Russian culture.[24]

We have seen that the demonic and the sacred consistently function together as a pair of interconnected and sometimes interchangeable opposites, inextricably linked in a close symbiotic relationship. We should now consider the question of the variable "value" which is attached to the demonic element of this duo: when is it regarded as a purely aesthetic category, and when is it invested with moral significance?

Demonism as an aesthetic category is closely related to the problem of artistic representation. In an ideal world, the individual's creative energies are in harmony with the will of God, fulfilment of the artist's divinely inspired intuition is possible, and artistic representation or analogy are part of a meaningful chain of being. When this link is broken, however, representation becomes demonic, leading to what Mallarmé described as the "démon de l'analogie,"[25] and to the substitution of demonic doubles for the original intuited ideal. The aesthetic dimension of demonism – as an aspect of the problem of artistic *voploshchenie* (embodiment) – can already be found in Gogol, or, even more prominently, in Dostoevsky's *The Double* (*Dvoinik*, 1846); it was extensively developed by Bely and Blok, whose poetry, prose and criticism abound in images of doubles, who function as the artist's demons and provide a false mirror reflection of his deeper intuitions.

Although this aesthetic dimension of demonism does not necessarily carry a moral value, it is often invested with one by the artist or his audience. A particularly vivid example of this phenomenon can be found in a telling episode from the life of one of Russia's most talented and demonically obsessed artists, the painter Mikhail Vrubel. One of his last, unfinished works was a portrait of Valerii Briusov, commissioned by the editor of *Zolotoe runo*. In 1905 Briusov made a series of trips to the psychiatric clinic in Moscow at which Vrubel was then confined, in order to sit for the portrait. After the painter's death in 1910, he wrote a short memoir, full of remarkable observations about his visits. He notes that on one occasion Vrubel was found entirely naked, circling his room in a squatting position; he explained to his doctor that he was obliged to perform this act a hundred times as a penance for the expiation of his sins. Vrubel was apparently also subject to hallucinations and heard voices; as he confessed to Briusov, he was tormented by the feeling that he had lived a sinful life and found that improper scenes were appearing of their own accord on his paintings to punish him for his sins. He was particularly worried about his recent painting *The Pearl* (*Zhemchuzhina*, 1904), in which an additional second figure had unexpectedly appeared. Briusov recorded Vrubel's hushed confession to him as follows: " 'It's him' (Vrubel meant the Devil), 'he is doing this to my paintings. He has been given this power because I, without being worthy, painted the Mother of God and Christ. He has distorted all my paintings...'."[26] Thus, the creation of artistic images came to be regarded by the artist as more than a problem of aesthetic representation: it was a form of demonic possession, the direct work of the Devil, sent to punish the artist for his unqualified and misguided attempts to represent the sacred.

This view was not just the product of Vrubel's own state of demented paranoia, it was shared by a number of his contemporaries. Shaliapin, for example, who took Vrubel's Demon as his inspiration when he sang the title role of Rubinshtein's opera *The Demon* in 1904, believed that Vrubel's demons were directly suggested to him by the archangels which he had earlier painted in churches – thus reinforcing the view that the pursuit of the sacred gives rise to the demonic.[27] Emilii Metner took the same point even further, warning Bely that he and Blok were both afflicted by the "demon of art," a form of divine punishment for their act of hubris in attempting to depict religious subjects.[28]

In general, therefore, it would appear that although the aesthetic dimension of demonism as a problem of artistic representation established a fairly firm footing for itself in the Russian tradition, leading to several interesting experiments in modernist literary techniques, it was all too often eclipsed by the predominant tendency to invest it with a moral value, particularly at times of personal or historical crisis. We should note, however, that the idea of demonic possession as a form of moral punishment was a fairly elastic one, open to a number of different interpretations. Sometimes it was viewed as an end in itself, as a purely negative, punitive experience, but more commonly it was seen as a stage of penitential, redemptive suffering. Although the demonic undoubtedly represents a hell of sorts, hell in the Russian tradition is a more fluid concept than in Catholic teaching. Because the Russian Orthodox church lacked the developed doctrine of Purgatory which exists in Catholic theology, hell often had to serve a dual function: while remaining a place of damnation and suffering, it could also acquire a certain purgatorial value and become a stage of transit rather than a complete dead end. Russian writers sometimes even adapted the Catholic tradition to reflect this perspective; as a licence for their approach, they would cite Dante's representation of his fictive poetic persona as a traveller, who descends into hell and emerges to climb Mount Purgatory and to ascend through the heavenly spheres of Paradise, while ignoring the fact that for the "real" sinners in Dante's inferno there is no hope of escape or possible redemption, only eternal torment.

The notion of demonic possession as a form of *redemptive* punishment becomes particularly prominent when viewed from a collective standpoint and linked up with the national idea – no doubt because the need to sustain faith in a better future even in the midst of the darkest experiences is magnified when projected onto the grand historical scale. This tendency towards a purgatorial interpretation of demonic suffering is noted in relation to the ages of Ivan the Terrible and Peter the Great by Kevin Platt, and also discussed by Rosalind Marsh in connection with literary treatments of Stalin and Stalinism. In between the periods covered by these two contributions, the same trend can be observed in the literary responses to one of the greatest

"demonic" upheavals of Russian history – the Revolution of 1917.
Among the many poems published in the immediate aftermath of the
Revolution, demonic motifs with a redemptive dimension proliferate,
no doubt as a legacy of the symbolist obsession with demonism, now
elevated onto a new plane of historical significance. Viacheslav
Ivanov's cycle "Songs of Troubled Times" (*Pesni smutnogo vremeni*,
first published in December 1917 and February 1918) was closely
echoed by Voloshin in several poems on Russian history, both past
and current, such as "Deaf and Dumb Demons" (*Demony glukhonemye*, 29 December 1917), "Petrograd" (*Petrograd*, 9 December 1917),
"Deaf and Dumb Rus" (*Rus' glukhonemaia*, 6 January 1918), and the
later "Severovostok" (Northeast, 1920).[29] Blok's enigmatic *The Twelve*
(*Dvenadtsat'*, first published in March 1918) was followed by Bely's
more explicit rejoinder, *Christ is Risen* (*Khristos voskres*, first published
in May 1918). Despite their considerable differences, these works are
united by the fact that they interpret historical events as a form of elemental, demonic possession, and place this in a wider, Christian,
redemptive context. In this, they are all following Dostoevsky's lead
in *The Devils* and perpetuating the myth of Russia's positive historical
development.[30] The common tendency to demonize the present in
order to provide a springboard for its translation into a projected,
holy future, confirms our earlier remarks about the interdependence
and even interchangeability of the two extremes of the sacred and the
demonic in Russian culture.

1. B. Kustodiev, *The Bolshevik*, 1920. Oil on canvas, 101 × 141 cm.

At the beginning of this introduction we posed a key question: how would the devils and demons of Orthodox and folk tradition make the transition into literature? In what forms or guises would they survive? One is tempted now to give the following answer: they survived, but were forced out of the relative "open" of religious and folk awareness into a literary underground. From the cells of monks and the marshes, woodlands and ravines of the peasant world, they migrated into literature and set about the business of adapting to this new habitat. Their main sphere of action became the literary world, their target – writers and readers, and their principal weapon – the creative process and the literary text. Although this shift of environment brought about various inevitable changes, many essential features were retained: literary demons remained ubiquitous and dangerous agents of temptation or manifestations of the unclean force, ambivalent in their many different guises, and highly elusive. The ease with which Blok was able to identify the literary demons which beset him as a writer with the spiritual demons described by the fourth-century monk Evagrius reflects his profound awareness of this thread of continuity, of the survival of "real" demons in the literary process.

That demonism is in a sense a literary phenomenon, constructed and conveyed through words, is nothing new. There are two principal reasons for this close association. Most obviously, one can point to the demonic power of literature as a corrupting force. Once detached from its traditional moorings in religious or moral values, literature can easily lead astray, distorting the reader's vision and inciting to sin. This aspect of the potentially demonic nature of literature is not a modern invention; it was already recognized in the Middle Ages, at a time when secular literature was just beginning to establish itself through popular courtly romances. A vivid illustration of the danger presented by the new literature is given by Dante in one of the most memorable episodes of the *Inferno*, concerning the fate of the carnal sinners Paolo and Francesca.[31] When Dante asks Francesca, "by what and how" she and her lover came to know their "dubious desires," she explains that the "first root" of their love was their joint reading of a romance (*Lancelot du Lac*), which, through its description of an adulterous kiss, brought them to sin. Thus a book, the very act of reading, reveals their love to them and causes them to sin. Francesca acknowledges this directly by describing the book and its author as a "Gallehault" or go-between. The power of the written or spoken word is demonstrated in three ways by Dante: firstly, in the explicit content of Francesca's account; secondly, in the impact that her tale has on Dante (he weeps from pity and, at the end of the canto, faints "as if in death");[32] thirdly, in the powerful effect it is designed to have on the reader. In each case it is *verbal* art, the way in which the story is told, which captivates, seduces, and distorts purity of judgement.

This particular aspect – apparent innocence and its fated corruption – has been well captured by the French artist Jean-Auguste-Dominique Ingres in his portrayal of the scene.[33] Francesca, attired in a long flowing pink robe, eyes modestly downcast, looks the very picture of demure and maidenly innocence; in her right hand she holds the book, still open at the fatal page. Paolo, seductively clad in matching pink tights and cap, his blue cape stretched out behind him, half kneels at her left side, while implanting the forbidden kiss on her cheek. Behind him, on the very edge of the picture, a sinister cloaked figure, only half revealed, crouches as he prepares to unsheathe his sword. Although this man clearly represents Francesca's husband, Giovanni Malatesta (the crippled brother of her lover, Paolo, who surprised the couple and killed them both), in the painting he comes to epitomize the demonic presence, the evil latent in the scene and so much at odds with its seeming charm and domestic intimacy.

In Russia the tale of Paolo and Francesca became one of the most popular episodes of the *Divine Comedy* (it was first translated in 1827 by A.S. Norov, whose versions of Dante were known to Pushkin).[34] Although it was frequently alluded to by critics and writers, attention was usually focused on the sin of forbidden erotic love, rather than on the role played by a literary text in determining the lovers' tragic fate. It was not until the early twentieth century that its relevance to the view of literature as demonic was highlighted in Blok's poem, "She came in from the frost..." (Ona prishla s moroza..., 6 February 1908).[35] The poet describes an encounter between a man (the narrator) and a woman, in which literary texts play a highly significant role. When the female visitor arrives in the man's room, she immediately drops a weighty volume of a literary journal on the floor. At her request, he begins to read *Macbeth* out loud to her. As he reaches the phrase "bubbles of the earth" (puzyrei zemli), they are both overtaken with excitement (volnenie). The sight of a large cat outside the window, watching over a pair of kissing doves, causes the narrator to regret that the doves, rather than he and his visitor, are kissing, and that "the times of Paolo and Francesca had passed" (proshli vremena Paolo i Francheski).

Since the narrator's description of his response to reading a particular passage from *Macbeth* is directly modelled on Francesca's account of her reaction to the scene of the fatal kiss in the romance,[36] one can assume that the allusion to the era of Paolo and Francesca having passed refers not so much to the intrinsic situation (revolving

in both cases around an act of reading which provokes erotic excitement), as to the possibility (or impossibility) of these erotic feelings
being realized. In Blok's poem the transition from reading to erotic
fulfilment does not take place; instead, with a distinct sense of anti-
climax, it is transferred from the living protagonists to the symbolic
image of the kissing doves outside the window (in Dante's account
Paolo and Francesca are compared to doves).[37] The change of the
couple's reading matter from medieval romance to Shakespearean
tragedy is significant in this context. *Macbeth* was one of Blok's
favourite works; the phrase "bubbles of the earth" (from *Macbeth*, 1.3)
was used by him as the title and in the epigraph of his cycle of
poems, "Bubbles of the Earth" (Puzyri zemli, 1904–1905),[38] where it
merges with the murky marshland world of the Russian folk devil.[39]
In Blok's poem, Dante's flesh and blood lovers, observed by the
murderous Malatesta, have been replaced by the symbolic image of
the kissing doves, watched over by a malevolent cat (an animal with
strong demonic connotations in Russian folklore). This substitution
suggests that, although the medieval tale of Paolo and Francesca is
still a reference point for the power of literature as demonic, it has
been overlaid by the later influence of Shakespeare's *Macbeth*, which,
through its association in Blok's verse with the Russian folk consciousness of the demonic, precludes the possibility of any resolution, whether erotic (through the kiss) or tragic (through death).
Times have changed, and so has the nature of the demonic power of
literature. In the age of Paolo and Francesca, literature corrupted
seeming innocence, but did not take away from life; in Blok's age, literature is demonic not only because it corrupts innocence, but, more
importantly, because it leads away from, or even excludes, real life.
The protagonists of Blok's poem are immured in a closed and bookish world, tainted by the folk demonic, where literary images
become a substitute for action, and real life only takes place in an
imagined outside world, on the other side of the window.

Blok's poem gives a modernist twist to a traditional theme, which
had already assumed a central importance in Pushkin's *Evgenii Onegin* (1823–31, published in full in 1833).[40] Throughout chapter three
the narrator makes it abundantly clear that Tat'iana's innate purity of
vision is tainted by her literary diet. When he rhymes the line "Chi-
taet sladostnyi roman" (Reads a sweet novel, 3:9.2) with "P'et
obol'stitel'nyi obman" (Drinks the seductive deception, 3:9.4), he
succinctly conveys the way in which deception, masked as sweetness, poisons the soul. Byron's "hopeless egotism" (beznadezhnyi
egoizm, 3:12.14), dressed up as "gloomy romanticism" (unylyi
romantizm, 3:12.13), has become a corrupting "idol" (kumir, 3:12.7).
Through Tat'iana, Pushkin also emphasizes the corrupting effect of

literature on the writer as well as on the reader, as is neatly demonstrated in the transition from Tat'iana the reader, wandering in the
woods "with a dangerous book" (s opasnoi knigoi, 3:10.5), to Tat'iana
the writer, reciting in a whisper her first composition – the letter
addressed to her hero (3:10.11–12). By implication, therefore, the
demonic power of literature affects the writer and the creative
process itself as much as the reader. It is in this context that Pushkin
the narrator makes an ironic reference to being possessed by the
"new devil" (novyi bes, 3:13.4) of prose.

In addition to the corrupting power of literature, there is a second,
even more fundamental reason for the close association between
demonism and literature. Perceptions of demons (testifying to their
very existence) have always depended on their description, whether
iconographic or verbal; the act of writing is a key instrument in articulating the awareness of demonic powers. In his well-known study,
Europe's Inner Demons, Norman Cohn has shown that the demonization of heretical Christian sects by Christians in the Middle Ages had
its sources in the pagan Graeco-Roman demonization of early Christians, regularly accused of such crimes as erotic orgies or the ritual
slaughter of babies. He surmises that these pagan accusations were
copied into early Christian manuscripts and from there picked up
and used by Christians against heretical Christian sects. The lack of
evidence of any *real* worship of Lucifer or Satan leads him to conclude that the persistence of the myth of demonic sects was a mere
"fantasy preserved in a literary tradition."[41] This awareness of the
fundamentally literary nature of demonism permeates the portrayal
of the hero of *Evgenii Onegin.* Tat'iana's "fateful tempter" (iskusitel'
rokovoi, 3:15.14) has the reputation of a "Satanic monster" (satanich-
eskim urodom, 8:12.6) or "Demon" (Demonom, 8:12.7). After studying his collection of books, however, Tat'iana comes to the
realization that "this angel, this arrogant devil" (sei angel, sei nad-
mennyi bes, 7:24.8) has crafted his identity out of fictional prototypes and is in many ways a purely literary phenomenon: a
"Muscovite in Harold's cloak" (Moskvich v Garol'dovom plashche,
7:24.11), an empty "imitation" (podrazhan'e, 7:24.9), an "interpretation" (istolkovan'e, 7:24.12), a "parody" (parodiia, 7:24.14), or even
a "complete lexicon of modish words" (slov modnykh polnyi lek-
sikon, 7:24.13). As all these phrases emphasize, Evgenii's demonic
identity is exposed as nothing more than a verbal construct.

These issues may be raised in a playful tone, but they are serious
ones nevertheless. Pushkin is demonstrating that demons have
moved into the sphere of literature, and may indeed be nothing but
a figment of the literary imagination. This does not, however, detract
from the very real danger which they present. Artistic representa-

tions of the demonic, as Pushkin shows, affect life as well as literature. In the Russian tradition they have often been treated as if they were of real historical substance, leading to debates about Pechorin's role as a demonic social type, or to earnest discussions of a novel such as Dostoevsky's *The Devils*, as if it were a factual source for the understanding of Russia's past history and future destiny. In similar fashion, arresting literary treatments of real historical figures, marked by extreme tendencies towards idolization or demonization, have frequently obscured or even supplanted the perception of their original prototypes in the public mind.

In the twentieth century these twin areas of association between literature and demonism (the power of the text to corrupt both reader and writer, and the demonic as a literary construct) have all been developed much more explicitly. Later essays in this volume will consider examples such as Rozanov's attacks on the latent demonism of the printed word, or Blok's seductive evocation of the Muse as a Demon.[42] To these one could add Remizov's comment that "books are from the Devil,"[43] or Kliuev's damning evocation of the literary world as a paper hell, in which writers are tormented by a horrible new type of devil, the very letters of the Church Slavonic alphabet:

Бумажный ад поглотит вас
С чернильным черным Сатаною,
И бесы: Буки, Веди, Аз,
Согнут построчников фитою.[44]

[A paper hell will swallow you
With a black ink Satan,
And the devils: *Buki*, *Vedi*, *Az*,
Will bend the scribblers into a *fita*.]

Not surprisingly, such an overriding preoccupation with the demonic powers of art infiltrated the very modes of narration, resulting in new literary techniques designed to convey the hallmark of the devil: shifting ambivalence or lack of coherent meaning. This trend was to a large extent (but not entirely) reversed by the advent of Stalinism, which brought about a return to social and moral concerns and to more "literal" forms of demonization. Although Stalin died almost half a century ago, Russian literature is still working through his legacy, and demonic themes related to the historical context accordingly continue to play a prominent role.

In the first part of this volume we saw that the devils and demons of Orthodox and folk tradition were renowned for their pervasive presence and ambivalent multiplicity of guises. In passing into literature, as demonstrated in the essays of part II, they succeeded in retaining these characteristics. The firm place which they were able to establish for themselves in their new habitat was due in large part to the ingrained religious orientation of Russian literature, further reinforced by historical circumstance. Whether welcome or unwelcome, these visitors adapted to their new environment so successfully that it is doubtful if they will ever be dislodged. One is reminded of Dostoevsky's description of Ivan Karamazov's shabby but respectable visitor: the devil is likened by him to a parasitic guest, who, rather than remaining upstairs in the room set aside for him, prefers to come downstairs to drink tea with his host and sits in silent expectation, ever ready to engage in conversation, should his host initiate it.[45] In the same way, demons are always a latent presence in the Russian literary tradition, just waiting for an opportunity to manifest themselves.

Merezhkovsky's claim, quoted as an epigraph to this introduction, that "all Russian literature is, to a certain degree, a struggle with the temptation of demonism" has so far been amply validated, and shows no signs of being disproved as this century draws to its close.[46] The tremendous upsurge of interest in various forms of occultism which Russia has witnessed, following the collapse of the Soviet Union, has led to a renewed preoccupation with the demonic, not unlike the one which took place at the turn of the last century; as before, this phenomenon will undoubtedly continue to have a strong impact on literature.[47] The popularity of occultism, reflected in the large sections devoted to this topic in the bookshops of Moscow and St. Petersburg, is developing even faster on Russian sites of the world wide web. Demons have evidently found an ideal new home in this protean environment. A recent browse through the web turned up a wide variety of demonic materials of mixed literary, political, historical, and religious orientation, a potent combination fuelled by millennial expectations.[48] Speculation as to what may lie ahead falls outside the scope of this book; however, the range and vitality of manifestations of the demonic throughout Russian literary history, as testified to by the contents of this volume, leads us to surmise that notions of the demonic will continue to play a central role in defining Russia's literary tradition.

Notes

1. D.S. Merezhkovskii, "M.Iu. Lermontov. Poet sverkhchelovechestva" (1909), in his *Polnoe sobranie sochinenii*, 17 vols. (St. Petersburg and Moscow: Izdanie T-va M.O. Vol'f, 1911–13), 10:287–334(315).
2. I.A. Goncharov, *Oblomov* (Moscow: Izdatel'stvo "Pravda," 1979), 144 ("Son Oblomova," part 1, chap. 9).
3. "Skazka ne nad odnimi det'mi v Oblomovke, no i nad vzroslymi do kontsa zhizni sokhraniaet svoiu vlast'." Ibid., 147.

4. "Ek.N. Ushakovoi" ("Kogda, byvalo, v starinu...") (1827), in A.S. Pushkin, *Sobranie sochinenii*, ed. D.D. Blagoi and others, 10 vols. (Moscow: Khudozhestvennaia literatura, 1974–78), 2:100.

5. For the text of "Besy," see ibid., 2:227–29. For further discussion of this poem in this volume, see Faith Wigzell, "The Russian Folk Devil and His Literary Reflections."

6. ["Podrazhanie italiianskomu"] ("Kak s dreva sorvalsia predatel' uchenik...") (1836), in Pushkin, *Sobranie sochinenii*, 2:380. For a discussion of Pushkin's reworking of "Sonnet de Gianni. Supplice de Judas dans l'enfer," a translation by Antoni Deschanns of "Sonetto sopra Giuda" by Francesco Gianni (1760–1822), see A.D. Grigor'eva and N.N. Ivanova, *Iazyk liriki XIX v.: Pushkin. Nekrasov* (Moscow: Nauka, 1981), 185–94.

7. Discussed in this volume in Rosalind Marsh, "Literary Representations of Stalin and Stalinism as Demonic."

8. See *Dvenadtsat' spiashchikh dev: Starinnaia povest' v dvukh balladakh* (comprising "Ballada pervaia: Gromoboi" and "Ballada vtoraia: Vadim"), in V.A. Zhukovskii, *Sochineniia v trekh tomakh*, ed. I.M. Semenko, 3 vols. (Moscow: Khudozhestvennaia literatura, 1980), 2:74–121 (text) and 2:464–66 (notes). For Zhukovsky's reference to this ballad in his letter to A.I. Turgenev of 7 November 1810, see ibid., 3:434.

9. On demonic themes in *The Brothers Karamazov*, see, for example, Victor Terras, "Turgenev and the Devil in *The Brothers Karamazov*," *Canadian-American Slavic Studies* 6 (1972):265–71; Victor Terras, "On the Nature of Evil in *The Brothers Karamazov*," in *Text and Context: Essays to Honor Nils Åke Nilsson*, ed. P.A. Jensen and others, Stockholm Studies in Russian Literature, no.23 (Stockholm: Almqvist and Wiksell, 1987), 58–64. For further references to critical discussion of *The Brothers Karamazov* see W.J. Leatherbarrow, *Fedor Dostoevsky: A Reference Guide* (Boston: G.K. Hall, 1990). On Sologub's *The Petty Demon*, see Milton Ehre, "Fedor Sologub's *The Petty Demon*: Eroticism, Decadence and Time," in *The Silver Age in Russian Literature*, ed. John Elsworth (Basingstoke: Macmillan, 1992), 156–70. On Bulgakov's *The Master and Margarita* see W.J. Leatherbarrow, "The Devil and the Creative Visionary in Bulgakov's *The Master and Margarita*," *New Zealand Slavonic Journal* 1 (1975):29–45; Elisabeth Stenbock-Fermor, "Bulgakov's *The Master and Margarita* and Goethe's *Faust*," *Slavic and East European Journal* 13 (Fall 1969):309–25; A.C. Wright, "Satan in Moscow: An Approach to Bulgakov's *The Master and Margarita*," *Proceedings of the Modern Languages Association* 88, no.5 (1973):1162–72; E. Ericson, "The Satanic Incarnation: Parody in Bulgakov's *The Master and Margarita*," *Russian Review* 33 (1974):20–36; Edward E. Ericson, *The Apocalyptic Vision of Mikhail Bulgakov's "The Master and Margarita"* (Lewiston: The Edwin Mellen Press, 1991), esp. 43–68 ("Satan and the Fallen Angels"); George Krugovoy, *The Gnostic Novel of Mikhail Bulgakov: Sources and Exegesis* (Lanham: University Press of America, 1991); the chapter on *The Master and Margarita* in David M. Bethea, *The Shape of Apocalypse in Modern Russian Fiction* (Princeton: Princeton University Press, 1989), 186–229; Andrew Barratt, *Between Two Worlds: A Critical Introduction to "The Master and Margarita"* (Oxford: Clarendon Press, 1987), esp. 133–72 ("Who the Devil?..."); J.A.E. Curtis, *Bulgakov's Last Decade: The Writer as Hero* (Cambridge: Cambridge University Press, 1987), esp. 168–76 ("Woland").

10. Aleksandr Blok, *Sobranie sochinenii*, ed. V.N. Orlov, A.A. Surkov, and K.I. Chukovskii, 8 vols. (Moscow and Leningrad: Gosudarstvennoe izdatel'stvo khudozhestvennoi literatury, 1960–63), 5:36–65, esp. 37, 49, 63–65.

11. ["Nabrosok stat'i o russkoi poezii"] (December 1901–January 1902), in Blok, *Sobranie sochinenii*, 7:21–37(28).

12. From the collection *Tol'ko liubov'* (1903), which, significantly, takes as its epigraph a quotation from Dostoevsky's *Besy*: "Ia vsemu molius'." K. Bal'mont, *Izbrannoe:*

Stikhotvoreniia. Perevody. Stat'i, comp. V. Bal'mont with notes by R. Pomirchii (Moscow: Khudozhestvennaia literatura, 1980), 194.

13. V.S. Solov'ev, "Lermontov" (1899), in *Sobranie sochinenii Vladimira Sergeevicha Solov'eva,* ed. S.M. Solov'ev and E.L. Radlov, 2d ed., 10 vols. (St. Petersburg: Prosveshchenie, [1911–13]), 9:348–67.

14. D.I. Pisarev, "Realisty" (1864), in his *Literaturnaia kritika v trekh tomakh,* ed. Iu.S. Sorokin, 3 vols. (Leningrad: Khudozhestvennaia literatura, 1981), 2:6–165(25).

15. *Skazka dlia detei* (3.5, 10), in M.Iu. Lermontov, *Polnoe sobranie stikhotvorenii,* introd. D.E. Maksimov, ed. E.E. Naidich, Biblioteka poeta, Bol'shaia seriia, 2 vols. (Leningrad: Sovetskii pisatel', 1989), 2:490. For further discussion of Lermontov's *Skazka dlia detei* and its influence on images of the demonic, see Tomas Venclova, "K demonologii russkogo simvolizma," in *Christianity and the Eastern Slavs,* vol. 3, *Russian Literature in Modern Times,* ed. Boris Gasparov and others, California Slavic Studies, no.18 (Berkeley: University of California Press, 1995), 134–60, and in this volume, Avril Pyman, "The Demon. The Mythopoetic World Model in the Art of Lermontov, Vrubel, Blok."

16. Blok, *Sobranie sochinenii,* 3:36–40 and 47–53, respectively.

17. See Evagrius's "To Anatolius: On Eight Thoughts," in the abridged English translation of *Dobrotoliubie: Early Fathers from the Philokalia,* selected and trans. E. Kadloubovsky and G.E.H. Palmer (London: Faber and Faber, 1954), 111–12.

18. For a study of the link between *acedia* and ennui, which traces the secularization of *acedia* back to Petrarch and the advent of the Renaissance, see Reinhard Kuhn, *The Demon of Noontide: Ennui in Western Literature* (Princeton: Princeton University Press, 1976), 39–64. On the "dark night of the soul" traversed by Saint John of the Cross and Saint Theresa of Avila, see ibid., 45.

19. On Dürer and Goethe, see ibid., 75–76 and 184–85, respectively.

20. On Blok's demon of dejection, see in this volume Pamela Davidson, "The Muse and the Demon in the Poetry of Pushkin, Lermontov, and Blok." Examples of the link between idleness (prazdnost') or boredom (skuka) and creativity can also be found in Pushkin's verse and are discussed in this volume in Pamela Davidson, "Divine Service or Idol Worship? Russian Views of Art as Demonic."

21. Kay Redfield Jamison, *Touched with Fire: Manic-Depressive Illness and the Artistic Temperament* (New York: The Free Press, 1993), analyses the overlapping natures of the artistic and manic-depressive temperaments and advances various psychological and biological arguments for this close relationship.

22. Viacheslav Ivanov, "Evrei i russkie," ed. K.Iu. Lappo-Danilevskii, *Novoe literaturnoe obozrenie* 21 (1996):191–93(191, 192).

23. M.S. Al'tman, *Razgovory s Viacheslavom Ivanovym,* comp. and ed. V.A. Dymshits and K.Iu. Lappo-Danilevskii (St. Petersburg: INAPRESS, 1995), 17.

24. Iu.M. Lotman and B.A. Uspenskii, "Rol' dual'nykh modelei v dinamike russkoi kul'tury (do kontsa XVIII veka)," in *Uchenye zapiski Tartuskogo gosudarstvennogo universiteta* 414, *Trudy po russkoi i slavianskoi filologii* 28 (1977):3–36.

25. On demonic analogy, see Gabriel Josipovici, *The World and the Book: A Study of Modern Fiction* (St. Albans: Paladin, 1973), 304–6, 308, 311–15.

26. Valerii Briusov, "Posledniaia rabota Vrubelia," in *Vrubel': Perepiska. Vospominaniia o khudozhnike,* comp. and ed. E.P. Gomberg-Verzhbinskaia and Iu.N. Podkopaeva (Leningrad and Moscow: Iskusstvo, 1963), 263–69(267). Briusov's memoir was first published in the journal *Iskusstvo* (Kiev) in 1912, and reprinted in his collection *Za moim oknom* (Moscow: Skorpion, 1913). For reproductions of Vrubel's portrait of Briusov and *The Pearl* (*Zhemchuzhina*), see Mikhail Guerman, ed., *Mikhail Vrubel,* comp. Alla Gaiduk and others, trans. John Greenfield and Valery Dereviaghin (Leningrad: Aurora Art Publishers, 1985), plates 148 and 132, respectively.

27. F.I. Shaliapin, *Maska i dusha: Moi sorok let na teatrakh* (Paris: Izd-vo "Sovremennye zapiski," 1932), 163.

28. On Bely's recollection of Metner's warning, see in this volume Davidson, "The Muse and the Demon."

29. The first three poems are in Maksimilian Voloshin, *Demony glukhonemye*, 2d ed., (Berlin: Knigoizdatel'stvo pisatelei v Berline, 1923; reprint, London: Flegon Press, 1965), 7, 17, 21, respectively. "Severovostok" was published in Maksimilian Voloshin, *Stikhi o terrore* (Berlin: Knigoizdatel'stvo pisatelei v Berline, 1923; reprint, Berkeley: 1983), 7–9.

30. See, for example, the article by Magomedova comparing Blok's *Dvenadtsat'* to Voloshin's "Severovostok." The author traces the myth of Russia's demonic possession back to Pushkin's "Besy" and to Dostoevsky's *Besy*, and argues that Blok and Voloshin develop it in two different directions: Blok's version is active, dependent on moral self-indictment and purification, while Voloshin's is based on a more passive, collective endurance of suffering, epitomized by the attitude of "terpen'e." D.M. Magomedova, "Blok i Voloshin (Dve interpretatsii mifa o besovstve," *Uchenye zapiski Tartuskogo universiteta* 917, *Blokovskii sbornik XI* (Tartu: TartuÜlikool, 1990), 39–49.

31. Paolo and Francesca are tormented in the second circle of hell, together with the other carnal sinners. Their story is told by Dante in *Inferno*, 5:73–142.

32. For quotations from Dante (in the order cited), see *Inferno*, 5:119, 120, 124, 137, 141. All translations from Dante's *Divine Comedy* are taken from *Inferno: 1: Italian Text and Translation*, the first part of volume one of the following edition: Dante Alighieri, *The Divine Comedy*, trans., with a commentary, by Charles S. Singleton, 2d ed., 3 vols. (in 6 parts), Bollingen Series, no.80 (Princeton: Princeton University Press, 1977).

33. Jean-Auguste-Dominique Ingres (1780–1867), *Paolo and Francesca*, oil on canvas, 35 × 28 cm, The Barber Institute of Fine Arts, The University of Birmingham. The picture is one of a group of small, brightly coloured "troubadour" works with medieval or Renaissance subjects, painted by Ingres mainly between 1814 and 1820.

34. For details of A.S. Norov's translation of the fifth canto of *Inferno*, see V.T. Danchenko, *Dante Alig'eri: Bibliograficheskii ukazatel' russkikh perevodov i kriticheskoi literatury na russkom iazyke 1762–1972* (Moscow: Kniga, 1973), 37 (item no.178). Norov was a minor writer and poet, who worked at the Ministry of Interior Affairs. Pushkin made good use of his excellent library, but took a dim view of his capacities as a translator of Dante (ibid., 8).

35. Blok, *Sobranie sochinenii*, 2:290–91.

36. Compare stanza 4 of Blok's poem with *Inferno*, 5:130–32.

37. *Inferno*, 5:82.

38. On Blok's love of *Macbeth*, see the extract from his letter to Ellis of 5 March 1907, quoted in Blok, *Sobranie sochinenii*, 2:436. For the cycle "Puzyri zemli" and its epigraph, see ibid., 2:8.

39. On folk motifs in this cycle, see in this volume Wigzell, "The Russian Folk Devil."

40. Pushkin, *Sobranie sochinenii*, 4:7–162. References to *Evgenii Onegin* are given in the text by chapter, stanza and line number.

41. Norman Cohn, *Europe's Inner Demons: The Demonization of Christians in Medieval Christendom*, revised edition (London: Pimlico, 1993 [first published in 1975]), ix.

42. See in this volume the essay on Rozanov by Liza Dimbleby, and the analysis of Blok's "K Muze" (1912) and "Demon" (1916) in Davidson, "The Muse and the Demon."

43. A.M. Remizov, "Chertik," in his *Izbrannoe*, ed. Iu.A. Andreev (Moscow: Khudozhestvennaia literatura, 1978), 96, cited in this volume in Adam Weiner, "The Demonomania of Sorcerers: Satanism in the Russian Symbolist Novel."

44. The opening quatrain of "Bumazhnyi ad poglotit vas..." (1916–17), from the cycle addressed to Sergei Esenin, in Nikolai Kliuev, *Sochineniia*, ed. G.P. Struve and B.A. Filippov, 2 vols. (Munich: A. Neimanis, 1969), 1:416–18(416). *Buki, Vedi, Az* and *Fita* are all names of letters of the Church Slavonic alphabet. In Kliuev's poem, the first three are represented as devils, who torment writers by bending them into the shape of a *Fita*, i.e. into a round circle. Unlike the other letters' names, *fita* is not capitalized in the poem; this suggests a possible allusion to a further meaning of *fita*, given in Dal's dictionary as "shkoliarnyi gramotei, doshlyi pisaka." *Tolkovyi slovar' zhivogo velikorusskogo iazyka Vladimira Dalia*, 2d ed., 4 vols. (St. Petersburg and Moscow: Izdanie knigoprodavtsa-tipografa M.O. Vol'fa, 1880–82; reprint, Moscow: Russkii iazyk, 1978), 4:683.

45. See "Chert. Koshmar Ivana Fedorovicha" (*Brat'ia Karamazovy*, part 4, book 11, chap. 9), in F.M. Dostoevskii, *Polnoe sobranie sochinenii v tridstati tomakh*, ed. V.G. Bazanov and others, 30 vols. (Leningrad: Nauka, 1972–90), 15:70–71.

46. Viktor Pelevin's recent novel *Chapaev and Emptiness* (*Chapaev i Pustota*), first published in *Znamia*, 1996, no.4:27–121, no.5:23–114, is rife with demonic characters and incidents; in chap.7 Baron Iungern, a demonic character somewhat reminiscent of Bulgakov's Woland, takes Petr Pustota to a Day of Judgement at a Satanic gathering. For further examples of recent works with demonic themes, see in this volume the section on "The Late and Post-Soviet Era" in Rosalind Marsh, "Literary Representations of Stalin and Stalinism as Demonic."

47. For a stimulating collection of essays on this important context for literary demonism, see Bernice Glatzer Rosenthal, *The Occult in Russian and Soviet Culture* (Ithaca and London: Cornell University Press, 1997); recent developments are covered in Holly DeNio Stephens, "The Occult in Russia Today," 357–78.

48. Internet publications, downloaded in October 1998, included the first twelve chapters of a novel by Aleksei Zikmund, *Doch' satany ili Po etu storonu dobra i zla* (http.://www.zhurnal.ru slova zikmund kniga 1.htm). This work deals with the struggle between good and evil, due to take place in Russia. Its main action takes place in Moscow in 1941. Flashbacks to Germany in 1921 include the account of how Georg/Lucifer turns his daughter, Lina, into Lilith during her childhood, following the advice of an old Rumanian witch. When she grows up, he arranges for her to be impregnated by a German professor of philosophy, who collects books on black magic. The twelfth chapter concludes with Lina/ Lilith asking for political asylum in Moscow as she is about to give birth. Many of the characters involved in black magic have Jewish names (e.g. the old *koldun* Miler, or Boris Solomonovich, who organizes a séance in which a demon is raised, using the blood of a freshly killed boy); this suggests an anti-Semitic slant to the novel's portrayal of the action of demonic forces in history. The novel also makes reference to early twentieth-century occultism, thereby hinting at its link with turn of the century Russian demonism. A further, non-literary work, entitled *Apokalipsis 2000* (http://www.apokalipsis.com/win/index.html, version of 7 July 1998), opens with a Dostoevskian epigraph ("Velichaishim dostizheniem D'iavola iavliaetsia obshchee mnenie o tom, chto D'iavola net") and draws on the Book of Revelation and the writings of Nostradamus; it sets out seven stages in the arena of international politics, which will lead to a final nuclear disaster and to the End of the World (predicted to start in January 2000 – will there be any readers left to read this note?). It is not clear whether the "Rezhisser Apokalipsisa" who controls this grim scenario represents God or the Devil. The journal *Anomaliia. Gazeta o neopoznannom* (http://www.dux.ru/anomalia, issue of 5 June 1998), produced in St. Petersburg with the help of the "Ufologicheskaia assotsiatsiia," contains an eclectic mix of articles. I am most grateful to my colleague Arnold McMillin and to Efim Slavinsky for providing me with these materials.

Part I

TRADITIONS
AND CONTEXTS

Chapter 1

Nostalgia for Hell:
Russian Literary Demonism
and Orthodox Tradition

Simon Franklin

> After Dostoevsky all the demons (*besy*) described by Gogol dispersed to
> their lairs, chuckling at the pathetic conceit of man, who used to shift the
> blame for all his human iniquities. In our age man acts on his own
> account and is responsible for himself (a jolly sight indeed!), and in liter-
> ature there's not a word about demons.
>
> Remizov, from the Introduction to *Demoniacs*[1]

A man of God is taken to visit a great city. It is a city which a *tsar* had
seen in a vision. And his guide shows the man the broad streets, and
the avenues bedecked with marble, and the great square, and the
palace glittering with gold and precious stones. And the man said: "If
this fine place exists by God's will ... then may it endure forever; but
if not, then may it come to nothing." And he made the sign of the
Cross, and his guide turned into a demon, and the palaces disappeared, and the place was nothing but a foul marsh. The tsar's vision
had been Satanic, brought to him by the devil "in the image of a
bright angel" (cf. 2 Cor. 11:14).[2]

What, in a Russian context, might this tale be taken to signify? It
is surely an allegory of St. Petersburg, full of the familiar encoded
elements: the tsar's vision, the magnificent city with squares and
palaces, its unreality, indeed its diabolical essence; and the clincher
– the marshland. We think perhaps of Gogol: "It's nothing but lies,

this Nevsky Prospect ... and a demon himself lights the lamps, just to show everything in a false aspect."[3]

Obvious, but wrong. For in fact this Russian text predates the founding of St. Petersburg. It appears in the late seventeenth century. For a mystic or theologian, so much the better: a splendidly prophetic warning, a prefiguration on the very eve of the event. Wrong again. The Russian *text* appears in the late seventeenth century, but the *story* originates much earlier, and is not even Russian. It is taken from the *Great Mirror* (*Velikoe zertsalo*), a Russian version (in this case actually the second Russian version) of a Polish edificatory collection published in 1633. And the Polish collection is itself a translation, from Latin, of the *Magnum Speculum Exemplorum* published at the start of the seventeenth century by the Belgian Jesuit Ioannes Maior. And *his* text is, in turn, based on a late-*fifteenth*-century anonymous Latin assemblage of tales, which included among its sources some stories which originate in early Christianity.[4]

Here lies the first problem in my theme: in a way, there is no such thing as "Orthodox" demonism, complete and self-contained and fixed. It is often inappropriate to describe something as belonging to an Orthodox tradition as distinct from broader Christian traditions, or to separate a specifically Russian tradition within Orthodoxy. However, in the wise words of Koz'ma Prutkov, "nobody can encompass the unencompassable."[5] For the purposes of the present survey "Orthodox" tradition is comprised of Church Slavonic and East Slavonic texts which were used in Rus and Russia before about 1700. The vast majority of such texts were translations from Greek, and were derived from Byzantine or Early Christian originals. Some were composed or compiled or edited locally. A few, like the *Great Mirror*, have still more complex histories. But since the focus is mainly on the response to a tradition, rather than on its formation, the provenance of any given text is not of crucial significance.

The second fundamental problem also emerges from the story in the *Great Mirror*. My paraphrase, rather in the spirit of its protagonist, was deliberately misleading. The original could not possibly be mistaken for a post-medieval narrative, except perhaps as an example of extreme stylization. The city may be unreal, but the demons are not. A modern reading might discount the "facts" and seek to treat such a tale primarily as allegory. In a medieval context the primary reading can and probably should be literal: the exemplary parable is also plausible as fact, simply as a true story. The aesthetics of narrative perspective cannot be fully disentangled from the assumed context of belief. There are many kinds of medieval resonances in post-medieval culture, but one must recognize the profound *dis*continuities. To put it crudely: in Orthodox tradition for most of the centuries of its existence, there is no such thing as demon*ism*. Instead, there are demons. There is no demonization; instead there is demonology. Demons are external, not externalizations. *We* may choose to psychologize them as, for example, ways of representing the Other, or the Other Self, or as equivalent to Jungian "shadow;" or we may choose to treat them as a store of imagery, as allegoric or metaphorical device, as oblique means of expression; but such choices would arise out of *our* ways of cultural modelling, not out of Orthodox understanding. Real demons are also morally unambiguous. They are not tragic or avuncular or nobly doomed free spirits. They are not Miltonic or Byronic. They can of course make themselves appear attractive, even affable and charming, but in no sense can they be presented as admirable, or as pitiable, or as providers of legitimate aesthetic interest and pleasure.[6] Their essence is thoroughly nasty. They are ceaselessly hostile. Their purpose, in their dealings with mankind, is to bring souls to damnation.

Who and what, then, were the Orthodox Devil and his demons? The difficulty with the Devil is that, although he incontestably exists and although there are recurrent features in his representation, he is very hard to pin down. His trademark is flexibility, adaptability, inconstancy. This is in part due to his nature, in part due to his provenance. There is no fixed, systematic, canonical Orthodox teaching on or description of the Devil.[7] Extensive theoretical demonology is rare in Byzantine writing; it was uninfluential even in Byzantium, and was virtually unknown to the Rus. Works such as the quasi-Platonic dialogue *On Demons*, spuriously attributed to the eleventh-century scholar Michael Psellos, did not make the transition into Slavonic. The Orthodox Devil – just as, more widely, the Christian Devil – was not created whole; he emerged over time, out of the accumulated and often disparate writings in which he is, by and large, not the main subject. The Devil is an extrapolation, a field of possibilities, a set of interwoven traditions.[8]

The Devil plays a surprisingly muted role in the Old Testament, barely perceivable in his own person except in his brief dialogue with God at the start of the book of Job.[9] By contrast, the writers of the New Testament clearly assume both in their audiences and in their protagonists a fairly elaborate demonological awareness, which seems to stem both from late Jewish apocrypha and from other regional cultures of the period during which the New Testament was composed. The Golden Age of growth in Christian demonology, when the repertoire was hugely expanded and when the main parameters of subsequent narrative and representation were set, was the Early Christian and patristic period. The context was polemical; the tradition was shaped in argument. There was argument within the Faith, about the nature of Creation and the status and powers of the Devil within it, leading to sophisticated distinctions between, on the one hand, what came to be regarded as Orthodox, and on the other hand various forms of dualist "heresy" which accorded the Devil greater authority and autonomy. And there were theoretical and practical polemics with those clearly outside the Faith, with those who accepted quite different deities, with classical and local paganisms.

If our interest is in literary history, then the main legacy of the anti-dualist polemic lies in cosmology, in a range of narratives which amplify the exiguous information in Genesis, to show how the Devil fits in the larger scheme: apocryphal accounts of Creation, for example, or of the fall of Adam and Eve. Several of these became embedded in Byzantine chronicles and historical compendia, and thence made their way into Slavonic and to the Rus.[10] However, the anti-dualist polemic was not actively pursued in Rus, for the simple reason that there was little to polemicize against. Bulgaria had had its very own dualist sect, the Bogomils. Bogomilism was one of the very few cultural phenomena which was exported by the Slavs back to Constantinople, and the charge of Bogomilism continued in Byzantine anti-heretical rhetoric well into the twelfth century, long after the official Conversion of the Rus. However, the search for substantive evidence of the spread of Bogomilism (or any other variety of Christian dualism) to the Rus themselves has yielded virtually nothing.[11] While man's struggle with his adversary the Devil in life can seem dualistic, the cosmological context for the Russian Orthodox Devil is consistently monistic: God *is* supreme and unthreatened, and when all is said and done, or tried and tempted, the Devil is a loser. He has no hold over the future; he can act only where God permits and where man loses vigilance; he can be resisted and expelled. It is sometimes assumed, wrongly, that apocryphal cosmologies in Slavonic must be heretical, hence associated with Bogomilism. In fact the apocryphal narratives were regularly transmitted in perfectly respectable Orthodox contexts (just as they were throughout medieval Christendom) by writers grateful for the supplementary information. The Rus received and recopied the narratives, but did little to amplify the tradition. The local literary and representational resonances were far more limited than those which were generated in the Christian encounter with paganism.

In Byzantine literature there were two main strategies for explaining and contextualizing pagan forms of worship: either to dismiss paganism as worship of the created rather than of the Creator (in which case pagan deities simply do not exist);[12] or to identify pagan deities as demons (and hence to acknowledge their existence but to reverse their evaluation, to authenticate and at the same time subordinate).[13] Both types of argument can be found in Slavonic sources from the very beginning,[14] but by far the most important is the latter, the assimilation of pagan deities to Christian demonology. The consequence is a vast, potentially limitless, expansion in the Devil's protean repertoire of forms and guises, a kind of colonization of paganisms by Christian discourse, and ultimately a blurring of boundaries between the Orthodox and the folkloric.

This leads (for us, if not for medieval writers) to a problem of demarcation. It would be misleading even to attempt to separate a notionally pure, learned, theologically self-contained Orthodox Devil, split off from his multiplicity of incarnations accumulated through Christianity's continuing encounters with paganism and folk beliefs. Early Christian and Byzantine demonology absorbed and adapted local folk demons, which became part of the received demonology as originally borrowed by the Rus.[15] The Rus, in turn, absorbed and adapted their own local demons into the Orthodox tradition. The assimilation works in both directions. Learned narratives can sound surprisingly "folksy" in many of the details; and, by contrast, an assumption of Orthodoxy can be implicit in authentic folk narratives. In the cycle of transmission teachings of the clergy address the experience of the flock, and tales from the monastery become oral lore among laymen. There is plenty here to disturb the sleep of textual genealogists: is a given version of a text a bookish reworking of an oral (folkloric) original, or a bookish original with folkloric accretions? Or simply a text, whose author would not have understood why anybody should be worried by such questions? The Orthodox Devil is a multiple hybrid, and the particular provenance of each of his guises is not especially relevant either to his own integrity or to his subsequent literary reception. Of course there are significant differences: in emphasis, in outlook, in language and, not least, in genre. But there are also significant areas of overlap, of common ground. One needs to bear in mind that post-medieval writers could encounter plenty of equivalent demonological figures and motifs across both sides of the conventional generic divide.

In narrative (and here we are concerned mainly with narrative representation) the multifariousness of Orthodox demonology is far more prominent than the singularity of *the* Devil. Neither in Byzantium nor in Russia was there much emphasis on a towering figure of Satan in splendour.[16] Though it was certainly possible in cosmology to describe, and in iconography to depict, hierarchies of infernal powers, nevertheless the most common narratives either focus on petty demons or else ignore the distinction. For the modern interpreter such representational flexibility poses a typographical dilemma: quite often it is impossible – and inappropriate – to deter-

mine whether the (anti-)hero of any given tale should be cast as
upper-case Devil or as lower-case devil or demon; or whether one
should use the definite or indefinite article (*a* devil, or *the* Devil).
Hitherto I have maintained upper-case convention, but as we pass
from cosmology to narrative a consistent adherence to the convention becomes misleading. Henceforth, therefore, the (or a) lower-
case devil will be the norm, except in those few instances where
Satan unambiguously intervenes in his own singular persona.

The lack of a consistent or unitary definition is reflected in vocabulary. The devil has many names, of many origins. Some are direct
transliterations from the Greek which was the immediate source of the
Slavs' Christianity (*sotona, diiavol, demon, supostat*); some are translated
(*vrag, lukavyi, nepriiazn'*);[17] others are native (in particular, *bes, chert*).
With the exception of *chert*, which – perhaps surprisingly, given that it
is the most common term in modern usage – does not seem to occur
in written texts before the seventeenth century,[18] all these names coexist in East Slav literature throughout its history. In theory one can
make distinctions between them: in descending order of bookishness
sotona is singular and *diiavol* tends to be so, whereas *demon* and *bes*
would more often be associated with an assumed plurality. In practice,
however, usage is fairly fluid and the various designations can substitute for each other. The terminological fluidity was inherited from
Greek and amplified in translation. In Old Church Slavonic texts, for
example, *sotona* can render *diabolos* as well as *satanas*; the Greek words
daimon and its diminutive *daimonion* can both be rendered either by
demon or by *bes* (different translators have different preferences), while
occasionally *bes* also renders *diabolos*.[19] As for native usage: in the *Primary Chronicle* the "philosopher's speech" – a potted history of the
world for the edification of the still-pagan Prince Vladimir – tells of the
fall of *Sotonail* (Satanael), first among angels; but in the ensuing narrative it is as *diiavol* that he tempts Eve, as *sotona* (the fallen Satanael
always loses his suffix)[20] that he enters Cain, as *diiavol* that he tempts
man to make and worship idols; and the Israelites were given over
into captivity for serving *besy*.[21] After baptism the Kievans beat the idol
of Perun, now unmasked as a *bes*, and they cursed *demony*.[22] All the
forms are masculine, always, although their bearers were quite adept
at disguising themselves as women.[23]

What did the demons look like? There are two answers to this
question. On the one hand they looked like demons; on the other
hand they looked like anything at all. Demons which look like
demons are described in some of the earliest native texts: they are
weedy and unappetizing to behold; they are "black, with wings and
tails."[24] The description is reinforced by narratives, icons, and wall-
paintings of the Last Judgement, used to scare pagans and children

2. "Demons Drag Kozmas to See Hell." Miniature from *The Vision of Kozmas*, late-eighteenth-century Russian manuscript.

3. "Ioann and Saint Benedict on the Ladder." Miniature from *The Vision of the Monk Ioann*, late-eighteenth-century Russian manuscript.

from Vladimir to Gogol.[25] From at least the twelfth century the Last
Judgement was the most common theme for the monumental fresco
at the western end of the nave, a reminder of the perils in store as the
worshipper passes out from the church into the world.[26] In what
eventually became one of the classic iconographic schemes of the
Last Judgement, the soul passes through a series of some twenty "cus-
toms-houses" or "tollbooths" (Greek *teloneia*; Slavonic *mytarstva*). At
each customs-house a demon checks the soul's baggage for the presence of a particular sin. At the end of the sequence the soul's total
contraband is placed on one side of a scales, while on the other side
an angel places the soul's virtues, converted into pure coinage.[27] The
demons do indeed tend to be somewhat spindly, and black, and with
wings and tails. Their hair usually stands on end. Unlike their West
European counterparts, Byzantine and Russian medieval demon-like
demons do not have horns or cloven hooves. These attributes were
acquired, together with others, in the more eclectic depictions dating
from the seventeenth century and later.[28] Prior to that the Russians
were quite conservative in their pictorial demonology, far less prone
to fantastic elaboration.[29] The basic iconographic scheme for the Last
Judgement was derived from Byzantine literary eschatology, specifically from the Vision of Theodora which forms part of the tenth-century *Life of Basil the New*.[30] The most widely known among
eschatological narratives is probably the *Descent of the Virgin into Hell*
(*Khozhdenie Bogoroditsy po mukam*), which Ivan Karamazov, when
introducing his own *poema* of the Grand Inquisitor, animatedly but
preposterously describes as a *poema* comparable to Dante's *The Divine
Comedy*.[31] But this brief and conventional text is entirely devoted to
the suffering souls and pays no attention to demons.

Usually, however, demons do not look like demons. Frontal
assault is not their normal style. They much prefer disguise. They
can appear in the shape of that which we detest and fear: sometimes
serpents and beasts, and especially foreigners; the Byzantine demon
was often an Ethiopian, Arab, or Turk. The Rus inherited the demon
as black,[32] and as early as the eleventh century Kievan demons had
added to their wardrobe when one of them turned up in the Caves
monastery disguised as a Pole, while in the Muscovite *Life of Saint
Sergii of Radonezh* (*Zhitie Sergiia Radonezhskogo*) the Devil enters a
church with a host of demons "in Lithuanian sharp-pointed hats."[33]
Conversely, demons can make themselves attractive, whether as
obviously dubious figures such as pagan deities or women, or in the
form of trusted allies such as "friends" or fellow-monks, even "bright
angels" or Christ himself.[34] They can be downright vicious or gently
coaxing. They can implant thoughts, or persuade through intermediaries. They can possess a person beyond that person's apparent

power to resist, hence to an extent remove responsibility from the human onto themselves; or they can slink from the scene, vanquished by prayer or the sign of the Cross, rendered impotent by human virtue or rendered redundant by human vice.[35]

The question "what are demons?" almost inevitably shades into the question "what do demons do?" Because there was no self-contained, systematic demonology, demons can only be described through the sum of their varied actions, through the accumulation of their appearances in narrative, exhortation, and edification. In this sense they are figures of literature more than of theology.[36] We must be selective. Demons have little respect for the boundaries of genre. They are pervasive literary figures of the Middle Ages, as ubiquitous in literature as they are in life.[37] Chroniclers explain their provenance and put the demonological "spin" on political narrative (erroneous or malevolent decisions are taken "at the devil's instigation"); sermonists rail against their noxious plots; even law-codes allow for their influence. But from a modern literary point of view the most productive field of inquiry is *hagiography*. Hagiography – writings about holy men and women – might seem an odd choice, almost the

4. "Margaret ('Marina') of Antioch Tussles with the Devil." Miniature from *The Life of Margaret of Antioch*, early- to mid-nineteenth-century Russian manuscript.

opposite of what is required. Yet it is appropriate and it has advantages. In the first place, hagiography is a theme, rather than a genre. It covers a broad spread of writings, from extensive Lives to brief anecdotes, from rhetorical eulogies to dramatic narratives, from martyrology to miracle-tale. Across time hagiography extends from stories of the early Desert Fathers (assembled into *paterika*) right through to seventeenth-century representations of new Russian candidates for sainthood. Hagiography is the most varied and vivid medieval repository of literary styles, devices, and themes.

Secondly, holy men and women have a special claim on the devil's attention. Good acquires definition and affirmation through its relations to evil.[38] Saints are the specialists; they expose themselves; they draw the devil's fire. Sometimes they meet him on his own territory: physically, in wildernesses, on mountains, on pillars.[39] Or by their very virtue they concentrate the devil's forces against them. The greater their devotion to the good, the more they excite the devil's envy and anger, hence the greater the danger to themselves, and the greater the benefit to the rest of mankind. Why does the *iurodivyi* (the holy fool, the fool for Christ's sake) throw stones at the houses of the virtuous yet kiss the walls of the houses of the wicked? His stones are not for the virtuous but for the envious demons who throng around them, and his kisses are not for the wicked but for the grieving angels who gather to them.[40]

The third reason for focusing on hagiography is its impact on post-medieval Russian literature. Despite Herzen's claim that "nowhere does religion play so modest a role in education as in Russia,"[41] there is no doubt that most of the "classic" writers of the nineteenth century were either brought up with or acquired a familiarity – ranging from superficial to intimate – with a fair spread of hagiographical narratives, whether through formal education, or through the rhythms of the ecclesiastical year as measured by saints' days, or through their own adult reading, or through nanny's stories.[42] For the seminarists, and those from a conventionally pious background such as Gogol, Leskov, or Dostoevsky this goes virtually without saying. Tolstoi's own heavily annotated copies of the *Synaxary* (*Prolog*, brief lives, and hagiographical excerpts) and *Monthly Readings* (*Chet'i minei*, extensive Lives for the full year, in twelve monthly volumes) survive in the Iasnaia Poliana library. In his *Confession* (*Ispoved'*) Tolstoi claims these as his "favourite reading" which had "revealed [to him] the meaning of life."[43] Leskov explicitly used the *Synaxary* (*Prolog*) as a store of plots and examples fit for adaptation and recycling. Even Herzen himself, in his youth, wrote his own version of the tale of Theodora, a transvestite nun whose feat of virtuous self-denial was to live unrecognized as a monk in a male monastery.[44] Indeed, the study of hagiographical sources and motifs in nineteenth-century Russian literature is well enough established to need no special justification.[45]

The devil's impressive array of weaponry against the stubborn holy man is prototypically displayed in the *Life* of Saint Antony of Egypt, by his fourth-century contemporary Athanasios of Alexandria. The main theme of the *Life* is the ascetic's ceaseless struggle against demons, and the multiplicity of their ruses and disguises. At first they gently tempt Antony by inducing alluring thoughts of material possessions, of comfort, home, family, and food. Then the devil, "as if succumbing, no longer attacked by means of thoughts," but assumed "the visage of a black boy" and spoke in a human voice, saying, "I am the friend of fornication." Antony resisted these first onslaughts. But for twenty years of his asceticism he was never left in peace. Crowds of devils came to beat him up; they would scream and shout at him, beguile him with bodily pleasures, set upon him in the form of wild beasts and reptiles. Not for a moment could Antony relax his vigilance. But eventually they "made fools not of him, but of themselves."[46]

The *Life of Antony*, and other tales of early ascetics (as recorded in translated *paterika*), were as authoritative in Rus as they were elsewhere, and the demonological themes were picked up with enthusiasm in native tales of asceticism. When local holy men appeared in Rus, demons were quick to follow. They were, at best, a perpetual irritant, almost playfully disruptive of monastic dignity and piety: induc-

5. "The Temptation of Saint Antony," 1820s or 1830s. Copper engraving, 28 × 38,2 cm.

ing drowsiness in church,[47] spilling the flour in the bakery, even unsettling the cattle.[48] At worst they could go through the full repertoire of strategies, as rehearsed against Saint Antony himself. The reminiscences of the *Life of Antony* are often implicit, but they can also be quite plain. For example, the thirteenth-century *Life of Avraamii of Smolensk* (*Zhitie Avraamiia Smolenskogo*) tells of how "at night ... [Satan] appeared in visions [standing] up to the ceiling, or falling upon [Avraamii] as a lion, or frightening him as wild beasts, or attacking and hacking at him as soldiers, or sometimes even hurling him from his bed... . During the day they [demons] afflicted him all the more, sometimes as themselves, sometimes in the guise of shameless women, in the same way as it is written about the great Antony." And when none of this succeeds, Satan tries his other main strategy, attack by proxy: "having tested the blessed one with all these attacks and failed ... Satan raised strife against Avramii... . [He] entered the hearts of disorderly people and moved them against him."[49]

Thus Orthodox demons quite comfortably made the transition from Byzantium to Rus. For seven centuries they flourished, as the principal agents of temptation and deception in East Slav written narratives, continually expanding their repertoire of multiple personae. How did they cope in the very different literary, aesthetic, and cultural environment of post-medieval Russia? The plain answer is that they fade almost entirely from plain view. Yet the manner of their fading is informative and revealing, even in a peculiar way influential. Mindful of Koz'ma Prutkov, and indeed of the specialist studies elsewhere in the present volume, I restrict the following discussion mainly to the nineteenth century, and mainly to remarks of a rather general nature. Broad issues, however, can emerge from specific examples, and we begin by considering what might be gleaned from one of the rare occasions on which apparently conventional demons do come out on public display.

The endangered species (the visible demon) found its most lush nineteenth-century sanctuary in Gogol's first collection of tales, *Village Evenings Near Dikanka* (*Vechera na khutore bliz Dikan'ki*, 1831–32). Demons cavort merrily through most of Gogol's early stories. I am not here concerned with the origins or functions of these demons in general (e.g. whether their immediate prototypes are mainly Ukrainian or Polish; whether they have travelled from *Kunstmärschen* or anywhere else).[50] Nor am I concerned to look at their place in the evolution of Gogol's demonology.[51] The limited purpose is to highlight just a couple of episodes which show instructive affinities and contrasts with similar episodes in pre-Petrine narrative. The relevant story is "Christmas Eve" (Noch' pered rozhdestvom).

"Christmas Eve" is a light piece, even a slight piece. Most of it reads as knockabout farce: the night sky teems with witches on broomsticks and folksy demons who tumble down chimneys to sow mildly sexual mild confusion among the bumbling, grumbling villagers of Dikanka. Much of the story is a comedy of errors, as the devil pockets the moon and blows up a blizzard so that the humans wander into the wrong places at the wrong times. But gradually the devil also loses control, becomes drawn into and subservient to the action against his will. From behind the farce there emerges a quasi-hagiographical tale of Vakula the blacksmith – perhaps not a saint, but a kind of *pravednik*, a righteous man – who is tested in life and by the devil and whose virtue is rewarded in the end.

Vakula is a "godfearing man," "the most pious man in the village,"[52] and as a practical application of his piety he paints icons, and his finest icon is of Saint Peter driving the devil from hell at the Last Judgement. This is why the devil detests him and schemes against him. While Vakula was painting the icon, the devil had tried to prevent him with the usual petty tricks, like jogging his hand or spilling ash in the smithy (rather like the devils knocking over the pots and pans in the monastic kitchen). But the icon was completed, and now, on Christmas Eve, the devil is looking for revenge. First he plays tricks to lead the villagers astray. Then, amid the resultant confusion, he gets his chance to strike. Vakula has declared his love to the pretty and flirtatious Oksana, who announces that she will marry him if he can bring her the slippers worn by the empress herself. Vakula is in despair, and decides that his only course is to seek the aid of the devil. So up pops the devil at his shoulder with a proposition: as Vakula's "friend and comrade" he will guarantee to obtain Oksana; and in return Vakula says he is prepared henceforth to belong to the devil.[53]

Pacts with the devil are comparatively rare in the Byzantine and Russian written tradition. When they occur, the motive tends not to be knowledge and power as in the "Faustian" variant of the theme. As often as not the stimulus is sexual, usually impure and illicit. In an apocryphal miracle attributed to Saint Basil of Caesarea, a young slave makes a pact with the devil in order to obtain the favours of a senator's daughter.[54] In the most expansive native Russian treatment of the theme – the seventeenth-century *Tale of Savva Grudtsyn* (*Povest' o Savve Grudtsyne*) – the young Savva and the wife of his unsuspecting landlord wallow in fornication "like pigs in dung."[55] These are murky areas for Vakula: the object of his desire (a woman) is conventional, but the nature of his desire has thus far, by contrast, been depicted as honourable, and the proposed means of fulfilment threatens to taint the quest.

Pacts with the devil have rules. Mere words are not enough. To be valid and binding, the agreement must be properly documented in writing. According to an apocryphal narrative (as told by Eve herself), the Devil demanded a written document (rukopisanie) to procure Adam's subservience.[56] The tale from the spurious *Life* of Saint Basil makes much of the fact that the misguided youth signed a written document with his own hand (*manu propria*), and the pact is only dissolved when the saint physically rips up the contract. The devil provides Savva Grudtsyn with parchment (khartiia) and ink, and Savva writes his pledge (rukopisanie) to the devil's dictation. Vakula's devil likewise knows the form: "Well, Vakula ... you know that nothing can be done without a contract."[57]

A curious feature of the tradition, however, is that most of the pacts are in some sense not real, not proper. Adam deceives the deceiver: he declares that he and his progeny will belong to the one who is "lord of the earth," and the delighted devil is victim of dramatic irony.[58] Savva's document is obtained by double deceit: he is unaware that his obliging "friend" is actually the devil; and – a point which is oddly stressed – Savva is only semi-literate, and he writes down the letters mechanically, to dictation, not actually stringing together the words himself.[59] It is as if there is resistance to the notion that any Christian might willingly, knowingly enter into a binding contract with the devil; or else the very idea of a written contract is perceived as somewhat alien in a Russian context, and hence as a source of confusion (for Savva)[60] or as an object of implied ridicule (in Gogol).[61]

The pious Vakula does not fall into the trap. Like Adam, he deceives the deceiver.[62] Making as if to reach for the implements of writing (a nail, for he has said he will sign in blood), he grabs the devil by the tail and makes the sign of the Cross to entrap him. The devil squeals (Vakula: "Ha! Now you're singing a different song, you cursed German!" – Vakula knows that the devil is a foreigner),[63] and the outcome is reversed: instead of Vakula serving the devil, the devil must serve Vakula. The twist in the action brings the story into contact with a new set of narrative motifs: from enslavement *by* the devil, to the entrapment and (temporary) enslavement *of* the devil. Vakula has not forgotten his main goal, to bring Oksana the empress's slippers, so the devil's task is to fly him "to Petemburg [i.e. St. Petersburg], straight to the tsaritsa." Which the hapless devil duly does.

Others before Vakula had taken advantage of night flight on the devil's back. The most notable was Ioann, bishop of Novgorod in the mid-twelfth century. The written narrative of Ioann of Novgorod's ride on the devil probably dates from no earlier than the fifteenth century (a late-fifteenth-century manuscript survives), and it was widely copied and adapted subsequently. A shortened version, preserving the principal episodes, was included in the *Synaxary (Prolog)*.[64] Oral derivatives have been recorded as folklore.[65]

One evening, as Ioann was at prayer in his cell, he heard a splashing in the wash-basin, and he realized that it must be the devil.[66] Like Vakula, he traps the devil with the sign of the Cross. As in Gogol's story the devil squeals. Like Vakula, Ioann makes the devil carry him at night to the distant place of his desires, the place of great wonders: Ioann flies to Jerusalem, to the Holy Sepulchre, where the doors miraculously open for him and the candles ignite of their own accord. Vakula flies to Petersburg (or rather, to "Petemburg"), where he meets Potemkin and Fonvizin and is given the empress's slippers by Catherine herself. The episode of Vakula's flight on the devil to "Petemburg" is a kind of comic or parodic mirror of Ioann's flight on the devil to Jerusalem.

After safe landings back home in Novgorod and Dikanka, the two narratives ostensibly diverge. Ioann releases the devil, who sets him a condition: that he should tell nobody of the events of that night. Some time later, however, Ioann cannot resist revealing some of the details.[67] The devil's revenge is to bring scandal upon the bishop. Visitors are shocked to see articles of women's clothing scattered around the bishop's chamber, and once a harlot (bludnitsa) is even spotted leaving his cell. Outraged at Ioann's apparently dissolute behaviour, and unaware that the harlot was in fact the devil in disguise, the Novgorodians cast Ioann out of office and set him adrift on a raft in the middle of the river Volkhov. Yet the bishop's true virtue is miraculously proved: instead of floating downriver into oblivion, the raft floats *up*stream to the Iur'ev monastery, the devil's schemes are undone, and Ioann is received back with honour and joy. One could interpret this episode (of the bishop and women's clothing) as a self-contained accretion,[68] but it also has important functions when linked to the story of flight on the devil. Why did Ioann suffer for breaking the devil's conditions? Several reasons might coexist: because the devil did not want his shame to be known; because to reveal such a victory is to be guilty of pride, and hence in effect to cede a kind of victory back to the devil; and because an ostensibly holy act, when achieved with the aid of the devil, remains ambiguous and perhaps tainted, until Ioann is justified through the subsequent authentic miracle. Meanwhile, back in Dikanka, Vakula presents the empress's shoes to Oksana and asks for her hand in marriage. The Happy Ending? Not quite, not yet. In Vakula's absence Oksana has realized how much she misses him. What she truly wants is Vakula, not the shoes; so she accepts him, and rejects them. The couple are married, and if you go into the local church you can still see, on a wall to one side, Vakula's fearsome painting of the devil in hell.

Thus in their respective denouements the two narratives seem to part company, although there are functional parallels. Like Ioann's trial by scandal and its conquest, Oksana's rejection of the empress's shoes serves more than one possible purpose: it is a sentimental touch, showing that Oksana commits herself out of true feeling rather than as a result of material gratification; generically it frees the narrative from dependence on the "impossible tasks" motif of courtship; and morally – even theologically – it denies the agency of the devil in contributing to virtue or happiness. Like the women's shoes seen in Ioann's chambers, the empress's shoes in "Christmas Eve" are revealed, ultimately, to be decoys.[69] The post-flight developments in both stories show how the devil's work is rejected even when he seems to serve man.

In nineteenth-century Russian literature Gogol's early stories are unusual in their explicit, literal demonology; and among Gogol's early stories the central episodes from "Christmas Eve" are unusual in their closeness to a couple of narrative motifs from hagiographical demonology. The exception proves the rule. Although it is perhaps an exaggeration to say that in "Christmas Eve" "the struggle between man and demons serves simply as raw material for the spinning of amusing tall tales"[70] – there is a quite careful and serious moral substratum, and the hagiographical resonances, though by no means predominant,[71] are there to be heard by those who have ears to hear – nevertheless the differences between Gogol's tale and its Orthodox precursors are at least as significant as the affinities. Even in this simple story there are elaborate layers of narrative perspective which serve to distance and de-authenticate superficial facts as presented. The narrative itself is saturated with demons; the narrator looks at that demon-filled world from within; but through comic stylization and parody the implied author is located firmly on the outside, sympathetic but not credulous; and the plot, which has played with the demonological, in the end casts it aside in favour of the human and the sentimental. There are no such contortions in the tale of Ioann. Here the explicit devil is vanquished – and the potential sinner redeemed – by explicit miracle, just as Savva Grudtsyn is redeemed through a miraculous vision of the Theotokos. In Gogol's story miracle and the Theotokos are replaced by Oksana, and the devil's gift is abrogated by true love (albeit set in a context of firm piety).

The loss of true demons is part of the same shift in aesthetic – reflecting an equivalent shift in the assumed context of belief – as the loss of true miracle. Crossing from Gogol into realism, for example, where cause and effect are supposed to be plausible by different criteria, the Orthodox devil is forced into greater contortions of self-concealment if he is to avoid becoming merely incongruous.[72] If external forces alone (whether *deus ex machina* or *Theotokos ex eikonos*) are unacceptable as narrative resolution, then an external force such as the *diabolus ex machina* is by itself unacceptable as the problem. Demons and miracles may still operate by allusion or implication, leaving indeterminate the question of whether or not they actually exist. Both demons and miracles are condemned to immanence or, at best, to ambiguity. At one end of the scale, the Orthodox devil provides no more than a store of suggestive imagery. A recent study of "hagiographical prototypes in *Anna Karenina*" devotes considerable space to the "diabolical" as a motif, claiming that "in *Anna Karenina* the 'devil' plays a role similar to that of his hagiographical predecessors." The manifestations of this role, apparently, are in images of black hair, scarlet clothes, whirlwinds of passion, Anna's flashing eyes, and the enigmatic smile playing about her face.[73] I doubt that the "hagiographical predecessor" would acknowledge any similarity of role whatsoever. The Orthodox devil is not confined to the role of a mere toy in the intertextualist's nursery.

At the other end of the scale, Dostoevsky chose to confront and test the literary dilemma rather than to submerge it. On the intellectual level, both Stavrogin's dialogue with Tikhon and Ivan Karamazov's dialogue with the *chert* include musings on whether one can believe in the devil without believing in God (the correct answer being: yes, such belief is possible, but false, hence diabolical).[74] On the representational level Ivan's *chert* is in many respects a worthy and adequate performer of his conventional role. He turns up in the guise of a would-be friend. He debates with Ivan at just the right intellectual level, with plausible arguments best calculated to sow confusion in Ivan's mind. He is smug about his "method," which is to lead Ivan to fluctuate "between belief and unbelief"[75] – a zone of uncertainty quite familiar to many a tormented hagiographical protagonist. Victor Terras speaks of the "novelty" of Ivan Karamazov's devil, as residing in the fact that he is, in Ivan's words to Alesha, "simply a *chert*, and not Satan with scorched wings, in thunder and lightning." But this is no novelty, nor (as Terras states in an equally mistaken footnote)[76] does the Russian tradition of such demons stem from Gogol. As we have seen, the shabby, smarmy, insinuating demon has an ancient pedigree in Orthodox demonology, and petty demons in general are the narrative norm. In this respect too, therefore, Ivan Karamazov's *chert* remains perfectly conventional.

The major departure, again, is in the arrangement of narrative perspectives. In hagiography the sense of ambiguity is confined to the protagonist. Dostoevsky extends it outwards. Hagiographers often use dramatic irony: the participants may be confused or temporarily deceived, but the implied author and reader see with knowledge and clarity from the outside. There is no doubt about the truth, only about how it will be demonstrated and manifested to those in the story. For Dostoevsky's demon the change of cultural environment has literary consequences, and the structures of deception implicate the reader.[77] There is a recurrent pattern of adaptation here. In Herzen's version of the legend of Theodora, Theodora's true identity (as a woman) is for most of the story concealed not merely from the other monks but also from the reader,[78] whereas in the traditional story a knowledge of Theodora's disguise is crucial to the reader's apprehension of her sanctity in the process of reading. Over a century later Remizov makes exactly the same type of adjustment in reworking the tale of Savva Grudtsyn: the identity of Savva's "friend" is concealed from the reader as well as from Savva.[79] Dostoevsky pushes ambivalence further, but the contrast with hagiographical perspectives is equivalent. Is Ivan Karamazov's devil a creation of Ivan's own intellect, or is Ivan's intellect (and perhaps sophisticated intellect in general) an implement of the devil? Ivan hurls a glass of tea at his visitor, who mocks him for imitating Luther's action with the inkwell. Ivan wakes up ("It's not a dream! No, I swear, this wasn't a dream")[80] and in his subsequent conversation with Alesha he sounds equally convinced. But his glass is undisturbed on the table, whereas Luther's inkstain remains on the wall to this day.

So, should medieval demonological narrative be characterized by its quaint simplicity, in contrast with post-medieval sophistication and complexity? Surely for the hagiographer all is straightforward: good is good, evil is evil, strive for one, fight the other, God is on your side and the devil is your enemy? This would be a travesty. Medieval demonologists were very well aware of ambivalence. Ambivalence was absolutely crucial to Orthodox demonological narrative: not, perhaps, in the status of the text as a whole, but in the deeply troubling hermeneutic dilemmas faced by the protagonists. Their problem was not whether demons existed, but how and where they could (or worse, could not) be recognized. And here, if we were in speculative mood, we might find greater affinities between the medieval and the modern. Devils deceive. Because they deceive, moral perception is fragile and uncertain. We can never fully trust anything that we see or think. There is always a potential gap between the outer and the inner, between appearance and essence. Evil can appear to be good, good can appear to be evil, and the consequences of error can be catastrophic.

Evil's propensity to disguise itself as good needs no special demon-stration. We recall the demons who appeared as "friends," as fellow-monks, as "bright angels," as Christ himself. They can urge such innocent, virtuous things: like diligent study,[81] or prudence with the monastery's belongings. Even a revered icon can turn out to be the work of the devil.[82] The greater the apparent virtue, the greater the hidden danger. For every tale of great feats of asceticism, there are tales of deluded asceticism, of conspicuous virtue which is no more than pride inflated by the devil. At the paradoxical extreme, even fighting the devil can be diabolical. In the tenth-century Byzantine *Life of Saint Nikon*, the saint at first declines to help a possessed woman, on account of his modesty (i.e. to avoid *philotimon*, the seek-ing after glory).[83] As late as the nineteenth century an Old Believer manuscript handbook for the exorcist consists mainly of long and detailed invocations to those who can help drive out Satan: the right sequences of prayers, the right lists of heavenly intercessors. But before all this, prominent and urgent, comes a section on the state of mind and soul of the exorcist himself: "First and above all [the exor-cist] must guard himself against pride and vainglory," he must remember at all times that devils are cast out not by him but by God, he must take no money for his labours, and he must truly and firmly believe all the tenets of the Orthodox faith.[84] One of the very earliest surviving dated manuscripts from Rus, the *Miscellany* (*Izbornik*) of 1076, includes a series of questions and answers on the actions of the devil. Among the hardy perennials (such as whether the devil is the cause of all sin, or why God permits the death of innocents and the prosperity of the wicked, or whether misfortunes should be attributed to God's wrath or to Satan's envy) we find a question which was highly topical in the Russian context: "how can some magicians drive out demons?" The answer is that they do not: "it is perfectly clear that it is not the magician who drives out the demon, but that the demon who lives in the possessed man leaves of his own accord in order to delude the man, so that instead of the man turning to God, the demon stimulates him to turn to the magicians."[85] A succinct enough riposte to the argument that alternative therapies appear to be effective; but mainly a reminder that the best of works may be the worst of works, that action and substance may be polar opposites.

Just as the seeming saint can be doing the work of the devil, so, more bafflingly, the seeming devil can be a saint. If virtue can be vice once it is made known, then some of the most virtuous virtues are so well hidden that you would never recognize them as such. A very simple version of this problem of recognition can be found at the start of the late-fifteenth-century *Tale of the Life of Mikhail Klopskii* (*Povest' o zhitii Mikhaila Klopskogo*). The abbot of a monastery goes to investigate a report that there is a stranger sitting in one of the cells, copying out the Scriptures. From the entrance to the cell he calls out "Who are you? Are you a man, or a demon (bes)? What is your name?" The stranger responds facetiously by merely shouting back the same question: "Who are you? Are you a man, or a demon? What is your name?" Again the abbot asks, and again the stranger replies with a facetious repetition of the question. And the same a third time. Eventually the abbot almost literally smoked him out: he ordered the cell to be fumigated with incense, whereupon the stranger made the sign of the Cross – sure proof that he could not be a demon.[86]

The stranger, Mikhail, is here behaving in the style of that odd category of holy men and women whose speciality is to be conspicuously unpleasant, even disgusting, an affront to decent behaviour. These are the *iurodivye*, the holy fools, or fools for Christ's sake. The tradition of *iurodivye* (the Greek *saloi*) is often assumed to be peculiarly Russian, although in fact it goes back to the Early Christian era and flourishes in Byzantium. Authentic *iurodivye* are not sweet simpletons. They offend, whether verbally, physically, or ethically. Nor is it enough merely to mimic the conventional and recognizable behaviour of the type. The offence must be real, the *iurodivyi* must truly be despised and rejected, or else he too becomes susceptible to the pride of display. The paradox of the *iurodivyi*, stressed from the very earliest Lives, is that to be recognized is, in a sense, to fail. When this category of holy man became popular in Russia, when certain kinds of offensive behaviour were accepted by tradition as being *potentially* valid signs of sanctity, there were continual uncertainties as to whether any particular foul-mouthed, foul-smelling vagrant was a true "fool for Christ's sake" or just a charlatan, or indeed as demonic as the appearance (the devil pretending to be good pretending to be evil).[87]

In principle, then, good and evil are clear and distinct; but in practice, in experience, anything may be the opposite of what it seems, and life is a continual anxiety of ambivalent surfaces. Thus in medieval writing, as in modern, demons (and Grace) can be immanent. One does not *have* to see the nasty little creatures prancing about. To this extent traditional demonological narratives can share with their modern counterparts an equivalent unease about problems of moral perception, about a reality beyond the visible, about the sheer inconsistency of the relationship between essence and appearance. We are not a very long way from Dostoevsky or Gogol. In these sorts of areas, rather than in specific narrative motifs, intertextual dialogue can be at its most productive. But it is not enough. One final speculative paradox. The dialogue is productive because it is doomed to irresolution. Orthodox demons can be deceptively immanent, but they are still real. And in their reality they, alongside the operations of Divine Grace, are part of the structures of cause and effect. And as such they provide for the possibility of fundamental inner change: unexpected, unpredictable, perhaps inexplicable. They make paradox itself normal: authentic paradox, in Greek *to paradoxon*, that which runs contrary to human reasoning or expectation. The possibility of possession, exorcism, and miracle is integral to what one might call the "poetics of transfiguration" in medieval literature. The poetics of transfiguration is integral to the main purpose of medieval demonological narrative, which is redemptive: to help bring mankind to salvation through tangible, demonstrable example.

Many post-medieval Russian writers shared, inherited, or reinvented a sense of an ideally redemptive function for their works, but they could no longer accept unmodified the poetics of transfiguration through which traditional Orthodox narrative had fulfilled that function. This dilemma was itself an immensely potent source of creative tension. A strong recurrent and characteristic quality of Russian literature, at least since Gogol, is a sense of yearning for a plausible, persuasive, new poetics of transfiguration adequate to the age. When Gogol's demons became serious, lurking beneath the surface rather than scampering around amusingly for all to see, then their author found to his anguish that he lacked the artistic means for persuasive exorcism. In Chernyshevsky's heavily hagiographical novel *What is to be Done?* (*Chto delat'?*)[88] Rakhmetov's asceticism is entirely practical, not metaphysical, and demons are simply abolished: for the archetypal seminarist, to taste the fruit of the tree of knowledge was the solution, not the problem, and the tree was of the knowledge of good. Chernyshevsky professed a breezy contentment that in his presentation of potentially transformed mankind he had to dislodge current notions of aesthetic coherence, but it is not surprising that in Dostoevsky's riposte (in *The Devils* [*Besy*]) the deficiency was recast in Orthodox terms: that the means of exorcizing evil was itself diabolical. Dostoevsky perhaps came closest to re-integrating the Orthodox devil into a new fabric of narrative, albeit with tantalizingly ambivalent status.[89] In his pursuit of a new redemptive poetics of transfiguration he incorporated the impasse of the devil's necessity and impossibility, and he also retrieved illogicality ("the unexpected") as a component of causation. Tolstoi most notoriously rejected his own realism as corrupt and corrupting, and abandoned it in search of an avowedly redemptive form. Yet Tolstoi, like Chernyshevsky, also explicitly rejected the received devices of transfiguration. In affirming his devotion to hagiography (because it revealed the meaning of life), he added the significant proviso: "except for the miracles; I regard them as stories used to express a thought."[90] So the problem remained. Reading Tolstoi's later stories, despite the power of ethical example, it is hard to avoid a sense that, unless one happens to have the good fortune to be a child or a peasant, one might be better off as a camel contemplating the eye of a needle.

It is tempting to conclude, therefore, that the strongest literary legacy of Orthodox demonology was not in its presence but precisely in the awareness of the literary consequences of its loss. The significance of the Orthodox devil becomes most keenly felt not in his rare personal appearances but in the gap which is created by his absence. Fished out of their own literary and cultural milieu, Orthodox demons became stranded in the wrong aesthetic. As Remizov pointed out (in the epigraph to the present survey) the demons were doubtless delighted at the moral, causational, and literary dilemmas posed by their own displacement. One solution, or quest for a solution, was to seek new aesthetics; another was to invent or borrow new demons, those diverse surrogates and impostors whose mask is demon*ism*.

Notes

1. A. Remizov, *Besnovatye* (Paris: Opleshnik, 1951), 9. All translations are mine throughout this paper, unless otherwise stated.
2. *Velikoe zertsalo*, chap.215. Text in O.A. Derzhavina, *Velikoe zertsalo i ego sud'ba na russkoi pochve* (Moscow: Institut mirovoi literatury Akademii nauk SSSR, 1965), 384–85.
3. The concluding phrases of "Nevskii Prospekt": N.V. Gogol', *Polnoe sobranie sochinenii*, ed. N.L. Meshcheriakov and others, 14 vols. (Moscow and Leningrad: Izdatel'stvo Akademii nauk SSSR, 1937–52) 3:46.
4. On the history of the text and its editions see Derzhavina, *Velikoe zertsalo*, 15–57.
5. "Nikto ne obnimet neob"iatnogo." See Prutkov's "Mysli i aforizmy," nos. 3, 44, 67, 104, 160: *Sochineniia Koz'my Prutkova*, ed. D.A. Zhukov (Moscow: Sovetskaia Rossiia, 1981), 79, 84, 86, 90, 96.
6. An aspect of the cultural gap is well symbolized in the semantic transformation of the word *prelest'*. Though now it denotes "charm" in a positive sense, in no pre-Petrine text can *prelest'* be a positive or even a neutral word. It is deception, sinful temptation, error, lies, transgression, sin itself, the most effective weapon in the devil's own arsenal; see *Slovar' russkogo iazyka XI-XVII vv.*, ed. S.G. Barkhudarov and others (Moscow: Nauka, 1975–), 18:259–60. Truth may be beautiful, beauty could even be powerful evidence of truth (as in the *Primary Chronicle*'s tale of the Conversion of the Rus to Christianity); but it was inconceivable that exterior attractiveness, mere delight for the senses, should be a self-sufficient, self-justifying cultural value.
7. Note the plural in the title of the most thorough recent investigation: R.P.H. Greenfield, *Traditions of Belief in Late Byzantine Demonology* (Amsterdam: Adolf M. Hakkert, 1988). In his analysis Greenfield treats "the beliefs of the standard Orthodox tradition" (3–148) separately from "alternative traditions" (153–302). Greenfield eventually posits an "overall tradition" in which, nevertheless, "the Byzantines in general seem to have shown little concern or felt little need to establish absolute consistency and to dispose of all anomalies" (312).

8. For a brief account of the emergence of Christian demonology see the first three chapters of Peter Stanford, *The Devil: A Biography* (London: Heinemann, 1996); also Alice K. Turner, *The History of Hell* (New York, San Diego, and London: Harcourt Brace, 1993), 1–88; in more detail the trilogy by Jeffrey Burton Russell, *The Devil: Perceptions of Evil from Antiquity to Primitive Christianity; Satan: The Early Christian Tradition;* and *Lucifer: The Devil in the Middle Ages* (Ithaca, N.Y.: Cornell University Press, 1977, 1981, 1984, respectively).

9. Job 1:6–12. Note that the Greek of the Septuagint (from which the Bible was translated into Slavonic) has *diabolos* rather than *Satanas.* Petty demons (Greek *daimonia*, Slavonic *besy*) are also conspicuous in their rarity: see Deut. 32:17; Ps. 105:37 (Septuagint numeration).

10. See e.g. Nikolai Tikhonravov, ed., *Pamiatniki otrechennoi russkoi literatury,* 2 vols. (St. Petersburg: Tipografiia Tovarishchestva "Obshchestvennaia Pol'za," 1863); É. Turdeanu, *Apocryphes slaves et roumains de l'Ancien Testament* (Leiden: E.J. Brill, 1981), 1–144.

11. For the few enigmatic fragments see D. Obolensky, *The Bogomils. A Study in Balkan Neo-Manichaeism* (Cambridge, 1948; reprint, Twickenham: Anthony C. Hall, 1972), 277–83.

12. For Byzantine exposition see the excursus in the chronicle of George the Monk: *Georgii monachi chronicon,* ed. C. de Boor, 2 vols. (Leipzig: Teubner, 1904), 1:58–92; a Slavonic translation of this chronicle was used in Rus by the compilers of more than one component of the *Primary Chronicle.* Note that the "created" need not be only an inanimate object: on the "Euhemerist" argument, which asserts that the gods of antiquity were in fact men, see D. Čiževskij, "Euhemerismus in den altslavischen Literaturen," in *The Religious World of Russian Culture,* ed. A.W. Blane (The Hague: Mouton, 1975), 23–42.

13. See also, in the wider medieval context, Richard Kieckhefer, *Magic in the Middle Ages* (Cambridge: Cambridge University Press, 1989), 34–41.

14. On mistaking the created for the Creator see e.g. the anti-pagan tracts in E.V. Anichkov, *Iazychestvo i drevniaia Rus'* (St. Petersburg, 1914), 26–80; on paganism as demon-worship see e.g. *Povest' vremennykh let,* ed. D.S. Likhachev and V.P. Adrianova-Peretts, 2 vols. (Moscow and Leningrad: Akademiia nauk SSSR, 1950), 1:80 (on the Kievans' treatment of the idol of Perun), 119 (on beliefs among the Chud) etc; or Metropolitan Ilarion's summary of the significance of Conversion: A.M. Moldovan, ed., *"Slovo o zakone i blagodati" Ilariona* (Kiev: Naukova dumka, 1984), 89; Simon Franklin, trans., *Sermons and Rhetoric of Kievan Rus* (Cambridge, Mass.: Harvard University Press, 1991), 15.

15. Russell, *Lucifer,* 62–91; on Byzantine demons contemporary with the newly-converted Rus see P. Ioannou, "Les croyances démonologiques au XIe siècle à Byzance," *Actes du VIe Congrès International d'Etudes Byzantines. Paris, 1948,* vol.1 (Paris: École des Hautes Études, 1950), 245–60; also Greenfield, *Traditions of Belief,* despite the emphasis on a somewhat later period.

16. See C. Mango, "Diabolus byzantinus," *Dumbarton Oaks Papers* 46 (1992):220–21; Greenfield, *Traditions of Belief,* 312–13, points to a proliferation of hierarchies in the "alternative traditions," but notes that they always involve a plurality of rule.

17. *Lukavyi* and *nepriiazn'* translate *ho poneros* – "the evil one," hence in the Lord's Prayer *Izbavi nas ot lukavago* – "Deliver us from the Evil One."

18. See I.B. Serebrianaia, "K istorii slova *chert* v russkom iazyke," *Slavianovedenie* 1998, no.3:65–73.

19. See e.g. R.M. Tseitlin and others, eds., *Staroslavianskii slovar' (po rukopisiam X–XI vekov)* (Moscow: Russkii iazyk, 1994), 107, 186, 188, 619. Derivatives from *bes* also translate the Greek *mania* and related forms.

20. See Harry E. Gaylord, "How Satanael Lost his 'el'," *Journal of Jewish Studies* 33 (1982):303–9.

21. Likhachev and Adrianova-Perretts, eds., *Povest' vremennykh let*, 1:62–64, 67.

22. Ibid., 1:80, 83.

23. Cf. Greenfield, *Traditions of Belief*, 182–90, on Byzantine Orthodox refutations of the idea that the female demons of the "alternative tradition" (i.e. folkloric demons) were authentic, rather than merely assuming female form. See also in this volume Faith Wigzell, "The Russian Folk Devil and His Literary Reflections."

24. Likhachev and Adrianova-Peretts, eds., *Povest' vremennykh let*, 1:119, in the context of an extensive set of demonological anecdotes in the entry for 1071.

25. On Vladimir's response to a portable depiction of the Last Judgement see ibid., 1:74; on Gogol's recollections of his own childhood response to his mother's accounts of the Last Judgement see Gogol', *Polnoe sobranie sochinenii*, 10:282; cf. the comments by F.C. Driessen, *Gogol as a Short-Story Writer. A Study of his Techniques of Composition*, trans. I.F. Finlay (The Hague: Mouton, 1965), 23.

26. From the earliest period only fragments remain: see V.N. Lazarev, *Old Russian Murals and Mosaics* (London: Phaidon, 1966).

27. On the history of this iconography see David M. Goldfrank, "Who Put the Snake on the Icon and the Tollbooths on the Snake? – A Problem of Last Judgement Iconography," *Harvard Ukrainian Studies* 19 (1995):180–99 and plates 6–12; also the detailed illustrations of one version in A.S. Kostsova, *Drevnerusskaia zhivopis' v sobranii Ermitazha* (St. Petersburg: Iskusstvo, 1992), 229–38 (plates), 391–95 (description).

28. On the physical variety of later demons (mainly with reference to their folkloric appearances) see N.I. Tolstoi, "Iz zametok po slavianskoi demonologii. 2. Kakov oblik d'iavol'skii?," in *Narodnaia graviura i fol'klor v Rossii XVII–XIX vv.*, ed. I.E. Danilova (Moscow: Sovetskii khudozhnik, 1975), 288–319.

29. Briefly on Western depiction see Russell, *Lucifer*, 129–33, 208–12.

30. On the *Life of Basil the New* and its reception among the Rus see S.G. Vilinskii, *Zhitie sv. Vasiliia Novogo v russkoi literature*, vol. 2 (Odessa: Imperatorskii Novorossiiskii universitet, 1913); G. Fedotov, *The Russian Religious Mind. I: Kievan Christianity from the 10th to the 13th Centuries* (Cambridge, Mass., 1946; reprint, Belmont, Mass.: Nordland, 1975), 169–75.

31. Text in *Pamiatniki literatury Drevnei Rusi. XII vek* (Moscow: Khudozhestvennaia literatura, 1980), 166–82 (hereafter volumes in this series will be abbreviated as *PLDR*); cf. F.M. Dostoevskii, *Polnoe sobranie sochinenii v tridtsati tomakh*, ed. V.G. Bazanov and others, 30 vols. (Leningrad: Nauka, 1972–90), 19:225; also V.E. Vetlovskaia, "Dostoevskii i poeticheskii mir drevnei Rusi (Literaturnye i fol'klornye istochniki 'Brat'ev Karamazovykh')," *Trudy Otdela drevnerusskoi literatury* 28 (1974):296–307. Note that the Eastern Church rejected the doctrine of Purgatory.

32. *Murin*, rendering the Greek *Aithiops*: e.g. in the anecdote of Saint Niphon, who encountered a "decrepit *murin*, who was the senior demon," as told in the twelfth-century manuscript known as the *Vygoleksinskii sbornik*, ed. S.I. Kotkov (Moscow: Nauka, 1977), 107.

33. Likhachev and Adrianova-Peretts, eds., *Povest' vremennykh let*, 1:126; *PLDR. XIV-seredina XV veka* (1981), 308.

34. See e.g. the tales of Isaakii, and of Feodor and Vasilii, in the *Paterik* of the Caves monastery: *PLDR. XII vek*, 572–76 (demon as fellow-monk), 608 (demons as angels and as Christ); M. Heppell, trans., *The "Paterik" of the Kievan Caves Monastery* (Cambridge, Mass.: Harvard University Press, 1989), 182–85, 206; also T.F. Volkova, "Khudozhestvennaia struktura i funktsii obraza besa v Kievo-pecherskom paterike," *Trudy Otdela drevnerusskoi literatury* 33 (1979):228–37, stressing the multiplicity of personae.

35. On demons as the lesser evil see Likhachev and Adrianova-Peretts, eds., *Povest' vremennykh let*, 1:92: "an evil man is worse than a demon; for demons fear God, but an evil man neither fears God nor feels shame before men" (apropos of Sviatopolk "the Cursed").

36. The more so since indigenous formal "academic" theology barely existed at all in medieval Rus, except insofar as – like demonology – it might be reckoned immanent in other genres: see, for example, the generic inclusivity of the "theological" in the standard textbook on the early period: Gerhard Podskalsky, *Christentum und theologische Literatur in der Kiever Rus' (988–1237)* (Munich: Beck, 1982).

37. The fullest thematic survey of demonological descriptions in medieval East Slav writings remains the slim volume by F. Riazanovskii, *Demonologiia v drevne-russkoi literature* (Moscow, 1915; reprint, Leipzig: Zentralantiquariat der DDR, 1974).

38. Ivan Karamazov's devil (chert) translates the point nicely for his own audience: "kakoi zhe zhurnal, esli net 'otdeleniia kritiki'? Bez kritiki budet odna 'osanna.' No dlia zhizni malo odnoi 'osanny,' nado, chtob 'osanna'-to eta perekhodila cherez gornilo somnenii, nu i tak dalee, v etom rode." Dostoevskii, *Polnoe sobranie sochinenii*, 15:77.

39. As the indignant demons expostulate to Saint Antony in the desert: "Get away from what is ours! What do you have to do with the desert?" See Athanasios, *The Life of Antony*, trans. Robert C. Gregg (London: SPCK, 1980), 41.

40. In a version of the *Life* of Vasilii Blazhennyi: I.I. Kuznetsov, *Sviatye blazhennye Vasilii i Ioann, Khrista radi moskovskie chudotvortsy*, Zapiski Moskovskogo arkheologicheskogo instituta, no. 8 (Moscow: Moskovskii arkheologicheskii institut, 1910), 72; see S.A. Ivanov, *Vizantiiskoe iurodstvo* (Moscow: Mezhdunarodnye otnosheniia, 1994), 145.

41. In *Byloe i dumy*; noted by Joseph Frank, *Dostoevsky. The Seeds of Revolt, 1821–1849* (Princeton: Princeton University Press, 1977), 42.

42. See Margaret Ziolkowski, *Hagiography and Modern Russian Literature* (Princeton: Princeton University Press, 1988), 16–32.

43. L.N. Tolstoi, *Sobranie sochinenii v dvadtsati dvukh tomakh*, ed. M.B. Khrapchenko and others, 22 vols. (Moscow: Khudozhestvennaia literatura, 1978–85), 16:158; also the notes on the library, ibid., 434–35.

44. "Legenda" (1836), in A.I. Gertsen, *Sobranie sochinenii v tridtsati tomakh* (Moscow: Akademiia nauk SSSR, 1954–66), 1:81–106; for an analysis see Ziolkowski, *Hagiography*, 84–89.

45. Besides Ziolkowski, *Hagiography*, see e.g. A. Opul'skii, *Zhitiia sviatykh v tvorchestve russkikh pisatelei XIX veka* (East Lansing, Mich.: Russian Language Journal, 1986); Marcia A. Morris, *Saints and Revolutionaries. The Ascetic Hero in Russian Literature* (Albany: State University of New York Press, 1993). The spread of writers is broad, though there are blankish spots: Pushkin's perception of native narrative tradition probably owes at least as much to Karamzin – plus his much-revered nanny Arina Rodionovna – as to authentic written sources.

46. Athanasios, *Life of Antony*, esp. 33–39.

47. Likhachev and Adrianova-Peretts, eds., *Povest' vremennykh let*, 1:126; cf. *PLDR. XII vek*, 470; Heppell, trans., *The "Paterik" of the Kievan Caves Monastery*, 109.

48. In Nestor's *Zhitie Feodosiia Pecherskogo*, *PLDR. XI-nachalo XII veka* (1978), 338, 368–70; Paul Hollingsworth, trans., *The Hagiography of Kievan Rus'* (Cambridge, Mass.: Harvard University Press, 1992), 56, 78; for an attempt to systematize the activities of demons in the Caves *Paterik* see Volkova, "Khudozhestvennaia struktura i funktsii obraza besa," 228–37.

49. *PLDR. XIII vek* (1981), 78, 80; Hollingsworth, trans., *Hagiography*, 145; cf. similar trials, also self-consciously allusive, in the *Life of Feodosii of the Caves*: *PLDR. XI-nachalo XII veka*, 334–36; Hollingsworth, trans., *Hagiography*, 55–56.

50. See esp. James M. Holquist, "The Devil in Mufti: the *Märchenwelt* in Gogol's Early Stories," *Publications of the Modern Language Association of America*, 1967, no. 5:352–62.

51. See in this volume Julian Graffy, "The Devil is in the Detail: Demonic Features of Gogol's Petersburg."

52. Gogol', *Polnoe sobranie sochinenii*, 1:203, 225.

53. Ibid., 223–25.

54. J.-P. Migne, *Patrologia graeca. Cursus completus*, 73:cols.306–9; in Slavonic both in the *Velikie chet'i minei* and in the *Prolog* for 2 January; note, however, that the progenitor of the "Faustian" variant – the sixth-century legend of Theophilos of Cilicia – was also known in the Eastern tradition.

55. *PLDR. XVII vek. Kniga pervaia* (1988), 44. For a detailed study of the literary sources of the *Tale* see O.D. Zhuravel', *Siuzhet o dogovore cheloveka s d'iavolom v drevnerusskoi literature* (Novosibirsk: Sibirskii khronograf, 1996) (see p. 58 for an analysis of the various reasons for seeking the devil's help). Note that Savva, like the man in the story from the *Velikoe zertsalo*, is also taken on a tour of the devil's city (*PLDR. XVII vek. Kniga pervaia*, 45–46); cf. another such visit, facilitated by the Constantinopolitan magician Mesitas, in the *Prolog* for 2 December, in O.A. Derzhavina, *Drevniaia Rus' v russkoi literature XIX veka (Siuzhety i obrazy drevnerusskoi literatury v tvorchestve pisatelei XIX veka). Prolog. Izbrannye teksty* (Moscow: Institut mirovoi literatury Akademii nauk SSSR, 1990), 250–51.

56. Tikhonravov, *Pamiatniki otrechennoi russkoi literatury*, 1:4 (from a seventeenth-century *sbornik*), 12 (from a sixteenth-century manuscript of the *Izmaragd*).

57. Gogol', *Polnoe sobranie sochinenii*, 1:225; cited from Nikolai Gogol, *"Village Evenings Near Dikanka" and "Mirgorod,"* trans. Christopher English (Oxford: Oxford University Press, 1994), 121.

58. Tikhonravov, *Pamiatniki otrechennoi russkoi literatury*, 1:4, 12.

59. *PLDR. XVII vek. Kniga pervaia*, 44: "Savva eshche i sovershenno ne umeiashe pisati, i eliko bes skazyve he emu, Savva zhe tako i pisashe, ne slagaia" (Savva was not yet able to write properly, so instead of composing he wrote down whatever the demon told him to write).

60. Written pacts are the devil's implements, whereas a true pledge needs no such device. Savva Grudtsyn's eventual release comes through an *un*written pact with the Theotokos, in which he undertakes to become a monk: *PLDR. XVII vek. Kniga pervaia*, 53.

61. This is by no means an exclusively Russian phenomenon, and mockery of the devil in such a context is a popular weapon in the Western tradition as well: Russell, *Lucifer*, 82, comments that "the typical pact story contains farcical elements."

62. The theme is underlined: "Thus, instead of corrupting, tempting and fooling others, the enemy of mankind was himself made a fool of" (Gogol', *Polnoe sobranie sochinenii*, 1:241; cited from Gogol, *"Village Evenings near Dikanka,"* trans. Christopher English, 139). This is a widespread topos; cf. the (almost certainly fortuitous) coincidence of expression with the summary in Athanasios's *Life of Antony*, above, n.46.

63. Gogol accentuated this motif while working on the story. In the rough draft, Vakula had called the devil "dog's spawn" (sobach'e otrod'e) rather than "cursed German" (nemets prokliatyi) (Gogol', *Polnoe sobranie sochinenii*, 1:433). Similarly, although in all versions the devil is introduced at the beginning of the story as looking like a German (draft – "speredi sovsem kak budto nemets"; final version – "speredi sovershennyi nemets"), the early draft lacked Gogol's additional footnote explaining that *nemets* denotes not specifically a German but "anyone from foreign parts" (ibid., 1:202, 406; Gogol, *"Village Evenings Near Dikanka,"* trans. Christopher English, 98). *Nemets prokliatyi* might therefore be rendered as "damned foreigner."

64. Full early text ed. L.A. Dmitriev in *PLDR. XIV-seredina XV veka*, 454–62; *Prolog* version in Derzhavina, *Drevniaia Rus' v russkoi literature XIX veka*, 196–97; textual history, noting also the link to Gogol's story, in L.A. Dmitriev, *Zhitiinye povesti russkogo severa kak pamiatniki literatury XIII-XVII vv.* (Leningrad: Nauka, 1973), 152–60. On Pushkin's use of motifs from the same source in the poem "Monakh," his earliest surviving work (1813), see S.A. Fomichev, "Poema Pushkina 'Monakh' i Povest' o puteshestvii Ioanna Novgorodskogo na bese," in *Novgorod v kul'ture drevnei Rusi* (Novgorod: Novgorodskii gosudarstvennyi universitet, 1995), 141–49.

65. See the version cited in the convenient thematic anthology by Linda J. Ivanits, *Russian Folk Belief* (Armonk, N.Y., and London: M.E. Sharpe, 1989), 156; also ibid., 164–66 for a tale associating a blacksmith, the devil, and icons.

66. Another example of the easy fusion between the Orthodox and the folkloric. One might assume here the presence of a Slav folkloric water-spirit, but the devil's association with water is also part of the Byzantine Christian tradition: e.g. the tenth-century *Life of Saint Nikon*, where a woman is possessed by a demon who enters her from a bucket of dirty water drawn from a well; see Mango, "Diabolus byzantinus," 220; cf. Ivanits, *Russian Folk Belief*, 157.

67. In the early version of the *Life*, Ioann tells of his trip as if it had happened to an acquaintance rather than to himself (*PLDR. XIV-seredina XV veka*, 456); the *Prolog* summary ignores this nicety (Derzhavina, *Drevniaia Rus'*, 196).

68. Cf. the almost identical sequence which forms the *Povest' o riazanskom episkope Vasilii*, written in the mid-sixteenth century by Ermolai-Erazm. Here the citizens of Murom (where Vasilii holds office initially) are shocked by sightings of dubious women in the bishop's house and aim to cast Vasilii adrift in a small boat on the Oka; but Vasilii spreads his robe on the waters and floats upstream to Riazan: *PLDR. Konets XV-pervaia polovina XVI veka* (1984), 648–50.

69. The shared imagery of women's footwear may be more than mere coincidence. See Dmitriev, *Zhitiinye povesti*, 154–56, on the cluster of linked demonological texts with similar emphasis on women's footwear: the tales of Ioann of Novgorod, Vasilii of Riazan, and Avraamii of Rostov.

70. Holquist, "The Devil in Mufti," 356.

71. For the range of conventionally adduced sources and prototypes see Gogol', *Polnoe sobranie sochinenii*, 1:539–42.

72. The Orthodox devil is of course not alone in facing this dilemma. Hannes Vatter, *The Devil in English Literature* (Bern: Francke Verlag, 1978), 179, baldly asserts, with reference to England, that "Romanticism was followed by a period of realism which, on the whole, considered the introduction of supernatural agents bad taste in literature."

73. A.G. Grodetskaia, "Agiograficheskie proobrazy v 'Anne Kareninoi' (Zhitiia bludnits i liubodeits i siuzhetnaia liniia geroini romana)," *Trudy Otdela drevnerusskoi literatury* 48 (1993):433–45, esp. 440–41.

74. Dostoevskii, *Polnoe sobranie sochinenii*, 11:9–10; 15:71–72.

75. Ibid., 15:80.

76. Victor Terras, *A Karamazov Companion. Commentary on the Genesis, Language, and Style of Dostoevsky's Novel* (Madison: University of Wisconsin Press 1981), 53.

77. George A. Panichas, *The Burden of Vision. Dostoevsky's Spiritual Art* (Chicago: Gateway Editions, 1985), 89–112, sweeps aside any view other than than that Stavrogin *is* the devil. We may or may not agree. And that – the very existence of a range of plausible, intelligent critical responses apparently legitimized by the text – is the point, which Panichas simply ignores. In hagiography, on such a fundamental issue of identity, the view from outside is unclouded, unequivocal, and any ambivalence (or even polyphony) is confined within the text.

78. Ziolkowski, *Hagiography*, 83–89: Ziolkowski comments that "in Herzen's hands, the legend of Saint Theodora becomes historical fiction rather than religious literature."

79. A.M. Gracheva, "Povest' A.M. Remizova 'Savva Grudtsyn' i ee drevnerusskii prototip," *Trudy Otdela drevnerusskoi literatury* 33 (1979):394; also Gracheva, "Drevnerusskie povesti v pereskazakh A.M. Remizova," *Russkaia literatura*, 1988, no. 3:110–17.

80. Dostoevskii, *Polnoe sobranie sochinenii*, 15:85.

81. See Simon Franklin, "Book-learning and Bookmen in Kievan Rus': A Survey of an Idea," *Harvard Ukrainian Studies* 12–13 (1988–89):830–48.

82. See S.A. Ivanov, "'Adopisnye ikony' v kontekste pozdnesrednevekovoi russkoi kul'tury," in *Chudotvornaia ikona v Vizantii i Drevnei Rusi*, ed. A.M. Lidov (Moscow: Martis, 1996), 385–91.

83. Mango, "Diabolus byzantinus," 220.

84. The manuscript is currently located in Cambridge.

85. See *Izbornik 1076 g.*, ed. S.I. Kotkov (Moscow: Nauka, 1965), 535–36, also 504–5, 512–13, 747 (Greek text); English translation in William R. Veder, trans. and introd., *The Edificatory Prose of Kievan Rus'* (Cambridge, Mass.: Harvard University Press, 1994), 81. These responses, which migrate through several manuscript miscellanies in Greek and Slavonic, are attributed to the seventh-century author Anastasios of Sinai.

86. *PLDR. Vtoraia polovina XV veka* (1982), 334–36; note that this episode dominates the much-abbreviated version of the Life in the *Prolog* for 11 January: Derzhavina, *Drevniaia Rus'*, 266–67.

87. Much has been written about Russian *iurodstvo* in relative ignorance of its wider context. By far the best and most thorough analysis of the phenomenon from its pre-Christian precursors down to the verge of modernity is Ivanov, *Vizantiiskoe iurodstvo*.

88. See e.g. Julia Alissandratos, "Hagiographical Commonplaces and Medieval Prototypes in N.G. Chernyshevskii's *What is to be Done?*," *St Vladimir's Theological Quarterly* 26 (1982); Morris, *Saints and Revolutionaries*, 136–47; Ziolkowski, *Hagiography*, 192–95.

89. A "pure" Orthodox reading of Dostoevsky is of course possible, but it is not the only possibility; and the alternatives are generated in the poetics of the text, not only by the perversity of readers. See above, n.77; also in this volume the analysis by W.J. Leatherbarrow, "The Devils' Vaudeville: 'Decoding' the Demonic in Dostoevsky's *The Devils*."

90. See above, n.43. The list of authors who use hagiography while stripping out the miracles could be extended: see e.g. E.V. Tyryshkina, "'Sinaiskii paterik' v 'Kryl'iakh' M. Kuz'mina (Khristianskii tekst v nekhristianskom kontekste)," in *Evangel'skii tekst v russkoi literature XVIII-XX vekov*, ed. V.N. Zakharov (Petrozavodsk: Izdatel'stvo Petrozavodskogo universiteta, 1994), 300–307

Chapter 2

The Russian Folk Devil and His Literary Reflections

Faith Wigzell

The topic of the devil or devils in Russian folklore is a broad or, perhaps better, a multifarious subject. This essay cannot encompass its diabolical variety. Furthermore, the image of the devil varies according to the oral genre in which he appears; for example, the type of folk tale which focuses on humour and satire often presents devils as pranksters who can be outwitted, while in the Russian equivalent of the ghost story, the fabulate (bylichka), they are commonly terrifying. Over and above this, the interpretation of perceived supernatural occurrences may differ according to either social milieu or individual perception. For example, the folklore of strongly religious individuals is more affected by Christian demonology than that of other social groups. Where many ordinary peasants in pre-Revolutionary Russia perceived a supernatural encounter as a manifestation of the unclean force (nechistaia sila), the exceptionally devout, steeped in the Orthodox hagiography of which Simon Franklin writes, were more likely to interpret the same thing as the work of the devil.[1] If one adds to these problems considerable regional variation, evolutionary changes in folk belief in the course of the nineteenth century, as well as different ways of talking about the same thing according to the nature of the audience (educated or fellow peasant), then the difficulties in generalizing become apparent. Nonetheless, the features of a folkloric devil can be discerned when he is placed in the context of a folk mythology of the supernatural.

What follows is based on broad generalizations, but is presented with an eye on the elements that link and those that distinguish the folk devil from his counterpart in Orthodox tradition (separation of the two is impossible). These elements are a *sine qua non* for a consideration of the significance of folklore for Russian literary demonism. In this last case, connections are not obvious; the folk devil is part of a complex of beliefs surviving among the peasants who still lived in a pre-modern world, while literary demonism stems primarily from European Romanticism, a facet of an essentially different world to which the educated creators of Russian literature belonged. In some instances, notably Gogol's Dikanka stories and other works by writers of the 1820s and 1830s, Russian writers deliberately created a direct link between élite and popular culture by recourse to folk demonic images, but, in general, nineteenth- and twentieth-century literary demonism exists without evident reference to oral tradition. Appearances can be deceptive, however, since, by acting as cultural sub-text, folk belief may well have affected either the form demonism took in Russian literature or its vitality. Judging this possibility requires a discussion of the general features of the folk devil and the mythological context in which he functioned.

Just as the repertoire of forms and guises of the Christian devil are "a kind of colonization of paganisms by Christian discourse, and ultimately a blurring of boundaries between the Orthodox and the folkloric,"[2] so, when transplanted in Russian soil along with Christianity, the devil was perceived by the Slavs refracted through their own mind-set and beliefs. Since beliefs in supernatural spirits in Russian or East Slav cultures generally bear a good deal in common with the pagan beliefs of the Mediterranean area, the concept of the devil proved easy for the East Slavs to absorb. Conversely, because of that closeness, it was natural that aspects of their own beliefs would be incorporated into the image with resulting changes of emphasis. The influence of native Slav beliefs is felt mainly in the beliefs and tales existing in the lay community, where Church control was naturally weaker than in the monastic circles that produced ecclesiastical literature. The Russian folk devil is, therefore, as much a product of a fluctuating set of traditions as the ecclesiastical Orthodox figure, but with local emphases, which, given the many similarities, cannot be delineated precisely.

Belief in the devil coexisted with belief in mythological spirits, and confusion between the two is evident even in Russian Orthodox hagiography. Mostly, it is simply a shift of emphasis, towards, say, the playful disruptiveness typical of folk spirits, found in the examples cited by Simon Franklin from Nestor's eleventh-century *Life of Feodosii of the Caves* (*Zhitie Feodosiia Pecherskogo*, after 1078).[3] Much more rarely, a folk spirit may actually replace the devil, as, for example, in a miracle account found in the *vita* of a minor Northern saint: "The Miracle of the Venerable Nikodim of Kozheezero about a Certain Elder and Shepherd, How he was Saved from the Wood Demon" (Chudo prepodobnogo Nikodima Kozheezerskogo o nekoem startse pastyre, kak ego izbavi ot lesnogo demona, 1688). Here the wood spirit or *leshii* replaces the usual *bes* (devil) of hagiography.[4] It is notable, however, that in the post-Petrine period, the influence of folk spirits diminishes, and through the nineteenth-century the reverse process develops; oral tradition is increasingly affected by the written, with folk spirits being slowly "diabolized," such that the functions and activities of various mythic personages, in particular the water spirit (vodianoi), are increasingly ascribed to the Christian devil.[5] Even more clearly, diabolization applied to the source of supernatural power in folk mythology.[6] Despite the ongoing processes of contamination, the folk devil remained a figure with distinct features, even if these may also be discerned in some form or other in Orthodox or general Christian tradition.

The Russian folk devil (or devils) is thus part of a complex of beliefs in mythological spirits.[7] Almost all of the extensive material relating to these beliefs was collected from peasants, mostly in the nineteenth century, though some in recent years.[8] In pre-Petrine Russia the whole population shared the same world-view (clerics, monks, and a handful of lay folk apart), but as Westernization led to an increasing gulf between the modernizing élite classes and the peasants, so belief in a set of non-Christian supernatural figures playing a role in human fate largely retreated to culturally conservative groups, above all to the peasants, for whom they remained as meaningful as ever. Among the élite classes, spirits ceased to be viewed from the inside with conviction, this being reserved solely for the supernatural beliefs connected with Orthodoxy (assuming the given individual believed in God). For them as for their West European counterparts, beliefs in spirits came to be regarded as foolish superstition, local colour, decorative rustic charm, or evidence of a distinctive national identity, depending on period or personality. The folk devil, on the other hand, by virtue of his connections with official religion, leapt the divide with agility. On the one hand, he might be perceived as part of a colourful folk world, on the other he could, ironically, be said to enjoy the protection of the Church, given his institutionalized role as number one Christian foe. Such a position allowed him to play a somewhat larger role in Russian culture and literature of the nineteenth and early twentieth centuries than folk spirits.

This role was limited by the absence of any demonism in the world of Russian folk belief, just as there was none in Orthodox tradition.⁹ In accordance with the mind-set of all pre-modern European societies, causation of events tended to be transferred to outside agencies rather than being sought in the psyche of the individual.¹⁰ These outside agencies were outside in the sense of being external to either individual or community. Agencies, generally if not exclusively, meant supernatural powers, either external figures seen as absolutely real, or forces conjured by humans with occult powers (witches, sorcerers, and so on). These last, it should be noted, were not generally seen as demonically possessed or inspired, nor in league with the devil in the same way as their counterparts in Western Europe in the early modern period; rather they were thought to possess the ability to tap into the supernatural power, known as the *nechistaia sila* or *nechist'* (unclean force). However, the Church always saw the unclean force and popular mythology as essentially demonic. It then took until the eighteenth and, more particularly, the nineteenth century before diabolization began to affect peasant views of the activities of the unclean force.¹¹ Believed to be ever present, if by no means always visible, the force manifested itself in specific forms, which made themselves known at will or when summoned. In a life situation in which the average person felt he or she had little control over capricious nature, weather, disease or death, the desire to find external scapegoats (witches and such like), whether for blame or punishment, is a natural one. Even when a person was deemed to have been invaded by evil forces, these remained distinct entities that could be expelled by appropriate measures, such as ritual actions and the use of spells. More important still were prophylactic measures designed to ward off hostility or attack in the first place.

It seems appropriate at this point to summarize the features of mythological spirits, before focusing on those elements relevant to the understanding of the folk devil, and, subsequently, to literary treatments and possible influence on literary demonism in Russia. As already mentioned, the unclean force normally took specific form, but it was habitat that explained their form and function; as Nikita Tolstoi has argued: "characteristic of the most ancient and of more recent pre-Christian mythological beliefs among the Slavs is the sense that the whole of surrounding nature is peopled by spirits, distinguished less by function than by place of habitation."¹² It is commonly assumed that these consisted solely of the house spirit (domovoi), the forest spirit (leshii), the water sprite (rusalka), favoured by the Romantics, and the water demon (vodianoi). However, innumerable others were believed to inhabit both natural locations in field, forest, or water as well as the human environment. For example, not just the house, but also farm buildings had their resident spirits with special names, the *ovinnik* (spirit of the threshing barn), *koniush-*

nik (spirit of the stable), and so on.[13] Some of these were little distinguished from the *domovoi*. Apart from the commonest spirits, local beliefs distinguished many others (such as the *lemboi* of the Olonetsk region, a form of devil or *leshii* whose name is of Finnic origin).[14]

In appearance spirits were generally anthropomorphic, though they might possess some powers of metamorphosis; for example, the *leshii* could on occasion turn into his favourite animal, the wolf, and the *domovoi* into a cat or dog.[15] Human in appearance, in their way of life they also replicated modes of human behaviour; thus, they were believed to have wives and children, to indulge in marital quarrels, go to war and even to play cards for money.[16] Though they possessed their own habitats, ultimately as manifestations of the unclean force they were connected with the Other World (tot mir), located above, beyond, or below our own.[17] It has been argued that the term "unclean" is Christian usage superimposed on the Russian folk concept, and that Christianity introduced new divisions into forces of good and evil, separating the Other World into upper (heavenly) and nether regions while attaching moral value to each.[18] This hypothesis is lent more substance when we note the attitudes to and the roles played by the various unclean spirits.[19]

Peasants' attitudes to the unclean force was one of profound fear coupled with a recognition that respect offered protection. Only the most benign, the *domovoi*, who was essentially a spirit-protector connected with ancestors,[20] was not feared, but he certainly had to be respected. Respect could take various forms, including following the correct ritual behaviour when in the spirit's domain. This was particularly necessary when asking a favour. Favours, such as requests for a prediction about an individual's fate, were best solicited at certain times and places, when the unclean force roamed the earth. Cross-roads, thresholds, and bathhouses were among the most dangerous places, particularly at certain liminal times of day or year. These included midnight and, by extension, night up to the first cock-crow, full moon and also dark moonless nights, as well as midday. The danger presented by the unclean force was also worse on unlucky days, either Wednesday or Thursday depending on which was regarded as the middle of the week.[21] But by far the most perilous were major festivals, most notably Yuletide (Sviatki), perceived as the threshold between the death of one year and the birth of the next, when the unclean force roamed the earth and could be tapped by the brave for predictions about the future.

One of the most striking characteristics of spirits is the large numbers of names by which they were known. For example, a recent dictionary of demonology lists forty-five different names for the *domovoi*.[22] Though some are simply regional variants of the basic name, it is evident that the main reason for the multitude of names for spirits arises out of the belief in the ubiquity of supernatural power and the consequent danger for man. One solution was to use flattering names such as *khoziain* (master of the house) for the house spirit, or else *batiushka* (father) or *dedushka-sosedushko* (grandad-neighbour) in recognition also of his origins in an ancestor cult. Another drew on the fear that mere mention of the name of the relevant mythological spirit caused him to appear, prompting the use of taboo names, such as *tot* (that one) or *on* (he) for the house spirit, or *kornoukhii* (one whose ear has been cut off) for the *leshii*.[23] The taboo on naming is part of a deep-seated belief in the power of words, which in themselves carried an inherent danger, and, as will be seen, affected other aspects of folk belief as well as literary attitudes to the demonic aspect of creativity.

Though the world was viewed as a place fraught with danger, the unclean force was essentially impersonal, not hostile *per se*, and not inherently evil. Thus, for example, the *leshii* was known for leading peasants astray in the forest to amuse himself, while the *domovoi* smashed crockery when in a bad mood.[24] As a corollary, spirits were not interested in castigating moral wrongdoing. They were not on the whole cunning, since they were not interested in trapping mortals into committing sins. Rather, it was external actions involving invasion of the spirits' territory, arrogant behaviour towards them, ignorance of ritual actions and prohibitions and other violations of the codes of peasant community life that might provoke attack. It was the unwary not the wicked who attracted their attention, and anybody in the community could slip up in this way. The fear peasants felt of the unclean force in part stemmed from the likelihood that it might attack or blight the lives of any of them, from the innocent to the worst reprobate. Attracting the unwelcome attentions of the unclean force in one of its manifestations could not, therefore, lead ultimately to redemption. Equally, since the unclean force was not inherently evil and might even be helpful, there was everything to be gained from treating it with respect, and/or using magic to deal with it.

Like the spirits, the Russian folk devil was usually "they" not "he." When peasants referred to a single devil (chert), they envisaged a small creature, one of a host of similar demons. Like the spirits devils were everywhere, places of worship included. But there was a difference; the forest spirit rarely left the forest (save, perhaps, to abduct a peasant child), and the house spirit did not visit his counterparts in pond, field, or wood. The very ubiquity of the devil was one of the factors that made him so frightening.[25]

He also resembled the spirits in that he was an external, potentially visible being. His ubiquity and his external existence led Russians (along with other European peoples) to treat the possibility of demonic attack in the same way as those from spirits, that is, to ward off potential trouble through ritual action and magic. Peasants believed, like their counterparts in Western Europe, that making the sign of the cross in front of one's mouth when yawning or sneezing was essential to stop devils creeping into the gaping aperture. Similarly, jugs or bowls of water were always covered, if only by two sticks in the form of a cross, to prevent them entering drinking water.[26] The mythological context in Russia seems to have reinforced the belief already found in Byzantine Christianity that the devil was anywhere and everywhere, and, furthermore, encouraged the application of a pre-existing deep-rooted belief in magic to him.

As already mentioned, both spirits and devils were connected with another world, but there was a difference, even if it was not always clearly articulated: spirits lived in this world while drawing their power from the Other World, whereas devils dwelt in hell (most graphically represented for the average peasant in icons of the Last Judgement). They emerged only to prompt evil deeds, trap the unwary, and inflict harm. It would seem to follow, then, that the folk devil differed from other spirits in not having a specific dwelling place in the world. The position is, in fact, somewhat more complex. Given the Christian location of devils in hell, it was necessary to explain how they effected their passage to and from the nether regions. Folk belief linked them with fissures in the earth's surfaces, caves, abysses, or ravines; it was devils' love of gaping holes that explained their proclivity for crawling into yawning mouths or through open doors. In a clear case of the intermingling of pre-Christian and Christian beliefs, folk belief also assigned devils a more precise habitat, apart from the yawning entrances: water, which in pre-Christian folk belief was believed to act as a boundary with and exit to the other world.[27] This choice also has a more prosaic explanation – its inherent danger for peasants who could not swim – but one does not exclude the other. Devils were more dangerous than spirits, and hence acquired not only a watery habitat but further preferred the most perilous places: bogs, swamps, and deep, dirty water: *v tikhom omute cherti vodiatsia* (devils lurk in deep, quiet pools), as the Russian version of "still waters run deep" has it.[28]

Danger also explains the equation of devil and unclean force and hence, the connection between devils and places within the man-made environment, such as cross-roads, which were originally favoured spots for the unclean force. Where places believed to be liminal were not the habitat of a specific spirit, there was a tendency over time to equate the two. The confusion between the concepts of the unclean force and the devil applied more generally as well, to the midsummer feast of Ivan Kupalo for example, as well as to liminal times of day, though here with one exception; thanks to the dualistic concepts of Christianity which associated light with good and darkness with evil, midday, the brightest time of day, when the *poludnitsa* (midday spirit) or the *polevoi* (field spirit) roamed the open fields, did not acquire demonic associations in the folk tradition.[29] Midsummer, another time associated with light, was less clearly associated with the devil than Yuletide, when extra care needed to be taken to protect oneself from demonic attack. The divinatory rituals deemed most effective required an encounter with the unclean force/devil; the symbolism of removing crosses together with sashes and belts (a pre-Christian form of magic protection) further indicates the mixture of Christian and pre-Christian in beliefs about occult power.

Parallels also exist between spirits and devils in the principles of naming and not naming. The folk tradition inherited many names from the Orthodox, while adding more of its own; thus the compiler of a recent dictionary of demonology gives more than sixty under *chert, Satana,* and *bes.*[30] However, names of biblical and Christian origin (e.g. *kniaz' t'my* [prince of darkness] or *demon*) are used mainly by the more educated or pious, with the term *lukavyi* (the cunning one) forming the sole exception. Its popularity depends less on the familiar words of the Lord's Prayer than its ability to express one of the defining characteristics of the folk devil, his guile. Overwhelmingly, however, the popular folk term for these ubiquitous imps is *chert* and, to a lesser extent, *bes.* The word *chert* is connected with *cherta* (a line) and the pre-Christian idea of drawing a magic circle as protection from evil spirits (as, for example, in Gogol's story "Vii," 1833–42).[31] *Bes,* by contrast, came through the Orthodox tradition, and tended to retain a more ecclesiastical feel. Both terms in popular usage referred not only to devils, but, as a consequence of the Church's designation of all spirits as *besy,* also to mythological spirits in general, as well as to the unclean force. Specific areas of linguistic usage might also determine the choice of *chert* or *bes,* notably profane language, which only invoked the *chert.*[32]

The terms *satana, d'iavol* and names like Satanael are also found in oral tradition, but mainly only in cosmological legends drawn from written apocrypha. Here is the only presentation of the Devil as the supreme figure in a diabolical hierarchy. But whereas, as Simon Franklin points out in this volume, "the cosmological context for the Russian Orthodox Devil is consistently monistic: . . . the Devil is a loser. He has no hold over the future; he can act only where God permits and where man loses vigilance," in folklore this impression is less consistent. One legend describes how kingdoms of darkness and light preceded the Creation while another tells how Satan creates his own habitat, in particular unfriendly trees like thorns and unclean animals like goats.[33] Satan here appears as co-creator and God's rival. It is not surprising that Russian folk belief adopted (and adapted) these legends since they are closer to the concept of an all powerful but impersonal supernatural force, albeit one divided into good and evil, than the idea of the Devil as a fallen angel, once the servant of God. The view of Satan's creative activities as a distorted version of the true Creator's may have engendered, albeit unconsciously, the concept common in Muscovite history and later of the diabolically inspired pretender or wicked ruler, to all appearances divinely ordained but in fact a pretender, Antichrist, or devil, as Kevin Platt explains in his contribution to this volume.

Other legends have been heavily adapted to fit the Russian cultural context, as in the aetiological tale about nature spirits and devils. Which spirit became which, it explains, depended on whether they fell into trees, water, or swamps when they were cast out of Heaven.[34] Such a legend reflects the concept of devils as one of many manifestations of the unclean force. In other respects, too, these creation legends are closer to folk concepts than their literary originals in that *Satana* is less an embodiment of evil than a jealous trickster who tries to cheat God, something like the folktale image of cunning devils.[35]

In as much as the folk devil differs from his ecclesiastical counterpart, the mythological folkloric context provides the key to those differences. Not that these should be overestimated; both folk and ecclesiastical devils are usually small and come in the plural, both are external beings, both look virtually the same, both live basically in hell but lurk everywhere, both aim to inflict harm, both are capable of metamorphosis in the pursuit of their nefarious purposes. The differences are slight and often simply a question of emphasis. The folk devil is often covered with shaggy hair (more like spirits); he is more likely to turn himself into an animal like a pig or a goat or an inanimate object than a seductive woman, since in the lay context the devil was, on the whole, more interested in terror than lust.[36] Peasants, unlike hagiographers, did not generally ascribe motivation for wicked actions to the devil, but on the other hand they conceived of mental and physical sickness as the incursion of an entity into the body, probably as the result of "spoiling," magic spells or curses placed by a sorcerer or witch whose powers came from the unclean force.[37]

Equally, the moral element is not quite so consistent or unambiguous. Firstly, the terror the folk devil invoked was quite often associated with the unknown rather than with sinful behaviour. He attacked those bold characters who left the safety of the village and went travelling on the high road (bol'shaia doroga); he was also associated with tobacco which arrived from the West in the seventeenth century and was viewed as alien as well as connected with smoke and hence hell.[38] He also preferred the unwary at least as much as the wicked, as the examples about protecting water and an open mouth show. Furthermore, the assumption that devils married, had families, frolicked in snowstorms, or enjoyed card and throwing games rendered them less unambiguously negative.[39] In the same way the stupid devil of the folk tale who could be outwitted diminished the sense of overwhelming diabolical power, even if peasants knew this to be mere wish fulfilment.[40] Comfort could be drawn from seeing the devil as spirit-like prankster.

The propensity for spirits to play jokes at the expense of man was also transferred to the folk devil; mocking laughter could often be heard as man was led astray. Indeed, one of the commonest euphemisms for the devil is "joker" (shut).[41] Reinforced by ecclesi-

6. "The Jester and the Female Jester," second half of the eighteenth century. Copper engraving.

Некоторыи чаловекъ пианица прописа накружале доныга иреч пианица незнаю
что пропить ащебы былъ купецъ продалъъ душу свою ириде кнему диаволъ вош
бразе чаловеческомъ а иреч ему что чаловече ухмаеши ато а думаю незнаю что сѣ
себа пропить аще бы купецъ продала бы душу свою иреч диаволъ дачто тебе
дати денегъ что хочешъ идавъ диаволъ денегъ пианица исела иначала пити ионъ
же Юкааныыи пианица нипомышлаше юдуше свои ныча пити ириближаса
вечеръ итогда реч диаволъ спротчими люди аще кто купилъ кона подобаетъ
взать изъду абы стороннии люди свидетели купиш усего чаловека душу поды
быстъ брати мне итело месе люди внезапу нападе нанихъ страхъ велии диавъ
олъ взалъ пианицу ипотыщилъ сквозъ полъ въ ддъ навечныа муки

7. "The Drunkard in the Tavern," second quarter of the nineteenth century.
   Copper engraving, 35,5 × 27,5 cm.

astical disapproval of secular enjoyment and levity, the view that
laughter was demonically inspired and, in general, impermissible is
one strand in folk belief.[42] It is one facet of the folk devil that, as we
shall see, is reflected in nineteenth-century Russian literature.

It would be wrong to suggest that the folk devil did not punish
mortals for their sins, but emphasis was often placed on social ills,
such as drunkenness or gambling (he could ruin mortals by playing
cards or dice with them, and loved to attack drunks), both of which
could destroy families.[43] The links between drink and gambling with
the devil can be traced back to the Church's strictures of 1551, contained in the *Book of a Hundred Chapters* (*Stoglav*),[44] and was seized
upon by those who produced popular tracts and *lubok* pictures in the

nineteenth century.[45] In one of these, as in the West, the devil appeared as "the distiller supreme."[46]

If it came to an incipient or actual encounter, prayer was naturally one of the chief ways of combatting the folk devil, but just as important was magic. We may perceive a clear difference between the drawing of a protective magic circle and the sign of the cross or use of holy water, but peasants, who saw themselves as good Orthodox, regarded both as equally valid and appropriate forms of protection against devils (as against other manifestations of the unclean force). Recourse to magic implies that good deeds and Christian behaviour are insufficient defence and further serves to diminish the role played by morality in combatting the devil.

Another feature of the folk devil which was more overt in folk belief than in Orthodox hagiography is the need to treat him with respect. Obviously influenced by attitudes to folk spirits, there was one difference; whereas folk spirits were not necessarily hostile and could be won over to assist if treated correctly, the devil was always man's enemy. Only where he was confused with the unclean spirit, as for example, in some Yuletide divinatory practices, could he be asked for help. Respect was reflected in the use of flattering names like guest (gost'), or the use of taboo names such as "that one" (tot) which avoided attracting his attention, or else in adopting measures to ward off attacks; "pray to God, but don't anger the devil" (Bogu molis', a cherta ne gnevi), as the proverb went. The sense of ubiquity that accompanied the figure of the folk devil ensured that his name was constantly on the lips of the average peasant.

Having as far as possible differentiated the folk devil from the "unclean force," while simultaneously indicating that vocabulary and social class played a major role in determining whether a phenomenon was to be attributed to the devil or the unclean force, I must now confess that these boundaries should be ignored when considering literary demonism (though not literary appearances by the devil/devils). Whatever their backgrounds, writers belonged to the intellectual élite which had rejected a traditional world-view. For them nice distinctions between devil and unclean force were largely irrelevant, a matter for ethnographers alone. Their vocabulary and perceptions naturally inclined them to merge the two and to describe them with demonological terms. I propose, therefore, to discuss traditional attitudes to magic and the word and art without distinguishing types of occult power.

Magic is a key concept in considering folk influence on literary demonism. It could be performed through actions, rituals, objects (such as amulets, or for harmful magic, such things as footprints), or with words. Verbal magic is of primary importance not only in the world of traditional Russian culture, but also for literary demonism. Common to most European cultures, Russia possessed (and, indeed, still possesses) a rich store of spells or, in scholarly parlance, charms (in Russian *zagovory*, or more rarely *zaklinaniia*). Their functions were numerous; ranging from the expulsion of human or animal illnesses, to curing or alleviating psychological disorders, soothing family strife, protection from weather or theft, ensuring success in love or business, as well as "spoiling" (porcha), that is causing harm, or putting the evil eye on someone. Harmful charms did not invoke Christian figures, and might directly invoke the devil. Often they were structured on a direct inversion of the invocations in the protective/curative charms. All charms were believed to draw on supernatural forces, acting through the person of the folk healer (znakhar'/ka) or that of the sorcerer (koldun) and witch (koldun'ia, ved'ma). In medieval times the separation between black and white magic practitioners seems to have been weakly developed, but by the nineteenth century, the folk healer was the purveyor of beneficial magic, regarding his, or more likely her, task as healing or protection and thinking of charms as prayers. The sorcerer, on the other hand, who was thought able to harness the unclean/demonic force through a pact with the devil, and who was assisted by demons, specialized, though not exclusively, in black or harmful spells. With time, these also came to be more closely associated with the devil. The sorcerer existed in every village; according to popular belief, his soul was claimed by the devil on death and his body might be peeled and consumed by devils leaving only the skin. As a representative of the unclean force he had to be placated and his attendance at every wedding was regarded as essential to prevent spoiling of the young couple.[47]

Healing or protective charms often had prayer-like introductions and conclusions but the main part did not necessarily possess Christian connotations. Since charms consisted of magic words, their structure, especially the opening and concluding formulae, conformed to fixed patterns. Not every word was understood by those who used them, but strict adherence to the words was essential if the charm was to work. Since they were magical, their text was not only sacrosanct but was believed to lose its efficacy if, firstly, not whispered, and, secondly, said to an uninitiated person. It would have been hard to find a Russian peasant in the pre-Revolutionary period who did not believe at all in the power of magic words to cause good or harm, and most believed absolutely in them as part of a hostile world where man was prey to attack from the unclean force/devil.

Fear of harmful charms has a long history in Russia. It is clear that from rulers downwards dread of spoiling in Muscovite Russia was intense. In a world where literacy was rare, and bookish activity seen as dangerous,[48] written versions of harmful magic were inevitably perceived as demonic and regarded with particular fear.[49] By the seventeenth century those who possessed books of charms were known by a special name, "black book men" (chernoknizhniki).[50] Such people were also believed to own books of black magic that conjured demons. In the early eighteenth century Iakov Brius (Bruce), astronomer to Peter the Great and promoter of the famous Brius calendar, was widely believed – because of his chemical experiments and collection of books – to dabble in sorcery and black magic. This reputation endured until the twentieth century in Moscow.[51] At least until the last quarter of the nineteenth century in rural society most books were held by the priest (who before this was often only semi-literate himself). In Jeffrey Brooks's words, "reading was often a religious experience for the ordinary people. The book was a religious symbol, and the process had religious connotations."[52] In the syncretic context of traditional Russian culture, it was little wonder that the power ascribed to religious books was also thought to reside in those books believed to draw on the supernatural/unclean force. Their magic was consequently regarded as demonic.[53] Widespread suspicion of literacy and belief in the magic power of the written word among peasants is reflected in the tale in Afanas'ev's collection about the illiterate soldier who, given a book by the devil, is immediately able to read.[54] *Chernoknizhniki*, those who possessed the ability to conjure with magic words, were feared, and also respected, at least as much as the ordinary sorcerer.

With the conclusion of this survey of attributes of and attitudes to the folk devil, we can turn to the demonic presence in Russian literature. As Simon Franklin remarks in the preceding essay in this volume, the visible demon becomes an endangered species in the literary, cultural, and aesthetic environment of the nineteenth century. Things do not start so badly for his folk variant (the Lermontovian Demon-seducer is essentially Western in origin despite folk legends on this theme and may be excluded here).[55] Pre-Romantic and Romantic interest in the fantastic, as well as in *narodnost'* (popular and/or national character), ensured him a few literary appearances. In the first phase of Romanticism and pre-Romanticism, the devil was presented through the eyes of an educated narrator or commentator who mocked or debunked the supernatural, and whose aim was local colour. Such eighteenth-century rationalist attitudes to superstition still prevailed, in, for example, Zhukovsky's popular ballad "Svetlana" (1812), where the heroine's attempt to tap the unclean demonic force at midnight on New Year's Eve concludes with authorial derision of her superstitious fancies. Even at the height of fashion for tales about folk belief, authors felt obliged to distance themselves by debunking folk demons. Thus in Orest Somov's story "Kikimora" (1829),[56] a frame narrative in which an educated traveller persuades his peasant coachman to tell the story of the havoc wrought by a *kikimora* (a troublesome female spirit, akin to the *domovoi*), the narrative is regularly interrupted by the educated traveller's derisive comments.

From the late 1820s the influence of Tieck and Hoffman led to Russian imitations which were more interested in the frisson of horror than in accurate reflections of folk belief (take, for example, Pogorel'sky's "The Poppyseed Cake-Seller of Lafertovo" [Lafertovskaia makovnitsa, 1825]). Others, such as Bestuzhev-Marlinsky's story "A Terrible Prophecy" (Strashnoe gadanie, 1831), attempted a fusion of the two. In the tale the officer narrator participates in a New Year ritual designed to conjure forth the unclean spirit/devil in a graveyard at midnight. A modest effort is made to evoke the horror involved, but the subsequent "sighting" is explained away as a dream. Mock horror at best. Suitably sanitized, the devil/unclean force occasionally featured in the nineteenth-century genre of the Yuletide story but since this literary form, like Dickens's "A Christmas Carol," was generally heart-warming rather than chilling, the devil received only bit parts.[57]

Even at the height of Romanticism, the artistic deployment of the folk devil was not restricted to simple ethnographic colouration or mock horror when in the hands of talented writers like Pushkin and Gogol. Gogol's devil-infested *Village Evenings near Dikanka* (*Vechera na khutore bliz Dikan'ki*, 1831–32) are an advance in terms of narrative stance. Though his own voice can certainly be detected from time to time, and the gap between reader and narrator is an essential part of the stories' charm, Gogol does not permit mocking interpolations, nor allow for the direct involvement of an educated narrator (the man in the pea-green coat is a townie whose misplaced scorn for the bumpkins is part of the humour for the reader). Furthermore, by using a variety of rural narrators, Gogol is able to shift between the two conventional contemporary modes of presentation of the folk devil, by combining the jolly treatment of devils as local colour (for example, "The Fair at Sorochintsy" [Sorochinskaia iarmarka]), where the reader can regard the antics of the characters with amused condescension, with the more terrifying "The Lost Letter" (Propavshaia gramota) and, particularly, "A Terrible Vengeance" (Strashnaia mest').

The stories are a further advance in that they contain such a broad variety of folk beliefs about the devil:[58] the ubiquity of small devils, their powers of metamorphosis (especially pigs in "The Lost Letter"), the danger of taking the devil's name in vain ("A Bewitched Place" [Zakoldovannoe mesto]), their fondness for cards and dancing

("The Lost Letter"), devils as pranksters, the smith as one who can combat the devil, devils in sacks (a well-known folktale type), Yuletide as a liminal time when the devil roams (the last four examples from "Christmas Eve" [Noch' pered rozhdestvom]), the other world beyond water ("The Lost Letter"), sexual relations between devils and witches ("Christmas Eve"), and the magic circle ("Vii," included in *Mirgorod*, 1835). Such details are combined in a manner untypical of folklore which focuses on one motif or belief at a time, though presented in the overall context of a demonically infested environment where, as J.M. Holquist noted, "the world of men and the world of spirits has many chinks in it."[59]

In his more terrifying tales, "Saint John's Eve" (Vecher nakanune Ivana Kupala, 1829–31), "A Terrible Vengeance," and "Vii," Gogol chose to intensify the horrific and the moralistic aspects of his folk sources. The fear felt by peasants for anything associated with the unclean force is magnified, and in "A Terrible Vengeance" given incestuous overtones. In "Saint John's Eve" Gogol reshapes the folk legend about the fern flower (tsvet paporotnika) by combining it with the motif of selling one's soul to the devil and adding details from a story by Tieck and features of his own.[60] Although oral tradition is familiar with soul-selling, the motif may be assumed to be ultimately of literary origin, because it always concerns the devil rather than mythological spirits.[61] Whereas the usual version of the folk legend describes an intrepid individual taking an unaided decision to challenge the unclean force/devils in the hope of acquiring treasure after plucking the fern flower on Saint John's Eve, here it is the Evil One in human disguise who urges the hero, Petrus, to seek out the flower. The ingredient added to the story by Gogol from Tieck's "Liebeszauber" is the condition to which Petrus agrees in order to obtain the treasure which will allow him to marry his beloved: the murder of his fiancée's young brother. Whereas in folk legend no blame is attached to the bold individual who is brave enough to challenge the devils who defend the treasure, Gogol, in adding the terrible condition imposed by the devil, emphasizes Petrus's obsessive greed and suggests that the pursuit of the fern flower is wicked rather than dangerous. Even more striking is the manner in which Gogol condemns not just Petrus, whose enjoyment of an affluent married life is destroyed a year later when he recalls what happened (a motif that can be found in folklore),[62] but also the whole village, which though moved to another site continues to be haunted by the devil. The moral condemnation of a whole community for the sins of one of its members is alien to the folk tradition, reflecting rather Gogol's own acute sense of demonic evil; his injection of morality into the folk tradition goes far beyond the usual treatment of the soul-selling motif, let alone the fern flower tale. Despite the general view that the unclean force lurked everywhere, communal guilt and punishment would end such a tale in the oral tradition only if it was deserved. Here an elemental malevolent force, not the more impersonal unclean force, continues active persecution against the innocent in a context where the heinous behaviour of one person can affect all. Perhaps if Gogol had been less imaginative and more steeped in Ukrainian folklore rather than relying on material from his mother and sister,[63] he would not have placed such a distinct slant on traditional motifs, thereby revealing so much of his own fear of an omnipresent destructive evil force, punishing moral lapses.

If Gogol's devils in his early stories reveal traits of a personalized view when compared with their folk originals, Pushkin's poem "The Devils" (Besy, 1830) overtly moves in this direction.[64] In it the poet finds himself lost in a snowstorm at night in the open countryside. His coachman complains that the devil is leading them astray, round and round, hoping that their exhausted horse will eventually stumble into a ravine. He points to where he believes the devil is playing, spitting and blowing at him. All these are common folk beliefs. In the second half of the poem (stanzas 5–7), the narrator himself seems to see endless hordes of hideous demons, reflecting folk belief that devils emerge in winter when their behaviour causes snowstorms. During blizzards, especially at night, they either perform devilish marriage ceremonies or conduct funerals to which they invite sorcerers and witches, the howling of the wind being their unholy lament.[65]

Interestingly, in the earliest drafts of the poem, the poet is alone, but as Pushkin introduced the figure of the coachman, so folk demonic details characterize the latter's voice. Subsequently these images are also presented as the poet's thoughts, and in later drafts are even more extended than in the final version, with additional references to, *inter alia*, the children of devils and animals with demonic associations. For example, in a variant of the draft stanza cited below, the kitten (kotenok) is replaced by another demonic animal, a goat (kozlenok):

> Что за звуки? … аль бесенок
> В люльке охает, больной;
> Аль мяукает котенок
> К ведьме ластится лихой –
> Али мертвых черти гонят –
> Не русалки ль там поют?
> Домового ли хоронят
> Ведьму ль замуж отдают – [66]

> [What sounds are these ?… is it a wee devil,
> Groaning in the cradle, taken ill;
> Or a kitten miaowing,
> Rubbing itself against an evil witch –

> Or are devils chasing the dead –
> Are those not *rusalki* singing there?
> Are they burying a house spirit
> Or marrying off a witch –]

The final version of the poem concludes not with cock-crow banishing the devils and the terrors of the night, nor with the discovery of a place of shelter, but with the horrible shrieking and howling which tears at the poet's heart. Although Pushkin maintains the folk imagery throughout his poem, it is by no means certain that poet and driver see the same devils. Pushkin, whose ability to perceive phenomena in psychologized and non-traditional symbolic terms divided him from his coachman, was certainly reflecting his personal feelings about more than the immediate snow-blown scene. Are the circles in which they are being led symbolic? Are the devils internal or external? Not surprisingly, the poem has been subject to a variety of interpretations (including political, implicit, as W.J. Leatherbarrow notes in his contribution to this volume, in its use as one of the epigraphs to Dostoevsky's novel of the same name). The creative and personalized use of folklore here indicates a step away from local colour or mere ethnographic realism to a more individualized and sophisticated approach.

Some further variation in treatment of the visible folk devil emerges in the Kunstmärchen of the 1830s, in particular in one of Vladimir Dal's early stories. *Russian Tales* (*Russkie skazki*, 1832), which contains a comic-satiric tale "About the Travels of the Devil's Assistant, Sidor Polikarpovich, on Land and Sea" (O pokhozhdeniiakh cherta-poslushnika, Sidora Polikarpovicha, na more i na sushe). In it a junior devil is despatched to earth to infiltrate the Russian army and navy.[67] Using a variant of the common folk theme of small devils and their encounters on earth, Dal offers a satirical picture of the cruelty and injustice of military life, implying that life in hell is distinctly preferable. It was one of two stories which precipitated Dal's arrest.

With the passing of Romanticism the folk *chert* makes fewer and fewer direct appearances in literature. References to the devil incorporate criticism of belief in the folk devil/unclean force, by presenting it as an indicator of backwardness. In Goncharov's novel *Oblomov*, for example, the description of the superstitious fear with which the inhabitants of remote Oblomovka view their ravine, a well-known devilish habitat, is couched in comic terms, designed to reveal the absurd benightedness of the hero's home milieu. One might have expected the devil to feature a little more in the works of a writer like Leskov, who was fascinated by traditional Russian culture and its bearers, the peasants, but the nature of that fascination excluded the devil. In general, but particularly in the 1860s and 1870s, Leskov was interested in traditional culture and peasant life either as an embodiment of traditional values, or as exemplars of Russian failings, both part of his search for a distinctive path for Russia. Typical of his time, he regarded superstition as a sign of backwardness (see, for example, "Vale of Tears" [Iudol', 1892]). Not surprisingly, then, the devil barely features in this writing, and when he does, in *Cathedral Folk* (*Soboriane*, 1872), he is not real, but simply one of the townsfolk from Stargorod down on his luck, in disguise. The comic episode reflects Leskov's view of the people as childish pranksters who need moral guidance. It owes much to satiric folktales about trapping the devil, but with the difference that here the demonic impostor is unmasked instead of an actual devil receiving his come-uppance – a reflection of Leskov's dismissive view of superstition. In later life, as Leskov became more concerned with moral values than with ethnic colouring, he only wrote about the devil in the context of his versions of Christian legends, of which one, "A Tale about the Devil's Granny" (Rasskaz pro chertovu babku, late 1880s, but not published in his lifetime), takes the form of a cosmological legend.[68] Its source (Danish) and its transformation into an indictment of moral and religious dogmatism ensure no input from the Russian folk devil.

Whereas the pragmatic Leskov tended to view evil in terms of human or specifically Russian failings, Dostoevsky's concern for a distinctive role for Russia, together with his ability to think in terms of general moral and aesthetic principles, allowed for a larger presence of the devil as symbol of evil. In *The Devils* (*Besy*, 1871–72) the Westernized radicals of Russia are seen as demonically possessed and inherently destructive of the country's values. As W.J. Leatherbarrow notes in his essay in this volume, though Dostoevsky's novel seeks to suggest the *nature* of the demonic "through discourses derived from Western European secular sources and biblical narrative," it "employs traditional Russian cultural symbols and discourses to alert us to the *presence* of the demonic," and he goes on to examine links with those traditional symbols. This presence is a lesser but far from unimportant feature of *The Brothers Karamazov* (*Brat'ia Karamazovy*, 1879–80), where in book XI, chapter 9 the devil visits Ivan Karamazov. Though evidently the product of Ivan's imagination, the form the demonic visitor takes reflects his culturally determined subconscious. This devil is clearly a folk *chert*, typical in his desire to tease and torment. Simultaneously, Dostoevsky draws on the folk use of flattering names by terming the diabolical visitor *gost'* (guest) and *dzhentl'men* (gentleman), while at the same time giving the names a basis in reality (if this is not a contradiction in terms) by presenting him not only as an (uninvited) guest but as a shabbily dressed gentleman. By emphasizing the folk demonic links Dostoevsky underlines Ivan's own alienation from the positive values the writer associated with his country, while suggesting that at some level his Russianness is present within him.

As the visible folk devil largely melts from sight, the folk demonic partly takes its place, most notably at first in the 1830s in Gogol's Petersburg tales. With the shift away from popular motifs, ethnographic settings, and folk humour or horror, Gogol largely left the visible folk devil behind (his appearances at dusk on Nevsky Prospect are an exception). In two general respects this statement underestimates the influence the folk imagination had on the writer. Firstly, the sense of the ubiquity of the devil, is, as Julian Graffy describes in his contribution to this volume, overwhelming in the Petersburg tales, and, one may add, also in works not set in Petersburg, such as *The Government Inspector* (*Revizor*, 1836). In all of these the devil is constantly invoked ("the devil only knows" [chert znaet] or "the devil take it" [chert poberi]).[69] While these exclamations do not, as in "A Bewitched Place," summon forth the devil/devils directly, they seem to activate the lurking demonic. The folk perception of devils as small malicious tormentors, whose tastes and way of life are deceptively like ours, would also seem to share a good deal with Gogol's devil, who is dangerous in his very ordinariness. Similarly, just as the folk devil catches out the unwary as well as attacking people for social failings as much as for great sins, many of Gogol's characters are enveloped in their own *poshlost'* (petty vulgarity and false values) and, unaware of this, are all too easily victims of the devil's snares. Other characters, like the artist Piskarev in "Nevsky Prospect" (Nevskii prospekt), find a world where the devil likes to make people lose their way (*chert poputal* [the devil led me/him etc astray], as folk speech had it). Here the loss of direction is spiritual rather than physical as we may find in folk *bylichki*. Furthermore, the sense that appearances are deceptive, which in Gogol extends beyond the diabolic metamorphoses of the early stories into a much more subtle and hence dangerous deceptiveness, owes something to both the ecclesiastical and the folk devil. Finally, one may note some other features of the folk devil in the Petersburg tales, such as his associations with liminal times of day, dusk when the devil lights the lamps on Nevsky Prospect, a time when all is deception, foreshadowing a moral and physical darkness.

In one further general respect, Gogol's view of his own talents and work may reflect folk views of the demonic. The writer came to see his own early work as too lighthearted, full of empty meaningless laughter. As he explained in his article written about *The Government*

Inspector, "On Leaving the Theatre after the Performance of a New Comedy" (Teatral'nyi raz"ezd posle predstavleniia novoi komedii, 1836), laughter possessed the ability to cleanse by deriding moral failings.[70] Reflected in his dismissal of empty laughter may be his innate sense that laughter was of the devil (note that the devil laughs at Piskarev in "Nevsky Prospect"). Only by allying laughter to moral purpose could he wrest it and his talents from the possibility of being engulfed by the demonic. The vision of laughter as moral or demonic may also reflect the dichotomy in traditional views of books as either spiritual or connected to black magic. Gogol increasingly perceived his own linguistic gifts as either one or the other, and since a talent for comedy was part of his linguistic gift, the antithesis between the demonic and the purificatory was easily extended to laughter. As is well known, he was incapable of dealing psychologically with the dichotomy.

Though negative views of laughter in the form of frivolity and buffoonery appear in Leskov's *Cathedral Folk* and *The Enchanted Pilgrim* (*Ocharovannyi strannik,* 1873) as indicators of the failure of ordinary Russians to realize the potential of the country,[71] this feature is not seen as demonically inspired. By contrast in Dostoevsky's *The Devils,* as W.J. Leatherbarrow notes in his contribution to this volume, destructive laughter and buffoonery surround the revolutionaries, indicating the persistence of traditional concepts in élite culture, even if these were often unrecognized.

From the late nineteenth century onwards, two important factors had a significant impact on the use of folkloric motifs in literature and, within this context, on references to the demonic. The first resulted from the rapid growth of scholarly research on folklore, initiated in the 1860s; this greatly superseded in breadth of coverage and depth the primarily literary and aesthetic interest which had earlier flourished at the time of Romanticism, and directly contributed to the heightened interest in the native folk tradition which was current at the turn of the century. A further factor, influential in shaping the approach to this newly discovered legacy, was the belief current in symbolist circles that the path to a national, spiritual, and cultural renaissance lay through a renewal of contact with primitive, pagan forces. This led to a fascination with myth which manifested itself in two areas: the revival of interest in classical pagan antiquity, spearheaded by figures such as Faddei Zelinsky, Viacheslav Ivanov, and Innokentii Annensky, and the focus on native Slav mythology, strongly evident in the prose of Remizov and in the work of poets such as Bal'mont, Konevskoi, Dobroliubov, Briusov, Ivanov, Blok, and Kliuev.[72] Great pains were taken to suggest a connection between these two mythological traditions, either by seeking to prove their historical continuity and archetypal similarity, or by interweaving them through artistic techniques. As an example of the first method one can cite Viacheslav Ivanov's extensive research on the ancient Greek cult of Dionysus. Far from being conducted in a scholarly void, it had an intensely practical application: Ivanov sought to establish a direct line of continuity between the ancient Greek god and the Slavs, as is evident from his description of Dionysus as "our god, a barbaric one, our Slav god."[73] Syncretic juxtaposition of the two traditions was another method, popular in the visual arts as well as in poetry. Vrubel's oil-painting *Pan* (1899) depicts the Greek god against the background of a typical Russian landscape complete with birch trees and moon; in this context he looks not unlike a Russian nature spirit.[74] A similar effect was achieved in verse by the constant blending of motifs from pagan antiquity and Slav folklore. This tendency can already be detected in Ivanov's first collection of verse, *Pilot Stars* (*Kormchie zvezdy*, 1903),[75] and was formulated by him as a programmatic principle in one of his earliest articles, "The Poet and the Rabble" (Poet i chern', 1904). Here he wrote of the poet's "inner need for a return to and communion with the native element," and advocated unlocking "the keys to the precious recesses of the people's soul"[76] as the source of true art.

Ivanov's words were echoed by several poets, most notably by Blok and Gorodetsky. In one of his first critical essays, Blok approvingly paraphrased Ivanov's dicta, even adding his own more explicit formulation: "the suffering path of symbolism is the 'submersion into the element of folklore'."[77] His practical implementation of this principle dates back to his early verse; it can be seen, for example, in his cycle of poems, "Bubbles of the Earth" (Puzyri zemli, 1904–1905), which includes numerous folkloric motifs related to the devils of the marshes.[78] Like Blok, Gorodetsky also came strongly under the influence of Ivanov in 1906; his first book of verse, *Spring Corn* (*Iar'*, 1907), was widely acclaimed for its innovative use of Russian folklore and was followed by a second collection in the same vein, named after the Slav thunder god, *Perun* (1907). In a later article on the immediate challenge facing Russian poetry, Gorodetsky specifically praised Ivanov's verse for its combination of classical images with Slav folklore: in his view this reflected the ideal progression from a return to classical antiquity through the attainment of universal principles to the subsequent revelation of the universal in the national.[79]

As well as responding to the desire to bring about the projected Slav renaissance on native soil, the deliberate incorporation of folkloric motifs into "high" culture was also generally perceived as a way of narrowing the gap between the intelligentsia and the people. A new urgency was lent to these issues by the widespread sense of historical crisis which developed in the aftermath of the Russo-Japanese war and revolutionary events of 1905. This brought about a marked increase in literary images of darkness and vengeance, some of which drew on the traditions of folklore. In Bal'mont's poem, "To Perun" (K Perunu), for example, the poet invokes the Slav god of thunder and vengeance as the source of his poetic gift and appeals to him for help in creating verses of revenge.[80]

In addition to these various historical and national factors, there was a further aspect of the folk tradition which made it a particularly attractive source to writers seeking images for the expression of their awareness of art as intrinsically demonic. Some of the underlying contexts of this attitude are examined by Pamela Davidson in this volume in her essay "Divine Service or Idol Worship?" The folk tradition provided a rich source for its expression: the popular view of words as a possibly dangerous source of power and the taboo surrounding naming linked up with literary views of art as demonic and paved the way for the association between the poet and the sorcerer, between the poetic text and magic charms. Little wonder then that Blok's discovery of folk charms prompted him to write "The Poetry of Charms and Incantations" (Poeziia zagovorov i zaklinanii, 1906).[81] The poet perceives charms as a reflection of primitive man's ability to be in unity with nature and sees the sorcerer or folk healer who knew them as empowered through his or her knowledge of the magic word to conjure the powers of nature (note that the unclean force manifested itself in the form of nature spirits). In the magic of the charms he saw true poetry which combined beauty, utility, and power. The parallels with the poet are obvious. As the sorcerer tapped the unclean force/demonic in his magic charms, so too the poet cast spells with words. But in both cases the activity was inherently dangerous: evil was always close by. The word might be demonically infected. The same trend is reflected in the symbolist novelists' tendency to associate their works of fiction with the legendary "black book" of the sorcerer, as discussed by Adam Weiner in this volume. For other instances of folk demonic appearances one must move from the symbolists to writers interested in the creative or parodic adaptation of folk belief such as Remizov, whose grotesque story "What Tobacco Is" (Chto est' tabak, 1908) uses the folk demonic associations of tobacco to concoct a mock, and indeed, mocking aetiological *bylichka*, discussed by Philip Cavendish in his contribution to this volume.

Thus, while one certainly could not claim that folklore (any more than Orthodoxy) was the primary source from which turn of the century literary demonism *derived*, one can say that it provided an important fund of images and concepts for the *articulation* of this obsession – a source which was particularly valued both because it was seen to be playing a role in the national revival of a pagan, primitive consciousness, and because it linked up with the symbolist preoccupation with the poetic word as a form of potentially demonic, incantatory magic. It can be no more than a hypothesis, but the folk cultural context of Russia may have helped literary demonism to enjoy a better run in Russia. The concept of a supernatural force that could equally harm or bring benefit, depending on the appropriateness or otherwise of human actions, may have led to a greater sense that good could turn to evil all too easily, certainly for a writer such as Gogol. In other instances it may be the ubiquity of the unclean force which found reflection in the near obsession of symbolist writers with the devil, while the sense that words and books were magic found numerous resonances. Though these aspects of possible folk demonic influence often cannot be demonstrated incontrovertibly, they may very well be at least as significant for the development of Russian literature as the overt appearances of the *chert* in the Romantic period and beyond.

Notes

1. Similar differences in perception explain the references to supernatural power as demonic throughout the medieval period in Russia; see W.F. Ryan, "The Witchcraft Hysteria in Early Modern Europe: Was Russia an Exception?," *Slavonic and East European Review* 76 (1998):49–84, esp. 55–59.
2. See in this volume Simon Franklin, "Nostalgia for Hell: Russian Literary Demonism and Orthodox Tradition," 35.
3. Ibid., 55 n.48.
4. O.A. Cherepanova, comp., *Mifologicheskie rasskazy i legendy russkogo Severa* (St. Petersburg: Izdatel'stvo S-Peterburgskogo universiteta, 1996), 186–87. The common variant name "vodianoi chert" reflects the blurring of the two figures.
5. Linda J. Ivanits, *Russian Folk Belief* (Armonk, N.Y., and London: M.E. Sharpe, 1989), 50, 62, 69, 73. She also notes an instance of reverse contamination, where the *leshii* takes on the role of the folk devil (69).
6. Ibid., 91–98.
7. Space obliges me to generalize and simplify, though beliefs varied from region to region, sometimes significantly.
8. For example, V.P. Zinov'ev, comp., *Mifologicheskie rasskazy russkogo naseleniia vostochnoi Sibiri,* ed. R.P. Matveeva (Novosibirsk: Nauka, 1987); Cherepanova, comp., *Mifologicheskie rasskazy*; V.P. Kuznetsova, ed., *Predaniia i bylichki (Pamiatniki russkogo fol'klora Vodlozer'ia)* (Petrozavodsk: Izdatel'stvo Petrozavodskogo gosudarstvennogo universiteta, 1997).
9. See in this volume Franklin, "Nostalgia for Hell."
10. A generalization that does not cover a sophisticated minority; Dante, for example, located causation in the individual psyche, allowing exploration of the related psychological dimensions of free will and choice.

11. It is commonly argued that in Russia witches were not seen as demonically possessed or inspired (e.g. Ivanits, *Russian Folk Belief,* 91–98, 124), but Ryan, "The Witchcraft Hysteria," 63–68, rejects this view, citing instances from the pre-Petrine period to show that the Church and official bodies certainly saw them as possessing demonic power, and arguing that most of the same factors were present in Russia. The explanation may well lie in Russian backwardness; Christianity penetrated the Russian countryside so much more slowly than in Western Europe that diabolization occurred much later. Certainly, French folk belief in the nineteenth century is much more heavily Christianized than Russian; see Judith Devlin, *The Superstitious Mind: French Peasants and the Supernatural in the Nineteenth Century* (New Haven and London: Yale University Press, 1987).

12. N.I. Tolstoi, "Otkuda d'iavoly raznye?," in his *Iazyk i narodnaia kul'tura: Ocherki po slavianskoi mifologii i etnolingvistike* (Moscow: Indrik, 1995), 245–49(249). Here and throughout this essay translations are mine.

13. See under *domovoi* in T.A. Novichkova, *Russkii demonologicheskii slovar'* (St. Petersburg: Peterburgskii pisatel', 1995), 130–31; O.A. Cherepanova, *Mifologicheskaia leksika russkogo Severa* (Leningrad: Izdatel'stvo Leningradskogo universiteta, 1983), 23–29.

14. M. Vlasova, *Novaia abevega russkikh sueverii* (St. Petersburg: Severo-zapad, 1995), 200–201, 325–26; Novichkova, *Russkii demonologicheskii slovar'*, 286–91, 543–44.

15. N.I. Tolstoi, "Kakov oblik d'iavol'skii?," in his *Iazyk i narodnaia kul'tura,* 250–69(256, 258); Ivanits, *Russian Folk Belief,* 52, 68.

16. Novichkova, *Russkii demonologicheskii slovar'*, 581, 585; Ivanits, *Russian Folk Belief,* 40; see also no.VI 10 in the motif index in Zinov'ev, comp., *Mifologicheskie rasskazy,* 305–20, which refers to the devil's wife and the birth of a child.

17. L.N. Vinogradova, "Kalendarnye perekhody nechistoi sily vo vremeni i prostranstve," in *Kontsept dvizheniia v iazyke i kul'ture,* ed. T.A. Agapkina (Moscow: Indrik, 1996), 166–84(171).

18. Tolstoi, "Otkuda d'iavoly raznye?," 249.

19. One should, however, note that the existence of ancient beliefs among the Slavs about such figures as vampires (upyr'), usually types of the unquiet dead, suggests that the Slavs did originally differentiate good from evil spirits of some kinds. It may therefore be that the hostile nature of some spirits, the *vodianoi* in particular, is not simply a result of Christian influence. This subject lies beyond the scope of this essay.

20. N.A. Krinichnaia, *Domashnii dukh i sviatochnye gadaniia* (Petrozavodsk: Karel'skii nauchnyi tsentr RAN, Institut iazyka, literatury i istorii, 1993).

21. B.A. Uspenskii, "K simvolike vremeni u slavian: 'chistye' i 'nechistye' dni nedeli," in *Finitis duodecim lustris: Sbornik statei k 60–letiiu prof. Iu.M. Lotmana,* ed. S.G. Isakov and others (Tallinn: Eesti Raamat, 1982), 70–75.

22. Novichkova, *Russkii demonologicheskii slovar'*, 130–31.

23. Ivanits, *Russian Folk Belief,* 66.

24. Ibid., 53–54, 170.

25. Peasants were, however, far more likely to attribute activities typical of a nature or house spirit to that spirit, rather than the Devil, when they found themselves in the relevant habitat.

26. S.V. Maksimov, *Nechistaia sila (Nechistaia, nevedomaia i krestnaia sila),* 2 vols. (Moscow: Russkii dukhovnyi tsentr, 1993), 1:4–5.

27. Vinogradova, "Kalendarnye perekhody," 171, 180–81; A. Toporkov, "Voda," *Rodina,* 1994, no. 1:108–12.

28. Tolstoi, "Otkuda d'iavoly raznye?," 248.

29. On the *poludnitsa,* see Felix J. Oinas, "Russian *Poludnica* 'Midday Spirit'," in his *Essays on Russian Folklore and Mythology* (Columbus: Slavica, 1985), 103–10; on the

polevoi, see Ivanits, *Russian Folk Belief,* 74; or, on both, Novichkova, *Russkii demonologicheskii slovar'*, 463–65.

30. Novichkova, *Russkii demonologicheskii slovar'*, 45, 495, 577.
31. Oinas, "The Devil in Russian Folklore," in his *Essays on Russian Folklore*, 97–102(97).
32. Russian profane language is connected to pre-Christian belief and was hence seen by the Church as demonic; see B.A. Uspenskii, "Mifologicheskii aspekt russkoi ekspressivnoi frazeologii," in his *Izbrannye trudy*, 2 vols. (Moscow: Gnosis, 1994), 2:53–128, esp. 56–65.
33. Ivanits, *Russian Folk Belief,* 41–42; Novichkova, *Russkii demonologicheskii slovar'*, 157–61, recounts a number of interesting cosmological legends. See also E.V. Pomerantseva, *Mifologicheskie personazhi v russkom fol'klore* (Moscow: Nauka, 1975), 124–30.
34. Tolstoi, "Otkuda d'iavoly raznye?," 245–46.
35. In yet another legend the devil is given the name of Gogol. Tantalizing as this may be to Gogolians, without any evidence that the devil-obsessed writer knew the legend or made some kind of link between himself and Satan, no connection should be assumed; see Ivanits, *Russian Folk Belief,* 41, 133.
36. A common motif in the folk tradition has the devil (sometimes in the form of a dragon) visiting a woman in the guise of her dead or absent husband (Zinov'ev, comp., *Mifologicheskie rasskazy*, motif nos.V 3, VI 47). At best the moral element is implied rather than stated.
37. For a subtle analysis of the connection between the Devil and the unclean force in sorcery, see Ivanits, *Russian Folk Belief,* 91–98.
38. Maksimov, *Nechistaia sila*, 1:9, notes that even tea and potatoes, which became widespread only in the early nineteenth century, were regarded by some as demonic in origin. The Old Believers ban tobacco to this day.
39. Maksimov, *Nechistaia sila*, 1:8; Ivanits, *Russian Folk Belief,* 40; E.A. Grushko and Iu.M. Medvedev, eds., *Slovar' russkikh sueverii* (Nizhnii Novgorod: Russkii kupets — Brat'ia slaviane, 1996), s.v. *perekrestok*.
40. Several stories about the devil tricked may be found in D.K. Zelenin, comp., *Velikorusskie skazki permskoi gubernii* (Petrograd: Orlov, 1914; reprint, Moscow: Pravda, 1991), 383–92. "The Devil as Moneylender" (Chert vzaimodavets) describes how a peasant borrows a thousand roubles from the devil promising to pay him "tomorrow." When tomorrow never comes, the peasant proposes that he hang a notice telling him when to come. The devil fails to check one day and the following day finds a notice saying "come yesterday."
41. Maksimov, *Nechistaia, nevedomaia i krestnaia sila*, 1:6–22.
42. S.S. Averintsev, "Bakhtin and the Russian Attitude to Laughter," in *Bakhtin: Carnival and Other Subjects*, ed. David Shepherd, Critical Studies, vol.3, no.2 and vol.4, no.1/2 (Amsterdam and Atlanta: Rodopi, 1993), 13–19. For a retelling of a *bylichka* with this theme, see Maksimov, *Nechistaia sila*, 1:23. See also Ju.M. Lotman and B.A. Uspenskij, "New Aspects in the Study of Early Russian Culture," in their *The Semiotics of Russian Culture*, ed. Ann Shukman, Michigan Slavic Contributions, no.11 (Ann Arbor: Department of Slavic Languages and Literatures, University of Michigan, 1984), 36–52.
43. See tale no.153 in A.N. Afanas'ev, *Narodnye russkie skazki*, ed. L.G. Barag and N.V. Novikov, 3 vols. (Moscow: Nauka, 1985), 1:272–75, in which the cunning soldier plays cards with the devil and outwits him. On the fondness of the devil for drunks, see motif nos.VI 12b, VI 45a and 45b.
44. Ch. 40, question 20, in I.P. Sakharov, *Skazaniia russkogo naroda*, ed. V.P. Anikin (reprint, Moscow: Gnosis, 1990), 391. See also the strictures contained in the sixteenth-century *Domostroi*: Carolyn Johnston Pouncy, ed. and trans., *The*

"Domostroi": Rules for Russian Households in the Reign of Ivan the Terrible (Ithaca and London: Cornell University Press, 1994), 186.

45. See the tale of the drunken tailor and the devil in Novichkova, *Russkii demono-logicheskii slovar'*, 610–11. The traditional link between the devil and treasure trove is similarly exploited to indict the "money devil" (556).

46. Ibid., 509.

47. For a recent edition of the standard collection of charms, see A.K. Baiburin, ed., *Velikorusskie zaklinaniia. Sbornik L.N. Maikova* (St. Petersburg: Izdatel'stvo evropeiskogo doma, 1994), with additional material in Sakharov, *Skazaniia russkogo naroda*, 47–76. For a useful survey of spoiling and sorcery, see Ivanits, *Russian Folk Belief*, 83–124; on sorcery and charms in Muscovite Russia, see Ryan, "The Witchcraft Hysteria."

48. See Pamela Davidson's essay in this volume "Divine Service or Idol Worship? Russian Views of Art as Demonic."

49. Ryan, "The Witchcraft Hysteria," 67, 71–72.

50. On *chernoknizhniki*, see Novichkova, *Russkii demonologicheskii slovar'*, 571–76.

51. On Brius's reputation and connections with divination, see Faith Wigzell, *Reading Russian Fortunes: Print Culture, Gender and Divination in Russia from 1765* (Cambridge: Cambridge University Press, 1998), 161–63.

52. Jeffrey Brooks, *When Russia Learnt to Read: Literacy and Popular Literature, 1861–1917* (Princeton: Princeton University Press, 1985), 22.

53. As in other traditional cultures. See Devlin, *The Superstitious Mind*, 165–66.

54. Tale no.154 in Afanas'ev, *Narodnye russkie skazki*, 1:275–77.

55. For example, tales nos.174–76 in Zinov'ev, comp., *Mifologicheskie rasskazy*; Ivanits, *Russian Folk Belief*, 43.

56. Published in N.A. Tarkhova, ed., *Literaturnye skazki pushkinskogo vremeni* (Moscow: Pravda, 1988), 85–94.

57. For more details on the genre, see E.V. Dushechkina, *Russkii sviatochnyi rasskaz* (St. Petersburg: Sankt-Peterburgskii gosudarstvennyi universitet, 1995).

58. Largely drawn from Ukrainian folklore. Differences certainly exist between Ukrainian and Russian folk belief, but many more beliefs about the devil are shared than are distinct. In the context of Russian literary demonism these differences are of little consequence. As is well known, some supernatural elements in the stories also stem from German Romanticism, but generally not those about the devil.

59. James M. Holquist, "The Devil in Mufti: The *Märchenwelt* in Gogol's Early Stories," *Publications of the Modern Language Association of America* 82 (1967):352–62(355).

60. Sakharov, *Skazaniia russkogo naroda*, 89–90; Zinov'ev, comp., *Mifologicheskie rasskazy*, nos.172, 173 (motif no.VI 51); Ivanits, *Russian Folk Belief*, 168. On the influence of Tieck's story "The Love Spell" (Liebeszauber), see Frederick C. Driessen, *Gogol as a Short Story Writer* (The Hague: Mouton, 1965), 76–85. The commentary in N.V. Gogol', *Polnoe sobranie sochinenii*, ed. N.L. Meshcheriakov and others, 14 vols. (Moscow and Leningrad: Izdatel'stvo Akademii nauk SSSR, 1937–52), 1:527–28, disputes the link with Tieck in favour of Ukrainian folk sources, but fails to explain the tone of horror which belongs much more to German Romanticism than to Ukrainian folklore.

61. It was known in early Russian literature in the form of one of the tales attached to the *Life of Saint Basil*, which was gradually russified, culminating in the seventeenth-century work, *The Tale of Savva Grudtsyn*; see R. Cleminson, "The miracle *De juvene qui Christum negaverat* in the pseudo-Amphilochian *Vita Basilii* and its Slavonic adaptations," *Parergon* 9, no.2 (1991):1–15.

62. Gogol', *Polnoe sobranie sochinenii*, 1:527.

63. Ibid., 10:142.

64. A.S. Pushkin, *Polnoe sobranie sochinenii*, ed. V.D. Bonch-Bruevich, 17 vols. (Moscow: Izdatel'stvo Akademii nauk SSSR, 1937–59), 3(book 1):226–27.

65. Novichkova, *Russkii demonologicheskii slovar'*, 397–98.

66. See variants a (cited) and b, in Pushkin, *Polnoe sobranie sochinenii*, 3(book 2):837.

67. Published in Tarkhova, ed., *Literaturnye skazki*, 284–97.

68. Text and commentary may be found in A.V. Rychkov, "'Umnyi i original'nyi chelovek...'," in *Vstrechi s proshlym*, ed. N.B. Volkova and others, Sbornik materialov Tsentral'nogo gosudarstvennogo arkhiva literatury i iskusstva SSSR, no.5 (Moscow: Sovetskaia Rossiia, 1987), 61–69. Leskov's last work, "The Devil's Dolls" (Chertovy kukly, 1890), with its theme of the artist whose creative freedom is seriously constrained by an oppressive ruler, owes little to folk devilry.

69. First discussed by Dmitrii Merezhkovsky in 1906; see his "Gogol and the Devil," in *Gogol from the Twentieth Century*, ed. Robert Maguire (Princeton: Princeton University Press, 1974), 57–102.

70. Gogol', *Polnoe sobranie sochinenii*, 5:149.

71. Deacon Akhilla in *Cathedral Folk*, who indulges in fisticuffs and pranks of various kinds, embodies these tendencies even more obviously than the hero of *The Enchanted Wanderer*, Ivan Fliagin.

72. The renewed focus on Slav mythology reflected the similar interests of the mythological school of folklore, best represented in Russia by A.N. Afanas'ev, notably in his *Poeticheskie vozzreniia slavian na prirodu* (1865–69). For a general survey of symbolist approaches to folklore, see Iu.K. Gerasimov, "Russkii simvolizm i fol'klor," *Russkaia literatura* 1985, no.1:95–109.

73. "O veselom remesle i umnom veselii" (1907), in Viacheslav Ivanov, *Sobranie sochinenii*, ed. D.V. Ivanov and O. Deschartes, 4 vols. (Brussels: Foyer Oriental Chrétien, 1971–87), 3:61–77(70).

74. For a reproduction, see Mikhail Guerman, ed., *Mikhail Vrubel*, comp. Alla Gaiduk and others, trans. John Greenfield and Valery Dereviaghin (Leningrad: Aurora Art Publishers, 1985), plate 116.

75. See, for example, the cycle "Raiskaia mat'" from *Kormchie zvezdy* (1903), and poems such as "Kitovras" or "Zharbog" from Ivanov's third collection *Eros* (1907); Ivanov, *Sobranie sochinenii*, 1:552–58 and 2:365, 367–68, respectively.

76. "Poet i chern'," in Ivanov, *Sobranie sochinenii*, 1:709–14(714).

77. Aleksandr Blok, "Tvorchestvo Viacheslava Ivanova" (1905), in his *Sobranie sochinenii*, ed. V.N. Orlov, A.A. Surkov, and K.I. Chukovskii, 8 vols. (Moscow and Leningrad: Gosudarstvennoe izdatel'stvo khudozhestvennoi literatury, 1960–63), 5:10.

78. See, for example, the poems "Bolotnye cherteniatki" (later dedicated to Remizov, with whom Blok shared a strong interest in folklore), "Boloto – glubokaia vpadina...," and "Starushka i cherteniata." Ibid., 2:10, 19, 20–21.

79. Sergei Gorodetskii, "Blizhaishaia zadacha russkoi literatury," *Zolotoe runo*, 1909, no.4:66–81(71–72).

80. From Bal'mont's collection *Zlye chary* (1906), in K. Bal'mont, *Izbrannoe: Stikhotvoreniia. Perevody. Stat'i*, comp. V. Bal'mont with notes by R. Pomirchii (Moscow: Khudozhestvennaia literatura, 1980), 235.

81. Blok, *Sobranie sochinenii*, 5:36–65.

Chapter 3

Antichrist Enthroned:
Demonic Visions of
Russian Rulers

Kevin Platt

I say to you [Ivan IV] again that when you secretly made your vow to the devil and his angels and gathered your devilish troops, establishing your accursed flatterers to lead them, you trampled on the commandments of Christ and rejected the evangelical law. Knowing the will of the Heavenly Lord, you have carried out the will of Satan.

Prince A.M. Kurbsky, History of Ivan IV[1]

And furthermore we have neither recognized nor obeyed any authority since the year 1666. We denounce, damn and trample Nikon the heretic, Aleksei the faithless and most of all the Emperor Peter the First as popes and Antichrists – as Satan himself and his steward – as well as your Emperor Nicholas as an oathbreaker and all of his godless legislation – the laws of Antichrist.

Old Believer manuscript of the early nineteenth century[2]

Sometimes it seems that the contradictions of the two elements dear to him [Peter I] – fire and water – have been fused in him into one being, strange and alien – whether good or evil, divine or devilish, I do not know – but certainly not human.

D.S. Merezhkovsky, from Antichrist (Peter and Aleksei)[3]

The Enigma of the Strong Russian Ruler

Russian culture harbours a peculiarly divided conception of its harshest rulers. Such figures as Ivan IV, Peter I and Joseph Stalin have been alternately elevated as earthly gods – intermediaries between mundane existence and sacred, transhistorical truths – and anathematized as personifications of evil, as Satan or even the Antichrist – who bring havoc and mayhem down upon the Russian people. This odd, dual tradition of interpretation regarding Russia's strong rulers reaches at least four centuries into the past, where it is rooted in late medieval writings regarding the sacral nature of the tsar and the associated hermeneutic quandary presented by a ruler who deviates from this sacral notion of authority. In this regard, Peter I and Ivan IV, for their departures from previous norms of policy and governance and for the harshness with which they pursued their innovations, earned places in the Russian historical consciousness both as glorious points of origin in the modern Russian political mythology and as prototypical tyrants. The centuries since their reigns have produced a large number of texts devoted to these rulers in various genres – history, literature, publicistic writing – some praising them as the apotheosis and grand initiators of Russian political and cultural institutions, some literally demonizing them as representatives of hellish, unholy forces, and some playing these various alternatives against one another. The function of texts belonging to this tradition of cultural and historical interpretation has likewise varied greatly, ranging from attempts to make sense out of the Russian cosmos and the place in it of the malicious tsar in chronicles of the late medieval period, to investigations of a Romantic historical-mythological nature such as A.K. Tolstoi's novel *Prince Serebrianyi* (*Kniaz' Serebrianyi*), to meditations on the role of coercion in social progress, charged with fully contemporary political import, such as A.S. Pushkin's masterpiece *The Bronze Horseman* (*Mednyi vsadnik*) or part two of S.M. Eizenshtein's magnificent film *Ivan the Terrible* (*Ivan Groznyi*). The present chapter constitutes an attempt to comprehend the demonic conception of Russia's tyrannical rulers, chiefly Ivan IV and Peter I, by describing the paradigm of significance associated with these figures in Russian historiography, literature, and popular culture and the evolution of this paradigm in modern Russia.

The Medieval Inheritance: Tsars, Saints, and Devils

I begin my overview of this complex network of interrelated topics with a consideration of the medieval texts which set the ground for later demonizing treatments of Russian rulers in modern historical and literary works. I should note at the outset that the significance of many of the writings which serve as crucial sources in traditional histories of medieval Russian political life is uncertain at best. In particular, Edward Keenan has cast considerable doubt on both the provenance and the representative character of many canonical texts and commonplaces of standard historical interpretations of the late medieval period I am concerned with here.[4] However, for the purposes of the present inquiry the undoubtedly serious problem of medieval Russian sources is largely moot. Regardless of the validity or invalidity of traditional histories of medieval Muscovy, my concern here is not medieval Russia *per se*, but rather the reception of the past germane to modern Russia, which is revealed precisely by the sources, canons, and narratives of traditional Russian historiography. The point of departure for my inquiry is that conception of the sacral nature of the Orthodox Christian tsar operative in a number of medieval and early modern texts which was later taken up in the vision of the Holy Russian past familiar from imperial Russian political and cultural traditions – a conception which played a crucial role in modern interpretations of harsh Russian rulers. As Michael Cherniavsky observed decades ago in his classic study of Russian political mythology, this conception of the tsar is in many ways reminiscent of Western doctrines concerning the dual nature of divinely ordained monarchs, for the tsar is viewed as possessing both divine and human qualities.[5] On one hand, as in the Western doctrine of kingship, the tsar is seen as a representative of heavenly power on earth, who therefore partakes of the authority and divinity of God above. In some late medieval texts this conception of the tsar is compounded by notions of the universal mission of the Russian state as the one true Orthodox kingdom, of Moscow as the "Third Rome" and therefore of the tsar as the protector of the Christian faith. Yet on the other hand, in distinction from Western ideological constructions in which the divine nature of the king's office is tempered by a recognition of the mortal and therefore potentially sinful nature of the person of the ruler, the human aspect of the Russian ruler is itself sacralized to the extent that the princes of medieval Russia were viewed as saints and frequently canonized.[6] In Cherniavsky's formulation: "While in the West it was possible … to distinguish between the king as man, mortal and sinful, and the king as King, the anointed of God, who was to be regarded and obeyed as God, this distinction would be meaningless in Russia; the prince as the vicegerent of God was contrasted with the man who was a saint, and as such, again, the image of Christ, possessed of eternal life."[7]

Under ordinary circumstances this model of cosmos and state would appear to present an admirably well organized conception of spiritual and political power: the tsar as human yet saintly is clearly a fitting temporal repository for heavenly authority. Yet this conception of the tsar presented difficulties in late medieval treatments of the extraordinary circumstances of a patently unjust or tyrannical ruler: for how is one to explain the actions of such a ruler if his nature as such does not allow for moral or spiritual corruption? Iosif Volotsky, the Abbot of Volokolamsk, devotes considerable energy to discussion of unjust rulers in what is one of the most well-known late medieval Russian pronouncements on political power, included in the final section of his didactic anti-heretical work *The Illuminator* (*Prosvetitel'*). Iosif concludes that such rulers are in fact not the representatives of Christ on earth at all, but quite the reverse: "Any King or Prince who lives in sinfulness, who does not care for those beneath him and does not fear God makes himself into a servant of Satan... . For a tsar who does not care for those under him is not a tsar, but a tormentor."[8] In a reversal that follows from the exalted sacral nature of the true tsar, it would seem that the false tsar can only be viewed as a Satanic figure. The Ivan IV-Kurbsky correspondence provides further examples of the application of this model of power to the malicious ruler. Much of Kurbsky's argumentation is calculated to demonstrate not only that Ivan IV is a tyrannical ruler, but that his failure to rule justly in fact renders him heretical and demonic: "O Tsar, most glorified by God and most radiant among the Orthodox; now – for our sins – having become opposite to this (let those comprehend who may), having a leprous conscience the likes of which can not be found among the godless pagans;" "O servant of the ancient beast and greatest dragon, who from time immemorial struggles against God and his angels and desires to destroy all divine creation and all human nature!"[9]

However, the situation is somewhat more complex than a conception of the legitimacy of saintly good tsars and the illegitimacy of Satanic bad ones. For despite Kurbsky's zeal in unmasking the demonic nature of Ivan, one may observe that the portions of the correspondence attributed to Ivan easily dismiss Kurbsky's accusations as lacking in the authority needed to judge the divinely appointed tsar. Indeed, late medieval Russian writings in general encounter great difficulty in suggesting how one might actually deal with a malicious ruler. In his efforts to formulate a consistent notion of the ruler's heavenly power and earthly duty Iosif Volotsky sought to temper the divine authority of the throne by cautioning that unimaginable punishment awaits the false ruler in the afterlife, and even goes so far as to grant to the subjects of such a ruler the right to disobedience – a concession of seemingly profound political significance. Yet as Marc Raeff has pointed out, Iosif Volotsky's formulations are rather contradictory, for he also maintains that the tsar is the highest authority in all matters, spiritual as well as temporal. Who, then, can legitimately pass judgement over the king's blasphemies or inequities?[10] In practice, the Abbot of Volokolamsk left

8. "The Secession of Satan and His Forces from the Angelic Order." Miniature from a late-sixteenth-century Russian manuscript. Pen, ink, tempera, 28,8 × 18,7 cm.

this question unresolved, preserving the unimpeachable authority of the tsar, no matter how unjust or heretical he might be, and extending to subjects only the right to suffer for their faith if they believed the tsar to be false. While one has a duty to resist evil, one must in any case submit to the divinely ordained powers, leaving the question of whether these might in fact derive from Satan rather than God to be sorted out in the afterlife. As Cherniavsky notes, it is this same ideological knot which is operative in the Ivan IV-Kurbsky correspondence. The only court of appeals is the Last Judgement, as Ivan points out when he invites Kurbsky to return and be martyred if he is so certain of the tsar's falsity.[11] The *vita* of Archbishop Filip casts the saint into a similar difficulty, which he solves by in fact accepting martyrdom at the hands of the terrible tsar.[12]

Texts concerning the tsar-pretenders of the Time of Troubles provide further examples of the consequences of the sacralized conception of the tsar for the treatment of malicious or illegitimate rulers.[13] Seventeenth-century writings on the Time of Troubles such as the *Tale* (*Skazanie*) of Avraamii Palitsyn or the *Chronicle* (*Vremennik*) of Ivan Timofeev contrast saintly true tsars such as Fedor Ivanovich or Mikhail Fedorovich with pretenders who are not only duplicitous usurpers, but emissaries of unholy powers and the instruments of divine retribution.[14] In these texts the pretenders possess powers of sorcery and engage in heretical behaviour such as disrespect for icons or disregard for dietary proscriptions. Their reigns are held to be heavenly punishment for the sins of the Russian people.[15] As in Iosif Volotsky's case, here it would seem that if the true tsar is elevated to the status of divinely appointed saint, the wrongful occupant of the Russian throne must therefore be regarded as Satanic. Yet writings concerning the tsar-pretenders also provide evidence concerning the fundamental uninterpretability of the Russian ruler by this mythology of power. Timofeev concedes the skill of Boris Godunov as a ruler and the lawfulness of his election to the throne, yet claims that his fundamental unsuitability to rule derived from his affirmation as tsar by an act of human will rather than by divine election. Alternatively, the same chronicler regards the Tatar sack of Moscow of 1571 as a retribution for the sins of Ivan IV, yet in the tsar's repentance and humble submission to God's punishment Timofeev recognizes him as the true tsar and the rightful bearer of divine authority.[16] As Cherniavsky observes, Timofeev's explanation of the legitimacy of the tsar is basically inoperable: the actions of the ruler in no way demonstrate his nature, but rather the proper interpretation of his actions depends on the truth or falsity of the tsar, which cannot be judged by any but God above.[17]

This late medieval conception of the sacral nature of the tsar provides a fundamental paradigm which later Russian political, historiographic, and cultural traditions would draw upon in constructing a politically useful image of the past. In sum, the sacral idea of the ruler leads to an exaggerated duality in the terms which are applied to certain key figures claiming the authority of the throne in the Russian historical imagination: either the tsar is true or he is false, he is divine or Satanic. Yet on a more complex level the sacralized conception of the monarch leads to a profound degree of ambiguity with regard to malicious rulers. In short, the tsar is himself the source of interpretive authority, and so in practice the distinction between the true tsar and the false tsar lies outside the realm of human judgement. Of course, this difficulty resonates in an interesting manner with the Christian and Orthodox tradition concerning demons, for, as Simon Franklin explains in his contribution to this volume, the evil one has a tendency to disguise himself as a friend or even a holy figure such as Christ. Thus the sheer indecipherability of the unjust ruler, who may oscillate between the divine and the diabolical in an unpredictable fashion, might be seen as a further demonic attribute of the false ruler. In late medieval texts this aspect of the paradigm of the demonic is adduced as retrospective proof of the true nature of the false tsar, as in Avraamii Palitsyn's remarks on the inability of the Russian ecclesiastical authorities to comprehend the perfidy of Boris Godunov, who masked his essential evil with seemingly good deeds: "Woe, woe is me, for I know not my left hand from my right and I am incapable of distinguishing bitter from sweet!"[18] But the full rhetorical potential of this implication of the Russian sacralization of the tsar would be fully exploited only in modern literature, with its greater technical and philosophical capacity to investigate ambiguity and inconclusiveness.

The Historiographic and Popular Memory of Tyranny: Sanctification and Demonization of Ivan IV and Peter I

The cultural paradigm regarding false tsars is particularly relevant for the reception in Russia of two figures of critical importance for the modern literary and political traditions: Ivan IV and Peter I. The interpretive conventions commonly associated with these two figures employ the features I have identified above as characteristic of the late medieval notion of the authority of the tsar, including both sacralization and association with unholy powers. Investigation of the reception of Ivan IV and Peter I in the Russian historical and cultural traditions is complicated by the extreme variance in the assessments of the two rulers in discrete areas of public discourse. Over the centuries since their reigns each of these two rulers has been alternately vilified and eulogized in folklore, historical writing, and artistic and literary works. Although particular sources or areas of public discourse often assess the two rulers in diametrically opposite manner (the Old Believer communities that viewed Peter I as Antichrist saw Ivan IV as a pious Christian tsar), when taken as a whole the overall range of assessments is remarkably similar for the two rulers. As I demonstrate below, this is due to the comparable role the two figures play in historical myths concerning the origins of modern Russian political institutions in the late medieval and pre-modern period.

I begin with the oral tradition concerning Ivan IV. On the basis of the early written record and later oral texts, folklorists such as Maureen Perrie and S.K. Rosovetsky have reconstructed a hypothetical late sixteenth-century and early seventeenth-century oral tradition of vilification of Ivan IV in terms of the paradigm of the malicious and

evil tsar.[19] Their sources include the Ivan IV-Kurbsky correspondence; the *History of Ivan IV* also attributed to Kurbsky (see the first
epigraph to this chapter); accounts of foreign travellers to Muscovy
such as Albert Schlichting, Ioganne Taube, and Elert Kruse, and later,
Samuel Collins; and seventeenth-century chronicles and historical
accounts (particularly of the northern regions which suffered bloody
repression during the reign of Ivan IV). Common in these sources are
stories of the confrontation of Ivan with evidence of his evil nature,
such as Schlichting's account of the tsar's execution of the "virtuous
man" Fedor Bashkin. When Bashkin refuses to obey Ivan's command
to convert from Lutheranism, the tsar, "animated by Satan," orders
the unfortunate to be burnt: "If you hold to the evangelical faith, then
let the fire take you."[20] Taube and Kruse recount the tale (repeated in
various other sources) of how the holy fool Mikula of Pskov accused
Ivan IV of godlessness ("how much longer will you spill blameless
Christian blood?"), thus frightening the tsar away from further bloodshed and saving Pskov from sharing the fate of Novgorod.[21] Often,
the unmasking of the evil of the tsar assumes a miraculous character,
as in the tale of the merchant Khariton Beloulin, who is put to death
in a mass execution of innocents on Red Square and whose head continues to denounce the tsar's injustices after being separated from his
body.[22] Rosovetsky and Ia.S. Lur'e have drawn attention to the parallels of this hypothetical early oral tradition with the cycle of tales
concerning the legendary figure of Dracula, based on the fifteenth-
century Wallachian prince Vlad Tepes. In this regard one may mention the tales of the "cruelly ingenious" punishments of the tsar that
directly echo the Dracula tales, such as nailing a hat to the head of a
dignitary who refuses to doff it in the royal presence, relieving the
poverty of the indigent poor by having them put to death, and
rewarding or punishing soldiers after battle according to whether they
are wounded on the front of their bodies or the back.[23] In composite,
these texts appear to draw on an early oral tradition which represented Ivan IV in terms of common folkloric motifs as a tyrannical
ruler allied with evil and often directly identified with Satanic forces.
It has been hypothesized that this conception of Ivan should be interpreted as the legacy of his political enemies and victims.[24]

However, despite the continued presence in the Russian oral tradition and written record of tales concerning the malicious and evil
nature of Ivan IV, the dominant folkloric image of the first tsar of
Muscovy is of the just yet harsh ruler. As Perrie has argued, from the
mid-seventeenth century forward historical songs and tales concerning Ivan cast him in a positive light. The most productive cycles of
tales and songs concerning Ivan describe the heroic capture of
Kazan, the relations of the tsar with the cossacks, the conquest of

Siberia and the destruction of Novgorod. If the tsar is seen to be harsh, his actions are often presented as either just in nature or the result of the deceptions of evil sorcerers or advisers. The majority even of tales concerning Ivan's cruel and inventive punishments describe these as the acts of a stern, yet just ruler against criminals, traitors, enemies, and marginalized groups (a repellent nineteenth-century version of the tale of nailing hats to heads concerns a yarmulke and the head of a Jew).[25] Furthermore, Old Believer writings concerning Ivan represent his reign as a golden age predating the Time of Troubles and later rulers who were associated with religious reform, civil unrest, and economic hardship. Thus the overall folkloric image of Ivan IV in later years presents him as a "hot-tempered and impulsive ruler, the scourge of overweening boyars and corrupt officials, who, although he was over-inclined to give credence to evil informers who falsely denounced fellow-citizens as traitors, was nevertheless quick to repent the consequences of his actions when he was brought to recognize that they had been unjust."[26]

Historical treatments of Ivan IV feature a similar wide range in interpretation.[27] Eighteenth-century Russian historians such as V.N. Tatishchev and I.N. Boltin viewed Ivan's reign in a positive light, justifying his policies as necessary measures to strengthen the autocracy. Similar reasoning was adopted by "statist" Hegelian historians of the nineteenth century such as K.D. Kavelin, K.N. Bestuzhev-Riumin, and S.M. Solov'ev (and by other notable members of the Hegelian camp, such as V.G. Belinsky) who viewed the terrible tsar's excesses as reflections of the "rational" and "progressive" struggle of the state against the conservative boyar class in the interests of the creation of a centralized modern state, a middle service class, and geopolitical and economic advantages for Muscovy. This view further evolved in the early twentieth century, when Soviet historians cast Ivan IV's policies as motivated by the transition from feudal to imperial political structures or, in M.N. Pokrovsky's version, from an agrarian to a merchant-capital economy. This approach reached its apogee in the work of official historians of the 1930s and 1940s, such as S.V. Bakhrushin and R.I. Wipper, who saw a "great predecessor" to Stalin in Ivan IV – a far-sighted military genius devoted to the creation and defence of a strong state who used terror as a calculated response to treasonous conspiracies.[28] A common thread running through this interpretive tradition, beginning with Tatishchev and continuing to the twentieth century, is the conception of Ivan IV as a predecessor of Peter I in that the former's northern and southern conquests and domestic policies were ostensibly motivated by aims of modernization and increased commerce with the West similar to those which animated the latter's military and political undertakings.[29]

However, an alternative and equally productive approach to the
history of Ivan IV presents a remarkable contrast to this apologist
version. Perhaps the most notable landmark in this other vision of
Ivan is the work of N.M. Karamzin, Russia's first "official historian,"
who stunned contemporaries with his outright condemnation of the
terrible tsar in the harshest possible terms as a "tormentor" and a
"tyrant" in the ninth volume of his monumental *History of the Russian
State* (*Istoriia gosudarstva rossiiskogo*); the future Decembrist Ryleev,
upon reading this volume, wrote "Well there's an Ivan! Well there's
a Karamzin!"[30] While the generic conventions of historical writing
clearly do not permit extensive development of the demonic potential of Ivan's character, Karamzin comprehended world history as
the unfolding of divine providence, and he clearly placed the mature
Ivan in the camp of unholy historical forces.[31] In this connection,
Karamzin's rhetoric calls directly upon the tradition of interpretation
of false tsars. He borrows much of his story-telling technique from
his seventeenth-century sources, as where he paraphrases chronicle
entries describing the terrors as an "alien storm, somehow sent from
the depths of hell to plague and torment Russia,"[32] or when he
relates the tale of the confrontation of Filip and Ivan in the terms of
the saint's *vita*, including his denunciation of the unholy nature of the
tsar's policies and of the "martyrdom" of innocents.[33] Karamzin
often adopts the rhetoric of the chronicle for his own, as where he
interprets Ivan's periods of repentance as the "implacable voice of
conscience" that "disturbed the troubled sleep of his soul, preparing
it for a sudden and terrible awakening in the grave!;"[34] where he
comments that "one cannot without trembling read in the accounts
of contemporaries about all the hellish inventions of the tyrant,
about all the ways of tormenting humanity!;" or tells the reader that
"we will a final time show Ivan as the baneful Angel of Darkness for
Russians, red with the sacred blood of the innocent."[35] Throughout
his discussion Karamzin refers as well to the late medieval situation
of interpretive ambiguity regarding tyrannical rulers, remarking
approvingly that the Russian people withstood "the terror of the
autocrat-tormentor" with "love for the autocracy, for they believed
that God Himself sends plague, earthquakes and tyrants."[36]
Karamzin's own analysis itself reflects a similar conception of the
indecipherability of Ivan, for: "In spite of all speculative explanations, the character of Ivan, a hero of virtue in his youth, a frenzied
bloodsucker in his maturity and old age, is a riddle for the mind."[37]
Karamzin's interpretation of Ivan, which discounts any rational
motivation for his bloody policies, was followed in its evaluative
position by a series of subsequent authors, including M.P. Pogodin,
N.I. Kostomarov, V.O. Kliuchevsky. These later historians, who

attempted to assume the academic stance of "scientific" historiography, allowed much less of the providential or supernatural to infiltrate their rhetoric than did Karamzin. Yet even so, the connection of Ivan with unholy forces sometimes bleeds through the causal explanations of his character and reign, as where Kostomarov, after a lengthy discussion of the psychology of the tsar, concludes that "the tyrant ... was frightened in earnest of the devils depicted on icons of the Last Judgement; truly, he clearly imagined what his soul was to experience upon parting with his body and meeting with demons ready to drag it with their hooks into the underworld."[38] And, of course, Karamzin's analysis and rhetorical example is of primary importance for subsequent Russian culture, both as a historical work of unparalleled authority, and as a cornerstone in the building of Russian narrative prose.

The reception of Peter I in Russia has been no less complex than that of Ivan IV. As with the "terrible" tsar, the "tsar-transformer" has had his admirers and detractors. The latter include such notables as Princess E.R. Dashkova, M.M. Shcherbatov, and Karamzin. The latter two, although recognizing the great importance of the Petrine reforms, condemned the tsar for his despotic methods and radical cultural innovations. In Karamzin's formulation, Peter's "passion for foreign customs surely exceeded the bounds of reason.... By uprooting ancient customs ... the sovereign of the Russians humbled Russian hearts. Does humiliation predispose a man to great deeds?"[39] Amplifying and modifying this view, Slavophile thinkers viewed the Petrine reforms as a demolition of the virtuous and uncorrupted Old Russian society and as the wellspring of the modern vices of bureaucratic rule and the associated alienation of "the people" from the gentry. Other, less Romantic critiques of Peter have included those of P.N. Miliukov, who, like Dashkova a century and a half earlier, viewed the first emperor as a tyrant given to grandiose schemes and drunken brawling. Late in the twentieth century some scholars, such as E.V. Anisimov, have formulated interpretations of Peter similar to those of Karamzin.[40]

Yet the majority of historical treatments of Peter stand in great contrast to these negative evaluations. Cultural mythology and official rhetoric contemporary to the "great reformer" exalted Peter as the founder of the modern Russian state and "re-creator" of the Russian people *ex nihilo* according to the ideals of rational law and service to the common good. This vision of Peter found later expression in the works of the "anecdotist" chroniclers of the eighteenth century, Iakov Stälin and Ivan Golikov, and later still in the rhetoric of Nicholas I's Official Nationality (Count E. Krankin, Nicholas's minister of finance, is supposed to have suggested that "If we consider the matter thoroughly, then, in justice, we must be called not *Russians*, but *Petrovians*").[41] One may mention as well the celebratory historical works of N.A. Polevoi and the Romantic philosophical works of P.Ia. Chaadaev ("All Peter the Great found at home was a sheet of white paper and, in his powerful handwriting, he wrote on it the words 'Europe' and 'The West'.").[42] In similar fashion, the Westernizers, like their Slavophile polemical opponents, perceived Peter and his policies as marking a complete break with Russia's native tradition of cultural isolation, although, in contrast, they approved of this break as the salvation of a "backwards" Russia. Later "scientific" historians, such as Kavelin, Solov'ev, and Kliuchevsky worked to modify the prevailing view of the radical nature of the Petrine reforms, tracing the precedents of Peter's policies in the seventeenth-century Russian political tradition, yet they continued to celebrate the genius of the tsar-reformer. In the immediate post-Revolutionary years the importance of the Petrine reforms for the evolution of Russian society was still recognized, yet Peter's despotic rule and personality were subjected to severe criticism, most notably in the works of the official historian (i.e. endorsed by Lenin) M.N. Pokrovsky (according to Lenin, Peter did not refrain "from using barbaric means to fight barbarism").[43] Yet, as in the case of Ivan IV, historical works of the "Soviet imperial" 1930s and 1940s redeemed Peter I, promoting him to the rank of forerunner to Stalin in specific areas of activity such as military leadership and foreign policy.[44]

However, the most pertinent feature of the historiographical and publicistic tradition concerning Peter I for this investigation is the rhetorical deification of the first emperor from the time of his reign through to the mid-nineteenth century. Chancellor G. Golovkin, in a celebrated speech of 1721 in which he begged the autocrat to take the title "Father of the Fatherland," proclaimed that Peter had brought the Russian people "from non-existence to existence."[45] M.V. Lomonosov declared that "if you must find a man like unto God, according to our understanding, you will find none but Peter the Great."[46] A.P. Sumarokov repeated Lomonosov's metaphor almost word for word.[47] And it was recalled many times in the next century as well, as in Belinsky's view that Peter "was a divine figure, calling us to life, breathing life into the colossal body of Old Russia, which was mired in deathly slumber."[48] As Cherniavsky observes, this brand of rhetoric reflects both an appropriation of late medieval formulations concerning the sacral authority of the tsar and a departure from them, in that the political image of Peter presents him not as the representative of divine authority on earth, but rather as an earthly god. The rhetorical claims surrounding Peter state not that he made possible the salvation of his subjects in the next world, but rather that he pointed the path towards salvation in this one.[49]

Given the heretical implications of this inflation of the medieval
vision of the divine *authority* of the ruler into the Petrine vision of the
divine *person* of the ruler, it is unsurprising that the Russian cultural
tradition reflects an equally remarkable escalation of the notion of
the diabolical false tsar in connection with Peter I. To usurp the place
of God is, after all, a rather devilish thing to do. Contemporary interpretations of Peter's departures from traditional policy and court
behaviour as sinful and even Satanic are well known. Prince I.I.
Khovansky, for instance, describes his forced participation in Peter
I's "Assembly" as a Satanic ritual in which he imperilled his immortal soul.[50] Many saw Peter not simply as the servant of evil, but as the
Antichrist himself – a tendency which was most fully developed and
long-lived, of course, among Old Believer and sectant groups (see
Illustration 9).[51] This vision of the tsar-reformer followed the prece-

9. "Three Unclean Spirits, Coming out of the Mouths of the "Beast"-Antichrist
    (in the Image of Peter the Great), of Satan-"Dragon," and of a False Prophet
    (in the Image of Patriarch Nikon). Miniature from a late-nineteenth-century
    Russian manuscript. Pen, ink, tempera, 24 × 15,8 cm.

dent of the Old Believer accounts of Peter's father Aleksei Mikhailovich and of the Patriarch Nikon, both also viewed as Antichrists for their roles in the church reforms of the mid-seventeenth century. Yet the apocalyptic conception of Peter I was more widespread during his reign, extending outside of the Old Believer population to Orthodox believers and clergy, and proved to have greater staying power in subsequent generations of Russians.[52] The suitability of Peter for this role is quite evident. His monstrous figure and frightening nervous tics, his disappearance in Europe, where he travelled incognito in 1697–98, the ruthlessness with which he resorted to coercive and bloody measures to further his goals – all contributed to legends that he was a changeling or an illegitimate child (some texts conjecture that his father was none other than Patriarch Nikon). The deification of the emperor in official rhetoric provided traditionalist religious thinkers with evidence that the emperor was usurping the place of God.[53] Peter's innovative cultural policies, of course, added more fuel to the fire. The shaving of beards, which had been anathematized by Patriarch Hadrian as late as the last decade of the seventeenth century, the adoption of heretical "German" clothing (the traditional dress of devils during carnival), abolition of the patriarchate and subordination of the church to the control of the Holy Synod with the tsar at its head, the death under torture of the tsarevich Aleksei; the branding of recruits (seen by sectants as the apocalyptic "mark of the beast"); Peter's assumption of the title of Emperor ("Imperator," by means of Russian numerological manipulation, could be brought into correspondence with "Antichrist") – all of these elements and more, as well as numerological, prophetic, and mystical "evidence," were mobilized to demonstrate that Peter I was the lord of darkness.[54]

Thus the modern Russian historical, publicistic, and cultural traditions have generated widely variable interpretations of Ivan IV and Peter I, with characterizations ranging from the Satanic to the divine. The notions of power associated with these figures draw alternately upon the late medieval model of the sacral authority of the tsar and upon the related diabolical conception of the harsh or malicious ruler. By the dawn of modernity these notions appear not only genetically connected, but rhetorically as well – for Peter's assumption of divinity serves to motivate and justify the diabolical vision of him. To a certain extent, the connection of this paradigm of authority to Ivan IV and Peter I is due to the role they both play in historical myths of origins associated with modern Russian political and cultural institutions. Ivan was assigned, perhaps largely retrospectively, the role of first Muscovite tsar, final victor over the remnants of the Mongol invaders – in later formulations, creator of the centralized Russian state or of modern economic forms. Peter, on the other hand, intentionally projected the idea of his initiation of a new "European" epoch in Russia as the central feature of his political rhetoric, and this idea was taken up wholeheartedly by subsequent historical mythology. The role of glorious initiator of a new epoch endowed each with highly equivocal characteristics in modern Russian historical discourse. They figure equally as heirs of the mythic past and as rebels against tradition. Their authority is seen to stem from the late medieval notion of sacral authority associated with the image of the Holy Russian past, yet at the same time their departures from these same "sacred" traditional social and political norms are open to diabolical interpretation. M.A. Voloshin's pithy epithet for Peter, the "first Bolshevik" ("pervyi bol'shevik," a term which, paradoxically, might be applied as well to Ivan IV) presents in distilled form the hermeneutic quandary associated with these figures: themselves the ostensible source of all authority, they nevertheless challenge the social and symbolic institutions supporting that very authority.[55] Throughout the last three centuries this conception of the originative status of the two rulers and the associated dynamic of interpretation has been broadly shared in the historical thought of both conservative and progressive groups, of various periods and various social strata. Each successive vision of the past has turned the unstable and therefore protean historical images of the two rulers to specific political ends, be they the denunciation or praise of modern Russia or of any of the grand historical missions that have been attributed to it. The result for later generations has been a highly volatile dual image of these two tsar-reformers, which has led to complex results in later artistic treatments of them.

Artistic Depiction of Ivan IV and Peter I: Variations on a Variable Theme

Perhaps needless to say, Ivan IV and Peter I have been perennial favourite subjects for artistic treatments of Russian history. The numerous literary, dramatic, operatic, and film treatments of these two figures (I will not address the visual arts here) range over the spectrum of available stances, often reflecting current debates in historiographic interpretation. To a certain degree, as Richard Taruskin has observed, the nineteenth-century popularity of Ivan IV as a topic for depiction on stage corresponds to the demands of the censor, which until late in the century forbade the dramatic treatment of members of the Romanov dynasty, thus increasing the artistic attention focused on the last tsars of the Riurik dynasty and the inter-

dynastic period.[56] Yet other factors more fully account for the popularity of Ivan IV and Peter I: namely, the inherent dramatic potential
of these figures, their importance in Russian historical mythology and
the continuing political relevance which they have therefore enjoyed
up to the present day. Although, in fact, most artistic visions of these
figures reflect some degree of both the positive and negative conceptions of the two rulers, artistic treatments of them may nevertheless be
roughly placed into three categories: primarily positive depictions,
primarily negative depictions, and thoroughly complex depictions.
Further, the artistic works of each of these three categories recall and
utilize the medieval Russian conception of sacral power and the
related demonic aspect of malicious or harsh rulers in different ways.

With regard to Peter I, the first category begins with the long tradition of eulogistic celebrations of the first emperor in verse, stretching
from the works of A.D. Kantemir (the lament *The Petride* [*Petrida*, 1731]
is his best-known work regarding Peter I), A.P. Sumarokov, M.V.
Lomonosov, G.R. Derzhavin (his "Monument of Peter the Great"
["Monument Petra Velikogo," 1776] is a particularly well-known exam-
ple), A.A. Petrov, and virtually every other literary figure of the eighteenth century to various of Pushkin's works, most notably his
"Stanzas" ("Stansy," 1826) and his epic poem *Poltava* (1828).[57] The
nineteenth-century genre of the historical novel contributed I.I.
Lazhechnikov's *The Last Recruit* (*Poslednii novik*, 1833), R.M. Zotov's
The Mysterious Monk (*Tainstvennyi monakh*, 1834), several novels by N.V.
Kukol'nik (as well as some shorter works on Petrine themes), M.N.
Zagoskin's *Russians at the Beginning of the Eighteenth Century* (*Russkie v
nachale XVIII-go stoletiia*, 1848), four of D.L. Mordovtsev's five historical novels treating Petrine material written during the 1870s and 1880s,
and other works.[58] In the twentieth century A.N. Tolstoi was the capable continuer of this positive interpretational tradition in the third volume of his classic novel *Peter the First* (*Petr Pervyi*, 1943–45). Tolstoi also
contributed to the Stalinist celebration of Peter I with the final versions
of his play and screenplay, both also called *Peter the First* (*Petr Pervyi*,
1937 and 1938, respectively). The nineteenth century contributed
comparatively fewer works of a laudatory nature regarding Ivan IV,
but I will mention M.Iu. Lermontov's *Song about Tsar Ivan Vasil'evich,
the Young Oprichnik, and the Valiant Merchant Kalashnikov* (*Pesnia pro tsaria
Ivana Vasil'evicha, molodogo oprichnika, i udalogo kuptsa Kalashnikova,*
1837), L.A. Mei's play *The Woman of Pskov* (*Pskovitianka*, 1860), adapted
by Rimsky-Korsakov for the operatic stage in 1872, A.N. Ostrovsky's
play *Vasilisa Melent'eva* (1867) and A.N. Maikov's poem "At the Tomb
of Ivan the Terrible" (U groba Groznogo, 1887), most of which reflect
to some degree Kavelin's and Solov'ev's views concerning the progressive significance of Ivan IV's reign, although all are also con-

cerned with the dramatic or psychological implications of the "terrible" nature of the tsar. However, the most significant artistic contributions to the positive literary image of Ivan IV were produced during the much later Stalinist vogue for Ivan, and include A.N. Tolstoi's "dramatic story in two parts" *Ivan the Terrible* (*Ivan Groznyi*, 1943), V.A. Solov'ev's tragedy *The Great Sovereign* (*Velikii gosudar'*, 1944), V.I. Kostylev's trilogy of novels concerning Ivan IV (1946), and, of course, the first part of Eizenshtein's acclaimed film *Ivan the Terrible* (*Ivan Groznyi*, film 1944; screenplay 1943).

All of these works celebrate Ivan IV and Peter I in terms of their grand accomplishments and their function as originative figures for Russian national history. Even in these primarily eulogistic or apologetic works, however, a negative and even demonic image of the two autocrats is sometimes evident beneath the triumphant façade. For example, as Richard Taruskin has observed, in Mei's *The Woman of Pskov* Ivan appears to debate the merits of Karamzin's and S.M. Solov'ev's views of his character, colourfully summarizing the former:

> Кем чаще: букой иль царем Иваном
> Тебя пугали в детстве?.. А когда
> Ты подросла, чай, наслыхалась притчей
> О некоем злодее, кровопийце,
> Гонителе бояр и слуг усердных,
> Мучителе, казнителе...
> Об изверге!.. От слова и до слова
> Готов я всю их песенку пропеть:
> «Он, мол, какой: чем только кто правее,
> Тем на суде его и виноватей;
> Кто житием, воистину молчальным
> И монастырским, Господу угоден,
> Тот у него – ханжа и лицемер;
> Кто лестию гнушается – завистник,
> А кто стоит за правду на присяге
> И целованью крёстному – отмётник,
> Злокозненный изменник и предатель!..
> И вот, мол, он мужей, толико доблих,
> Преславных царства русского сингклитов,
> Всеродно истребляет, аки зверь,
> О нем же нам гласит Апокалипсис...
> Ни возраста, ни пола не жалеет:
> Грудных младенцев, старцев беспомощных,
> Невинных дев терзает лютой мукой
> И тешится их кровью, со своею
> Кромешной тьмой, что сатана с бесами...»[59]

[With whom did they frighten you more often as a child:
The bogeyman or Tsar Ivan?.. And when
You grew up, no doubt you heard your fill of tales
Of a certain bloodthirsty villain,
The persecutor of the boyars and of devoted servants,

A tormentor, a hangman…
A monster!.. From beginning to end
I am prepared to sing their whole song through:
"This," they say, "is what he's like: the more righteous a person,
The more guilty in *his* judgement he is found;
Whoever through a life of true monastic discipline
Finds favour with the Lord
In *his* eyes is a fake and a hypocrite;
He who hates flattery is an envier,
And whoever stands by the truth sworn to
Over the cross is a renegade,
A perfidious traitor and a turncoat!..
"And just look," they say, "such virtuous men,
Glorious defenders of the Russian realm,
He is destroying them one and all, like a wild beast;
It is he of whom the Apocalypse speaks to us…
He pities neither age nor sex:
Babes in arms, the helpless aged
And innocent maidens – he torments all with cruel tortures
And takes pleasure in their blood, with his
Hellish pack, like Satan with his devils…"]

Mei's Ivan goes on to explain and justify his policies in terms recalling Solov'ev's teleological vision of history, as necessary measures in the grand project of state-building.[60] This "justification of evil," one might suggest, represents a Miltonic revision of the demonic conception of Ivan, in which his "Satanic" harshness is reconfigured as a Promethean rebellion against the constraints of an outworn past.

A comparable (although more pragmatic than Miltonic) apologetic scheme may be found in Maikov's "At the Tomb of Ivan the Terrible," and a similar, although much less explicit, dynamic is visible in Pushkin's "Stanzas." In this latter work, a reference to Peter I's bloody suppression of the *strel'tsy* uprising serves to remind Nicholas I, the addressee of the poem, that Peter I only achieved greatness by overcoming his cruel and arbitrary side:

> В надежде славы и добра
> Гляжу вперед я без боязни:
> Начало славных дней Петра
> Мрачили мятежи и казни.
>
> Но правдой он привлек сердца,
> Но нравы укротил наукой,
> И был от буйного стрельца
> Пред ним отличен Долгорукой.
>
> . . . .
>
> Семейным сходством будь же горд;
> Во всем будь пращуру подобен:
> Как он, неутомим и тверд,
> И памятью, как он, незлобен.[61]

[In hope of glory and of bliss
I glance ahead without misgiving:
The start of Peter's glorious days
Was dark with riot and execution.

By truth, though, he attracted hearts,
By learning, though, he gentled manners,
Before the wanton janissary
Was honored by him Dolgoruky.

. . . .

Be proud, then, of the kinship semblance;
In all be like unto the forbear:
Like him unfaltering and firm,
And in memory, like him, unspiteful.]

Pushkin's poem instructs Nicholas that to be true to the legacy of his ancestor he must progress along an analogous path, from the execution of the Decembrists towards enlightened rule.[62] Finally, a related approach may be found in A.N. Tolstoi's later works on both Peter I and Ivan IV, where the author does not baulk at examination of the harshness and even cruelty of the policies of the two rulers, but where these policies are seen to reflect the devotion of the autocrat to the greater goals of the economic, military, and political development of Russia. In these works one may discern an interesting evolution of the late medieval conception of the harsh or malicious autocrat. Whereas in early writings such as Timofeev's chronicle account or the Ivan IV-Kurbsky correspondence the actions of the tsar are insulated from the judgement of human institutions by virtue of the sacral nature of the tsar's office, in these nineteenth- and twentieth-century works the great cause of progressive history results in a similar brand of ineffability. As Maikov puts it:

Сведен итог его винам и преступленьям;
Был спрос свидетелей; поставлен приговор,
Но нечто высшее все медлит утвержденьем,
Недоумения толпа еще полна,
И тайной облечен досель сей гроб безмолвный...

. . . .

О, если б он предстал, теперь, в загробной схиме,
И сам, как некогда, народу речь держал:
«Я царство создавал и создал, и доныне, –
Сказал б он, – оно стоит четвертый век...
Судите *тут* меня. В паденьях и гордыне
Ответ мой Господу: пред Ним я – человек,
Пред вами – царь!»[63]

[Account has been given of his sins and crimes;
Witnesses have been questioned; a sentence has been pronounced,

But something higher still delays the confirmation,
The crowd is still filled with doubts,
And this silent tomb still remains clothed in mystery...

. . . .

O, if he were to rise now, in his funeral robe,
And address the people, as of old:
"I strove to create this kingdom and created it, and to this very day,"
He would say, "it is still standing in its fourth century...
Judge me *on this*! In all my falls and pride
My answer to God is as follows: before Him I am a man,
Before you – a tsar!"]

My second category of primarily negative artistic treatments of the two autocrats includes, with regard to Ivan IV, such works as A.K. Tolstoi's classic novel *Prince Serebrianyi* (1862) and the same author's play *The Death of Ivan the Terrible* (*Smert' Ioanna Groznogo,* 1866) and ballad *Prince Mikhailo Repnin* (*Kniaz' Mikhailo Repnin,* 1840s), and Lazhechnikov's *The Oprichnik* (*Oprichnik,* 1834), adapted as an opera by P.I. Tchaikovsky in 1874 (although the tsar could not be depicted in the opera for reasons of censorship).[64] All of these works take Karamzin's portrait of Ivan IV as their inspiration and all paint horrific and dark portraits of the tsar. Later in the century the historian Kostomarov, who, as noted above, was a late follower of Karamzin in his interpretation of Ivan IV, was moved to address his audience in *belles lettres* with a historical novel *Kudeiar* (*Kudeiar,* 1882) which depicts the tsar as a bloodthirsty tyrant. The twentieth century saw fewer purely negative depictions of Ivan IV, perhaps the only one of note being M.A. Bulgakov's comedy *Ivan Vasil'evich* (1935), later adapted for the big screen in the well-loved late Soviet classic *Ivan Vasil'evich Changes Profession* (*Ivan Vasil'evich meniaet professiiu,* 1973).[65] Primarily negative artistic depictions of Peter I are in general a rarity. From the nineteenth century one may name K.F. Ryleev's positive treatments of Hetman Mazepa's armed resistance to Peter I as a reflection of the Decembrist critique of the first Russian emperor's tyrannical authority. Mordovtsev, who, as noted above, wrote four novels that depict the tsar-reformer in a positive light, also authored a novel *Idealists and Realists* (*Idealisty i realisty,* 1878), which depicts the conservative followers of the tsarevich Aleksei as virtuous opponents of the villainous, greedy, and self-serving camp of Peter I and his followers. In the immediate post-Revolutionary period Boris Pil'niak and A.N. Tolstoi wrote shorter prose works that depict Peter I as a tyrant given to barbarity and cruelty both in his personal habits and in his methods of government: "His Majesty Kneeb Piter Komondor" ("Ego velichestvo Kneeb Piter Komondor," 1919) by the former author and "Peter's Day" ("Den' Petra," 1918) by the latter. The novels of K.G. Shildkret of the early 1930s also reflect the general early Soviet hostility to Peter I.

As far as diabolical images of Ivan IV and Peter I are concerned, the works of this second category, while certainly critical of the two rulers, do not delve deeply into the metaphysical dimensions of the two figures, preferring to impeach them on moral grounds or to examine their psychological complexity. Nevertheless, the demonic element does play a certain role in the works of this category as an available rhetorical tool or an interpretive stance attributed to characters rather than to the authorial or readerly perspective. In A.K. Tolstoi's *Prince Serebrianyi*, for instance, Ivan IV himself harbours a conception of his reign as an expression of Satanic evil, as well as a vision of his saintly mission to cleanse Muscovy of traitors. These two notions appear to do battle for the conscience of the tsar, the Satanic version taking the lead when his aged nanny warns the tsar that numberless sins will: "drag you down to the depths of hell, and devils will skip up to you and catch you on their hooks," following which the autocrat sees a nightmare-vision in which all the wrongfully executed rise before him and call him to a final reckoning at the Last Judgement.[66] Satanic characteristics are ascribed directly to the tsar or to his servants by other characters, such as the boyar Morozov, who in telling the story of Ivan's brief renunciation of the throne in 1654 and creation of the *oprichnina* remarks that the autocrat seemed to be "the tsar, and yet not the tsar" and describes the *oprichniki* as "bloodthirsty, devilish regiments."[67] The central protagonist of Mordovtsev's *Idealists and Realists* is the historical monk Varlaam, executed in 1722 for disseminating the belief that Peter was the Antichrist. Mordovtsev devotes considerable space to filling in the details of this Old Believer vision of the tsar-reformer, although implied authorial and readerly perspectives in this straightforwardly realistic novel give this view no actual credence. The same monk makes an appearance in A.N. Tolstoi's "Peter's Day" to make an apocalyptic announcement. For most of these works, the notion of the demonic influence on Ivan IV and Peter I is little more than a colourful historical curiosity. The more discerning historical thinkers, such as A.K. Tolstoi, explore the logic of this interpretive stance and capture some features of the late medieval Russian dilemma with regard to harsh rulers. The positive characters of the boyar Morozov and Prince Serebrianyi choose to suspend judgement concerning the devilish evils of Ivan IV out of their loyalty to the sacral office of the tsar – a self-contradictory stance which Tolstoi exploits for its tragic and dramatic potential to great effect. Thus the works of the second category generally take a pragmatic approach to the characters, deeds, and policies of Ivan IV and Peter I which obviates the need for metaphysical explanation, yet they recreate with greater or lesser thoroughness the demonic interpretation as an object of representation.

The third category of works treating Ivan IV and Peter I, those that combine the positive and negative characterizations of the two rulers in complex manner, constitutes by far the most interesting group with regard to the investigation of the figure of the demonic ruler, but also with regard to historical interpretive subtlety and sheer artistic merit. I include relatively few works in this group, but many are acknowledged masterpieces: Pushkin's *The Bronze Horseman* (1833) (and V.Ia. Briusov's 1923 variations on Pushkin's poem), the third novel in D.S. Merezhkovsky's historical trilogy *Christ and Antichrist* entitled *Antichrist (Peter and Aleksei)* (*Antikhrist [Petr i Aleksei]*, 1905), various poetic works of Maksimilian Voloshin, most notably his "Petersburg" (Peterburg, 1915), "Northeast" (Severovostok, 1920), and "Russia" (Rossiia, 1924), Andrei Platonov's masterful short story "The Epifan Locks" (Epifanskie shliuzy, 1927), the first two volumes of A.N. Tolstoi's *Peter the First* (1929–34), Iu.N. Tynianov's novella *The Waxen Effigy* (*Voskovaia persona*, 1931), and the second part of Eizenshtein's film *Ivan the Terrible* (1946). All of these works are deeply ambivalent in their treatment of Ivan IV and Peter I. The equivocal treatment of Peter in Pushkin's poem is a familiar topic of critical discussion. On the one hand, one finds in the introduction a eulogy of Peter and of the modern Russia he created, both of which are metaphorically represented in St. Petersburg, the object of the poet's intense adoration. On the other hand the reader confronts an unsympathetic portrayal of this same emperor, represented in the "idolatrous" monument to him, as the ultimate cause of the degradation and devaluation of human life characteristic of this same modern Russia and St. Petersburg. Merezhkovsky's, Tolstoi's, Platonov's, and Tynianov's works all strike a similar balance between positive and negative evaluations of Peter – between a vision of the positive role of the first emperor as "transformer" and the brutal methods and dubious results of his modernizing effort. Needless to say, each author puts his particular spin on this formula, ranging from Merezhkovsky's mystical vision of the Nietzschean battle of the spiritual values of Old Russia against Peter's creative annihilation of moral constraints, to Tolstoi's more thoroughgoing "realistic" vision of the costs and benefits of the Petrine epoch to the Russian people.[68] Eizenshtein's film brings an analogous interpretive strategy to bear on Ivan IV, whom he presents in terms of the Stalinist historiographic vision of the progressive role of the first tsar in his struggle with the conservative boyar élite, yet with the addition of an unflattering portrait of the psychology of terror with obvious resonance with the realities of Soviet Russia of the 1930s and 1940s.

To a greater degree than with regard to my initial two categories of works, those of this last group make use of the demonic resonance of these two figures, especially in the case of three of these works: those of Pushkin, Merezhkovsky, and Eizenshtein. At the conclusion of Pushkin's work the crazed Evgenii challenges the Bronze Horseman:

И, зубы стиснув, пальцы сжав,
Как обуянный силой черной,
«Добро, строитель чудотворный! –
Шепнул он, злобно задрожав, –
Ужо тебе!..»[69]

[And, grinding his teeth, clenching his fists,
As if possessed by a dark power:
"All right, miraculous builder,"
He whispered, shaking with rage,
"Just you wait!.."]

Evgenii's possession by a "dark power" suggests that opposition to the deified emperor must be seen as heretical. Yet the subsequent scene throws into question precisely who represents the forces of impiety. In Evgenii's hallucination the horseman abandons his pedestal, arm still raised in a grotesque parody of his former immobile pose, to pursue the poor madman all night. This final transformation completes the trajectory of Pushkin's treatment of Peter in the course of the poem, from the great transformer, godlike in his power and majesty, to a "false god" to whom one builds "idols" in the body of the poem, to an image that, as David Bethea has recently observed, represents the unholy forces of innovation and revolution that challenge the unity and sanctity of the Old Russian world, and recalls nothing so much as a rider of the apocalypse.[70] Pushkin's poem thus recapitulates the entire spectrum of possible assessments of the cosmological significance of Peter – from deified emperor to crowned Antichrist – and points to the logical and rhetorical fabric that ties these interpretations together. For it is the hubristic assumption by Peter of divinity that leads to his downfall as a heretical deity, idol, and servant of the dark forces of history and damnation.

In a similar vein, Merezhkovsky's Peter appears to have a split identity, alternately the good father, benevolent and far-sighted ruler, and the maddened, bestial personification of evil on earth. The very dense metaphorical apparatus of the novel, communicated in dreams, visions, and authorial narrative, identifies Peter half the time with God, who sacrifices his own son in order to move human history forward towards universal love, and half the time with the Antichrist, who demolishes Christianity itself in pursuit of dehumanizing material progress. At one point, in an inverted echo of Pushkin's poem, the tsarevich observes as his father seemingly works miracles to save his subjects during a flood of Petersburg, and recalls how his teacher instructed him that miracles are not only from God but from the devil as well, musing: "for the laws of nature may be defied by the will of ... by the will of whom: God or Satan?"[71] Merezhkovsky's comprehension of the integral relationship between the Satanic and divine aspects of Peter's character reframes Pushkin's vision of the diabolical nature of Peter's assumption of divinity, adding a touch of modernist counterpoint. While the novel's conclusion projects the necessity for Christian humility and for an end to the hubristic struggle against God, Merezhkovsky's portrait of Peter recalls the stock formulae of Russian Nietzscheanism: Peter was superhuman by virtue of his rejection of past morality – he became the man-god of the future by becoming the Devil of the past.

Eizenshtein's work similarly contains a dense fabric of metaphoric connections, especially in the film's use of iconographic elements of the sets, that alternately substantiate and refute the accusations of the Archbishop Filip that Ivan's administrative reforms "come not from God ... but from the Devil!"[72] Particularly interesting in this regard is the scene of the confrontation of Ivan and Filip in the cathedral, in which Eizenshtein straightforwardly suggests the equivalence of Ivan and the figure of Nebuchadnezzar of the Furnace Play about three pious youths, miraculously saved from the fires into which the evil ruler cast them. Another example of this tendency of Eizenshtein's work is the banquet scene, which is orchestrated to produce an image of hell, over which reigns a demonic Ivan.

In each of these three works, the generally ambivalent assessment of the ruler contributes additional punch to the demonic paradigm: the most unnerving elements in these works are the moments of transformation, where the image of the ruler seems to shift horrifically from one extreme to another. (Merezhkovsky titles a key chapter in his novel *oboroten'*, or "shape-shifter" – a rough equivalent of the English "werewolf".) In this, these works reconstruct the late medieval paradigm regarding the harsh tsar more comprehensively than the works of the other categories delineated above, placing the reader into the position of Avraamii Palitsyn (cited above): "Woe, woe is me, for I know not my left hand from my right and I am incapable of distinguishing bitter from sweet!" The treatment of the demonic conception of Peter and Ivan in these three works further departs from such works as A.K. Tolstoi's *Prince Serebrianyi* in that demonism figures as a fundamental aspect of the metaphoric structure of the artistic text, reflecting the agency of the artist, rather than rhetorical material that is merely depicted by the author. This is to say, whereas for Tolstoi the idea of the demonic tsar was an interesting element of the fictional world and characters that he sought to portray, for Eizenshtein, Pushkin, or Merezhkovsky this concept forms part of the author's own understanding of their subject.

This is not to say, of course, that these authors believed that Ivan IV or Peter I were demonic rulers or personifications of the Antichrist. (Merezhkovsky, in fact, did believe that Peter was the embodiment of a certain historical principle, which he termed "Antichrist." Yet Merezhkovsky's view of Russia's first emperor, I would offer, is actually closer to Pushkin's and Eizenshtein's visions of their subjects than to the apocalyptic interpretation of Peter I from which Merezhkovsky drew inspiration and much raw material for his novel.) What these three visions of modern Russia's mythic founders share is a use of the paradigm of the demonic ruler as a lens to focus their meditations on the historical process in Russia, and in particular on the perennial problematic of coercive state power and social progress. In *The Bronze Horseman*, opposed interpretational possibilities with regard to Peter aid Pushkin in his exploration of the significance of the autocracy as a tool for instituting progress: as Iu.M. Lotman succinctly described the poetics of Pushkin's "Petersburg Tale," Petrine absolutism appears as a truly beneficial force in its capacity to bring about advances in civilization and culture, to ensure the victory of the human spirit over the limitations of the material world. Yet the institutional structures of the state, like the dead weight of a statue, also crush down the individual human being who should be the ultimate beneficiary of such social progress.[73] The uncanny, demonic aspect of the image of Peter I conveys the ultimately tragic lack of resolution in this vision of history: the state that he built is both the saviour and the tormentor of the Russian people. For Merezhkovsky, the Petrine epoch embodies the conflict between the pagan, earthly, and rational values which Peter sought to introduce into his land and the Christian morality, love, and otherworldliness of Old Russia, a conflict which, once again, is charged with irony. Merezhkovsky considered that both of these elements satisfy fundamental needs of humanity, yet that the two are irreconcilable, opposed forces: the Promethean, revolutionary rationalism of Peter's state allowed no room for the faith of the Russian people; *raison d'état* dictated that Peter must sacrifice his son and thus reject Christian love and humility.[74] Once again, for Merezhkovsky the demonic image of Peter – seemingly of two natures, holy and unholy – serves to crystallize the irresolution of this historical conflict. Finally, Eizenshtein's depiction of Ivan faces a similar historical quandary which he also leaves unresolved: when is bloodshed and terror, even against the innocent, necessary and even justified by the exigencies of historical progress? One of Eizenshtein's villains, the scheming boyar's wife Efrosin'ia, pronounces that "a sovereign should not stray from the path of righteousness if he can help it, but he must be prepared to tread the path of evil if necessary."[75] In a poetic twist characteristic of these works, this sentiment appears to unite Ivan with his enemies in a dissolution of the simple distinction between good and evil. History itself, it would seem, is the ultimate demon that renders those figures who embody the crucial moments in the Russian historical process diabolical in their disruption of basic evaluative categories. Space does not permit me to explore here the significant evolution in the use of the paradigm of the demonic ruler in these three important works, which clearly belong to separate cultural periods and have distinct intellectual and political affiliations. Yet one may conclude in general that the works of my third category contribute to a unified tradition in the poetic interpretation of power and history in Russia that employs the late medieval sacralized conception of autocratic authority and the associated vision of the demonic ruler – in which the primary concern was the evaluation of the essential nature of the ruler, be it good or evil – to organize a modern vision of the unresolvable complexity of the historical process and of the subjective consequences of this complexity.

Conclusion: Later Rulers and Later Demons

In the course of the centuries since Peter I the interpretive paradigm of the demonic ruler has undergone later development and application to subsequent Russian rulers in several ways. First of all, the simple application of the idea of the demonic or unholy ruler has been continuously recycled at various levels of public discourse. The Old Believer community has proven to be remarkably persistent in interpreting every Russian ruler after Peter I as the Antichrist. Thus the middle nineteenth century saw both Alexander I and Nicholas I portrayed as Antichrists in Old Believer written and graphic works (see the second epigraph to this chapter).[76] In the twentieth century one finds examples of apocalyptic interpretations of Soviet leaders, such as that of the Old Believer Dorofei Utkin, who saw the Bolsheviks as the "masters of the fate of the world – a union of the warring godless," and Marx, Engels, Lenin, and Stalin as the "four unbound angels" who would "destroy one third of the people of the earth" as prophesied in the Apocalypse of Saint John.[77] One may propose that such political cosmological interpretations among the Old Believers will continue to be a productive genre as long as the community itself remains viable: the domination of the world by the forces of the Antichrist and the identification of the Antichrist with the powers that be are, simply, the bread and butter of apocalyptic thinking in Russia.

The literary tradition has also extended the idea of the demonic ruler to later Russian historical figures. First of all, many of the works that I have reviewed above, which take as their overt subject matter Ivan IV and Peter I, clearly also have direct relevance to modern Russian rulers, in particular Nicholas I and Stalin. The notion that Peter I was the model and prototype of Nicholas I was an enormously significant feature of the "Official Nationality" of the latter's reign. As Nicholas Riasanovsky puts the matter, in the era of Nicholas I Peter was seen as "the founder and, so to speak, the patron saint of imperial Russia."[78] As an example of this identification, one might cite N.A. Polevoi's remarks concerning his *History of Peter the Great* (*Istoriia Petra Velikogo*) in a letter to A.Kh. Benkendorf: "I will tell you here of my most private idea: the history of the last *ten years* has revealed to us the secret of Peter's great, great grandson – of Him, Who ascended the throne *exactly one hundred years later* (1725–1825). We know *Who* is reincarnate in *Him.*"[79] A more tenuous connection might be posited between Nicholas and Ivan IV, arising from the conception in the statist historiography of the middle nineteenth century of Ivan IV as the predecessor of Peter I. K.D. Kavelin, for instance, pronounced in 1846 that "in fact, the reign of Peter was a continuation of the reign of Ivan."[80] By this equation it appears that at least some may have considered Ivan to be, like Peter, an originative figure for imperial Russia under Nicholas I – to cite Kavelin once again: "everything that the contemporaries of Ivan defended has fallen in ruin and disappeared; everything that Ivan IV defended has grown and been realized. His conceptions were so much alive that they have outlasted not only his life but centuries, and with each passing age they grow and expand."[81] In a similar historical-mythological construction, the 1930s and 1940s saw the close linkage in Soviet public discourse of Stalin with both Ivan IV and Peter I. According to Robert Tucker, Stalin "consciously emulated Peter," revolutionizing Russian social, economic, and military life through a "revolution from above."[82] At other times he "thought of himself as a latter-day Ivan": crushing sedition and treason through use of terror, fighting with the great powers of Europe for dominance in the theatre of the Baltic, and fusing together an enormous, administratively centralized empire.[83] This folding of the present into the past reflects the significant reliance of modern Russian political structures on ideas of authority derived from a largely mythical medieval and pre-modern past. At moments of national crisis such as the Napoleonic Wars or the great revolutions and wars of this century, it seems, political institutions have reinforced and legitimated the autocratic principle by means of its "ancient" and "sacred" provenance.

Writers have been among the engineers of this legitimizing process and among its most perceptive critics. The artistic depiction of Ivan and Peter has often served not only as a means to comment on the historical processes and figures of the past, but as an allegorical exposition of contemporary problems and persons. The artistic works of my first and second categories, as I have described them above, adopt relatively straightforward political positions with regard to their contemporary political circumstances. At the laudatory extreme, one may mention Pushkin's *Stanzas* of 1826, which, as I have already noted, are a well-known example of commentary on the present by means of exposition of the past. Maikov's "At the Tomb of Ivan the Terrible," in part reproduced above, echoes the remarks I have just cited from Kavelin on the longevity of Ivan's accomplishments nearly verbatim, and might be seen as an excursus (albeit an obscure one) into praise of Nicholas by means of reference to his predecessors. In the twentieth century, examples of allegorical eulogy of Stalin through the figures of Ivan and Peter are well-known: Tolstoi's *Peter the First*, especially the final volume, or his pair of plays *Ivan the Terrible*, the first of which is titled *The Eagle and his Mate* (*Orel i orlitsa*) – an obvious reference to Stalin, the "Mountain Eagle" of Soviet public rhetoric. All of these positive representations of Peter and Ivan work to legitimate their respective contemporary regimes (and often, contemporary applications of coercion and bloodshed) as the just continuation of the Russian political tradition, and as necessary bastions of historical progress and social well-being. The analogical interconnection of past and present serves to place contemporary rulers into a seemingly inevitable historical pattern, proper to the Russian national experience. However, at the opposite end of the spectrum, this same strategy of historical analogy serves as an equally powerful method of critical commentary on political realities. Thus A.K. Tolstoi's *Prince Serebrianyi* and A.N. Tolstoi's "Peter's Day" were clearly intended to denounce the archaic violence inherent in the autocratic political structures of later epochs, just as Karamzin's representation of Ivan serves as a didactic exposition of the ever-present dangers of tyranny (although it was clearly not intended as an allegorical representation of Tsar Alexander I).

The works of my third category present more interesting – from a "demonic" perspective – meditations on the relationship of the later Russian political tradition to its tyrannical progenitors. As I demonstrate above, works like Pushkin's *The Bronze Horseman* and the second part of Eizenshtein's *Ivan the Terrible* hold up for consideration the diabolical complex of relations that binds the benefits of progress to the evils of bloodshed, coercion, and human misery. Yet an additional characteristic of the Demon of History, as he is portrayed in these works, is precisely the frightening prospect of historical return. Evgenii's protest against the monument to the autocrat on the Senate Square clearly recalls the Decembrists who gathered on the same square to be similarly crushed;[84] Eizenshtein's meditation on whether Ivan's terror was justified by progressive political aims applies equally well to the Stalinist terror.[85] Ironically, Evgenii, and by allegorical extension the Decembrists, are crushed by the same intractable historical logic that governed Peter's pursuit of a better and more enlightened future. Eizenshtein's Ivan likewise evokes the eerie resurgence of archaic cruelty in Stalin, the world's most "modern" leader. Here, the resonance of past and present shows Russian history as a perpetual repetition of cycles of terror and mayhem in the service of transcendent ideals which may never be attained. The imagery of Pushkin's work aptly captures the horror of this conception of history: just as the inanimate monument comes to life to pursue Evgenii, the distant and buried past may rise again to crush later generations.

In *The Waxen Effigy* Tynianov pays homage to Pushkin's demonic "animation of the monument." The novella is devoted to the treatment of the wax figure of Peter that was housed after the first Russian emperor's demise in his own Museum of Curiosities, the *Kunstkamera*. In Tynianov's work, the mechanical figure of Peter endlessly jumps up from its throne to menace whoever comes before it in a grotesque repetition which epitomizes Freud's conception of the uncanny. At the time of publication of Tynianov's novella, this image of the effigy of Peter must certainly have evoked the embalmed corpse of Lenin, newly installed in its Mausoleum on Red Square as a reminder that "Lenin is more alive than the living."[86] Platonov's "The Epifan Locks" calls forth a similar recognition of the Petrine period as a precursor to or allegorical double of the early Soviet period. Platonov tells the tale of Perry, an English engineer who contracts with Peter I to oversee the construction of a system of canals to connect the Oka and the Don rivers. Confounded by uncooperative and incapable Russian labourers and local administrators, as well as by the harsh and unpredictable climate, Perry's project devolves into a nightmarish sisyphean labour, overshadowed by a steadily growing fear of the cruel and godlike tsar's reprisals for failure. Ultimately, the canal system is completed, yet proves to be so shallow that it is unnavigable, and Perry is tortured to death (rather horribly) by an executioner characterized in the narrative as a "Satan."[87] As in the case of Tynianov's novella, Platonov's short story draws troubling parallels between the Soviet present and the Petrine past. However, as is so often the case with Platonov's works, the significance of his tale is rather obscure. Platonov perhaps intended the work to enable a recognition of the superiority of the present over the past: the Soviet era would achieve a grand sweep of modernization which

the Petrine era could only dimly imagine. Yet in light of the subsequent history of both the author and of Soviet development of water-
ways, "The Epifan Locks" seems to function just as well as a
revelation of the Soviet era's awful resurgence of centuries-old barbarity and folly.

Even earlier than Platonov and Tynianov, Voloshin had presented
in his poem "Northeast" (1920) a similarly horrible vision of the
demonic force of history, which eternally returns Russia to its tyrannical past:

> Расплясались, разгулялись бесы
> По России вдоль и поперек –
> Рвет и крутит снежные завесы
> Выстуженный Северовосток.
>
> Ветер обнаженных плоскогорий,
> Ветер тундр, полесий и поморий,
> Черный ветер ледяных равнин,
> Ветер смут, побоищ и погромов,
>
> . . . .
>
> В этом ветре – гнет веков свинцовых,
> Русь Малют, Иванов, Годуновых –
> Хищников, опричников, стрельцов,
> Свежевателей живого мяса –
> Чертогона, вихря, свистопляса –
> Быль царей и явь большевиков.
>
> Что менялось? Знаки и возглавья?
> Тот же ураган на всех путях:
> В комиссарах – дурь самодержавья,
> Взрывы Революции – в царях.[88]

> [Devils have broken into dance, have gone wild
> From one end of Russia to the other –
> The frozen northeast
> Tears and twists snowy curtains.
>
> The wind of barren plateaux,
> The wind of the tundra, of woodlands and coastlines,
> The black wind of icy plains,
> The wind of troubles, of slaughters and pogroms,
>
> . . . .
>
> In this wind is the crushing weight of leaden ages,
> The Rus of Maliutas, Ivans and Godunovs –
> Predators, *oprichniki, strel'tsy*,
> Flayers of living meat –
> Of deviltry, whirlwind, cavorting –
> The past of the tsars and the reality of the Bolsheviks.

What has changed? The symbols and leadership?
The very same hurricane is on all paths:
The idiocy of autocracy is in the commissars,
The explosions of revolution in the tsars.]

Tynianov, Voloshin, and Platonov (the last perhaps unwittingly) take
the implications of the works of my third category regarding history
(writ large) to their fullest extension. These works suggest that Russia is condemned to a cyclical recurrence of tyranny and suffering;
and that the true nature of the tyrant – whether divine or diabolical,
redeemed by progress or damned by bloodshed – can be revealed
only when (and if) history itself comes to an end. As Voloshin concludes his poem:

> Сотни лет навстречу всем ветрам
> Мы идем по ледяным пустыням –
> Не дойдем... и в снежной вьюге сгинем,
> Иль найдем поруганный наш храм –
> Нам ли весить замысел Господний?
> Все поймем, все вынесем любя –
> Жгучий ветр полярной Преисподней –
> Божий Бич, – приветствую тебя![89]

> [For centuries we have advanced into all winds
> Through icy wastelands:
> We will falter and vanish in the snowy blizzard,
> Or we will find our desecrated temple.
> Is it for us to judge the divine plan?
> We shall comprehend all, bear all in love.
> O, burning wind of the polar nether regions,
> Scourge of God – I welcome you!]

As is indicated by the common allegorical correlation of later
Russian rulers and political regimes to Ivan IV, Peter I, and their
respective reigns, the representations of these medieval and early
modern figures which I have reviewed above are the central elements of a longstanding and productive tradition in modern Russian
cultural life. According to this tradition, Russian political authority
has been constituted, comprehended, and contested in terms of the
divine and the diabolical, and Russian history has been envisioned
as the unfolding of superhistorical spiritual imperatives. By way of
conclusion, one may note that the paradigm of the demonic ruler has
been developed and applied directly in Russian literature to at least
one later ruler, Stalin himself. Given that Stalin fulfilled Voloshin's
"prophecy" by self-consciously stepping into the role of the infallible
and divinely inspired ruler inherited from imperial and early modern Russian political culture, and that his adulators and flatterers
praised him in nearly hagiographical terms, it is perhaps unsurprising that he has been the target of demonization in a series of works

of the late twentieth century, including V.E. Maksimov's *Quarantine* (*Karantin*, 1973), A.I. Solzhenitsyn's *The First Circle* (*V kruge pervom*, 1968) and others.[90] However, as these works are the subject of Rosalind Marsh's contribution to the present volume, I will refrain from examination of them here. Suffice it to say that this series of literary works demonstrates that the dual tradition of sacralized and demonic visions of authority apparently remains an available paradigm for political explication in the Russian cultural tradition up to the present day. Further evidence of the continued resonance of this tradition in contemporary Russia may be seen in the recent rash of mass-market republications of many of the (greater and lesser) portrayals of Peter and Ivan which I have examined above. One hopes, however, that the more extreme manifestations of this cultural tradition are no longer operative elements of Russian political rhetoric and institutional symbolism.

Notes

1. J.L.I. Fennell, ed. and trans., *Prince A.M. Kurbsky's History of Ivan IV* (Cambridge: Cambridge University Press, 1965), 290–91. I have adjusted Fennell's translation slightly with regard to syntax.

2. N.S. Gur'ianova, *Krest'ianskii antimonarkhicheskii protest v staroobriadcheskoi eskhatologicheskoi literature perioda pozdnego feodalizma* (Novosibirsk: Nauka, 1988), 116. All translations in this chapter, unless otherwise noted, are my own.

3. D.S. Merezhkovskii, *Antikhrist (Petr i Aleksei)*, in his *Sobranie sochinenii v chetyrekh tomakh* (Moscow: Pravda, 1990), 2:317–759(414).

4. See Edward L. Keenan, *The Kurbskii–Groznyi Apocrypha: The Seventeenth-Century Genesis of the "Correspondence" Attributed to Prince A.M. Kurbskii and Tsar Ivan IV* (Cambridge, Mass.: Harvard University Press, 1971); Edward L. Keenan, "Muscovite Political Folkways," *The Russian Review*, 1986, no. 1:115–181.

5. Cherniavsky's work, dependent on the very corpus of canonical sources and interpretive approaches that has been subjected to such serious recent critique, might be seen as an unsuitable secondary source regarding the medieval Russian tradition. However, his original and often insightful analyses of individual texts retain much validity. Further, by the logic outlined above in the body of this chapter regarding medieval sources, Cherniavsky's conception of medieval Russian political "mythology" may be seen, *mutatis mutandis*, as relevant not to medieval Russian political life but rather to the modern Russian historical vision which served as the basis for his work on the more remote past and which generated the traditional canon of historical sources. Michael Cherniavsky, *Tsar and People: Studies in Russian Myths* (New Haven: Yale University Press, 1961). On Western doctrines concerning the dual nature of kings, see Ernst H. Kantorowicz's classic work *The King's Two Bodies: A Study in Mediaeval Political Theology* (Princeton: Princeton University Press, 1957).

6. For more on the sacralization of Russian rulers, see V.M. Zhivov and B.A. Uspenskii, "Tsar' i bog: semioticheskie aspekty sakralizatsii monarkha v Rossii," in *Iazyki kul'tury i problemy perevodimosti*, ed. B.A. Uspenskii (Moscow: Nauka, 1987), 47–153; Ihor Shevchenko, "A Neglected Byzantine Source of Muscovite

Political Ideology," in *The Structure of Russian History: Interpretive Essays*, ed. Michael Cherniavsky (New York: Random House, 1970), 80–107.

7. Cherniavsky, *Tsar and People*, 29.

8. Iosif, Igumen Volotskii, *Prosvetitel', ili Oblichenie eresi zhidovstvuiushchikh*, 4th ed. (Kazan: Tipografiia Imperatorskogo universiteta, 1903), 546–49.

9. Ia.S. Lur'e and Iu.D. Rykov, eds., *Perepiska Ivana Groznogo s Andreem Kurbskim* (Leningrad: Nauka, 1979), 7, 117 (from the first and third epistles of Kurbsky, respectively).

10. See Marc Raeff, "An Early Theorist of Absolutism: Joseph of Volokolamsk," in *Readings in Russian History From Ancient Times to the Abolition of Serfdom*, ed. Sidney Harcave, 2 vols. (New York: Thomas Y. Crowell, 1962), 1:177–87, esp. 185–86.

11. Cherniavsky, *Tsar and People*, 50. For the relevant passages of the Ivan IV–Kurbsky correspondence, see Lur'e and Rykov, eds., *Perepiska Ivana Groznogo s Andreem Kurbskim*, 13–14.

12. See Shevchenko, "A Neglected Byzantine Source," 93–97.

13. On the Time of Troubles and early modern political traditions see Boris Uspenskij, "Tsar and Pretender: *Samozvanchestvo* or Royal Imposture in Russia as a Cultural-Historical Phenomenon," in Ju.M. Lotman and B.A. Uspenskij, *The Semiotics of Russian Culture*, ed. Ann Shukman, Michigan Slavic Contributions, no. 11 (Ann Arbor: Department of Slavic Languages and Literatures, University of Michigan, 1984), 259–92. Compare Maureen Perrie, *Pretenders and Popular Monarchism in Early Modern Russia: The False Tsars of the Time of Troubles* (Cambridge: Cambridge University Press, 1995).

14. See Uspenskij, "Tsar and Pretender," 262–64.

15. See Avraamii Palitsyn, "Skazanie," in *Pamiatniki drevnei russkoi pis'mennosti otnosiashchiesia k Smutnomu vremeni*, Russkaia istoricheskaia biblioteka, no.13, 2d ed. (St. Petersburg: Imperatorskaia arkheograficheskaia komissiia, 1909), 473–523, esp. 490–97; V.P. Adrianova-Peretts, ed., *Vremennik Ivana Timofeeva* (Moscow: Akademiia nauk, 1951), 83–98. As Uspensky has indicated, historical songs collected in later centuries concerning the false Dmitriis converge significantly with these seventeenth-century texts in their treatment of the Time of Troubles. See "Grishka Otrep'ev" and "Na nas, brattsy, gospodi razgnevalsia," in *Russkaia istoricheskaia pesnia*, Biblioteka poeta, Bol'shaia seriia, ed. L.I. Emel'ianov (Leningrad: Sovetskii pisatel', 1987), 123–25, 391–92; Uspenskij, "Tsar and Pretender," 274–75.

16. Adrianova-Peretts, ed., *Vremennik Ivana Timofeeva*, 16–17.

17. Cherniavsky, *Tsar and People*, 55.

18. Palitsyn, *Skazanie*, 488.

19. S.K. Rosovetskii, "Oral Prose of the 16th–17th Centuries about Ivan the Terrible as a Ruler," *Soviet Anthropology and Archeology* 23(3) (1984):3–49; Maureen Perrie, *The Image of Ivan the Terrible in Russian Folklore* (Cambridge: Cambridge University Press, 1987).

20. A.I. Malein, ed. and trans., *Novoe izvestie o Rossii vremeni Ivana Groznogo: "Skazanie" Al'berta Shlikhtinga*, 3d ed. (Leningrad: Izdatel'stvo Akademii nauk, 1934), 42.

21. I. Taub and E. Kruz, "Velikogo kniazia moskovskogo neslykhannaia tiraniia," *Russkii istoricheskii zhurnal* 8 (1922):50; cited and translated in Perrie, *The Image of Ivan the Terrible*, 77. Also see Rosovetskii, "Oral Prose," 27–29; D.S. Likhachev and A.M. Panchenko, *"Smekhovoi mir" drevnei Rusi* (Leningrad: Nauka, 1976), 176–78. Other, more detailed versions of this tale relate how Mikula first offers Ivan IV a piece of raw meat and, when the tsar refuses with revulsion, objecting that only dogs eat raw meat, the holy fool tells him that he is worse than a dog, because "a dog would not eat live human flesh, but that's what you eat!" See Perrie, *The Image of Ivan the Terrible*, 54.

22. D.N. Al'shits, "Drevnerusskaia povest' pro tsaria Ivana Vasil'evicha i kuptsa Kharitona Beloulina," *Trudy Otdela drevnerusskoi literatury* 17 (1961):255–71. Also see Rosovetskii, "Oral Prose," 30–31; Perrie, *The Image of Ivan the Terrible*, 104–5. In another tale, Ivan IV orders the wealthy Novgorod merchant Fedor Shirkov bound with rope and thrown into the Volkhvov river, then dragged out when he begins to drown. The tsar asks, "Tell me, Fedor, what you saw at the bottom of the river," and the merchant answers, "I saw many devils, who live in this river … ; if only they would tear the soul out of you, tormentor, and throw it into the fires of hell, just as you throw us innocents into your rivers." See Malein, *Novoe izvestie*, 30; Rosovetskii, "Oral Prose," 26.

23. Rosovetskii, "Oral Prose," 21–25; Ia.S. Lur'e, *Povest' o Drakule* (Moscow: Nauka, 1964), 65–66. Also see Perrie, *The Image of Ivan the Terrible*, 96–101.

24. Perrie, *The Image of Ivan the Terrible*, 108.

25. Ibid., 179.

26. Ibid., 108.

27. For a partial summary of Russian historiographic interpretations of Ivan IV see Richard Hellie, "In Search of Ivan the Terrible," in S.F. Platonov, *Ivan the Terrible*, ed. and trans. Joseph L. Wieczynski (Gulf Breeze, Fla.: Academic International Press, 1974), ix–xxiv.

28. An interesting recent contribution to the "rationalist" interpretation of Ivan IV's policies may be found in the work of R.G. Skrynnikov, who has reversed the traditional evaluative stance associated with the thesis of the legitimate political motivations of the terror, arguing that while Ivan did indeed have a political "method in his madness," his purpose was simply to prevent the political and intellectual development of institutions of civil governance and legalized authority such as those which were then taking shape in Western Europe. See his *Tsarstvo terrora* (St. Petersburg: Nauka, 1992).

29. For what is perhaps the first extensive historiographical equation of Ivan IV and Peter I see K.D. Kavelin, "Vzgliad na iuridicheskii byt drevnei Rossii," in his *Sobranie sochinenii*, 4 vols. (St. Petersburg: M.M. Stasiulevich, n. d.), 1:9–66, esp. 46–56(47). For summary discussion of this view in nineteenth-century Russian historical works, see N.K. Mikhailovskii, "Ivan Groznyi v russkoi literature," in his *Sochineniia*, 6 vols. (St. Petersburg: Russkoe bogatstvo, 1896–97), 6: 127–220, esp. 147–63. This historiographical connection corresponds in part to the ideological constructions of Peter I's day, which occasionally represented Ivan IV as the predecessor of the later tsar-transformer. On this latter connection, see A.M. Panchenko and B.A. Uspenskii, "Ivan Groznyi i Petr Velikii: kontseptsii pervogo monarkha," *Trudy Otdela drevnerusskoi literatury* 37 (1983):54–78, esp. 54–55.

30. K.F. Ryleev, *Polnoe sobranie sochinenii* (Moscow: Academia, 1934; reprint, The Hague: Europe Printing, 1967), 458. Cited in Iurii Lotman, "Kolumb russkoi istorii," in his *Izbrannye stat'i* (Tallinn: Aleksandra, 1992), 2:206–227(221). The impression on contemporaries was in part due to the restrained and apologetic approach to the autocracy of the earlier volumes of the *History*, that drew heavy criticism from the Decembrist camp. For discussion of the evolution of the official historiographer's views on Russian history see Lotman, "Kolumb russkoi istorii," and his "'O drevnei i novoi Rossii v ee politicheskom i grazhdanskom otnosheniiakh' Karamzina – pamiatnik russkoi publitsistiki nachala XIX veka," in his *Izbrannye stat'i*, 2:194–205.

31. On Karamzin's conception of history see Lotman, "Kolumb russkoi istorii," 2:206–27.

32. N.M. Karamzin, *Istoriia gosudarstva rossiiskogo*, 12 vols. (St. Petersburg: Izdanie Evg. Evdokimova, 1892; reprint, The Hague: Mouton, 1969), 9:13.

33. Ibid., 9:65–69, 93.

34. Ibid., 9:15.

35. Ibid., 9:167.

36. Ibid., 9:273.

37. Ibid., 9:274.

38. N.I. Kostomarov, "Lichnost' Ivana Vasil'evicha Groznogo," in his *Sobranie sochinenii*, 21 vols. (St. Petersburg: M.M. Stasiulevich, 1903–6), 13:431.

39. N.M. Karamzin, "A Memoir on Ancient and Modern Russia," in Richard Pipes, *Karamzin's Memoir on Ancient and Modern Russia: A Translation and Analysis* (Cambridge: Harvard University Press, 1959), 121.

40. See, for instance, Evgenii V. Anisimov, *Vremia petrovskikh reform* (Leningrad: Lenizdat, 1989). The volume has been translated as *The Reforms of Peter the Great: Progress through Coercion in Russia*, trans. John T. Alexander (Armonk, N. Y. and London: M. E. Sharpe, 1993).

41. F. Bulgarin, *Vospominaniia*, 6 vols. (St. Petersburg: D.M. Ol'khin, 1846–49), 1:200. Cited and translated in Nicholas V. Riasanovsky, *The Image of Peter the Great in Russian History and Thought* (New York: Oxford University Press, 1985), 109.

42. P.Ia. Chaadaev, "Apologiia sumasshedshego," in his *Sochineniia* (Moscow: Pravda, 1989), 143. For an analysis of Chaadaev's views see Andrew Baruch Wachtel, *An Obsession with History: Russian Writers Confront the Past* (Stanford: Stanford University Press, 1994), 134–35.

43. V.I. Lenin, "O 'levom' rebiachestve i o melkoburzhuaznosti," in his *Polnoe sobranie sochinenii*, 5th ed., 55 vols. (Moscow: Izdatel'stvo politicheskoi literatury, 1958–70), 36:283–313(301).

44. Stalin, in one of his few public statements on Peter I, denied the validity of this historical parallel in particular and of historical analogies in general. Yet the widespread elevation of Peter I in the thirties and forties as ideal leader could not but be viewed as related to the elevation of Stalin himself. See I.V. Stalin, "Beseda s nemetskim pisatelem Emilem Liudvigom," in his *Sochineniia*, 13 vols. (Moscow: Gosudarstvennoe izdatel'stvo politicheskoi literatury, 1949–53), 13:104–23, esp. 104–5.

45. Cited in S.M. Solov'ev, *Istoriia Rossii s drevneishikh vremen*, 15 vols. (Moscow: Sotsial'no-ekonomicheskaia literatura, 1960–66), 7:321. For discussion of the metaphor of creator as applied to Peter I, see Stephen Lessing Baehr, *The Paradise Myth in Eighteenth-Century Russia: Utopian Patterns in Early Secular Russian Literature and Culture* (Stanford: Stanford University Press, 1991), 41–64.

46. M.V. Lomonosov, "Slovo Pokhval'noe blazhennye pamiati Gosudariu Imperatoru Petru Velikomu" (1755), in his *Polnoe sobranie sochinenii*, 11 vols. (Moscow and Leningrad: Izdatel'stvo Akademii nauk, 1950–83), 8:584–612(611). Also see his "Oda na den' Tezoimenitstva Ego Imperatorskogo Vysochestva Gosudaria Velikogo Kniazia Petra Feodorovicha 1743 goda," in stanza 13 of which one finds the oft-quoted reference to Peter I, "On Bog, on Bog tvoi byl, Rossiia," in Lomonosov, *Polnoe sobranie sochinenii*, 8:103–10(109).

47. See A.P. Sumarokov, "Nadpis' k statue gosudaria imperatora Petra Velikogo," in his *Stikhotvoreniia*, Biblioteka poeta, Bol'shaia seriia (Moscow: Sovetskii pisatel', 1935), 281.

48. V.G. Belinskii, review of: I.I. Golikov, *Deianiia Petra Velikogo, mudrogo preobrazovatelia Rossii*, 2d ed. (Moscow, 1837–40); Veniamin Bergman, *Istoriia Petra Velikogo*, trans. E. Alad'in, 2d ed. (St. Petersburg, 1840); G. Kotoshikhin, *O Rossii v tsarstvovanie Alekseia Mikhailovicha* (St. Petersburg, 1840), in V.G. Belinskii, *Sochineniia v chetyrekh tomakh*, 4th ed. (St. Petersburg: Izdatel'stvo M. A. Aleksandrova, 1911), 2:184.

49. Cherniavsky, *Tsar and People*, 101–27.

50. See Panchenko and Uspenskii, "Ivan Groznyi i Petr Velikii," 58.

51. On sectant and Old Believer conceptions of Peter I as Antichrist, see Michael Cherniavsky, "The Old Believers and the New Religion," *Slavic Review* 1 (1966):1–39; reprinted in Cherniavsky, ed., *The Structure of Russian History*, 140–88 – this article is especially interesting for its reproductions of graphic representations of Peter I as the Antichrist. Also see K.V. Chistov, *Russkie narodnye sotsial'no-utopicheskie legendy XVI–XIX vekov* (Moscow: Nauka, 1967), 96–109; B.A. Uspenskii, "Historia sub specie semioticae," in *Kul'turnoe nasledie Drevnei Rusi (Istoki, stanovlenie, traditsii)*, ed. V.G. Bazanov (Moscow: Nauka, 1976), 286–92; N.N. Pokrovskii, "Sledstvennoe delo i vygovskaia povest' o tsarskikh sobytiiakh 1722 g.," in *Rukopisnaia traditsiia XVI–XIX vv. na vostoke Rossii*, ed. N.N. Pokrovskii and E.K. Romodanovskaia (Novosibirsk: Nauka, 1983); Riasanovsky, *The Image of Peter the Great*, 76–85; Gur'ianova, *Krest'ianskii antimonarkhicheskii protest*, 17–60, 115–152. The last citation includes publications of Old Believer writings regarding Peter I, from which I have drawn the second epigraph to this chapter.

52. My gratitude goes to Lindsey Hughes for her remarks on the extent to which this conception of Peter was shared among his contemporaries. See J. Cracraft, "Opposition to Peter the Great," in *Imperial Russia, 1700–1917: State, Society, Opposition. Essays in Honor of Marc Raeff*, ed. Ezra Mendelsohn and Marshall Shatz (DeKalb, Ill.: Northern Illinois University Press, 1988), 22–36; Daniel L. Schafly, "The Popular Image of the West at the Time of Peter the Great," in *Russia and the World of the Eighteenth Century*, ed. R.P. Bartlett, A.G. Cross, and Karen Rasmussen (Columbus: Slavica, 1988), 2–21.

53. As T.A. Krasotkina and G.P. Blok note in their excellent commentary to the Lomonosov eulogy to Peter cited above, that particular work was adduced in at least one Old Believer tract as evidence of the unholy nature of Peter I. See Lomonosov, *Polnoe sobranie sochinenii*, 8:901. Also see the particular Old Believer composition in question in *Chtenie v obshchestve istorii i drevnostei rossiiskikh*, 1863, no. 1:60–61 (3d pagination, "Smes'").

54. On the significance of the Petrine cultural reforms in the eyes of his contemporaries, see esp. Uspenskii, "Historia sub specie semioticae."

55. Maksimilian Voloshin, "Rossiia" (6 February 1924), in his *Stikhotvoreniia i poemy*, ed. B.A. Fillippov, G.P. Struve, and N.A. Struve, 2 vols. (Paris: YMCA Press, 1982–84), 1:339–51(344); cited in Robert C. Tucker, *Stalin in Power: The Revolution from Above, 1928–1941* (New York: Norton, 1990), 61.

56. Richard Taruskin, "'The Present in the Past': Russian Opera and Russian Historiography, ca. 1870," in *Russian and Soviet Music: Essays for Boris Schwartz*, ed. Malcolm Hamrick Brown (Ann Arbor: UMI Research Press, 1984), 77–146(79).

57. For comparative and in some instances excellent analyses of many of the literary depictions of Peter I, see Xenia Gasiorowska, *The Image of Peter the Great in Russian Fiction* (Madison: The University of Wisconsin Press, 1979); Riasanovsky, *The Image of Peter the Great*.

58. R.M. Zotov also wrote a play on Peter I, the name of which says it all: *Saardamskii korabel'nyi master, ili net imeni emu!* (1841).

59. L.A. Mei, *Pskovitianka*, in his *Izbrannye proizvedeniia*, Biblioteka poeta, Bol'shaia seriia (Leningrad: Sovetskii pisatel', 1972), 530–31.

60. For an analysis of *Pskovitianka* in comparison to contemporary historical thought, see Taruskin, "The Present in the Past," 93–96.

61. I cite the original and the translation from: A.S. Pushkin, *Pushkin Threefold: Narrative, Lyric, Polemic, and Ribald Verse*, ed. and trans. Walter Arndt (New York: E.P. Dutton, 1972), 210–12.

62. On Pushkin's "Stanzas" and Nicholas I, see Riasanovsky, *The Image of Peter the Great*, 88.

63. A.N. Maikov, "U groba Groznogo," in his *Polnoe sobranie sochinenii*, ed. P.V. Bykov, 9th ed., 4 vols. (St. Petersburg: Izdanie T-va A.F. Marksa, 1914), 2:166.

64. According to an imperial decree of 1837, while Russian rulers prior to the Romanov dynasty could appear in drama, they could not be depicted in opera. Richard Taruskin cites Rimsky-Korsakov's amusing recollection of his inquiry as to the rationale behind the decree at the censorship bureau, where he was told: "And suppose the Tsar should suddenly sing a ditty? Well, it would be unseemly." Cited and translated in Taruskin, "The Present in the Past," 97.

65. My categorization of Bulgakov's play *Ivan Vasil'evich* and of its later film version as negative depictions of Ivan IV no doubt constitutes something of an oversimplification. The tsar's bloodthirsty tendencies are amply illustrated in these works, where his reaction to any difficulty is to attempt removal of its cause by violent means. Yet there is no indication that the audience is intended to judge negatively the tsar's murderous assaults on various other characters or his accounts of the painful tortures and executions he has inflicted on his enemies. Rather, his taste for bloodshed is exploited in these works for cartoonish slapstick effects, reminiscent, for instance, of the painful antics of the three stooges. Of course, the author's assumption that Ivan IV was given to outbursts of grotesque violence at the slightest provocation reveals the fundamentally negative conception of the tsar on which the play and film are based. For a stronger reading of the play as a satire on arbitrary power and in particular on Stalin (in my opinion, an incorrect reading), see Peter Doyle, "Bulgakov's *Ivan Vasil'evich*: Light Hearted Comedy or Serious Satire?," *Journal of Russian Studies* 43 (1982):33–42. Compare A. Colin Wright, *Mikhail Bulgakov: Life and Interpretations* (University of Toronto Press: Toronto, 1978), 207–8.

66. A.K. Tolstoi, *Kniaz' Serebrianyi: Povest' vremen Ioanna Groznogo* (Moscow: Sovremennik, 1993), 79–86.

67. A.K. Tolstoi, *Kniaz' Serebrianyi*, 43. In Tolstoi's novel Ivan IV's reign also serves as the vehicle for explorations of other forms of literary demonism, as in the case of Tolstoi's fictional characterization of the historical Prince A.I. Viazemsky. The formerly virtuous boyar Viazemsky, tormented by unrequited love for Elena Pleshcheeva-Ochina, turns to evil and enlists as an *oprichnik* in the hopes of claiming Elena by force (he also resorts to black magic). He has "imperilled his soul" on the theory that "in the depths of hell it can be no worse than it is here!" In this rejection of virtue out of unrequited love Viazemsky clearly has more to do with the Romantic demonic rebellious soul than with the historical demonology of rulers. A.K. Tolstoi, *Kniaz' Serebrianyi*, 21.

68. It has been observed that the ambivalent assessment of Peter I in Tolstoi's "Petrine" works of the early and middle 1930s reflects the general evolution of Soviet views of the first emperor, as the Pokrovsky school of historiography was eclipsed by more conservative Stalinist views of Russian history. See Riasanovsky, *The Image of Peter the Great*, 280–82.

69. A.S. Pushkin, "Mednyi vsadnik. Peterburgskaia povest'," in his *Polnoe sobranie sochinenii v desiati tomakh*, 4th ed. (Leningrad: Nauka, 1977–79), 4:273–287(286).

70. David Bethea, *The Shape of Apocalypse in Modern Russian Fiction* (Princeton: Princeton University Press, 1989), 44–61.

71. Merezhkovskii, "Antikhrist," 473–74.

72. I have worked with the American release of *Ivan the Terrible, Part II* by Corinth video (1988) and the printed script of the film published and translated in Sandra Wake, ed., *Ivan the Terrible: A Film by Sergei Eisenstein* (New York: Simon and Schuster, 1970), cited on 135. Also see the original film script (of the entire project): S.M. Eizenshtein, "Ivan Groznyi, kino-stsenarii," *Novyi mir*, 1943, no. 10–11:61–108.

73. Iu.M. Lotman, "Zamysel stikhotvoreniia o poslednem dne Pompei," in his *Pushkin: Biografiia pisatelia; Stat'i i zametki; 'Evgenii Onegin' – kommentarii* (St. Petersburg: Iskusstvo-SPB, 1995), 293–99, esp. 295.

74. On the historical and cosmological construction of Merezhkovsky's novel, see Bernice Glatzer Rosenthal, *Dmitri Sergeevich Merezhkovsky and the Silver Age: The Development of a Revolutionary Mentality* (The Hague: Martinus Nijhoff, 1975), · 86–105.

75. Wake, *Ivan the Terrible*, 184–85.

76. See Robert O. Crummey, *The Old Believers and the World of Antichrist: The Vyg Community and the Russian State, 1694–1855* (Madison: University of Wisconsin Press, 1970), 211; Gur'ianova, *Krest'ianskii antimonarkhicheskii protest,* 116.

77. M.M. Beliakova and T.V. Chertoritskaia, "Krug chteniia staroobriadtsa-spasovtsa pervoi poloviny XX v., ili tri biblioteki Dorofeia Utkina," in *Traditsionnaia dukhovnaia i material'naia kul'tura russkikh staroobriadcheskikh poselenii v stranakh Evropy, Azii i Ameriki,* ed. N.N. Pokrovskii and R. Morris (Novosibirsk: Nauka, 1992), 306–12(309).

78. Nicholas V. Riasanovsky, *Nicholas I and Official Nationality in Russia, 1825–1855* (Berkeley: University of California Press, 1959), 105–16(115).

79. Polevoi's rhetorically obtuse and rather mystically inspired idea is that the enthronement of Nicholas I one hundred years after the death of Peter serves as evidence of the close identification of the two emperors. The emphases are in the original. Cited in M.K. Lemke, *Nikolaevskie zhandarmy i literatura 1826–1855: Po podlinnym delam Tret'ego otdeleniia Sobstv. E.I. Velichestva kantseliarii,* 2d ed. (St. Petersburg: S.V. Bunin, 1909), 102.

80. Kavelin, "Vzgliad na iuridicheskii byt," 1:47.

81. Cited in Mikhailovskii, "Ivan Groznyi v russkoi literature," 6:161.

82. Tucker, *Stalin in Power,* 60–64(63).

83. Ibid., 276–82(278).

84. Waclaw Lednicki, *Pushkin's "Bronze Horseman": The Story of a Masterpiece* (Westport, Conn.: Greenwood Press, 1978), 81.

85. See Anthony R. Guneratne, "History as Propaganda: The Portrait of Stalin as Medieval Hero, and its Epic Frame," *Cinefocus,* 1990, no. 2:33–40.

86. For an insightful reading of Tynianov's treatment of Russian history and the allegorical relationship between Peter and Lenin, see: Dragan Kujundzic, *The Returns of History: Russian Nietzscheans After Modernity* (Albany: State University of New York Press, 1997), 135–79.

87. Andrei Platonov, "Epifanskie shliuzy," in his *Povesti. Rasskazy* (Moscow: Khudozhestvennaia literatura, 1989), 85–118(118).

88. Voloshin, *Stikhotvoreniia i poemy,* 1:310–12.

89. Ibid., 1:311–12.

90. On the demonic image of Stalin in *The First Circle* see Vladimir Grebenschikov, "Les cercles infernaux chez Soljénitsyne et Dante," *Canadian Slavonic Papers* 13 (1971):147–63. On the representation of Stalin in post-Stalinist literature in general, see Gary Kern, "Solzhenitsyn's Portrait of Stalin," *Slavic Review* 33 (1974):1–22; Rosalind Marsh, *Images of Dictatorship: Portraits of Stalin in Literature* (London and New York: Routledge, 1989); Margaret Ziolkowski, "A Modern Demonology: Some Literary Stalins," *Slavic Review* 50 (1990):59–69.

Chapter 4

Divine Service or Idol Worship?
Russian Views of Art as Demonic

Pamela Davidson

Oppose the devil and try to discern his wiles. He usually hides his gall under an appearance of sweetness, so as to avoid detection, and he fabricates various illusions, beautiful to look at – which in reality are not at all what they seem – to seduce your hearts by a cunning imitation of truth, which is rightly attractive. All his art is directed to this end – to oppose by all possible means every soul working well for God.

Saint Antony the Great, from the *Philokalia*[1]

Волшебный демон – лживый, но прекрасный
[An enchanting demon – false, but beautiful]

Pushkin[2]

The first three contributions to this volume have dealt with the perception of demons, as evident in the traditions of Russian Orthodoxy, folklore, and historiography. The present chapter concludes part I with an analysis of the way in which the understanding of the demonic shaped by these traditions infiltrated the perception of art itself. This process is central to the tradition of literary demonism, and its investigation forms a natural bridge to part II, which considers reflections of the demonic in individual works.

This essay does not therefore deal with demonism as a *theme* in Russian literature; it traces some of the sources and the historical development of the view of literary activity as intrinsically demonic, that is to say as deriving from evil forces which somehow possess the artist and obstruct the pursuit of higher goals. Art in this sense can be understood in the light of the epigraph cited above as one of the many beautiful illusions or cunning imitations of truth by which the devil seduces the hearts of men. The study of this topic is by no means new; its history goes back to debates in the early Church on the relationship of Christianity to pagan culture. Surprisingly, however, its development and ramifications within the Russian tradition have never been the subject of a special investigation, despite its central importance for a literary culture which persistently emphasizes its preoccupation with religion.

The purpose of this chapter is to set out in very broad terms some of the pre-literary contexts for the view of art as demonic, and to consider the characteristic ways in which this view has manifested itself in Russia. Three main questions will be addressed. Firstly, what are the main sources for the notion of art as demonic? This will require an examination of two key traditions which have shaped Russian thinking on art – the Bible and classical antiquity – with particular reference to their differing views of art and its relation to divinely inspired revelation. Secondly, what were the particular historical circumstances surrounding the reception of these traditions in Russia, which resulted in the formation of a strong national preoccupation with the demonic potential of literature? This will entail a brief excursion through the development of Russian views of secular culture with particular reference to the impact of Peter's reforms. Thirdly, what were the typical approaches to art and its demonic attributes which emerged from this complex of cultural and historical influences? Here we shall consider some literary manifestations of the view of post-Petrine culture as inherently demonic; by way of a closing illustration, we shall examine the reflection of these issues in a thought-provoking poetic fragment by Pushkin, which resonates interestingly with Chaadaev's analysis of Russia's distinctive historical path.

We should note in passing that the various formative areas of influence considered in this article were, of course, supplemented by a further important strand: that of Western European literature, which, through writers such as Dante, Milton, Goethe, Byron, and Baudelaire – to name but a few salient examples – shaped the reception of the biblical and classical traditions in Russia and exerted an important influence on literary perceptions of the demonic. Despite its very considerable role, the study of this mediating channel of influence lies outside the scope of this essay, which concentrates on the pre-literary context leading up to the inception of modern Russian literature after Peter's reforms (even in the case of the earliest of these writers, Dante and Milton, the process of assimilation of their legacy through critical discussion, translation, and imitation did not begin until the late eighteenth century).[3] Furthermore, the works of

these writers (with the possible exception of Baudelaire) were generally more concerned with the nature of evil as a moral, philosophical, or religious category than with the question of art itself as
demonic – a preoccupation which, as we shall argue below, was
peculiarly specific to the Russian literary tradition for a variety of historical and cultural reasons.

It should also be emphasized at the outset that this essay is
intended only as a general introduction to a very large topic, which
on its own could easily fill an entire book. This has necessarily led to
a very selective approach and to a certain degree of schematization
and simplification in the presentation of its argument. The issues
raised aim to provide some contextual background for the study
undertaken in part II of individual literary works which served to
build up the tradition of art as demonic.

Biblical Views of Art and the Artist

Attitudes to the question of whether or not art is intrinsically
"demonic" depend on a broader underlying issue: that of the relationship between art and religion, between beauty and the truth of revelation, or, in Shestov's phrase, between Athens and Jerusalem. Is
artistic activity compatible with the pursuit of religious goals, or does
it represent at best an unnecessary diversion, at worst a dangerous,
potentially undermining threat? In order to set this question in its
proper historical perspective, that of the Judaeo-Christian tradition
which has shaped European attitudes to culture, it is necessary to
return to the primary source of the Bible and to consider its treatment
of this issue – particularly as many of the texts discussed below in part
II allude directly to this tradition. First, however, a *caveat* concerning
the use of the words "art" and "artist" throughout this section. These
terms come to us laden with classical and post-medieval connotations,
and, strictly speaking, are not applicable to biblical usage, which deals
with the quite distinct concepts of the craftsman and his skill. They are
nevertheless used in this section in a retroactive sense, as we are concerned here not so much with the original biblical text as with the various ways in which it could be interpreted by later artists as a source
and model for their own understanding of the creative vocation.

Two distinct attitudes to the artist and artistic activity can be
derived from a study of biblical references – one positive, and one
negative. For the positive biblical image, for art to be viewed as supportive of religion, two conditions must be met: the work of art must
be dedicated to the service of God and holy in purpose, and the artist
called upon to execute it must be filled with an appropriate spirit of

wisdom. The original biblical prototype of the work of art is the Tabernacle with all its elaborate appurtenances, and the first model of the artist is provided by its maker, Bezalel.[4] The terms in which Bezalel is described on first appearance make it unambiguously clear that both the source of the artist's manifold gifts and the purpose of their deployment come from God: "And the Lord spoke unto Moses, saying: See, I have called by name Bezalel the son of Uri, the son of Hur, of the tribe of Judah; and I have filled him with the spirit of God, in wisdom, and in understanding, and in knowledge, and in all manner of workmanship. … in the hearts of all that are wise-hearted I have put wisdom, that they may make all that I have commanded thee" (Exod.31:1–3,6).[5]

The precise details of the construction of the Tabernacle and its contents were given directly by God, and constant stress is placed upon their holiness of purpose. The artist is therefore primarily a craftsman, endowed by God with a spirit of wisdom to appreciate this sacred purpose and with the necessary knowledge and skill to understand the instructions and to implement them. This is quite distinct from the modern image of the artist as an independent creator, following his own fantasy and devising his own techniques. Significantly, in the biblical account, the divine plan for the Tabernacle is first described in consummate detail (Exod.25–30); only then, in second place, is the artist designated (Exod.31) and the actual execution of the work described (Exod.35–39).

Biblical attitudes to verbal forms of expression, both oral and written, emphasize the divine origin and tremendous power of language. Through the spoken word of God the universe was created: "And God said: 'Let there be light.' And there was light" (Gen.1:3). The spoken language with which man was endowed was originally a very powerful force, as can be seen from the fact that Adam is entrusted with the task of naming the animals; after creating the animals and the birds, God "brought them unto the man to see what he would call them; and whatsoever the man would call every living creature, that was to be the name thereof" (Gen.2:19). Both the Tabernacle and the temple were built to house the stone tablets on which the ten commandments were engraved; these artefacts, inscribed by God with a divine message and given directly to Moses, provide the first and most striking example of the divine origin of the written word in the Bible. If we look beyond the tablets to the text of the Pentateuch, we see that Moses received the written law directly from God; his job was to write down that which was communicated from above, to be a faithful scribe rather than a writer of his own text.[6] Likewise the later prophets received and conveyed a message which was not of their own making.

10. M. Chagall, *Literature*, 1920. Oil on canvas, 212 × 79 cm. The Hebrew letters coming out of the animal's mouth spell the name Chagall.

Christian theology provided a strong further impetus to the original biblical emphasis on the divine, creative power of language. Although already known both in pagan and Jewish antiquity, the concept of *Logos*, the Creative Word or Reason, was developed in the Johannine writings of the New Testament (John 1:1, 14; 1 John 1:1; Rev.19:13) and in subsequent Patristic teachings with particular reference to the Second Person of the Trinity. When "the Word was made flesh" (John 1:14) through incarnation in the man, Jesus Christ, the gap between the Divine Word and the poetic word was potentially narrowed and the basis for a closer association between human and Divine creativity was strengthened.

Under what circumstances is art viewed as a negative force in the Bible? The answer to this question is important as it provides part of the context for the later literary view of art as demonic. Whenever artistic activity is divorced from its true source and goal in God, it is invariably associated with idol worship and condemned (in other words, from a biblical perspective, there is no "neutral" middle ground secular art). The Old Testament is full of passages which decry and curse the makers of images and idols, the works of cunning craftsmen.[7] The fundamental difference between God – who cannot be represented – and man-made idols or images is constantly stressed, in both the Old and New Testaments. The spiritual danger which artists can present is spelled out in the Book of Revelation: an angel rejoices at the fall of the corrupt city of Babylon, from which all musicians and craftsmen will henceforth be excluded (Rev.18:22).

What of speech and the written word? The power of language with which God originally endowed man can be abused. Adam is corrupted through the subtle speech of the cunning serpent to Eve and loses his privileged status as a result (Gen.3:1–5). The expulsion of Adam and Eve from paradise later becomes a key image of the exiled artist's or fallen angel's loss of intimate contact with the divine source of creativity.[8] This regression culminates in the account of the building of the Tower of Babel; when men strive to take the place of God ("let us make us a name," Gen.11:4), God restrains them by causing them to lose their "one language" (Gen.11:6), clearly a dangerous source of power, susceptible to misuse, and removed in the verbal confusion which ensues. That language, the gift of speech, and its power to curse or to bless, is ultimately controlled by God is clearly demonstrated by the tale of Balaam whose ass could talk and whose curses were turned into blessings against his will.[9]

The positive and negative images of art outlined so far might cause one to think that this distinction is always pleasingly black and white. Although the biblical distinction is not in fact inherently ambiguous, it is important for an understanding of the way in which it was developed in later literary tradition to recognize that it depends on a delicate balance which is easily subject to distortion. The artist does indeed derive his creative powers from God, and is therefore not an autonomous creator in his own right; however, the considerable powers with which he is endowed can lead to his being viewed as a mirror image of God the Creator.

If we return to our first example of Bezalel and the Tabernacle, we can see how such a view might arise. Jewish tradition teaches that Bezalel, although only thirteen when chosen for his task, knew the art of combining the sacred letters with which heaven and earth were created, and possessed a degree of wisdom similar to that with which God created the universe.[10] This suggests a symmetrical relationship between God the Creator and Bezalel the artist, a significant extension of the parallel between their two creations (the Tabernacle as the dwelling place of God can be viewed as a microcosm of the creation). This close association between the artist and God, the supreme Creator, was one which, as we saw above, had to be denied to avoid the danger of idol worship; and yet the Bible and traditions of biblical exegesis almost invite it.

Furthermore, the artists involved in making the Tabernacle clearly had the power of conferring holiness on their creation. Any reader of the account of the construction of the Tabernacle is struck by the fact that, as noted above, its details are first enumerated in the form of instructions, and then reiterated in equal fullness in the course of two further chapters describing their execution. Why was the concluding sentence that Bezalel and his helpers carried out the instructions as God had commanded them not deemed sufficient? Commentators suggest that the repetition comes in order to stress the vital importance of the artist's constant awareness of the sacred and symbolic holiness of the Tabernacle and its utensils. The original holiness of purpose could only be preserved if the artist bore it in mind all the time whilst engaged in his creative task; in this sense (as a mediator rather than originator) he has the power of conferring holiness on to the physical world through his art – an idea which the religious symbolists, following Vladimir Solov'ev, would later take up enthusiastically.

The pitfall of equating the holy powers of the artist with those of God can, of course, be avoided by remembering that the artist's gifts, however great, ultimately derive only from God, who chooses a fit vessel for his wisdom. This is aptly conveyed by the meaning in Hebrew of the name Bezalel, "in the shade of God,"[11] inviting the association, but at the same time establishing its hierarchical nature.

God is therefore in an absolute sense the only true artist, past, present, and future, both as the Creator of the universe and as the builder and maker of the ideal city (Heb.11:10). The human artist's gaze should be directed above at his Maker, rather than below at his own creation. In this upward-looking hierarchy of reverence, man is creature rather than creator. When he assumes the role of creator, he runs the danger of losing sight of his Creator and of his subordinate position in this vertical hierarchy; hence the link between artistic activity and idol worship.

Although considerably obscured by centuries of cultural accretions and sometimes lost from view, this is the original root in the modern Russian literary tradition of the demonic view of art. The analogy between the artist and the Supreme Creator, which was originally a reflection of the deep harmony perceived in the order of Creation, once divorced from a sense of hierarchy, led to the view of the artist as a demonic usurper of divine creativity. The gradual transformation which this analogy underwent in Russian literature can be briefly illustrated by citing examples representing three different cultural periods: the late eighteenth century, early nineteenth century Romanticism, and post-symbolist modernism. Derzhavin's ode "God" (Bog, 1784) was the first work of Russian literature to acquire a substantial international reputation, and provides a striking early treatment of the parallel between artist and Creator.[12] In the third stanza God is described in terms which underline his role as Supreme Creator, past, present, and future:

> Создавый все единым словом,
> В твореньи простираясь новом,
> Ты был, Ты есь, Ты будешь ввек!

> [You who created everything with one word,
> Spreading throughout the new creation,
> You were, You are, You will be forever!]

The key question "And what before You am I?" (I chto pered Toboiu ia?) is introduced in the central stanza and marks the midway turning-point of the ode. The apparently straightforward answer "But I before You am nothing" (A ia pered Toboi – nichto) is then developed. Although man is nothing, because he is made in the image of God, he is a vessel for the divine and his "nothingness" becomes endowed with supreme significance. This leads to the arresting paradox at the heart of the poem: "I am a tsar – a slave, a worm – a god!" (Ia tsar' – ia rab, ia cherv' – ia bog!). The impact of this line was even more striking in the original manuscript versions of the poem, in which the word "god" was written by Derzhavin with an initial capital.[13] This controversial statement is followed, however, by an unquestioning affirmation of the hierarchy of creation and of the poet's dependent position within it:

> Твое созданье я, Создатель!
> Твоей премудрости я тварь!
> Источник жизни, благ податель,
> Душа души моей и царь!

> [I am Your creation, Creator!
> The creature of Your wisdom!
> Source of life, bestower of blessings,
> Soul of my soul and ruler!]

Some fifty years later, in the age of Romanticism, a similar parallel was drawn by Tiutchev. In his "Dream at Sea" (Son na more, 1830) the strong sense of hierarchy and explicit references to God which we noted in Derzhavin have been replaced by a more evenly balanced mirroring of man as microcosm and the Macrocosm, symbolized by the natural element of the sea. Man is presented as a builder of precarious dreams or artistic visions who strides "like a god" over the world which he has created:

По высям творенья, как бог, я шагал,
И мир подо мною недвижный сиял.[14]

[Over the summits of creation, like a god, I strode,
And the world beneath me, motionless, shone.]

Almost a century later, in a modernist poem by Khodasevich, "Dactyls" (Daktili, 1927–28), the demonic implications of the audacious image of man as god are taken one stage further:

Мир созерцает художник – и судит, и дерзкою волей,
Демонской волей творца – свой созидает, иной.[15]

[The artist contemplates the world – and judges, and with the daring will,
With the demonic will of a creator – he builds his own, a different one.]

In Derzhavin's ode, the artist, like Bezalel, only gains significance because of the divine spark inherent in him and does not hope to rival his Creator. Tiutchev shows how the godlike artist or dreamer attempts to impose his own fragile vision on the created universe, while Khodasevich, developing themes already latent in Lermontov and made plain by Blok, uncovers the demonic drive behind this creative impulse, viewed as an attempt to rival the work of the Supreme Creator. As Blok wrote, quoting the folklorist E.V. Anichkov: "without poetry man was nothing, but with poetry he became almost a god."[16]

Classical Images of Art and Inspiration

Not surprisingly, the biblical view of the artist as divinely inspired (and its demonic, idol-worshipping counterpart) strongly coloured Russian responses to the classical tradition. A revealing insight into this process of interaction can be found in a comment from the unpublished diary of Tat'iana Gippius about the leading religious poet and classical scholar, Viacheslav Ivanov. In her description of an all-night discussion held at the Tower in 1907, Gippius noted that "Viacheslav Ivanov upheld the incompatibility of art with religious ritual and, for the sake of preserving art, again [upheld] his mythopoeia (*mifotvorchestvo*)."[17] Her concise formulation pinpoints one of the ways in which an attempt was made to bridge the gap between both traditions: the creation of a new mythopoeic art form at the turn of the century was seen as a means of preserving the classical ideal of art without entirely relinquishing its links with religious ideals originally inspired by the Bible.

To understand the ways in which biblical and classical influences combined to nurture the Russian view of art as demonic, we first need to establish the key areas of difference and overlap between the two traditions and their approaches to art. The classical tradition offered a quite distinct set of images from the Bible for the understanding of artistic inspiration and its relation to divine prophecy. Apollo was the god of all the fine arts (including music, poetry, and eloquence) and also received from his father Zeus the divine gift of prophecy. Although the two gifts of prophecy and artistic inspiration were thus united in one person, when it came to passing them on to humans, the lines of transmission diverged. Prophecy was communicated through the sibyls who presided over the oracles, whereas different forms of artistic inspiration were under the aegis of the nine muses, daughters of Zeus (according to most opinions) and of Mnemosyne. Under the guidance of Apollo, they elevated art to the level of the sacred and conferred this blessing on mortals who would invoke them before embarking on their creative work.

Two additional points are of particular significance for our topic. A part of the Apollo myth presents him as a figure who was banished by Zeus from the heavens (in other words a classical equivalent of the biblical Lucifer or the figure of the fallen angel). The act of expulsion or fall, viewed as irretrievable, thus plays a part in bringing about the transition from divine prophecy to the mediating of this prophecy to humans through art and oracles. It is also worth noting that in the classical tradition as in the biblical tradition humans cannot and should not attempt to rival the gods in the sphere of artistic inspiration. Two legends illustrate the dangers of any such attempt: the Sirens, who invited the muses to a contest in singing which they lost, and most vividly, the Pierides, the daughters of the king of Boetia, who challenged the muses to a trial in music and were changed into magpies following their defeat.

There is one further paradigm for artistic inspiration in the classical tradition, which differs quite substantially from the serene harmony of Apollo and his cortège of modest, virginal muses. This is provided by the altogether plumper, more sensual and less disciplined god, Dionysus, descended from the same father, Zeus, and usually surrounded by a group of half-naked and orgiastic female consorts, the Bacchantes or maenads. Although Dionysus is most commonly thought of as the god of wine and intoxication, he was also the god of tragic art and the protector of theatres (since Greek drama had grown out of the dithyrambic choruses recited at the festival of Dionysus). This allowed the link to be made in his cult between the states of intoxication and inspiration.

Whereas Apollo and the muses confer their gifts on man through a vertical hierarchy of patronage (the artist may invoke them in order to receive their gifts, but may not imitate them), the Dionysian paradigm of inspiration allows man to merge with the god, to enter the state of intoxication which brings about inspiration. The fairly passive and upward-looking hierarchy of receiving a divine gift is replaced by an active descent into chaos, which in turn can become an image for art as demonic (dark, chaotic, initiated by man). Therefore, while the Apollonian and Dionysian myths both reinforce the biblical view of the divine origin of artistic inspiration, they offer very different methods for attaining this state. The Apollonian reception of grace from above is more easily assimilated into the biblical tradition of the artist as prophet, whereas the Dionysian descent into chaos is subversive in its promotion of individual initiative over divine grace and accordingly more closely allied with idol worship.

Indeed, a possible reason for the increased emphasis on art as demonic in turn of the century Russia may well have been the switch of emphasis from Apollo to Dionysus, following the popularization of Nietzsche's ideas in Russia from the 1890s onwards. Although Pushkin describes one of the incarnations of his muse as a frisky "little Bacchante,"[18] in his understanding the Bacchic spirit of the muses was closely allied with the "holy sun" of reason and therefore had little in common with later post-Nietzschean connotations of darkness and chaos.[19] Such references are in any case not typical – Apollo and the muses generally provide the norm up until the turn of the century, after which artistic inspiration is increasingly viewed as Dionysian and accordingly demonic.

An example of this shift in emphasis can be found in the description of the creative process given by Viacheslav Ivanov in an essay of 1905. His analysis is of particular relevance to our subject as his views on aesthetics were widely influential, both on the symbolist, acmeist, and futurist poets of his own time and on the writers, literary theorists, and philosophers of culture of subsequent generations. Ivanov distinguished three stages of artistic creation: a first stage, male, linked to Apollo, and termed "the feat of ascent" (*podvig voskhozhdeniia*); a second stage, female, linked to Aphrodite, referred to as the "grace of descent" (*milost' niskhozhdeniia*), and a third stage, the sphere of the bisexual Dionysus, representing the chaotic element of inspiration, and described as follows: "This sphere is indeed a shore 'beyond good and evil.' It is demonic in the demonism of its elements, but not evil. It is a fruitful source, not a diabolical numbness."[20] Although some writers, including Blok,[21] later took issue with Ivanov's attempt to define creativity in terms of a purely aesthetic, Dionysian demonism, far from the biblical view of demonism as immoral, this approach, once popularized, was remarkably enduring. A seductive visual expression of the equation of the demonic with the Dionysian was provided by Nikolai

Kalmakov in a painting of 1913 entitled *The Awakening of Bacchus* (Illustration 11). In sinuous outlines of green, grey, and brown, the artist depicted a naked and bearded Dionysus, goblet in hand, sitting astride a panther and above a serpent. His portrait evokes a curiously hellenized *Koshchei bessmertnyi* (Koshchei the Deathless), whose traditionally demonic features have been toned down and rendered aesthetically pleasing.[22]

We should also mention the figure of Orpheus, not only because he was the prototype of the singer, musician, and poet and widely represented as such in early twentieth-century Russian verse,[23] but also because he brought his Apollonian gift of poetry into a

11. N. Kalmakov, *The Awakening of Bacchus,* 1913. Mixed media, 64 × 48 cm.

Dionysian engagement with the demonic forces of death and the underworld, and, through the early Orphic mysteries, acted as a bridging figure between the classical and Christian traditions. In a short but profound essay on Orpheus Viacheslav Ivanov specifically emphasized Orpheus's relation to all three worlds, describing him as the "two-faced mysterious incarnation of both [Dionysus and Apollo]" and as "the creative Word which moves the world," who "represents the God-Word in early Christian symbolism of the first centuries."[24]

The points of overlap between the biblical and classical traditions illustrated by the myth of Orpheus are important: in both the gifts of prophecy and inspiration are linked by their common divine origin. In the biblical tradition there are no intermediaries; in the classical tradition the intermediary figures of muse, maenad, or Orphic poet open up different paths of access. The fundamental difference clearly revolves around the ontological status and moral content of the imparted revelation. The biblical vision is based on the revelation of pure truth, from above to below, whereas the classical tradition brings inspiration from above for the poet to express his own dreams and visions.

In this respect it is worth recalling the difference between the original meaning of the Greek term *daimon*, best translated as a "divinity," and the later significance which it acquired in Christian tradition. The Greek *daimon* was a being of intermediate nature between that of gods and men, sometimes identified with an individual's guiding force or destiny, whether for good or for evil. In *The Symposium* Plato uses the term of Eros, a divinity which has the power of "interpreting and conveying things from men to gods and things from gods to men;" through its realm "moves all prophetic art and the art of priests having to do with sacrifices and rituals and spells, and all power of prophecy and enchantment."[25] Elsewhere, in the *Phaedrus*, prophetic art is linked with the muses' gift of poetic inspiration, since both depend on a god-sent madness.[26] In the context of the creative process, the *daimon* of Eros can therefore be viewed as a positive mediating power through which divine madness possesses the poet. Later Greek tradition began to shift the emphasis towards the *daimon* as a malevolent, evil spirit, and, with the advent of Christianity and the translation of pagan gods into devils, this process was completed.[27] Although the distinction between the two types of spirit has been partially preserved in English (through the survival of the two variant spellings *dæmon* and *demon*), the existence of only one form of the word in Russian (*demon*) has blurred the difference and led to a greater degree of ambivalence in the use of the term. This confusion directly contributed to the gradual merging of the amoral dæmon of inspiration or guidance with the malignant demon of later Greek and Christian tradition – a process which can be traced through its literary manifestations in the poetry of Pushkin, Lermontov, and Blok.[28]

The dual legacy of the biblical and classical traditions, intertwined through these various areas of overlap and confusion, played an important role in forming the self-image of Russian writers and the expectations which they brought to the literary vocation. It raised several important questions and challenges. Could literature serve as a means for retrieving the two "lost" golden ages of biblical revelation and classical inspiration (thereby carrying out a redemptive or transfiguring function)? Were these two traditions mutually exclusive or could they be reconciled? The longstanding debate over the proper interpretation of Pushkin's "The Prophet" (Prorok, 1826)[29] is just one instance of the fertile polemics surrounding the relation of these two traditions. Does the poem, saturated with biblical imagery, refer only to the figure of the prophet, or do its textual links with "The Poet" (Poet, 1827),[30] whom Pushkin depicts as summoned by Apollo, justify its common interpretation in the Russian tradition as an image of the poet? Is the muse's divine status an assurance of her purity and truth, or is she a freelance agent, a channel of artistic inspiration but not a medium of revelation, accountable only to the poet's fantasy and not to any higher truth? As we shall argue in the next essay of this volume, part of the Russian answer to these questions resulted in a most peculiar and unorthodox union, sanctioned by neither biblical nor classical precedent, but deriving from both: the marriage of the muse and the Demon.

The Historical Context in Russia

So far we have been looking at the background to literary demonism non-chronologically, in terms of essential issues and shaping traditions. The Russian reception of these influences cannot, of course, be properly understood without reference to the historical dimension. If one were to investigate the relationship of biblical revelation to Hellenic culture against the unfolding background of Western European history, one would have to trace its development through the heated discussions among the early Church fathers on the right place for classical culture and literary endeavour in a Christian context, and then in the transition from medieval culture to Renaissance humanism. One would note, for example, that Augustine (354–430) devoted large sections of *The City of God* to inveighing against the spiritual dangers of classical culture, regarded by him quite literally as the work of devils (he severely condemned the stage plays of the Romans as one of the main methods adopted by "wily devils" – the pagan gods – for the corruption and blinding of men's souls).[31] By the late Middle Ages, however, the process of assimilation was much further advanced. Theologians and poets had a fairly sophisticated grasp of classical culture and ancient Greek philosophy (through Latin translations) and had succeeded in integrating these much more smoothly into the Christian faith, while nevertheless preserving a clear line of demarcation between the two. Dante, for example, inherited from Aquinas a body of Christianized Aristotelian and Platonic thought on which he was able to draw freely; indeed, he quotes Aristotle more frequently than any other body of writings apart from the Bible.[32] For him Aristotle was quite simply "the Master of those who know," while Virgil was dubbed "the great Poet."[33]

The same transition, played out on the Russian historical map, looks entirely different. Russia had no Renaissance and was more or less catapulted from medieval Rus into modern post-Petrine culture. There was no strong tradition of theological debate; arguments of any substance on the question of correct attitudes to secular culture and learning only began to emerge in the sixteenth century and did not gather much momentum until the mid-seventeenth century onwards,[34] largely because of a lack of systematic secular learning before this period. Simon Frankin has put the point succinctly: "There was no debate over classical learning because there was no classical learning to debate."[35]

Franklin notes only three times when book learning is represented as controversial in Kievan Rus. Two of these are relevant to our subject. The first concerns Nikita of Novgorod, an eleventh-century monk from the Monastery of the Caves at Kiev, who locked himself up in his cell to enjoy a bout of eremitic asceticism (despite having been denied permission). The devil appeared to him in the guise of an angel and instructed him to give up prayer and to pass his time reading books in order to converse with God. Nikita applied himself diligently to reading and soon had acquired quite a reputation for his learning, even for prophecy. However, he was faulted on two counts: his learning was not pious but vainglorious, and his erudition was suspiciously idiosyncratic. The brethren prayed for Nikita and, mercifully, the Lord intervened and reduced him "almost to a state of primal ignorance,"[36] thus ensuring his salvation. This story can perhaps be regarded as the first source in the Russian tradition for the "demonic" view of bookish activity (here reading, later translated into writing), regarded, quite literally, as inspired by the devil and as representing a false path to God.

The second example concerns Klim Smoliatich, a twelfth-century metropolitan of Kiev, who was charged with "abandoning the Scrip-

tures and citing instead from Homer, Aristotle, and Plato."[37] This is
apparently the only example in Kievan Rus of an attack against classical culture, and one might begin to get quite excited about it. But
there was in fact no real debate over the issue; in his defence Klim
evaded the attack rather skilfully, leading Franklin to conclude that
"this apparent twelfth-century Kievan controversy over the classics is
a hollow form," borrowing "the terms, but not the substance" of an
argument from Constantinople.[38]

For our purposes, it is important to note the following point. The
accusation levelled against both Nikita and Klim that they are using
book learning to promote their own personal glory rather than that
of God is an ingrained and recurrent theme which can be directly
related to the biblical differentiation between art as divine service
and idol worship outlined above; thus it provides a link between the
Bible and later literary representations of writing as a demonic form
of self-aggrandizement.

These views persisted and were considerably amplified in the
debate on the merits or perils of secular culture, which gradually
established a firmer place for itself throughout the sixteenth and seventeenth centuries. In an illuminating survey of attitudes to grammar
and rhetoric during this period Boris Uspensky argues that opposition to the study of these subjects among the Russian clergy and
monks was not the result of ignorance or obscurantism. It was motivated by two factors: the desire to resist Latinate influences (closely
bound up with the traditional academic syllabus) and – on a much
more fundamental level – by the perception of grammar as a tool by
which language could be manipulated, thereby making it possible
for man not only to distort the meaning of sacred texts, but also,
eventually, to become the author of his own texts. Such an approach
runs counter to the traditional reverence for the authority of Holy
Scripture as the sole source of learning and medium through which
all other subjects (including grammar) could be passively absorbed.
Grammar and rhetoric constitute the foundation of modern literary
studies, and opposition to them goes hand in hand with resistance to
the concept of literature as an independent sphere of activity. This
link is made clear by Evfimii, a monk from Chudov writing in
1684–85, whose trenchant formulation of the issues at stake interestingly includes reference to the art of poetry and leaves little doubt as
to his own opinion on the matter: "Is it more useful for us to study
grammar, rhetoric, philosophy and theology and the art of poetry
and from there to get to know the Divine Scriptures, or, and without
studying these subtleties, in simplicity to please God and by reading
to get to know the meaning of Holy Scriptures?"[39] The demonic
dimension of the study of such "subtleties" emerges from a letter in

which Avvakkum berates a young lady for her pursuit of secular knowledge, mentioning grammar, rhetoric, dialectics, and philosophy; he warns her that all worthwhile knowledge can be found in the teachings of the Church and that leanings towards any other branches of learning should be resisted as the work of the devil: "Evdokeia, Evdokeia, why will you not shake off from yourself the proud devil? You are looking for high learning, from it people fall away from God, unnourished, like leaves. ... Fool, fool, great fool!"[40]

These attitudes to secular learning were mirrored in early views of what constituted correct art. Clearly, the only sort of art which could exist in a religious context was devotional art. The representation of holy truths in plain and unadorned fashion required the total effacement of the artist's individuality – hence the emphasis on collective or anonymous authorship (perceived as a sign of artistic humility), and on translation, compilation, or the imitation of existing models, rather than on original composition or invention. In the field of icon painting, which perhaps best exemplifies the ideal of devotional art, the strict instruction to maintain tradition went hand in hand with a deep-seated distrust of innovation; the artist was obliged to adhere to a formal canon with fixed rules of composition, which left no room for imagination or conjecture. The Church formulated numerous strictures against the deployment of any element of fantasy, issuing a stern warning to painters in the *Book of a Hundred Chapters* (*Stoglav*, 1551) "to create nothing from their own fantasy" (ot svoego zamyshleniia nichtozhe predtvoriati).[41] The medieval *ikonopisets* was therefore much closer to the biblical ideal of a craftsman, executing a holy design, than to the image of a modern artist, creating works out of his own imagination. The icon painter's talent was regarded as a God-given gift, to be used for holy purposes, and failure to lead a pure life (modelled on the monastic ideal) disqualified him from his appointed task.[42]

In theory, therefore, the issue of art as a form of demonic idol worship was unlikely to arise in relation to devotional art. Although devils made frequent appearances in icons and hagiographic literature, the purity of the *medium* of their artistic depiction, whether visual or verbal, was not to be questioned: absolute loyalty to a hallowed tradition, based on biblical precedent and safeguarded by the Church, guaranteed freedom from contamination by the demonic, even allowing the artefact itself, in the case of icons, to acquire the status of a holy object of veneration.

In practice, however, this was not always the case: the canon of iconographic representation was surrounded by a considerable amount of controversy, and revered icons were occasionally even regarded as the work of the devil.[43] Viktor Bychkov's fascinating account of the historical development of the aesthetics of the icon highlights a constant tension between official theory and evolving artistic practice. By the mid-sixteenth century, numerous innovations had been introduced into the traditional canon of icon painting; these included the depiction of real historical people, allegorical subjects, and symbolic representations of Christ, not based on scenes from his real life. These innovations aroused deep feelings of indignation among traditionalists such as Ivan Viskovaty, who brought his worries to the attention of Ivan IV. The Council of 1554 was convened to deal with this crisis, but was not able to do much more than condone and legitimize existing practice. Some ten to fifteen years later, the controversy resurfaced on an even more fundamental level in a lively debate between Feodosii Kosoi and the monk Zinovii Otensky. Feodosii opposed icons on the grounds that they were forbidden by the biblical prohibition against idol worship. Zinovii countered this charge by invoking a different scriptural precedent; he argued that the verse which describes God showing Moses the design of the candlestick for the Tabernacle (Exod.25:40) was in actual fact a reference to icons and included the command that Moses should make them (as further support for the creation of icons Zinovii also cited the commandment to fashion two cherubs for the cover of the ark [Exod.25:18]).[44] This example is of particular interest in the context of our opening discussion of attitudes to art in the Bible, as it demonstrates the continuing relevance of biblical tradition to the Russian debate on art as divine or idolatrous.

We can see from the foregoing that the notion of secular learning and even of devotional art as potentially demonic or idolatrous was already present in latent form in early Russian culture, from the times of Nikita of Novgorod in the eleventh century through to the debates of the late sixteenth century. For the wider application of this attitude to Russian culture as a whole, we must look ahead to the time of Peter the Great and to later perceptions of this important turning-point in Russian history. During Peter's reign various changes already set in motion during the seventeenth century[45] came to fruition and altered the existing situation radically. Two areas of Peter's reforms were destined to have a particular impact on later views of culture and its "demonic" associations. The first concerns the reform of the Russian Orthodox church. The weakening of its autonomous authority and the subordination of all its values to the needs of autocracy totally undermined its role as a preserver of spiritual principles.[46] This in turn opened the way for a fundamental shift in the focus of faith from traditional orthodoxy to sectarian movements. Peter was widely denounced as Antichrist by Old Believers and other conservative traditionalists because of his

endorsement of Nikon's liturgical reforms and enforced modernization of religious ritual.[47] As a consequence, the new culture which
grew up in the wake of Peter's reforms later came to be regarded as
tainted by the demonic attributes of its founder; furthermore, the
subjection of church to state and the resulting disengagement of religious aspirations from their traditional moorings in Orthodox teaching facilitated the subsequent adoption of these aspirations by other
"oppositional" groupings, whether sectarian (in the first instance) or
literary (in later developments).

The second area concerns various steps which marked a move
towards the eventual secularization of culture. It is interesting to note
in relation to our earlier examples that a substantial section of the
Spiritual Regulation (Dukhovnyi reglament, 1721) was devoted to refuting the notion that education and book learning undermine faith
and lead to heresy.[48] Peter clearly did not aim to establish a new culture independent of the Church, nor was this achieved under his
reign (society and culture without God and the Church were
unthinkable in early modern Russia, and churchmen played a central role in elaborating the new culture for Peter). Nevertheless several of the reforms which he introduced contributed both directly
and indirectly to the gradual process of secularization. These reforms
are well-documented; they ranged from institutional changes, such
as the foundation of secular schools and of the Academy, to numerous practical measures, including the publication of new textbooks
and translations, the introduction of the civic script (grazhdanskii
shrift), which to a large extent (although not completely) relegated
the superseded alphabet to specifically ecclesiastical use,[49] and the
general undermining of the prestige of Church Slavonic (according
to some opinions, "the most fruitful of all languages and most dear to
God").[50] All these changes "helped to lay the foundations of a literacy ... no longer focused on religious purposes and the reading of
sacred texts."[51]

At the same time the existing barrier between the domains of the
secular and the religious was further reinforced by the introduction
of new measures. At Peter's personal direction an article was added
to the *Supplement to the Spiritual Regulation (Pribavlenie k Dukhovnomu
reglamentu),* which forbade monks from keeping ink and paper in
their cells or from writing anything in private, subject to severe cor-
poral punishment.[52] Although this measure was originally undertaken for political reasons (to stem the flow of seditious attacks on
Peter emanating from the monasteries) and was not in any case
intended to apply to the upper clergy, who spearheaded educational
reform, one can nevertheless appreciate the effect which it had on
the development of Russian culture, where, unlike the West, secular

literature was effectively cut off from the potential input of monks or members of the lower clergy, leaving little or no space in which the secular and the devotional could mingle.[53]

Literary Views of Post-Petrine Culture as Demonic

The combined effect of Peter's reforms was to prepare the ground for what would eventually become a new "secular" culture, paradoxically both sustained and burdened by the weight of displaced religious aspirations. Russian writers were heirs to a tradition which restricted the function of literacy to religious purposes; in this respect they were no different from their Western counterparts. However, rather than breaking free from this precedent and creating an alternative secular culture, devoid of religious content, in the main they chose to harness the existing tradition to their own sphere of activity. They appropriated the notion of literature as sacral, instead of challenging or rejecting it, and came to regard their mission in this light as the re-creation of moral and religious values through literature. This attitude has been remarkably persistent in the Russian tradition, finding one of its most extreme manifestations in the symbolist movement with its theory of theurgic art. The poet Aleksandr Blok – whose own art was entirely shaped by the legacy of this approach – went so far as to state that its uncritical acceptance in his country was the principal source of the Russian artist's tragic predicament.[54] And yet the attitude was so well entrenched that it became a prism through which works of literature were not only conceived but also read; this use of works of imaginative literature as a source of historical and religious "truths" for the definition of the nation's spiritual identity is a curious and typically Russian phenomenon, taken for granted and largely unquestioned within the native tradition. Blok's friend Evgenii Ivanov, for example, in an unpublished essay entitled "The Demon and the Church" (Demon i Tserkov', 1906), elaborated an entire interpretation of Lermontov's *The Demon* (*Demon*, 1839) in terms of the historical relationship between culture and religion in Russia. According to his reading, the Demon represents the tragedy of the Russian intelligentsia, seeking knowledge and freedom while striving for union with the Church, represented by Tamara. The tragedy lies in the fact that the Church has rejected the intelligentsia and its gifts of culture because it wrongly considers culture to be the work of the devil. Yet "the Demon is not a devil," it is also "a Church, but one which has descended into Hell," a holy martyr abandoned by God. The arresting solution envisaged by Ivanov is for the Church to "become a Tamara who loves the Demon."[55]

As is evident from this example, the transfer of the functions of religion into the literary domain created an optimum climate within which the demonic could flourish. From the writer's point of view, frustrated literary aspirations to transcendence would often result in an undue emphasis on the demonic, as the sublimated inner urge to prayer resolved itself through curses; in the words of Bely, writing in 1907 of Pushkin and Lermontov, "secretly they prayed, outwardly they cursed."[56] From the historical point of view, just as Peter was regarded as Antichrist in the religious sphere, so in the cultural sphere he came to be seen as the initiator of a new phase of antichristian, secular, hence "demonic" culture.[57] He had, after all, not only appropriated the biblical greeting formerly reserved for the Patriarch, but was also in triumphal processions "cast in the personae of Mars or Hercules, pagan gods who owed their victories to their own strength or valour."[58] Significantly, in the draft notes for his unfinished *History of Peter I (Istoriia Petra I*, 1831–37) Pushkin noted several features of Peter's rule which were relevant to the ruler's heretical, idolatrous image: the popular view of him as Antichrist, his attempt to suppress this opinion by denying monks the right to keep ink and paper in their cells, his unceremonious acceptance of the manifold new titles bestowed on him, and his refusal to appoint a new Patriarch (including anecdotal evidence, excised by the censor, that in 1721 he slapped himself on the chest, bared his dagger, and announced "Here's your new Patriarch").[59]

This idol-like image already carried within it the seed of its own dissolution into one of demonic hubris. The dynamics of this process of transformation can be traced through the fluctuating styles of various literary treatments of Peter. In the eighteenth century, the tendency to compare the tsar to God and to mix pagan and biblical images in panegyric eulogies of his virtues was widely practised by writers, but without any heretical intent; it was not until the time of Romanticism that the idolatrous implications of this trend were treated as problematic in literary texts. The transition from Lomonosov's tones of hyperbolic adulation to Pushkin's ambivalent and demonically tainted portrait of Peter provides an apt illustration of this shift of perspective. In an ode of 1743, which disconcertingly mixes pagan and Christian motifs, Lomonosov has Minerva and Mars describe Peter as a God (*Bog,* with an initial capital), who descended from the heavenly regions to Russia, took on fleshly form, and then returned to shine among the stars for all eternity.[60] In *The Bronze Horseman (Mednyi vsadnik,* 1833)[61] Pushkin continued this tradition of representing Peter as an idol (translating rhetorical conceit into literal image through the device of the statue), but gave it a new polemical twist. His portrayal of Peter in this work is of particular significance for our purposes, in that it unites in one person the historical figure and the image of the *artist-creator*, and hints at the way in which the transition from deified mortal to demonic idol operates in the spheres of both history and artistic creation. The parallel drawn in the introduction between God, the Creator of the universe, and Peter, referred to simply as "He," the creator *ex nihilo* of a new city and a potent symbol of the artist contemplating his impending act of creation, can be read in two ways: as an extreme form of praise for Peter, or as an indictment of his idolatrous pretensions. The source on which Pushkin modelled his opening in fact made the link between Peter the *artist* and God the creator even more explicit: in a prose work of 1814 K.N. Batiushkov described Peter surveying the swamps on which he would build his "wonder of the world" and emphasized that the projected city was conceived specifically as a demonstration of the triumph of *art* over nature.[62] Batiushkov was in turn drawing on a much earlier tradition, well developed in Peter's day, of comparing the tsar in his role of historical transformer to an artist-creator (as in the depiction of Peter as Pygmalion, carving the image of New Russia as Galatea), and, by extension, even to the Supreme Creator.[63] Pushkin, however, was the first poet to bring out the demonic implications of this analogy so clearly. His description of the subsequent flood suggests that Peter's attempt to usurp the role of Creator was indeed an act of hubris which unleashed the wrath of God (in a letter to his brother written at the time of the catastrophe, Pushkin openly compared the flood to the biblical deluge of Noah's generation, now visited upon "cursed Petersburg").[64] It was perhaps this dimension of divine retribution which the poet was alluding to at the end of various drafts of his introduction, when he expressed the not entirely convincing hope that his narrative would be "just an evening tale" (vechernii lish' rasskaz) for his readers, "and not an ominous legend" (a ne zloveshchee predan'e).[65] It has even been suggested that "Pushkin's use of the unnamed 'he'" in the poem's introduction "implies an identification of Peter not with God but with the devil, who by tradition was left unnamed and who challenged the good works of God."[66]

We can see, therefore, that a key aspect of Pushkin's tale in the context of our topic was the subtle link which it established between the demonic forces which operate in history and those which inform the creative impulse. This association of historical and artistic demonism in one work played an important role in laying the foundation for a specifically Russian, historically defined, tradition of literary demonism, linked to the figure of Peter and to the city of St. Petersburg, a fitting image of the new culture which he created. Some of the works which developed the demonic dimension of the theme of Peter and his city, building directly on the precedent set by Pushkin, are explored later in this volume. These include Gogol's story "The Portrait" (Portret, 1835, second version 1842), Merezhkovsky's novel *Antichrist (Peter and Aleksei) (Antikhrist [Petr i Aleksei]*, 1904), Bely's *Petersburg (Peterburg,* 1916), and Akhmatova's *Poem Without a Hero (Poema bez geroia,* 1940–62). The discussion could also be extended to numerous other works, including the representation of Petersburg in the poetry of the symbolists. An interesting development of *The Bronze Horseman* occurs, for example, in Blok's *The Twelve (Dvenadtsat',* 1918). Whereas Pushkin portrays a cycle which leads from an opening vision of the natural elements through the imposition of artistic order (Peter as creator of his new city) to the final release of demonic forces (Peter as Bronze Horseman), Blok's poem opens with blackness and wind, an intensified vision of elemental chaos, tinged with the demonic, and yet brings forth from this dark picture a closing image of redemption in the person of Jesus Christ. Blok's line "a man cannot stand on his feet" (na nogakh ne stoit chelovek)[67] ironically echoes Pushkin's anonymous introduction of Peter through the phrase "He stood" (stoial On), as well the ruler's plans "to stand by the sea with a firm foot" (nogoiu tverdoi stat' pri more).[68] The forceful figure of Peter portrayed by Pushkin has been swept away in Blok's demonic wind, but this is only in order to prepare the ground for a new figure of salvation. This late symbolist development of the demonic forces already latent in Pushkin's portrayal of Peter and his city testifies once more to the innate Russian tendency to magnify the demonic in order to create a springboard for the sacred.

Pushkin's "Enchanting Demon" and Russia's Historical Path

Peter's reforms and his associated public image came to be regarded by writers and historians as marking a decisive turning-point in Russian history, and a highly accelerated version of the shift from medieval Christianity to the humanist revival of paganism which Western Europe went through more gradually. Many of the same issues were at stake, including the problematic status of art as idol worship or divine service within the context of the relation of secular culture (based on the classical model) to religious revelation (based on the biblical model). The fact that Peter came to be seen as the focus of these issues was no doubt a simplification from the strictly historical point of view; nevertheless, from the broader, literary/cultural perspective which Russian writers adopted, the figure of

Peter appeared as pivotal and all-embracing; as Pushkin put it in a letter to Chaadaev, "à lui seul est une histoire universelle!"[69]

This complex of cultural and historical influences produced a wide range of approaches to the demonic properties of art. Among these, the intriguing lyric fragment by Pushkin, "At the beginning of my life I remember a school..." (V nachale zhizni shkolu pomniu ia..., 1830)[70] is of exceptional interest for our topic. It occupies a unique place in Pushkin's *œuvre* and merits our close attention at this point, as it raises the issue of art as demonic in the context of the cultural and historical factors discussed above. It offers a stylized, yet highly personal exploration of the relationship between secular culture and religious values in its twin philosophical and historical dimensions. The autobiographical tone which it adopts blends with what we shall argue is in effect an allegorical representation of the transition from medieval Christianity to Renaissance humanism, with particular emphasis on the question of the relation of artistic beauty to religious truth. Dante achieved a similar combination of personal autobiography, philosophical enquiry, and historical perspective in *The Divine Comedy*, and Pushkin signals his debt to this work in a number of ways, most obviously by adopting the same verse form of *terza rima* in his poem.[71]

The lyric persona of Pushkin's poem recalls his early life at school: strict order was kept by a "stately woman" (velichavaia zhena), described in one early variant as a "wondrous woman" (divnaia zhena), whose "veil" (pokryvalo) and "eyes clear as the heavens" (ochi svetlye, kak nebesa) he remembers with particular clarity. This female figure is clearly associated with religion and spiritual guidance, and may be a personification of Divine Wisdom or Theology.[72] Her speech is described as "words full of holiness" (polnye sviatyni slovesa) and her role in the hero's spiritual salvation is made even more explicit in an earlier variant, which refers to her "saving reproaches" (spasitel'nye ukory) and to the "deep meaning of spiritual conversations" (glubokoi smysl dukhovnykh razgovorov) held with her. While the autobiographical elements of the poem place her in a Russian context, other features link her with the world of medieval Catholicism and suggest a more specific analogy with Beatrice, Dante's "dolce guida,"[73] his teacher in matters of faith and the instigator of his spiritual journey, also regarded as an allegory of Divine Wisdom or Theology.[74]

The truthful teachings of this lady are distorted by her errant pupil who prefers to escape to the "splendid gloom of an alien garden" (velikolepnyi mrak chuzhogo sada) where, in an environment shaped by human artifice (iskusstvennyi), he begins to dream idle thoughts (prazdnomyslit'). Pushkin, in keeping with many artists, regarded the state of idleness (prazdnost') as highly conducive to poetic inspiration, and it is the link between this fruitful creative idle-

ness and the arid spiritual state of boredom (skuka), in which the
devil traditionally makes his entrance, which allows for the possibility of pure art becoming contaminated by the demonic.[75] In
Pushkin's poem, this connection is demonstrated with economic precision: it is just at the moment of idle thoughts that the sight of statues, referred to as *kumiry*, the biblical word for pagan idols, brings
about "tears of inspiration" (slezy vdokhnoven'ia). The transition
from aesthetic inspiration to the demonic follows. Two further statues
in particular captivate him with their "enchanting beauty" (volshebnaia krasa); significantly, these are described as "images of two devils" (dvukh besov izobrazhen'ia), a phrase which underlines their
demonic connotations more strongly than the earlier variant,
"images of two gods" (dvukh bogov izobrazhen'ia). In a variant of an
earlier line they are referred to as "the artists' other two creations"
(khudozhnikov drugie dva tvoren'ia), a description which brings out
the specific link between the statues as works of *art* and the demonic.
The first statue, a Delphic idol, exudes awesome pride:

> Один (Дельфийский идол) лик младой –
> Был гневен, полон гордости ужасной,
> И весь дышал он силой неземной.

> [One (a Delphic idol) of youthful face –
> Was angry, full of terrible pride,
> And breathed all over with unearthly power.]

This is evidently a statue of Apollo, patron of the arts, nurtured by
pride, the root of all sin and of demonic (Luciferian) art. The second
statue is described as follows:

> Другой женообразный, сладострастный,
> Сомнительный и лживый идеал –
> Волшебный демон – лживый но прекрасиый.

> [The other was of womanly form, voluptuous,
> A doubtful and false ideal –
> An enchanting demon – false, but beautiful.]

Although most commentators have interpreted this as a reference to
Aphrodite, the goddess of beauty and love, the use of the adjective
zhenoobraznyi (would a female goddess be described as "*like* a
woman" in form?), the terms "demon" (demon) and "devil" (bes), as
well as a variant of the tercet's middle line which describes the statue
as "the false ideal of naked nature" (nagoi prirody lzhivyi ideal)
make it more likely that it represents Dionysus, the effeminate and
sensual god of intoxication and inspiration.[76] Alternatively, it is possible that the statues are purely allegorical representations of the two
sins or "devils" which gained particular ascendancy during the
Renaissance: pride, fuelled by anger, and unbridled sensuality.[77]

The flight from the humble, modestly attired lady to the seductive statues of the garden suggests a move from medieval Christian culture to Renaissance humanism with its revival of pagan idols and attendant shift of values. This allegorical landscape is crossed by an unidentified narrator, who has been linked by several commentators with Pushkin.[78] Autobiographical elements are indeed suggested by the intimate, personal tone, as well as by close textual echoes of other poems in which Pushkin evokes the gardens and statues of Tsarskoe Selo, where he went to school, as the backdrop to his first encounter with poetic inspiration.[79] If so, we have a curious amalgam – a Russian poet trying to find his bearings in a "philosophical" landscape defined by the evolution of Western European culture. This is altogether different from the more purely "Russian" experience of demonic disorientation which Pushkin had evoked immediately before in "The Devils" (Besy, 1830).[80] There the traveller's journey lay through "unknown plains" (nevedomykh ravnin) devoid of mileposts (apart from demonic ones), and any attempt at establishing a linear sense of direction is sabotaged by the swirling scores of swarming devils which fill the night. By contrast, "At the beginning of my life…" introduces a philosophical and historical perspective into this picture of elemental chaos and dark forces. Its setting, described by Annensky as the "garden of Tsarskoe Selo transformed,"[81] already contained the necessary elements for such an approach: from its original conception to the details of its execution, Tsarskoe Selo was a literal and visual embodiment of the renaissance of classical antiquity on Russian soil.[82] Sculpture, which was a particularly prominent feature of its landscape, was not an accepted art form in the Russian Orthodox tradition and was therefore a particularly fitting symbol of pagan resistance to religous values, embodied in aesthetic form. Pushkin's poem exploits this ready-made, richly suggestive allegorical setting to raise the key issue of the relation of artistic inspiration and beauty (associated with the demonic "idols" of classical culture) to revealed religion and truth (the sphere of the "stately woman") – and also of Russia's relation to the historical unfolding of this relationship in Western Europe. However, both issues are left unresolved:[83] the fragment ends with the hero wandering gloomily all day, a Russian Dante of the modern age, lost in a dark garden in which the original certainties of faith are overshadowed by later artistic images:[84]

> …всё кумиры сада
> На душу мне свою бросали тень.
>
> [… still the idols of the garden
> Cast their shadow on my soul.]

The link between the state of artistic inspiration and demonic idol worship or possession, which we have highlighted in this relatively late poem, is not one which most readers would normally associate with Pushkin's view of art. And yet, as we can see from the elusive, haunting quality of the poem, many of the biblical, classical, and historical contexts for the view of art as demonic examined in this essay, as well as the problematic issues which arise from their interaction, had an intimate, personal resonance for Pushkin. His poem suggests an awareness of the spiritual danger presented by following the path of art, devoid of religious purpose, together with a strong sense of the magnetic attraction of this path for the artist. If the faith in pure ideals (represented by the "stately woman") is forsaken, and if, as a consequence, the pursuit of art is divorced from the source of spiritual guidance that nourishes it, and becomes an end in itself (signalled by the flight into the enclosed space of the garden), then art will become a form of demonic idolatry (hence the description of the statues as demons or idols). This is entirely consonant with the conflict outlined earlier in this essay between the biblical ideal of art (subject to religious revelation) and the classical ideal of art (dependent on aesthetic rather than moral values). In his formulation of the problem, Pushkin reveals a deep understanding of its central significance for the modern Russian poet, depicted as standing at a crossroads, torn between the two traditions to which he is heir. His poem provided an important precedent for later treatments of this issue, anticipating by almost eighty years Viacheslav Ivanov's explicit characterization of the post-medieval artist as a "maker of idols" (kumirotvorets).[85]

Pushkin's poem is so distinctive and rich in historical and philosophical insights that one is tempted to speculate on what external influences might have prompted its genesis. Several factors point to the role of Petr Chaadaev, who, as Pushkin's early mentor, encouraged him to think deeply about historical issues. In a letter of March-April 1829, Chaadaev wrote to Pushkin that his "most fiery wish" was to see his friend "initiated into the mystery of time," adding pointedly that "there is no more distressing spectacle in the world of morals than the spectacle of a man of genius, who does not understand his time (vek) and his calling." Chaadaev appealed to Pushkin to retire into himself in order to discover the inner light within his soul, and expressed his faith that Pushkin could bring "infinite blessing to this poor Russia, wandering lost on the face of this earth."[86] Pushkin's poem, written in the following year, may be seen as a response to this challenge: it takes up the consideration of Russia's plight from a religious and historical perspective, adopting a tone of spiritual introspection. In this context, we should also note the significance of the poem's setting, as Pushkin was closest to Chaadaev during his years at the Lyceum in Tsarskoe Selo.

For more specific evidence of the impact of Chaadaev's ideas on Pushkin's poem, we need to turn to Chaadaev's first philosophical letter, dated 1 December 1829 by its author, but thought to date from 1828 or early 1829.[87] We know that Pushkin had read the original French version of this letter by June 1830,[88] a few months before he wrote "At the beginning..." in October. Chaadaev's letter is cast in the form of a personal address to a friend (E.D. Panova), who is urged to develop her religious feelings by turning to the practice of Christian ritual; Chaadaev advises her to take up the contemplative life and to don the "robe d'humilité" which suits her sex so well.[89] From these individual admonitions, Chaadaev moves on to a general consideration of Russia's spiritual needs as a nation. He argues that Russia has no place in history, because she is excluded from European history, represented as one unified march towards the realization of a single Christian ideal.[90] As a result, the Russian people is well and truly lost ("égaré dans le monde");[91] it has no awareness of the past or memories to treasure, no meaningful present or individual identity, and no sense of the future: "Nous ne vivons que dans le présent le plus étroit, sans passé et sans avenir, au milieu d'un calme plat. ... nous n'avons rien d'individuel sur quoi asseoir notre pensée; mais, isolés par une destinée étrange du mouvement universel de l'humanité, nous n'avons rien recueilli non plus des idées traditives du genre humain."[92] Russia cannot appropriate or transfer to her own experience the slow process of historical maturation which Europe has been through, nor is she free to develop her own independent path towards civilization, because she has no meaningful Christian heritage of her own to develop.[93] The only solution, therefore, is for her to turn to the path of true religion (although Catholicism is not named, it is clearly implied).

If we return to our suggested reading of Pushkin's poem as an allegorical description of a Russian trying to find his bearings in a "philosophical" landscape defined by the evolution of Western European culture, we can now see that it takes as its point of departure the very same problem posed by Chaadaev: Russia's place in relation to the development of European history. By contrast, however, Pushkin's poem suggests that Russia *does* have a place in history, including a strong sense of her own past and interest in the future. Chaadaev's accusation that Russia has no clear identity or memories to treasure is countered by Pushkin's allegorical representation of Russia through an individual lyric voice, together with the emphasis which he places on the memory of his teacher's voice ("I remember" [ia pomniu] is repeated twice within the first ten lines of the poem, and the teacher's voice is described as "lovely, sweet" [priiatnym, sladkim]).

Pushkin also challenges Chaadaev's views on two related issues. Although he would doubtless agree that Russia cannot easily assimilate the historical process which Europe has been through, he shows his lyric hero grappling with this problem and lost in deep reflection. Chaadaev's idea that Russia has no independent path towards civilization, because she lacks a meaningful Christian heritage, is also disputed through the portrait of the wise woman, who embodies a rich legacy of deep spirituality, on which Russia can draw. Pushkin echoes Chaadaev's use of the predicament of an individual person to mirror national preoccupations, but reinstates the dimension of faith by replacing Chaadaev's move from a *lack of faith* to the need to discover true faith with a move from a *faith once held* to its subsequent overshadowing.

Pushkin, therefore, is taking up the issues raised by Chaadaev, but suggests a different answer, based on the belief that Russia does have its own form of spirituality and distinctive place in history. Furthermore – and here we return to the question of art as demonic – in this very distinctiveness there is perhaps a positive virtue. Chaadaev argued that Europe's synthesis of Christianity and classical antiquity had enabled it to elaborate an ideal of beauty, but that Russia had missed out on this opportunity: "en se repliant sur l'antiquité païenne, le monde chrétien avait retrouvé les formes du beau qui lui manquaient encore. Relégués dans notre schisme, rien de ce qui se passait en Europe n'arrivait jusqu'à nous."[94] The fact that Pushkin places his lyric hero in an allegorical setting evocative of Tsarskoe Selo, replete with classical statues, not only demonstrates that Russia has had her own encounter with pagan antiquity, but also puts a new slant on this encounter: his hero, as we saw, is troubled by the demonic connotations of the statues, which he recognizes as idols, representing "an enchanting demon – false, but beautiful" (volshebnyi demon – lzhivyi, no prekrasnyi). This raises a question mark over the European synthesis of Christianity and pagan antiquity advocated by Chaadaev: is this the best path, or does the Russian tendency to regard this synthesis as potentially problematic, and to dwell more closely on the demonic properties of art, point to a different spiritual path of superior value?

Pushkin's lyric fragment does not, after the manner of prose, refute Chaadaev's arguments directly; it engages with them obliquely, using poetry, the language of faith, to repudiate philosophy. A more explicit confirmation of its underlying drive can be found in the fuller response which Pushkin elaborated in his letter to Chaadaev of October 1836,[95] shortly after the publication of the first

philosophical letter in Russian translation.[96] Many points of
Pushkin's letter echo the ideas that he expressed earlier in his poem.
One senses that he is feeling his way towards a positive definition of
Russia's national identity and historical development in relation to
the two pivotal points of Chaadaev's critique, Europe and Christianity. His letter argues more openly than the poem that Russia does
have a clearly defined history, marked by a growing closeness
towards Europe, and also defends Russian spirituality as a basis for
national identity.

Although the influence of Chaadaev's letter on Pushkin's poem
cannot be proven indisputably, there is enough internal textual evidence to suggest a real connection.[97] This points to an important further dimension, initiated by Pushkin, which the discussion of art as
demonic acquired in the context of polemics over Russia's distinctive historical path and relation to the European tradition.

The biblical, classical, and historical contexts, outlined in this essay,
combined to produce a strong Russian emphasis on the demonic
properties of art, which manifested itself in a wide variety of
approaches. These can be summarized, according to the main
sources of non-literary influence, as follows:

Biblical influences. In the first instance, literature was regarded as
demonic because of its inability to live up to the religiously inspired
ideal of the writer as prophet, or of the written word as an echo of
the sacred *Logos.* Failure to meet this lofty ideal resulted in its inversion: if the writer was no prophet, he was a Demon, a victim of his
own hubris; if the literary word was not sacred, it was seen as
demonically tainted and corrupting. The writer therefore became a
demonic double of his ideal self, and the word was reduced to a
demonic travesty of its sacred origins. Prayers give way to curses,
revelations are displaced by solipsistic dreams, and intuitions by
parodic doubles. Literature, divorced in this way from its ideal
source in religion and morality, came to be seen as a form of
demonic idol worship, spreading false teachings and corrupting true
values, as described by Pushkin in "The Demon" (Demon, 1823).
Although this version of literary demonism had its source in the
negation of *moral* values, it subsequently gave rise to many manifestations of a purely *aesthetic* character, particularly in the productive area of literary experimentation.

Folk influences. An alternative model for the demonic attributes of
literary activity was provided by the folk tradition. Its view of the
word as incantation led to the representation of the writer as sorcerer
or "black book man" (chernoknizhnik), manipulating language in
order to cast spells.

Classical influences. Literature was further seen as demonic in the classical sense, by dint of its ability to "possess" the artist. Pushkin also wrote of this demon, the morally neutral demon of poetic inspiration. This form of artistic demonism later gained particular popularity as a result of the impact of Nietzsche on the Russian tradition; it was extended to include a religious dimension by Viacheslav Ivanov, whose theory of a fruitful form of chaotic Dionysian demonism could be used as a way of overcoming the "negative" connotations of demonism, defined as immoral by the Bible, or as dangerous by folk tradition.

Historical influences. Finally, on a historical level, superimposed upon the preceding traditions of influence, literature was viewed as demonic simply by virtue of the fact that it forms a part of post-Petrine culture and thereby, following the popular view of Peter as Antichrist, becomes invested with the demonic attributes of its founder. Pushkin laid the literary foundation for a recognition of Peter's role as a demonic figure in both history and artistic creation – a fatal combination for which the city of Petersburg served as a potent symbol.

The many ways in which these varied approaches to art as demonic were interwoven and developed within the Russian literary tradition are investigated in relation to different authors and their works in part II of this volume. The evolution of the relationship between the muse and the Demon in the poetry of Pushkin, Lermontov, and Blok, is traced in the next essay by Pamela Davidson. Gogol's early development of the theme of art as demonic is studied by Julian Graffy with particular attention to the relevance of Petersburg as demonic city. Rozanov, whose ideas on art are discussed by Liza Dimbleby, perhaps represents the furthest (and most paradoxical) extreme to which Russian writers took the concept of the very act of writing as demonic. A similar awareness informs the works of the symbolist novelists, whose literary techniques for portraying their metaphysical vision of the demonic were increasingly infiltrated by the disorientating, illusory nature of their subject, as demonstrated by Adam Weiner. Michael Basker shows how Akhmatova, through her reading of Gumilev's creative path, attempted to overcome the legacy of symbolist demonism but was unable to achieve a complete exorcism. A secularized version of the literary techniques elaborated by the symbolists found its way into the work of later prose writers such as Zamiatin, who, as Philip Cavendish argues, used demonic methods to describe and undermine notions of the sacred and demonic. All these contributions provide ample evidence of the deeply ingrained Russian conviction that "art is Hell,"[98] a conviction shaped by the interaction of the different cultural traditions and historical contexts examined in this essay.

Notes

1. Saint Antony the Great, "Directions on Life in Christ," in *Early Fathers from the Philokalia*, selected and trans. from the Russian text *Dobrotoliubie* by E. Kadloubovsky and G.E.H. Palmer (London: Faber and Faber, 1954), 50.

2. From "V nachale zhizni shkolu pomniu ia..." (1830), in A.S. Pushkin, *Sobranie sochinenii*, ed. D.D. Blagoi and others, 10 vols. (Moscow: Khudozhestvennaia literatura, 1974–78), 2:252–53(253). For a detailed discussion of this poem, see the concluding section of this essay. Unless otherwise stated, all translations in this essay are mine.

3. The first reference to Dante in Russia occurs in 1762; the first translation from his works did not appear until 1798. See M.P. Alekseev, "Pervoe znakomstvo s Dante v Rossii," in *Ot klassitsizma k romantizmu: Iz istorii mezhdunarodnykh sviazei russkoi literatury*, ed. M.P. Alekseev (Leningrad: Nauka, 1970), 6–62; V.T. Danchenko, *Dante Alig'eri: Bibliograficheskii ukazatel' russkikh perevodov i kriticheskoi literatury na russkom iazyke 1762–1972* (Moscow: Kniga, 1973), 6, 51. Milton's *Paradise Lost*, although first translated in 1745, was not published in Russian until 1780, the date at which the first Russian imitations also began to appear. See Valentin Boss, *Milton and the Rise of Russian Satanism* (Toronto: University of Toronto Press, 1991), 16–17, 20. On the early reception of Goethe in Russia, see André von Gronicka, *The Russian Image of Goethe*, 2 vols. (Philadelphia: University of Pennsylvania Press, 1968–85), 1:7–59 (chaps. 1 and 2), and V.M. Zhirmunskii, *Gete v russkoi literature*, ed. N.A. Zhirmunskaia (Leningrad: Nauka, 1981), 30–126 (chaps. 2 and 3); although translations of Goethe began to appear from 1780 (30), it was not until Zhukovsky's translations of 1818 that Goethe entered Russian poetry (77–78). On the Russian reception of Byron, see V.M. Zhirmunskii, *Bairon i Pushkin. Pushkin i zapadnye literatury* (Leningrad: Nauka, 1978), esp. 397–407 for a bibliography of translations from 1822. The Russians were remarkably quick off the mark in their response to Baudelaire, whose first essay on Edgar Allan Poe appeared in Russian in 1852 (the earliest translation of Baudelaire into any language); the first Russian translation of a poem from *Les Fleurs du Mal* (1857) was published in 1869. See Adrian Wanner, *Baudelaire in Russia* (Gainesville, Fla.: University Press of Florida, 1996), 10.

4. The example of Noah, also a divinely inspired builder, provides a precedent. However, the biblical description of the construction of the ark is purely technical and does not make reference to the specifically artistic attributes of craftsmanship, wisdom, and beauty, constantly stressed in the account of the building of the Tabernacle by Bezalel.

5. In order to convey the meaning of the original Hebrew as closely as possible, all quotations from the Old Testament have been taken from the authoritative translation *The Holy Scriptures*, 2 vols. (Philadelphia: The Jewish Publication Society of America, 1955). For similar descriptions of Bezalel and his helpers, see Exod.35:30–35, 36:1–4. Quotations from the New Testament are given from the King James Authorized Version.

6. Moses tried several times to get out of the job for which he was chosen, invoking lack of eloquence as his final excuse: "'Oh Lord, I am not a man of words, neither heretofore, nor since Thou hast spoken unto Thy servant; for I am slow of speech, and of a slow tongue'" (Exod.4:10). God's reply – "'Who hath made man's mouth? or who maketh a man dumb, or deaf, or seeing, or blind? Is it not I, the Lord? Now therefore go, and I will be with thy mouth, and teach thee what thou shalt speak'" (Exod.4:11–12) – makes it clear that God is the source of both the content of the message and its eloquent form.

7. See, for example, the well-known lines: "Their idols are silver and gold, / The work of men's hands. / ... / They that make them shall be like unto them; / Yea, every one that trusteth in them" (Ps.115:4,8).

8. This view directly informs the treatment of the artist-Demon in the works of Lermontov and Blok; see in this volume Pamela Davidson, "The Muse and the Demon in the Poetry of Pushkin, Lermontov, and Blok." The subject also became popular among modernist painters; see, for example, Kuz'ma Petrov-Vodkin, *The Expulsion from Paradise* (1911) and Nataliia Goncharova, *The Expulsion from Paradise* (1912–13), reproduced in Valerij Aleksandrovič Dudakov, ed., *Il Simbolismo russo: Sergej Djagilev e l'Età d'argento nell'arte* (Milan: Olivetti/ Electa, 1992), 110, 153.

9. "And the Lord opened the mouth of the ass" (Num.22:28). "And the angel of the Lord said unto Balaam: 'Go with the men; but only the word that I shall speak unto thee, that thou shalt speak,' ... And Balaam said unto Balak: 'Lo, I am come unto thee; have I now any power at all to speak any thing? the word that God putteth in my mouth, that shall I speak'" (Num.22:35,38).

10. *The Babylonian Talmud,* Sanhedrin 69b, Berachos 55a.

11. *The Babylonian Talmud,* Berachos 55a.

12. Although not published until 1784, "Bog" was already substantially completed by 1780. The text is cited from *Sochineniia Derzhavina s ob"iasnitel'nymi primechaniiami,* ed. Ia. Grot, 2d ed., 7 vols. (St. Petersburg: Tipografiia Imperatorskoi Akademii nauk, 1868–78), 1:130–33 (text), 133–48 (notes). For a close analysis of the poem's non-linear structure, which emphasizes the centrality of the parallel between God and the poet Derzhavin, see Anna Lisa Crone, "The Chiasmatic Structure of Deržavin's 'Bog': Poetic Realization of the 'Chain of Being'," *Slavic and East European Journal* 38, no.3 (1994), 407–18.

13. The daring comparison of the poet to God in this line was debated in 1838 by Shishkov and a professor of Kazan University. After citing their discussion, Grot defends his editorial decision to change Derzhavin's original capital "B" to a lower-case "b" on the grounds that Derzhavin always wrote "Bog" with a capital letter, even when referring to pagan gods, and was hardly likely to have intended to compare the poet with the Supreme Creator (Grot, ed., *Sochineniia Derzhavina,* 1:143). This editorial intervention is, however, highly questionable, as it destroys the symmetry between man and God which informs the rest of the poem.

14. F.I. Tiutchev, *Polnoe sobranie stikhotvorenii,* ed. V. Gippius and K. Pigarev, Biblioteka poeta (Leningrad: Sovetskii pisatel', 1939), 44. The poem was first published by Pushkin in *Sovremennik* in 1836. Although previously dated 1833, it is now thought to date from 1830; see *On the Heights of Creation: The Lyrics of Fedor Tyutchev,* trans. with introduction and commentary by Anatoly Liberman (Greenwich, Conn. and London: JAI Press, 1993), 197. In some editions "kak bog, ia" is replaced with the more muted "ia gordo."

15. Vladislav Khodasevich, *Stikhotvoreniia,* ed. N.A. Bogomolov and D.B. Volchek, Biblioteka poeta, Bol'shaia seriia (Leningrad: Sovetskii pisatel', 1989), 189.

16. "Poeziia zagovorov i zaklinanii" (October 1906), in Aleksandr Blok, *Sobranie sochinenii,* ed. V.N. Orlov, A.A. Surkov, and K.I. Chukovskii, 8 vols. (Moscow and Leningrad: Gosudarstvennoe izdatel'stvo khudozhestvennoi literatury, 1960–63), 5:36–65(53).

17. M. Pavlova, "Ivanovskie 'sredy' i upominaniia o Viach. Ivanove v dnevnikakh T.N. Gippius," an unpublished paper read at an International Symposium on Viacheslav Ivanov, held at the University of Vienna in July 1998. M. Pavlova is currently working on the unpublished diaries of T.N. Gippius, housed at Amherst University. I am grateful to her for allowing me to quote this fragment from the entry headed "27 January [1907], midnight."

18. "I kak Vakkhanochka rezvilas'," from *Evgenii Onegin* (8:3.9), in Pushkin, *Sobranie sochinenii*, 4:141.

19. In "Vakkhicheskaia pesnia" (1825) the description of Bacchanalian revelries is associated with the muses, reason, and the light of the holy and immortal sun of the mind, directly opposed to darkness. See Pushkin, *Sobranie sochinenii*, 2:33.

20. "Simvolika esteticheskikh nachal" (1905), in Viacheslav Ivanov, *Sobranie sochinenii*, ed. D.V. Ivanov and O. Deschartes, 4 vols. (Brussels: Foyer Oriental Chrétien, 1971–87), 1:823–30(829).

21. See in this volume Davidson, "The Muse and the Demon."

22. Reproduced in Dudakov, ed., *Il Simbolismo russo*, 155.

23. On representations of Orpheus in poetry of this period, see Lena Szilard, "'Orfei rasterzannyi' i nasledie orfizma," *Studia Slavica* 41 (1996):209–46.

24. "Orfei" (1912), first published in the opening issue of *Trudy i dni* 1912, no.1:60–63, cited from Ivanov, *Sobranie sochinenii*, 3:706.

25. *The Dialogues of Plato*, vol. 2, *The Symposium* (202d–203a), trans. with comment by R.E. Allen (New Haven and London: Yale University Press, 1991), 146.

26. Plato, *Phaedrus* (244a–245a), with translation and commentary by C.J. Rowe (Warminster: Aris and Phillips, 1986), 57, 59. On Plato's daemons, see the "Excursus on the History of the Doctrine of Daemons," in *The Myths of Plato*, trans. J.A. Stewart, ed. G.R. Levy, 2d ed. (London: Centaur Press, 1960), 384–401.

27. See the article on δαίμων in Hermann Cremer, *Biblico-Theological Lexicon of New Testament Greek*, trans. from German by William Urwick, 4th ed. (Edinburgh: T.& T. Clark, 1895, reprint, 1977), 168–71.

28. See in this volume Davidson, "The Muse and the Demon."

29. Pushkin, *Sobranie sochinenii*, 2:82–83. For examples of the debate surrounding this poem, see the essays by Vladimir Solov'ev, "Znachenie poezii v stikhotvoreniiakh Pushkina" (1899), Mikhail Gershenzon, "Mudrost' Pushkina" (1917), Viacheslav Ivanov, "Dva maiaka" (1937), Sergei Bulgakov, "Zhrebii Pushkina" (1938), and the response to the latter in Vladislav Khodasevich, "'Zhrebii Pushkina,' Stat'ia o. S.N. Bulgakova", in *Pushkin v russkoi filosofskoi kritike: Konets XIX- pervaia polovina XX vv.*, comp. R.A. Gal'tseva (Moscow: Kniga, 1990), esp. 55–81, 219–20, 254–55, 282–83, 489–91.

30. Pushkin, *Sobranie sochinenii*, 2:110.

31. See, for example, Saint Augustine, *The City of God (De Civitate Dei)*, trans. John Healey, ed. R.V.G. Tasker, Everyman's Library, no. 982, 2 vols. (London: J.M. Dent, 1945), 1:37 (book 1, chap.31).

32. See David Knowles, *The Evolution of Medieval Thought* (London: Longman, 1962), esp. 221–23 and 255–68; R.W. Southern, *The Making of the Middle Ages* (London: Hutchinson, 1967), esp. 164–77. On Dante's knowledge of Aristotle, see Lorenzo Minio-Paluello, "Dante's Reading of Aristotle," in *The World of Dante: Essays on Dante and his Times*, ed. Cecil Grayson (Oxford: Clarendon Press, 1980), 61–80(64).

33. *Inferno*, 4:131, 80, respectively. All quotations and translations from Dante's *Divine Comedy* are taken from the following edition: Dante Alighieri, *The Divine Comedy,* trans., with a commentary, by Charles S. Singleton, 2d ed., 3 vols.(in 6 parts), Bollingen Series, no. 80 (Princeton: Princeton University Press, 1977).

34. See B.A. Uspenskii, "Otnoshenie k grammatike i ritorike v Drevnei Rusi (XVI–XVII vv.)," in his *Izbrannye trudy*, 2 vols. (Moscow: Gnozis, 1994), 2:7–25. Uspensky's first example of a critical attitude to secular learning is taken from the early sixteenth-century epistle of the monk Filofei of Pskov (7); he notes that the polemics surrounding this question subsequently became particularly acute at the time of Nikon's reforms (10).

35. Simon Franklin, "Echoes of Byzantine Elite Culture in Twelfth-Century Russia?," in *Byzantium and Europe. First International Byzantine Conference*, ed. A. Markopoulos (Athens: European Cultural Center of Delphi, 1987), 177–87 (184), cited in Francis J. Thomson, "The Distorted Mediaeval Perception of Classical Antiquity: The Causes and the Consequences," in *Medieval Antiquity*, ed. A. Welkenhuysen, H. Braet, and W. Verbeke, Mediaevalia Lovaniensia, 1st ser., no. 24 (Leuven: Leuven University Press, 1995), 303–364(303). I am grateful to Simon Franklin for his helpful suggestions on this essay.

36. Simon Franklin, "Booklearning and Bookmen in Kievan Rus': A Survey of an Idea," *Harvard Ukrainian Studies* 12–13 (1988–89):830–48(837).

37. Ibid., 838. Franklin is quoting Klim's own description of the charge levelled against him.

38. Ibid., 839.

39. Uspenskii, "Otnoshenie k grammatike," 13.

40. Ibid.

41. For the phrase cited, and on the *Stoglav* and its views on icons, see V.V. Bychkov, *Dukhovno-esteticheskie osnovy russkoi ikony* (Moscow: Nauchno-izdatel'skii tsentr "Ladomir," 1995), 179–84(180). See also Robin Cormack, "Moscow between East and West," in *The Art of Holy Russia: Icons from Moscow, 1400–1660* (London: Royal Academy of Arts, 1998), 25, and in the same volume Yuri Malkov, "The Icon Painter in Medieval Russia," 79–85.

42. Bychkov, *Dukhovno-esteticheskie osnovy russkoi ikony*, 182.

43. See in this volume, Franklin, "Nostalgia for Hell," n.82.

44. For these examples, see Bychkov, *Dukhovno-esteticheskie osnovy russkoi ikony*, 184–90.

45. Victor Zhivov emphasizes the extent to which the seventeenth century was an age of crucial changes, a "critical," not an "organic" epoch in Russian history, and credits it with establishing the distinction between the secular and spiritual spheres; Victor Zhivov, "Religious Reform and the Emergence of the Individual in Russian Seventeenth-Century Literature," in *Religion and Culture in Early Modern Russia and Ukraine*, ed. Samuel H. Baron and Nancy Shields Kollmann (Dekalb: Northern Illinois University Press, 1997), 184–98(187–88).

46. For a detailed account see James Cracraft, *The Church Reform of Peter the Great* (London and Basingstoke: Macmillan, 1971). See also Evgenii V. Anisimov, "Reforming the Clerical Rank," a chap. in his *The Reforms of Peter the Great: Progress through Coercion in Russia*, trans. John T. Alexander (Armonk, N.Y. and London: M.E. Sharpe, 1993), 203–216, esp. 216, and Robert K. Massie, "Supreme under God," a chap. in his *Peter the Great: His Life and World* (London: Abacus, 1982), 783–94. On Peter's own approach to religion see L.R. Lewitter, "Peter the Great's Attitude towards Religion: From Traditional Piety to Rational Theology," in *Russia and the World of the Eighteenth Century*, ed. R.P. Bartlett, A.G. Cross, and Karen Rasmussen (Columbus: Slavica, 1988), 62–77.

47. On views of Peter as the Antichrist, see Lindsey Hughes, *Russia in the Age of Peter the Great* (New Haven and London: Yale University Press, 1998), 451–53; Robert O. Crumney, *The Old Believers and the World of Antichrist: The Vyg Community and the Russian State. 1694–1855* (Madison: The University of Wisconsin Press, 1970), 63. For further discussion in this volume see Kevin Platt, "Antichrist Enthroned: Demonic Visions of Russian Rulers." I am grateful to Kevin Platt for his helpful suggestions and critical comments on this essay.

48. *The Spiritual Regulation of Peter the Great*, trans. and ed. Alexander V. Muller (Seattle and London: University of Washington Press, 1972), 30–37.

49. On the civic script, introduced in 1708–10, see A.P. Vlasto, *A Linguistic History of Russia to the End of the Eighteenth Century* (Oxford: Clarendon Press, 1988), 39, 375. Lind-

sey Hughes (to whom I am most grateful for her helpful and perceptive comments on this essay) points out that "it is hard to agree that the two 'opposing' scripts were 'linked with the opposition of two cultures, Petrine and anti-Petrine' in an entirely consistent way" as "a third of the titles printed in the old script during Peter's reign were actually secular in content." Hughes, *Russia in the Age of Peter the Great*, 319.

50. The words of Ioann Vishenskii, cited in Uspenskii, "Otnoshenie k grammatike," 8.

51. M.S. Anderson, *Peter the Great*, 2d ed. (London and New York: Longman, 1995), 130.

52. Muller, ed., *The Spiritual Regulation*, 78–79, 118 n.138. This measure was first introduced in 1701; see Anisimov, *The Reforms of Peter the Great*, 211.

53. This point is made in general terms by Victor Terras in *A History of Russian Literature* (New Haven and London: Yale University Press, 1991), 116. One should not, however, exaggerate the specific impact of Peter's article, which was clearly impossible to enforce in a systematic way.

54. "O Merezhkovskom" (21 March 1920), in Blok, *Sobranie sochinenii*, 6:393–95(393).

55. E.P. Ivanov, "Demon i Tserkov'" (1906), from the collection of M.S. Lesman. Extracts from this article are published in L.A. Il'iunina, "A. Blok i E. Ivanov v gody pervoi russkoi revoliutsii (K voprosu o genezise obraza Khrista v poeme 'Dvenadtsat')," *Uchenye zapiski Tartuskogo gosudarstvennogo universiteta* 881, *A. Blok i russkii simvolizm: Problemy teksta i zhanra. Blokovskii sbornik X* (Tartu: Tartuskii gosudarstvennyi universitet, 1990), 21–31(30–31 n.12). My thanks to Avril Pyman for drawing my attention to this extract.

56. "Nastoiashchee i budushchee russkoi literatury" (written 1907, first published 1909), in Andrei Belyi, *Simvolizm kak miroponimanie*, ed. L.A. Sugai (Moscow: Respublika, 1994), 350.

57. This view was later extensively popularized by Merezhkovsky in the third volume of his historical trilogy, *Antikhrist (Petr i Aleksei)* (1905), discussed in this volume in Platt, "Antichrist Enthroned."

58. Geoffrey Hosking, *Russia: People and Empire. 1552–1917* (London: HarperCollins, 1997), 82.

59. See Pushkin, *Sobranie sochinenii*, 8:12, 80–81, 304. After Pushkin's death, Nicholas I forbade the publication of this work, which remained unprinted until 1938.

60. See M.V. Lomonosov, "Oda na den' Tezoimenitstva Ego Imperatorskogo Vysochestva Gosudaria Velikogo Kniazia Petra Feodorovicha 1743 goda" (stanza 13), in his *Polnoe sobranie sochinenii*, 8 vols. (Moscow and Leningrad: Izdatel'stvo Akademii nauk SSSR, 1950–83), 8:109, and other examples cited in this volume in Platt, "Antichrist Enthroned."

61. A.S. Pushkin, *Mednyi vsadnik*, ed. N.V. Izmailov, Seriia "Literaturnye pamiatniki" (Leningrad: Nauka, 1978). For further discussion of this work in this volume, see Platt, "Antichrist Enthroned."

62. "I voobrazhenie moe predstavilo mne Petra, kotoryi v pervyi raz obozreval berega dikoi Nevy, nyne stol' prekrasnye! ... velikaia mysl' rodilas' v ume velikogo cheloveka. Zdes' budet gorod, skazal on, chudo sveta. Siuda prizovu vse khudozhestva, vse iskusstva. Zdes' khudozhestva, iskusstva, grazhdanskie ustanovleniia i zakony pobediat samuiu prirodu. Skazal – i Peterburg voznik iz dikogo bolota." K.N. Batiushkov, "Progulka v Akademiiu khodozhest" (1814), in Pushkin, *Mednyi vsadnik*, ed. Izmailov, 130–34(132).

63. The image of Peter as Pygmalion was used by Peter on his personal seal in the 1710s, included in a panel on C.B. Rastrelli's bronze bust of Peter (1723), and echoed by Feofan Prokopovich in his eulogy after Peter's death: "All Russia is your statue, transformed by you with skilful craftsmanship" (1726). See Hughes, *Russia in the Age of Peter the Great*, 470, 563 n.159. For a discussion of views of Peter as divine, including reference to G.I. Golovkin's declaration in 1721 that Peter

brought Russia "from nothingness into being" (like God in Genesis), and raised Russia as from the dead (like Christ), see ibid., 96, 452. For further discussion of the analogy between tsar and God, including comments on Peter as the "planter" and "gardener" of Russia (and occasionally St. Petersburg), represented as a new Eden, see Stephen Lessing Baehr, *The Paradise Myth in Eighteenth-Century Russia: Utopian Patterns in Early Secular Russian Literature and Culture* (Stanford: Stanford University Press, 1991), 16–18, 27–29, 65–66.

64. "Chto eto u vas? potop! nichto prokliatomu Peterburgu! voilà une belle occasion à vos dames de faire bidet. ... Chto pogreba? Priznaius', i po nikh serdtse bolit. Ne naidetsia li mezhdu vami Noia, dlia nasazhdeniia vinograda?" Letter to L.S. Pushkin of November 1824, in Pushkin, *Sobranie sochinenii*, 9:114.

65. See the first and second drafts of the poem in Pushkin, *Mednyi vsadnik*, ed. Izmailov, 64, 73.

66. Baehr, *The Paradise Myth*, 166.

67. *Dvenadtsat'*, in Blok, *Sobranie sochinenii*, 347–59(347).

68. Pushkin, *Mednyi vsadnik*, ed. Izmailov, 9.

69. Letter to P.Ia. Chaadaev of 19 October 1836, in Pushkin, *Sobranie sochinenii*, 10:285–87(286).

70. The poem is an incomplete fragment of fifty-one lines, assumed to date from October 1830, and unpublished in Pushkin's lifetime. The received text is based on two sources: a final manuscript version (ll. 1–42) and a second draft version (ll. 43–51). For the text and earlier variants, see Pushkin, *Polnoe sobranie sochinenii*, ed. V.D. Bonch-Bruevich, 17 vols. (Moscow: Izdatel'stvo Akademii nauk SSSR, 1937–59; reprint, Moscow: Voskresen'e, 1994–97), 3(book 1):254–55 (text), 862–66 (variants) and 1222 (note). Hereafter the poem will be referred to in the text and notes by an abbreviated version of its first line.

71. This association was given particular prominence by Zhukovsky who first published the poem in 1841 as one of Pushkin's "Podrazhaniia Dantu."

72. As, for example, is argued by Viacheslav Ivanov in his essay on Pushkin, "Dva maiaka" (1937); Ivanov, *Sobranie sochinenii*, 4:330–42(334).

73. "The light of the sweet guide (dolce guida), whose holy eyes (occhi santi) were glowing as she smiled" (*Paradiso*, 3:23–24). The analogy with Beatrice is developed in a number of ways. The most memorable features of Pushkin's lady, her veil and heavenly eyes, are constantly emphasized attributes of Beatrice. When Dante first glimpses her at the scene of their climactic meeting in Purgatory, her veil is mentioned several times and linked with the mention of her eyes which she directs at Dante (*Purgatorio*, 30:31, 65–67); later in the same canto, in her famous speech of rebuke, she reminds Dante of the role of her eyes in ensuring his spiritual salvation: "showing him my youthful eyes I led him with me toward the right goal" (*Purgatorio*, 30:122–23).

74. One of Beatrice's names is Sapientia (Wisdom); a hint at this allegorical role is found in the olive-green crown worn over her veil (*Purgatorio*, 30:31), which links her with Minerva, the goddess of wisdom, whose tree is the olive. See the commentary on this line in Dante, *The Divine Comedy*, 2(part 2):738.

75. An example of the link between idleness (prazdnost') and poetic inspiration occurs in a poem of the same year, "K vel'mozhe" (1830), addressed to Prince N.D. Iusupov. Pushkin expresses his certainty: "Chto blagosklonstvuesh' ty *muzam* v tishine, / Chto imi v *prazdnosti* ty dyshish' blagorodnoi." The association is reinforced in the later line: "Tak, vikhor' del zabyv dlia *muz* i negi *prazdnoi*" (emphasis mine). See Pushkin, *Sobranie sochinenii*, 2:222. The associated link between boredom (skuka) and the demonic is wittily captured in the memorable opening lines of Pushkin's "Stsena iz Fausta" (1825). To Faust's complaint "Mne skucho, bes," Mephistopheles replies "Chto delat', Faust?," thus making it clear

that boredom provides the cue for the devil's entrance (Pushkin, *Sobranie sochinenii*, 2:43). The connection between ennui and artistic creativity in Western literature is explored in Reinhard Kuhn, *The Demon of Noontide: Ennui in Western Literature* (Princeton: Princeton University Press, 1976) from antiquity through the Middle Ages to contemporary literature; regrettably, although Kuhn points out the need for a special study of this important theme in Russian literature, he includes no discussion of Russian authors apart from a few pages on Leskov.

76. The adjective *zhenoobraznyi* does not occur anywhere else in Pushkin's verse; see *Slovar' iazyka Pushkina*, 4 vols. (Moscow: Gosudarstvennoe izdatel'stvo inostrannykh i natsional'nykh slovarei, 1956–61), 1:783–84. The closely related adjective *zhenopodobnyi* is used in "Safo" ("Schastlivyi iunosha, ty vsem menia plenil...," 1825) to characterize the beauty of a *male* youth (Pushkin, *Sobranie sochinenii*, 2:35). As a counter-argument to the Dionysus interpretation, one could cite the fact that the variant phrase "nagoi prirody" replaced an even earlier variant "prirody zhenskoi," suggesting a woman. For a discussion of different interpretations of the identity of this god see B.A. Vasil'ev, *Dukhovnyi put' Pushkina* (Moscow: Sam and Sam, 1994), 182–83.

77. As suggested in Ivanov, "Dva maiaka," 4:334.

78. See Vasil'ev, *Dukhovnyi put' Pushkina*, 182.

79. See, for example, the early "Vospominaniia v Tsarskom Sele" (1814), "Tsarskoe Selo" (1817–19), in which Pushkin describes the "volshebnye mesta" where he first experienced love and came to know poetry, "Dubravy, gde v tishi svobody..." (1818), and the later revival of this theme in "Vospominaniia v Tsarskom Sele" (1829) and "Tsarskosel'skaia statuia" (1830), both dating from the period shortly before "V nachale zhizni..." was written (Pushkin, *Sobranie sochinenii*, 1:9–14, 49, 510; 2:192–93, 233, respectively). The autobiographical reading of "V nachale zhizni..." is given a particularly literal application by Vasil'ev; in an ingenious but not altogether convincing attempt to relate the poem to the realia of Pushkin's experience, he identifies the "velichavaia zhena" with the figure of the Virgin Mary depicted on the seventeenth-century miracle-working icon known as the "Bogomater' Znamenie" in the Znamenskaia Church near the *litsei* at Tsarskoe Selo. See Vasil'ev, *Dukhovnyi put' Pushkina*, 185–92.

80. Pushkin wrote the first version of "Besy" in October and early November 1829, and completed it on 7 September 1830, just before composing "V nachale zhizni..." in October. See Pushkin, *Polnoe sobranie sochinenii*, 3(book 1):226–27(text), 830–37 (variants), 1211–12 (note).

81. "Pushkin i Tsarskoe selo" (1899), in Innokentii Annenskii, *Kniga otrazhenii*, ed. N.T. Ashimbaeva, I.I. Podol'skaia, and A.V. Fedorov (Moscow: Nauka, 1979), 304–21(312).

82. "Bringing antiquity to life here took on a concrete meaning. ... A considerable part of the Tsarskoye Selo park had been turned into an allegory." Dimitri Shvidovsky, *The Empress and the Architect: British Architecture and Gardens at the Court of Catherine the Great*, trans. from Russian (New Haven and London: Yale University Press, 1996), 105. On the way in which Catherine II's intention to build a "Greco-Roman rhapsody" in the garden of Tsarskoe Selo was put into practice, see Dmitri Shvidovsky, *St. Petersburg. Architecture of the Tsars*, trans. from French by John Goodman (New York, London, and Paris: Abbeville Press, 1996), 224–26. For a survey of literary treatments of Tsarskoe Selo, see N.P. Antsiferov, *Prigorody Leningrada. Goroda Pushkin, Pavlovsk, Petrodvorets* (Moscow: Gosudarstvennyi literaturnyi muzei, 1946), 7–79 (44–46 on "V nachale zhizni..."), and the more recent collection, Lev Losev and Barry Scherr, eds., *A Sense of Place: Tsarskoe Selo and its Poets* (Columbus: Slavica, 1993).

83. The same unresolved quality marks another poem composed in the same month, "Stikhi, sochinennye noch'iu, vo vremia bessonnitsy" (October 1830), in Pushkin, *Sobranie sochinenii*, 2:248. The experience of night-time insomnia generates an obscure metaphysical or religious anxiety in the poet's soul and expresses itself through a series of stark questions, growing in intensity, and supplanting his earlier attempt to "explain" the night through poetic metaphors (in ll.5–7). If "V nachale zhizni…" describes the way in which the lyric hero is diverted from the pursuit of religious truths by the false idols of art, "Stikhi, sochinennye noch'iu, vo vremia bessonnitsy" evokes – albeit in a totally different manner – the attempt to reverse this process, to recover contact with a deeper level of religious enquiry. Although the two poems are quite different in style, it is possible that they were informed by similar preoccupations.

84. The link between Pushkin's lyric hero and Dante rests on the fact that they both deserted the straight path of faith. Just as Dante received his first spiritual guidance from Beatrice but was then sidetracked to his dark wood by "false images of good" (*Purgatorio*, 30:131), so Pushkin's lyric persona was initially under the tutelage of a wise woman but escaped to a dark garden where he was seduced by false ideals. Since Pushkin's poem is only a fragment, it is possible that he intended to develop this analogy more fully. As it stands, his poem functions on several different levels simultaneously: the poet's autobiographical experience is filtered through the prism of Dante's spiritual journey, and both are given an allegorical treatment which projects them on to a broader historical canvas and raises universal philosophical issues. Critics who read the poem wholly in terms of Pushkin's autobiography, or who go to the opposite extreme and regard its narrator and subject as Dante (D.D. Blagoi, *Tvorcheskii put' Pushkina* [Moscow: Sovetskii pisatel', 1967], 519) significantly reduce its profound complexity.

85. Ivanov characterizes the artist as a "kumirotvorets-genii" in "Khudozhnik," a poem from the collection *Eros* (1907); Ivanov, *Sobranie sochinenii*, 2:380. His essay "O veselom remesle i umnom veselii" (1907) includes a section entitled "Khudozhnik-kumirotvorets," dealing with the transition from the medieval craftsman artist (khudozhnik-remeslennik) to the modern artist; ibid., 3:64–66.

86. Letter to A.S. Pushkin of [March-April] 1829, in P.Ia. Chaadaev, *Polnoe sobranie sochinenii i izbrannye pis'ma*, ed. Z.A. Kamenskii and others, 2 vols. (Moscow: Nauka, 1991), 2:66–67(66).

87. For the original French text of the first letter of "Lettres philosophiques adressées à une dame" and for a discussion of its date, see ibid., 1:86–106, 695 n.23.

88. See Pushkin's letter to M.P. Pogodin, dated second half of June 1830, in Pushkin, *Sobranie sochinenii*, 9:321. Pushkin asks Pogodin's opinion of "Chaadaev's letter," but does give any more detailed description of it. The editors of Pushkin's letters identify it as Chaadaev's first philosophical letter (ibid., 9:455), as do the editors of Chaadaev's works (Chaadaev, *Polnoe sobranie sochinenii*, 1:690).

89. Chaadaev, *Polnoe sobranie sochinenii*, 1:88.

90. Ibid., 1:100–101.

91. "Il est dans la nature de l'homme de se perdre quand il ne trouve pas moyen de se lier à ce qui le précède et à ce qui le suit; toute consistance alors, toute certitude lui échappe; le sentiment de la durée permanente ne le guidant pas, il se trouve égaré dans le monde. Il y a de ces êtres perdus dans tous les pays; chez nous, c'est le trait général." Ibid., 1:94.

92. Ibid., 1:91. For related points of Chaadaev's argument, see ibid., 1:92, 96.

93. Ibid., 1:98–100.

94. Ibid., 1:98.

95. Letter to P.Ia. Chaadaev of 19 October 1836, in Pushkin, *Sobranie sochinenii*, 10:285–87.

96. *Teleskop* 24, no.15 (October 1836).
97. Chaadaev may have had Pushkin's poem in mind, and, in particular, its Dan-
     tesque allusions, when, after expressing his approval of Pushkin's plan to write a
     history of Peter the Great, he wrote to him "Mne khochetsia skazat': vot,
     nakonets, iavilsia nash Dant." Although the text of this letter is torn at this point,
     it seems likely that Chaadaev is referring to Pushkin; see his letter to Pushkin of
     18 September 1831, in Chaadaev, *Polnoe sobranie sochinenii*, 69–73(73).
98. Aleksandr Blok, "O sovremennom sostoianii russkogo simvolizma" (1910), in his
     Sobranie sochinenii, 5:433.

Part II

LITERARY DEMONS

Chapter 5

The Muse and the Demon in the Poetry of Pushkin, Lermontov, and Blok

Pamela Davidson

Он звал прекрасное мечтою;
Он вдохновенье презирал;

[He called the beautiful a dream;
He held inspiration in contempt;]

Pushkin, "The Demon" (1823)[1]

И муза кротких вдохновений
Страшится неземных очей.

[And the muse of gentle inspirations
Fears his unearthly eyes.]

Lermontov, "My Demon" (1829)[2]

Я пронесу тебя над бездной,
Ее бездонностью дразня.
Твой будет ужас бесполезный –
Лишь вдохновеньем для меня.

[I will carry you above the abyss,
Tantalizing you with its infinite depth.
Your futile terror will be
Only an inspiration for me.]

Blok, "The Demon" (1916)[3]

Following the survey of cultural and historical approaches to art
which concluded part I, this chapter considers one of the ways in
which the view of art as demonic shaped by these contexts took root
in the Russian literary tradition. In verse, the notion of art as demonic
crystallized around the muse's relations with the Demon, giving rise
to a rich collection of interrelated poems, through which one can
trace the evolution of this theme. By considering a triad of authors
pivotal to the whole tradition, I hope to uncover the path which led
from Pushkin's "holy lyre"[4] through the "magic voice" of Lermontov's Demon[5] to Blok's assertion that "art is *Hell*,"[6] and thereby to
illustrate the progression of the notion of art as demonic from nineteenth-century Romanticism into early twentieth-century modernism.

The distance that separates perceptions of the demonic in these two
periods is far more than one of just time. The dark forces which
threaten the journey undertaken by the traveller in Pushkin's "The
Devils" (Besy, 1830) are presented through the prism of a guiding
human consciousness which, however disorientated it may be, still
strives to maintain a sense of direction. By the turn of the century,
however, demonic forces have infiltrated literary representations of
human consciousness to such an extent that this sense of direction or
broader perspective is often submerged or lost. Sologub's novel *The
Petty Demon (Melkii bes,* 1907) evokes a totally enclosed demonic world,
and the lyric hero of Blok's poem "There is No Way Out" (Net
iskhoda, 1907)[7] is trapped in a "charmed circle" (ocharovannyi krug),
where death is welcomed and the call to rise from the dead rings hollow. In the same year a memorable iconographic image for this new
type of static, circumscribed hell can be found in Mstislav Dobuzhinsky's depiction of the devil as a giant spider (Illustration 12), trapped
within prison walls, at whose feet huddles a group of barely distinct
human beings, condemned to trudge round and round in an endless
circle.[8] Although the stars can be seen shining in the sky through the
prison windows, they are so remote and inaccessible (high above the
human heads and invisible to the spider's gaze) that they only intensify the horror of this powerful image of the solipsistic and demonic
nature of modern art, cut off from any meaningful contact with the
created universe. This essay will attempt to uncover the demonic trail
which led from Pushkin's threatened journey into such a dark impasse.

Pushkin: The Muse's Encounter with the Demon

Although Pushkin was eminently capable of light-hearted references
to the demonic qualities of art, describing himself when he was a sev-
enteen-year-old student at the *litsei* as a "poor hermit of Tsarskoe

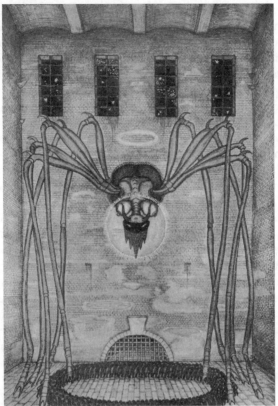

12. M. Dobuzhinsky, *The Devil*, 1907. First published in the journal *Zolotoe runo*, which organized a competition for literary and artistic representations of the devil.

Selo ... harassed by the maddened demon of graphomania" (besh-enyi demon bumagomaraniia),[9] or referring to his lyre in a poem of 1821 as a "sinful gift of fate" (greshnyi dar sud'by) which, in typical Russian fashion, he has swopped for some dried mushrooms,[10] his fundamental attitude to the poetic vocation was undoubtedly based on a deep reverence for the "spirit of pure beauty" (genii chistoi kra-soty)[11] which inspires the poet's "holy lyre" (sviataia lira), and on a full recognition of the "sacred sacrifice" (sviashchennaia zhertva) which this divine gift requires.[12] The innate purity of the artistic impulse is constantly stressed throughout his early verse. In "To Zhukovsky" (Zhukovskomu, 1818),[13] for example, the poet's journey to the world of dreams is inspired by his "elevated soul" (vozvyshen-naia dusha) and can only be shared with like-minded friends of the "sacred truth" (sviashchennaia istina). "Enjoyment of the beautiful" (naslazhdenie prekrasnym) is the ultimate aim and art inspires an

"ardent and clear delight" (vostorg plamennyi i iasnyi). The only
hint at a darker dimension comes in the reference to the poet's
visions which "change ... in an enchanted gloom" (smeniaiutsia ... v
volshebnoi mgle); inconstancy, enchantment, and darkness are
attributes of the demonic view of the creative process which Blok
and Bely were later to develop, but in Pushkin's poem they are only
a passing detail, which barely impinges on the general mood of lofty
idealism. In a poem of 1824, the muse is described as a "wayward
enchantress" (svoenravnaia volshebnitsa), who roams a world of
pagan spirits with total freedom. She is the poet's "innocent, simple
/ And somehow sweet" (nevinnuiu, prostuiu / No chem-to miluiu)
friend (podruga),[14] and her status as *neporochnaia* (pure, chaste)[15]
remains inviolate, beyond contamination.

One is entitled to ask, therefore, what sort of connection can exist
between a muse as pure as this and the concept of the demon. Can
the muse's innocence in any way be tainted by demonic influence?
The answer to this question is complicated by the fact that, as we
shall see, Pushkin associated his muse with not one, but two quite different demons, whose subsequent confusion was the source of a fruitful and enduring tradition of art as demonic in Russian literature.

Pushkin's first type of demon makes his initial appearance in "The
Demon" (Demon, 1823).[16] This early and influential poem is well
known as a personal statement of the way in which the demon,
described as a "wicked genius" (zlobnyi genii), insinuates himself
into the soul and poisons all pure aspirations and feelings. What is
particularly interesting for our purpose, however, is to determine
whether this demon also corrupts artistic inspiration. A close reading
indicates that the demon strikes precisely at the time when sensory
impressions of existence and elevated emotions culminate in a
heightened receptivity to art:[17]

> Когда возвышенные чувства,
> Свобода, слава и любовь
> И вдохновенные искусства
> Так сильно волновали кровь, –
> Часы надежд и наслаждений
> Тоской внезапной осеня,
> Тогда какой-то злобный гений
> Стал тайно навещать меня.
>
> [When elevated feelings,
> Freedom, glory, and love,
> And inspired arts,
> So strongly stirred my blood, –
> Hours of hopes and delights
> Overshadowing with sudden anguish,
> Then did a certain wicked genius
> Begin to visit me in secret.]

Even before he appears or is named, the demon's shadow has already fallen. By placing the gerund clause before the key syntactical turning-point of *togda* (then), Pushkin underlines the insidious nature of the demon, who steals up on the soul and spreads his pervasive poison. In his apologue "The New Demon" (Novyi demon, 1824), V.F. Odoevsky rightly commented that Pushkin's personification of "those incomprehensible feelings which chill our soul in the midst of the most ardent delights" revealed a remarkably deep grasp of the most secret recesses of the human heart.[18]

The key lines

> Он звал прекрасное мечтою;
> Он вдохновенье презирал;
>
> [He called the beautiful a dream;
> He held inspiration in contempt;]

reveal the indissoluble link for Pushkin between faith in pure ideals and artistic inspiration – when the first is corrupted, the second is also tainted. The closing couplet

> И ничего во всей природе
> Благословить он не хотел.
>
> [And nothing in all nature
> Did he desire to bless.]

leads one to conclude that the effect of this demon on the pure source of inspiration is either to destroy it entirely (blessing being the original power of the word and source of poetry), or to corrupt it through his main weapon, his "poisoned speech" (iazvitel'nye rechi), in itself a demonic art form, later developed by Lermontov and Blok, as we shall see below.

In 1825 Pushkin wrote a brief commentary on his poem to counter an incorrect interpretation, which was in circulation, and to reassert its essentially "moral" purpose.[19] The passage, like the poem, highlights the intrinsic connection between pure faith in an ideal and poetic inspiration. The heart is at first tender and "open to the beautiful" (dostupno dlia prekrasnogo),[20] but the contradictions of life gradually give rise to painful doubts. The demon is the personification of this "spirit of negation or doubt" (dukh otritsaniia ili somneniia), regarded by Goethe as the eternal enemy of mankind. In a variant, Pushkin also uses the term *razlad* (disintegration) to denote the resulting moral collapse. Eventually the feeling of doubt passes, but only after it has "destroyed forever the best hopes and *poetic predisposition* of the soul" (unichtozhiv navsegda luchshie nadezhdy i *poeticheskie predrassudki* dushi; emphasis mine). The demon therefore saps and corrupts both faith in the ideal and the pure sources of poetic inspiration – the result is not so much "demonic art" as the destruction of art, which cannot survive when faith in the ideal which nurtures it has been corrupted.

The word "forever" in this fragment has a terrible ring of finality. However, "The Demon" was not Pushkin's last word on this score, nor did it in fact fundamentally alter his original view of the muse's intrinsic purity. Zhukovsky, with whom, as we saw above, Pushkin associated his faith in the close alliance of purity and poetic inspiration,[21] was quick to recognize this. In a letter of 1 June 1824, written on the eve of Pushkin's name-day (den' angela), he thanks him for "The Demon" and continues, as if anxious to ward off any malevolent influence, by reminding Pushkin of the divine nature of his poetic genius: "I embrace you for your 'Demon.' To hell with the devil! This is your motto for now. You were made to join the gods – go forward. The soul does have wings! It will not fear the heights, its true element is there! Give those wings freedom, and the heavens are yours. This is what I believe. When I begin to think what sort of a future you can concoct for yourself, my heart glows with hope for you. Farewell, little devil, be an angel."[22]

Zhukovsky was right: Pushkin's muse was not inherently demonic; the demon represented a moral threat to the individual, not an essential aspect of the creative process. This is an important distinction because, as we shall see later, in the modernist period art was often viewed as intrinsically and unavoidably demonic, and the figures of the muse and demon merged into a new androgynous being of ambivalent morality. Pushkin's treatment of the problem is different. His first type of demon is a force threatening the moral integrity of the individual, and therefore only indirectly, through this channel, able to affect the inspiration which informs art.

Despite this distinction, Pushkin's "The Demon" came to be regarded as the source text for the view of art as inherently demonic. This creative "misreading" of Pushkin began very early: with Lermontov's poem of response of 1829, as we shall see in the next section of this essay, and also with Gogol's short story "The Portrait" (Portret, 1835, second version 1842), one of the first prose works in the Russian tradition to develop the idea of art as tainted by the demonic. Significantly, as noted by Julian Graffy in his discussion of this story in this volume, Gogol describes Chartkov, the Petersburg demonic artist, as a personification of Pushkin's demon, thereby effecting the fusion of artist and demon (Gogol's enthusiasm for Pushkin's "The Demon" apparently even extended to joking that he had written the poem himself).[23]

Although Pushkin would not have equated his demon with artistic inspiration or the figure of the artist, he may nevertheless have unwittingly contributed to the formation of the tradition of the "demonic muse" by introducing a second type of demon, who subsequently became confused with features of the first. This second demon makes a brief appearance together with the muse in "The Conversation of a Bookseller with a Poet" (Razgovor knigoprodavtsa s poetom, 1824),[24] written just one year after "The Demon." In this dialogue in verse a poet recalls the time when, carefree and full of hope, he would invite the muse to a "feast of the imagination" (pir voobrazhen'ia). At such times, a certain demon would take full possession of his creative fantasy:

> Какой-то демон обладал
> Моими играми, досугом;
> За мной повсюду он летал,
> Мне звуки дивные шептал,
> И тяжким, пламенным недугом
> Была полна моя глава;
>
> [A certain demon possessed
> My games, my leisure-time;
> After me everywhere he flew,
> Whispered wonderful sounds to me,
> And with a heavy, fiery sickness
> My head was full;]

This second type of demon is more akin to the amoral Greek concept of *daimon* than to Pushkin's earlier demon of corruption, loosely based on Christian tradition; he personifies the poet's guiding spirit and is linked with what Plato extolled as the "possession and madness" from the Muses which arouse a "tender, virgin soul ... to a Bacchic frenzy of expression" without which true poetry cannot exist.[25] Such a demon is the natural ally and companion of the muse, aiding her in the production of her "sweet gifts" (muzy sladostnykh darov), mentioned by the poet later on in his speech; the "fiery sickness" is a positive indication of inspiration, not a threatening danger. In this respect the second type of demon has little but his name in common with the first type described in "The Demon."

"The Conversation of a Bookseller with a Poet" was first published as a preface to the opening chapter of *Evgenii Onegin* in February 1825. This link is significant for our subject because the next stage in Pushkin's view of the relations between his muse and the demon can be found in the veiled encounter which he engineers between them in the last chapter of *Evgenii Onegin*. However, on this occasion, it is not the benign demon of poetic inspiration who appears, but the old, negative demon of doubt, whose memory is evoked by the return of Evgenii.

The eighth chapter of *Evgenii Onegin*, composed in 1829–30, begins with an extended description of the poet's muse, through which Pushkin offers a profound interpretation of his own creative development. Significantly, the opening of the first stanza is directly modelled on the beginning of "The Demon," but instead of the demon, the muse appears.[26] This deliberate echo serves two purposes: it indirectly prepares the reader for the later appearance of the demon, and it reinstates the supremacy of the muse, who, from here until stanza 7, is described at length in the various guises which she has assumed throughout Puskhin's peregrinations and changes of poetic style and subject. After detailing her movements from revelries in Petersburg to the Caucasus and Crimea, on to the wilds of Moldavia, and back to the garden of Mikhailovskoe, Pushkin brings her to the scene of the ball, where Evgenii, newly returned from his travels abroad, is about to meet Tat'iana once more, and this time to be spurned by her. The muse disappears at the first appearance of Evgenii (four lines into stanza 7) and the narrator then moves on to a series of musings about Evgenii and the reader's opinion of him, culminating in stanza 12, which enumerates various views of human lives and pointedly juxtaposes a reference to the demon with the name of Onegin:

> Несносно (согласитесь в том)
> Между людей благоразумных
> Прослыть притворным чудаком,
> Или печальным сумасбродом,
> Иль сатаническим уродом,
> Иль даже Демоном моим.
> Онегин (вновь займуся им),
> > (*Evgenii Onegin*, 8:12.2–8)

> [It is unbearable (you will agree with that)
> Among sensible people
> To pass for a sham eccentric
> Or a sad crackbrain,
> Or a Satanic monster,
> Or even for my Demon.
> Onegin (let me take him up again)][27]

The immediate switch back to Evgenii, coupled with the fact that in the previous chapter Tat'iana herself had thought of Evgenii in similar terms as an eccentric or arrogant devil (7:24.6–8), makes it possible to read into this scene a meeting not just between the muse and Evgenii, but between the muse and the erstwhile source of her threatened corruption, the demon, now exposed as a hollow mask. Is Pushkin not suggesting by this final confrontation between his muse and the demon that the former has triumphed over the latter? She moves on and survives, while the Evgenii-demon figure is bid a firm "farewell," along with the other characters, as signalled in the epigraph from Byron which heads this last chapter – not unlike the way in which Akhmatova's muse revisits the scene of turn-of-the-century symbolist demonism in *Poem Without a Hero* (*Poema bez geroia*) in order to mark a final break with it.[28]

The lyric fragment, "At the beginning of my life I remember a school ..." (V nachale zhizni shkolu pomniu ia ..., October 1830), which we discussed in the concluding section of the previous essay, forms an interesting sequel to the vision of the pure muse triumphing over the demon with which *Evgenii Onegin* concludes. It probes deeper into the underlying issue from a philosophical and historical perspective and explores an alternative scenario: if the demon had gained the upper hand, the connection between art and faith in the ideal would be severed, and art itself would become a form of demonic idol worship.[29]

In a lecture of January 1836 Pushkin returned once more to the subject of the relationship between art and the ideal. He was responding to the views of Mikhail Lobanov (1787–1846), a dramatist and translator, who decried the immoral content of recent Russian literature, ascribing it to the pernicious influence of foreign writers, particularly of the French.[30] As well as defending French literature from this charge, Pushkin went further and defended the right of literature to deal with any subject, however improper, without overt moralizing. However, he drew the line at a significant point. In his view, as a reaction to their previous, narrowly moral and utilitarian approach to literature, the French had espoused an opposite but equally misguided view: that the sole aim of literature was henceforth to be the pursuit of an indeterminate "ideal," no longer bound by moral strictures. In such a case, Pushkin comments, even "moral depravity can be the aim of poetry, that is to say an ideal." Pushkin regards this new brand of writing as a transient literary fashion which will not last, referring to it as a "literature of despair" (slovesnost' otchaiania) or "Satanic literature" (slovesnost' satanicheskaia) – phrases which he attributes to Goethe and Southey respectively.[31] This is essentially, in a different form, a projection of his own personal experience of "overcoming" the demon and conveys a similar message to that suggested by the ending of *Evgenii Onegin*, where the fashionable demon of yesterday is left behind, unmasked and exposed as an empty parody, and the muse moves on, unscathed.

It is perhaps an irony of literary history that Pushkin, who entertained such a pure vision of the muse, and whose work reflects a profound understanding of the dangerous process of inner corruption by which art can degenerate into a form of idol worship, should have laid the foundation for the tradition of art as demonic in Russian literature. This came about through the later merging of his two types of demons: the benign demon, an ally of the muse, closely associated with the sacred madness of poetic inspiration, and the destructive demon, a spirit of doubt and negation, who undermines the pure faith which sustains art. Although these two demons were distinct for Pushkin, we shall see below in our discussion of Lermontov and Blok that they subsequently fused into a single composite figure, with the result that the muse's demon of artistic inspiration ended up being seen as a potent force for spiritual and moral perdition. This superimposition of one type of demon on another echoed and transferred into the Russian literary tradition the Christian tendency to "demonize" all pagan gods, including the morally neutral *daimon* of classical tradition. It is also consonant with the innate Russian tendency, highlighted in the introduction to this volume, to endow aesthetic demons with moral value.

Lermontov: The Muse's Seduction by the Demon

Although Pushkin provided the initial impetus, it was Lermontov's development of the image of the Demon which served as the main springboard for later modernist views of art as demonic. This was no doubt in the first instance because, as Merezhkovsky commented, Lermontov was the first figure in Russian literature to raise "the religious problem of evil."[32] Indeed, according to Vladimir Solov'ev, whereas Pushkin drew inspiration from a mere "playful baby devil" (igrivyi besenok) or "joker gnome" (shutnik gnom), Lermontov was possessed by a "true demon of impurity" (nastoiashchii demon nechistoty).[33] His magnificent Demon provided a commanding figure of evil to fill the void left by the relative lack of emphasis "on a towering figure of Satan in splendour"[34] in Russian Orthodox tradition. A second reason for Lermontov's impact was his particular focus on the artist's subjective personality with all its inherent contradictions. Pasternak saw this emphasis on the individual personality as the essence of Lermontov's contribution to Russian literature: for him, Lermontov was the very "personification of creative adventure and discovery."[35] It was this combination of an interest in the metaphysical problem of evil, together with a focus on the contradictions of the individual personality, which led Lermontov to explore the demonic potential inherent in the creative process.

Lermontov's vision of the human condition was fundamentally divided. In his verse man is presented as a split, dual creature; his soul binds him irrevocably to the world of the spiritual, while through his bodily existence he remains rooted in the domain of the material. As the spiritual realm is his true home, in this earthly world he can never be more than a prisoner or exile. Although such a world-view is positive in so far as it rests on an underlying belief in the existence of a Supreme Being and higher spiritual world, there is a negative, tragic aspect to its portrayal of the condition of man, who remains excluded from this world; his only link with it is through past memory, present intuition, or future hope. There are two possible responses to the quandary of this split existence. The first is the path of ascent or reversal, trying to regain the lost paradise, the spiritual homeland. Nature, love, faith, and prayer all provide different avenues. However, the upward striving contains the germ of its own dissolution. When frustrated, its own inner momentum can lead to a reverse swing of the pendulum, to a dynamic embracing of evil. This is the second common response: the path of descent.

These factors directly inform Lermontov's view of art and its potentially demonic qualities. On a simple thematic level, art will of course reflect all the conflicts of the condition outlined above, including the demonic descent into sin or negative spiritual state which results. On a more complex level, however, can it be said to be intrinsically demonic? In a sense, it cannot, as the creative impulse originates in the divine.[36] However, as in Lermontov's general view of the human condition, this ideal source and level is in fact impossible to achieve. Art may have its roots in the upper realms, but it is forced to take form in a material way which is imperfect due to two factors: the inadequacy of language as a means of expression of spiritual insight, and the limitations of the reader's understanding.

A vivid illustration of this is provided by Lermontov's poem "The Angel" (Angel, 1831),[37] which serves as a paradigm of the parallel relationship between the divine Creator and the holy Word on the one hand, and the human soul and human art on the other hand. An angel singing a "holy song" (pesnia sviataia) about God carries a newborn soul to earth; this soul is forever tormented by a "wondrous thirst" (zhelaniem chudnym) and as a result can find no satisfaction in the songs of this world:

> И звуков небес заменить не могли
> Ей скучные песни земли.

> [And the sounds of the heavens could not be replaced
> For it by the boring songs of the earth.]

The importance which Lermontov continued to attach to this poem many years later is reflected in the fact that it was the only one of his early works which he published under his name during his lifetime. It is clear that although Lermontov adopted the biblical ideal of divinely inspired art as his model, he regarded it as one which could never be realized on earth. The artist is therefore a fallen angel, whose deepest intuitions and aspirations are formed in a paradise from which he is irretrievably exiled: poetry cannot fulfil the function of prayer. Among modern poets this attitude finds its fullest development in the work of Blok, who used Lermontov's "The Angel" as a condensed expression of his poetic credo.[38] In his edition of Lermontov, opposite the phrase "wondrous thirst," Blok copied out Lermontov's variant "vain thirst" (zhelan'em naprasnym), emphasizing the impossibility of fulfilment.[39]

There is a further, more sinister dimension, to this issue – one which leads directly on to the symbolists and is already foreshadowed in Lermontov. Since the real intuition cannot be expressed or understood, and since the poet wants to write (like Pushkin, Lermontov refers to himself as gripped by the "démon de la poésie"),[40] he comes to substitute dreams for deeper intuitions, or the expressible for the inexpressible. In "A Russian Melody" (Russkaia melodiia, 1829)[41] the poet's created world of images is exposed as a false delusion:

> В уме своем я создал мир иной
> И образов иных существованье;
>
> . . . .
>
> И рушилось неверное созданье!..
>
> [In my mind I created another world
> And of other images an existence;
>
> . . . .
>
> And the untrue creation collapsed!..]

A later poem, "Do Not Trust Yourself" (Ne ver' sebe, 1839)[42] advises the young dreamer not to trust his dreams or inspiration:

> Не верь, не верь себе, мечтатель молодой,
>   Как язвы, бойся вдохновенья…
> Оно – тяжелый бред души твоей больной[43]
>   Иль пленной мысли раздраженье.
> В нем признака небес напрасно не ищи:
>
> [Do not trust, do not trust yourself, young dreamer,
>   Like an ulcer, fear inspiration …
> It is the heavy delirium of your ill soul
>   Or the irritation of a captive thought.
> Do not search vainly in it for a sign of the heavens:]

The ending, in which the suffering poet appears to the crowd as a rouged actor waving a cardboard sword, strikingly anticipates Blok's "Puppet Booth" (Balaganchik, 1905) and reveals the extent to which the sources of symbolist demonism are already latent in Lermontov.

This was the general context in which Lermontov's elaboration of the theme of the demon took place. He was only fifteen years old when he composed "My Demon" (Moi demon, 1829)[44] in response to Pushkin's "The Demon" of six years earlier. His poem shows what happens when the "imperfect," limited vision (as that of the fallen angel or demon) is built up into a universal principle or ideal (precisely the process against which Pushkin warned). Here we have the final stage of the masking of the substitution which has taken place. Pushkin's demon was quite chatty and personable by comparison: he spoke, if only in "poisoned speech," and although he takes over completely half way through the poem (the point at which references to the lyrical "I" cease), he is nevertheless described in terms of his interaction with a human protagonist. In Lermontov's poem, this human dimension has entirely disappeared. The Demon has become an abstract deity on his throne, an impersonal cosmic force. Inspiration is no longer simply despised, it withers at source (hence the arid landscape); pure art cannot survive in this climate, as we see from the striking final lines, more explicit than in Pushkin:

> И муза кротких вдохновений
> Страшится неземных очей.

> [And the muse of gentle inspirations
> Fears his unearthly eyes.]

The muse, who was only an implied presence in Pushkin's "The Demon," is now openly juxtaposed with the Demon. This marks the beginning of the process by which Pushkin's association of the muse with the benign demon of inspiration was eventually transformed into the symbolists' association of the muse with the demon of corruption or destruction. Significantly, the two key lines from Lermontov's poem cited above were sidelined by Blok in his edition of the poet's works;[45] they clearly influenced his vision of the muse as demonic and formed a bridge linking Pushkin through Lermontov to the symbolists.

The theme of the demon was one which continued to preoccupy Lermontov for many years. In a second, expanded "My Demon" (Moi demon, 1830 or 1831)[46] he developed it in a more personal vein, stating in the last verse that the demon would never release the poet: he will deprive him of happiness by first showing him an "image of perfection" (obraz sovershenstva) and then removing it forever. Blok also marked the whole of this verse;[47] it encapsulates the notion, central to the symbolist experience, that the demonic in art as well as in life has its deepest roots in the soul's aspiration to a perfect, transcendent ideal, frustrated at its source.

The culmination of the theme – and the source of its transformation into a potent and lasting myth – came in *The Demon* (*Demon*,

completed in 1839, published in fragments in 1842, and in full in
1856).[48] For over ten years Lermontov worked on eight successive
versions of this narrative poem, essentially a dramatic enactment of
the process by which innocence and purity are corrupted. Significantly for our purposes, this process can be extended to the field of
art by regarding the Demon's seduction of Tamara as an image of the
artist's corruption of the "muse of gentle inspirations" alluded to at
the end of the first "My Demon."[49] Because of the centrality of Lermontov's narrative poem to the modernist view of art as demonic, it
is worth investigating the basis for such a reading in some detail.

The starting-point lies in the common ground which exists
between the predicament of the hero of *The Demon* – a fallen angel, a
"fugitive from Eden" (beglets Edema) or exile from Paradise (izgnannik raia),[50] who seeks to recover his lost unity with the divine – and
the task of the modern artist, as outlined by Lermontov in poems
such as "The Angel" and subsequently elaborated by Vladimir
Solov'ev and his disciples. Although the symbolists differed in their
individual responses to this view of the artist's predicament, they all
shared a common view of its origin which defined their approach to
The Demon. We saw above that Lermontov's poetry offers three main
avenues for the recovery of this ideal union: nature, love, faith or
prayer. The Demon tries all three, with particular emphasis on the
path of love. When he first glimpses Tamara he recognizes that she
alone can offer him the possibility of spiritual regeneration; later, during the climactic scene of seduction, he bases his main argument to
her on this plea.[51] Union with Tamara would restore him to oneness
with the sacred essence of the universe. For the symbolists this quest
for the realization of an ideal through love later became an image of
the artist's quest for the embodiment of spiritual intuitions in art.

Although such a reading of *The Demon* undoubtedly reflects modernist preoccupations with the status of art, there is some support for
it in Lermontov's text. One of the most striking and explicit passages
in this respect comes in the Demon's second main monologue to
Tamara, in which he draws a link between his ideal image of his
beloved and the Creator's vision of the spirit of the created world
before its embodiment in matter:

> Люблю тебя нездешней страстью,
> Как полюбить не можешь ты:
> Всем упоением, всей властью
> Бессмертной мысли и мечты.
> В душе моей, с начала мира,
> Твой образ был напечатлён,
> Передо мной носился он
> В пустынях вечного эфира.
>   (*The Demon*, 2:10.645–52)[52]

[I love you with an unearthly passion,
In a way you cannot love:
With all the abandon, with all the power
Of immortal thought and dream.
In my soul, since the beginning of the world,
Your image was imprinted,
Before me it hovered
In the expanses of the eternal ether.]

Following the well-established parallel between the Creator of the universe and the artist-creator, the Demon's ideal image of his beloved and craving for its realization through love can be read as an allegory of the artist's intuition of his created work and desire to embody it through creation. The act of erotic seduction therefore becomes a mirror image of the act of artistic creation. Both derive from an initial yearning for purity and wholeness, but suffer from the concomitant danger of embracing a false, illusory form of embodiment, which could eventually lead to the corruption or destruction of the original impulse.

This view of the Demon as a figure of the artist is reinforced in the text by frequent references to the power and enchantment of his verbal artistry. His evil work in the world is referred to as his "art" (iskusstvo, 1:2.28) and his main tools are those of the poet: his "speech" (rech'), his "words" (slova), and the "sound" (zvuk) of his "magic voice" (volshebnyi golos).[53] In the course of the poem he delivers several long monologues and his voice accordingly comes to assume an increasingly prominent position. Within the conventions of a literary text, this gradual encroachment on the function of the omniscient narrator suggests the artist usurping the role of the supreme Creator. The Demon even takes over some of the narrator's language and words, thereby transposing assumed narrative authority into the realm of subjective, solipsistic rhetoric.[54] His vision of the world replaces the broad landscapes which are sketched in at the beginning of the poem and only return in muted form at its very end; indeed, his proud indifference to nature as "the creation of his God" (tvoren'e Boga svoego, 1:3.57) is based on the "cold envy" (zavisti kholodnoi, 1:4.83) of the impotent exile, who, like the figure of the demonic artist, desires to rival God by supplanting his Creation. His growing dominance is underlined by the extraordinarily powerful musical rhythms and cadences which mark his main monologues, rich in sound effects and replete with repetitions of key words, constructions, and verbal forms.[55] This tendency is also highlighted through a change of metre; during his opening speech the Demon introduces a section in trochees (1:15.329–44), which temporarily overrides the standard iambic metre used in the rest of the poem.

We shall see below how several of these features were later developed by Blok in his poems of 1910 and 1916 on the Demon. In both texts the process of demonic takeover is completed, the narrator's voice can no longer be heard and only the Demon speaks. Furthermore, in Blok's second poem, the path of artistic creation is explicitly portrayed in terms of an ultimately destructive act of demonic seduction.

The role of the Demon's verbal art is also closely linked to a problem of crucial importance in Lermontov's work: the conflict between prayer and poetry. Both use the same medium and may even stem from the same source, but they are essentially different and vie with each other for supremacy. In "The Angel," as we saw, Lermontov suggested that poetry was a form of surrogate prayer, which could never succeed in fulfilling the function of its displaced source. *The Demon* illustrates the destructive dynamics of attempting to effect such a substitution. Throughout the poem words and speech, the language of poetry, are pitted against prayer, the language of faith. A brief prefiguration of the destructive consequences of preferring dream to prayer is offered by the fate of Tamara's bridegroom, whose death is directly linked to the fact that he despised the traditional roadside prayer (which would have ensured his salvation) and gave himself up instead to a private, erotic reverie, instigated by the Demon: the word "prayer" (molitva) is repeated twice and contrasted with the "insidious dream" (kovarnaia mechta) and thoughts inspired by the Demon (1:11.220–31). (We shall see below how Blok later took up these lines as a key image in "The Demon" of 1910.) The Demon usurps the language of prayer and litany, but uses it for unholy purposes. His speech frequently obstructs prayer or attempts to rechannel it. In the second part of the poem, after Tamara has retired to the convent, the Demon's words come to her precisely at the moment of prayer;[56] later, when he seduces her with the "miraculous tenderness of his *speech*" (chudnoi nezhnost'iu *rechei*, 2:6.496; emphasis mine), this not only stops her from praying, but diverts the impulse to Demon worship.[57] Tamara recognizes this danger; she realizes that the Demon's words are a poison, which prevents her from praying,[58] and she fears the temptation of his cunning speech, just as Eve was wary of the serpent's subtle tongue.[59] Finally, a close look at the wording of the lines cited below makes it clear that the act of seduction (symbolized by the burning kiss) is essentially an act of verbal artistry, which displaces prayer by providing a false response to the spiritual impulses of the soul:

И он слегка
Коснулся жаркими устами
Ее трепещущим губам;

Соблазна полными *речами*
Он отвечал ее *мольбам.*

(*The Demon,* 2:11.872–76; emphasis mine)

[And he slightly
Touched with his hot mouth
Her trembling lips;
With *speeches* full of seduction
He answered her *entreaties.*]

Lermontov's Demon is not only carrying out the demon's traditional function (as defined from a Christian perspective) by obstructing the prayers of the faithful,[60] he is also adding a new literary twist by using art or poetic rhetoric to achieve his ends. In this sense he is the true prototype of the modern "literary" demon. It would therefore seem fair to conclude that, although *The Demon* does not deal in explicit terms with the issue of demonic art, there is ample support both in the plot and in the mode of its narration to support a further level of reading in terms of the artist's predicament with specific reference to the problematic relationship between poetry and prayer or, more broadly, between art and religious faith. Ultimately, the Demon's verbal artistry cannot lead to union with the divine, it can only entice and destroy, for art does not represent a path to salvation.

A similarly negative conclusion was reached by Lermontov in an intimate, confessional lyric on the same subject, written in the same year as he began work on *The Demon.* "A Prayer" (Molitva, 1829)[61] is one of Lermontov's most open and direct poems on the conflict between the spiritual path of salvation (service to God) and the artistic drive (sinful and demonic). It opens with a prayer to God:

Не обвиняй меня, Всесильный,
И не карай меня, молю,
За то, что мрак земли могильный
С ее страстями я люблю;
За то, что редко в душу входит
Живых речей Твоих струя;
За то, что в заблужденье бродит
Мой ум далёко от Тебя;
За то, что лава вдохновенья
Клокочет на груди моей;
За то, что дикие волненья
Мрачат стекло моих очей;
За то, что мир земной мне тесен,
К Тебе ж проникнуть я боюсь,
И часто звуком грешных песен
Я, Боже, не Тебе молюсь.

[Do not accuse me, Almighty,
And do not punish me, I beg,
For the fact that the sepulchral gloom of the earth

I love with its passions;
For the fact that the stream of Your living words
Rarely enters my soul;
For the fact that in confusion
My mind wanders far from You;
For the fact that the lava of inspiration
Bubbles on my chest;
For the fact that wild emotions
Darken the glass of my eyes;
For the fact that the earthly world is too narrow for me,
I am afraid to penetrate into You,
And often with the sound of sinful songs
I, Lord, pray not unto You.]

Here we have not only a restatement of the same hierarchical distinction between the two levels of the divine word and human art as in "The Angel," but also a powerful expression of the link between song or poetry and sinful earthly passions; the impulse to human art blocks out the receptivity to the divine word and must be quelled in order to achieve spiritual growth. The poet therefore asks the Creator to extinguish "this miraculous flame" (sei plamen' chudnyi), the lava of his poetic inspiration, and to turn him into stone, concluding with the prayer:

От страшной жажды песнопенья
Пускай, Творец, освобожусь,
Тогда на тесный путь спасенья
К Тебе я снова обращусь.

[From the terrible thirst of poesy
Let me, Creator, free myself
Then on the narrow path of salvation
To You I will turn once more.]

This is in some sense a modern literary version of the problem which faced the eleventh century monk Nikita of Novgorod, whose spiritual salvation depended on a retreat from the world of culture.[62] It is also precisely the same conflict as we find in Blok, who, not surprisingly, marked key sections of this poem in his edition of Lermontov.[63] By endowing Pushkin's demon of negation with a powerful new dimension of verbal artistry and enchantment, Lermontov released the demon's creative potential and laid the foundation for the association between the demons of inspiration and corruption – an association later developed by Blok, in whose verse the muse and the Demon merge into a potent force for spiritual perdition. When Pasternak put into the mouth of Lermontov's Demon the words "Sleep, my friend, – I will return as an avalanche" (Spi, podruga, – lavinoi vernusia), he may well have had Blok's poetry in mind.[64]

Blok: The Muse's Metamorphosis into Demon

Of all the symbolists, Blok was perhaps the most acutely aware of the threat which the artistic vocation could present to life and the pursuit of religious goals. This temperamental predisposition underlay his vision of art as demonic and was reinforced by the strong sense of affinity which he felt with Lermontov, who occupies a central position in his work.[65] His deep inner feeling for Lermontov's verse is well captured in a comment which he jotted down opposite a poem in his edition of the poet's works: "It failed to be said, he wanted to say more, I know about what."[66] This intuitive understanding led Blok to clarify and develop themes and tensions which remained latent in Lermontov's verse. In both his essays and his poems he provided a new interpretation of Lermontov's Demon, refashioned as an image of the modern artist.

Blok's reading of Lermontov was superimposed on his response to the biblical and classical traditions and also drew on the legacy of Vladimir Solov'ev, reinterpreted in a novel manner. All these factors played a crucial role in shaping his understanding of art and its demonic qualities. His essay of 1910 in memory of the recently deceased artist Mikhail Vrubel provides a good starting-point for examining the multi-layered palimpsest produced by these different traditions.[67] It presents a vision of art and its goals directly modelled on the biblical ideals of prophecy and revelation. Genius is defined as the quality of a person, who can hear and form a coherent phrase from the snatched fragments brought by a "muffled wind from other worlds" (5:422–23).[68] Three examples follow: Moses on Sinai, the Virgin Mary at the crucifixion, and the artist in his studio. All three hear the same phrase: "Search for the Promised Land" (5:423). The order in which they are named is significant. The first two figures belong to the Judaeo-Christian tradition and represent the sphere of revealed religion. The artist is presented as their natural successor; in the modern era, he is the chosen channel for the communication of divine messages, a latter-day substitute for the prophet or bearer of divine revelation. All three figures are united by a common endeavour, the search for a promised land. This goal transcends individual needs and requires considerable sacrifice; the artist must be prepared to "burn in the fire of his own inspiration" (5:423).

The framing of the artist's task in this way prepares the ground for the view of art as demonic. The transferring of religious aims to the sphere of literature, coupled with the manifest inadequacy of the artist to the role of the prophet, leads to a situation where the artist is inevitably regarded as a Demon-like "fallen angel and artist-enchanter" (padshii angel i khudozhnik-zaklinatel', 5:424), whose creations can be no more than a flawed substitute for divine revelation.[69] From the outset the modern artist is therefore in a quandary. Blok compares him to Lermontov's exiled angel: once he has heard the "sounds of the heavens" he can no longer find any satisfaction in the "boring songs of the earth."[70] Although driven by the same impulse (the recovery of the promised land, based on a message of divine revelation), he is denied the necessary tools to achieve this goal. Instead, he must conjure up visions of his own making, a process which involves a dangerous game with demonic forces: "the heart of the prophet awakens in the artist; alone in the universe, understood by no one, he invokes the very Demon in order to enchant the night with the brightness of his sad eyes" (5:423–24). As no other means apart from art are available, this is the path which must be embraced, despite its risks.[71] It follows that Lermontov and Vrubel are among the main models for the contemporary artist to emulate.

In an earlier essay, "Stagnant Times" (Bezvremen'e, 1906),[72] Blok had already made the point that the demonic tendency – for which he then chose the image of the whirlwind (smerch) – is the inevitable accompaniment of the characteristic Russian preoccupation with the mystery of transformation (prevrashchenie) and transfiguration (preobrazhenie).[73] This phenomenon of demonization occurs because of the problematic nature of artistic embodiment (voploshchenie). In searching for appropriate forms for the expression of his vision, the artist comes up against the inadequacy and profound ambivalence of any attempt at artistic realization. The created forms are no more than doubles and masks, demonic mirror images of a deeper intuited truth which eludes expression. There is a further danger. The artist may become so enchanted by the play of his fantasy that he loses sight of his original ideals. Eventually, he may even abandon his faith in their objective existence. If so, he will perish, a victim of his own creative imagination. (Elsewhere Blok interprets the deaths of both Lermontov and Vrubel in this light.)[74] We have already noted this fated progression from unattainable ideal to demonic mask in our discussion of Lermontov's poetry; in his essays Blok is merely clarifying and making more explicit some of the central underlying themes of Lermontov's poetry.

On this basis Blok continues to elaborate a genealogy of Russian demonic authors, variously referred to as demons (demony) or sorcerers (kolduny), and ranked according to the degree of their success or failure in achieving an adequate form of expression for their innermost visions. The greater the urge to transcendence, the greater the risk of demonic fall at the moment of artistic realization. Lermontov and Gogol are depicted as two demons, who failed to fulfil their dreams and perished in the attempt; they lead a third blind and mighty demon, Dostoevsky, whose vision was embodied prematurely, and who therefore sank back into nothingness. Gippius and Sologub carry the legacy of Lermontov and Gogol forward to the present generation. The key question is whether the artist's imperfect images, described as doubles (dvoiniki) and phantoms (prizraki), can ever break through to a higher level of true incarnation. Like a demon high on a mountain peak, Lermontov towers above this literary landscape, mirrored in his work as a double which longs to burst into flower. The poet-demon watches this "icy phantom" (5:77) in horror – will the longed for transformation ever come about?[75]

Blok's response to this question varied according to his mood and medium. As we shall see below, he tended to be more optimistic in his essays than in his verse. However, this was not always the case. An essay written in the following year, "On the Lyric Poet" (O lirike, 1907),[76] gives a generally sombre portrayal of the poet's predicament. Art is described as an intoxicating dark wine which destroys the appetite for pure "transparent water" (5:132). The first lyric poet is a "fallen Angel-Demon" (5:131), who inhabits a "cursed den" (5:131); he is imprisoned within the "enchanted, magic circle" (5:134) of his own solipsistic world of false images (the legend of this fallen angel has been captured by Lermontov in song and by Vrubel in colour). God-fearing Christians pass by, cross themselves, and keep a safe distance. Their attitude illustrates the first of three possible responses to art which Blok outlines. One may refuse to listen (the path of rejection); one may listen and believe (the path of wholehearted acceptance leading to inevitable death); or one may listen but not believe. Whereas the first two options are characterized by an all or nothing maximalism, the last one depends on achieving a difficult balance of involvement and distance – a tightrope which Blok tried to walk, while remaining acutely aware of the attractions of either extreme. In fact, in his essay he classifies the poet together with the one who listens and believes, regarding them both as partners at the same demonic feast: "And here for him is all the tenderness of our cursed lyric soul. And all the cursed victuals from our demonic table" (5:131).

A more positive perspective on the demonic character of art is offered by Blok in "On the Present State of Russian Symbolism" (O sovremennom sostoianii russkogo simvolizma, 1910).[77] According to the somewhat utopian dialectic argument advanced in this essay, the original ideal or paradise (the thesis) has been lost and has given way to the present state of demonic art (the antithesis); however, through this intermediary stage the lost ideal will eventually be recovered (the final stage of synthesis). The dangerous game with doubles and masks is therefore justified as a necessary and inevitable phase on the way to apocalyptic redemption. The first two stages are encapsulated in the telling phrase: "We were 'prophets,' we desired to become 'poets'" (5:433); they will be followed by a return to the original sacred ideal of theurgic prophecy. Nowhere does Blok explain how this will come about; it is simply posited as an article of faith, following the eschatological pattern of the Book of Revelation.

The fact that this projected resolution became a particularly prominent theme in Blok's writing around the year 1910 was no accident. The anniversary of Vladimir Solov'ev's death ten years earlier coincided with the crisis of symbolism and the deaths of Vrubel and Komissarzhevskaia in 1910; this combination of factors evidently provided a renewed impetus for the reassertion of faith in the eventual triumph of the theurgic ideals of the movement. We will see later, however, that Blok's work as a whole remained firmly grounded in the middle stage of the demonic antithesis; the positive resolution was a superimposed frame, elaborated to a large extent under the influence of Viacheslav Ivanov, and much less marked in his verse than in his essays.

The great attraction of the dialectical scheme was that it provided a model for promoting and understanding the significance of the demonic in contemporary art, and also for interpreting the diachronic development of Russian literature since Pushkin (building on the genealogy of demonic authors set out in "Stagnant Times"). In both areas Blok's reading of the classical tradition exerted an important shaping influence – in particular, his understanding of the Apollo-Dionysus polarity, popularized by Nietzsche and reinterpreted for Russians at the turn of the century by Viacheslav Ivanov.[78] Many of Blok's remarks on the demonic occur in his essays of 1906, a peak period in his cult of the Dionysian, when he came strongly under the influence of Ivanov. Significantly, Blok identified Pushkin, the founder of modern Russian literature, with Apollo. By contrast, he linked Lermontov and Tiutchev with images of the night and *bezdna*, a dark abyss with Dionysian overtones.[79] The Dionysian paradigm was also based on a cyclical progression leading through darkness and death to spiritual rebirth. This lent further support to the view that the demonic was the inevitable prelude to the recovery of the sacred and provided a historical context for the central endeavour of Blok's generation: to carry through the legacy of Lermontov by completing the stage of the antithesis (which could be seen as culminating in the deaths of Vrubel and Komissarzhevskaia) and thereby to bring about a final return to the sacred origins of art.

So far, we have been tracing Blok's attitude to art as demonic through his essays. It is important to remember, however, that Blok was a reluctant theorist and committed his deepest intuitions to poetry. Although the essays played a significant role in creating a climate of debate for the popularization of new ideas on aesthetics and in providing a context for the verse, they did not constitute the backbone of the demonic tradition which was built up and in the long term survived through the poems.

Ever since Blok abandoned the Beautiful Lady as a subject for his verse (though not as a tenet of faith), the way was opened for demonic themes to enter his work. In renouncing the attempt to create a new poetic language for the expression of his spiritual intuitions, he turned instead to describe that which could be described, using the "masks of speech" (rechi maski).[80] Many cycles of poems written after the *Verses about the Beautiful Lady* (*Stikhi o Prekrasnoi Dame*, 1901–1902, first published in 1905) deal explicitly with demonic images such as the devils of the marshland, the demons of the modern city, masks, doubles, or the snow and ice imagery of the Dionysian whirlwind of erotic passion. However, we are concerned here not with demonic themes as such, but with a more specific area: the expression in verse of Blok's growing awareness of the creative process itself as inherently demonic. We shall therefore consider in detail two particular poems which are crucial to this theme and have played a key role in its development within the Russian tradition. Both eventually came to form part of "The Terrible World" (Strashnyi mir), the opening cycle of Blok's third book of poems, and occupy significant positions within it. "To the Muse" (K Muze, 1912) is the first poem of the cycle and "The Demon" (Demon, 1916), together with one other poem, forms its conclusion.[81]

Before embarking on the discussion of these two poems, it is worth noting that there is in general a significant difference between Blok's treatment of the demonic in his essays and in his verse. The genre of the essay was linked to a culture of public debate involving disputations with formidable opponents such as Viacheslav Ivanov; this led Blok to advance dialectic arguments in prose, which presented a more dogmatic or positive vision of future synthesis than one would normally find in his verse. An interesting example of this difference can be seen in the contrast between the relative optimism of the essay discussed above, "On the Present State of Russian Symbolism" (1910), and his altogether much bleaker poem, "The Demon" (Demon, 1910), written just a few days later.[82]

Blok's essay was originally conceived as a rejoinder to a talk given by Ivanov.[83] His notebook record of this talk indicates that his initial response was fairly sceptical. After summarizing Ivanov's conclusion that the next stage of symbolism would be the great art of myth, he listed some of the questions which he put to him: "1) About the *terrible* (*uzhasnom*) in art – about its curse. 2) Consequently, about

whether that which is desired will be *art* (true theurgy, myth)."[84]
Blok's acute awareness of the demonic character of art could not be
lightly dispelled by Ivanov's assurance of an imminent new form of
theurgic art. Even if one were to accept this promise, would the
envisaged ideal in fact count as art? For Blok the distinction between
the revealed truth of religion (sacred) and the subjective artistic
vision (cursed) was absolute and could not easily be bridged.

These questions were clearly uppermost in Blok's mind. They
found their way into his essay in a somewhat watered-down form
(5:431), but retained a much stronger presence in his poetry. His essay
concluded with a vision of two alternative paths facing the artist: either
perdition (gibel') or the recovery of the lost thesis, represented by the
golden sword (zolotoi mech). As a striking image of the first path, Blok
quoted the lines from Lermontov's *The Demon* on the bridegroom's
headlong ride to death, but inscribed them within the dialectic of a
promised future synthesis.[85] By contrast, in his poem "The Demon"
(19 April 1910)[86] he chose the same image of fated death, but lent it a
quite different emphasis. Death has now become the focal point, the
key image with which the poem concludes. In the midst of an erotic
embrace, the thoughts of the Demon-like narrator are invaded by a
vision of the bridegroom's death. Through recollection and dream, an
incident from the narrative of Lermontov's poem is transformed into
an inexorable law of the human condition; Blok's cryptic final lines
suggest that all earthly aspirations are fated to end in death:

> Пусть скачет жених – не доскачет!
> Чеченская пуля верна.
>
> [Let the bridegroom gallop – he will not arrive!
> The Chechen bullet is true.]

As this example indicates, the sense of the demonic and its association with death is generally rendered more intensely in Blok's
poetry than in his essays. Although Blok's poem of 1910 on the
Demon does not directly raise the question of art (unlike the essay of
the same year), it does suggest within a broad context that the fulfilment of an ideal based on individual dreams is doomed. If one
recalls the fate of Lermontov's bridegroom, whose dreams, instigated by the Demon, took the place of prayer, one can begin to see
the link between the figure of the individual dreamer and the artist.[87]

The application of this theme to the creative process was taken up
and developed in "To the Muse," written two years later.[88] The lingering doubts which Blok had voiced at Ivanov's talk are now articulated much more forcefully, not simply as queries or reservations,
but as part of a programmatic statement, which comes down firmly
on the side of art as either immoral or at best amoral, as not only dis-

tinct from religion but as explicitly anti-religious. The muse is portrayed as a Siren-like figure, an intoxicating, Dionysian seductress, who, like the Demon in Blok's poems of 1910 and 1916, leads only one way – to death or perdition.[89] She represents the "curse of sacred precepts" (prokliat'e zavetov sviashchennykh) and evokes the *Neznakomka* (Stranger) of 1906 through the purple-grey radiance which lights up around her when she mocks faith. In fact, when describing the figure of the *Neznakomka* in 1910, Blok confessed that he would have created a Demon if he had had the technical means of Vrubel[90] (there is an interesting precedent for this association in Lermontov, who used the term *Neznakomets* [Stranger] to refer to the Demon in early drafts of his work).[91] Here, in his poem on the muse, Blok is creating another female incarnation of the Demon, this time directly related to artistic creation. This blurring of boundaries marks a significant departure from the distinction preserved by Pushkin[92] and still maintained, although less rigidly, by Lermontov. There is, however, a clear visual antecedent for Blok's ambivalent image in Vrubel's compelling oil-painting *The Muse* (*Muza*, 1896; Illustration 13), which depicts the muse with the mesmerizing features of the Demon.[93] As in the case of Lermontov's *The Demon*, Blok's poem is

13. Mikhail Vrubel, *The Muse*, 1896. Oil on canvas, 106 × 96 cm.

disorientating, in that the danger which it warns against is partially obscured by the seductive rhythms of its cadences.[94]

The fourth verse places art outside moral categories in a sphere of its own:

> Зла, добра ли? – Ты вся – не отсюда.
> Мудрено про тебя говорят:
> Для иных ты – и Муза, и чудо.
> Для меня ты – мученье и ад.[95]

> [Are you evil or good? – You are all from beyond.
> Enigmatically they speak of you:
> For some, you are both Muse and miracle.
> For me, you are torment and hell.]

For some, art may possess a miraculous transforming power (this was a fundamental tenet of the theurgic aesthetics initiated by Vladimir Solov'ev). The poet's personal experience, however, teaches him otherwise. Through an ingenious transmutation of sounds (*Muza* [Muse] and *chudo* [miracle] become *muchen'e* [torment] and *ad* [hell]), the anticipated transformation is reversed and the miracle-working Muse of theurgic aesthetics is moved back into the closed world of a personal inferno.

The central theme at issue here – the ambivalent relation of beauty and art to the moral and religious values of redemption and transfiguration – builds on the well-known discussion of this subject which occurs in *The Brothers Karamazov* (*Brat'ia Karamazovy*, 1879–80):[96]

> Beauty is a fearful (*strashnaia*) and terrifying (*uzhasnaia*) thing! Fearful because it is indefinable, and it cannot be defined because God sets us nothing but riddles. Here the shores meet, here all contradictions live side by side. ... Beauty! It makes me mad to think that a man of great heart and high intelligence should begin with the ideal of Madonna and end with the ideal of Sodom. What is more terrible is that a man with the ideal of Sodom already in his soul does not renounce the ideal of Madonna, and it sets his heart ablaze, and it is truly, truly ablaze, as in the days of his youth and innocence. ... What appears shameful to the mind, is sheer beauty to the heart. Is there beauty in Sodom? Believe me, for the great majority of people it *is* in Sodom and nowhere else – did you know that secret or not? The awful thing is that beauty is not only a terrible (*strashnaia*), but also a mysterious, thing. There God and the devil (*d'iavol*) are fighting for mastery, and the battlefield is the heart of man.[97]

The points of overlap with Blok's poem are numerous.[98] Both texts share a view of beauty as a fearful mystery which lies beyond rational definition, encompasses unfathomable contradictions, and confuses the boundaries between good and evil. Dostoevsky distinguishes between two aspects of beauty: its spiritual aspect, represented by the ideal of the Madonna, linked with God, and its purely aesthetic aspect, bound up with a deep inner attraction to evil, represented by the ideal of Sodom, and linked with the devil. Both the heart and the mind are sensitive to the spiritual aspect of beauty, but only the irrational impulses of the heart respond to its aesthetic appeal. The purer aspirations of the mind towards holiness or spiritual beauty can therefore be undermined insidiously by the heart's attraction to evil, by the substitution of one ideal for another.

On the surface, this has a great deal in common with Blok's view of the process by which art may come to substitute a false image for an originally pure intuition, leading to its corruption. And yet there is much more to Blok's poem than a simple affirmation of solidarity with Dostoevsky. It contains a strong underlying polemical thrust, directed against a reading of Dostoevsky advanced by Viacheslav Ivanov during the previous year. In 1911, Ivanov published an influential essay which presented Dostoevsky's muse in a Dionysian light: "Dostoevsky's muse, with her ecstatic and clairvoyant penetration into another *I*, resembles both the mindless (obezumevshuiu) Dionysiac Maenad, rushing headlong 'with loudly beating heart,' and the other countenance (lik) of the same Maenad – the daughter of Darkness, the bloodhound-bitch of the goddess of Night, the snake-haired Fury …"[99]

Ivanov's characterization of Dostoevsky's muse as Dionysian has important implications, which were later incorporated by him into a more extended theory of demonology. According to his view of the process of artistic creation, the initial Dionysian descent (niskhozhdenie) leads to a second stage of Apollonian ascent (voskhozhdenie).[100] The dark, demonic Dionysian aspect of artistic activity is therefore only a prelude to a new stage of renewal. Blok, however, disputes this approach; although he accepts the view of the muse as Dionysian, he no longer agrees that this will automatically lead on to a higher stage. This is made particularly clear in the second verse:

> Будто ангелов ты низводила,
> Соблазняя своей красотой…

> [It is as if you brought down angels,
> Seducing by your beauty…]

By using the word *nizvodila* (brought down) Blok is subverting the sense of Ivanov's *niskhozhdenie* (descent). The descent in Blok's poem is not a prelude to ascent, it is merely a *bringing down* of the sacred to the level of art.

Blok's underlying polemic with Ivanov's Dionysian view of artistic creation was even more explicit in the first published version of "To the Muse." This originally concluded with an additional verse describing the destructive power of the muse over the soul:

И доныне еще, безраздельно
Овладевши душою на миг,
Он ее опьяняет бесцельно –
Твой неистовый, дивный твой лик.[101]

[And still hitherto, after totally
Possessing the soul for an instant,
It intoxicates it aimlessly –
Your frenzied, your marvellous countenance.]

The terms used to describe the muse's countenance and its effect on the poet's soul – "frenzied" (neistovyi) and "intoxicates" (op'ianiaet) – are usually associated with the worship of Dionysus. For Ivanov the state of Dionysian intoxication was part of a process which led to a higher goal; for Blok it has no goal (bestsel'no) and leads nowhere – this is a direct refutation of the more optimistic premise of his earlier essay of 1910, "On the Present State of Russian Symbolism," which had suggested that demonic or Dionysian intoxication (the stage of the antithesis) would somehow bring about a new synthesis.

"To the Muse" therefore represents a significant turning-point in the development of Blok's view of art as demonic. On the one hand, he has taken over from Ivanov the view that art is essentially Dionysian and has conflated this with his own Lermontov-inspired view of art as demonic. On the other hand, he no longer accepts Ivanov's attempt to square Dionysus with the theurgic aesthetics of Vladimir Solov'ev by regarding the Dionysian stage as a prelude to spiritual regeneration; this marks his arrival at a more sober recognition of the irreconcilable differences between the paths of art and religion.[102] In this respect the closest antecedent of his poem is perhaps Baudelaire's "Hymne à la Beauté," which conveys a similar mood of willing surrender to the intoxicating power of beauty, coupled with a full awareness of its moral ambivalence and curse.[103]

Blok's approach is clarified by a conversation about art and religion which he had with M.I. Tereshchenko at about the time when he started work on "To the Muse."[104] Blok objected to his friend's view that art could offer the same benefits as religion and recorded his reasons in his diary: "I began in reply to develop my *customary view: what* in art is *infinity*, unclear 'about what,' beyond everything, but empty, destructive (pustoe, gibel'noe), perhaps, *that same thing* in religion is the *end*, clear about what, plenitude, salvation" (7:162–63). In response to Tereshchenko's view that art could bring happiness, Blok's feelings were painfully divided: "I argued because I once knew something greater than art, i.e. not infinity, but the End, not worlds (miry), but the World (Mir); I did not argue, because I have lost That, probably for ever, *I have fallen, betrayed*, and am now, indeed, an 'artist,' I do not live by that which fills life, but by that which makes it black, terrible (strashnoi), which pushes it away" (7:163).[105]

These extracts are extremely relevant to both "To the Muse" and "The Demon" (1916). They reflect Blok's conscious identification with art as his chosen vocation, made in full awareness of its infinite but ultimately "empty, destructive" worlds, distinct from the sphere of religion and life, which was paradoxically perceived as finite by virtue of its relation to a time scale governed by the truth of revelation, past and future. This vision of art as empty and destructive is brought out very clearly in Blok's magnificent late poem, "The Demon," completed on 9 June 1916.[106] His second lyric on this subject provides a much fuller poetic reworking of those elements in Lermontov's narrative poem which, as we saw above, could contribute towards an interpretation of the Demon as artist. It achieves this by building on the interpretation of Lermontov advanced by Blok in his essays and by synthesizing this with elements from the earlier "The Demon" (1910) and "To the Muse."

The immediate source of Blok's poem is the second of the two highly persuasive monologues which Lermontov's Demon delivers to Tamara, now a nun, in order to convince her of his integrity and thereby complete the act of seduction (2:10). His speech leads up to the fatal burning kiss (2:11) after which Tamara's soul is irrevocably lost. Blok has reproduced several aspects of Lermontov's monologue, including its metre, rhyming scheme, central themes, and formal structure.[107] It was evidently for this reason that the manuscript of the poem carried the subtitle of "Exercise" (Uprazhnenie, 3:515). And yet the poem is far more than a simple exercise in imitation: it amounts to a profound interpretation of the story of Tamara's seduction by the Demon in terms of Blok's understanding of the creative process.

Two changes in particular stand out as most significant. Lermontov's Demon paints a purely positive picture to Tamara in order to overcome her last reservations; it is only after he falls silent that the kiss ensues and her spiritual destruction becomes plain. Blok's Demon, however, reveals his innate character from the outset. He not only promises his companion a giddy ascent to the higher regions; he also tells her that at the end of their journey he will drop her "into a shining emptiness" (v siiaiushchuiu pustotu). Thus, the tantalizing ambivalence of Lermontov's Demon (were there genuine elements in his hope of regeneration?) is resolved in Blok's poem into a passionately sincere, but ultimately negative statement by a Demon, who entertains no illusions about the final outcome of his actions.[108]

The second major change concerns the move from the particular to the abstract and universal. One can safely assume that the lyrical voice which speaks in Blok's poem is that of the Demon, but who is the addressee? Although she is female, she is never actually named as Tamara. This lack of explicit identification invites an allegorical interpretation. One could, for example, see the Demon and his female companion as symbolic of two aspects of the artist's personality. The Demon represents the artist's creative drive; he is a conflated amalgam of Pushkin's two demons: the "daemon" of inspiration and the demon of corruption (this is consistent with Blok's earlier definition of the fallen Angel-Demon as the "first lyric poet" and with his statement that every person involved in cultural activity is a "demon who curses the earth and invents wings so as to fly away from it").[109] His female companion represents the artist's pure spirit or soul (previously allied with the pure muse), striving to regain a lost intuition of the heavenly or infinite.[110] Accordingly, Blok's poem could be read as a dramatization of the fated outcome of an inner conflict between the two divided aspects of his creative personality which he was unable to reconcile (Akhmatova may have had this in mind when she referred to Blok as "the Demon himself with Tamara's smile" (Demon sam s ulybkoi Tamary).[111] This represents a further development of the dilemma articulated earlier in his conversation with Tereshchenko; it also continues the debate over the divergent spiritual and aesthetic aspects of beauty, initiated by Dostoevsky and echoed in "To the Muse."

The same conflict can also be applied to Blok's poetic development. The Tamara figure suggests the early, pure muse of his Beautiful Lady period, subsequently displaced by a darker form of Dionysian inspiration. This later muse, addressed in "To the Muse," gradually merges with the figure of the Demon, whose voice eventually takes over completely in "The Demon" of 1916. This echoes and develops some of the nineteenth-century precedents discussed earlier in this essay, in which such tensions were adumbrated but generally left unresolved. Although Pushkin's muse was brought into a carefully engineered confrontation with the demon, and although Lermontov's "muse of gentle inspirations" even took fright at the Demon's eyes, the two figures always remained distinct and autonomous in the work of both authors. Blok was the first poet in the Russian tradition to recognize that the encounter between muse and Demon might result in the final erosion of the muse's autonomous identity and in the severance of her links with the artist's pure soul.

"The Demon" of 1916 also continues Blok's long-standing polemic with Ivanov's positive reading of the Dionysian roots of artistic inspiration. This can be sensed particularly strongly in the second verse:

> Я пронесу тебя над бездной,
> Ее бездонностью дразня.
> Твой будет ужас бесполезный –
> Лишь вдохновеньем для меня.

> [I will carry you above the abyss,
> Tantalizing you with its infinite depth.
> Your futile terror will be
> Only an inspiration for me.]

Blok's notion of terror as the source of inspiration is reminiscent of Ivanov's view of *terror antiquus* (drevnii uzhas) as the Dionysian force which fuels true art. Just under a fortnight before Blok completed "The Demon," Ivanov's essay, "The Inspiration of Terror" (Vdokhnovenie uzhasa), was published.[112] It dealt with Bely's recently published novel *Petersburg (Peterburg)* and argued that the spirit of ancient Dionysian terror with which this work was imbued would help to bring about the spiritual regeneration of Russia through Christ. In his poem, Blok has taken up several terms used by Ivanov in his essay ("terror" [uzhas], "inspiration" [vdokhnoven'e], "emptiness" [pustota]),[113] but has shown that Dionysian terror is an end in itself, devoid of any apocalyptic or redemptive dimension, and leading only to emptiness. This was in keeping with his view, expressed in discussion with Tereshchenko, that the apocalyptic dimension belonged only to the sphere of religion, not of art. A similar perspective informs the advice which he gave to O.A. Kaufman, an aspiring poet, in the spring of 1916, warning her not to call poets prophets on the grounds that this demeans a great word. Poets are poets, not prophets, and have their own distinct language and sphere of truth (8:462). This is a clear revocation of the earlier description which Blok had given of the two stages preceding his vision of the ideal future synthesis: "we were 'prophets,' we desired to become 'poets'" (5:433).

Our reading of "The Demon" (1916) has suggested that the intoxicating path of artistic inspiration leads to a spiritual void. If art cannot carry the burden of a displaced religious quest, and is in fact detrimental to the latter, then what is its role and ultimate justification? Blok could no more abandon the initial spiritual premise of his art than he could deny the artist within himself, and yet he came to see the two paths as mutually hostile and incompatible. Perhaps this inner sense of impasse, as well as the more commonly cited personal and historical factors, go some way towards explaining what Nadezhda Pavlovich described as Blok's "feeling of being finished as a poet" towards the end of his life.[114]

Tentative confirmation of this suggestion can be found in one of Blok's rare late essays. In March 1920 he wrote a short piece on Merezhkovsky in which he briefly summed up the attitude which he had come to espouse: that art and life should be kept entirely separate, and that the Russian tendency to harness art to life (i.e. to religion or social causes) was detrimental to both. The fundamental plight of the Russian artist in Blok's view was the way in which art encroaches on life: "The *curse* which every artist carries on him lies in the fact that art takes too much away from his life. ... In Europe they know about this *curse*; there they *understand* and *respect* this simple and painful human tragedy.[115]

By contrast with Europe, in Russia the artist has traditionally been expected to be a jack of all trades, a prophet, a social activist, a politician. Blok seems to accept this as an inevitable part of the Russian character ("What can we do – we're Russian ...," 6:394) and therefore as the source of the Russian artist's tragic and inescapable predicament. Interestingly, it does not occur to him to challenge this attitude; the displacement of religious ideals into the sphere of art, which, as we argued in the previous essay, was partly a consequence of the reforms of Peter the Great, was evidently accepted by him as a final and binding legacy.

In support of this view of art, Blok quoted the following lines from Lermontov:

> ... Жалкий труд,
> Отнявший множество минут
> У Бога, дум святых и дел:
> Искусства горестный удел!..[116]

> [... A wretched work,
> Taking away a multitude of minutes
> From God, from holy thoughts and deeds:
> The sorry destiny of art!..]

Lermontov, whose maximalist approach to life and art caused him to portray any less elevated substitute as inherently demonic, is now called upon to voice the logical outcome of this line of reasoning: art is a flawed substitute for man's spiritual aspirations, from which it can only detract. By quoting the cited lines out of their original context, Blok is making Lermontov appear as the spokesman for his more sober late view of art as a temptation and distraction – a far cry from his earlier reading of Lermontov as a mystic poet of Sophia.[117]

Blok's Literary Demons and the Demons of Orthodox Tradition

We have seen that Blok was indebted to the biblical tradition (filtered through Vladimir Solov'ev) for his view of the spiritual source and prophetic mission of art, and to the classical tradition (assimilated through Nietzsche and Viacheslav Ivanov) for his view of the Dionysian qualities of the artistic experience. Lermontov was read by him in the light of both traditions; in fact the secret of his particular appeal to Blok probably lay in the fact that, as a poet who was "seraphic ... and at the same time demonic,"[118] he could reflect both traditions in a way that Pushkin could not. However, Blok's reading of Lermontov evolved in the light of his own shifting awareness of the relationship between these two traditions. As he became increasingly aware of their fundamental incompatibility, the figure of Lermontov's "muse of gentle inspirations" was gradually taken over by doubles tainted with features of the Demon, whose guise she eventually assumed.

Lermontov's Demon thus provided Blok with the perfect voice to articulate the triumphant awareness of art in its demonic (and irredeemable) aspect; this perspective "from within" on the artist's espousal of his chosen path in full knowledge of its fatal consequences is conveyed in exhilarating form in "The Demon" of 1916. There is, however, a second possible perspective "from without" on the artist's predicament, judged from the point of view of the spiritual quest which the doomed flight into creativity frustrates. From this angle art is a purely negative diversion, deflecting the soul from its true path; the intoxicating Demon sheds his grandeur and aura of attractiveness and is stripped down to reveal a plainer, unadorned demon of destructive temptation. Although Blok, as an artist, was naturally more given to articulating the first perspective, part of him clearly strove to make room for the second point of view, to find a voice which would reflect the discipline of the spiritual life. This desire is reflected in a note which he made in the spring of 1916: after commenting on the one path of spiritual insight (which he felt that he had abandoned), he remarked that he should stop writing poetry because he found it too easy and needed to bring about an inner transformation of self.[119]

Blok did find a voice for this second approach, but, significantly, only in a non-literary, religious source. Just five days after completing "The Demon," feeling low, he wandered into a secondhand bookshop and bought a copy of the first volume of the Russian translation of the *Philokalia (Dobrotoliubie)*; on the same day he noted that this was perhaps a "great discovery."[120] Two days later he explained the reason for his excitement in a letter to his mother: "the chapters on the struggle with devils contain very simple and useful observations, often, of course, also familiar to artists – of the type to which I too belong. ... Evagrius's attitude to demons is exactly the same as my attitude to doubles, e.g. in my essay on symbolism."[121] We know from Blok's marginalia on his copy of this book that two particular aspects of Evagrius's acute analysis of demons and their manifold wiles caught his attention. One was the way in which a demon, described as a "thought which can suitably be called the wanderer" distracts and corrupts the mind by drawing it into conversation: "Thus, little by little, it [the mind] falls away from consciousness of God and virtue, and forgets its calling and its vow."[122] Opposite this passage, Blok wrote: "I know, I know it all." The other was the description of the closely related "demon of dejection" (demon pechali), which, unlike the other demons which teach the soul to love pleasure, cuts off every pleasure of the soul and dries it up through dejection: "The symbol of this demon is the viper. When used in moderation for man's good, its poison is an antidote against that of other venomous creatures, but when taken in excess it kills whoever takes it."[123] Opposite this passage Blok noted that "this demon is essential to the artist."[124] (At the time of writing "The Demon" and reading the *Philokalia*, he was suffering from a state of severe depression and apathy.)[125]

One can infer from these various sources that Blok drew a parallel between the insidious thoughts which distract the spiritual seeker from union with God, and the false doubles, generated by the creative process, which divert the artist from his goal and corrupt his original purity of intuition. There are two possible ways of interpreting this parallel, one negative, the other positive. According to the first, artistic activity is a demonic illusion, tempting in its beauty but spiritually destructive. According to the second, just as the early Christian ascetic monks used to go out into the desert and deliberately confront demons in order to rise higher on the ladder of spiritual perfection through such trials, so in the same way the invocation and exorcizing of artistic demons can be viewed as a tool for spiritual growth.[126] The demonic game of art could therefore be a spiritual dead end or a method for self-advancement. Although this latent ambiguity was not clearly resolved in Blok's work, on balance it seems likely that he had the first, negative interpretation in mind when drawing this parallel.

Towards the end of his life Blok gave his copy of the *Philokalia* to Nadezhda Pavlovich.[127] A few weeks after his death she met with Bely in order to show him Blok's comments on the volume. Bely copied out the description of the demon of dejection as a viper, compared it to the Demon of Lermontov and Vrubel, and noted Blok's comment that it is essential to the artist.[128] When he later wrote up these notes for his published memoir of Blok, he gave them an interesting slant, identifying the demon of dejection highlighted by Blok with Emilii Metner's understanding of the "demon of art" as a form of punishment sent to Blok and Bely "for the attempt to go outside the sphere of pure art."[129] This provides a curious further twist to the convoluted history of symbolist interpretations of traditional demons, now seen as instruments of divine punishment for the hubris of theurgic aspirations.[130]

While it may, therefore, not be possible to pinpoint precisely what Blok and Bely meant by identifying the literary demons of symbolist culture with the moral demons which beset the fourth-century Christian monk, Evagrius, one thing is clear. Evagrius may not have known the demon of artistic creativity, but he did know and could describe the reality of the spiritual quest and the factors which detract from it, and this provided a language which Blok and Bely latched on to, particularly at a time when the earlier confident assertions of theurgism were no longer seen as adequate. Their sense of close affinity with Evagrius was symptomatic of their desire to find a language outside the perspective of the artist, by which to describe and evaluate his underlying spiritual quest.

By tracing the complex evolution of the muse's relations with the Demon in the work of three poets, this essay has highlighted one strand in the progression of the notion of art as demonic from nineteenth-century Romanticism into early twentieth-century modernism. We have seen how Pushkin's pure muse was associated with two quite different demons – one evil, linked with the individual's moral corruption, the other benign, inspiring the artist's creative process. These two distinct demons were subsequently merged in the figure of Lermontov's Demon, whose combination of evil intent with verbal artistry overshadowed the poet's gentle muse. From here, it was but one more step to the final metamorphosis of muse into Demon, which we witness in the essays and poetry of Blok. Thus, the purity of art, which, although threatened, was still posited as an ideal at the time of Romanticism, gives way to the modernist perception of art as intrinsically demonic: the muse and the Demon are no longer two separate figures, but have fused into a new, androgynous demonic being. For Blok the artist, there was no way out of this hell; for Blok the man, the only alternative was to equate his literary demons with the demons of Orthodoxy, thus completing the circle from his early theurgic aspirations to their "demonic" negation in religious tradition. The key link in this chain from Pushkin to Blok was Lermontov's Demon, who became for Russian literature what Harold Bloom has argued that Milton's Satan was for Western European literature: the "archetype of the modern poet at his strongest."[131]

Notes

1. A.S. Pushkin, *Sobranie sochinenii*, ed. D.D. Blagoi and others, 10 vols. (Moscow: Khudozhestvennaia literatura, 1974–78), 1:212. Translations throughout this essay are mine, unless otherwise indicated.

2. M.Iu. Lermontov, *Polnoe sobranie stikhotvorenii,* introd. D.E. Maksimov, ed. E.E. Naidich, Biblioteka poeta, Bol'shaia seriia, 2 vols. (Leningrad: Sovetskii pisatel', 1989), 1:88.

3. Aleksandr Blok, *Sobranie sochinenii,* ed. V.N. Orlov, A.A. Surkov, and K.I. Chukovskii, 8 vols. (Moscow and Leningrad: Gosudarstvennoe izdatel'stvo khudozhestvennoi literatury, 1960–63), 3:60–61(60).

4. From "Poet" (1827), in Pushkin, *Sobranie sochinenii,* 2:110.

5. The reference to the Demon's "volshebnyi golos" occurs in Lermontov's *Demon* (1:15.311), in Lermontov, *Polnoe sobranie stikhotvorenii,* 2:446.

6. "O sovremennom sostoianii russkogo simvolizma" (1910), in Blok, *Sobranie sochinenii,* 5:433.

7. Blok, *Sobranie sochinenii,* 2:250.

8. *Zolotoe runo,* 1907, no.1, 7. This issue was devoted to a competition on the devil for which Blok was one of the judges. As well as reproducing works of art, it contained poems, stories, and critical essays on the devil in literature, music, and the visual arts. Kuzmin, Remizov, Rozanov, and Bely were among the contributors. Dobuzhinsky's illustration is also reproduced in Michael Raeburn, ed., *The Twilight of the Tsars: Russian Art at the Turn of the Century* (London: South Bank Centre, 1991), 147.

9. Letter to P.A. Viazemsky of 27 March 1816, in Pushkin, *Sobranie sochinenii,* 9:8. See also the reference to deserting poetry for the "novyi bes" of humble prose in *Evgenii Onegin* (3:13.4), in Pushkin, *Sobranie sochinenii,* 4:52. Hereafter references to *Evgenii Onegin* will be cited from this edition and given in the text and notes by chapter, stanza, and line number.

10. "V.L. Davydovu," in Pushkin, *Sobranie sochinenii,* 1:146–47.

11. From "K ****" ("Ia pomniu chudnoe mgnoven'e …," 1825), in Pushkin, *Sobranie sochinenii,* 2:23–24(23). The phrase "genii chistoi krasoty" is borrowed from Zhukovsky with whom Pushkin closely associated his ideal of pure art. Zhukovsky used it in "Lalla Ruk" (written in 1821, published in 1827) and in "Ia Muzu iunuiu, byvalo …" (written in 1822 or 1824, published in 1824); see V.A. Zhukovskii, *Sochineniia v trekh tomakh,* comp. I.M. Semenko (Moscow: Khudozhestvennaia literatura, 1980), 1:118–19(119), 300, respectively.

12. The last two phrases are from "Poet" (1827), in Pushkin, *Sobranie sochinenii,* 2:110.

13. Pushkin, *Sobranie sochinenii,* 1:59.

14. "O bogi mirnye polei, dubrov i gor …," in Pushkin, *Sobranie sochinenii,* 1:593.

15. In a letter to A.A. Del'vig of 16 November 1823, Pushkin uses this term of Baratynsky's muse. Pushkin, *Sobranie sochinenii,* 9:75.

16. Pushkin, *Polnoe sobranie sochinenii,* ed. V.D. Bonch-Bruevich, 17 vols. (Moscow: Izdatel'stvo Akademii nauk SSSR, 1937–59; reprint, Moscow: Voskresen'e, 1994–97), 2(book 1):267 (text); 2(book 2):760–61 (variants), 1076–77 (note). The poem is dated from October to 10 November 1823 and was first published under the incorrect title of "Moi demon" in *Mnemozina,* part 3 (Moscow, 1824), 11–12. For a brief survey of this and later images of the devil (covering the Romantic demon, folk demons, the demon of ideology, and the demon of decadence) in nineteenth-century Russian poetry, see Andrzej Dudek, "The Devil in 19th Century Russian Poetry," *Slavia Orientalis* 41 (1992), no.1:19–26. Dudek places Pushkin's poem at the start of this tradition; he does not, however, distinguish between Pushkin's two types of demons, or between the concept of the demon and the devil.

17. Exactly the same transition from aesthetic excitement to demonic corruption occurs in Pushkin's "V nachale zhizni shkolu pomniu ia …" (1830), discussed in the previous essay in this volume, Pamela Davidson, "Divine Service or Idol Worship? Russian Views of Art as Demonic."

18. V.M. Odoevskii, "Novyi demon," in *Mnemozina*, part 4 (Moscow, 1824; not in circulation until October 1825), 35–41(35), cited in Iu. Oksman's note in Pushkin, *Sobranie sochinenii*, 6:453–54.

19. ["O stikhotvorenii 'Demon'"], in Pushkin, *Polnoe sobranie sochinenii*, 11:30 (text), 300–301 (variants), 531 (note). The fragment is dated 1825, but was not published until 1874. Pushkin was refuting the opinion of contemporary readers who identified his demon with A.N. Raevsky.

20. An early variant emphasized the need for faith by adding at this point: "Emu [serdtsu] nuzhno verit'."

21. See the discussion of "Zhukovskomu" and n.11 above. In the additional stanzas on the muse from the draft of chap. 8 of *Evgenii Onegin* Pushkin later referred to Zhukovsky as the "gluboko vdokhnovennyi / Vsego prekrasnogo pevets" who offered him support and summoned him "k slave *chistoi*" (emphasis mine). Pushkin, *Sobranie sochinenii*, 4:417.

22. Zhukovskii, *Sochineniia v trekh tomakh*, 3:447. In the letter Zhukovsky plays on the link between his instructions to Pushkin to be an angel ("bud' angelom") and Pushkin's impending name-day ("zavtra zhe tvoi angel").

23. See in this volume Julian Graffy, "The Devil is in the Detail: Demonic Features of Gogol's Petersburg," n.77.

24. Pushkin, *Sobranie sochinenii*, 1:229–34 (cited on 229–30).

25. Plato, *Phaedrus* (245a), with translation and commentary by C.J. Rowe (Warminster: Aris and Phillips, 1986), 57, 59. For a fuller discussion of the term *daimon*, see in this volume Davidson, "Divine Service or Idol Worship?"

26. See the identical opening words ("V te dni, kogda ...") and the ensuing parallel between "Togda kakoi-to zlobnyi genii / Stal taino naveshchat' menia" ("Demon") and "Iavliat'sia Muza stala mne" (*Evgenii Onegin*, 8:1.8). Nabokov notes the coincidence of the opening words and intonation as "curious" but does not expand any further. See Aleksandr Pushkin, *Eugene Onegin. A Novel in Verse*, trans., with a commentary, by Vladimir Nabokov, rev. ed., 4 vols., Bollingen Series, no. 72 (Princeton: Princeton University Press, 1975) 3:129. Lotman makes the same observation and develops its significance more fully; see A.S. Pushkin, *Evgenii Onegin. Roman v stikhakh*, ed. Iu.M. Lotman (Moscow: Izdatel'stvo Atrium, 1991), 566–67.

27. Pushkin, *Eugene Onegin*, trans. Nabokov, 1:287.

28. On Akhmatova's "overcoming" of symbolist demonism, see in this volume Michael Basker, "Symbolist Devils and Acmeist Transformation: Gumilev, Demonism, and the Absent Hero in Akhmatova's *Poem Without a Hero*."

29. This parallel is supported by a thread of textual echoes which link "Demon" (1823), chap. 8 of *Evgenii Onegin* (1829–30), and "V nachale zhizni ..." (1830). The various stanzas on the muse, which were subsequently omitted from drafts and the fair copy of chap. 8 of *Evgenii Onegin*, repeat the opening construction of "Demon" ("V te dni, kogda ...") and include a much more extensive description of Pushkin's early encounter with his muse at the *litsei*, many details of which are echoed in "V nachale zhizni ...," composed in October 1830, soon after *Evgenii Onegin* was completed on 25 September 1830 (see Pushkin's chronology of his work on the novel in Pushkin, *Evgenii Onegin*, ed. Lotman, 655). These details include references to the poet's hours of lazy dreaming in the garden of the *litsei*, to his escape into this garden by jumping over the fence, and to his characteristic mood of longing and "smutnaia pechal'." See Pushkin, *Sobranie sochinenii*, 6:415–17.

30. Pushkin's lecture was delivered on 18 January 1836 at the Imperial Russian Academy and published in the same year in *Sovremennik*. See "Mnenie M.E. Lobanova o dukhe slovesnosti kak inostrannoi, tak i otechestvennoi," in Pushkin, *Sobranie sochinenii*, 6:120–28.

31. Ibid., 6:124.

32. D.S. Merezhkovskii, "M.Iu. Lermontov. Poet sverkhchelovechestva" (1909), in his *Polnoe sobranie sochinenii*, 17 vols. (St. Petersburg and Moscow: Izdanie T-va M.O. Vol'f, 1911–13), 10:287–334(312). Although Merezhkovsky was anxious to redeem Lermontov from Vladimir Solov'ev's severe condemnation (on moral grounds) of 1899, he admitted that "v Demone byl eshche ostatok d'iavola" (329). His essay was first published in 1909 in *Vesy* and *Russkaia mysl'*. In his (highly debatable) view, Pushkin, unlike Lermontov, was content with a purely aesthetic resolution of the problem of evil.

33. V.S. Solov'ev, "Lermontov" (1899), in *Sobranie sochinenii Vladimira Sergeevicha Solov'eva*, ed. S.M. Solov'ev and E.L. Radlov, 2d ed., 10 vols. (St. Petersburg: Prosveshchenie, [1911–13]), 9:348–67(362).

34. See in this volume Simon Franklin, "Nostalgia for Hell: Russian Literary Demonism and Orthodox Tradition," 35.

35. Pasternak's letter of 22 August 1958 to his American translator, Eugene Kayden, in Boris Pasternak, *Poems*, trans. Eugene M. Kayden (Ann Arbor: University of Michigan Press, 1959), ix, cited in Pasternak's original English from Henry Gifford, *Pasternak: A Critical Study* (Cambridge: Cambridge University Press, 1977), 49.

36. This attitude is expressed in many of Lermontov's lyrics. See, for example, "Poet" (1838), "Zhurnalist, Chitatel' i Pisatel'" (1840), "Prorok" (1841), in Lermontov, *Polnoe sobranie stikhotvorenii*, 2:27–29, 43–48, 85–86, respectively.

37. Ibid., 1:222 (text), 595 (variants), 658 (note).

38. See, for example, Blok's essay "Pamiati Vrubelia" (1910), in Blok, *Sobranie sochinenii*, 5:423–24.

39. See the detailed record of Blok's notes on his edition of Lermontov, in K.P. Lukirskaia, ed., *Biblioteka A.A. Bloka. Opisanie*, comp. O.V. Miller, N.A. Kolobova, and S.Ia. Vovina, 3 vols. (Leningrad: Biblioteka Akademii nauk SSSR, 1984–86), 2:49 (notes relating to p.284 of Blok's edition of Lermontov).

40. Letter to S.N. Karamzina of 10 May [1841], in M.Iu. Lermontov, *Sobranie sochinenii*, ed. I.L. Andronikov, 4 vols. (Moscow: Khudozhestvennaia literatura, 1975–76), 4:461.

41. Lermontov, *Polnoe sobranie stikhotvorenii*, 1:76.

42. Ibid., 2:32–33. For a discussion of this poem's use of several distinct voices see Efim Etkind, "Poeticheskaia lichnost' Lermontova ('Dialektika dushi' v lirike)," in Efim Etkind, ed., *Mikhail Lermontov. 1814–1989*, Norwich Symposia on Russian Literature and Culture, no.3 (Northfield, Vt.: The Russian School of Norwich University, 1992), 11–38(28–33).

43. This line is slightly adapted from Lermontov's "Posviashchenie" (1838) to the sixth version of *Demon*, in which he refers to his work as "bol'noi dushi tiazhelyi bred" (Lermontov, *Polnoe sobranie stikhotvorenii*, 2:590). This link is evidence of the intimate connection between Lermontov's own reflections on the creative impulse and the indirect treatment of this theme in *Demon*.

44. Lermontov, *Polnoe sobranie stikhotvorenii*, 1:88. The poem was not published until 1859.

45. Lukirskaia, ed., *Biblioteka A.A. Bloka*, 2:46 (notes relating to pp.69–70 of Blok's edition of Lermontov).

46. Lermontov, *Polnoe sobranie stikhotvorenii*, 1:184.

47. Lukirskaia, ed., *Biblioteka A.A. Bloka*, 2:49–50 (notes relating to pp.299–300 of Blok's edition of Lermontov).

48. For the text of the different versions of *Demon* see Lermontov, *Polnoe sobranie stikhotvorenii*, 2:436–68 (eighth version of 1839), 533–92 (first six versions of 1829–38). References to the final version are given from this edition in the text and notes by part and stanza numbers, followed by the line number within the work as a whole.

49. In this respect the link between Tamara and the muse develops the parallel association in Pushkin's *Evgenii Onegin* between Tat'iana and the muse, also both threatened by the figure of the demon.

50. The phrase "beglets Edema" is used of the Demon in the first three and in the fifth versions of the poem; in the final version it is replaced by the broader "izgnannik raia" (1:3.32). In the fourth version, the fact that the Demon is unlikely to regain his lost paradise is given special prominence ("Ne voskresiv dushevnoi chistoty, / Ty ne naidesh' poteriannyi svoi rai!"). See Lermontov, *Polnoe sobranie stikhotvorenii*, 2:535, 536, 547, 558, 560.

51. "Nemoi dushi ego pustyniu / Napolnil blagodatnyi zvuk – / I vnov' postignul on sviatyniu / Liubvi, dobra i krasoty!.." (1:9.165–68). "Menia dobru i nebesam / Ty vozvratit' mogla by slovom. / Tvoei liubvi sviatym pokrovom / Odetyi, ia predstal by tam, / Kak novyi angel v bleske novom" (2:10.609–13). A similar plea was expressed by Lermontov: in his "Posviashchenie" of 1831 to the third version of *Demon* he compares himself to his Demon, seeking spiritual regeneration through his "madonna," to whom he offers his poem as a gift (Lermontov, *Polnoe sobranie stikhotvorenii*, 2:545–46).

52. This image was later identified with Sophia by the symbolists who regarded love and poetry as a means of bringing about the realization of Sophia in this world. In his late essay of 1947 on Lermontov (first published in Italian in 1958), Viacheslav Ivanov quoted the last four lines of the passage cited alongside biblical verses on Wisdom (Prov. 8:22–23, 27–28) as an example of Lermontov's nascent intuition of Sophia. See Ivanov, "Lermontov," in Viacheslav Ivanov, *Sobranie sochinenii*, ed. D.V. Ivanov and O. Deschartes, 4 vols. (Brussels: Foyer Oriental Chrétien, 1971–87), 4:364–65 (Italian original), 380–81 (Russian translation).

53. When the Demon first speaks to Tamara, the magic of his voice is stressed ("volshebnyi golos," 1:15.311) and later echoed by the "magic word" at which the created world falls silent ("volshebnoe slovo," 1:15.347), thus reinforcing the link between the Demon-artist and the Creator of the universe. It is specifically the lingering sounds of the Demon's words ("Slova umolkli v otdalen'e, / Vosled za zvukom umer zvuk," 1:16.363–64) and his voice ("etot golos chudno-novyi," 1:16.372) which penetrate and poison Tamara's dreams.

54. For example, when the narrator testifies to the beauty of Tamara, he repeats the word "klianus'" twice (1:7.131, 144). Later the Demon takes over this device and amplifies it, using the same word ten times in the opening part of his third and longest monologue to Tamara (2:10.773–92). The narrator's apparently "objective" vow is thereby subsumed into the Demon's rhetoric of seduction.

55. Repetitions are particularly abundant in the central scene of seduction (2:10). The Demon's first monologue opens with a series of majestic self-definitions "Ia tot ..." (2:10.593–603). His third monologue moves from ten vows ("klianus'") to four expressions of the wish for love and faith ("khochu"), and then continues with a series of future perfective verbs and imperatives, starting with "voz'mu" (2:10.814) and ending with "dam" (2:10.871).

56. "Znakomaia, sredi *molen'ia*, / Ei chasto slyshalasia *rech'*" (2:2.424–25; emphasis mine).

57. "Sviatym zakhochet li molit'sia – / A serdtse molitsia *emu*" (2:6.499–500).

58. "Ostav' menia, o dukh lukavyi! / *Molchi*, ne veriu ia vragu... / *Tvorets* ... Uvy! ia ne mogu / *Molit'sia* ... gibel'noi otravoi / Moi um slabeiushchii ob"iat! / Poslushai, ty menia pogubish'; / Tvoi *slova* – ogon' i iad..." (2:10.631–37; emphasis mine).

59. The climactic scene of seduction opens with Tamara's words to the Demon; she specifically identifies his dangerous attractiveness with his use of language ("O! kto ty? Rech' tvoia opasna!," 2:10.589); in her last speech before her death she reiter-

ates her fear of his powers of speech ("No esli rech' tvoi lukava," 2:10.754). In the second version of *Demon* (1830) Tamara's words before her death (addressed to the Demon although spoken in the presence of the confessor) make it plain that it was the Demon's sweet speech which brought a curse upon them and caused their joint spiritual downfall: "Svoimi sladkimi rechami ... / Ty ... bednuiu ... zavorozhil... / Ty byl liubim i ne liubil, / Ty b mog spastis', a pogubil... / Prokliat'e sverkhu, mrak pod nami!"). See Lermontov, *Polnoe sobranie stikhotvorenii,* 2:544.

60. The word used by Lermontov, "mol'ba," translated here as "entreaty," comes from the same root as "molitva" and is closely associated with the concept of prayer. For Christian sources on demonic interference in prayer, assimilated into the Russian tradition through translation, see the *Philokalia,* a collection of ascetic and mystical writings dating from the fourth to the fifteenth centuries, compiled by two Greek monks in the eighteenth century, first published in Greek in 1782, in a Slavonic translation in 1793, and in Russian in several editions from 1877 (under the title *Dobrotoliubie*). The texts on prayer ascribed to Saint Nilus of Syria (now recognized as the work of Evagrius) offer many cautionary insights on this theme: "The demon is greatly envious of a man who prays, and uses many wiles to disturb his intention; so he does not cease to provoke, through memory, thoughts of various things, while through the body he sets all the passions in movement; his one aim is somehow to spoil the excellence of the man's progress and his ascent (by attention) to God;" "If you strive after prayer, prepare yourself for diabolical suggestions and bear patiently their onslaughts; for they will attack you like wild beasts and will riddle your body with wounds." See the abridged English translation of *Dobrotoliubie: Early Fathers from the Philokalia,* selected and trans. E. Kadloubovsky and G.E.H. Palmer (London: Faber and Faber, 1954), 133, 138. On Blok's discovery in 1916 of the demons of *Dobrotoliubie,* see below.

61. Lermontov, *Polnoe sobranie stikhotvorenii,* 1:96 (I have reinstated the original capitals for terms relating to God). First published in 1859.

62. See in this volume Davidson, "Divine Service or Idol Worship?"

63. Lukirskaia, ed., *Biblioteka A.A. Bloka,* 2:46 (notes relating to p.78 of Blok's edition of Lermontov).

64. Pasternak dedicated his collection *Sestra moia – zhizn'* (written in the summer of 1917, first published in 1922) to Lermontov and opened it with "Pamiati demona," from which I have quoted the closing line. Boris Pasternak, *Stikhotvoreniia i poemy,* ed. L.A. Ozerov, Biblioteka poeta, Bol'shaia seriia (Moscow and Leningrad: Sovetskii pisatel', 1965), 110–11(111).

65. For a thoughtful study of Blok's reception of Lermontov, see the chapter "Lermontov i Blok (K postanovke voprosa)," in D.E Maksimov, *Poeziia Lermontova* (Moscow and Leningrad: Nauka, 1964), 247–65. Useful sources include the detailed record of Blok's notes on his copies of Lermontov's works in Lukirskaia, ed., *Biblioteka A.A. Bloka,* 2:44–69, and two related articles, O. Miller, "Pomety Aleksandra Bloka na Polnom sobranii sochinenii M.Iu. Lermontova," in *V mire Bloka: Sbornik statei* (Moscow: Sovetskii pisatel', 1981), 503–516, and O.V. Miller, "Pomety Bloka na knigakh po istorii russkoi literatury XIX v.," *Literaturnoe nasledstvo,* vol. 92, *Aleksandr Blok. Novye materialy i issledovaniia* (Moscow: Nauka, 1987), 4:57–74 (68–71 on Lermontov).

66. Lukirskaia, ed., *Biblioteka A.A. Bloka,* 2:46 (noted opposite "Russkaia melodiia").

67. "Pamiati Vrubelia" was a reworked version of the speech which Blok read at the funeral on 3 April 1910. The text was published in the same year and is reprinted in Blok, *Sobranie sochinenii,* 5:421–26 (references to this edition will hereafter be given in the text and notes by volume and page number). For the draft text of the original speech, see 5:689–91.

68. Blok's image of the muffled wind may be related to Lermontov's description in "Moi demon" (1829) of the Demon sitting enthroned "sred' vetrov one-mevshikh," particularly as this phrase was underlined by him in the first volume (printed in March 1910) of his edition of Lermontov: *Polnoe sobranie sochinenii M.Iu. Lermontova*, ed. D.I. Abramovich, Akademicheskaia Biblioteka Russkikh Pisatelei, no.2, 5 vols. (St. Petersburg: Izdanie Razriada iziashchnoi slovesnosti Imperatorskoi Akademii nauk, 1910–13), 1:69. See Lukirskaia, ed., *Biblioteka A.A. Bloka*, 2:46.

69. This view is encapsulated in an entry of 26 February 1905 in the diary of Blok's friend, Evgenii Ivanov: "Tragediia bibleiskogo tsaria Saula, lishennogo Dukha, tragediia poeta, pisatelia, lishennogo svoego dara, potomu chto tak nadobno, i tragediia Demona – vse odno." "Vospominaniia i zapisi Evgeniia Ivanova ob Aleksandre Bloke," ed. E.P. Gomberg and D.E. Maksimov, in *Blokovskii sbornik* (Tartu: Tartuskii gosudarstvennyi universitet, 1964), 392.

70. 5:424, quoted from Lermontov's poem "Angel" (1831), discussed above.

71. "Inykh sredstv, krome iskusstva, my poka ne imeem" (5:424).

72. 5:66–82. The essay was first published in *Zolotoe runo*, 1906, no.11–12, the issue immediately preceding the issue of January 1907, devoted to a competition on the devil for which Blok was one of the literary judges (see n.8 above).

73. 5:76. On demons and the poetics of transfiguration, see in this volume Franklin, "Nostalgia for Hell."

74. In "Bezvremen'e" Blok only hints at this interpretation of Lermontov's death (5:77). In "O sovremennom sostoianii russkogo simvolizma" (1910) he explicitly interprets the deaths of Lermontov, Gogol, Vrubel, and Kommissarzhevskaia in this light (5:434). In "Pamiati Vrubelia" (1910) he attaches the same significance to Vrubel's death (5:424).

75. For a striking poetic treatment of this theme, see Bely's poem "Demon" (March 1908), in Andrei Belyi, *Sobranie sochinenii. Stikhotvoreniia i poemy*, ed. V.M. Piskunov (Moscow: Respublika, 1994), 251–52, and the related passage on the poet staring at his reflection in a mirror in Andrei Belyi, *Mezhdu dvukh revoliutsii*, ed. A.V. Lavrov (Moscow: Khudozhestvennaia literatura, 1990), 287.

76. 5:130–59. This essay is closely related to Blok's poem of the previous year, "Ty byl osypan zvezdnym tsvetom…" (19 March 1906; 2:100), in which he addressed the young German poet, Johannes von Guenther, as an "angel padshii," associated with deception, betrayal, and doubles. This was the first projection of the figure of the Demon onto the image of the poet in Blok's verse. For Guenther's understanding of this poem as an invitation for him to join Blok in the host of Lucifer, see "Iogannes fon Giunter i ego 'vospominaniia'," ed. and trans. K.M. Azadovskii, in *Literaturnoe nasledstvo*, vol.92, *Aleksandr Blok. Novye materialy i issledovaniia*, 5 vols. (Moscow: Nauka, 1980–93), 5:330–61 (335–36, 342). Azadovsky notes that Guenther later transferred Blok's poetic portrait of him as a Luciferian figure to his own characterization of Blok.

77. 5:425–36. A similar perspective also informs "Pamiati Vrubelia" (1910).

78. On Blok's reception of Nietzsche, filtered through Ivanov, see V.M. Papernyi, "Blok i Nitssche," *Uchenye zapiski Tartuskogo gosudarstvennogo universiteta* 491 (1979):84–106. On the significance of the Apollo-Dionysus polarity for the view of art as demonic, see in this volume Davidson, "Divine Service or Idol Worship?"

79. In a letter of 31 January 1906 to Pertsov Blok interprets M. Tchaikovsky's libretto for *Pikovaia dama* in terms of a transformation into their opposites of the two sources of Petersburg culture: Pushkin, linked with Apollo, and Lermontov, linked with the abyss (8:150). In "Pedant o poete" (1906), a scathing review of N. Kotliarevsky's study of Lermontov, Blok stresses Lermontov's role as the

main source for the revitalization of contemporary literature and links his role in this respect to that of Tiutchev, "samaia 'nochnaia' dusha russkoi poezii" (5:25), who was able to pick up and echo Lermontov's message of inner mystery and chaos.

80. Blok uses this phrase in an intriguing poem on the links between art and life, "Oni chitaiut stikhi" (10 January 1907), 2:245. For a study of the relationship between Blok's love poetry and his rejection of fundamental assumptions about the powers of language, see Gerald Pirog, "The Language of Love and the Limits of Language," in *Aleksandr Blok Centennial Conference*, ed. Walter N. Vickery with Bogdan B. Sagatov (Columbus: Slavica, 1984), 225–36.

81. "Demon" (1916) precedes the last poem of the cycle "Golos iz khora" (1910–14). The final arrangement of poems within the cycle was not fixed until the second and third editions of Blok's *Stikhotvoreniia. Kniga tret'ia* appeared in 1916 and 1921. For further discussion of "K Muze" and the two "Demon" poems see in this volume, Avril Pyman, "The Demon. The Mythopoetic World Model in the Art of Lermontov, Vrubel, Blok."

82. A similar contrast could be drawn between the same essay and the unrelieved pessimism of the poem which follows "Demon," "Kak tiazhelo khodit' sredi liudei…" (1910, 3:27).

83. Ivanov's talk was given on 26 March 1910 and published in essay form as "Zavety simvolizma" in *Apollon*, 1910, no.8 (May-June):5–20 (first pagination); reprinted in Ivanov, *Sobranie sochinenii*, 2:589–603. Blok's response was delivered as a talk on 8 April 1910; the resulting essay was published in the same issue of *Apollon*, 21–30 (first pagination); reprinted in 5:425–36. In his essay Ivanov elaborated a dialectic scheme which incorporated a brief genealogy of the development of Russian literature and included reference to the places of Lermontov and Blok within this dialectic. Blok took up the structure of Ivanov's argument and illustrated it with examples of his own verse (thereby earning himself the ironic epithet of Ivanov's Baedeker; see Valerii Briusov's rejoinder, "O 'rechi rabskoi,' v zashchitu poezii," *Apollon*, 1910, no.9 (July–August):31–34 (first pagination).

84. Entry of 26 March 1910, in Aleksandr Blok, *Zapisnye knizhki*, ed. V.N. Orlov, A.A. Surkov, and K.I. Chukovskii (Moscow: Khudozhestvennaia literatura, 1965), 169.

85. 5:436. The lines from Lermontov's *Demon* (1:13.284–87) are slightly misquoted by Blok.

86. The poem was written eleven days after Blok gave the talk on which his essay was based; it was first published in *Russkaia mysl'*, 1910, no.11, and later included in the "Strashnyi mir" cycle alongside "K Muze" and "Demon" (1916). For the text, early drafts, and Blok's own note on the link between the demons of Lermontov and Vrubel reflected in the poem, see 3:26, 504–6. See also the recent edition: A.A. Blok, *Polnoe sobranie sochinenii i pisem v dvadtsati tomakh* (Moscow: Nauka, 1997–), 3:215–16 (variants), 598–99 (notes).

87. This connection was discussed in the section above on Lermontov's *Demon*.

88. The poem was evidently composed over a period of a few months at the end of 1912; although published versions carry the date of 29 December 1912, the manuscript is dated "Autumn – 29.xii.1912." It was first published in *Russkaia mysl'*, 1913, no.11, and included in the second edition of *Stikhotvoreniia. Kniga tret'ia* (1916). For the text and variants, see 3:7–8, 501. See also the recent edition: Blok, *Polnoe sobranie sochinenii i pisem*, 3:201 (variants), 585–86 (notes).

89. The word *gibel'* plays a key role in the two essays of 1910 ("Pamiati Vrubelia" and "O sovremennom sostoianii russkogo simvolizma") and is taken up twice in the poem; it is introduced in the second line as a fundamental characteristic of the Muse ("Rokovaia o gibeli vest'") and recurs in its verbal form in connection

with the suggestion of the poet's death in the fifth verse ("Ne pogib ia, no lik tvoi zametil").

90. "O sovremennom sostoianii russkogo simvolizma," 5:430. For the text of "Neznakomka" (24 April 1906), see 2:185–86.

91. See versions 3 (1831) and 5 (1833–34) of *Demon* in Lermontov, *Polnoe sobranie stikhotvorenii*, 2:553–54, 564–66. See also the edition owned by Blok: *Polnoe sobranie sochinenii M.Iu. Lermontova*, ed. Abramovich, 2:406–8 (it includes the full text of version 5, identified as version 4).

92. It is possible that Blok's reference in verse 6 to the muse's gift of a "lug s tsvetami" is a deliberate echo of the "tsvetushchii lug," mentioned in Pushkin's "Razgovor knigoprodavtsa s poetom," and serves to mark his relation to and yet distance from Pushkin's treatment of the muse and the demon. In Pushkin's poem, the image of the flowering meadow is associated with the poet's early encounters with the muse of pure inspiration and followed three lines later by the description of the benign demon of inspiration, quoted above. In Blok's poem, the same flowering meadow (the promise of beauty and pure inspiration) becomes the gift by which the muse seduces the poet and condemns him to the curse of beauty, associated with a destructive demon.

93. This painting, originally from the F. Shekhtel collection in Moscow, is now held in the M. Umnova collection in Moscow and is seldom reproduced. It was shown at exhibitions in Moscow in 1902–1903, 1916, and later. For further details, see Mikhail Guerman, *Mikhail Vrubel. Paintings. Graphic Works. Sculptures. Book Illustrations. Decorative Works. Theatrical Designs*, catalogue compiled by Alla Gaiduk and others, trans. John Greenfield and Valery Dereviaghin (Leningrad: Aurora Art Publishers, 1985), 236 (catalogue no.111).

94. This effect was noted by the poet Naum Korzhavin, who wrote of his failure for many years to grasp the full import of the warning against art expressed in the poem: "Zhivuchest' ego korenitsia v ego dvoistvennosti. V tom, chto … govorit ono odno, a poet drugoe, priamo protivopolozhnoe." N. Korzhavin, "Igra s d'iavolom (Po povodu stikhotvoreniia Aleksandra Bloka 'K Muze')," *Grani* 95 (1975):76–107(104). I would, however, dispute Korzhavin's view that the poem contains "two" contradictory messages; it conveys a single message, concerning the paradoxical properties of art, which combines spiritual danger with magnetic attraction.

95. These lines recall Tamara's question to the demon at the beginning of the climactic scene of seduction: "O! kto ty? Rech' tvoia opasna! / Tebia poslal mne ad il' rai?" (2:10.589–90). This echo reinforces the implied association in "K Muze" between Tamara and the poet's soul, seduced by a Demon-like Muse. In "Demon" (1916) this pattern of symbolic association is developed further; the poet's pure soul is once more linked with Tamara, while his artistic impulse is represented by the Demon (no longer disguised as Muse).

96. The link between Blok's poem and the passage from Dostoevsky has been pointed out by several commentators. See, for example, V. Zhirmunskii, *Poeziia Aleksandra Bloka* (Petersburg: Kartonnyi Domik, 1922), 28–29 (reprinted as a separate offprint from the collection of articles *Ob Aleksandre Bloke*, Petersburg: Kartonnyi Domik, 1921).

97. F.M. Dostoevskii, *Polnoe sobranie sochinenii v tridstati tomakh*, ed. V.G. Bazanov and others, 30 vols. (Leningrad: Nauka, 1972–90), 14:100. The passage occurs in Dimitrii's first confession to Alesha (part 1, book 3, chap. 3) and is cited here in translation from Fyodor Dostoyevsky, *The Brothers Karamazov*, trans. David Magarshack (Harmondsworth: Penguin Books, 1972), 1:123–24.

98. The key words of Dostoevsky's passage, "krasota," "strashnaia," "serdtse," and "um," are all taken up and directly echoed in Blok's poem; see, for example,

Blok's phrase "bezumnaia serdtsu uslada." The dialogue with Dostoevsky runs throughout the poem and is highlighted by numerous other textual echoes (see, for example, Dimitrii Karamazov's words, "popiranie vsiakoi sviatyni, nasmeshka i bezverie," in Dostoevskii, *Polnoe sobranie sochinenii*, 14:417). Dostoevsky's view of beauty as terrible is also alluded to by Blok in the opening line of a slightly later poem, "'Krasota strashna' – Vam skazhut ..." ("Anne Akhmatovoi," 16 December 1913, 3:143). A discarded variant of the first line, "Krugom tverdiat: 'Vy – demon, Vy – krasivy'" (3:550), makes more explicit the association of the Muse and beauty with the demon, a link which is already suggested in "K Muze" and subsequently developed more fully in "Demon" (1916).

99. Ivanov, *Sobranie sochinenii*, 4:417. For the original Russian essay of 1911, see "Dostoevskii i roman-tragediia," *Russkaia mysl'*, 1911, no.5:46–61 (second pagination) and no.6:1–17 (second pagination). Blok's poem "K Muze" (as previously his "Demon" of 1910) was later published in the same journal. The extract from Ivanov makes a similar distinction between the heart and the mind as the passage quoted from *The Brothers Karamazov*, echoed in "K Muze."

100. Ivanov, *Sobranie sochinenii*, 1:828–29. The link between the Dionysian principle and Dostoevsky was also drawn by Ivanov in "Drevnii uzhas" (1909), which dwells on the need to revive the principle of ancient Dionysian terror in art and to reconcile it with Dostoevsky's promise that beauty will save the world (Ibid., 3:97–98). On Ivanov's related theory of demonology, see Tomas Venclova, "K demonologii russkogo simvolizma," in *Christianity and the Eastern Slavs*, vol. 3, *Russian Literature in Modern Times*, ed. Boris Gasparov and others, California Slavic Studies, no.18 (Berkeley: University of California Press, 1995), 134–60, and Andrzej Dudek, "Demonologia Wiaczesława Iwanowa," in *Wizja człowieka i świata w myśli rosyskiej*, ed. Lucjan Suchanek (Krakow: Wydawnictwo Uniwersytetu Jagiellońskiego, 1998), 87–106 (article in Polish) and 181–84 (summary in Russian).

101. 3:501. The "lik" is that of the Muse, first mentioned in verse five. This quatrain, subsequently deleted, contains the kernel later developed in Blok's "Demon" (1916).

102. In this sense "K Muze" can be linked to an earlier poem of the same year, "Viacheslavu Ivanovu" (18 April 1912, 3:141–42), in which Blok signals his parting of the ways "na pyl'nom perekrestke" with Ivanov, described as a "tsar' samoderzhavnyi." Significantly, Blok uses lines in this poem which echo Lermontov's "Moi demon," thereby drawing an implicit comparison between Ivanov's role in his artistic life and that of the demon in the life of the pure muse. Compare Blok's "I ia, dichivshiisia dosele / Ochei pronzitel'nykh tvoikh" with Lermontov's "I muza krotkikh vdokhnovenii / Strashitsia nezemnykh ochei" (lines sidelined by Blok in his edition of Lermontov; see Lukirskaia, ed., *Biblioteka A.A. Bloka*, 2:46).

103. Both poems take the form of an address to a female seductress (Beauty or the muse), and use images of erotic love and intoxicating wine to convey her dangerous power. Compare "K Muze" with the opening quatrain of Baudelaire's poem: "Viens-tu du ciel profond ou sors-tu de l'abîme, / O Beauté? Ton regard, infernal et divin, / Verse confusément le bienfait et le crime, / Et l'on peut pour cela te comparer au vin." Also see the lines "Sors-tu du gouffre noir ou descends-tu des astres?", "Que tu viennes du ciel ou de l'enfer, qu'importe," "De Satan ou de Dieu, qu'importe? Ange ou Sirène," in Charles Baudelaire, *Les Fleurs du Mal*, ed. Enid Starkie (Oxford: Basil Blackwell, 1966), 21–22. Baudelaire's poem was included in the second edition of *Les Fleurs du Mal* (1861); on Russian responses to this collection, as well as translations from it (dating from 1869), see Adrian Wanner, *Baudelaire in Russia* (Gainesville, Fla.: University Press of Florida, 1996).

104. Blok's diary entry is dated 11 October 1912. "K Muze" was begun in the autumn of 1912 and finished on 29 December 1912. The link between the poem and the diary extract has been pointed out by Avril Pyman in the excellent notes to Alexander Blok, *Selected Poems*, ed. Avril Pyman (Oxford: Pergamon Press, 1972), 234.

105. Blok's use of the words "mir" and "strashnyi" in this passage casts interesting light on the title of the cycle "Strashnyi mir," in which the poems under discussion appeared.

106. For the text, see 3:60–61. The poem was first published in the almanac *Tvorchestvo* (Moscow and Petrograd, 1917), 1:18–19, and included in the third edition of *Stikhotvoreniia. Kniga tret'ia* (1921). Although the published text is dated 9 June 1916, the manuscript is dated "1916.20.iii (-9.vi)," suggesting that "Demon" (like "K Muze") was composed over a period of about three months (3:515). For further details, see the recent edition: Blok, *Polnoe sobranie sochinenii i pisem*, 3:259–60 (variants), 633 (notes).

107. In both texts the demon's address is constructed in the form of a rising series of cumulative promises, all voiced in the first person future perfective. Blok has even reproduced (in verse 5) Lermontov's thematic shift to a digression on the inadequacy of human passion.

108. Blok's poem can be read as an extension and answer to a question posed but left open in Lermontov's *Demon*: "Siial on tikho, kak zvezda; / Manil i zval on ... no – kuda? ..." (2:2.430–31).

109. Blok, "O lirike" (June–July 1907), 5:131; "Stikhiia i kul'tura" (December 1908), 5:356.

110. In support of this reading, see two poems by Baudelaire, elements of which are combined and closely echoed in Blok's "Demon." In "Élévation" the poet addresses his spirit as it soars through the air ("Par delà le soleil, par delà les éthers, / Par delà les confins des sphères étoilées, / Mon esprit, ... / Tu sillonnes gaiement l'immensité profonde"); in "Le Vin des Amants" a man invites his lover to join him "dans un délire parallèle" on a flight to an imagined paradise ("Comme deux anges ... / Dans le bleu cristal du matin / Suivons le mirage lointain!"). Baudelaire, *Les Fleurs du Mal*, 6–7, 113. "Demon" takes the image of the lovers' intoxicating flight from the second poem, and combines it with the poet's address to this spirit from the first. This reading does not exclude other interpretations; on a biographical level, for example, L.A. Del'mas claimed that Blok's poem was addressed to her. See Blok, *Polnoe sobranie sochinenii i pisem*, 3:633.

111. In *Poema bez geroia* (2:312), in Anna Akhmatova, *Stikhotvoreniia i poemy*, ed. V.M. Zhirmunskii, Biblioteka poeta, Bol'shaia seriia (Leningrad: Sovetskii pisatel', 1976), 364.

112. "Vdokhnovenie uzhasa: O romane Andreia Belogo 'Peterburg'," *Utro Rossii*, 28 May 1916, 5–6; reprinted in Ivanov, *Sobranie sochinenii*, 4:619–29. Blok received a copy of Bely's *Petersburg* on 4 May 1916 and had met with Ivanov in Moscow a few weeks earlier on 5 April (see Blok, *Zapisnye knizhki*, 297, 294).

113. See, for example, Ivanov's use of the phrases "pustota," "polnoe vdokhnovenie uzhasa," "fleita uzhasa," "gubitel'nyi dukh," "demon," and his description of Bely as a "russkii poet metafizicheskogo uzhasa;" Ivanov, *Sobranie sochinenii*, 4:619, 623, 627, 629.

114. N.A. Pavlovich, "Vospominaniia ob Aleksandre Bloka," in *Blokovskii sbornik* (Tartu: Tartuskii gosudarstvennyi universitet, 1964), 495. A similar period of poetic silence affected Viacheslav Ivanov in the 1920s, when he also came to reconsider his view of the relationship between art and religion; after a period of recantation, he eventually returned to poetry. See Pamela Davidson, "Hellenism, Culture and Christianity: The Case of Vyacheslav Ivanov and His

'Palinode' of 1927," in *Russian Literature and the Classics,* ed. Peter I. Barta, David H.J. Larmour, and Paul Allen Miller (Amsterdam: Harwood Academic Publishers, 1996), 83–116.

115. "O Merezhkovskom" (21 March 1920), 6:393–95(393). The essay was not published until after Blok's death.

116. By quoting a few lines from the original work by Lermontov out of context, Blok has succeeded in imparting to them a broader, more universal significance which fits well within his argument. In the original *Boiarin Orsha* (an early work of 1835–36, first published in 1842), the lines quoted by Blok are more limited in reference; they serve as a passing comment on an incidental background detail, the description of the ceiling of the monastery refectory, painted by an "userdnyi inok." See *Boiarin Orsha* (ll.332–35) in Lermontov, *Polnoe sobranie stikhotvorenii,* 2:325; here cited in the form quoted by Blok (6:393). These lines had evidently caught Blok's eye; they were sidelined by him in his edition of Lermontov. See Lukirskaia, ed., *Biblioteka A.A. Bloka,* 2:52.

117. The view of Lermontov as a poet of Sophia was widespread among the symbolists who regularly quoted the fifth stanza of Lermontov's "Kak chasto, pestroiu tolpoiu okruzhen ..." (1840) in support of this approach. The tradition was started by Vladimir Solov'ev who incorporated a reworked version of the key lines from this poem in his autobiographical poem on his visions of Sophia, "Tri svidaniia" (1898). Briusov quoted a line from the same poem by Lermontov as an epigraph to his poem "Mon rêve familier" (1903), and Blok discussed this poem and the Lermontov-Solov'ev-Briusov connection in his 1904 review of Briusov's *Urbi et Orbi* (5:543). The same lines from Lermontov are quoted once more by Blok in his 1906 review "Pedant o poete" (5:29) in order to counter N.A. Kotliarevsky's more pedestrian approach to the poet. For Viacheslav Ivanov's view of Lermontov as the first Russian poet of the Eternal Feminine, see his "Zavety simvolizma" (1910), in Ivanov, *Sobranie sochinenii,* 2:597.

118. Ivanov, "Zavety simvolizma," 4:597.

119. "Vse 'ukhody' i geroizmy – tol'ko zakryvanie glaz, zhelanie 'zabyt'sia' ... krome odnogo puti, na kotorom glaza otkryvaiutsia i kotoryi ia *zabyl* (i on menia). Na dniakh ia podumal o tom, chto stikhi pisat' mne ne nuzhno, potomu chto ia slishkom umeiu eto delat'. Nado eshche izmenit'sia ..., chtoby vnov' poluchit' vozmozhnost' preodolevat' mater'ial." Entry of 25 March 1916, in Blok, *Zapisnye knizhki,* 292–93.

120. Entry of 14 June 1916 in Blok, *Zapisnye knizhki,* 306. On the *Philokalia* see n.60 above.

121. Letter of 16 June 1916, 8:463–64. Blok is referring to his essay of 1910 "O sovremennom sostoianii russkogo simvolizma," in which he discusses the artist's struggle with the demons or doubles of his creative fantasy (5:429–30).

122. *Early Fathers from the Philokalia,* ed. and trans. Kadloubovsky and Palmer, 119.

123. This passage was not included in the English version of the Russian *Dobrotoliubie* cited in the previous note. For an English translation from the original Greek, see *The Philokalia: The Complete Text compiled by St Nikodomus of the Holy Mountain and St Makarios of Corinth,* trans. from the Greek and ed. G.E.H. Palmer, Philip Sherrard, and Kallistos Ware, 4 vols. (London: Faber and Faber, 1979–95), 1:45.

124. For both of Blok's comments, see the record of his notes in his copy of *Dobrotoliubie,* 4th ed., vol.1 (Moscow: Tip. I. Efimova, 1905), in Lukirskaia, ed., *Biblioteka A.A. Bloka,* 1:267–69(269).

125. In a letter of 16 January 1916 to S.N. Tutolmina (8:453–55) Blok wrote of his lack of feeling for human relationships and of the emotional aridity which resulted from his maximalist approach to life, causing him to demand either too much or nothing at all from life, and in either case to receive nothing. A few

months later, on 29 May 1916, he broke off his diary after noting a feeling of total inertia ("apatiia takaia, chto nichego ne khochetsia delat'"); the diary was not resumed until November 1916 (7:250).

126. *Dobrotoliubie* contains numerous instances of monks strengthening their spirit through demonic trials. See, for example, *Early Fathers from the Philokalia*, ed. and trans. Kadloubovsky and Palmer, 101, 138–39. On the same phenomenon in hagiography, see in this volume Franklin, "Nostalgia for Hell."

127. N. Pavlovich recorded in the book that it was given to her by Blok in the winter of 1921 (i.e. 1920–21); Lukirskaia, ed., *Biblioteka A.A. Bloka,* 1:267. She also noted the fact in her memoirs; Pavlovich, "Vospominaniia ob Aleksandre Bloka," 494.

128. The meeting took place on 31 August 1921. Andrei Belyi, "Dnevnikovye zapisy," ed. S.S. Grechishkin and A.V. Lavrov, in *Literaturnoe nasledstvo,* vol.92, *Aleksandr Blok: Novye materialy i issledovaniia,* 5 vols. (Moscow: Nauka, 1980–93), 3:803, 807. Bely erroneously attributes Evagrius's description of the demon of dejection to Antony the Great.

129. Andrei Belyi, "Vospominaniia ob Aleksandre Aleksandroviche Bloke" (1922), in *Aleksandr Blok v vospominaniiakh sovremennikov,* ed. Vl. Orlov, 2 vols. (Moscow: Khudozhestvennaia literatura, 1980), 1:269.

130. This approach was later developed in an unusual article attributed to P. Florensky: "O Bloke," *Vestnik russkogo khristianskogo dvizheniia* 114 (1974):169–92. The author argues that Blok's verse is deeply demonic in that it parodies and undermines the sacred; in support of his view, alongside Blok's poetry (including "K Muze" and "Demon" of 1916) he quotes extracts from *Dobrotoliubie,* suggesting that Blok was himself possessed by various demons (176–77, 183–84). For a discussion of this article and refutation of its attribution to Florensky, see A. Paiman, "Tvorchestvo Aleksandra Bloka v otsenke russkikh religioznykh myslitelei 20–30–kh godov," in *Blokovskii sbornik XII* (Tartu: Izdatel'stvo TOO "ITs-Garant," 1993), 54–70.

131. Harold Bloom, *The Anxiety of Influence: A Theory of Poetry,* second edition (New York and Oxford: Oxford University Press, 1997), 19. Bloom offers an experimental reading of *Paradise Lost* "as an allegory of the dilemma of the modern poet, at his strongest. Satan is that modern poet, while God is his dead but still embarrassingly potent and present ancestor, or rather, ancestral poet. ... Poetry begins with our awareness, not of a Fall, but that *we are falling.* ... When this consciousness of self is raised to an absolute pitch, *then* the poet ... comes to the bottom of the abyss, and by his impact there creates Hell. ... There and then, in this bad, he finds his good; he chooses the heroic, to know damnation and to explore the limits of the possible within it" (20–21). Bloom's model only partly fits the Russian literary tradition, which has not usually made of the state of damnation an absolute value, preferring instead to balance it against the sacred. On Milton's influence on Russian literature, including "Milton's Satan and Lermontov," see Valentin Boss, *Milton and the Rise of Russian Satanism* (Toronto: University of Toronto Press, 1991), 102–18.

Chapter 6

Lermontov's *The Demon*: Identity and Axiology

Robert Reid

When the Demon first sees Tamara he appears to undergo a sudden enlightenment:

> И вновь постигнул он святыню
> Любви, добра и красоты!..
>   (*The Demon*, 1:9.167–68)[1]
>
> [And once more he understood the holiness
> Of love, goodness and beauty!..]

Two of the objects of this experience fall into established philosophical categories – the ethical (goodness) and the aesthetic (beauty). Whether love can be philosophically contextualized in the same way is a moot point and, apart from its obvious role in the plot of *The Demon* (*Demon*, 1839), I am inclined to see it rather as the dynamic or facilitating paraclete of this trinity, producing love-of-beauty (*philokalia*) and love-of-goodness. It is these two thematic areas of the poem – the aesthetic and the ethical – which the present study seeks to explore, and I have used the term *axiology* (literally "the study of value") to characterize them both and to stress the valuational element crucial to each. A discussion of this kind cannot be undertaken without reference to the identity, status, and motives of the chief conduit of these values – the Demon himself. Here, however, an initial and major problem is encountered: who or what *is* the protagonist – what is his ethical and ontological status? Thus discussion of the axiological dimension of the poem is necessarily prefaced by a characterizational one – the nature of the Demon's identity.

Demonic Identity

General Considerations

The question of the hero's identity has always been at the centre of interpretative approaches to *The Demon*.[2] This is partly because the Demon is a double fiction, the fictional embodiment of a pre-existing fictional archetype, or, more generally, the reconfiguration of one of the pre-existing figurative representations of evil. It is equally true that vagueness of identity is explicitly sustained by characterization, the Demon being

> … похож на вечер ясный:
> Ни день, ни ночь, – ни мрак, ни свет!..
> (*The Demon*, 1:16.390–91)

> [… like a clear evening:
> Neither day nor night, neither dark nor light!..]

This equivocal representation of such a culturally significant religio-mythological figure has, as we shall see, profound philosophical and ethical implications. Three principal answers have generally been given to the question of the Demon's identity: 1. the Demon is a supernatural being (this answer subdivides according to the identity of the being);[3] 2. the Demon is a self-portrait of Lermontov; 3. the Demon is an allegorical portrait of post-Decembrist man (this answer presupposes at least part of 2). As well as these quasi-personalistic rationalizations of the protagonist's identity, we should note two more strictly literary-critical approaches to the poem itself, which, owing to the eponymous nature of the work, are effectively answers to the same question of identity: 1. *The Demon* is wrought intertextually out of predecessors by Goethe, Byron, Milton, Vigny, and others; 2. it is an auto-intertext, an example of Lermontov's literary "self-imitation."[4]

The present paper is premised on an acceptance of the relative validity of each of these approaches, but seeks to address that "fuzziness" of definition which has given rise to such a plurality of interpretations in the first place. The demonic persona is so constructed by Lermontov that it can only be resolved by *reductio ad humanum*, a process which constantly conflicts with the indisputably numinous qualities which the Demon possesses. Meanwhile, the numinous dimension of the Demon's identity is safeguarded by a calculated *aporia* or ambiguity: we cannot identify the Demon because we cannot place him in the demonic table of ranks – C.S. Lewis's "lower-archy": is he indeed only a demon, or a fallen archangel, or is he Satan himself?[5] This resistance, in particular, to ordination, to exact location in a meaningful scale of power and moral influence, links *The Demon* to otherwise generically and thematically remote works such as Pushkin's *Mozart and Salieri* (*Motsart i Sal'eri*) – though there are indeed other analogies in that work – and the civil service stories of Gogol, the early Chekhov, and Dostoevsky. In works such as these knowledge of a man's rank is equivalent to knowledge of his identity (Chekhov's "Fat and Thin" [Tolstyi i tonkii] and "The Chameleon" [Khameleon]) and, by corollary, loss of rank, or its appropriation by others, jeopardizes personal identity (Gogol's "The Nose" [Nos]; Dostoevsky's *The Double* [*Dvoinik*]).[6] From a logical point of view *The Demon* may be said to maximize denotation at the expense of connotation: our inability to define what is meant by "Demon" in the poem facilitates a plurality of speculative understandings of the term; these would be considerably reduced had the poet defined it more clearly. There are clear stylistic advantages in Lermontov's approach: for instance, it is the a priori non-definition of the Demon which justifies the rhetorical grandeur of the language which he uses when attempting to identify himself to Tamara (in 2:10). It will be necessary, then, to establish a critical context in which it will be possible to work with this vagueness as a textual reality and on this basis to investigate the philosophical, ideological, and psychological implications of the poem and its protagonist.

As a prelude to what follows I would point out one particular strand of the Demon's genealogy which, though less thematically prominent than his theological or literary ancestry, is crucial to an understanding of the philosophical background to Lermontov's demonism. This pedigree runs from Plato, through Descartes, down to the scientific thought of Laplace and Maxwell in the nineteenth century. The demon first becomes associated with philosophical enquiry with Socrates, the uniqueness of whose demonic familiar lies in the fact that it made itself known as a voice of prohibition whenever the philosopher was about to reach a wrong decision or faulty conclusion.[7] It was therefore, in effect, a personification of the negative principle without which logical and philosophical thought is impossible. Descartes refined this negative inheritance with his *démon malin*, the imaginary being which threatened the validity of the *cogito*.[8] One's thinking proves one's existence (*Cogito ergo sum*: I think, therefore I am) unless some malign entity is deliberately intervening to misrepresent reality or is simply inventing it, causing one to doubt even self-evident truths. Descartes is *par excellence* the philosopher of doubt and thus he was perceived, particularly by thinkers of the anti-rationalist Russian tradition.[9] The Demon's philosophical heritage had thus come to include both negativity and doubt by the time Lermontov had begun to elaborate his theme and both of these qualities were clearly intended by Pushkin when he wrote his identically named poem, "The Demon" (Demon, 1823), the lyric which is generally thought to have introduced the concept in this form both to Russian literature and to Lermontov in particular.

A rather different form of philosophical demon was implied by Laplace in his treatise *Philosophical Essay on Probability* (*Essai philosophique sur les probabilités*), published in 1819, but formulated by him over twenty years earlier. As a heuristic device aimed at showing that stochastic phenomena are merely an illusion created by ignorance of the processes of causation, Laplace envisages "an intelligence which could comprehend all the forces by which nature is animated" and from whose supernatural perspective, therefore, the causative origins of all phenomena would be perfectly plain.[10] For such a being all events, both past and future, would be locked into a single structure related by the principle of sufficient reason and there would be no place, either, for chance or free will. This intelligence is not the deity; rather it is a projection of positivist scientific effort – a vision of the omniscience which the scientific mind might aspire to. That pretending to such knowledge might have evil consequences, or be in itself evil is, of course, the underlying axiom of the dystopian misgivings about human progress which began to emerge in the nineteenth century. Commentators on Laplace, rather than the writer himself, established the now conventional "demon" epithet for his imaginary being (as indeed for a similar fiction of the physicist James Clerk Maxwell capable of following the motion of all atomic particles during a reaction).[11] The philosophical demon, then, in his maturity, lays claim to phenomenal powers of perception and cognition which must presuppose ubiquity and trans-temporality. Such qualities, I would suggest, along with the Socratic and Cartesian heritage of negation and doubt, do indeed characterize the Demon, but only at the prologic stage of the poem, before the romantic drama begins. The Demon's encounter with Tamara leads him away from these demonic characteristics towards their opposites of faith, and voluntary self-disempowerment:

> Я враг небес, я зло природы,
> И, видишь, – я у ног твоих!
>
> . . . .
>
> Я раб твой, – я тебя люблю!
> (*The Demon*, 2:10.602–3,615)

[I am the enemy of heaven, I am nature's evil,
And, look, – I am at your feet!

. . . .

I am your slave, – I love you!]

The discrepancy between the demonic essence, whether understood, as here, philosophically, or in terms of religious tradition, and the whole nature and course of the Demon's relationship with Tamara is productive of rich irony, for a demonic or fallen "reality" always shadows the Demon's romantic fiction of salvation through love. All of these elements – doubting, negativity, supernatural power, and romantic irony – while enriching the ideological content of the theme, contribute to the *aporia* surrounding the Demon's identity.

Fictional Identity

"O! Who are you? Your words are dangerous!" (O! kto ty? Rech' tvoia opasna!, 2:10.589). Though in a quite different way, the hero of *The Demon* is just as problematical as that of *A Hero of Our Time* (*Geroi nashego vremeni*): both confront the reader with the paradox of fictional identity, created in the latter case by the rival demands of multiple narrative, and, in the former, by the ontological status of the hero. On one level the Demon partakes in a problem created, to a greater or lesser extent, by all fictional characters: how is it possible for an avowedly fictional character to evoke real emotions in the reader?[12] In *The Demon* this question is broached, on the reader's behalf by Tamara: "Why should I know your sorrows?" (Zachem mne znat' tvoi pechali?, 2:10.742). On the other hand, it is precisely by means of his emotions that the Demon impinges on Tamara as a real being, so that it may indeed be the case that, whatever else a fictional character lacks in comparison with a real one, it does at least "really" possess those aspects of personality capable of provoking emotional response. This is in effect to adopt towards the Demon, albeit in modified form, Strawson's view of the logical priority of the concept of a person.[13] Personal identity is independent of ontological status and it is possible to discuss the psychological essence of a personality which is either fictitious or mythological or, in the case of the Demon, both. This view presupposes that these real traits in fictional characters are essentially human and, indeed, the effectiveness of Lermontov's Demon resides precisely in the intense and recognizable human emotions which he manifests, while still remaining a demon – something other than human. The anthropomorphism of this portrayal allows human and numinous qualities to exist side by side, the numinous being supernatural mobility, ability to exist both inside and outside the perceiver (Tamara), the possession of super-

human powers etc. These qualities too, however, are, in a Feuer-
bachian sense, essentially maximalizations of human faculties, and
thus, in turn, they facilitate the maximal realization of the Demon's
human attributes: the Demon's supernatural mobility, for instance,
makes him a more effective wooer and also a deadlier threat to his
rival in love than any mortal.[14]

Nonetheless, it is the numinous quality of the Demon which
greatly complicates the question of his identity. As we have already
suggested, information which would allow us to locate the Demon in
a traditional hierarchical context is wanting. Even leaving this aside,
the fictionality of a demonic personality differs from the fictionality
of human personality in that we have real models for the latter
whereas the models for demonic fictional personality are themselves
fictional (unless we can claim first-hand experience of the demonic!),
since mythological. However, as mythological or folkloric "facts"
demons are real, much as other anthropological facts are real, and,
in this sense, one might try to construct Lermontov's Demon less as
fiction than as a *sortal*, an instance, that is, of known demonic archetypes in culture and folklore.[15] However, it is as difficult to define
what *sort* of demon Lermontov has created as to answer the narrower but related question of his status within a hierarchical model.
Moreover the cultural prototypes themselves seem disconnected, if
not mutually contradictory: thus the Socratic-Cartesian theme in *The
Demon* seems to have no point of contact with that of demonic possession which, as an interpretation of Tamara's encounter with the
Demon, would point to a demonic deep structure in folk and religious belief.

On the more orthodox religious level it is true that, while we cannot identify the Demon as an actor in traditional Christian
demonology, Lermontov does offer us an impressionistic prehistory
of his hero which suggests his participation in Lucifer's rebellion,
without defining the precise role. Thus there is at least also a Miltonic premise in the poem, if little else. Beyond this there is no hint
of the Fall of man nor of the incarnation and subsequent redemption.
And whether the "assumption" of Tamara at the end of the work and
the re-confirmation of the Demon's damnation is to be taken as an
event of cosmic proportions or merely the conclusion of two tragic
personal histories again depends on the status of the being who has
sought redemption through the poem's heroine.

Finally, there is a not insignificant linguistic component to the
problem of identity. It is worth pointing out that the absence of an
article in Russian intensifies the question of whether a unique entity
is envisaged or one of many. We are not shown other demons at
work in the poem, nor are we shown the hero's exploits elsewhere

(with other Tamaras, for instance). Furthermore, since the Demon is given every opportunity to introduce himself onomastically, we must treat the Russian word "Demon" as his proper name; indeed, "Demon" has more significance as a proper name than as a descriptor since we are not clear what is being described: "Demon," therefore is a true proper name, having reference but no necessary *sense*.[16] This is not to say that "Demon," by which we mean the name of Lermontov's fictional entity (designated by a capital letter) has no more than a coincidental relationship to "demon" (the term which persists in cultural and linguistic tradition, designated by the lower case). It is simply that "Demon" is indexical: it names *this* representation of the demonic phenomenon, "demon"-for-Lermontov, and to this extent it is resistant to interpretation based upon "demon." Accordingly "Demon" must be understood in the first instance analytically, in terms of what is predicated of it textually in the poem as a whole. This inevitably points to a Formalist or a phenomenological approach to the protagonist of Lermontov's poem.

Phenomenology and Identity

The sort of approach to the Demon outlined above has the merit of directing attention to the Demon as he manifests himself in the poem. It does not mean that reductive critical approaches are not possible or without value. For instance, it has been suggested that the Demon is essentially an emanation of Tamara's troubled psyche,[17] a view which could provide the basis of a feminist reading of the poem. However, this, like most reductive readings, has difficulty integrating all the demonic phenomena in the poem (such as those in which Tamara does not herself participate), nor is it easy to define in psychological terms the precise nature of the experience which Tamara undergoes in connection with the Demon. Since there are unbridgeable contradictions between the Demon as someone's subjective experience, as a spiritual being, and as a force capable of acting physically in the world,[18] there is heuristic merit in simply discounting the question of how, or indeed whether, the Demon exists. The common factor throughout the poem is that he is an *intentional* being, both for Tamara, writer, reader and, not least, himself.[19] In this sense *esse est percipi* (to be is to be perceived); the Demon is a phenomenal presence in the poem.

To bracket the Demon's existence in this way and to forgo the empirical direction of reductive enquiry is not to balk the critical process. The phenomenological processes which are everywhere at work in a poem so dominated by such a protagonist posit their own perceptual laws. Among these are criteria of expectation and coherence. Tamara is confronted not merely by an apparition but a speaking one and so, logically, treats what confronts her as a personality with an identity to be discovered. That the Demon attempts to satisfy her curiosity further consolidates this impression. On the other hand her initial interpretation of her first demonic visitation, made in the hysterical, superstitious aftermath of her bridegroom's death, is somewhat different although perfectly coherent under the circumstances:

> Ты сам заметил: день от дня
> Я вяну, жертва злой отравы!
> Меня терзает дух лукавый
> Неотразимою мечтой;
>
> *(The Demon,* 2:1.401–4)

> [You yourself have noticed it: day in day out
> I fade, victim of an evil poison!
> A cunning spirit is tormenting me
> With an irresistible dream;]

I would suggest, too, that the reader, during the reading process, is willing to suspend judgement on the ontological contradictions thrown up by the Demon because these do not threaten the emotional coherence of a story which has its own compelling consistency. Reader expectation at crucial points in the story is essentially conventional; the horizon of expectation at such moments as the Demon's first sight of Tamara, or his lover's vigil outside her nun's cell, is the same for both Demon and reader: it is not implausible for him (or us) to hope for his redemption in the first case or for reciprocation in the second. Plot, too, underlies another important property of the phenomena described in *The Demon*: whatever the status of the demonic actor they are real events inasmuch as they exhibit properties in time and are consecutive. They are also intimately related to real "empirical" events so that in most cases a phenomenal event shadows a real one: Tamara dances in anticipation of her physical bridegroom but is watched by his spiritual counterpart; the bridegroom dies thinking of his future bride, but he is also inveigled into such thoughts by the Demon; Tamara feels grief for the dead bridegroom but is comforted by his supernatural rival; Tamara's body is buried but her soul is squabbled over by the powers of good and evil. The thematic essentiality of the phenomenal element of the poem is thus underwritten by a plot structure which points to a parallelism between the real and phenomenal worlds. Why should this be? I would suggest that the phenomenal dimension of *The Demon* itself facilitates the incorporation into the poem of ideological themes which are themselves, if not phenomenal, then profoundly abstract in nature and idealistic in their metaphysical foundation. These are the axiological trinity with which the Demon hopes to establish contact through Tamara: "the holiness / Of love, goodness and beauty" (sviatyniu / Liubvi, dobra i krasoty, 1:9.167–68). *The Demon* is thematically dominated by a meditation on this *summum bonum* of Platonic thought and, more pertinently for Lermontov, the German idealist philosophy of Kant, Fichte, and Schelling. The rest of this paper is devoted to a consideration of the paradoxes and implications of Lermontov's treatment of this theme.

Beauty

The aesthetic is thematically prominent in *The Demon.* The author makes beauty a central issue in the poem by 1. lyrically asserting the beauty of the Caucasian landscape; 2. having the Demon reject this beauty;[20] 3. asserting the exceptional beauty of Tamara; 4. having the Demon accept Tamara's beauty; 5. linking Tamara's beauty to the possibility of redemption for the Demon. It can be seen, therefore, that the principal functional areas of the poem's structure are explicitly associated with beauty: characterization, setting, plot and, more narrowly, psychological motivation, poetic language and narrative suspense and reader expectation. Furthermore, the aesthetic in the poem has to be understood in the broad Hellenic sense which had become available to European thought again through the German idealist philosophers, who put a high premium on beauty as a Good as well as through the romantic ideology of the artist more generally.

For Schelling, for instance, the aesthetic was the master sense, art the culmination of philosophy.[21] Kant had argued for the universal validity of aesthetic value.[22] In *The Demon* the aesthetic process is shown as essentially phenomenal, as an act of intentionality by subject upon object. What ensures that *The Demon* is an essentially philosophical poem is the polemical paralleling of intentionalities: the Demon's, the poet's, and the reader's. In the case of the Demon himself the intentional process is, as it were, laid bare. It conforms well to Brentano's threefold model of the intentional process which, presupposing the presence and mutual accessibility of subject and object of perception, begins with the initial act of perception, followed by an effective judgement of the perceived object by the perceiving subject, and culminates in emotional response.[23] The Demon contemplates the Caucasian landscape, judges it to be God's world and despises it. The poet also contemplates the landscape, makes the same judgement, but, we must infer, experiences a different emotional response from the Demon.

However, that there is any real point of intersection between what the Demon perceives and what the poet perceives is a rhetorical illusion. Lermontov's descriptions are themselves the end product of an intentional process between the poet and the Caucasian landscape,

which convey the former's pleasurable aesthetic response and imply
the generalized validity of that response; central therefore to the
poem's aesthetics is that one can have a correct or incorrect emotional response to an aesthetic stimulus. However we ourselves are in
no position to judge the comparative correctness of the Demon's and
the poet's responses, because we perceive only a phenomenal Caucasus and an aestheticized one at that: we cannot get at a real landscape or a real Tamara in order to verify the poet's point of view. The
narrating voice's claims are therefore incorrigible, or, more correctly,
a-corrigible. One of the by-products of this situation is the reinforce-
ment of the Kantian notion of a universally valid aesthetic standard:[24]
indeed in order to read the poem at all we must accept that the Caucasian landscape confronting the Demon is self-evidently beautiful
and that he is wrong to reject this truth. At the same time this self-evi-
dence is undermined by the rhetorical effort which is put into the natural description and that of Tamara: there is indeed a performative
flavour to them and in them the narrative voice of the poem comes
closest to asserting its own personal presence:

> Клянусь полночною звездой,
> Лучом заката и востока,
> Властитель Персии златой
> И ни единый царь земной
> Не целовал такого ока;
>   (*The Demon*, 1:7.131–35)

> [I swear by the midnight star,
> The rays of dawn and sunset,
> The Lord of golden Persia
> Nor any earthly king
> Has ever kissed such an eye;]

It is the performance itself which creates the aesthetic, not the aesthetic which creates the performance.[25]

Despite the conceptual deep structure of the poem's aesthetic
polemic, it is one which can only be conducted *ad hominem* (or *ad
daemonem*); for the intentional processes which give rise to differing
aesthetic responses are by definition deictic, referring as they do to
this subject's response and the correctness or otherwise thereof. The
aesthetic polemic in *The Demon* is not merely a by-product of the
plot; plot, or at least the elenctic engagement of fictional voices, is
the only means by which such a polemic can be conveyed.

Failure to acknowledge self-evident beauty is also a major impediment to the Demon's potential spiritual progress; indeed, by corollary,
as long as he remains impervious to it, he locks himself into an endless
cycle of rejection in which he continues to fulfil his demonic role.
While it is not difficult to appreciate why a demon might reject a nat-

ural world which is the product of a Schellingian divine artist,[26] it is
hard to understand why he might make exception for a Georgian
maiden, who though transcendently beautiful, is still nevertheless
wholly a product of that world. One possible explanation requires us
to see beauty almost as a force with varying strengths: weaker applications such as those represented by the nature descriptions in 1:3 and
1:4 can be withstood but that represented by Tamara is irresistible.
Accordingly the poet ironically tempts the tempter incrementally until
he succumbs, and indeed flaunts his conviction that this will happen:

> ... если б Демон, пролетая,
> В то время на нее взглянул,
> То, прежних братий вспоминая,
> Он отвернулся б - и вздохнул...
>   (*The Demon*, 1:8.158–61)

> [... if the Demon, flying by,
> Had glanced upon her then,
> Remembering his lost brethren,
> He would have turned away – and sighed...]

Another more comprehensive explanation is that Tamara prevails
where landscape does not because the phenomenal experience is
qualitatively rather than just quantitatively different. The aesthetic
response is here neither an end in itself nor an expression of the
acceptance of divine power; it is the trigger which sets off a complex
of psychic events, some mnemonic, some intellectual, and some voli-
tional; it is irresistible because it leaves no level of the Demon's psyche untouched, no inner fastness from which to repel it. The poet has
established Tamara as transcendently beautiful; in acquiescing the
Demon proceeds to access two further manifestations of *ton kalon* –
goodness and love. These, like the beauty of landscape, we must take
on trust (indeed we must trust the Demon's judgement in this regard
– a paradox of which we have more to say below) since no characterizational apparatus has been supplied to show that Tamara is the
embodiment either of moral goodness or love. Again this articulates
a very explicit view of the nature of the aesthetic: it is part of the trinity which comprises also goodness and love, but without it these
other two remain inaccessible. Aesthetic response is a precondition
for both morality and love. Awareness of the beautiful stimulates
other positive human responses and impulses, not least moral goodness. Such a position implies the aestheticization of morality and
therefore a philosophy of moral sense[27] which connects moral
response with feeling rather than (as with the Kantians) reason. Perhaps less obviously it also implies the ethicization of the aesthetic: we
are shown no aesthetic response in the poem which is not conditional on the recognition of some non-aesthetic good, whether this

be God's creation or the possibility of reciprocated love. There is no
such thing in *The Demon* as that which is commonly termed aesthetic
distance whereby subjective emotions are restrained in the interests
of balanced critical response; indeed the Demon is shown to have
"got it wrong" the first time precisely because

> ... на челе его высоком
> Не отразилось ничего.
> (*The Demon*, 1:3.58–59)
>
> [... nothing was expressed
> On his lofty brow.]

Finally there is a quite distinct aesthetic dimension in *The Demon*,
one moreover quintessentially romantic, that of the Sublime. This
aesthetic category, Kantian in its mature formulation, but English in
origin, is clearly applicable to the Demon.[28] For Kant, whereas the
aesthetic appeals to our understanding ("And once more he *understood*" [I vnov' *postignul* on, 1:9.167; emphasis mine]), the sublime
defies understanding and can be grasped rationally only by the paradox that it is beyond our comprehension. Two distinct intentionalities in the poem correspond to the aesthetic and the sublime. On the
one hand there is the poet as subject contemplating first the landscape and then Tamara as paragons of earthly beauty; with him, by
way of a fortiori corroboration, is the intentionality of the Demon,
who comes at length to accept the poet's perspective. Ironically this
corroborating subject, the Demon, himself becomes the object of a
rival intentionality, again with two subjects: the poet and Tamara.
Tamara finds the Demon terrifying and fascinating; the poet, though,
as narrative voice, who must mediate all aspects of the Demon's
character and activities, also presents him as a sublime spectacle,
particularly when he reveals his true self after Tamara's death:

> Он был могущ, как вихорь шумный,
> Блистал, как молнии струя,
>
> . . . .
>
> Каким смотрел он злобным взглядом,
> Как полон был смертельным ядом
> Вражды, не знающей конца, –
> (*The Demon*, 2:16.1015–16,1025–27)
>
> [He was powerful like a loud whirlwind,
> He shone like a streak of lightning,
>
> . . . .
>
> His gaze was so malign,
> He was so full of the fatal poison
> Of enmity without end, –]

Sublimity, in the romantic sense, is indeed one of the constants in Lermontov's evolution of the Demon, being present in his earliest adumbration of the figure, and it is just as strongly present in the Pushkinian prototype. The importance of intentionality in the overall aesthetic system is illustrated by the absence in the poem of aesthetic reflexivity or self-consciousness: the principal aesthetic foci in the poem – Tamara, the Demon, the natural landscape – do not function as both subject and object within a single act of aesthetic intentionality. There is no suggestion that they enjoy *themselves* as aesthetic object. Though the Demon can describe, or perform his own sublimity for Tamara, he experiences himself only in terms of boredom and longing. There is no clear evidence that Tamara is aware of herself as an object of aesthetic enjoyment before her encounter with the Demon, after which the plot allows her little scope, amidst her confusion and apprehension, to develop the kind of aesthetic self-awareness of which we are speaking here. Even the narrative voice is not found here either praising poetry directly or suggesting that beauty resides anywhere than in the non-verbal object of contemplation. The aesthetic experience is exclusively synthetic in *The Demon.* It is conditional on the existence of an Other to impact forcefully on the sometimes unwilling subject. It is an aesthetics which conveniently dovetails into the demands of romantic plot and, as we shall see, with its juxtaposition of oppositions, into romantic ethics.

Goodness

Whereas the Demon is but one component in the aesthetic system of the poem, its ethical or moral theme revolves in large measure round the protagonist, his character, actions and status. Crucial to the ethical interest of the work is *akrasia,* the moral paradox generated by the Demon's decision to seek salvation through Tamara's love: how can a demon, by nature evil and drawn to evil, find it in himself to desire what is good? This question also has religious repercussions if the Demon is identified not merely as a moral instance but as a source of evil in himself. Less obvious, however, is that the paradox of the Demon merely reproduces *in negativo* an ethical problem of wholly human relevance which has been debated from Plato onwards: since man is a rational animal who will inevitably be drawn to what is good or beautiful (or truthful, according to the axiological context), how then is it possible (indeed *is* it possible?) for man to choose what is evil? The Socratic solution to this question, later elaborated by the Stoics, was that man is not willingly deprived of the truth and that all evil acts are merely instances of ignorance or error: the perpetrator simply thought that the act was good (however evil it might appear in the light of common sense or collective opinion or hindsight).[29] The Demon would seem to present us with the Socratic problem in reverse. A being by definition evil and drawn to evil is tempted by goodness: the Socratic analogy would require us to conclude that he is drawn to goodness because he mistakes it for evil.

In fact, however, there is no way in which we can meaningfully construct such a consciousness even fictitiously. While it may be possible to speak rhetorically of a being for whom it is, for instance, evil to love and good to hate, this does not dissociate such a being from the basic desiderative categories of the Socratic model. The paradox lies in the fact that, however evil the being, we have to find some way of defining that which draws him to one action and repels him from another and, whether this be defined as desire, aversion, pursuit, or avoidance, it is difficult not to define the criteria for judgement in such actions as those of good and evil.

The Demon falls far short of any attempt to construct a truly evil being. Once an angel himself, and exiled for no stated reason, he is not a whole-hearted malefactor:

> Он сеял зло без наслажденья.
>
> . . . .
>
> И зло наскучило ему.
>   (*The Demon*, 1:2.27,30)
>
> [He sowed evil without enjoyment.
>
> . . . .
>
> And evil bored him.]

Indeed the Demon embodies evil in a traditionally tragic way; it is something which befalls him rather than something which he actively desires. Even the idea of redemption comes to the Demon unbidden and, once grasped, obsesses him like a true tragic passion, obscuring the impossibility of its realization. The Demon's situation, then, remains recognizably human in its tragedy, but the evil dimension introduced by his demonic status is sufficient to raise and problematize a range of recognizable moral situations. We can verify this by reference to the most basic ethical position: the so-called "golden rule." If the Demon were to treat others as he would wish to be treated himself, what would ensue? This problematic relationship between the basic demonic nature of her lover and his ability to truly love her is felt keenly by Tamara. The reader, however, who knows more of the Demon than her, is probably willing to let him pass this basic ethical test: the Demon does at least possess the protasis of the golden rule – he wishes to be treated in a way which is consonant with our notions of human rights and is driven by a desire to recover lost happiness, however foreign the context of this ambition may be to human experience. Thus, the Demon shares with humanity a common ethical frame of reference; the function of his demonic identity is to cast doubt on whether he can ever act within that framework and deliver the apodosis.

The classical notion that the goal of ethics is happiness, rather than, as in the Judaeo-Christian tradition, the service of God, is thematically prominent in *The Demon*. Interestingly, without this pagan ingredient, there would be no plot, for, as long as the Demon carries out his demonic functions in accordance with the divine scheme, there is only endless repetition, which the Demon experiences as boredom. Construed as a search for happiness, the entire plot may be seen as ethically charged, its dynamics determined by the presence or absence of those things which might make the Demon happy. Putting it more systematically we can say that there are four possible modes for the Demon to experience happiness or unhappiness in terms of their source: 1. joy at the presence of the source; 2. sorrow at the absence of the source; 3. joy at the absence of the source; 4. sorrow at the presence of the source.[30] If Good is that which evokes joy at its presence and sorrow at its absence, and Evil is that which evokes joy at its absence and sorrow at its presence we may represent the "ethical plot" of *The Demon* as follows: 1. happiness at the presence of the Good (at one with God); 2. sadness at the absence of this Good (memory of the past) and sadness at the presence of Evil (boredom with exile); 3. happiness at the presence of the Good (Tamara) and happiness at the absence of evil (hope; repentance); 4. sadness at the presence of evil (the re-assertion of his exile) and sadness at the absence of good (Tamara's spirit taken to God).

This schema illustrates very well that good and evil are temporally indexed in *The Demon*: since goodness is the primal and undifferentiated situation, it is marked mnemonically throughout the poem. Evil, by contrast, makes itself known as an event, a *creatum*, the fact that it persists after its emergence, being, at least according to some definitions of "an event," no impediment to its being defined as such.[31] Yet the long event, or state, of the Demon's exile is not entirely inert; objective changelessness is not matched subjectively: recollection of the past perpetuates a counter-model to the status quo; boredom, a cumulative reaction to changelessness, is itself a prelude to change, or at least a condition.[32] The effect of the subjectivization of a time sequence is to change it from what McTaggart called an A-series to a B-series, to transform it, that is, into a hierarchized temporal scheme in which time is modelled according to its relation to a climactic event or *kairos*, in this case the exile of the Demon.[33] A psychology dominated by such a time scheme will be typically romantic: nostalgia for the past combines with a tragic attempt to recover lost innocence.

This temporal model also suggests, though without detail, the post-lapsarian view of the human condition and broaches the philosophical question of ethical naturalism. Interestingly, the poem manages to address simultaneously two mutually contradictory traditions of ethical naturalism: on the one hand there is the Rousseauan and broadly Christian image of a being once good and estranged by sin from its natural state (which raises the corollary possibility of a return to the primal innocence); on the other there is the Hobbesian notion of the natural state as inherently savage and brutish, with society and civilization acting as necessary restraining forces. A demonic or diabolic dimension is easily integrated into the latter view and it is precisely as an antisocial, destructive force that the Demon has functioned in the course of his long exile from heaven. This is how the Demon impacts on Tamara's family and on her future husband, and this is how Tamara herself instinctively conceives him: as a being incapable of adhering to the most basic rules of social conduct – honesty and trust. On the other hand it is by no means the case that the Demon conceives his own nature in such wholly unrelieved terms: from his own perspective he believes in the possibility of reform. Ironically, he is the only such believer in the poem, for, if Tamara wavers, the divine powers are resolute in perpetuating his fallen state.

Although the points so far touched upon are of considerable thematic importance in *The Demon*, it is arguable that the core ethical confrontation in the poem is between voluntarist and consequentialist values as foundations of conduct; this suggests that *The Demon* is, at least in part, concerned with the problems raised by Kantian or Kantian-inspired ethics.

A consequentialist reading of the poem would stress the fact that the hero is goal-orientated. He starts from a position of helpless dissatisfaction with his lot and when he perceives his opportunity for escape and for the restoration of his former status he applies all his ingenuity to achieve this end, not scrupling over the implementation of immoral means. Such conduct has predictable results. The direct means used – Tamara and her bridegroom – both die, and these calamities involve Tamara's family, presumably that of the bridegroom and (we are told) neighbours as well:

> Толпой соседи и родные
> Уж собрались в печальный путь.
> (*The Demon*, 2:15.971–72)

> [In a crowd neighbours and relatives
> Had already gathered for the sad journey.]

Indeed, since Tamara's family and funeral guests are the only community to which we are introduced in the poem, and these may stand microcosmically for that wider human community among which the Demon has for long ages "sown evil" (seial zlo, 1:2.27), we may conclude that his willingness and ability to sacrifice means for ends appears limitless. Albeit in highly figurative form, the teleological fanaticism of the Demon anticipates the excesses of some of the mature Dostoevsky's creations and contributes prematurely to the later nineteenth-century critiques of utilitarianism and social engineering.

It may be argued, however, that the means/end relationship is hopelessly confused by the Demon's amatory interest. If this is the case, love, as well as orientating the Demon towards higher values and providing a conventional plot dynamic, is a relativizing ethical force in *The Demon*. Thus whereas the bridegroom may be held to be a means to an end, Tamara herself is clearly both means *and* end, the traditional role allotted to the beloved by the lover. Under these conditions the lover's motivation becomes all-important and points us towards a voluntaristic reading. According to such a reading the Demon has good intentions in his pursuit of Tamara. He was once a perfectly good being and he sees in Tamara and the possibility of her love a real chance of recovering his former goodness. In his imagination Tamara will rule alongside him as his queen; she is not so much a means to an end as part of that end herself. His hesitation outside her nun's cell is in effect an access of doubt wherein he does indeed for a moment fear that she may be *just* an end, but he is able to overcome this hesitation through the conviction of the genuineness of his love. The Demon's role in the death of the bridegroom is problematical for such a voluntarist interpretation, but it is possible to downplay his culpability in this, reducing it by stressing the bridegroom's insouciance and ritual negligence (in not stopping at a wayside shrine) or even excusing it as a kind of clumsy residue of demonic reflex in the hero, the demonic equivalent of Sobakevichism. What is important is that the Demon's intentions are good; it is not his fault that, in the event, things go terribly wrong: indeed the responsibility here is God's, for he it was who originally imposed on the Demon a baneful form which burns up all with which it comes into contact, and it is he who scoops up the object of the Demon's desire just as the latter is about to possess her.

The voluntaristic motifs in *The Demon* are clearly major guarantors of its tragic effect, just as the consequentialist elements are largely responsible for perpetuating the impression of evil. However if the voluntarist argument is given a Kantian spin, something likely to happen in the case of readers contemporary to Lermontov, important deconstructive features are brought to light. Kantian ethics stressed not merely good will but also obligation, an obligation which obtained even when it ran counter to a subject's wishes or self-interest. The most celebrated Kantian maxim is the categorical imperative which expresses itself across the whole range of ethical action: 1. the subject's relationship to others; 2. the subject's self-definition as a moral being; 3. the nature of obligating utterances (such as promising, swearing etc.).[34] I would argue that, in each of these areas, the demonic status of the subject problematizes or invalidates the efficacy of the ethical position. Thus, if we formulated the incident of the death of the bridegroom in terms of the categorical imperative, we would expect under normal circumstances to find it absolutely condemned: can it be right to arrange the death of one's rival in love? Could such action ever be expanded into a general law? On the other hand, if the Demon is a being divinely charged with the task of human temptation, the rhetorical force of the question is diminished. The Demon is still obedient to the commission given to him by God, both in the case of the bridegroom and in the case of his visitations to Tamara which also take the form of temptations, even if, in the latter case, they have a good intent. So it is with all the other guiding criteria for action: if the Demon is to relate to others in accordance with the demonic relationship established for him by the divine order there will inevitably be tragic consequences; if he attempts to act as a moral being, he is transgressing against the divine order.

The situation is the same with obligating speech acts. Demonic visitors are by tradition mendacious (in accordance with such precedents as the Serpent of Eden and the Mephistopheles of the Faust legend); therefore the normal expectations concerning the veridical status of their utterances cannot apply. However, this locutionary aspect of ethics is particularly complex in *The Demon* and merits closer examination. The Demon's own words play a central role in the plot of the poem; they constitute its complication, as the action leads up to the central question of whether Tamara will accept the Demon's love or not. Even a superficial glance at his direct speech shows that the Demon's words are not necessarily or invariably untruthful: when asked who he is by Tamara he does not lie. It is true that he is

> ... тот, которому внимала
> Ты в полуночной тишине,
> (*The Demon*, 2:10.593–94)
>
> [... the one to whom you listened
> In the midnight silence,]

However this is also the kind of evasive reply which infuriates those who interview the politicians of our time. The Demon is being rhetorically elusive, "a cunning spirit" (dukh lukavyi, 2:1.403) as

Tamara rightly apprehends. The Demon instead characterizes himself grandly, not concealing his demonic credentials, but formulating them in such a way that they will impress his hearer:

> Я тот, чей взор надежду губит;
> Я тот, кого никто не любит,
> Я бич рабов моих земных,
> Я царь познанья и свободы,
> Я враг небес, я зло природы,
> И, видишь, – я у ног твоих!
> *(The Demon,* 2:10.598–603)

> I am he whose glance destroys hope;
> I am he whom none will love,
> I am the chastisement of my earthly slaves,
> I am the king of knowledge and freedom,
> I am the enemy of heaven, I am nature's evil,
> And, look, – I am at your feet!]

We need to add a Cartesian warning: "And it is a demon who is telling you this." This is precisely what is left unsaid: a subtle form of lying. The question of veracity is thrown more clearly into focus when Tamara asks the Demon to swear to her that he will "renounce forthwith" (otrech'sia nyne, 2:10.770) his evil-doings. Tamara herself articulates the problem this raises:

> Ужель ни клятв, ни обещаний
> Ненарушимых больше нет?..
> *(The Demon,* 2:10.771–72)

> [Are there really no more inviolable
> Oaths or promises left?..]

Swearing is a form of reflexive promise. In swearing we assert that what we say is true by exposing ourselves to divine wrath should the case be otherwise. Like promising, it is underpinned by a conditional consisting of a protasis and apodosis, for instance: "if what I say is untrue (protasis), may my soul be damned (apodosis)." However, whereas a promise reaches forward beyond the moment of utterance, the oath refers to the utterance itself. For this reason oaths are less verifiable than promises. A promise is validated when the apodosis "I will do this" (to the protasis "if I say I will do this") is fulfilled. However, the apodosis of an oath cannot be so clearly validated: how are we to *know* whether the oath-taker's soul has been damned (and without this knowledge the oath retains only hypothetical force)? Swearing is therefore basically incorrigible: there is a normative expectation of truth but no reliable supportive criteria of correspondence to confirm it at the moment of utterance. Typically the Demon's complex oath that he has "renounced old vengeance" (otreksia ot staroi mesti, 2:10.793) is both true and untrue: although his actions relating to the bridegroom are in the (albeit recent) past, they bear sharply on the validity of what he is swearing to. The main issue, however, is that in the Demon's case swearing can only amount to a rhetorical emphasis. Tamara is right; as a demon, he is already damned and can swear on what he likes.

For the reader the entire discourse divides itself into constative and performative domains. Into the latter fall such eloquent incidents as the Demon's reaction to earthly beauty, his killing of the bridegroom, his vigil outside the convent; these help to throw the constative discourse, all that is available to Tamara, into true rhetorical relief.

Since the Demon's nature and role in the universe have been created and sustained by the deity, the Demon's actions from first to last can never be autonomous. But, since God enforces evil in the poem's universe, and reasserts this status quo at the end of *The Demon*, the Demon himself can be portrayed as an unwilling perpetrator of evil. There is a marked contrast between reluctant and embraced activity, both mental and physical, in *The Demon* and we are allowed to see the difference between an act carried out (or emotion expressed) unwillingly and one wholeheartedly subscribed to.[35] Thus, there is a qualitative difference between the temptation of the bridegroom and all the other temptations which the Demon has carried out in his long career; there is a difference between the Demon's passionate courtship of Tamara and that carried out from afar by her arranged bridegroom. There is a difference between the Demon's ardent concern for Tamara and the merely dutiful care for her displayed by her guardian angel. None of the divine activities in the poem are particularly impressive or meritorious because they are required actions, God being by nature good; on the other hand, whatever goodness we can detect in the Demon's intentions and actions seems all the more impressive or meritorious because goodness is not required of the Demon – quite the contrary.[36] On the negative side we make a similar comparison between the Demon's relationship to evil and that of God Himself: we may argue of the Demon that his evil-doing is excusable because he is required to do it, or, by corollary, is required not to do good. On the other hand God's insistence on sustaining an agent of evil in the universe is scarcely excusable in a being of whom only goodness is required. The divine perspective suggested by the poem is utterly different from the human. From the human perspective there is a meaningful distinction between the alethic universe, which runs between the extremes of the *necessary* and the *impossible*, and the deontic universe, which runs between the *obligatory* and the *impermissible*. For God, however, the two universes are identical. God reasserts the obligation of the Demon to continue as a fallen being by asserting the impossibility of its being otherwise. The whole drama, in fact, lies in the temporary suspension of these certainties in a moment of the *possible* or, in deontic terms, the *permissible*. However, while we cannot deny the fact that God has established the impossibility of the Demon's reform, we can entertain subversive doubts about its impermissibility. This is because the deontic universe is essentially a human construct and its polar positions are not empirical facts, but simply ethical assents: obstats or fiats.

The Demon has all the instincts of a true believer, perhaps even of a maker of religion. Like Pelagius, he dares to imagine that salvation may be won both with and without God's help. Once this is allowed, however, the latter position supplants the former, as something higher on the spiritual scale of values. *The Demon* is therefore a theomachy (rather than a theodicy), as writers like Zakrzhevsky and Vladimir Solov'ev were right to point out.[37] The Demon is engaged in an eternal, heroic Sisyphean struggle against the God of the poem, a vindictive absentee, who like a Gnostic archon, holds the universe in thrall. Comparisons between the Demon and the Nietzschean superman were also (perhaps inevitably) made by such fin-de-siècle critics; but even this is to rationalize and reduce. The philosophical power of Lermontov's Demon, like those of Descartes and Laplace, lies precisely in the demonic, non-human, elements, whether these are epistemological, ethical or even mathematical.

Nevertheless, it is probably true to say that anthropomorphic interpretations of the poem have in general prevailed in determining its critical reception in the course of the nineteenth century. In this context *A Hero of Our Time* became a crucial intertext through which the demonic *fabula* could be read in more human terms. The demonism of Pechorin was asserted with explicit reference to his demonic predecessor and there is no doubt that the equation between Lermontov's two heroes – the first supernatural, the second human – was an essential stage in the process of secularizing demonism, so that it became available to later writers, Dostoevsky and the symbolists in particular, as a kind of generalized anti-model, capable of multiple fictional incarnations. There are, as we have seen, other anthropomorphic aspects to the Demon which must have spoken directly to the concerns of the nineteenth-century Russian intelligentsia: like his Miltonic predecessor the Demon is a revolutionary and, in his problematic relationship to beauty and rhetoric, also an aesthetically conscious being. None of these things – his rebellion, his aesthetic sense, his verbal facility, indeed his passion – are in themselves problematical; they become so only when a demonic attribution is applied to them. As several contributions to the present volume show, awareness of the complexity of this problem intensifies in the course of the nineteenth century, culminating in the symbolist preoccupation with demonic poesis. If Lermontov's contribution to the development of the demonic tradition in Russian literature is fundamental, this is due in large measure to the unconcretized nature, the "fuzziness" of his demonic creature: it fell to later writers to gradually fuse together Demon, Pechorin, and Lermontov himself, as lyric hero, into the romantic *fons et origo* of the concept.

Notes

1. This and all subsequent quotations from *The Demon* are from the following standard edition: M.Iu. Lermontov, *Polnoe sobranie stikhotvorenii*, ed. E.E. Naidich, Biblioteka poeta, 2 vols. (Leningrad: Sovetskii pisatel', 1989), 2:437–68. References to quotations in the text and notes are by part and stanza numbers, followed by the line number within the poem as a whole. Translations are my own.

2. For a full discussion of this subject see my "Lermontov's *Demon*: A Question of Identity," *The Slavonic and East European Review* 60 (1982):189–210.

3. Among those who consider that Lermontov intended the Demon to be Lucifer himself or, at least, the personified source of evil, are A. Pozov, *Metafizika Lermontova* (Madrid: n.p., 1975), Iu.V. Mann, *Poetika russkogo romantizma* (Moscow: Nauka, 1976), and J. Harvie, "Lermontov's *Demon*," *Journal of the Australasian Universities' Language and Literature Association* 29 (1968):25–32. Nestor Kotliarevskii, *Mikhail Iurevich Lermontov: Lichnost' poeta i ego proizvedeniia* (St. Petersburg: Tipografiia M.M. Stasiulevicha, 1909) and Elena Loginovskaia, *Poema M.Iu Lermontova "Demon"* (Moscow: Khudozhestvennaia literatura, 1977) opt for a definition of the Demon which falls short of definitive Satanic identity.

4. Lermontov's tendency to redraft and reprocess the same or closely related themes is not confined to *The Demon*: *Mtsyri* also has closely related predecessors in *Boiarin Orsha* and *Ispoved'*. A.L. Bem saw self-imitation as a fundamental principle of Lermontov's creativity: A.L. Bem, "Samopovtoreniia v tvorchestve Lermontova," in *Istoriko-literaturnyi sbornik*, (Leningrad: Rossiiskaia Akademiia nauk, Otdelenie russkogo iazyka i slovesnosti, 1924), 268–90.

5. Reference here is to Lewis's *The Screwtape Letters* which, in its (humorous) treatment of diabolical axiology, provides an interesting comparison to *The Demon*; C.S. Lewis, *The Screwtape Letters* (London and Glasgow: Fontana Books, Collins, 1942; reprint, 1960), e.g. 102.

6. I would suggest that what is common here is a preoccupation among Russian nineteenth-century writers not so much with the demonic principle as with the hierarchical principle of which the Satanic or diabolic is but one, figurative, example. I have suggested elsewhere that such works "reveal hierarchy as an aspect of consciousness, as much as a quantifiable social structure," associating, as they do, "the hierarchized power structure of society and the hierarchized structure of the individual psyche": Robert Reid, "Cechov's *Tolstyj i Tonkij*: The Disclosure of Hierarchy," *Russian Literature* 36 (1994):387–402(389).

7. On Socrates' demon, see Barry S. Gower and Michael C. Stokes, eds., *Socratic Questions: New Essays on The Philosophy of Socrates and its Significance* (London and New York: Routledge, 1992), 156–57. Sometimes this "daemon" is equated with the voice of conscience: William Lillie, *An Introduction to Ethics* (reprint, London: Methuen, 1966), 74.

8. See *The Philosophical Writings of Descartes*, trans. John Cottingham, Robert Stoothoff, and Dugald Murdoch, 3 vols. (Cambridge: Cambridge University Press, 1984–91), 2:15: "I will suppose, therefore, that not God, who is supremely good, and the source of truth, but rather some malicious demon of the utmost power and cunning has employed all his energies in order to deceive me."

9. So, for instance, the hostility of the Intuitivists towards Cartesianism (for which see the present author's "Russian Intuitivism," *Irish Slavonic Studies* 1 [1980]:43–59). Significantly dream is the other major threat to epistemological certitude in Descartes. The oneiric quality of Tamara's visions of the Demon is very striking in the poem.

10. I quote from P.S. Laplace, *A Philosophical Essay on Probabilities*, trans. Frederick Wilson Truscott and Frederick Lincoln Emory (New York: Dover Publications, 1951; reprint, 1995), 4.

11. There is no direct evidence that Lermontov read Laplace, although it would be surprising if he had not some acquaintance with his theory of probability. In particular *The Fatalist* seems to be a classic post-Laplacian work which, interestingly, echoes the theme and tone of chap. 2 of Laplace, *A Philosophical Essay*: "Concerning Probability."

12. For an interesting discussion of the validity of fictional emotion see Colin Radford and Michael Weston, "How Can We Be Moved by the Fate of Anna Karenina?," *Proceedings of the Aristotelian Society* 49 (supplementary volume, 1975):67–93, which takes the form of a polemic. Radford argues that we are only partially moved by the predicaments of fictional characters (and less than by real ones) because we are simultaneously distracted by other sensations as audience, reader etc. (enjoyment, excitement, aesthetic appreciation) (70). He concludes therefore that being moved by real characters and being moved by fictional characters are two distinct types of emotion (75). He links "being moved" to the possibility of our imagining fictitious people as real: "Perhaps we are and can be moved by the death of Mercutio only to the extent that, at the time of the performance, we are 'caught up' in the play, and see the characters as persons, real persons, though to see them as persons is not to believe that they are real persons" (78). Thus being moved by a work of art "involves us in inconsistencies and incoherence" (78). Weston sees emotional responses being evoked from a much wider range of human-related sources including such abstracts as man's inhumanity to man: "such responses are part of a conception of what is important in life and will vary with differences in what is perceived" (86).

13. Strawson, as I understand him, asserts the conceptual priority of personhood, while insisting that a person must always be conceived with reference to both body and mind. The corporeal attributes of the Demon, however precariously defined (involving position, vision, touch, hearing etc.) are as much a condition of his personhood as the more obvious evidence that he has thoughts and feelings. Strawson places dead persons (merely bodies) and imaginary "disembodied persons" (e.g. souls after death) in a secondary category "retaining the logical benefit of individuality from having been a person": each has its personhood supplemented by what it once had and now lacks. In the case of fictional persons (not dealt with by Strawson) this supplementation must be hypothetical and mimetic (i.e. aesthetic) rather than historic. See P.F. Strawson, *Individuals: An Essay in Descriptive Metaphysics* (London: Methuen, 1959), 103.

14. Ludwig Feuerbach, *The Essence of Christianity*, trans. George Eliot (New York and London: Harper and Row, 1957), passim, esp. 14.

15. I follow Strawson's terminology here and his differentiation between universals which *instantiate* (sortals) and those which *characterize* a subject. Significantly for the present discussion most of the universals by which we can characterize the

Demon (is bored, in love, desires, is angry, jealous, hopeful, nostalgic) are also attributable to human beings. By contrast the sortal predication remains uncompromisingly supernatural: the hero is a sort of demon, not a sort of human being. See Strawson, *Individuals*, 168 ff.

16. On the question of sense and reference in proper names see A.W. Moore, ed., *Meaning and Reference* (Oxford: Oxford University Press, 1993), especially the Introduction (Part I) and Gottlob Frege, "On Sense and Reference," 23–42.

17. By G. Kondr, *Novaia liubov': "Demon," tragicheskaia poema M.Iu. Lermontova* (Kiev: Nezhin, 1893).

18. See, for example, the lines "Naskvoz' prozhzhennyi … kamen' / … / Nechelovecheskoi slezoi!.." (2:7.544–46).

19. Intention is used here and subsequently to designate the process whereby the knowing subject directs its attention towards an object of knowledge.

20. "I vse, chto pred soboi on videl, / On preziral il' nenavidel" (1:4.87–88).

21. See F.W.J. von Schelling, *System of Transcendental Idealism* (1800), Section VI: "Deduction of a Universal Organ of Philosophy, or Main Propositions of the Philosophy of Art According to Principles of Transcendental Idealism," in *German Aesthetic and Literary Criticism: Kant, Fichte, Schelling, Schopenhauer, Hegel*, ed. David Simpson (Cambridge: Cambridge University Press, 1984), 122. For Schelling art fulfils philosophy: "If aesthetic intuition is only intellectual intuition become objective, then it is evident that art is the sole true and eternal organon as well as document of philosophy, which sets forth in ever fresh forms what philosophy cannot represent outwardly" (129).

22. See *The Critique of Judgement*, Part 1 ("Critique of Aesthetic Judgement"), Section 6, in Simpson, ed., *German Aesthetic and Literary Criticism*, 38: "where anyone is conscious that his delight in an object is with him independent of interest, it is inevitable that he should look on the object as one containing a ground of delight for all men. … the judgement of taste … must involve a claim to validity for all men."

23. See Maurice Roche, *Phenomenology, Language and the Social Sciences* (London: Routledge and Kegan Paul, 1973), 7.

24. See n.22.

25. One may argue that this is always the position of the reader with regard to textual discourse. While it is arguable that an author may first experience emotion and then set it down on paper, the reader's emotion, even allowing for narrative suspense, must be a posteriori. According to one view, however, this is the universal causal relationship between emotional response and stimulus: "we feel sorry because we cry, angry because we strike, afraid because we tremble, and not that we cry strike or tremble because we are sorry, angry or fearful, as the case may be." William James, "What Is an Emotion?," *Mind* 9 (1884):188–205, reprinted in Carl Georg Lange and William James, *The Emotions* (New York: Hafner Publishing, 1967), 11–30(13). Be that as it may, in *The Demon* it is not merely the evocation of emotional response which is at issue, but the assertion of unverifiable truths, aesthetic in the case of the authorial voice, moral in the case of the Demon.

26. "Ves' Bozhii mir … / … / Tvoren'e Boga svoego" (1:3.55–57).

27. In origin an eighteenth-century English tendency. Shaftesbury, in particular, "assumed the existence of a 'moral sense' in man, a sense of right and wrong, an emotional reaction, based on the fact that the mind of man is itself in harmony with the cosmic order;" Erich Fromm, "Conscience," in *Moral Principles of Action*, ed. Ruth Nanda Anshen (New York: Harper and Bros., 1952), 77.

28. Originally formulated by Burke: "Whatever is fitted in any sort to excite the ideas of pain, and danger, that is to say, whatever is in any sort terrible, or is conversant about terrible objects, or operates in a manner analogous to terror, is a source of the *sublime*; that is it is productive of the strongest emotions which the

mind is capable of feeling." See Edmund Burke, *A Philosophical Enquiry into the Origin of our Ideas of the Sublime and Beautiful*, ed. Adam Phillips (Oxford: Oxford University Press, 1990), 36.

29. See Laszlo Versenyi, *Socratic Humanism* (New Haven: Yale University Press, 1963), 81–82; also Epictetus, *Moral Discourses* (1:18.1), trans. Elizabeth Carter, Everyman's Library (London: J.M. Dent and Sons, 1910; reprint, 1966), 39.

30. I use Alexius Meinong's concepts here; see J.N. Findlay, *Meinong's Theory of Objects and Values*, 2d. ed. (Oxford: Clarendon Press, 1963), 295ff.

31. The Demon's exile is, strictly speaking, a state or fact, rather than an event. Jonathan Bennett, *Events and Their Names* (Oxford: Clarendon Press, 1988), 7, argues that "any philosophical theory of events should be extended to cover states as well" because of the only superficial differences between the two categories. Bennett (22–24) also discusses the causal interrelationship of facts to facts, events to events, facts to events and vice versa. In *The Demon* events are marked by their emergent quality: they are unforeseen by those who suffer them or simply happen without explanation (the Demon's exile; his seeing Tamara; Tamara's first encounter with the Demon; the killing of the bridegroom). Facts or states are marked principally by sharp psychological awareness on the part of the relevant subject: boredom (the Demon's exile); love (his relationship with Tamara); mixed emotions (Tamara, between meeting the Demon and her death).

32. In this sense boredom is the opposite of habit and the Demon's rejection of habituation to evil is part of a general pattern of alienation to be found in Lermontov's plots, whereby characters resist or reject the forces of social conditioning: both the novice in *Mtsyri* and Pechorin provide examples of this in different social contexts.

33. See John McTaggart Ellis McTaggart [*sic*], *The Nature of Existence*, ed. C.D. Broad (Cambridge: Cambridge University Press, 1927; reprint, 1968), 2:9–31 (esp.10).

34. Promise-keeping in particular, and its opposite, lying, are consistently used by Kant in testing the categorical imperative: "I can indeed will to lie, but I can by no means will a universal law of lying; for by such a law there could properly be no promises at all, for it would be futile to profess a will for future action to others who would not believe my profession, or who, if they did so over-hastily, would pay me back in like coin; and consequently my maxim, as soon as it was made a universal law, would annul itself." *The Moral Law: Kant's Groundwork of the Metaphysic of Morals*, trans. and ed. H.J. Paton (London: Hutchinson Universal Library, 1964), 71.

35. The distinction between reluctant and embraced desires is developed by Ted Honderich, *A Theory of Determinism: The Mind, Neuroscience, and Life-Hopes* (Oxford: Clarendon Press, 1988), 394: "*Reluctant* desires and intentions, we can say, are those which operate in situations to which the agent is somehow opposed. *Embraced* desires and intentions satisfy the condition that they operate in situations which the agent at least accepts. These two types of situation (there is more than one subtype of each) can also be called *frustrating* or *obstructing* situations and *satisfying* or *enabling* situations."

36. Based on Meinong's model of required and meritorious actions; see Findlay, *Meinong's Theory of Objects and Values*, 275–76.

37. Aleksandr Zakrzhevskii, *Lermontov i sovremennost'* (Kiev: Izdatel'stvo I.I. Samonenko, 1915), 18 and passim; V.S. Solov'ev, "Lermontov," in *Sobranie sochinenii Vladimira Sergeevicha Solov'eva*, ed. S.M. Solov'ev and E.L. Radlov, 2d ed., 10 vols (St. Petersburg: Prosveshchenie, [1911–13]; reprint with 6 additional vols., Brussels, 1966–70), 9:364.

Chapter 7

The Devil is in the Detail: Demonic Features of Gogol's Petersburg

Julian Graffy

In February 1827, the eighteen-year-old Gogol wrote to his mother from high school in Nezhin: "If I think of anything now, then it is always about my future life. Both waking and sleeping I dream of Petersburg."[1] Later that same year, in a letter to his friend Vysotsky, he expressed himself more precisely: "in my thoughts I place myself in Petersburg, in that jolly little room looking out over the Neva, since I have always thought of finding myself such a place. I don't know if my ideas will come to fruition, and whether I really shall live in a such a paradisaical place" (v etakom raiskom meste, 10:101). Dreams of Petersburg, for the young Gogol, were dreams of paradise.

The imagery used here, imagery of looking out from a high place, pervades Gogol's writing, and in his world model the vertical axis, expressive of a polarity between high and low, is ubiquitous. In the article from *Arabesques* (*Arabeski*, 1835), the collection in which three of his Petersburg stories were first published, entitled "On Contemporary Architecture" (Ob arkhitekture nyneshnego vremeni), he suggests that: "In building towns you must pay attention to the position of the earth. Towns are built either on an elevation and hills, or on plains. A town on an elevation demands less art, because nature herself is already at work there. ... But where the lie of the land is completely flat (gladko), where nature sleeps, then art must work with all its strength. It must variegate, if I can put it that way, dig up and conceal the plain, bring to life the deadness of the flat desert" (8:72–73). The same image recurs in a letter to Konstantin Aksakov of 1841, in which he encourages his addressee to "get out on to the Russian path, and use it as scaffolding, to raise yourself up to a certain height, from which you can start a building which will fly to the heavens, or simply to a rocky hill, from which views will open to you wider and further" (11:338). The desire for a distanced vantage point also characterizes Gogol's writing about Rome,[2] and is recurrently invoked as his reason for leaving Russia in the 1847 "Author's Confession" (Avtorskaia ispoved', 8:441–42, 449, 451–52). For Gogol, vertical polarity is infused with religious significance. Down beneath is the "unclean spirit which emerges from below" (8:415), the devil (chort), who wishes to: "bring [us] down from that lofty (vysokogo) calm, which is essential for living a higher (vysshei) life, the life which man ought to live (Letter to A.O. Smirnova, 14:154). Man's understanding is vitiated, writes Gogol, in "The Rule for Living in the World" (Pravilo zhitiia v mire, 1844), "because we hold our eyes down and do not wish to raise them aloft. For if we raised them up for a few minutes, we would see above all only God and the light which emanates from Him, illuminating everything in its real form (v nastoiashchem vide), and we would ourselves laugh then at our blindness. … God is light, and therefore we too must strive towards the light."[3] Thus the vertically based vision is pervasive in Gogol's writings, and central to his world-view. Above is heaven, associated with harmony, light, and vision; below is hell, the realm of the devil and darkness.

In December 1828 Gogol left for the Petersburg he had imagined as paradise. Vertical imagery continued to preoccupy him. At the end of 1829 he moved into a fifth-floor flat in the Zverkov house, famous in the 1830s as the first five-storey house in St. Petersburg.[4] To his mother's concern about his living so high up, he replies: "That means nothing here, and believe me, it doesn't make me at all tired. The Tsar himself occupies rooms that are no lower than mine; on the contrary, higher up the air is much cleaner and healthier" (10:184).[5] In general, though, he found Petersburg a disappointing place. Soon after his arrival, on 3 January 1829, he admits to his mother: "I must tell you that Petersburg has turned out to be not at all the way I expected. I imagined it to be much more beautiful and grander, and the tales which others told of it are false" (10:136–37). In another letter to her, of April 1829, he describes the city as "quite unlike other European capitals. … Petersburg has no character." Its inhabitants are "neither one thing nor the other.[6] There is an unusual silence in it, no spirit sparkles in its people." This depression is also expressed in spatial terms: "everything is crushed," Petersburg's houses are "large … but not tall" (10:139).

The disillusionment of these early impressions will be extensively developed, and its demonic implications articulated, in the articles Gogol later writes about the city, and in the stories he sets there. In this context it is especially remarkable that in this letter Gogol breaks off from his description of St. Petersburg to ask his mother for information on the "habits and customs of our Little Russians," including information about "spirits or house spirits" and "beliefs, terrible tales and traditions" (10:141).[7] For though the visibly participant devils of the stories collected as *Village Evenings near Dikanka* (*Vechera na khutore bliz Dikan'ki*, 1831–32), described by Faith Wigzell in her contribution to this volume, have all but disappeared from the Petersburg writings, manifestations of their influence, expressed in actions and phenomena rooted in folk consciousness, remain ubiquitous. Demonic forces are just as powerful in St. Petersburg, even though the devil is not a named participant, and their influence, asserted through the atmosphere and the values of the city itself, is strongly felt, and repeatedly acknowledged, both by the characters and by the narrators of the tales.

While earlier studies have established demonic traits in individual characters and individual Petersburg tales, the purpose of this article is to reveal how a concern with the demonic is in fact imbricated in the very nature of the city and informs the essence and structure of Gogol's Petersburg world.

The Space of Petersburg

The Petersburg of Gogol's writings is a kind of anti-space, in which, in "The Overcoat" (Shinel', 1842), a policeman's sentry-box stands on "the edge of the world" (3:161), an image that describes the entire city in the first sentence of "Petersburg Notes of 1836" (Peterburgskie zapiski 1836 goda, 1837, 8:177). At the start of the draft version of "Nevsky Prospect" (Nevskii prospekt, 1835) one is forced to "suspect and doubt the very existence" of Petersburg society (3:339), and the image of a desert (pustynia) is used to describe both the streets (3:158) and an "endless square" (3:161) in "The Overcoat."[8] The space of this world is regularly described as being broken up. In the fragment "1834" (1833) Petersburg is "this pile of houses thrown one upon the other" (9:17); in "Petersburg Notes of 1836" the town is inhabited by "completely separate circles, who rarely mix," and each class "if you look more closely, is made up of a number of other little circles who also do not mix" (8:180); on the Nevsky Prospect you can encounter parts of bodies, side whiskers, moustaches or waists (3:12), whereas in "The Overcoat" "everything in Petersburg, all the

streets and the houses have merged and mixed so much" in the narrator's head "that it is extremely difficult to get anything out of there
in an orderly fashion" (3:158). In "The Portrait" (Portret, 1835, second version 1842) the artist Chartkov sees the money-lender's portrait "double and quadruple before his eyes" while "the room
widened and continued to infinity" (3:116); and, most famously, in
"Nevsky Prospect" "some demon has shredded the whole world into
a large number of small pieces and mixed all these pieces up
together, without sense or meaning" (3:24), so that the destruction of
spatial coherence is also a destruction of significance. The devil's
association with cutting things up is reiterated in the barber's exclamation that "the devil knows how it happened" when he finds a nose
in his bread in "The Nose" (Nos, 1836, 3:50).[9]

Because of these demonic interventions, Petersburg space is characterized by an alarming disorder and instability: "Our world is
organized in a miraculous way. ... Everything happens in reverse"
(Nevsky Prospect, 3:45). In this unstable world "houses grew and
seemed to rise out of the earth at every step; bridges trembled; carriages flew," in "Christmas Eve" (Noch' pered rozhdestvom, 1832),
the only one of the early Dikanka stories to be set partly in Petersburg (1:232); and "the pavement moved under him [the artist
Piskarev], the carriages with their galloping horses seemed motionless, the bridge stretched and snapped on its arch, a house stood on
its roof, a sentry-box rolled towards him" (3:19), while later "myriads
of carriages fall from the bridges" (Nevsky Prospect, 3:46),[10] bridges
which have explicitly demonic connotations in "The Tale of Captain
Kopeikin," the one section of *Dead Souls* (*Mertvye dushi*, 1842) set in
St. Petersburg, in which "some sort of spire hangs in the air; the
bridges hang like the devil, you can imagine, without touching anything" and when he tries to rent a flat "it all bites terribly; the cur-
tains, the blinds, all that devilry" (chertovstvo, 6:200).

Instability is echoed in the very lack of solidity of the surface of
the place, and in the fragment "The Rain Was Continuous" (Dozhd'
byl prodolzhitel'nyi, 1833) the endless precipitation "seems to want
to crush down this swampy town even lower" (3:333). This wetness
is also present in "The Overcoat," where as Bashmachkin crosses a
square on the way home from the party "he looks back and to the
sides: it was as if he was surrounded by sea (3:161), and is itself an
indication of demonic presence, since, as L.N. Vinogradova points
out, water is a "median place," to which devils repair when they
leave this world.[11]

Another sign of demonic intervention in the very essence of the
Petersburg world is the instability of conventional dimensions. That
the ability to change in size is a demonic attribute is evident from the

episode in "Christmas Eve," where, upon Vakula's instruction, "the devil grew thin in a single minute, and became so small that it had no difficulty in climbing into his pocket" (1:233). The motif is repeatedly used in the "Petersburg Tales": in the enormous shadows, and the man with a mouth "the size of the arch of the General Head Quarters" in "Nevsky Prospect" (3:15, 45), and most obviously in "The Nose," where the nose is first found inside a loaf of bread, then seen walking and driving around the town and finally returned wrapped in paper in a policeman's pocket (3:67). The same instability characterizes Bashmachkin's overcoat, for it, too, is both worn by its buyer and wrapped in Petrovich's handkerchief (3:156), and the displacement motif is developed in "Notes of a Madman" (*Zapiski sumasshedshego*, 1835) by the hero's contention that the human brain is not to be found in the head, but "is brought by the wind from the direction of the Caspian Sea" (3:208). Conventional spatial oppositions also fail to apply. In Russian folklore the house (*dom*) is conventionally opposed to the wood, the "forest home" (*lesnoi dom*) which is inhabited by the devil, and this opposition is effectively used by Gogol in the *Mirgorod* story "Old World Landowners" (*Starosvetskie pomeshchiki*, 1835) where the cat's escape into the wood brings destruction to the idyll.[12] But, as Iurii Lotman has pointed out, in the Petersburg tales, the devil infiltrates the inner world of home, creating a demonic "anti-home" (*antidom*) in the brothel of "Nevsky Prospect" (which is described as a kind of microcosm of the capital, 3:21) or the offices of the various bureaucracies.[13] That Petersburg is, indeed, hell, is apparent from its smell. The narrator exclaims of merchants in "The Rain Was Continuous": "God, what a hellish (*adskuiu*) stream of cabbage and onion they left behind them in the air" (3:332), and the same "hell" "seeps from under the gates of every house" in "Notes of a Madman" (3:200), where later "a terrible stench spreads through the earth" and Poprishchin's very treatment is described as "such hell" as he has never experienced before (3:212, 313). The motif is also taken up in the smell of the staircase and the smoke in the kitchen of the tailor Petrovich's house in "The Overcoat" (3:148) and in the "terribly thick air" of the newspaper office in "The Nose" (3:60).

But perhaps the most notable demonic distortion of spatial coordinates concerns the treatment of the vertical axis, in the demolition of the stable spiritual significance afforded to it by Gogol in his earlier vision of paradise. In "Christmas Eve," as Vakula flies on the devil's back through the air to St. Petersburg, he discovers that the heavens are full of devils: a sorcerer rushes by; an "entire swarm of spirits swirls around to one side;" a devil doffs his caps, a witch returns from a trip on a broomstick, and there is "a great deal more rubbish" (1:232).[14] But the heavens are no longer the domain of spiritual knowledge, for when Chartkov becomes a successful painter he takes to denying the existence of "inspiration from above" (3:110).[15] Heaven itself is degraded in the erotic surrogates of "Nevsky Prospect" and "Notes of a Madman," as will be seen in the section below on women. The negation of the significance of the up-down opposition is adumbrated in various other ways: in the actual typographical inversion of the last entry, for "February 349," of Poprishchin's diary (3:214); and in the "open-ended potential ascent heavenwards or descent to the bottom among the moustachioed thugs of the pseudospirit world" which Priscilla Meyer detects at the end of "The Overcoat."[16] Iurii Lotman, in a posthumously published article, recalls Gogol's fondness for "a landscape reflected in water, that is to say a space in which the concept of above and below has been practically removed;"[17] and in similar vein O.G. Dilaktorskaia discusses "The Nose" revealingly in the context of the "vice-versa paintings" (kartinki-oborotni) of the Russian *lubok* popular print in which "changes of down and up (niza i verkha) … overturn the content of the painting."[18] Vertical instability is also expressed through the recurrence of the motif of falling, the demonic significance of which is apparent in Chartkov's desire to paint a "fallen angel" (otpadshego angela, 3:113). The motif is further developed in the first version of "The Portrait," in which the deaths of both the wife and the son of the holy artist are explicitly falling deaths (3:438, 439), occasioned by his decision to impart the portrait's terrible secret.[19]

The central example of the spiritual significance of the vertical axis is the image of the ladder or stairway (lestnitsa), which has as its source the image of Jacob's ladder in Genesis 28, an image later developed by the early Church fathers. Gogol frequently invoked the ladder in his spiritually informed writings. For example, in the "Easter Sunday" section of the *Selected Passages from Correspondence with Friends* (*Vybrannye mesta iz perepiski s druz'iami*, 1847) he suggests that "God knows," the human desire for spiritual reconciliation may perhaps cause "a ladder (lestnitsa) to throw itself down to us from the heavens, and a hand to stretch out, to help us to fly up along it," before concluding that nineteenth-century man does not want to act in this way (8:416). The image is echoed in "The Rule for Living in the World," where a "feat (podvig) of Christian bravery, any feat supplies us with a new step (stupen') to the achievement of the heavenly kingdom,"[20] leading Geir Kjetsaa to conclude that "scarcely a single Gogolian homily does not include a mention of the 'ladder'."[21] The image is echoed in another recurrent motif, that of the tower (bashnia) or belvedere, which serves as a beacon to the traveller, and from which one can see far and wide.[22] And Gogol's dying words were reported by A.T. Tarasenkov as being "A ladder, quickly, give me a ladder!" (Lestnitsu, poskoree, davai lestnitsu!).[23]

The image of the *lestnitsa* is repeatedly used in all the Petersburg stories, but its fate is to be sullied and debased. It is overwhelmingly described as an enclosed, oppressive, inner stairwell, rather than the spacious aerial staircase or ladder of other settings. The stairwell that leads to Chartkov's lodgings at the start of "The Portrait" is "covered in slops and decorated with the traces of cats and dogs" (3:83); the stairs which Piskarev "soars up" in "Nevsky Prospect" (3:19) lead to a brothel; while those that lead to Petrovich's fourth-floor flat in "The Overcoat" are "steeped in water and slops, and give off a smell of spirits (spirtuoznyi) which eats your eyes and which, as is well known, is an inevitable feature of all the backstairs of Petersburg houses" (3:148). There is an "airy staircase with shining banisters and smelling of perfume" (3:23) in "Nevsky Prospect," but it is revealed as the stairway of a dream,[24] and in the same story another kind of *lestnitsa*, a ladder, is clambered up to light the city's deceptive lamps (3:14). The same theme of disappointment and deception is taken up in the stairway of the Zverkov house, climbed to the sixth floor by Poprishchin (3:200), for this is the stairway of hierarchy and social exclusion.[25]

Thus this key Gogolian image of spiritual striving is consistently travestied in the Petersburg world,[26] a fate which connects it with the treatment of the city's central image, that of Nevsky Prospect itself. That the Nevsky is the finest thing in Petersburg is stated explicitly in the first sentence of the story (3:9), which is also the first sentence in all editions of the "Petersburg Tales," and both the position of the story and its title announce it as setting an agenda for Gogol's examination of the city, in which the street plays as dominant a role as it does in the city itself. Its very name suggests extended vision,[27] a function echoed in its description as "the general communication of Petersburg" (vseobshchaia kommunikatsiia Peterburga, 3:9). Its centrality in the life of the capital's denizens is apparent in the stories. It is the place where Piskarev and Pirogov stroll in "Nevsky Prospect," the place where the successful Chartkov rents a smart flat and has his studio in "The Portrait" (3:97) and where Kovalev "has the habit of strolling every day" (3:53) in "The Nose," the home of expensive tailors in "The Overcoat" (3:156). Yet this street which "is everything" for Petersburg, and whose "brightness" earns it the sobriquet "the beauty of our capital" (3:9) has a more sinister side. It is the place where dogs talk in "Notes of a Madman" (3:200), where a "swift phantasmagoria" (bystraia fantasmagoriia, 3:10) unfurls every day, and where the brunette bewitches Piskarev and carries him away (tak okoldovala i unesla ego na Nevskom prospekte, 3:21). These qualities lead Dilaktorskaia to call it a "mythological creature which dies away and revives by the hour ... a werewolf image" (obraz-oboroten').[28] And the chief manipulator of all these forces, the presiding genius of the street, the destroyer of its "visionary" aspirations, is, of course, the devil himself, for in one of the most famous passages of Gogol's Petersburg writings, at the end of "Nevsky Prospect," the narrator abjures us: "Oh, don't trust that Nevsky Prospect! ... It tells lies at all times (on lzhet vo vsiakoe vremia), that Nevsky Prospect, but above all at the time when night falls on it in a thick mass ... and when the demon himself (sam demon) lights the lamps for one reason only, to show everything in an unreal form" (3:45–46).[29]

Light and Darkness

Images of light are repeatedly invoked in Gogol's paradisaical visions, and the fate of light and darkness in his descriptions of St. Petersburg is another register of the mood of the place. The image of light is fundamental, for example, to several of the sections of the *Selected Passages*. In the section "Enlightenment" the word "enlightenment" (prosveshchenie) is said (with startling braggadocio) to exist in no other language than Russian, and is opposed to "all the darknesses and glooms of ignorance (vse mraki i nevezhestvennye t'my) which surround it from all sides" (8:285) as the "Light of Christ illuminates everyone!" (8:286). In "Four Letters to Various People About Dead Souls" he speaks of the "terrifying ... form" in which "darkness and the frightening absence of light can be presented to man" (8:294), and in the "Fears and Terrors of Russia" section (8:343–46) the imagery is similarly pervasive. In "The Rule for Living in the World": "Love is light and not darkness. In love there is God and not the spirit of darkness: where there is light there is calmness, where there is darkness there is resentment."[30]

The strange hybrid text, half literary criticism and half story, "Boris Godunov. A Poem by Pushkin" (Boris Godunov. Poema Pushkina) which Gogol wrote in 1831 and which is one of the first of his texts to be set in Petersburg, also begins with images of light, as "lamps throw a warm light" on walls of books, "sharply illuminating the titles" (8:148), but this light is later replaced by the "light of the moon, agonizing as the merging of joy and sadness" (8:149) and by a room "lit by a solitary flickering lamp" (8:149–50), and this anxious, weak and deceptive light is far more typical of the Petersburg texts and their battle between the forces of light and darkness. That there is something odd about the Petersburg light is apparent from Vakula's exclamation: "My God, what a light! ... where we live it is

not this light even during the day" (1:234). Natural sources of illumination cannot function in Petersburg where, in "Notes of a Madman," the sun is present only in Sophie's gaze ("and her glance: the
sun, good heavens, the sun!," 3:196) and the "unstable" moon is
made by a lame cooper in Hamburg "and made extremely badly"
(3:212). In "The Portrait" the moon's light brings with it "the delirium of dream" (3:88). They are replaced by artificial light that is
associated, throughout Gogol's Petersburg writings, with the key
emblem of nineteenth-century Petersburg, the street lamp (fonar').[31]
In the fragment "The Terrible Hand" (Strashnaia ruka, 1831–33) "a
single street lamp cast a capricious light on the street and threw a terrible brightness (blesk) on the stone buildings" (3:329) and in "A
Street Lamp Was Dying" (Fonar' umiral, 1832–33) because of this
weak light, "only the white stone houses were picked out here and
there. The wooden ones turned black and merged with the thick
mass of darkness hanging over you" (3:329). Bashmachkin wanders
similarly murky streets on his way to and from the party (3:158, 161),
and in "Nevsky Prospect" it is "good fortune if you can get away with
it [the street lamp] spilling its stinking oil over your foppish frock-
coat" (3:46). And the cause of this mayhem, the reason why the
reader is advised: "Keep away, for God's sake, away from the street
lamp!" (3:46) is that it is the devil's object, for it is "the demon himself" (sam demon) who lights it (3:46).[32]

Time and Weather

As a recent dictionary of Russian demonology displays, devils are
associated in the popular imagination with particular times of the
day and year.[33] The same point is made by L.N. Vinogradova, who
refers to the "dependence of the behaviour of the unclean spirit (the
strengthening or weakening of its malevolence, the period of its
being on the earth, contacts with human beings) on the concrete sea-
sons and feast days of the time of year."[34] During the year, devils are
particularly active in the time of cold weather, associated with the
bringing of wind, frost, and snowstorm. In the day, they favour the
liminal times between light and dark, particularly dusk.[35] It is
remarkable to what extent events in Gogol's Petersburg writings take
place at these times, and thus temporal factors are another register of
their demonic coding.

Dusk (sumerki) is repeatedly invoked in "Nevsky Prospect." It is
the time at which the policeman lights the street lamp (3:14), a "mysterious time, when the lamps give everything a kind of seductive,
miraculous light" (3:15). The motif of the mysterious, deceptive time

is made explicit at the end of the story when, as noted above, the demon lights the lamps and the street is at its most mendacious. Dusk is also the time when Kovalev returns home and confirms that his nose is, indeed, missing (3:64–65), when Chartkov comes home with the terrible portrait,[36] when the money-lender appears to the portrait painter (3:437 [first version]), and when he learns of his death (3:129). In "The Overcoat," attention is repeatedly paid to the cold, frosty setting, to the extent that the story seems mired in an eternal winter. It is the "northern frost" (3:147) that first announces to Bashmachkin that he needs a new overcoat. He then spends several months visiting the tailor, Petrovich, starving himself to save money for it, and checking the cloth, after which Petrovich takes two weeks making it. Yet when Bashmachkin finally begins to wear the coat "rather strong frosts" are beginning (3:156). The impression of permanent winter is adumbrated by other indications of life outside of time. The word "eternal" (vechnyi) is applied both to Bashmachkin and to his future overcoat, and, however many directors come and go, Bashmachkin remains "in one and the same place and the same position" (3:143). His mother is repeatedly described, at the time of his birth, as "the deceased" and "the old woman."[37] Indeed it is precisely Bashmachkin's attempt to escape from this sinister inertia that brings about his demise.[38] In a similar way Poprishchin's decline is expressed in temporal terms, as the dates of his diary entries cease to make sense with "January of that same year, which happened after February" (3:212), and, most tellingly, "I do not remember the date. There was no month either. There was the devil knows what (bylo chort znaet, chto takoe, 3:210). And, as O.G. Dilaktorskaia points out, the striking precision about the date of the events in "The Nose" can be seen to be motivated for the same reason. The very first words of the story indicate that the "unusually strange event" (not just an ordinarily strange one!) took place on 25 March (3:49), and we later learn (3:65) that Kovalev notices the loss of his nose on a Friday morning. These days, too, have demonic implications.[39]

Sinister times are associated with sinister weather, and, as Vinogradova and others have noted, wind and whirlwind, snowstorm and frost can all be shown to be manifestations of the devil's wiles.[40] The extremism of the geographical position of Petersburg is signalled by Gogol at the very beginning of "Petersburg Notes of 1836," where he suggests that the Russian capital may pull off the trick of joining up to the North Pole (8:177). He then describes the fog (tuman) that fills the Petersburg air, a fog that in stories such as "The Nose" engulfs both the city and the narration so that "what happened next is absolutely unknown" (3:52).[41] The inhabitants of the city are also assailed by rain, both in the fragment "The Rain Was Continuous," where the rain forces people to "run home like a damp rat" (3:332), and in the "Notes of a Madman," when the crucial event of Poprishchin's hearing the dogs talking takes place on a day of "non-stop drizzle" (prolivnoi dozhdik, 3:194). In Petersburg "everything is damp, smooth, flat, pale, grey, misty" (3:16). Most terrible of all is the weather in "The Overcoat," at the start of which "the Petersburg climate is guilty" (3:141) for all Bashmachkin's woes, assailing him with the "terrible enemy of everyone," the "northern frost," which "gives such strong and pricking slaps indiscriminately on everyone's noses that the poor clerks really don't know where to put them" (3:147). This is followed by attacks by wind and snow, and, when he returns from supplicating the important personage, by a snowstorm (v'iuga), a "wind which, according to Petersburg custom, blew on him from all four directions at once" (3:167, another indication of its unworldly power) and leads directly to a fever, which, in turn, "thanks to the magnanimous help of the Petersburg climate" (3:167) ends in his death. Later, when the important personage goes to visit his lady friend, Katerina Ivanovna, a "gusting wind … God knows from where … cuts into his face, hurling scraps of snow at him" (3:172). Petersburg seems to be defenceless against nature's demonic armoury.

The Devil and His Representatives

The behaviour of the denizens of this demonically tinged city is affected by their awareness of the devil's influence upon their environment, and also by their numerous encounters with the devil and his surrogates. Gogol frequently attempts to define the devil in his writings, particularly in his letters. Though he tells S.T. Aksakov that the devil is "*the devil knows what*" (*chort znaet chto*) and that "I call the devil the devil straight" (chorta nazyvaiu priamo chortom (12:300, 301), he makes many specific statements about the devil's qualities, in letters and essays as well as in his stories, and these are both internally consistent and consistent with popular belief. Thus his suggestions to Aksakov that the devil "will run away and then come up from the other direction, in another form" (12:300) and to A.O. Smirnova that his tactic is "to hide his snout" (14:154) are consistent with popular tradition.[42] The devil is not usually a directly visible presence in Gogol's Petersburg texts in the way that he is in several of the Dikanka stories, though he does appear as an "enormous red-haired devil with an axe in his hand" on a sign at a corner show-booth in "Petersburg Notes of 1836" (8:189). He is also ever present in the consciousness of both the narrators and the participants of the stories, and his interventions are freely acknowledged. Indeed, the holy artist in "The Portrait" reminds his son that the devil is ubiquitous: "he strives to penetrate into everything" (3:443 [first version]).[43] His interventions are frequently invoked by characters such as Chartkov in "The Portrait," Poprishchin in "Notes of a Madman," and both Kovalev and the barber in "The Nose," and though these are usually just ritual expressions, they suggest a certainty that the devil is somehow at the bottom of any "unusually strange event."

More frequently, however, in the Petersburg tales, the devil is represented by his surrogates, whether in human or object form, and in this context it is necessary to look for identifying features. Thus Gogol's suggestion to S.T. Aksakov that the devil is just a "petty functionary" (melkii chinovnik, 12:300), and to Zhukovsky that he is a "horned functionary" (rogatyi chinovnik) who has "put on a green uniform with heraldic buttons" (10:207) may explain Poprishchin's description of the cashier as a "grey devil" (3:193). Certain features have led a number of commentators to identify in particular three characters (Petrovich in "The Overcoat," the money-lender in "The Portrait," and the barber in "The Nose") as the "devil's disciples." One of these is the presence of an unusual, and often deforming physical feature. At the time he was working on the Dikanka tales, Gogol wrote a brief text entitled "The Lame Devil" (Khromoi chert, 1830–31) in which he recorded a Ukrainian folk anecdote that suggests that the lame (*khromoi* or *kryvyi*) devil is the most cunning and wisest in hell.[44] The same contention about the lame devil is made in "Christmas Eve" (1:225). The widespread popular belief that devils are distinguished by "the absence of a prominent organ of the body," or its deformation, has been recorded by Afanas'ev and informs Toby Clyman's illuminating analysis of Petrovich, who is described as being boss-eyed (krivoi glaz) and pock-marked (3:148), has a damaged big toe, and is even called "a one-eyed devil" by his wife (3:149).[45] The cooper who makes the moon in "Notes of a Madman" is also lame (khromoi, 3:212), and an interesting hint about the character of the clerk who replaces Bashmachkin is that he makes his letters "far more slanting and crooked" (gorazdo naklonnee i kosee, 3:169). Another common folkloric belief about devils is that they are "of another faith" (inovertsy) or "of another land" (inozemtsy),[46] a feature which characterizes a number of demonically connected Gogolian characters. Petrovich "sits with his legs under him like a Turkish Pasha" (3:149). The money-lender, in "The Portrait," is described as wearing "a sort of wide Asiatic cassock" (3:89) and later "wide Asiatic clothes; the dark colour of his face indicated his southern origin, but precisely what nation he came from: an Indian, a Greek or a Persian, no one could say precisely" (3:121), before being called "the devil, the absolute devil!" by the holy artist (3:126) and being "buried according to the rights of his religion" (3:129). Further details are supplied in the first version of the story. Here the money-lender "sits with his legs under him on a blackened divan" (3:433), and when advised by the artist to "repent before the Almighty" is reduced to convulsions (3:434), leading the artist to be able to identify him to his son as "the Antichrist himself" (3:443).[47] These features are also directly echoed in "Nevsky Prospect" in the lascivious Persian art collector found "sitting on a divan with his legs under him" (3:29), and in the sorcerer Patsiuk in "Christmas Eve" who "knows all the devils" and "sits on the floor in Turkish fashion" (1:222). A third key identifying feature for demonic figures is the name Petr, which connects the tailor, Petrovich, and the money-lender, Petromikhali, directly to the city of Petersburg and its founder, thus further adumbrating the city's own demonic qualities. We recall that Petrovich had recently been a serf called Grigorii and "began to call himself Petrovich after he received his freedom and began drinking relatively heavily" (3:148). Priscilla Meyer, in her discussion of Petrovich as pretender (samozvanets, literally "self-namer"), has reminded us that the pretender to the Russian throne, the "False Dmitrii," was also a Grigorii, the unfrocked monk Grishka Otrep'ev, and Toby Clyman has produced an interesting interpretation of the change of name, reminding us that the name Grigorii means "watcher."[48] New light on the symbolic significance of this change can be shed by the recurrence of the two names in "The Portrait." Here, the artist Chartkov, who, suborned by the devil, pretends to a talent he does not have, is revealed in his vainglorious newspaper article to be Andrei *Petrovich* (3:99); while the holy artist, when he enters the monastery, becomes Father Grigorii (3:441 [first version]).

The demonic characteristics of Ivan Iakovlevich, the barber in "The Nose," have been brilliantly revealed in the work of Mikhail Vaiskopf and O.G. Dilaktorskaia. Vaiskopf speaks of the barber's "theft of Kovalev's soul," and shows how he, too, is connected to Petrine themes, while Dilaktorskaia, in a lengthy analysis of the connection between barbers and unclean spirits, stresses that his wife calls him a "wild animal" (3:50), that his hands are notoriously unclean (3:51), and that the only words on his shop sign are "they also let blood" (i krov' otvoriaiut, 3:49).[49]

Encounters with the Devil and His Surrogates

That the devil is primarily a tempter and deceiver is widely attested by Gogol. In "The Rule for Living in the World" he calls despair "the true temptation (istoe iskushenie) of the spirit of darkness,"[50] and in his let-

ter to Smirnova he accuses the devil of spreading slander and reminds
her that "everything in the world is deceit" (vse na svete obman,
14:154). He ends his "Author's Confession" in horror that people have
called him "a liar and a cheat" (lzhetsom i obmanshchikom, 8:466).[51]
The themes of deceit and temptation are central to Gogol's demonic
vision of Petersburg. In "Nevsky Prospect" the street lamp casts a
deceptive light (obmanchivyi svet, 3:18) and everything is deceit and
dream (vse obman, vse mechta, 3:45), leading Lotman to contend that
"thus deceit in this case is really creativity, but devilish creativity, that
is false, seeming creativity. It is *pseudo-creativity, creating a pseudo-
world.*"[52] The same theme is taken up in "The Portrait" where
Chartkov's teacher warns him that the chance to be a fashionable
painter may seduce (zamanit, 3:85) him, and Chartkov later wonders
"Have I not been deceived?" (ne obmanulsia li ia? 3:114). The connected theme of *iskushenie* (temptation) is used both in "The Portrait,"
where it describes the influence of Petromikhali's image on the holy
artist (3:439 [first version]), and in "Notes of a Madman," where it is
used by Poprishchin of attempts by the Capuchins to get him to
renounce the throne of Spain (3:211). Though Gogol told Malinovsky
that the devil "sits astride him [man] without ceremony and controls
him like the most obedient horse,"[53] he advised Shevyrev to make a
fool of the devil and to laugh at him (13:293).[54] Vakula, in "Christmas
Eve," another text in which the whole world's attraction to trickery is
invoked (1:204), manages to follow Gogol's instructions, outwitting the
devil and travelling astride him to Petersburg, but in Petersburg itself
Kovalev complains that the devil has played a trick on him (3:60).[55]
He later writes to Podtochina accusing her of responsibility for his
nose's "sudden separation from its place, flight and masking
(maskirovanie), now in the form of a certain functionary, now finally
in its own form" (3:70). The idea of masking "in its own form" is highly
paradoxical, but the devil's penchant for masking is widely attested,
despite Gogol's complaint in the "Easter Sunday" section of the
Selected Passages that "the devil has already stepped out without a mask
into the world. The spirit of pride has already stopped appearing in
various forms ... he has appeared in his own form" (8:415).

Another characteristic of the devil's surrogates is their ability to
impart a terrible secret, as does Piskarev's Bianca (3:26), and, most
terribly, the money-lender, who cautions the artist: "But do not
reveal this secret to anyone – neither to your wife, nor to your children, or you will die and they will die" (3:436), a prophecy that is fulfilled when the artist attempts to inform a priest (3:438, 439).
Characters will run away in horror from demonic encounters, as
does Piskarev from the brothel ("he rushed off at full speed, like a
wild she-goat, and ran out into the street," 3:21, and again 3:33).

Encounters with the terrible painting and with the money-lender repeatedly provoke the same reaction in Chartkov and the artist in "The Portrait." But the devil can also cause you to lose your way. In a letter to Zhukovsky of September 1831, Gogol complained that the devil was to blame for the quarantine that had closed the road between them (10:207). Demonically- inspired bad weather causes a similar loss of one's path in "Christmas Eve."[56] In "The Overcoat" Bashmachkin's first visit to Petrovich in quest of the coat leads him "in a dream" "instead of going home to go in the opposite direction, without suspecting it" (3:152) and his acquisition of it also causes him "not to notice the way at all and suddenly to end up at the department" (3:157). On being made a general the important personage "somehow got confused, lost his way" (kak-to sputalsia, sbilsia s puti, 3:165), a phrase that is echoed in the artist's injunction to his son: "Your path is pure. Do not turn from it" (3:135).

The importance of unimpeded vision in the Gogolian scheme has already been alluded to. Though for Gogol man's eyes are "fragile" (brennye),[57] he stresses to Smirnova the need to see people "the way that Christ orders us to see them" (14:154) so as not to be deceived. But he tells S.T. Aksakov that the devil will "throw dust in everyone's eyes" and warns him not to look at him (12:300, 301), and complains to Danilevsky that "some devil is sitting in my stomach, and stopping me seeing everything the way I would like to" (11:179).[58] The image of terrible seeing is widespread in Gogol's writings about Petersburg. It is the intimidating habit of the sinister *znachitel'noe litso* (important personage) in "The Overcoat" "usually to look very meaningfully into the face of the person to whom he is talking (3:164), and in "The Portrait" the ghastly, "murderous" and "magnetic" (3:409 [first version]) eyes of both the money-lender and his portrait affect all who see them, especially Chartkov and the holy artist. That this maleficent gaze can be transmitted to its victims is clear from the "basilisk stare" with which Chartkov looks at talented work (3:115).[59] In fact, spoilt vision is prevalent throughout the Petersburg stories. The kaleidoscope of clothes on Nevsky Prospect is "blinding" (3:12). On the same street Piskarev "has seen a wonderful woman just like Perugino's Bianca" (3:15), but later this woman's "single glance" causes the whole cityscape to break up and makes Piskarev chase after her "not hearing, not seeing, not sensing" (3:19). The policeman to whom Bashmachkin appeals after he has been robbed "has seen nothing" (3:162), and the police official in "The Nose" is short-sighted (as is his mother-in-law!), but fortunately has his glasses with him (3:66).[60] Both Chartkov (3:97) and Lise's mother (3:99) use a lorgnette (but see nothing), and in "Notes of a Madman" a woman aims her lorgnette at the devil (3:209). And

Petrovich, as noted earlier, is a "one-eyed devil" (3:149). In this context there is a striking aptness to Bely's remarks that "from his second phase a particularity of Gogol's vision cries out: one eye is long-sighted, the other short-sighted; one distances; the other brings close; one is a telescope; the other a microscope."[61]

But often the reality of Petersburg is so terrible that characters prefer not to see at all. Thus Bashmachkin decides that it is "better not to look" as he crosses the "endless square" on the way back from the party (3:161); Kovalev, having confirmed that his nose is, indeed, missing, "decided, against his usual habit, not to look at anyone" (3:54); and Poprishchin, at the very end of "Notes of a Madman," wishes to be taken "further, further, so that nothing can be seen, nothing" (3:214).[62]

Demonic forces attack not just the eyes, but the whole face and body. In "The Overcoat" Petrovich has a tobacco tin with the portrait of "some general" whose identity is unclear, since "the place where his face once was had been poked through with a finger (3:150), and Sergei Bocharov has drawn attention to the frequency with which the faces of Gogol's characters are absent or deformed, leading him to contend that in Gogol God fights the devil on men's faces.[63] But the battle also spreads to the body. In a fascinating recent study of the "convulsive body" in Gogol and Dostoevsky, Mikhail Iampol'sky has referred to the "negative body" of the devil, and drawn attention to the frequency of convulsive or automatic "desemanticized" movement in, for example, Bashmachkin, Chichikov, and Khlestakov, as well as reminding us that Boris Eikhenbaum, in his classic study "How Gogol's Overcoat is Made," describes Bashmachkin as speaking in "the language in which marionettes might speak."[64] The death of Piskarev causes his arms to extend convulsively (sudorozhno, 3:33) and the same phenomenon is widely recorded in "The Portrait," where the "convulsive movement" (sudorozhnoe dvizhenie, 3:82) which Chartkov notices in the portrait is echoed in the refusal of the hands and head in his own painting to take on the desired position (3:423 [first version]), in the "convulsions" (konvul'sii, 3:434 [first version]) of Petromikhali at the point of death, and in the convulsive death (sudorogi) of the artist's wife (3:438 [first version]).[65]

In the "The Meaning of Illnesses" section of the *Selected Passages* Gogol exclaims: "O! How necessary are our ailments!" and seeks the words to "thank heavenly providence for my illness" (8:228–29), interpreting this trial as a test of his will to moral betterment. He advises his addressee to pray to God to reveal the "miraculous meaning" of her own ailments. The popular belief that devils are responsible for illness is widely attested.[66] The characters in the Petersburg tales are assailed by a succession of demonically inspired symptoms ranging from fever to madness and death. Chartkov, in "The Portrait," is worst afflicted, becoming a "moving stone coffin with a corpse in it instead of a heart" (3:110), and experiencing fury and madness (beshenstvo i bezumie), a terrible illness (bolezn'), fever (goriachka), and consumption (chakhotka, 3:116) before his horrific death, but the young art patron also experiences "strange madness and fury" (3:124), as do Prince R. (3:125) and the holy artist, both of whom it almost causes to kill their wives (3:125, 130). Both Bash-machkin (3:167–68) and Piskarev (3:30–33) suffer a similar succession of ordeals. Though Pirogov and Kovalev are eventually restored to health, Pirogov experiences fever (likhoradka) and madness (3:44), and Kovalev, taken ill on the Nevsky, "almost went mad" (3:55), later deciding that Podtochina has "resolved to spoil (isportit') him and hired some sorceress-women to do it" (3:65).[67] The worst fate of all is the violent death and suicide that befalls so many of the characters in these stories – Chartkov, the holy artist's family, the young art patron and Prince R. in "The Portrait," Bashmachkin in "The Overcoat," and Piskarev in "Nevsky Prospect." Chartkov's corpse is described as terrifying (3:116), as is the "terrifyingly dis-torted aspect" of the dead Piskarev (3:33), and awareness of the demonic associations of suicide causes the narrator to assert that "I don't like corpses and dead people, and I always find it unpleasant when a long funeral procession crosses my path (3:33).[68]

Gogol writes widely of the moods induced by the devil. In "The Rule for Living in the World" the spirit of darkness induces "despon-dency" (unynie).[69] In a letter to Aksakov, the devil is described as causing alarm (volnenie), and his business is "in a word to frighten, to blow up (naduvat'), to bring to despondency (unynie)" (12:300–301). In the *Selected Passages* he is "the father of presumption" (8:298). These moods are also visited upon the heroes of the Peters-burg tales. Under the influence of the demonic painting Chartkov wants to become a glorious artist (3:97). His attempt to "catch glory … by the tail" (skhvatit' slavu … za khvost, 3:98) shows that he knows that it is a devil, but stolen glory gives him no joy and he searches for money (another demonic temptation) instead (3:110). Later he is assailed by the hellish thought (adskaia mysl', 3:417 [first version]), the "crazed envy" (3:115, 424 [first version]), the "hellish intention" (adskoe namerenie, 3:115, 424 [first version]), the "hellish enjoyment" (adskoe naslazhdenie, 3:424 [first version]), the "hellish desire" (adskoe zhelanie, 3:115, 424 [first version]) that eventually lead to his death. The same hellish moods attack the young Maece-nas, who becomes an informer; Prince R., who is plunged into terri-ble jealousy; and even the holy artist, to whose art Petromikhali wants to give a "hellish direction (adskoe napravlenie, 3:437 [first version]), and in whom he causes "a demonic feeling of envy"

(3:131). The friend he passes the portrait on to feels melancholy (toska), wants "to slit someone's throat," and is afflicted by dreams and insomnia (3:132). For these too are a gift of the devil.

Writing to his mother in November 1835, Gogol accuses her of paying too much attention to her dreams (mechty), and cautions her: "Please, mama, we dream all sorts of rubbish. … Dream (son) is a reflection of our disordered thoughts" (10:376). He gives her a lengthy description of how dreams work, concluding: "So you see, mama, that dream (son) is nothing more than unconnected, senseless fragments of our thoughts, which then stick together and make a salad (vinegret, 10:376–77). To his female correspondent in the "Woman in Society" section of *Selected Passages*, he insists that a number of social ills have their root cause in the "emptiness of the domestic life" of women, which is "given over to some ideal dreams (mechtam) and not to the essence of their duties, which are several times finer and more elevated than any dreams" (8:224). Several of Gogol's Petersburg characters are assailed by the temptation of dream. Piskarev finds it increasingly difficult to distinguish between dream (son) and reality (iav'). He becomes a typical Petersburg dreamer (mechtatel', 3:18), but "his own dreams make fun of him" (3:18–19). Eventually he chooses to induce dreams artificially ("Oh, how repulsive is reality!

14. "The Money-Lender's Blissful Dream," 1858. Lithographic transfer from a copper plate, 35 × 44 cm.

What is it by comparison with dream?" 3:27). For Chartkov, too, dreams of the old money-lender are a mesmerizing temptation. Chartkov does not know what he is experiencing, "the crushing weight of a nightmare or a house spirit (domovogo),[70] the raving (bred) of fever, or a living vision" (3:91). Eventually, in the last sentence of the story, people wonder whether the ominous painting itself was but a dream (prosto mechta, 3:137). For both these artist heroes, dreams are an eventually fatal temptation, the devilish implications of which are half intuited by Chartkov.[71]

The Fate of the Heavenly in Petersburg: Art and Women

For Gogol both art and women are potentially expressions of heavenly perfection, especially when encountered in Italy or the classical world generally. But neither art and artists nor women can survive the demonic forces that pervade St. Petersburg, and his treatment of them in his Petersburg writings is a catalogue of treachery and the dissolution of ideals.

Art

The importance of the subject of art for Gogol's Petersburg stories is apparent from the fact that the second version of "The Portrait" has no fewer than four artist protagonists: Chartkov; his contemporary who has "perfected himself" (3:110) in Italy; the "Artist B.," who recognizes the portrait of the money-lender; and his father, the holy artist who painted it and then withdrew to a monastery. The heavenly qualities of true art are explicitly discussed in the story, both by the holy artist, and earlier by the narrator in his description of Chartkov's contemporary. He describes this artist's work, directed by his "heavenly brush" (nebesnaia kist') as "pure, immaculate (neporochnoe), fine as a bride. ... Modestly, divinely (bozhestvenno), innocently and simply as genius it soared above everything. It seemed that the heavenly figures" lowered their eyes before the public gaze, "but the picture meanwhile seemed every minute loftier and loftier (vyshe i vyshe) ... and it was all turning into a single moment, the fruit of a thought which has flown down from the heavens on to the artist, a moment for which all human life is but a preparation." Before it everything merges "into some silent hymn to the divine work" (3:111–12). This intuition of the divine nature of art is articulated again at the end of the story by the holy artist. When his son is reunited with him his father's face shines "with the brightness of heavenly joy" (3:134). He describes art as a journey and talent as "the most precious gift of God." He tells his son that "a hint of divine, heavenly paradise is contained for man in art, and for that single reason it is already loftier than anything." By as much as an angel is "loftier than all the countless forces and proud passions of Satan, by so much is a lofty work of art loftier than anything that exists in the world," for art "strives eternally towards God" (3:135).

It is of fundamental importance that both of these artists paint their heavenly works outside of Petersburg; indeed, this very same point is made in "Nevsky Prospect," where the narrator exclaims of Piskarev at the beginning of a long passage about artists: "he was an artist. Is it not true that this is a strange phenomenon? A Petersburg artist! An artist in the land of snows, an artist in the country of Finns, where all is damp, smooth, flat, pale, grey, misty" (3:16). Such figures are explicitly contrasted with Italian artists. When speaking of the latter he refers directly to the sky and air that make them free and expansive, just as in "The Portrait" the artist works in Italy "in sight of the fine heavens" (3:110).

In Petersburg, even artists who are sentient of their holy mission encounter temptation. Thus the painter of the money-lender's portrait is explicitly described as a "godly" (nabozhnyi, 3:433) man, whose "inner feeling and own conviction turned his brush to Christian subjects, to the loftiest and last stage of the lofty" (3:127). His paintings are intended for the church. In this he is like the blacksmith Vakula, in "Christmas Eve," another God-fearing (bogoboiazlivyi, 1:203) man, who frequently paints for the church. The greatest of Vakula's paintings is of Saint Peter on the day of the Last Judgement expelling the evil spirit from hell. This terrifies the devil, who swears vengeance on the blacksmith (1:203–4).[72] Later, desperate to win Oksana's love, Vakula is tempted to give his soul to the devil, who is delighted that "the most godly man in the entire village is in my hands" (1:225). But Vakula soon repents of this weakness, yanks the devil by the tail, cows him by repeatedly making, or threatening to make, the sign of the cross (1:225, 232), and rides him to Petersburg. Though he here acquires what Oksana desires, the Tsaritsa's slippers, the story ends outside Petersburg, and the Petersburg gift is deemed unnecessary by Oksana. The final paragraph of the story describes the extraordinary power of a new church painting by Vakula of the devil in hell, a devil "so foul that everyone spat as they passed by" (1:243). Since Vakula is not a Petersburg artist, he manages to resist temptation with relative ease.

Things are not as simple for the portrait painter. He is struck by the forceful features of the money-lender, whom he calls "the devil, the perfect devil!" (3:126), and feels that he would be a perfect model for a church commission of a portrait of the "spirit of darkness" (3:127–28). When the money-lender asks for his portrait to be painted ("What could be better? He himself is asking to become a devil in my painting," 3:128), he notices an extraordinary power: "if I paint him in half the way he is now he will kill all my saints and angels. ... What devilish force" (3:128). He is gradually overwhelmed by alarm. Discarding his brush and palette he runs from the room. Driven by professional pride, he has failed to notice what a man of the cloth later observes, that the demonic has entered his art (3:130). He disposes of the painting to a friend, who quickly passes it on, since "the devil take it, there is something strange about it. ... I don't believe in witches, but say what you will, it has the evil spirit (nechistaia sila) in it." He likens the effect of owning the painting to being suffocated by a house spirit (domovoi), adding "well, brother, you have cooked up a devil" (sostriapal ty chorta, 3:132).[73] Thus, in Petersburg, art is particularly susceptible to being invaded by demonic forces of pride. The artist's brush has served as the "devil's tool" (3:133); unlike the "heavenly brush" of Italy, it is "sullied" (3:133). The life of the money-lender has entered the portrait "and alarms people, inspiring devilish (besovskie) impulses and seducing the artist from his path" (3:133). It is only after suffering and lengthy repentance that he can return to his art in a remote monastery. As he warns his own son: "Be amazed, my son, at the terrible power of the devil (besa). It tries to get into everything:

15. "The Money Devil," second quarter of the nineteenth century. Copper engraving, 30,5 × 37 cm. The corruption of art by money is indicated by the inclusion of a painter, armed with a gun, among the figures pursuing the money devil.

into our affairs, into our thoughts, and even into the very inspiration of the artist. The victims of this hellish spirit which lives unseen without image on the earth will be numberless" (3:443–44).

For artists who remain in Petersburg there can be no hope. Piskarev betrays his art both in reality, by agreeing to draw a "beauty" with "black brows, and eyes big as olives" (3:29) for a Persian in exchange for opium, and in his dreams. His "most joyous" dream is a complacent vision of his wife and himself in his studio. He sits palette in hand while his wife looks on adoringly. "He had never had a better dream," "everything in the room breathed of paradise" (3:30), but the disparity between this fantasy and coarse reality will destroy him. In general, Petersburg is not a place where art can flourish. The vulgarity of the artistic tastes of its officer class is described at length (3:35), and in Petersburg Schiller and Hoffmann are "not the Schiller who wrote *William Tell*" and "not the writer Hoffmann," but a tinsmith and cobbler (3:37).

But of course the most potent example of the Petersburg artist is Chartkov in "The Portrait." Though his name is changed in the second version of the story, both its original form, Chertkov, and a play on words in the original version give direct etymological evidence of his devilish inclinations and of the devil's hidden presence in Petersburg. Discussing Chertkov, the narrator writes: "is there for man some boundary (cherta), which higher cognition leads to, and crossing which he is already stealing something not created by the work of man. … Why is the crossing of this boundary (chertu), placed as a limit for the imagination, so terrible?" (3:405–6 [first version]).[74] More than any other Petersburg artist, Chartkov is driven by the spirit of vanity, as is shown by the article he commissions about himself (3:98–99). His professor is aware that he risks ruining his talent, and the terms he uses to express his concern are morally tinged: "it will be a sin (greshno) if you ruin (pogubit') it" (3:85), a word directly repeated by Chartkov (3:113) when he realizes the extent of his fall. In his pride he has denied "inspiration from above" (3:110) and the achievements of great artists,[75] and his consciousness that he has repeated the sin of Lucifer is made explicit both in his failed attempt to paint a "fallen angel" (otpadshego angela, 3:113),[76] and in the narrator's description of him in his final madness as a Harpy and as the personification of "that terrible demon which was portrayed ideally by Pushkin" (3:115).[77] So, in Petersburg, art can be the very devil.[78]

Women

Gogol's early writings often refer to women as idealized, heavenly creatures. At the beginning of his first published work, "Hans Küchelgarten" (Gants Kiukhel'garten, 1829) the beautiful heroine Luisa is described as "an inhabitant of heaven-paradise" (zhilitsei neba-raia, 1:62).[79] It was followed, in January 1831, by his first publication under his own name, "Woman" (Zhenshchina), a brief philosophical dialogue between Plato and his pupil Telecles on the nature of woman. The dialogue begins with Telecles' bitter complaint about his betrayal by the beautiful Alcinoe, but Plato insists that Telecles had found "life and happiness" in her embraces, and wonders whether "you would have wanted to take all the precious stones of the Shahs of Persia, all the gold of Libya for those heavenly (nebesnye) moments." He further insists she has "established heaven with its light, heavenly inhabitants in your soul;" that he has "read eternity in the heavenly features of Alcinoe;" that this has caused him to attain "new mysteries ... new revelations." "What is woman?" he asks, and replies: "The language of the gods! We are amazed by the meek, bright brow of man: but we do not see the likeness of the gods in it [man's brow, J.G.]; we see in it woman, we are amazed by woman in it, and only in her are we amazed by the gods. She is poetry, she is thought, and we are only her embodiment in reality" (8:145). He further describes the role of the artist as "to embody woman in man" (8:146). Persuaded, the rapturous Telecles throws himself at her feet.[80]

A similarly dazzling vision is presented by the beauty of Annunziata in the story "Rome" (Rim, 1842): "It was a miracle (chudo) in the highest degree. Everything must fade before this brilliance. ... It was the sun itself. Beauty in its fullness. . ... Believer and unbeliever would both fall down before her as before the sudden appearance of the godhead" (3:248). Woman as heavenly creature is also present in the "Woman in Society" section of *Selected Passages*. Here Gogol tells his female correspondent that "the beauty of woman is still a mystery. It was not for no reason that God ordered some women to be beauties" (8:226). But he stresses the good that beautiful women can do, describing his addressee as exuding "heavenly concern about people ... angelic yearning about them" in her soul, and as having a voice "in which man hears his sister who has flown down from the heavens" (8:227).

It is, nevertheless, striking that the very first words of "Woman" are Telecles' exclamation "Creature of hell!" (adskoe porozhdenie!) and that he accuses his teacher of being but a "baby in knowledge of the boundless depths of [her] treacherous heart" (8:143), for such is also the experience of women that attends upon Petersburg's bachelor clerks as they walk the Nevsky in search of erotic encounters.[81] The aerial imagery found in Gogol's other works is also present here. The narrator of "Nevsky Prospect" avows that "a lady would suddenly rise into the air if a man did not hold on to her" (3:13). Piskarev views his Bianca in the same way: she has "flown down from heaven straight on to the Nevsky Prospect and will probably fly off who knows where"

(3:16); she has "divine features" (3:18, 22), "a heavenly gaze" (3:19) and "a voice like a harp" (3:20). In his dreams she is "a pearl, the whole world, the whole paradise (ves' rai)" (3:22) of her husband, and the image of paradise is repeated to describe her setting (3:25, 30), as it is in Poprishchin's description of Sophie's boudoir as "a paradise the like of which does not exist in heaven" (3:200). But the infernal city has had a predictable effect upon the character of these women, and they are revealed to be seductive artificers, merely masquerading as the angelic innocents of their admirers' dreams. As the narrator of "Nevsky Prospect" warns: "Trust ladies least of all. … God forbid that you look under their hats" (3:46), an activity whose erotic potential he has already mentioned (3:15).[82] Both Piskarev and Poprishchin are betrayed by their heavenly creatures. Using the same words as Tele-cles, Poprishchin describes woman as "a perfidious creature," and con-tinues: "I have only now realized what woman is. Nobody has yet discovered whom she loves: I am the first to discover it. Woman is in love with the devil. … And she will marry him" (3:209).

In this context one notes the ubiquitousness of images of bewitch-ment in these stories. Bianca has "bewitched (okoldovala) and car-ried off" Piskarev on the Nevsky (3:21). Kovalev, too, repeatedly accuses Podtochina of employing sorceresses (koldovki-baby, 3:65) and soothsaying (volkhvovaniia, 3:70); and the aristocratic lady has "charmed" (ocharovala) Chartkov.[83] And even Bashmachkin, once he has got his new overcoat, is distracted by a picture of a woman discarding her boot (3:159), and makes to follow a lady down the street (3:160), only to be brought down to earth by the parodic re-evocation of the lady in the picture in his old landlady (3:162). So, in Petersburg, there is no hope for the heavenly, or for the naive and self-deluding men who continue to search for it. For art and women have made their pact with the devil, and the sinister price of this pact is paid by the doomed Petersburg bachelors.

The Devil and Vanity: Clothes and Mirrors

In his lascivious imaginings, Poprishchin describes Sophie's dress as "more like air than a dress" and her stocking as "white as snow" (3:199–200), just as Alcinoe's garments had seemed like "thin, light ether" (8:147). As Poprishchin says, when he sees Sophie: "Tell me now that women do not have a great passion for all these rags" (tri-apok, 3:194). But in this respect they are true inhabitants of Peters-burg, for the city itself is a fop (shchegol', 8:177), constantly dressing up and admiring itself (8:178). The word *shchegol'stvo* (foppery) and the descent into foppery are extraordinarily widespread in Gogol's

Petersburg tales. Piskarev, Poprishchin, and even Bashmachkin, once he acquires his new coat, show a hypertrophic interest in how they are dressed, but the most extensive use of this imagery concerns the young artist Chartkov in "The Portrait." As soon as he becomes successful "he visited a tailor, dressed from head to toe, and, like a child, started looking himself over all the time" (3:97). He rents a grand flat (foppish in the first version, 3:413, where he also lolls on a "Turkish divan"), and "changed his clothes several times a day" (3:107). In a reference to Gogol's own abiding interest in clothes, he is described as "walking up and down the pavement like a golden-eye (gogolem), aiming his lorgnette at people" (3:97).[84]

But for all these men, the move into foppery parallels their descent into perdition, and this is unsurprising since Gogol's devil also fancies himself, in "Christmas Eve," as a "handsome fellow" (krasavets, 1:204), and is described by the narrator as a "nimble dandy with a tail" (frant s khvostom, 1:215), which casts a sinister light on the "ladies in satin dresses with long trains" (s dlinnymi khvostami, 1:236), whom Vakula glimpses in Petersburg.[85] The devil can use clothes as a disguise for his nefarious purposes. In "Notes of a Madman" he hides in a fat man's star decoration (3:209), and in a letter of Gogol to Zhukovsky he "put on a green uniform with heraldic buttons, hung a sharp-pointed sword at his side and became a quarantine supervisor" (10:207). Chartkov's false, fashionable portrait of Lise is made by dressing her up as Psyche (3:105). Nevsky Prospect is also the setting for a fashion parade where you can meet "thousands of sorts of hats, dresses and scarves, light and multi-coloured" (3:12), but where a gentleman in a finely tailored frock coat "consists entirely of his frock-coat" (3:45).

Clothes are a sinister temptation. Annette,[86] in "The Portrait," wears an expression that craves the chance to discuss the decorations that the *modiste* Madame Sikhler has made for Princess B.'s dress (3:414 [first version]); but in the "What a Wife Can Be for Her Husband in Her Simple Domestic Life ..." section of the *Selected Passages* Gogol warns his correspondent not to worry about "comme il faut," because "real comme il faut is what is demanded from man by Him who created him ... and not by Madame Sikhler herself" (8:340).

This explicit contrast of the Almighty and a dress-designer emphasizes that those associated with clothes, and their accoutrements, have demonic implications. The tailor Petrovich's demonic qualities have already been discussed, and it may be an apprehension of this that leads Poprishchin to exclaim in horror that he does not come from a line of tailors (3:198), and that tailors are "donkeys" and "scoundrels," who may "spoil" (isportit') his royal costume if he gives it to them to make (3:210). Though Gogol described himself in a letter to his uncle in 1828 as a "good tailor" (khoroshii portnoi, 10:133), his vision of contemporary hell in the "Easter Sunday" section of the *Selected Passages* is of a world in which "seamstresses (shvei), tailors (portnye) and all sorts of craftsmen rule the world, and God's anointed sovereigns have been left to one side" (8:415). That the tailor can be metonymically represented by his needle is apparent from the use for both of them of the same epithet. Just as Petrovich shows "barbarian (varvarskoe) calm" (3:151), so his needle is a "barbarian" (varvarka, 3:149).[87] And it is "ten needles" that kill the artist's wife in "The Portrait" when he attempts to reveal the demonic secret (3:438 [first version]).[88]

Mirrors, too, are widely held to be a demonic invention, since the shades of the dead can appear in them.[89] It is therefore striking just how widespread they are in Gogol's Petersburg writings. In "Petersburg Notes of 1836" the city itself is made up of mirrors: "There are mirrors before it on all sides: there is the Neva, there is the Gulf of Finland. It (foppish Petersburg) has somewhere to look at itself in" (8:177). This narcissism is echoed in the use of mirrors in the tales. The first thing Kovalev does on waking is "to call for the small mirror that stands on his table" (3:52); when Poprishchin bursts into Sophie's dressing-room he finds her "sitting at her mirror" (3:209); when Piskarev enters the brothel a prostitute "was sitting in front of a mirror … and did not think at all of abandoning her toilette when a stranger entered" (3:20); and when Chartkov acquires his fashionable flat with its "mirrors and French windows" he "constantly adjusts his newly waved curls against the mirror" (3:97) and "walks around the grand rooms, constantly looking in mirrors" (3:98). The only one of these narcissists not to be doomed is the village girl Oksana. She too "lengthily smartened herself up and preened in front of a small pewter-framed mirror" and "holding the mirror a little further away from herself she shrieked: 'No, I am pretty! Oh, so pretty! A marvel!'" (1:207), but the prospect of losing Vakula's love brings her to her senses, and she insists that she does not need his gift of the Tsaritsa's slippers, "waving her hands and unable to keep her eyes off him" (1:243). The Petersburg characters, fixated by *their own* reflections, are incapable of such good sense. Thus the city, in all its manifestations, in its physical space, its temporal cycles, its climate, and in the character and behaviour of its inhabitants, is, to an extent that is without parallel in any other spaces described by Gogol, the realm of the demonic.

The Devil and Sense

Because the devil is at the invisible centre of the Petersburg world, space, time and other referential categories are fragmented and dismantled. Because, in infinite regression, "*everything* is not what it seems" (3:45; emphasis mine), the characters have no stable system of values to act by, and the narrators no stable heuristic system to interpret by. It is remarkable how many of the endings of the tales are open and how much of their plot is frustratingly unexplained, a fact which the narrator of "The Nose" acknowledges, only to dismiss it with his final, lame contention that "such events happen in the world; rarely, but they happen" (3:75).

Several of the most challenging of recent critics of Gogol's Petersburg writings stress that this is a world without sense. Gary Saul Morson calls the adventures of the nose "not *explicable in any way.* ... What we have here is *absolute* nonsense, nonsense that conforms not even to a system of nonsense;" while Donald Fanger says that in the story "Gogol has created a puzzle that many keys may fit, but none open."[90] O.G. Dilaktorskaia concludes that "in 'Notes [of a Madman]' the principle of alogicality acts in the word, in the syntactical construction, in the building of motif and image, in the building of the consciousness of the hero, of all the atmosphere of life, striking in its unfantastic fantasticness."[91]

This alogicality, too, is caused by the devil. Ann Shukman, quoting the phrase in "Nevsky Prospect" in which "the devil broke up the whole world into a multiplicity of little pieces and mixed all these pieces together without sense and without point" (bez smysla, bez tolku, 3:24), concludes that "the struggle between man and the devil then is perhaps the struggle between the principle of sense-making and the principle of sense-destroying nonsense."[92] Cathy Popkin, in a section of her study of Gogol entitled "The Devil Only Knows What to Make of It," suggests that in Gogol the devil is "an agent provocateur, one who inflames desire only to sabotage its satisfaction," and links the demonic frustration of desire to the demonic generation of frustrating discourse, concluding that "the rampant devilry, then, is both source and object of the rampant storytelling and all the complaints it inspires."[93]

In the "About What the Word Is" section of *Selected Passages* Gogol insists: "You must treat the word honourably. It is the highest gift of God to man. ... It is dangerous for a writer to joke with the word." He warns against the foppish use of words (poshchegoliat' slovom), and adds that "our language is our betrayer" (8:231–32).[94] But this advice is undermined in Petersburg, where "complete nonsense happens in the world" (3:73).

Bashmachkin's words "mean decidedly nothing" (ne imeiut nikakogo znacheniia, 3:149), he speaks "complete nonsense, so that you could not understand a thing" (3:168). The expression of the demonic Petrovich is "meaningful" (znachitel'noe, 3:155); the important personage, however, while glad that a word from him may "even cause a man to lose consciousness" (3:167), is concerned that joining an interesting conversation may mean that he will "drop (uronit) ... his significance" (znachenie, 3:165), as if meaning were merely one friable object among others. In "The Nose" both the characters and the narrator regularly "do not understand" what is happening, culminating in the narrator's admission: "I confess it is already quite incomprehensible, it's just like ... no, no, I just don't understand ... I simply don't know what it is" (3:75). The same confusion reigns in "Notes of a Madman," where near the end Poprishchin confesses: "I don't understand, I don't understand, I decidedly don't understand a thing" (3:213). Kovalev and the barber repeatedly insist, on the other hand, that "the devil knows" what is going on, that "only the devil will make this out!" (tol'ko chert razberet eto!, 3:71).[95] For in this quintessentially confused world, where dogs talk and even the cats are senseless (bessmylennye koshki, 3:329), the devil has subverted the rules that govern the generation and reception of meaning itself.

Gogol's Legacy

Gogol's achievement in his treatment of the demonic in his Petersburg writings is unobtrusively to blend the folkloric consciousness of the devil that informed his earlier writings with a modern sensibility that finds the demonic expressed through elements of the illogical and of existential alienation. This demonic vision of the city, this shadow cast by Gogol's overcoat, becomes a fundamental constituent feature of the "Petersburg text" in the work of later writers. Thus the vision of the fantastic city, now so routinely invoked as a quintessential domain of contemporary urban unease, has its roots in Gogol's anxious retreat into the familiar world of the "habits and customs of our Little Russians" (10:141).

Dostoevsky, it seems, did not in fact say that "we all came out from under Gogol's 'Overcoat'," but he obsessively rewrote Gogolian texts and episodes in his writings, and repeatedly invoked Gogolian moods and atmospheres. His description of Petersburg in "Notes from Underground" (Zapiski iz podpol'ia, 1864) as "the most abstract and intentional city in the entire world" (samom otvlechennom i umyshlennom gorode na vsem zemnom share) is only the most concise of his re-evocations of a Gogolian world.[96]

Of the Russian symbolists, Merezhkovsky and Briusov, Blok, Bely, and Remizov have all written absorbing critical analyses of the Gogolian world, as well as showing his influence deep in the structures and motifs of their writings. Blok's cycle "The Terrible World"

(Strashnyi mir, 1909–16), to take but one example, not only uses an essentially Gogolian term for its title, but structures its picture of Petersburg round Gogolian motifs of lostness, senselessness, the meaninglessness of time and space, where doomed encounters take place in a climate of dankness, fog and contamination lit by a mocking street lamp. Bely provides detailed analyses of the Gogolian legacy in the work of a number of nineteenth- and twentieth-century writers in chapters at the end of his *Gogol's Mastery* (*Masterstvo Gogolia*, 1934). Writing of the influence of Gogol on his novel *Petersburg* (*Peterburg*, 1913–14), he shows how the noses, side-burns, and moustaches of Gogol's clerks, the terrible Petersburg weather they have to endure, and the illnesses and fevers they suffer have all migrated into the crazed atmosphere of his own work. He concludes: "Bely's prose, in its sound, image, range of colours, plot elements, is the summation of work on Gogol's linguistic imagery; this prose renews in the twentieth century Gogol's *school*."[97] The achievements of a later generation of Russian writers, particularly of Bulgakov and Zamiatin, are also unthinkable without their dependence on Gogol's urban demonism.[98]

Gogol did not find the paradise he sought in Petersburg. Perhaps because by its very nature the search for paradise on earth was doomed to failure, he was destined to find only the demonic. In this lies a microcosmic parallel of the frustration of other hopes: of Gogol's repeated searches for something to believe in, of the historical creation of the city itself, and of the long, baulked Russian obsession with utopian visions. Nevertheless, without the sights that Gogol saw there, our own vision of this "most intentional city in the world" would be occluded.

Notes

1. N.V. Gogol', *Polnoe sobranie sochinenii*, ed. N.L. Meshcheriakov and others, 14 vols., (Moscow and Leningrad: Izdatel'stvo Akademii nauk SSSR, 1937–52), 10:83. Henceforth references to this edition will be by volume and page number within the text and notes. All translations are my own.

2. On this see Robert Maguire, *Exploring Gogol* (Stanford: Stanford University Press, 1994), 102–7, the section "Distanced Height."

3. N.V. Gogol', "Pravilo zhitiia v mire," publ. G. Kjetsaa, in *N.V. Gogol'. Materialy i issledovaniia*, ed. Iu.V. Mann (Moscow: Nasledie, 1995), 6–10(8–9).

4. On this house see Ksana Blank, "Po zakoldovannym mestam Gogolia," *Novoe literaturnoe obozrenie* 11 (1995):177–79 (177). The house also plays a role in the story "Notes of a Madman," where the hero Popryshchin describes it as "Eka mashina!" (3:196).

5. A similar concern over the floor he lives on in St. Petersburg is exhibited by the boastful Khlestakov in *The Inspector General*: "You rush up the stairs to your fourth-floor flat ... oh, what am I saying, I forgot that I live on the first floor" (4:49).

6. Compare this description with that of the Petersburg suburb of Kolomna in "The Portrait" (3:119). "The Portrait" exists in two versions, the first "Arabesques" version of 1835 and the second version of 1842. Reference in this article will be to the second version unless specifically indicated.

7. Compare Iu.M. Lotman's contention that: "Gogol is a writer who synthesized the most various elements of national life. The sharp modernity of his works was combined with the capacity to penetrate into the deepest layers of the archaic consciousness of the people. Thus the works of Gogol can serve as the basis for the reconstruction of the mythological beliefs of the Slavs, going back to the most ancient times, and, of course, unknown to Gogol on the conscious level." Iu.M. Lotman, "Gogol' i sootnesenie 'smekhovoi kul'tury' s komicheskim i ser'eznym v russkoi natsional'noi traditsii," in *Materialy vsesoiuznogo simpoziuma po vtorichnym modeliruiushchim sistemam 1(5),* ed. Iu.M. Lotman (Tartu: Tartuskii gosudarstvennyi universitet, 1974), 131–33(132). The recourse to the familiarity of folk belief as a reaction to disappointment with the city is echoed in the returns of Gogol's narrator from Petersburg to the "joy" of country life in the story "Old World Landowners" (Starosvetskie pomeshchiki, 1835). On this see Julian Graffy, "Passion versus Habit in *Old World Landowners,*" in *Nikolay Gogol. Text and Context,* ed. Jane Grayson and Faith Wigzell (Basingstoke and London: Macmillan, 1989), 34–49(39–40).

8. On the ubiquitousness of the cognate image of emptiness (pustota) in Gogol's descriptions of Petersburg, see V.N. Toporov, "Peterburg i peterburgskii tekst russkoi literatury," *Uchenye zapiski Tartuskogo gosudarstvennogo universiteta 664, Trudy po znakovym sistemam* 18 (1984):4–29 (20). The image of a town as the quintessence of emptiness is also used by Gogol in his drafts for *Dead Souls*: "The idea of the town. Emptiness brought to the highest degree. Empty words" (6:692).

9. The idea of cutting off a nose is also present in "Nevsky Prospect," 3:38. On "fragmentation as demonism" in the earlier Dikanka stories, see Mikhail Vaiskopf, *Siuzhet Gogolia* (Moscow: Radiks, 1993), 58–59, a pioneering study which is full of brilliant insights about Gogol's use of demonic themes, and to which I am greatly indebted.

10. This image is strikingly used to suggest chaos in a famous sequence in Sergei Eizenshtein's film about the Russian Revolution *October* (*Oktiabr'*, 1927). For Eizenshtein's continuing interest in Gogol see his "Gogol' i kinoiazyk," introd. N.M. Kleiman, *Kinovedcheskie zapiski* 4 (1989):94–112; the "Masterstvo Gogolia" section of his *Memuary,* 2 vols. (Moscow: Redaktsiia gazety "Trud" and Dom kino, 1997), 2:172–78; and his plan for an unfinished book, "Pushkin i Gogol'," *Kinovedcheskie zapiski* 36–37 (1997–98):180–220.

11. L.N. Vinogradova, "Kalendarnye perekhody nechistoi sily vo vremeni i prostranstve," in *Kontsept dvizheniia v iazyke i kul'ture,* ed. T.A. Agapkina (Moscow: Indrik, 1996), 166–84 (171). See also the discussion of this topic in this volume by Faith Wigzell, "The Russian Folk Devil and His Literary Reflections."

12. On this see Graffy, "Passion versus Habit," 39.

13. On the house-wood opposition and its destruction, see Iu.M. Lotman, "Zametki o khudozhestvennom prostranstve," *Uchenye zapiski Tartuskogo gosudarstvennogo universiteta 720, Trudy po znakovym sistemam* 19 (1986):25–43(36). On the "iron house" as the dark abode of the devil and of vice, see Vaiskopf, *Siuzhet Gogolia,* 252–54.

14. On examples of the demonic capture of the heavens in Gogol's early stories, see Vaiskopf, *Siuzhet Gogolia,* 84–85, 120–21.

15. The use of the word "revelation" rather than "inspiration" in the first version of "The Portrait" (3:420) makes the spiritual implications even clearer.

16. Priscilla Meyer, "False Pretenders and the Spiritual City: 'A May Night' and 'The Overcoat,'" in *Essays on Gogol. Logos and the Russian Word,* ed. Susanne Fusso and Priscilla Meyer (Evanston, Ill.: Northwestern University Press, 1992), 63–74(72).

17. Iu. Lotman, "O 'realizme' Gogolia," *Trudy po russkoi i slavianskoi filologii. Literaturovedenie* 2 (n.s.) (1996):11–35(12).

18. O.G. Dilaktorskaia, "Khudozhestvennyi mir Peterburgskikh povestei N.V. Gogolia," in N.V. Gogol', *Peterburgskie povesti*, ed. O.G. Dilaktorskaia (St. Petersburg: Nauka, 1995), 207–57(224). Dilaktorskaia also alludes here to the frequency of the motif of the barber (tochil'shchik nosov) in the *lubok*, another possible source of Gogol's inversions in the story.

19. On the use of the up-down division and of falling imagery, and on the connections of this imagery both with Lucifer and Saint Paul, in the first half of *Dead Souls*, see A.Kh. Gol'denberg and S.A. Goncharov, "Legendarno-mifologicheskaia traditsiia v 'Mertvykh dushakh'," in *Russkaia literatura i kul'tura novogo vremeni*, no editor indicated (St. Petersburg: Russkaia Akademiia nauk, 1994), 21–48(38).

20. Gogol', "Pravilo zhitiia," 8.

21. Geir Kjetsaa, "Gogol'-propovednik: Novye materialy," in Mann, ed., *N.V. Gogol'. Materialy i issledovaniia*, 11–21(16). See also Liza Knapp, "Gogol' and the Ascent of Jacob's Ladder. Realization of Biblical Metaphor," in *Christianity and the Eastern Slavs*, vol. 3, *Russian Literature in Modern Times*, ed. Boris Gasparov and others (Berkeley: University of California Press, 1995), 3–15, which discusses the use of the motif particularly in "A May Night" and *Dead Souls*; and N.V. Khomchuk and A.S. Ianushkevich, "Otzvuki pritchi o bludnom syne v Peterburgskikh povestiakh N.V. Gogolia," in *"Vechnye" siuzhety russkoi literatury. "Bludnyi syn" i drugie*, ed. E.K. Romodanovskaia and V.I. Tiupa (Novosibirsk: Rossiiskaia Akademiia nauk. Sibirskoe otdelenie, 1996), 68–78(68).

22. On the use of the "tower" image and the motif of looking down from a high place, in such texts as "On Contemporary Architecture" in *Arabesques*, and also in "On Leaving the Theatre" and *Dead Souls*, see Leon Stilman, "The 'All-Seeing Eye' in Gogol," in *Gogol from the Twentieth Century. Eleven Essays*, ed. Robert A. Maguire (Princeton: Princeton University Press, 1976), 376–89.

23. Cited from V. Veresaev, *Gogol' v zhizni. Sistematicheskii svod podlinnykh svidetel'stv sovremennikov* (Moscow: Moskovskii rabochii, 1990), 566.

24. There is another beautiful staircase in "Christmas Eve," one which Vakula thinks it would be "a shame to trample with one's feet" (1:234), but it should be noted that this story is set in the eighteenth century, in the time of Catherine, and that its hero returns from Petersburg soon after.

25. Ksana Blank argues persuasively that the "ladies" whom Poprishchin follows are in fact maidservants. Blank, "Po zakoldovannym mestam," 177–78.

26. For the symbolic use of the image in the oppressive *lestnitsy* climbed by Pushkin's German in "The Queen of Spades" and Dostoevsky's Raskol'nikov in *Crime and Punishment*, thus placing Gogol at the centre of a symbolic tradition, see V.N. Toporov, "O strukture romana Dostoevskogo v sviazi s arkhaichnymi skhemami mifologicheskogo myshleniia (*Prestuplenie i nakazanie*)," in *Structure of Texts and Semiotics of Culture*, ed. Jan Van der Eng and Mojmír Grygar (The Hague and Paris: Mouton, 1973), 226–302(248, 246).

27. Compare the word *prospekt* with the use of the semantically comparable word *krugozor* (horizon) in the description of an ideal capital city in the "On Contemporary Architecture" essay in *Arabesques* (8:62). On the history of the term *prospekt*, see Elena Hellberg-Hirn, "Nevskii prospekt v svete postmodernizma," in *Modernizm i postmodernizm v russkoi literature i kul'ture*, Studia Russica Helsingensia et Tartuensia 5, *Slavica Helsingensia* 16 (1996):323–34(324). On its semantics, see Toporov, "Peterburg," 24–25 n.29.

28. Dilaktorskaia, "Khudozhestvennyi mir," 215.

29. In the context of the devil's thraldom over the Nevsky, it is interesting that Chartkov, when he sets himself up there, struts the street "ready to take on the devil" (chortu ne brat, 3:97).

30. Gogol', "Pravilo zhitiia," 6.

31. Compare the use of the street lamp in the Petersburg texts of such writers as Pushkin and Dostoevsky, Blok and Bely; and see, for example, A.L. Toporkov, "Iz mifologii russkogo simvolizma. Gorodskoe osveshchenie," in *Uchenye zapiski Tartuskogo gosudarstvennogo universiteta* 657, *Mir A. Bloka. Blokovskii sbornik V* (Tartu: Tartuskii gosudarstvennyi universitet, 1985), 101–12.

32. For another example of the devil's deceptive treatment of a source of light, see the episode in Dikanka at the start of "Christmas Eve" in which the devil steals the moon so that humans will lose their way (1:203). In the context of the devil's relationship with light, see the assessment of the devil as Lucifer in the entry on "Satan" in *The Oxford Companion to the Bible*, ed. Bruce M. Metzger and Michael D. Coogan (New York and Oxford: Oxford University Press, 1993), 678–79, and S.S. Averintsev, "Liutsifer," in *Mify narodov mira*, ed. S.A. Tokarev, 2d ed., 2 vols. (Moscow: Sovetskaia entsiklopediia, 1987–88), 2:84; and, in the Gogolian context, S.A. Pavlinov, *Filosofskie pritchi Gogolia. Peterburgskie povesti* (Moscow: authorial publication, 1997), 52–53. On the devil and light in Gogol's stories see the "Temnyi svet" and "Bor'ba za lunu" sections of Vaiskopf, *Siuzhet Gogolia*, 285–87, 301. On deceptive light, see also Mikhail Epshtein, "Ironiia stilia: Demonicheskoe v obraze Rossii u Gogolia," *Novoe literaturnoe obozrenie* 19 (1996):129–47 (134–35), and compare Bely's description of Gogol's "rare ability to make a picture from light, darkness and glimmerings in only two strokes," in Andrei Belyi, *Masterstvo Gogolia* (reprint, Ann Arbor: Ardis, 1982), 132.

33. See the calendar of the activities of devils in the *nechistaia sila* section of T.A. Novichkova, *Russkii demonologicheskii slovar'* (St. Petersburg: Peterburgskii pisatel', 1995), 393–443(397–435).

34. Vinogradova, "Kalendarnye perekhody," 166.

35. "The most popular and ubiquitous … is the belief about the division of *the time of day* into 'one's own' (svoe) time, which has been made its own by human beings (the day time, before the sun goes down) and 'alien' (chuzhoe) time (dusk, midnight until the first cock-crow) as the most malevolent and dangerous, belonging to the unclean spirit." Vinogradova, "Kalendarnye perekhody," 166–67. Compare: "periodically in the course of the year there is a repetition of times of the 'opening' of the boundary between the worlds, times intended on each occasion for a particular category of spirits." Ibid., 182.

36. In the first version of "The Portrait": "The shadows thickened at that time, in order, it seemed, to make this unfathomable phenomenon even more terrible" (3:405). In the second version the demonic connotations are made more explicit: "The red light of dusk remained in part of the sky … and at the same time the cold blueish light of the moon was already becoming stronger. Semi-transparent light shadows fell tail-like (teni khvostami padali) on to the earth" (3:83). On *ten'* see Novichkova, *Russkii demonologicheskii slovar'*, 540–42. On Gogol's awareness that the devil has a tail, see his letters to Aksakov (12:300) and to Smirnova (14:154).

37. On the hypertrophic use of the word *vremia* in "The Overcoat," see M. Vaiskopf, "Poetika peterburgskikh povestei Gogolia (Priemy ob"ektivatsii i gipostazirovaniia)," *Slavica Hierosolymitana* 3 (1978):8–54 (53), where he finds it to be used thirty-one times.

38. On the link of the coat to "the world of contingency" see Donald Fanger, *The Creation of Nikolai Gogol* (Cambridge, Mass., and London: The Belknap Press of Harvard University Press, 1979), 158ff.

39. Dilaktorskaia, "Khudozhestvennyi mir," 275 n.28. On the demonic implications of Friday, see also the entry on *piatnitsa* in Novichkova, *Russkii demonologicheskii slovar'*, 471–77. The same timelessness noted in the other stories may also be at work in "The Nose," which begins on 25 March (3:49) and ends on 7 April (3:73). The striking insistence on naming these two dates may be motivated by the fact that a transference from the Julian to the Gregorian calendar would mean that the story's events took place "outside time," over a single night and were, perhaps, a (devilish) dream, something further indicated by the fact that the Russian title of the story, *Nos* is an inversion of the Russian word for dream, *son*. On "null time" in the story, see Vaiskopf, "Poetika," 23.

40. On the demonic implications of bad weather, see the entries on *veter, vikhr', metel'*, and *moroz* in Novichkova, *Russkii demonologicheskii slovar'*, 78–86, 86–88, 383–84, and 388–89, respectively, and Vinogradova, "Kalendarnye perekhody," 167–68, for the devil's association with the *sviatki* period between Christmas and Epiphany. On the workings of climatic and meteorological forces in Petersburg, see also Toporov, "Peterburg," 18–19 and, on the horizontality of Petersburg climatic phenomena, 23–24; and Vaiskopf, *Siuzhet Gogolia*, 200–201, 246–47, 318. On the link of Poprishchin's madness to the wind, and on a similar affliction affecting Hamlet, see Dilaktorskaia, "Khudozhestvennyi mir," 250. For an example of direct demonic climatic intervention, see the scene in Dikanka in "Christmas Eve" where the devil causes a snowstorm (1:212), leading Chub to exclaim: "What a pile of snow Satan has thrown in our eyes!" (1:213).

41. The Gogolian fog is one of the key elements taken up by later writers in their evocation of the fantastic, unstable qualities of Petersburg. In Dostoevsky's novel *Podrostok* (1875), for example, the hero calls the Petersburg morning "chut' li ne samym fantasticheskim v mire," and dreams a dream in which, on such a "peterburgskoe utro, gniloe, syroe i tumannoe," the fog will disperse and "ne uidet li s nim vmeste i ves' etot gniloi, sklizlyi gorod, podymetsia s tumanom i ischeznet, kak dym." F.M. Dostoevskii, *Podrostok*, in his *Polnoe sobranie sochinenii v tridtsati tomakh*, ed. V.G. Bazanov and others, 30 vols. (Leningrad: Nauka, 1972–90), 13:113.

42. See the entries on *besy* and *demon* in Tokarev, ed., *Mify narodov mira*, 1:169–70, 366–67.

43. On the devil's ubiquitousness for Gogol, see Robert Maguire's remarks about Dmitrii Merezhkovsky's article "Gogol and the Devil": "The devil exists 'outside space and time, he is omnipresent and eternal'." Robert Maguire, "Introduction," in Maguire, ed., *Gogol from the Twentieth Century*, 31. See also Merezhkovsky's remarks on the demonic Khlestakov as a "moral and mental *median* incarnate, a mediocrity." Ibid., 63.

44. On this text see K.Iu. Rogov, "Gogol' i 'khromoi chert' (K tvorcheskoi istorii 'Vecherov na khutore bliz Dikan'ki')," in *Sed'mye Tynianovskie chteniia*, ed. M.O. Chudakova (Riga and Moscow, 1995–96), 130–34.

45. Toby W. Clyman, "The Hidden Demons in Gogol''s *Overcoat*," *Russian Literature* 7 (1979):601–10(602–3). Both Clyman and Alexis E. Emerson-Topornin in his "*Šinel'*. The Devil's Ovals. Motif of the Doubles," *Forum at Iowa on Russian Literature* 1, no.1 (1976):34–56, consider the demonic aspects of Petrovich and offer useful surveys of the large number of earlier discussions of the subject. We also note here the "abyss" (bezdna) that separates Petrovich from other tailors (3:156).

46. On this see the entry for *besy* in Tokarev, ed., *Mify narodov mira*, 1:169–70.

47. On the terrible death of the miser "whose body and soul are taken over by the devil," see the *chert* section of Novichkova, *Russkii demonologicheskii slovar'*, 591. On the devil's links with money and treasure, see ibid., 594.

48. Meyer, "False Pretenders," 69; Clyman, "The Hidden Demons," 602. Compare a passage in a later Petersburg text profoundly concerned with questions of iden-

tity and deception, Dostoevsky's *The Double*. Mr Goliadkin senior accuses Mr Goliadkin junior in the following terms: "'A samozvanstvom i besstydstvom, milostivyi gosudar', v nash vek ne berut. Samozvanstvo i besstydstvo, milostivyi moi gosudar', ne k dobru privodit, a do petli dovodit. Grishka Otrep'ev tol'ko odin, sudar' vy moi, vzial samozvanstvom, obmanul slepoi narod, da i to nenadolgo'." Dostoevskii, *Polnoe sobranie sochinenii*, 1:167–68. For a Dostoevskian Grigorii who watches, see *The Brothers Karamazov*. For the demonic connotations of the name Petr in Dostoevsky's character Petr Verkhovensky in *The Devils*, see in this volume W.J. Leatherbarrow, "The Devils' Vaudeville: 'Decoding' the Demonic in Dostoevsky's *The Devils*."

49. See especially Vaiskopf, "Poetika," 19–22; Vaiskopf, *Siuzhet Gogolia*, 537–38 n.348; Dilaktorskaia, "Khudozhestvennyi mir," 217–24. The demonic connotations of barbers are also alluded to in "Christmas Eve" where the snowstorm aroused by the devil whips around Chub's face like the tyrannical activities of a barber who has grabbed his victim by the nose (1:215).

50. Gogol', "Pravilo zhitiia," 7. On devils as *iskusiteli*, especially of monks and ascetics, see the entry for *besy* in Tokarev, ed., *Mify narodov mira*, 1:169–70.

51. In this context it is striking that the first sentence of Iurii Lotman's last article on Gogol reads, categorically: "Gogol was a liar" (Gogol' byl lgun), and that he goes on to refer to "lying and seeming" as the key theme of Gogol's work. Lotman, "O 'realizme' Gogolia," 11, 18.

52. Ibid., 29.

53. Cited from V. Veresaev, *Gogol' v zhizni*, 441.

54. For Nikolai Osipov's contention that Gogol's "main idea" was "how to make a fool of the devil," see Alexander Etkind, *Eros of the Impossible* (Boulder, Col. and Oxford: Westview, 1997), 222.

55. On Kovalev and the barber Ivan Iakovlevich as the reverse of the smith Vakula (*kovat'*, meaning "to forge," plus reversal of the consonants vkl/kvl), see Vaiskopf, "Poetika," 35.

56. For meeting the devil at a crossroads, see Novichkova, *Russkii demonologicheskii slovar'*, 395. For the way a demonically-inspired snowstorm can make you lose your way, see the entry on *metel'*, ibid., 383–84. For examples of fantastically inspired loss of one's way in other Gogolian texts, see Iu. Mann, *Poetika Gogolia*, 2d ed. (Moscow: Khudozhestvennaia literatura, 1988), 113–14.

57. Gogol', "Pravilo zhitiia," 10.

58. On the devil's capacity for blinding people, see the entry on "demons" in Metzger and Coogan, eds., *The Oxford Companion to the Bible*, 162–63.

59. On the maleficent gaze of the basilisk, see, for example the entries on *vasilisk* in Tokarev, ed., *Mify narodov mira*, 1:218, and Novichkova, *Russkii demonologicheskii slovar'*, 63. On the source of the theme of seeing as demonic temptation in Genesis, see Epshtein, "Ironiia stilia," 132, and see this article passim for Gogolian images of seeing. On the malevolent gaze see also Stilman, "The 'All-Seeing Eye'."

60. On the anomaly of an official wearing glasses, and the need to obtain special permission to do so, see Dilaktorskaia, "Khudozhestvennyi mir," 276 n.30.

61. Belyi, *Masterstvo Gogolia*, 267. On Gogol's use of telescope and microscope imagery, see Susanne Fusso, "The Landscape of *Arabesques*," in Fusso and Meyer, eds., *Essays on Gogol*, 112–25(114–15).

62. On the relationship of seeing and not seeing in Gogol, see Viach.Vs. Ivanov, "Kategoriia 'vidimogo' i 'nevidimogo' v tekste: Eshche raz o vostochnoslavian-skikh fol'klornykh paralleliakh k gogolevskomu 'Viiu'," in Van der Eng and Grygar, eds., *Structure of Texts*, 151–76. For important recent contributions to the theme of vision in Gogol, see B.M. Gasparov, "'Suddenly All the Distant Ends of

the Earth Became Visible.' (The Theme of Mystical Revelation in Gogol's Work and Life)," in *O Rus! Studia Litteraria Slavica in Honorem Hugh McLean*, ed. Simon Karlinsky, James L. Rice, and Barry P. Scherr (Berkeley: Berkeley Slavic Studies, 1995), 219–32; and chap.7, "The Art of Seeing," in Maguire, *Exploring Gogol*, 97–114.

63. Sergei Bocharov, "Around 'The Nose'," in Fusso and Meyer, eds., *Essays on Gogol*, 19–39(24, 23). On the idea of facelessness as meaninglessness in "The Nose," see Dilaktorskaia, "Khudozhestvennyi mir," 225–26.

64. Mikhail Iampol'skii, "Konvul'sivnoe telo: Gogol' i Dostoevskii," chap.1 of his *Demon i labirint (Diagrammy, deformatsii, mimesis)* (Moscow: Novoe literaturnoe obozrenie, 1996), 18–51. On the "negative body," 41; on "desemanticized movement," 36; on Eikhenbaum, 22.

65. On mechanized movement, compare Vasilii Rozanov's remarks about *Dead Souls*: "They are tiny wax figures, but they all make their grimaces so skilfully that for a long time we suspected that they may be moving. But they are unmoving ... all the others move their arms and legs, but not at all because they want to do so; it is the author moving their legs for them." V.V. Rozanov, *Legenda o velikom inkvizitore. Dve stat'i o Gogole* (reprint, Munich: Wilhelm Fink, 1970), 261. And compare Iurii Mann, "Gogol's Poetics of Petrification," in Fusso and Meyer, eds., *Essays on Gogol*, 75–88.

66. On demonic causes of illness, see, for example, the entry on *besy* in Tokarev, ed., *Mify narodov mira*, 1:169–70; and the entry on *likhoradki* in Novichkova, *Russkii demonologicheskii slovar'*, 343–52. On the calendar of *dukhi boleznei*, see Vinogradova, "Kalendarnye perekhody," 172, and the calendar in Novichkova, *Russkii demonologicheskii slovar'*, 397–435.

67. On "spoiling" (porcha), see the entry on *besy* in Tokarev, ed., *Mify narodov mira*, 1:169; and consider the meaning of the verb *podtochit'*, to undercut, undermine health, in *Russko-angliiskii slovar'*, ed. A.I. Smirnitskii (Moscow: Russkii iazyk, 1989), 446.

68. On devils and violent death and suicide, see the entries on *zalozhnye, mertvetsy, samoubiitsa*, and *ten'*, in Novichkova, *Russkii demonologicheskii slovar'*, 183–86, 365–82, 491–95, and 540–42, respectively. On Petersburg as necropolis see Toporov, "Peterburg," 21, and Vaiskopf, *Siuzhet Gogolia*, 316–17.

69. Gogol', "Pravilo zhitiia," 7; and see Geir Kjetsaa, ibid., 13. See also Vaiskopf, *Siuzhet Gogolia*, 251, on despair.

70. On the *domovoi*, see Novichkova, *Russkii demonologicheskii slovar'*, 130–54.

71. On the demonic connotations of dream (mechta) in Gogol, see also Lotman, "O 'realizme' Gogolia," 35 n.15.

72. On the particular interest of devils in blacksmiths, and their jealousy of their work with fire, see Novichkova, *Russkii demonologicheskii slovar'*, 591–93.

73. For an interpretation of this phrase, see Epshtein, "Ironiia stilia," 144.

74. Gogol's attraction to names with demonic implications is apparent, too, in the protagonist Chertokutsky in the story "The Carriage" (Koliaska, 1836). For his play on words sounding like *chert*, including *chetyre, chernyi*, and *cherepakha*, in "The Overcoat," see Clyman, "The Hidden Demons," 604–5; and compare Bely's contention that in the Petersburg tales "the devil (chort) of *Evenings* has become a boundary (chertoi), beyond which are both the madman Poprishchin and the maniac and vulgarian Kovalev ... as if on the way from Dikanka to the capital it had turned into the bureaucrat 'devil' (v chinovnika 'chort')." Belyi, *Masterstvo Gogolia*, 186. For a discussion of the passage quoted from "The Portrait," see Robert Louis Jackson, "Gogol's 'The Portrait': The Simultaneity of Madness, Naturalism and the Supernatural," in Fusso and Meyer, eds., *Essays on Gogol*, 105–11(108). Lermontov indulges in similar word games, with different

ends, in *A Hero of Our Times*, where the romantically inclined narrator disabuses his reader of an initial surmise that the "Chertova dolina" may be "the nest of the evil spirit," explaining that "this was not the case: the name 'Chertova dolina' comes from the word 'cherta' (boundary) and not from 'chert' (devil), since this was once the border of Georgia." M.Iu. Lermontov, *Sobranie sochinenii v chetyrekh tomakh*, 4 vols. (Moscow and Leningrad: Izdatel'stvo Akademii nauk SSSR, 1958–59), 4:307. But see also Roman Jakobson, "Marginalia to Vasmer's Russian Etymological Dictionary (R-Ia)," *International Journal of Slavic Linguistics and Poetics* 1–2 (1959):266–78(276), for a suggestion that the words *chert* and *cherta* are, in fact, etymologically connected, as well as in this volume Wigzell, "The Russian Folk Devil."

75. According to Robert Maguire: "Although Chertkov has not literally painted the portrait of the money-lender, his paintings have all been 'demonic' because they have been copies of one another while pretending to be unique." Maguire, *Exploring Gogol*, 166.

76. For an extended discussion of the money-lender and Chartkov as Faust and Mephistopheles, see Dilaktorskaia, "Khudozhestvennyi mir," 229–36.

77. On Gogol's enthusiasm for Pushkin's 1823 poem "The Demon" and his jocular pretence that he had written it himself, see Pavlinov, *Filosofskie pritchi Gogolia*, 17. For a discussion of the contribution of this poem to the Russian tradition of art as demonic, see in this volume Pamela Davidson, "The Muse and the Demon in the Poetry of Pushkin, Lermontov, and Blok."

78. On the theme of Peter and his city as the prime context for the view of art as demonic in the Russian literary tradition, see in this volume Pamela Davidson, "Divine Service or Idol Worship? Russian Views of Art as Demonic."

79. On "Hans Küchelgarten" see, for example, Pavlinov, *Filosofskie pritchi Gogolia*, 13–16.

80. On "Woman" see ibid., 18–19.

81. According to Toporov: "In the year of Pushkin's death women made up only 30% of the population of Petersburg. This is the reason for the enormous percentage of unmarried and childless men in the lowest, and partly also in the middle stratum of society (the poor clerk of Russian literature usually has no family), and the strong development of prostitution." Toporov, "Peterburg," 21 n.24.

82. For further instances of this dangerous glance under a lady's hat, see Kovalev in "The Nose," who espies part of a lady's cheek "the colour of the first rose of spring," but then jumps back as if scalded (3:57); later, offered tobacco by the newspaper clerk, he notices another portrait of a lady in a hat on its lid and exclaims: "the devil take your tobacco!" (3:63); and the plainness of Petrovich's wife (explicitly a "mirskaia" [secular] woman) which so disappoints the guardsmen who look under her cap (3:148). The motif of the dangerous glance from under a large hat is deployed very effectively in the 1926 film *The Overcoat* (*Shinel'*), directed by Grigorii Kozintsev and Leonid Trauberg, which draws upon a number of Gogol's Petersburg stories.

83. On Podtochina as spoiler and on the etymology of her name as underminer, see above, n.67. Compare the use of the cognate *podtachivanie* (patching, 3:147) to describe the demonic Petrovich's attentions to Bashmachkin's overcoat. On *ved'ma* see Vinogradova, "Kalendarnye perekhody," 172–73, and Novichkova, *Russkii demonologicheskii slovar'*, 64–78. On the etymological connection between the words *chary* and *chert*, see the entries for these two words in Maks Fasmer (Max Vasmer), *Etimologicheskii slovar' russkogo iazyka*, 2d ed., 4 vols. (Moscow: Progress, 1986–87), 4:317, 347–48.

84. In this context, *gogolem* can be interpreted almost as a homonym of *shchegolem*. For Gogol's interest in clothes, see Simon Karlinsky, *The Sexual Labyrinth of Nikolai Gogol* (reprint, Chicago and London: University of Chicago Press, 1992), 22.

85. On Blok's use of similar features, including trains (shleify) and silks, as the "attributes of the demonic woman of the 1900s" in Petersburg, see Lidiia Ginzburg, *O lirike*, 2d revised ed. (Leningrad: Sovetskii pisatel', 1974), 269.

86. The daughter of the fashionable lady, called Annette in the first version of the story, becomes Lise in the second.

87. On devils' hatred of the Orthodox and espousing the cause of the "enemy-infidel," see Novichkova, *Russkii demonologicheskii slovar'*, 605; and see above, n.46.

88. See Vinogradova, "Kalendarnye perekhody," 178, for the ban on sewing (motat', krutit', snovat', tkat', priast', shit') during periods of mourning and on major feast days as a defence against mythological creatures. See also Vaiskopf, *Siuzhet Gogolia*, 328–31, 334, on the significance of cloths and threads in other works by Gogol.

89. See the entry on *ten'* in Novichkova, *Russkii demonologicheskii slovar'*, 540–42, and compare Vaiskopf, *Siuzhet Gogolia*, 84–85, on the world beyond the mirror.

90. Gary Saul Morson, "Gogol's Parables of Explanation: Nonsense and Prosaics," in Fusso and Meyer, eds., *Essays on Gogol*, 200–39(233); Fanger, *The Creation of Nikolai Gogol*, 120.

91. Dilaktorskaia, "Khudozhestvennyi mir," 256; compare the section on "utrata logosa" in Vaiskopf, *Siuzhet Gogolia*, 241–42.

92. Ann Shukman, "Gogol's *The Nose* or the Devil in the Works," in Grayson and Wigzell, eds., *Nikolay Gogol. Text and Context*, 64–82(75); and compare Epshtein's reference to the "demonism of the very style" in Epshtein, "Ironiia stilia," 145.

93. Cathy Popkin, *The Pragmatics of Insignificance. Chekhov, Zoshchenko, Gogol* (Stanford: Stanford University Press, 1993), 178, 180. The chapters of this book concerned with Gogol are full of interesting ideas about the nature of meaning in his stories.

94. In Rozanov's view, Gogol was the main writer in the Russian tradition guilty of this very act of betrayal of the sacred function of language. See in this volume Liza Dimbleby, "Rozanov and His Literary Demons."

95. For an interpretation of their insistence that "the devil alone knows," see Pavlinov, *Filosofskie pritchi Gogolia*, 45–50; and compare Poprishchin's assertion at the start of "Notes of a Madman" that "Satan himself will not make it out" (sam satana ne razberet, 3:193).

96. Dostoevskii, *Polnoe sobranie sochinenii*, 5:101.

97. Belyi, *Masterstvo Gogolia*, 309.

98. For an analysis of Gogol's influence on Zamiatin, and evidence of the way he obsessively reworked a Gogolian obsession plot, see Julian Graffy, "Zamyatin's 'Friendship' with Gogol," *Scottish Slavonic Review* 14 (1990):139–80.

Chapter 8

The Devils' Vaudeville: "Decoding" the Demonic in Dostoevsky's *The Devils*

W.J. Leatherbarrow

Devils undoubtedly exist, but our understanding of them can vary considerably.

Tikhon to Stavrogin, "At Tikhon's"

The Devils (*Besy*), serialized in *Russkii vestnik* between January 1871 and December 1872, is a political novel that outgrew itself. Conceived during Dostoevsky's protracted and painful stay in Western Europe, during which he dreamed of earning enough to pay off his Russian creditors and thus return home, it was designed as a "pamphlet-novel," a polemical catharsis in which he would have his say about the spread of "nihilism," i.e. revolutionary activity, in Russia, as well as warning of the dangers inherent in the Russian liberal intelligentsia's apparently unconditional love affair with Western European ideas and civilization. By the time he began work on the novel in late 1869, his own earlier liberal sympathies had all but disappeared and his political views had hardened into an uncompromising religious nationalism and an intolerant aversion to Westernism in both its liberal and radical embodiments. In a letter to his friend A.N. Maikov (9 October 1870), he recalls with distaste his own past association with the Petrashevsky circle, remembering how he was then "under the strong ferment of the mangy Russian liberalism preached by turd-eaters such as the dung-beetle Belinsky and his ilk."[1] This loss of respect for his erstwhile mentor of the 1840s goes hand in hand with contempt for the generation of monstrous radicals that had followed in the 1860s. Citing to Maikov the parable of the Gadarene swine that was to serve as one of the epigraphs to *The Devils*, Dostoevsky concludes his vituperative account of the Russian revolutionary movement with the observation: "the devils have departed from the Russian man and entered into the herd of swine, that is into the Nechaevs" (29/i:145). The reference is, of course, to the infamous "Nechaev affair" of November 1869, when the student Ivanov was suspected of informing and was murdered by members of a group of conspirators led by Sergei Nechaev, an event dramatized by Dostoevsky in the Shatov-Petr Verkhovensky plot line of *The Devils*.[2] The Nechaev affair provided a focus for Dostoevsky's anti-radicalism and gave impetus to the polemical purpose of his novel. "The nihilists and Westernizers need a decisive thrashing," he wrote to his friend N.N. Strakhov. "You're far too soft on them. With them you must write with a whip in your hand" (29/i:113).

We need not rehearse here the creative process by which *The Devils* outgrew its original, narrowly polemical design. Suffice to say that while it retained its political immediacy and reliance on events of the Nechaev affair, the emergence of Stavrogin as primary hero brought with it an enlargement of the novel's philosophical grasp that enabled it to transcend its origins in polemics of the 1860s and to retain its impact on the imagination of succeeding generations of readers. Its enduring vitality is suggested by the fact that it has been translated into English on several occasions, the most recent being in 1994.[3] Interestingly though, the authors of the various English versions have not established a canonical translation of the novel's title. Constance Garnett's original English translation was called *The Possessed*; subsequent versions have used *The Devils*, simply *Devils*, and *Demons*. Even the presence/absence of the definite article slightly shifts the semantic weighting, and the range of titles is suggestive of conceptual uncertainty on the part of Dostoevsky's translators. We may apply Tikhon's warning to our reading of the novel: *besy* certainly exist in this work, but they are likely to mean different things to different people. Dostoevsky's Russian title is neutral enough to promote interpretational uncertainty even among readers drawing upon the same cultural tradition and discourse; the problem is enlarged to unmanageable proportions when we start to ask ourselves not only whether *besy* carries the same cultural semantics as the English words *devils* or *possessed*, but also how, if at all, these correspond to those implicit in the German *dämonen*, the Spanish *demonios*, or the French *possédés* (all found in the titles of translated versions of *The Devils*). Pursuit of this line of enquiry is likely to prove akin to the traveller's pursuit of the *besy* in the poem by Pushkin also used by Dostoevsky as an epigraph to his novel: we shall end up in a dark field, going round in circles. Instead the present essay seeks to discuss some of the cultural traditions and discourses upon which Dostoevsky appears to have drawn in his treatment of the demonic in *The Devils*. We shall see how some of these, particularly those employed in the depiction of the activities of Petr Verkhovensky and his followers, are drawn from carnival traditions such as folklore, the Russian puppet theatre and the cultural-historical phenomenon of imposture and role-play, traditions which are structured on the breakdown or inversion of established hierarchies. Other discourses, however, drawn from Romantic and Christian traditions, surround the tragedy of Stavrogin and serve to establish an apocalyptic and redemptive purpose which forms the core of the author's ideological design.

The place to start might appear to be with the two epigraphs already mentioned. The tradition of epigraph as coded signifier, or clue, is well established in literature. Unfortunately, so is the tradition of epigraph as red herring. As interpretational signposts the epigraphs to *The Devils* appear to point in different directions: Pushkin's poem, with its references to house sprites and witches, towards the pagan world of popular superstition and folk tradition; and Saint Luke's story of the Gadarene swine to a biblical parable of demonic possession and redemption through Christ. Moreover, we must at least recognize the possibility that Dostoevsky intended his epigraphs to be read only at a superficial level, and that their references to demonic possession and enticement by devils merely introduce a conveniently "diabolical" rhetoric for the expression of a straightforwardly political point on Dostoevsky's part: that Russian Westernized liberals and radicals are "possessed" by evil ideologies, and that they have used these to entice Russia from its proper path. This is the interpretation that Stepan Trofimovich Verkhovensky attaches to the parable of the Gadarene swine in the novel's closing pages. Moreover, the nihilists had themselves used demonic rhetoric to express their opposition to the established order and instil fear in their opponents: for example, the student Dmitrii Karakozov, who attempted the assassination of Tsar Alexander II in 1866, belonged to an organization that termed itself "Hell."[4] Equally, as Harriet Murav has pointed out, the tradition of the anti-nihilist novel, to which *The Devils* contributes, had attempted to demonize the radicals by attaching to them diabolical symbolism.[5]

Dostoevsky's employment of demonic motifs certainly serves such a directly metaphorical function in *The Devils*, but this function alone is not enough to account for the complex cultural and ideological implications with which he invests his "devils," and which are perhaps signalled in the epigraphs; nor indeed does it explain what appears to be the literal, as opposed to merely figurative, presence of the demonic in the novel. Tikhon's warning holds true again: devils *do* exist in this work. The Russian provincial town, whose topographical and social credentials the narrator seeks so eagerly to establish in Part 1, is soon transformed into a fissure in the Russian earth, a turnstile to hell through which pass sundry demons, great and small. As befits a sociopolitical novel, the characters in *The Devils* possess social and ideological identities and they articulate positions in the polemical exchanges of their time. Stepan Trofimovich Verkhovensky is invested with the generalized characteristics of a liberal Westernizer of the 1840s; his son Petr caricatures the revolutionary nihilist of the 1860s; Stavrogin, somewhat anachronistically, suggests the Byronic nobleman of the 1820s;[6] Shatov is a messianic Slavophile; his neighbor Kirillov is a Westernizer; and so on. But all these sociopolitical identities vie with the demonic physical characteristics manifested by the majority of the novel's characters. Attention is consistently drawn, for example, to the bestiality that breaks through Stavrogin's aristocratic veneer. He is described as possessing the mask-like face, supernatural strength, predatory instincts, and death-like demeanour of a vampire; his very presence arouses supernatural alarm in children; and one description of him alone in his room conveys the impression of an "undead" ghoul who arouses dread in his mother:

> Seeing that Nicholas was sitting somehow unnaturally still, she cautiously approached his divan with a beating heart. It was as though she were struck by how quickly he had fallen asleep and how he could sleep thus, sitting upright and so motionless; even his breathing was hardly perceptible. His face was pale and stern, but immobile as though it had completely frozen; his brows were slightly drawn together and frowning; he looked decidedly like a soulless wax figure. She stood over him for about three minutes, hardly drawing breath, and suddenly she was seized with terror. She withdrew on tiptoe, stopped in the doorway, hurriedly made the sign of the cross over him, and went away unobserved, her heart heavy with a new despair. (10:182)

The passage leaves little doubt that we are approaching the realm of the supernatural, and Varvara Petrovna's apparent blessing of her son – the sign of the cross – must also be seen as a traditional response to the presence of evil, a ritual popularly believed to immobilize or trap the Devil.[7]

The initial description of Petr Verkhovensky, when he arrives in town to begin the process of luring the unwary into his schemes, is also physically suggestive of the demonic. It occurs in a chapter appropriately titled "The Wise Serpent," and it is remarkable for its elusiveness, as though we were witnessing some intangible and diabolical mirage. It is littered with contradictions and imprecision, as well as with the sort of evasive particles, phrases, and adjectival suffixes that dissolve all semantic certainty:

> At first glance it was as though (kak budto) he were sort of stooped and rather awkward (sutulovatyi i meshkovatyi), but, however, not at all stooped and even free-and-easy. It was as though (kak budto) he were some sort of (kakoi-to) eccentric, but, on the other hand, we all then found his manners entirely becoming, and his conversation always to the point.
>
> No one will say that he was ugly, but nobody liked his face. His head was elongated at the back and as though (kak by) flattened at the sides, so that his face seemed pointed. His forehead was high and narrow, but his facial features were small. His eyes were sharp, his nose small and pointed, his lips long and thin.

The description – so reminiscent in its evasiveness of that of another collector of souls, Gogol's Chichikov – continues in this vein until the demon reveals his distinctive trademark:

> His speech was remarkably clearly articulated; his words tumbled out like large, smooth grains, always well chosen and always at your service. At first you found this appealing, but then it became repulsive, precisely because of that too clearly articulated speech and those pearls of ever-ready wisdom. Somehow or other, you began to imagine the tongue in his mouth as being surely of a special sort of shape, somehow unusually long and thin, terribly red and exceedingly pointed, with a tip that flickered constantly and involuntarily." (10:143)

We thus find ourselves suddenly confronted not just by a Nechaev-intriguer who has arrived in town to begin his political machinations, but also by the Serpent-tempter and Father of Lies, about to embark on the gathering of souls and the dissemination of destruction. In this role Petr is helped by his circle of dupes, some of whom also bear the Devil's mark. There is something ghoulish, for example, about the ears possessed by Shigalev, the group's theoretician: they are "of an unnatural size, long, broad and thick, and somehow sticking out in a peculiar way," like the ears of a beast. The narrator is further struck by the "ominous impression" Shigalev makes (10:110). The same motif of concealed bestiality, with all its diabolical connotations, attaches also to Liamshin, who in the aftermath of Shatov's murder lets loose an "unbelievable scream" and displays classic symptoms of demonic possession, such as speaking in tongues, bulging eyes, and uncontrollable convulsions:

> There are extreme moments of alarm when a man, for example, suddenly starts to cry out in a voice that is not his own, the sort of voice no one could have suspected he possessed beforehand, and this can sometimes be very frightening. Liamshin started to scream in a voice that was not human, but somehow animal. Squeezing Virginsky from behind with his arms ever tighter in a convulsive fit, he screamed without pausing or

stopping, staring at everyone with his eyes popping out of his head, his mouth hanging open extremely wide, and his feet tapping lightly on the ground, as if beating out a drum rhythm. (10:461)

Kirillov too appears to lose his humanity and undergo an analogous process of bestial transformation in the scene leading up to his suicide. The hideously possessed engineer frightens even the usually imperturbable Petr Verkhovensky, almost severing his finger with his teeth (10:476). What is more, there is a strange and general irritability distributed among many of the characters we encounter: the narrator is at a loss to account for the "strange irritability" (strannaia razdrazhitel'nost') displayed by Kirillov, while in the same scene Shatov is also described by Stepan Trofimovich as "notre irascible ami" (10:76). Liputin refers to Captain Lebiadkin as "an irritable fellow" (chelovek razdrazhitel'nyi, 10:79), Stavrogin is described as the victim of "a kind of constant anxiety" (nekotoroe postoiannoe bespokoistvo, 10:81), while the initial description of Lizaveta Nikolaevna emphasizes her "constant, morbid, nervous anxiety" (boleznennoe, nervnoe, bespreryvnoe bespokoistvo), which gives the impression that "everything within her was as if permanently seeking its level and was unable to find it, everything was in chaos, agitated and anxious" (10:88–89). The same pattern, so suggestive of possession of some kind, is emphasized in several other characters.

This all contributes to the creation of an implicitly diabolic matrix against which the action of *The Devils* unfolds. It is reinforced by the very verbal texture of the novel: constant and apparently casual references to the devil assume a menacing and incantatory value by the very frequency of their repetition. Linguistically formulaic expressions such as "the devil only knows what…" (chert znaet chto…), "go to the devil" (k chertu), "the devil take…" (chert voz'mi…), or, on Stepan Trofimovich's lips, "au diable," acquire a more than conventional resonance against the novel's demonic background. The same is true when Stavrogin refers to Fed'ka the convict as a "little devil" (besenok) immediately after confessing to Dasha Shatova that he sees visions of the Devil (10:230), when we learn that the Governor's morose assistant Blum has red hair, popularly regarded as a sinister characteristic, and when we are told that the Governor himself courted popularity at school by his ability to play the overture to Daniel Auber's comic opera *Fra Diavolo* through his nose, an orifice with diabolical connotations in Russian folklore (10:242). When Stavrogin undertakes his pilgrimage about the town in the chapters entitled "Night," Fed'ka offers to guide him through the maze of alleys, adding that the town is so confusing, "just as though the devil had carried it around in a basket and shaken it all up" (10:206). We cannot expect conscious literary references from Fed'ka, but the reader will surely sense an oblique echo here of the image in Gogol's story "Nevsky Prospect" (Nevskii prospekt) of a world presided over by the Devil, "some sort of demon" who has "crumbled up the world into pieces and mixed them all together without rhyme or reason."[8] In his final conversation with Petr Verkhovensky, Kirillov raises such a prospect of a world abandoned by God, in which "the very laws of the planet are a lie and a devils' vaudeville" (diavolov vodevil', 10:471). The carefully constructed matrix of demonic references in *The Devils* sets the scene for the novel's own account of a contemporary Russia in which all tradition has been sacrificed, all authority has broken down, and all sense is lost in the devils' vaudeville that has overwhelmed it.

The ability of *The Devils* to function as a sociopolitical novel while simultaneously accommodating a "devils' vaudeville" points to the sort of generic enrichment that Leonid Grossman saw as characteristic of the "adventure novel" (avantiurnyi roman). It was, according to Grossman, Dostoevsky's debt to the tradition of the adventure novel that permitted his art to express "the impulse to introduce the extraordinary into the very thick of the commonplace, to fuse into one, according to Romantic principles, the sublime with the grotesque, and by an imperceptible process of conversion to push images and phenomena of everyday reality to the limits of the fantastic."[9] Bakhtin, however, has shown how the adventure novel in turn can be seen as only one branch of the generic tradition of the serio-comic, a tradition reaching deep into the past and characterized by a folkloric-carnival "sense of the world" that encourages the breakdown of generic boundaries.[10] Each new contribution to the generic tradition represents a "contemporization" (osovremenenie) that "lives in the present, but always *remembers* its past"[11] in the sense of addressing the present while renewing archaic elements of the genre. In considering the credentials of *The Devils* as a contemporization of the serio-comic genre we shall seek to examine how it "remembers" past tradition and how such remembering contributes to its depiction of the demonic.

At the risk of rehearsing the already over-familiar, we might begin by testing *The Devils* against the primary generic characteristics of the serio-comic identified by Bakhtin. These are, firstly, a starting point in "the living present ... without any epic or tragic distance" and a presentation that is consequently provisional and reliant on experience, rather than one validated by time and distance. The presentation of *The Devils* as a contemporary chronicle narrated by a participating and often bemused "chronicler," who only occasionally resorts to devices of the "as we later found out" sort, is clearly important in this respect (although it is arguable that a more "distanced" and authoritative set of values is introduced into the novel by its ultimately tragic form and its pervasive religious symbolism). Second, Bakhtin draws attention to "the deliberately multi-styled and hetero-voiced nature" of the serio-comic genres: "Characteristic of these genres are a multi-toned narration, the mixing of high and low, serious and comic; they make wide use of inserted genres – letters, found manuscripts, retold dialogues, parodies on the high genres, parodically reinterpreted citations; in some of them we observe a mixing of prosaic and poetic speech, living dialects and jargons (and in the Roman stage, direct bilingualism as well) are introduced, and various authorial masks make their appearance."[12]

Of these features we recognize in *The Devils* the mixture of the serious and comic, the reliance on inserted genres (most notably, Stavrogin's letter and the manuscript of his confession), parodies of high genres (Lebiadkin's poetry, Karmazinov's "Merci"), and a variety of speech characteristics (including, in Stepan Trofimovich's constant recourse to French, the bilingualism referred to by Bakhtin).

The Devils exhibits in a much more overt way than Dostoevsky's other great novels those folkloric-carnival features that Bakhtin held to be characteristic of the serio-comic genre. Space does not permit – nor, indeed, necessity demand – rehearsal of Bakhtin's analysis of carnival and carnivalized literature.[13] What is appropriate here is discussion of those carnival elements "remembered" in *The Devils* that underpin the novel's presentation of the demonic. The primary characteristic of carnival – its setting in a "public square" that permits familiarity and intermingling, with a consequent suspension of normal hierarchical barriers – is met most obviously in *The Devils* in the drawing-room scandal scenes and the culminating grand scene of the fête organized by the Governor's wife Iuliia von Lembke, a fête significantly designed to be non-exclusive and open to all. It is this "openness" that transforms what Iuliia intends to be a dignified affair into a public spectacle, where people let their hair down, where respect and distance between the classes are broken down, and where all kinds of eccentric and inappropriate behaviour take place. But the spirit of carnival is not confined to such scenes. The novel suggests what Bakhtin terms "life drawn out of its usual rut" (zhizn', vyvedennaia iz svoei obychnoi kolei) and "life turned inside out" (zhizn' naiznanku)[14] in a much more fundamental way through its preoccupation with social breakdown and revolutionary ideas and activity. Indeed, in a sense revolution is carnival in its most concentrated form, resulting in social clashes and inversions, the relativizing of moral and social principles and ideologies, destruction and renewal, and the crowning-decrowning of kings, described by Bakhtin as the primary carnivalistic act. This act is particularly

prominent in *The Devils* through the destruction of administrative
authority in the figures of the Governor and his wife, as well as
through Petr Verkhovensky's plan to install Stavrogin in power as
"Ivan the Crown-Prince" (Ivan-Tsarevich) and Mar'ia Lebiadkina's
subsequent decrowning of Stavrogin as "Grishka Otrep'ev," a pretender to the Russian throne during the Time of Troubles in the
early seventeenth century. Further echoes of carnival tradition may
be discerned in the novel's use of parodistic doubles (e.g. the relationship of Lebiadkin to Karmazinov, and that of Kirillov and Shatov to Stavrogin), its preoccupation with masks, role-play, and
disguises (Stavrogin's mask-like face, the "masks" worn by the narrator-chronicler, the role of civic martyr played by Stepan Trofimovich, and the figures in the literary quadrille), its references to the
profanation of the sacred (a desecrated icon and an abused Bible-
seller), and the function of Petr Verkhovensky as carnival jester.

The discussion of carnival features in *The Devils* could be
extended, but what is important for our purposes is that the carnivalized world of the novel provides an ideal breeding-ground for the
demonic. The breakdown of social hierarchies leads to the sort of
erosion of order which the Devil traditionally exploits, while the suspension of generic boundaries permits the intrusion of the para-
phernalia of the supernatural into the world of the
nineteenth-century sociopolitical novel. These features of carnival
were seen by Bakhtin as essentially positive, promoting an atmosphere of "joyful relativity" (veselaia otnositel'nost'), "a mighty life-
creating and transforming power, an indestructible vitality."[15]
Recently, however, Harriet Murav has argued that the carnivalized
world of *The Devils* is designed instead to promote a "frightening
chaos" and thus to serve its author's polemical aim of alerting his
readership to the dangers of nihilism.[16] The role played by laughter
in the novel is the clearest confirmation of this inversion of emphasis. For Bakhtin the ritual laughter that attended carnival was liberating; it debunked established institutions and released the
participant from the pressures of normal hierarchical structures. Lotman and Uspensky, however, have pointed out that in medieval
Russia laughter possessed a demonic and blasphemous significance
that went beyond a merely liberating function. In their essay "New
Aspects in the Study of Early Russian Culture" they write:

> Russian medieval Orthodox culture is organized around the opposition
> holiness vs. Satanism. Holiness excludes laughter (cf.: "Christ never
> laughed" – [a saying from Saint John Chrysostom]) ... The Devil (and the
> whole demonic world) is held to possess the features of "holiness inside
> out" and belongs to the inverted, "left-hand" [i.e. "sinister"] world. There-
> fore this world is blasphemous in its very essence, that is, it is not serious.

This is a world that guffaws; it is no accident that the Devil may be called the "jester" (shut) in Russian. The kingdom of Satan is the place where sinners groan and gnash their teeth while the devils laugh.[17]

Lotman and Uspensky go on to say that "the external sign of this kind of laughter is that it is not infectious. For those who are not in league with Satan, it is terrifying rather than comical." Such non-infectious laughter (non-infectious, that is, outside the circle of the possessed) is widespread in *The Devils*, and it contributes a distinctively hysterical quality to the novel's mood. It originates primarily in the demon-jester Petr Verkhovensky, who even refers to himself as a clown (shut, 10:408). "Il rit. Il rit beaucoup, il rit trop…Il rit toujours," complains Stepan Trofimovich of his son (10:171), while elsewhere we note that the book under which Stepan Trofimovich hides a letter from Mrs Stavrogina is Victor Hugo's *L'homme qui rit* (10:73). Lizaveta Nikolaevna is disposed to a malignant form of laughter particularly suggestive of loss of self-control and hysteria: "From the moment that the Captain went out and collided in the doorway with Nikolai Vsevolodovich, Liza had suddenly started to laugh – at first quietly and intermittently, but then her laughter grew ever greater, becoming louder and more distinct. Her face turned red. The contrast with her gloomy mood of a short time ago was extraordinary… She was visibly trying to regain control of herself and put her handkerchief to her mouth" (10:156).

Destructive laughter becomes symptomatic of Petr's growing hold over the town and of the breakdown of propriety and social and moral values. In the build-up to the fête a carnival mood prevails in the town, but it is a mood in which frivolity is tempered by the threateningly unpleasant:

> The state of mind among people at that time was strange. Particularly in female society a certain frivolous attitude manifested itself, and it cannot be said that it appeared gradually. It was as though certain extremely free-and-easy notions were carried on the wind. A mood of light-heartedness and merriment set in, but I cannot say that it was always pleasant. Some sort of mental disarray was in vogue. Afterwards, when everything was over, the blame was attached to Iuliia Mikhailovna, her circle and her influence. But all this could hardly have been the fault of Iuliia Mikhailovna alone. (10:249)

Iuliia's circle of intimates, reflecting the hold Petr has over their patroness, resorts to a behavioural pattern structured on the sort of pranks and practical jokes that arouse an exclusive form of laughter based upon the discomfiture of those outside the circle. The laughter arises from a carnivalistic/blasphemous disregard for established institutions and moral codes: a Bible-seller is compromised when obscene photographs are introduced into her bag of holy books; a poor but worthy lieutenant's wife is acutely embarrassed when her debts are disclosed to her violent husband; a newly married couple are hounded and mocked when it emerges that the young wife was not a virgin on her wedding night; and the room where a young man has taken his own life after a final meal of cutlet and Château d'Yquem is invaded by irreverential scoffers (surely a world ruled by the inappropriate when a bottle of sweet Bordeaux is deemed suitable accompaniment for a cutlet!). All these events remind us that in Russian folklore the devil traditionally plays the role of prankster.

Bakhtin is careful to point out that the carnival elements in Dostoevsky's novels entered his work indirectly and unconsciously, not through the influence of carnival itself, which had diminished in importance as a public spectacle in Dostoevsky's day and of which he had little personal experience, but through the tradition of carnivalized literature. Bakhtin's discussion of this tradition is illustrated by references primarily to high culture (he cites, for example, Cervantes's *Don Quixote* and the works of Rabelais).[18] Dostoevsky's depiction of demons and demonism in *The Devils* is, however, inscribed with formulae derived also from low cultural forms such as folk literature, popular theatre, and historical legend; and it is in this regard that the significance of the Pushkin epigraph begins to emerge. His presentation of the demonic is, for example, deeply indebted to the typology of the Devil and his world established by Russian folk tradition. We must leave aside the conventional physical form of the Devil as shaggy with horns and a tail; such characteristics can have no place in a nineteenth-century novel with pretensions to realism (except, of course, in dreams and hallucinations, such as those experienced by Stavrogin. Even here, though, the Devil assumes a more modest and down-at-heel guise). Other features of the folk tradition are, however, embraced in *The Devils*: folk belief that it is dangerous to mention the Devil by name for fear of summoning up his presence is, as we have seen, suggested in the consequences that follow his repeated invocation in the novel. Lameness is another characteristic popularly attributed to Satan, the result apparently of his fall from grace. Linda J. Ivanits has drawn our attention to Dostoevsky's extensive use of the motif of lameness in *The Brothers Karamazov* (*Brat'ia Karamazovy*),[19] but the same motif is equally prominent in *The Devils*. The venomous schoolmaster in Petr's circle is lame; Stavrogin's wife, Mar'ia Lebiadkina, is a cripple (khromonozhka); Lizaveta Nikolaevna hysterically anticipates breaking her legs in a fall from her horse and becoming a *khromonozhka*; and Captain Lebiadkin dedicates to her a poem on the theme of lameness. Mental disturbances, such as the hysteria and uncontrollable laughter displayed by Lizaveta and the members of

Iuliia von Lembke's intimate circle, are also ascribed in folklore to the work of the Devil, as is the epilepsy attributed to Kirillov. Further behaviour typical of popular conceptions of the Devil and discernible in *The Devils* include the seduction of other men's wives (cf. Stavrogin), the abduction of young children from their parents (suggestive of Stavrogin's seduction of Matresha), a predilection for hooks with which to snare souls (cf. the metaphorical hooks with which Petr Verkhovensky captures the von Lembkes), and responsibility for suicides, another motif common in the novel. We have already referred to the death of the young man who takes his life after a meal of cutlet and wine, but suicide is also a particular preoccupation of Kirillov, who however sees it not as a sign of the Devil, but as the means of man's deification. His own terrifying demonic transformation in the minutes before his death suggests that he is wrong and that folk tradition is right.

Felix J. Oinas has drawn attention to the importance of the magic circle in folk belief about the devil. He argues that *chert*, the most commonly used word to denote the devil in Russian, is derived from the word-family that includes *cherta* ("line" or "limit"), as well as the verb *chertit'* ("to draw"), and that this denotes an origin in the ritual of drawing a circle to protect oneself from the devil. "Once the magic circle has been drawn, anybody inside it will supposedly be unable to get out and anyone outside will be unable to get in."[20] It is just conceivable that this notion has a tangential relevance to the two "circles" (kruzhki) we encounter in *The Devils*: the *exclusive* social circle gathered around Iuliia von Lembke, and the *inclusive* political circle managed by Petr Verkhovensky, from which Shatov is unable to detach himself.

"Petrusha," the affectionate diminutive form of "Petr" that Stepan Trofimovich sentimentally addresses to his son, is morphologically adjacent to "Petrushka," the name of the hero of the Russian carnival folk theatre, the equivalent of Punch and Judy. This suggests the possibility of another cultural inscription carried by this jester-demon, one equally deeply embedded in popular tradition. As Catriona Kelly has shown, Petrushka was largely a nineteenth-century Russian adaptation of the Italian Pulcinella tradition, and it enjoyed great popularity from about the 1830s onwards.[21] It was initially performed by foreigners, usually German and Italian puppeteers whose command of Russian – and therefore that of their puppet-characters – was imperfect. (We might remember at this point Kirillov's stilted use of Russian, as well as Stavrogin's stylistic and grammatical inadequacies in his letter to Dasha, although both of these devices were primarily intended to serve Dostoevsky's polemic against the West-

ДЛЄ ТИНДНЄ БОГАТОН ДИМЄÑО НОСЪ ГОРБАТОЙ
СОБОНОВЕСМА ВАЖНЕБАЛОН ЗОБУТЪ МЕНА
ФАРНОГЪ КРАСНОН НОСЪ ТРИДНИ
НДАЗУВАЛСА КАКЪ ВТАНЦАВ
АЛНЫЕ ВАШМАИН ОБЗУВАЛСА
АКОЛПАКЪ СПЕРОМЪ НАДЕЛЪ
ПОЛНЫ ШТАНЫ Ч Г ЛЕЛЪ СОВ
СЕМЪ ОБОЛОКСА НАВИНОХОД
НОИ СВИНЬЕ ПОВОЛОКСА
ВИНЬА МОД ХРЮКАЕКЪ
АКОМТВА СВОЕГО НЮ
ХАЄТЪ

16. "The Jester Farnos the Red Nose," second half of the eighteenth century. Woodcut, 36,5 × 29 cm. The character Farnos was a popular *lubok* jester, who later came to be associated with Petrushka in the Russian puppet theatre.

ernized nobleman-intellectual.) Dostoevsky knew and enjoyed puppet shows from childhood, and this early familiarity almost certainly included the Pulcinella (Russian – Pul'chinel') text in which the figure of Petrushka appeared initially as a clown, a secondary figure.[22] Later the Petrushka figure acquired greater prominence and developed "an aggressive and unpleasant character."[23] Between the 1840s and 1870s the names Pul'chinel' and Petrushka became interchangeable and denoted the play's central character. The two figures are still distinct, however, in Dostoevsky's draft for his *Diary of a Writer* (*Dnevnik pisatelia*) for 1876, where he writes:

> What a character, what a complete artistic character! I am speaking of Pul'chinel'. He is something like Don Quixote, and at the same time Don Juan. How trusting he is, how merry and straightforward; how angry he gets and how he is unwilling to believe evil and deceit. How quickly he gets worked up and sets about injustice with his stick, and how triumphant he is when he thrashes someone with that stick. But what a scoundrel that Petrushka, his constant companion, is. How he deceives him and makes fun of him, and Pul'chinel' never notices. Petrushka is like a Sancho Panza or Leporello, but completely Russianized, a folk character. (22:180)

One is tempted to discern in this description echoes of the trustingly Quixotic Stepan Trofimovich, defending his values in the face of nihilism, and his deceitful scoundrel of a son, Petr.

Petrushka reflected the suspension of hierarchies characteristic of carnival. The hero triumphs over and outwits his superiors, even murdering some of them, and in some versions he even escapes the retribution symbolized in the final appearance of the Devil. As Kelly has pointed out, this "subversive" quality encouraged some members of the radical intelligentsia in the 1860s to discern in the spectacle a reflection of the potential for popular rebellion in Russia.[24] Kelly concedes that, in its depiction of violence without retribution, Petrushka indeed expressed, and perhaps encouraged, "a fragmented sense of morality,"[25] and she cites descriptions of this "entertainment for hooligans by hooligans" that recoil from its antisocial and subversive implications, including a reference of 1908 by M. Braunschweig to "the Petrushka theatre with its ugly, mangled, caricature figures, violent gestures, absurd squeaking, which can communicate nothing but crude foolery."[26] These are qualities that we also find in *The Devils*, with its recounting of social disruption, political murders, and gross caricatures of revolutionary figures. The primary function of Petrushka was to make people laugh, but the kind of laughter it sought to evoke was the same disruptive laughter, challenging all social and moral conventions, that fills Dostoevsky's novel. In other words, the disruptive carnival mood invited collusion: it passed beyond the puppet booth and infected the audience, just as Petr Verkhovensky's "pranks" extend beyond the immediate circle of his activities and infect the townsfolk with destructive laughter.

There is no canonical version of Petrushka, but despite textual variations the play always begins with the arrival of Petrushka, who launches immediately into a wordy monologue, often with his legs dangling from the booth in a gesture of familiarity with the crowd. We remember the arrival of Petr Verkhovensky and his breathless and verbally hypnotic ensnarement of his audience: "His speech was remarkably clearly articulated; his words tumbled out like large, smooth grains, always well chosen and always at your service." Petr's sugary over-familiarity with his superiors is a persistent feature of his behaviour throughout the novel, and at times it is conveyed through reference to his tendency to curl his legs up on a sofa. See, for example, the following scene with his father: "Stepan Trofimovich sat stretched out on the sofa. Since last Thursday he had grown thin and sallow. Petr Stepanovich settled down alongside him in a most familiar manner, unceremoniously tucking his legs beneath him and occupying much more of the sofa than respect for his father demanded" (10:238). And, in the presence of the Governor: "Petr

Stepanovich sprawled out on the sofa, and in a flash drew his legs up under him" (10:272).

Certain physical and moral characteristics of Petrushka appear to have passed, with varying degrees of modification, into the figure of Petr Verkhovensky. For example, the puppet's deformed physical appearance – he is hunch-backed, with an unattractive physiognomy that includes pointed nose and chin and button eyes – is suggested in the initial evasive physical description of Petr, which alludes to the impression of round-shoulderedness he conveys, his sharp eyes, and his pointed nose. His movements are hurried and jerky, like those of a puppet, a feature that acquires additional resonance in the light of comments Dostoevsky makes in the draft for *Diary of a Writer*, referred to above. Here he considers the possibility of translating Petrushka to the conventional theatre using human actors who would retain the "wooden and doll-like" movements of the original (22:180). Petrushka's moral characteristics coincide quite strikingly with those manifested by Petr. As Elizabeth Warner has written: "In many cases Petrushka is no more than a bully and a hooligan, using violence for its own sake or to get out of an awkward situation... . Petrushka is violently disposed towards anyone in authority, whether civil, military or ecclesiastic. Although keen enough to belabour those weaker than himself, Petrushka is at heart a coward and some-times his bravado and effrontery break down... . But in spite of his cowardice, his greed and his dishonesty Petrushka has a very high opinion of himself and is inordinately vain and cocksure."[27]

This description could be applied without modification to Petr, even the reference to greed and gluttony (which Kelly also mentions). Greed may well be a general and familiar human trait and thus in itself not carry a particular semiotic charge, but on several occasions this feature of Petr's behaviour is given a surprising prominence: we recall the scene where he demands a cutlet, wine, and coffee during a morning visit to Karmazinov, much to his host's surprise and dis-pleasure (10:285); he insensitively finishes off the supper Kirillov has left as the latter contemplates the hour of his suicide; and on his way to convince Liputin of the willingness of Kirillov to take responsibil-ity for the murder of Shatov, he still finds time to call into a tavern where he consumes steak with a gusto that repels Liputin (10:423).

Many critics have commented on the use made in *The Devils* of the motif of *samozvanstvo* ("pretendership" or "royal imposture"). It is a motif Dostoevsky exploits for its demonic connotations. Bakhtin, for example, remarks that in the novel "all life that is penetrated by dev-ils is portrayed as a carnival nether world. The entire novel is thor-oughly permeated by the theme of crowning-decrowning and pretendership," and he cites the examples of Stavrogin's exposure as a Grishka Otrep'ev by Mar'ia Lebiadkina and Petr's plan to crown him as "Ivan the Crown Prince," a later pretender to the Russian throne who appeared in 1845.[28] More recently, Murav has devoted an entire essay to the theme, claiming that the novel "is permeated with a vision of the past. Its vision of the political upheaval of late nineteenth-century Russia is refracted through the prism of the early seventeenth century, a period known as the 'Time of Troubles,' when the Ryurikid dynasty came to an end and a series of pretenders took the throne, most notably False Dmitrii, believed by historians to be Grishka Otrep'ev, a runaway monk."[29] Apart from such overt references to Grishka Otrep'ev and other historical pretenders, *The Devils* seeks to alert its readership to the presence of this theme through a network of motifs and incidents that focus attention on the cognate ideas of pretence, role-play, masquerade, imitation, and imposture. In the opening passage we are told that Stepan Trofimovich has always played a "civic role," that of a martyr to the liberal cause, but later we are warned that "to tell the truth, he was merely an imitator (podrazhatel') of such figures" (10:12). "Captain" Lebiadkin turns out to be not a staff-captain, as he claims, but rather a villain once caught up in an incident involving *counterfeit* banknotes (10:29, 79). The virtuoso Liamshin imitates animals at the piano (10:30–31). Petr Verkhovensky's deception of the von Lembkes and others is repeatedly referred to as "role-play." The fête includes a literary quadrille, danced in masks and costumes, in which participants *pretend* to be literary journals. And the "silver" chin-setting of Saint Nikolai the Miracle-Worker (note the coincidence of name with that of Stavrogin), stolen from a church by Fed'ka, turns out to be a fake (similerovyi, 10:220). The implication carried by this final detail – that Stavrogin himself might turn out to be a comparable "fake" – is encouraged by passages in *The Devils* that appear to align him with Danila Filippov, the false god of the heretical sect of Castrates,[30] as well as with that paradigm of imposture in nineteenth-century Russian literature, Khlestakov in Gogol's *The Government Inspector* (*Revizor*). The notebooks for *The Devils* refer to Khlestakov by name, but in connection with the arrival of Petr Verkhovensky; in the novel itself it is left to the narrator-chronicler to suggest indirectly a link with Stavrogin. He dutifully reports rumours in the town to the effect that Stavrogin is secretly a government official who has arrived incognito on a secret mission and who reports back to Petersburg (10:168). The motif is taken up later when Petr and Stavrogin discuss whether or not the latter is secretly an inspector (revizor), albeit one working for the revolutionary movement (10:299). In neither case do the participants appear to be alert to the literary resonance of the role ascribed to Stavrogin, but the novel's readership surely is. The same readership might also recall that the theme of imposture carries a demonic charge in Gogol's comedy too.

The more specific historical motif of royal imposture is also sustained by similar supporting references. The madness that follows the fête is described by the chronicler as "our time of troubles" (nashe smutnoe vremia), using the same linguistic formula applied to the historical interregnum (10:354). And Mrs Stavrogina dresses Stepan Trofimovich in the fashion of the poet and dramatist N.V. Kukol'nik, whose portrait, we are told, is one of her most cherished possessions (10:19). Kukol'nik was a contemporary of Dostoevsky and the author of a historical drama about the Time of Troubles.[31]

The significance for our purposes of the theme of imposture and, in particular, royal imposture is suggested by Boris Uspensky, who has argued that it is a phenomenon carrying a particular cultural-historical significance in Russia, and one that is popularly associated with the demonic. Recollection of the fête in *The Devils* is evoked by the following observation:

> It should be borne in mind that any kind of masquerade or dressing up was inevitably thought of in early Russia as *anti-behavior*: i.e. a sinister, black-magic significance was attributed to it in principle. This is quite plain from the example of the mummers of Yuletide, Shrovetide, Saint John's Night and other festivals, who, it was assumed (by participants in the masquerade as well as spectators!) depicted devils, or unclean spirits; correspondingly, the dressing up was accompanied by extremes of disorderly behavior, often of an overtly blasphemous character.[32]

The most extreme form of this anti-behaviour was to masquerade as tsar. Citing the historian Kliuchevsky, Uspensky points out that royal imposture was a "chronic malady" of the Russian state, with hardly a single reign before the mid-nineteenth century not throwing up a pretender. Clearly, how such pretenders were viewed by Russians is inextricably bound up with Russian attitudes to royal power, for they represent an inversion of such power. As Uspensky writes: "If true Tsars receive power from God, then false Tsars receive it from the Devil. Even the church rite of sacred coronation and anointing do not confer grace on a false Tsar, for these actions are no more than outward appearances; in reality the false Tsar is crowned and anointed by demons acting on the orders of the Devil himself. It follows therefore that if the real Tsar may be likened to Christ [i.e. a creation of God, not man] and perceived as an image of God, a living icon, then a pretender may be regarded as a false icon, i.e. an *idol*."[33]

This passage provides a particularly graphic template, allowing us to recognize several of the cultural symbols surrounding Stavrogin and his relationship with Petr Verkhovensky. First of all, of course, it

serves to clarify the demonic resonances in both characters: Stavrogin is the false tsar – in Mar'ia Lebiadkina's terms "Grishka
Otrep'ev" masquerading as a "Prince" – who derives his power from
Satan, and Petr is the demon that anoints him. The presence of the
demonic is suggested during Mar'ia's final interview with Stavrogin
in the supernatural terror that overcomes her on his entrance, in her
attempts to protect herself by holding up her arms, and in her unwill-
ingness to look Stavrogin in the face. Her fate is perhaps sealed by
the symbolic gesture of inviting him into her *circle*: "'I would ask you,
Prince, to get up and come in,' she said suddenly in a firm and insistent voice. 'What do you mean, *come in?*' [Stavrogin replied]. 'Come
in where?'" (10:217). Petr's complementary role emerges in the chapter "Ivan the Crown-Prince," during which he confesses that he is a
rogue rather than a socialist, before unfolding his plan to reap the
harvest of the moral disorder that afflicts contemporary Russia:

> "Then, sir, the troubles (smuta) will begin. There'll be an upheaval such
> as the world has never seen… Rus will be shrouded in mist, and the earth
> will cry out for its old gods… Well, sir, then we'll unleash… do you know
> who?"
> "Who?"
> "Ivan the Crown-Prince."
> "*Who?*"
> "Ivan the Crown-Prince; you, you!"
> Stavrogin was silent for a moment.
> "A Pretender?" he asked suddenly, staring in astonishment at the mad-
> man. "Ah, so that's your plan in the end." (10:325)

Stavrogin is central to Petr's design as a usurper, a *false icon* attracting the worship of a morally confused populace, and this iconic
imagery is also rich in meaning. For a start, it amplifies the significance
of the desecration of real church icons by Fed'ka, another of Stavrogin's demon-doubles. It also allows Petr to reveal the nature of his own
aesthetic stance, one founded upon blasphemy and the sin of *idolatry*:

> "Stavrogin, you're beautiful!" Petr Stepanovich cried, almost in ecstasy.
> "Don't you know that you're beautiful! … I love beauty. I'm a nihilist, but
> I love beauty. Do nihilists really not love beauty? It's only idols they
> don't love, but I even love idols! You are my idol! … You're just what I
> need. I particularly need someone like you. I know of no one like you.
> You are my leader, my sun, and I am your worm…"
> He suddenly kissed Stavrogin's hand. A chill ran down Stavrogin's spine,
> and he tore his hand away in alarm. They stopped.
> "You're mad!" whispered Stavrogin. (10:323–24)

We are here close to the core of Dostoevsky's own polemic with
the aesthetic views of the nihilists, who had largely rejected the value
of beauty in favour of an uncompromising utilitarianism. As early as
1861, Dostoevsky had addressed the issue in his article "Mr –bov

and the Question of Art" (Gospodin −bov i vopros ob iskusstve), where he defended ideal beauty from the attacks of the radical critic Nikolai Dobroliubov (Mr −bov) in terms similar to those employed by Stepan Trofimovich Verkhovensky, when in his outburst at the fête he insists that Shakespeare and Raphael are more important for man's development than petroleum or a good pair of boots: "Don't you see, mankind can still get by without the Englishman, without Germany, and certainly without the Russian. It can survive without science, without bread. Only it can't survive without beauty, for then there would be absolutely no purpose to its existence on earth! The whole secret lies in this, the whole of history! Science itself would not last a minute without beauty – it would turn into loutishness; you wouldn't be able to invent a nail!" (10:373). For Dostoevsky it was man's sense of ideal beauty that elevated him above bestiality and gave spiritual purpose to his existence, and the primary image of such beauty was that of Christ.[34] He did, however, recognize that in times of moral confusion man's instinct for ideal beauty, which comes from God, could be compromised by corrupt aesthetic instincts deriving from the Devil. In "Mr −bov and the Question of Art" he wrote:

> We have seen examples where man, having achieved the ideal of his desires and not knowing what else to aim for, being totally satiated, has fallen into a kind of anguish, has even exacerbated this anguish within himself, has sought out another ideal in life, and out of extreme surfeit has not only ceased to value that which he enjoys but has even consciously turned away from the straight path, and has fomented in himself strange, unhealthy, sharp, inharmonious, sometimes even monstrous tastes, losing measure and aesthetic feeling for healthy beauty and demanding instead of it exceptions. (18:94)

It is Dmitrii who, in *The Brothers Karamazov*, links such aesthetic confusion to the influence of the Devil, an influence which encourages the illusion that evil can be beautiful. Dmitrii admits to possessing an equal receptiveness to both "the beauty of the Madonna" and "the beauty of Sodom," and he concludes that beauty is a terrible mystery: "Here God and the Devil struggle for mastery, and the battlefield is the heart of man" (14:100). The "beauty of Sodom," intoxication with the aesthetics of evil, was for Dostoevsky a characteristic of the late-Romantic, Byronic temperament, and it is therefore understandable that we should witness such confusion in *The Devils* in the person of Stavrogin, himself a Byronic figure gone to seed who deliberately marries the crippled Mar'ia Lebiadkina partly in order to revive his perverted but flagging aesthetic sense. Shatov recognizes this when he confronts Stavrogin in the chapter "Night": "'Is it true you claimed that you saw no aesthetic difference between some voluptuous, bestial prank and any kind of heroic feat, even the sacrifice of one's own life for mankind? Is it true that you found identical beauty, the same pleasure, in both extremes? … I don't know either why evil is squalid and good is beautiful, but I do know why the sense of distinction between them is erased and lost in gentlemen like Stavrogin!'" (10:261).

The loss of the same sense of distinction afflicts Petr too and allows him to mistake the sterile, mask-like countenance of Stavrogin for beauty, and to present this demon of non-being as a false icon, a focus for idolatry. The terms in which Petr couches his idolatry – "You are my leader, my sun (solntse), and I am your worm" – are also significant, for Uspensky reveals that the description "sun of righteousness" (pravednoe solntse), applied to Christ in liturgical texts, was also used of the False Dmitrii.[35] The term is repeated elsewhere: for example in Stavrogin's description of his relationship with Shatov: "'Forgive me,' Nikolai Vsevolodovich said with genuine surprise, 'but you appear to look upon me as some sort of sun (solntse) and yourself as some sort of insect in comparison'" (10:193); and in Lebiadkin's admission to Stavrogin that he has been waiting for him "as one awaits the sun" (10:210). This use of "sun" to link Stavrogin with the theme of imposture and with the False Dmitrii in particular is supported by other verbal and thematic symbols such as, for example, the cross. The sign of the cross was the most common of the "royal signs" popularly held to be found on the body of a true (i.e. divinely ordained) tsar.[36] Stavrogin's name conceals the Greek word for "cross" (stavros), but he is a false tsar and the fact that this "royal sign" fails to penetrate beyond his name emerges most clearly in the chapter "At Tikhon's" and in its draft and variant material. This chapter was, of course, excluded from the published version of the novel when Dostoevsky proved unable to tone down its shocking content to the censor's satisfaction. As a result, there is no truly canonical version, although the editors of the Academy Edition have sought to establish one (11:5–30). In one variant of the chapter, the narrator refers to Stavrogin's written confession as driven by "the need for punishment, the need for a cross to bear," but goes on to point out that this need for a cross is manifested by a man "who does not believe in the cross" (12:108). Tikhon does urge Stavrogin to take up the "cross of shame" (11:26) and to seek redemption, significantly by entering a monastery (Grishka Otrep'ev was a runaway monk); but Stavrogin refuses to bear this cross and leaves, the variants describing how he accidentally breaks Tikhon's crucifix before storming out of his cell (12:114).

The accusation of anti-behaviour and imposture was frequently levelled at Peter the Great by those who saw in the Westernization of Russia begun in his reign a demonic reversal of true Russian tradition. Dostoevsky himself saw the subsequent absorption of Western culture by Russia's educated classes as a form of demonic possession; and this encourages us to recognize that while *The Devils* employs traditional Russian cultural symbols and discourses to alert us to the *presence* of the demonic, it seeks to suggest its *nature* through discourses derived from both Western European secular sources and biblical narrative. Moreover, this new cluster of cultural inscriptions pivots primarily on the figure of Stavrogin, confirming his centrality in the novel's compositional and ideological design. Stavrogin's eventual role as the compositional centre of *The Devils* was recognized by Dostoevsky in the drafts for the novel where he described the "Prince," the draft character from which Stavrogin evolved, as the point around which all the rest turns "as in a kaleidoscope" (11:136). Elsewhere in the notebooks he wrote: "Everything is contained in the character of Stavrogin. Stavrogin is *everything*" (11:207). In the novel this centrality is suggested in the way that Stavrogin serves as both the source and the object of the emotional, psychological, or ideological aspirations of the other characters. Admittedly, at first he seems to have little bearing on the novel's initial polemical purpose as a "whip" with which to lash the nihilists, in that he actively has little to do with the political machinations of Petr and his group, and in any case he enters the flow of events at quite a late point. When he does appear, however, it soon becomes clear that he is a major player in this vaudeville of devils and a figure of genuinely tragic stature when seen against the activities of the lesser prankster-devils. Stavrogin is, of course, also guilty of prank-playing – he bites the old Governor's ear, pulls Gaganov's father by the nose, and subjects Liputin's wife to a minor sexual assault. But these are joyless acts disguising an inner inertia and lack of purpose. Ultimately, there is a bleakness about Stavrogin, a spiritual desolation, a death-like stillness at the core of his being that set him apart from the "enthusiasm" of Petr, the mad conviction of Kirillov, or Shatov's desperate fanaticism. His "demonism" derives from the spirit of non-being that has consumed him, and it is articulated primarily through the symbols of European Romantic tradition that are attributed to him.

E. Loginovskaia has made a distinction in this respect between the notions in Russian literature of *bes* (devil) and *demon* (demon). She argues that the former, usually envisaged in the plural as a collective horde and derived from biblical origins (e.g. the devils in the parable of the Gadarene swine), have been conventionally used in a negative sense to denote the forces of evil that possess man and distort his spiritual make-up; however, this negative function has prevented their becoming symbols capable of giving expression to "man's rich and complex nature." The figure of the *demon*, however, draws upon a literary tradition stretching through Milton's Satan and Byron's Lucifer, in order to provide, in works such as Lermontov's poem *The Demon* (*Demon*, 1839), a symbolic expression of "man's complex individualism, in conflict and tragically fated, but filled with force and grandeur."[37] Loginovskaia is perhaps wrong to imply that this distinction may be reduced to one of vocabulary, for in Russian Orthodox and folk tradition the terms *bes* and *demon* are often used interchangeably. What she does draw attention to, however, is a duality in the literary depiction of the demonic that emerges clearly in nineteenth-century Russian literature and which may be illustrated by comparing the anonymous and mischievous collection of spirits in Pushkin's "The Devils" (Besy, 1830) with the seductively rebellious individualism and irony of the "malignant spirit" (zlobnyi genii) in the same poet's "The Demon" (Demon, 1823).

The spirits tempting and deceiving the traveller in Pushkin's "The Devils" are the anonymous and multitudinous petty devils of folkloric and Orthodox tradition. As Simon Franklin argues in the present volume, hagiographic tradition played down the depiction of *the* Devil in favour of devils, and its demonology gave little emphasis to "a towering figure of Satan in splendour."[38] This tradition of depicting devils is absorbed in the work of Gogol. What we see in Pushkin's "The Demon," however, is an attempt to "psychologize" the devil/demon, to treat him as an allegory, an externalization of Romantic revolt and individualism. In this form he transcends the pedestrian nastiness, and indeed perceived cosmological *objectivity*, of the traditional petty devil (remember Tikhon again: "devils undoubtedly exist"); he becomes instead an aesthetically potent, *subjective* projection of man's rebelliousness.

A typology of the demon in this incarnation is provided in Lermontov's narrative poem *The Demon*. He is the "spirit of exile" (dukh izgnan'ia, 1:1.1),[39] possessed by an ironic despondency; excluded from paradise by his pride, "he sowed evil without enjoyment" (on seial zlo bez naslazhden'ia, 1:2.27); he smoulders with the desire for reconciliation, but on his terms; he is "a tsar of knowledge and freedom" (tsar' poznan'ia i svobody, 2:10.601), but this brings him nothing but an all-consuming boredom, his soul an "indestructible mausoleum / Of hopes and passions that have perished" (Nadezhd pogibshikh i strastei / Nesokrushimyi mavzolei, 2:10.740–41). Because the demon was a projection of essentially human qualities, Lermontov was able to extend the typology almost unchanged into Pechorin, the central figure of his novel *A Hero of Our Time* (*Geroi nashego vremeni*, 1840). In *The Devils*, as many critics have pointed out,[40] a consistent system of both overt and oblique references point to Lermontov and his hero as a yardstick against which we must measure the demonism of Stavrogin. Apart from similarities in the spiritual and psychological make-up of the respective heroes, and a certain overlapping of plot motifs (e.g. duelling and seduction), the novel offers a lengthy discourse on Stavrogin as an inheritor of Lermontovian malice (10:165), as well as references to him as a "Pechorin-ladykiller" (10:84) and a "vampire," a term Pechorin applies to himself (10:401). Other similarly suggestive details include the attribution of his behaviour to "the demon of irony" and mention of a book he is reading called *The Women of Balzac* (10:180), the latter recalling a description of Pechorin as "like a thirty-year-old Balzacian coquette after a particularly exhausting dance."[41] Such implied comparisons are intriguing, but we must approach them circumspectly. Like so much else in the relativistic world of Dostoevsky's polyphonic narrative, these details lack authority: they are contaminated by what Gary Saul Morson has termed "the irony of origins," in that they arise not from direct authorial discourse but from the voices of other characters.[42] The reference to the "demon of irony" is by Stepan Trofimovich, and it points as much to his own penchant for inflated Romantic rhetoric and desire to win favour with Stavrogin's mother as to any objective assessment of Stavrogin himself. The description "Pechorin-ladykiller" is offered sarcastically by Liputin, whose wife Stavrogin has assaulted, and the vampire motif is the product of the inflamed passions of a local lady smitten by the hero. Even the extended discussion of Stavrogin's place in the gallery of Romantic heroes is offered by a narrator-chronicler whose partiality and perceptual lacunae are well documented. Stavrogin's own description of the demon that possesses him contributes to the process of compromising Romantic expectations. The spirit that visits him is a far cry from Lermontov's Demon, "shining with an unearthly beauty" (krasoi blistaia nezemnoi, 1:16.379): he confesses to Dasha that it is "a petty, repulsive, scrofulous little devil (besenok) with a runny nose" (10:231). Thus is Stavrogin's demonism subverted, and we are alerted to the possibility that this proud spirit of Romantic revolt might be only a deflated demon, a Lucifer with the air let out.

The presentation of Stavrogin's "demonism" through the accumulation and simultaneous subversion of Romantic motifs is not neutral in ideological terms. It coincides with views Dostoevsky expresses elsewhere to the effect that the "evil" represented by figures like Stavrogin is one not indigenous to Russian culture, but was imported along with the cult of Byron and "Byronism" during the 1820s. In an entry in *Diary of a Writer* for December 1877 Dostoevsky acknowledges Byron and the mood of Romantic despair that attended his popularity as legitimate responses to the cultural and spiritual collapse that overtook Western Europe in the wake of the

French Revolution, when "the old idols lay shattered" and the poet articulated "the dreadful anguish, disillusionment and despair" of his age (26:113–14). But the cult of Byron among Europeanized Russian noblemen, and the assimilation by them of the same spirit of despair and revolt, carried no such legitimacy, for it symptomized the alienation of the Russian upper classes from native tradition and the rupture of the organic unity of Russian society. The results were: the estrangement of the Westernized intellectual from Orthodox spiritual culture in favour of rational Western civilization; the gulf that opened between such men and the Russian masses, still steeped in the traditions of pre-Petrine Russia; and the emergence in Russia of social and political disharmony, as the absorption of Western scepticism led to the questioning of the traditional Russian order. The phenomenon of the Russian educated man thus cut off from his own national identity was referred to by Dostoevsky as that of the *obshchechelovek*. This word translates conventionally as "universal man," but the translation carries a positive charge that Dostoevsky did not intend. His *obshchechelovek* was a wraith-like being, a ghost drifting without the anchor of national identity, in whom the erosion of nationality had led to the erosion of personality.[43]

The concept of the *obshchechelovek* was central to Dostoevsky's conception of *The Devils* and to the demonism of its hero, Stavrogin. To Maikov in 1870 he wrote: "a man who loses his people and his national roots also loses the faith of his forefathers and his God. Well, if you really want to know, this is essentially the theme of my novel. It is called *The Devils*, and it describes how the devils entered the herd of swine" (29/i:145). The long discussion with Shatov in "Night" reveals the extent to which Stavrogin has lost his own national roots, and in the working drafts for the novel Dostoevsky refers to the Stavrogin-Prince character as an *obshchechelovek* whose very being has disintegrated along with his Russianness (11:134–5). The point to grasp is that for Dostoevsky Russianness was inseparable from Orthodoxy; being Russian was not merely a matter of jingoistic national pride; it also meant being part of the only true God-bearing nation. Alienation from Russian national identity meant alienation from God. The tragedy of Stavrogin the *obshchechelovek* is thus not confined to his psychological and national estrangement: it is a religious tragedy transcending the sociopolitical. It is thus appropriate that our attempts to decode the demonic in *The Devils* should conclude with discussion of a pattern of symbolic inscriptions that enlarge the scale of Stavrogin's demonism and reveal its true significance by setting it in the context of the most potent biblical account of the struggle between good and evil – the Book of Revelation.

The apocalyptic patterning of *The Devils* is clear to the attentive reader, and its detail has been drawn out in the critical literature: Karmazinov compares the collapse of Europe to the fall of Babylon; Kirillov reads the Apocalypse at night to Fed'ka and cites its prophecy that "there will be time no more;" the Stavrogin estate, from which so much evil emanates, is called Skvoreshniki, a name derived from *skvorechnik*, a wooden bird-box, suggesting an analogy with Revelation's description of Babylon as "a cage for every unclean and hateful bird," an analogy further implied by several references to the members of Petr's circle as "birds about to flee the nest" and by characters whose names are derived from birds (Lebiadkin, Gaganov, Drozdov); Stavrogin's indifference is described as being "neither cold nor hot," the formula used in Revelation to describe the Church of the Laodiceans; the novel's account of outbreaks of incendiarism and cholera in the district recall the scourges of fire and plague that accompany the Last Judgement; and so on.[44] Dostoevsky's heavily annotated copy of the New Testament makes clear just how inspirational and suggestive he found the evocative but elusive imagery of the Revelation of Saint John. His annotations to chapter 13 of Revelation suggest a particular interest in the predicted advent of a "beast," whose name is Mystery, and who will rule over the earth with supreme power. Revelation describes how the way is paved for this beast by a false prophet, a lesser devil with two horns and a dragon's tongue, who "exerciseth all the power of the first beast before him, and causeth the earth and them which dwell therein to worship the first beast." The false prophet, moreover, "maketh fire come down from heaven on the earth in the sight of men," "deceiveth them that dwell on the earth," and causes "that as many as would not worship the image of the beast should be killed" (Rev.13:12–15). It is not extravagant to discern behind these devils the figures of the mysterious "wild beast" Stavrogin and the serpent-tongued deceiver Petr Verkhovensky. Petr's first appearance in the novel is when he comes on ahead to announce the advent of Stavrogin, whom he plans to make men worship. On the night of the fête he too makes fire come down to earth by organizing the incendiarism that claims the lives of the Lebiadkins. He practises the systematic deception of the Governor's wife and members of his own circle. And he arranges the murder of Shatov when the latter ceases to believe his fabrications.

Alongside a passage in Revelation 17:11 referring again to "the beast that was, and is not," Dostoevsky has written the single word *obshchechelovek*,[45] a concept closely related, as we have seen, to his critique of the Westernized Russian intellectual and to his notebook conception of Stavrogin. In this way the devils' vaudeville of *The Devils* gives way to apocalyptic warning of the dangers facing Russian society in its unnatural espousal of Western European values and a prophecy of the salvation to be found only through that society's rediscovery of native Orthodox culture. This duality at the heart of the novel returns us neatly to the point from which we started: the two epigraphs, pointing in different directions in their implied interpretations of the demonic. It is clear now that the Pushkin epigraph anticipates the carnival strand of the novel and goes with the revolutionary activities of Petr Verkhovensky and his circle as they seek to lure Russia from its proper track. The discourses through which Dostoevsky approaches this aspect of the novel, with their gleefully disruptive disregard for conventions drawn from carnival tradition, perfectly match Dostoevsky's own ambiguous attitude to Petr and what he represents. He is a demon, certainly, but what he creates dissolves into vaudeville. In a letter to Katkov, dated 8 October 1870, Dostoevsky referred to Petr as a "pitiful freak" who, despite his monstrous criminality, was emerging as a half-comic figure "unworthy of literature" and incapable of carrying the weight of the novel's import (29/i:141). Petr is caught in the same demonic trap as his victims: the breakdown of order he orchestrates offers the freedom only to go around in circles in a dark field. Like the travellers in Pushkin's poem, who cannot see where they are going (sbilis' my), the Russian revolutionary has no inkling of what lies ahead. As Dostoevsky remarked in 1873 to Varvara Timofeeva, his co-worker on the journal *Grazhdanin*, following a discussion about the penetration of European influences into Russia: "They don't suspect that soon it will be the end of everything, of all their 'progress' and idle chatter. They have no inkling that the Antichrist has already been born… and *he is coming!*.. The Antichrist is coming among us! And the end of the world is close – closer than people think!"[46]

The epigraph from Saint Luke, however, anticipates the apocalyptic/redemptive theme with which Dostoevsky overlays the carnival strand of the novel. It clearly points to the tragedy of Stavrogin, sick with the devils that have laid low several generations of Europeanized Russians who have lost the anchor of salvation offered by their nationality. It also prefigures the "cleansing" of the liberal-Westernizer Stepan Trofimovich Verkhovensky, who at the end of the novel and shortly before his death revives the redemptive theme through espousal of those native Russian values that elude the *obshchechelovek* Stavrogin.

Notes

1. F.M. Dostoevskii, *Polnoe sobranie sochinenii v tridtsati tomakh*, ed. V.G. Bazanov and others, 30 vols. (Leningrad: Nauka, 1972–90), 29/i:145. All further references to

Dostoevsky's works are to this edition and appear in the text. Translations from Dostoevsky's works are my own.

2. For a fuller account of the Nechaev affair see Joseph Frank, *Dostoevsky. The Miraculous Years, 1865–1871* (Princeton: Princeton University Press, 1995), chap. 23.

3. Fyodor Dostoevsky, *Demons*, trans. Richard Pevear and Larissa Volokhonsky (New York: Random House, 1994).

4. Franco Venturi, *Roots of Revolution*, trans. Francis Haskell (Chicago: Chicago University Press, 1960), 331–53.

5. Harriet Murav, *Holy Foolishness. Dostoevsky's Novels and the Poetics of Cultural Critique* (Stanford: Stanford University Press, 1992), 115.

6. For a discussion of Stavrogin's anachronism see Frank, *Dostoevsky. The Miraculous Years*, 467–70, 478.

7. Felix J. Oinas, *Essays on Russian Folklore and Mythology* (Columbus: Slavica, 1985), 101.

8. N.V. Gogol', *Sobranie sochinenii v semi tomakh*, 7 vols. (Moscow: Khudozhestvennaia literatura, 1966–67), 3:21.

9. L. Grossman, *Poetika Dostoevskogo* (Moscow: Gosudarstvennaia Akademiia khudozhestvennykh nauk, 1925), 61–62. Cited in M. Bakhtin, *Problems of Dostoevsky's Poetics*, ed. and trans. Caryl Emerson (Manchester: Manchester University Press, 1984), 103.

10. Bakhtin, *Problems of Dostoevsky's Poetics*, 107.

11. Ibid., 106.

12. Ibid., 108.

13. See Bakhtin, *Problems of Dostoevsky's Poetics*, chap. 4, and *Rabelais and His World*, trans. Hélène Iswolsky (Bloomington, Ind.: Indiana University Press, 1984).

14. Bakhtin, *Problems of Dostoevsky's Poetics*, 122.

15. Ibid., 107.

16. Murav, *Holy Foolishness*, 9.

17. Ju.M. Lotman and B.A. Uspenskij, *The Semiotics of Russian Culture*, ed. Ann Shukman, Michigan Slavic Contributions, no.11 (Ann Arbor: Department of Slavic Languages and Literatures, University of Michigan, 1984), 40.

18. Bakhtin, *Problems of Dostoevsky's Poetics*, 131.

19. Linda J. Ivanits, "Folk Beliefs About the 'Unclean Force' in Dostoevskij's *The Brothers Karamazov*," in *New Perspectives on Nineteenth-Century Russian Prose*, ed. George J. Gutsche and Lauren G. Leighton (Columbus: Slavica, 1981), 137.

20. Oinas, *Essays on Russian Folklore and Mythology*, 98.

21. Catriona Kelly, *Petrushka. The Russian Carnival Puppet Theatre* (Cambridge: Cambridge University Press, 1990).

22. James L. Rice, *Dostoevsky and the Healing Art. An Essay in Literary and Medical History* (Ann Arbor: Ardis, 1985), 75.

23. Kelly, *Petrushka*, 48–49.

24. Ibid., 160.

25. Ibid., 90.

26. Ibid., 55.

27. Elizabeth A. Warner, *The Russian Folk Theatre* (The Hague and Paris: Mouton, 1977), 115–16.

28. Bakhtin, *Problems of Dostoevsky's Poetics*, 180.

29. Harriet Murav, "Representations of the Demonic: Seventeenth-Century Pretenders and *The Devils*," *Slavic and East European Journal* 35, no.1 (1991):56.

30. 10:326. See also Richard Peace, *Dostoyevsky. An Examination of the Major Novels* (Cambridge: Cambridge University Press, 1971), 171, 323.

31. Murav, "Representations of the Demonic," 59.

32. Lotman and Uspenskij, *The Semiotics of Russian Culture*, 272.

33. Ibid., 263.

34. I have developed these ideas more fully than is possible here in *Fedor Dostoevsky* (Boston, Mass.: Twayne, 1981). For a further treatment of Dostoevsky's aesthetic views see Robert Louis Jackson, *Dostoevsky's Quest for Form. A Study of His Philosophy of Art* (New Haven: Yale University Press, 1966).

35. Lotman and Uspenskij, *The Semiotics of Russian Culture*, 261.

36. Ibid., 264–65.

37. E. Loginovskaia, "Motiv demonizma v *Besakh* Dostoevskogo. Tekstovye i vnetekstovye koordinaty," *Scando-Slavica* 26 (1980):35–36.

38. See in this volume Simon Franklin, "Nostalgia for Hell: Russian Literary Demonism and Orthodox Tradition," 35.

39. For the text of *Demon*, see M.Iu. Lermontov, *Polnoe sobranie stikhotvorenii*, introd. D.E. Maksimov, ed. E.E. Naidich, Biblioteka poeta, Bol'shaia seriia, 2 vols. (Leningrad: Sovetskii pisatel', 1989), 2:436–68. References are given from this edition in the text by part and stanza numbers, followed by the line number within the work as a whole.

40. See, for example, Elisabeth Stenbock-Fermor, "Lermontov and Dostoevskij's Novel *The Devils*," *Slavic and East European Journal* 17 (1959):215–30.

41. M.Iu. Lermontov, *Polnoe sobranie sochinenii v piati tomakh*, ed. B.M. Eikhenbaum, 5 vols. (Moscow and Leningrad: Akademiia, 1935–37), 5:224.

42. Gary Saul Morson, *The Boundaries of Genre. Dostoevsky's "Diary of a Writer" and the Traditions of Literary Utopia* (Austin: University of Texas Press, 1981), 77.

43. For a fuller discussion of these ideas than is appropriate in the present essay see Frank, *Dostoevsky. The Miraculous Years*, chaps. 21 and 24.

44. W.J. Leatherbarrow, "Apocalyptic Imagery in *The Idiot* and *The Devils*," *Dostoevsky Studies* 3 (1982):43–52, and Geir Kjetsaa, *Fyodor Dostoyevsky. A Writer's Life* (London: Macmillan, 1987), 253–61.

45. Geir Kjetsaa, *Dostoevsky and His New Testament* (Oslo and New Jersey: Humanities Press, 1984), 77.

46. A. Dolinin, ed., *F.M. Dostoevskii v vospominaniiakh sovremennikov*, 2 vols. (Moscow: Gosudarstvennoe izdatel'stvo khudozhestvennoi literatury, 1964), 2:170

Chapter 9

Rozanov and His Literary Demons

Liza Dimbleby

Rozanov did not claim that he knew the company of demons, he gives no account of metaphysical torment or temptation. In a period of great fascination with the supernatural and occult, he protested his ordinariness,[1] and claimed to value the gentle, homely details of everyday life far more than any knowledge of other worlds. Merezhkovsky saw this as a shortcoming. In his view, Rozanov "was never attracted by intimations of the 'so-called Satanic profundities'" and suffered "not from an excess, but rather from a lack of such intimations."[2] Yet intimations and imagery of devilry and demonism are a recurrent feature of Rozanov's work. These demonic evocations are closely linked to his views on the contemporary state of literature, and should be understood in the context of his "battle" for the life of the word in Russian writing.

The notion of the life of the word as a powerful source of spiritual renewal is as central to the tradition of religious thought in Russia as it is to an understanding of the Russian literary tradition.[3] The ideal of a living, concentrated, energetic word, capable of opposing dead and ossified language, was a focus of both religious and literary thought, in particular at the time when Rozanov was writing most prolifically. Rozanov's own writing is very conversant with both traditions. This is evident in his articles on religion, his literary criticism, and his own creative work in the "fallen leaves" genre.[4] Throughout his writing, he repeatedly returns to the ideal of verbal activity as an ultimately religious act, privileging such "spoken" gen-res as prayer and prophecy against more artificially constructed "lit-erary" vestiges. He seeks to portray the writers he favours as participating in these more sacred genres. His own development of an intimate "spoken" genre of writing "for oneself"[5] was a bid to align his work with this sacred, as opposed to purely literary, tradi-tion. In this context, his presentations of the demonic acted as a cat-alyst to the elucidation of his own role as a writer.

In this essay I look at the conflicts between Rozanov's aims and the means by which they were expressed; at his own battle, as a suc-cessful literary figure, with the "demonic" temptations of print and publication; and at his evocation of the demonic aspects of his writer contemporaries, Vladimir Solov'ev and Merezhkovsky. Rozanov's criticism of the spirit in which these writers used words extended beyond the details of phrasing and punctuation in their articles into an attack on all aspects of their physical being, including their appearance, habits, and sexuality. His eccentric defence of Lermon-tov as an anti-demonic writer was similarly a polemic against the separation between the verbal and the physical aspects of contem-porary life that he believed lay at the root of the malaise in Russian verbal culture. His portrayal in his late writings of Gogol as the ulti-mate embodiment of the literary demonic set Gogol up as a force of negation, to which Rozanov opposed his own role as a writer-prophet, seeking to redeem Russia and Russian literature with his words. Finally, I attempt to assess how far Rozanov believed that he had been successful in his role, and how much he himself continued to be tormented by inner demons of literary temptation that he embodied in the various devils of print, journalists, and writers.

Literary Demonism and Russian Attitudes to the Word

The literary demonism of Dostoevsky, Vladimir Solov'ev and of the religious symbolists was closely connected to their understanding of the nature of the word. All had some sense of a sacred origin of the word that informed their ideas about the tasks of literature and art. The role of the demonic in their writing was closely linked to a sense of literature as potentially redemptive. For Solov'ev, and in particular Dostoevsky, the faith in the redemptive power of the word fuelled a faith, more constant than that of the symbolists, in the redemptive, regenerative power of literature. Dostoevsky's literary demonism had such a redemptive purpose, yet the agency of redemption was the work of literature, whose status was unquestioned. Rozanov's images of the demonic owe much to Dostoevsky, yet for him the relation between demonism and the work of literary art was more complex. Demonism was not only something to be addressed through literature. Demons lurked unsummoned in the very mechanism of writing, printing, and publishing one's inventions. Rozanov went further than any of his near contemporaries in questioning the process of literary production itself, in which he sensed a demonic threat.

Rozanov's writing is marked by a deep anxiety about the purpose of literature. He claimed that his own writing was an attempt to overcome an artifice in literature that he saw as demonic, to return men to the thoughts and feelings of life, freed from the authority of books. Yet he sought to achieve this through writing that was printed and published. His awareness of the devilish ambiguity in the process of writing and publication is a tension that runs throughout his life and even the stages of his death (an account of which he dictated to his daughter so that it too became a printed and published work).[6] Like the symbolists, he was acutely aware of the moral ambiguity involved in literary activity.[7] However he did not court spiritual transgression in the hope of a metaphysical and artistic transcendence. He went further than his contemporaries in pushing literature to its limits – yet it was the boundary between literature and the everyday, not the supernatural, that he pushed against in his persistent questioning of the limits of the expressible. He sought to expose the artifice and false pretensions of literature by making his most intimate thoughts and day-to-day habits "immortal" in print. Rejecting received ideas of literary language, content, and form, he shocked even the supposedly more daring of his contemporaries with his "intimate" genre of "fallen leaves." This fragmentary and seemingly haphazard assembly of statement and reflection was his bid to counteract the "demonic" tyranny of the printing press and a predominantly journalistic civilization by making the last domestic incident or private thought into a "literary" statement, publishable alongside political and literary gossip or thoughts about Dostoevsky's heroes and Pushkin's effect on the nervous system. *Fallen Leaves* (*Opavshie list'ia*, 1913) was a literary success, yet Rozanov remained obsessed by the need to "overcome" literature. Perversely, this obsession itself furthered the cause of purely literary activity. In his attempt to return to the original intimacy of the spoken, spontaneous word, rooted in life, Rozanov achieved supremely literary and stylistic innovations, making use of devices of print and punctuation with great sophistication.[8] In this exploitation of print, he enlists his demons in order to exorcize them. While pointing out, in print, the demonic potential of printed words and publication, Rozanov recognizes that he himself is tainted by the devilish associations of the printing press.[9] Yet this attempt to resolve the ambiguities of his role as a writer was itself a spur to further literary activity.

Rozanov presented his writing as a return to spontaneous, spoken forms of utterance, to its physical surroundings of warmth and intonation, to something that was close to breathing, and to the first cries of prayer. The distancing of words from this fiery inspired origin was fatal to the life of a culture. Words hold together the gap between man and the world only insofar as they contain the heat and spontaneity of the first impulse to reach out to God and the world, to engage directly with things. Rozanov claimed that literature was failing to fulfil this role. With increasing intensity, he characterized agents of the separation of the word from its origins as "demonic" threats to the life of the word. Words, like man after the fall, had fallen away from God into a demonic coldness and separation.[10] He valued spoken intonation and manuscripts for containing a redemptive warmth that might counteract the icy demonism of the printing press: "Where exactly lies the magic of book-printing, its negative magic? The letters, each one printed out, have lost their distinct character and with that their soul. ... A book without soul!!! – the devil knows what this is. A corpse, decay, stench. ... The magic of writing has vanished. A book is a manuscript without magic – a manuscript 'in which the spirit has been killed'."[11] The banal godlessness of contemporary life was seen by Rozanov as the fate of a civilization remote and distanced from its religious instincts and from reality, whose words had gone cold. He feared that print imposed a pseudo-objectivity and uniformity on words that distanced them from their origins in each individual impulse towards speech. He explained the immensity of contemporary literary and journalistic output as an attempt to compensate for the loss that people experienced because they could not achieve this immediate contact with reality through their words. They are condemned to live a life of words without value, to keep pouring out words that resist their original purpose.

The Satanic character of Gutenberg, the German inventor of the printing press, is attacked throughout Rozanov's writing as the personification of the evils of print, the demonic possession of writing that has "lost its soul" to print: "It's as though that cursed Guttenberg [*sic*] licked all the writers over with his copper tongue, and they all lost their soul 'in print,' they lost their individuality, their character."[12] Rozanov even refers to Gutenberg as "Mephistopheles-Gutenberg"[13] and describes his malevolent legacy in *After Sakharna* (*Posle Sakharny*, 1913): "Gutenberg destroyed the common need to touch one another. People began to touch 'by cable,' 'by telephone' (the book): this is the evil black point in Gutenberg. Gutenberg alone brought more death to the earth than anyone before him. After him the freezing-up (of the planet) began."[14] Love had been replaced by literary consciousness. Print and the mass circulation of journals and newspapers threatened to suffocate and eventually to kill all live thought and feeling, replacing it with a pervasive nihilism. Rozanov frequently evoked a past golden age in his writing, free of the authority of printed words, in which people were naturally loving and connected, full of a celebratory joy in living that he contrasted with the pessimistic and over-literary contemporary culture. This nostalgia shaped his apocalyptic anticipations for a new dawn, where people would be freed from their awe of print, abandon their newspapers and journals, and start to "simply live."[15] Literature would then be returned to its original sacred status as something occasional, uplifting, but no longer regarded as a replacement for life.

Rozanov claimed that by "publishing his soul," in all of its intimacy, confusion, and last details, an unheard-of subject for literature, he might further this literary apocalypse by a subversion of the proud and public, published domain with a display of what normally defies transcription.[16] He argued that by pushing the expressible in literature to its limits, its artifice and false authority would collapse through its own contradictions. He would be the last writer, after whom people would return to their lives:

> I "publish my soul," like Gershenzon "published Pushkin," with the same detachment, objectivity and bibliographical detail.
> How terrifying: a living, burning soul – and I lay it on the cold typographer's press.
> The soul feels cold. But the press "feels nothing."
> Why am I doing this and how is it even in any way possible?
> I think that I can overcome literature (my dream). My soul will not freeze up from print, but "the leaden column" … will *no longer exist* (it will melt down).
> Manuscripts again … yellowing, old.
> How good it would be.
> Man will be free again: free from a MONSTROUS ENSLAVEMENT to books.
> Oh, what an enslavement … demeaning, oppressive; destroying everything (culture). (*Mim.*, 263)

Yet the battle against the demonism rife amongst words had itself to take place through the agency of words. Rozanov recognized that words are fraught with potential for good and bad. Literature was thus increasingly becoming the battleground of good and evil, of the use and abuse of the word. This concern with the use of words was central to Rozanov's view of writers, both famous ones, already canonized in Russian literature, and more obscure or neglected writers. Writers who made use of words in an artificial, literary, or journalistic way, unrelated to the physical presence of things, were condemned as demonic incursors on the essential life of words and things.

Rozanov takes up many features of Dostoevsky's "demonic" in his indictment of the isolation of most Russian writers and intellectuals from their country's people and traditions. In *Fleeting* (*Mimoletnoe*, 1915), he argues that the inevitable consequence of a literature so dominated by a foreign Western tradition could only be nihilism and revolution, culminating in the annihilation of Russia.[17] He describes Dostoevsky as the one writer who had attempted to overcome this self-destructive tendency of Russian writing, and claims that by taking up Dostoevsky's "method" of warmth and intimacy in a radically personal way, he would "overcome" the terrifying immanent nihilism of Russian literature that had penetrated the whole of Russian life.[18] Yet Rozanov's solution was more extreme than Dostoevsky's; he sought the demise of the novel itself in his bid to reassert a "truly" Russian religious verbal culture, whose kernel is to be found in the genres of prayer, prophecy, and the psalms. He saw his own "fallen leaves" genre as a continuation of this tradition and increasingly came to regard writing that was linked to this tradition of the (sacred) word as the only way forward. Rozanov's intimations of an imminent apocalypse in Russia become increasingly strident in his writing, culminating in *Apocalypse of Our Time* (*Apokalipsis nashego vremeni*, 1917–18). In *Fleeting*, he praised Dostoevsky's prophetic vision of the Russian people, crowding in anticipation of the final revelation, but in *Apocalypse of Our Time*, written after the Revolution of 1917, it is the bathos of a godless vaudeville that he evokes.[19] He came to see his own fate as a writer as the literary incarnation of the apocalypse taking place in Russian life, describing himself as perhaps the last ever writer.[20] In 1918, he describes himself no longer as a writer, but as a prophet, doing battle with the forces of negation in literature and the press.[21]

Lermontov's *The Demon*

Rozanov's articles on Lermontov of 1901 and 1902 introduce the idea of the demonic in close connection to verbal activity.[22] Lermontov was, and remains, a central reference point for the exploration of the demonic in Russian writing. Rozanov engages with him in his own idiosyncratic manner. His articles were a conscious refutation of Solov'ev's warnings against the perilous legacy of Lermontov.[23] However, in contrast with his symbolist contemporaries, he does not explore the potential of moral transgression in Lermontov's *The Demon* (*Demon*, 1839). Lermontov's Demon is not interpreted as an evil, nor even ambiguous figure, but as a misunderstood force for the regeneration of life and the sacred in words and in the world.

Rozanov sought to make Lermontov's writing exemplary of the spontaneous qualities that he claimed need to be restored to the word. Throughout these articles the emphasis is on the pre-literary, pre-printed life of the word. Rozanov describes the approach of the ancient Egyptian and Judaic cultures to God through the sigh (vzdokh)[24] and ties of blood. The emphasis is on an unnamed God. He describes the Jewish rite of circumcision and the blood sacrifice of ancient religions as a communication with God that is wordless and invigorating: "Through the sacrificial blood man was united with God. What is blood? The current of life, living, creative, wordless and formative."[25] The juxtaposition of this direct blood-connection to God with cultures whose only approach to God is through the more remote access of words was central to Rozanov's writing.[26] Man compensates for the loss of this instinctive connection to God by a faith in the intellect, in verbal abstractions, as Rozanov claims: "We are no longer able to love. ... But we think like gods."[27] He argued that it was this replacing of an instinctive religious culture by an increasingly intellectualized and literary existence that prevented a reliable identification of the truly malevolent influences in contemporary life: "In an age, when people revere God only *in books*, and no longer in living experience, they begin, first and foremost, to mix up 'the devil' and 'God'."[28] Such intellectually based confusion was evident, according to Rozanov, in the reception of Lermontov's *The Demon*. His critique emphasizes that Lermontov's supernatural perceptions were rooted in sexuality, which for Rozanov was the central act of religious communication, but which society, and Lermontov himself, feared as "demonic": "Lermontov called it 'the demon,' but the ancients called it 'a god.' ... They called this feeling of love and phenomenon of sex, inexplicable to us or to anyone else, 'miraculous,' 'sacred,' 'unknowable' and 'frighteningly powerful' (o, boundlessly!), and finally magical in its activity."[29] Cultures that were immanently religious revered this physical power which in turn empowered their words. The lasting importance of Lermontov's *The Demon* was its engagement with this central religious issue: "Everything depends on how we look at love and birth, whether we see them as the source of sin or the source from which all truth springs. Here the religious rivers converge. Yet the historical and metaphysical interest of *The Demon* lies in the fact that he [Lermontov] stood at this point of convergence and once more thoughtfully posed the question about the origin of evil and the origin of good, not in the narrow moral sense, but in its wider, transcendental implications."[30] As Rozanov wrote, everything depends on one's view of the sexual impulse – on whether it is seen as a disintegrating, destructive force or as the source of all life – everything, not least words and writing. Words can equally be forces for fiery regeneration or cold disintegration. The life of the word was dependent on the life of the sexual impulse within a culture, and Rozanov believed that both were inextricably in peril. He claimed that the writing of Lermontov and Dostoevsky had a sense of this power of ancient cultures, that was so lacking in contemporary life: "The theology of the ancients, and the theology of Dostoevsky's vision, is like a sort of poured-out milk, rather like the pouring into all of our veins of a gentle, soft, loving substance, something that is wordless, that lifts up our hearts, without any names ..."[31]

Lermontov's wrongly named *The Demon* is presented as an example of a much needed spiritual energy that is contrasted with the true demonism of contemporary life in its distrust of the physical.[32] Fearful of immediate sensual experience, so vividly evoked in Lermontov's writing, readers condemned the writer as demonic.[33] Rozanov claims that this view of the demonic was so integral to contemporary morality that it had penetrated even the writer's interpretation of his experience. The demons of both Lermontov and Gogol were the expression of acute religious insight, inextricable from the sexual, but had been wrongly named by their authors, who recognized that they were at odds with prevailing ideas about the sacred:

> These phenomena – as far as we can judge from their writings – were so unlike the conceptions that they had grown up with of the religious and the sacred, that they gave them a label to bear witness to their revulsion and indignation: "sorcerer," "demon," "devil" (bes). This was merely a mark of their incompatibility with accustomed, expected or conventional ideas. In *The Demon* Lermontov essentially expounds an entire myth about the "gentleman" (gospodin) tormenting him. ... But, I repeat, the name "devil" is a mark of what is incompatible, a memory of fright.[34]

Yet Rozanov suggests that it is but a small "philological" leap from the devilish *gospodin* (gentleman) to the holy *Gospod'* (Lord).[35] He argues that the fear of and contempt for the true sources of life stem from the Christian Middle Ages.[36] The tempting devils of the Middle Ages summoned man from the Christian religion of death to a real experience of life.[37] It is this same summons to life that Lermontov was making in his poetry. In society's fear and rejection of the flesh Rozanov saw a demonic tendency that threatened contemporary existence with an absolute loss of substance. The rejection of life in the name of religion was a denial and perversion of life's innate religious vitality. Rozanov's views challenged both religious orthodoxy, which identified the demonic with sexual temptation, and the decadent "God-seekers," whose exploration of the demonic and the erotic he dismissed as overwhelmingly literary. He focused in particular on the Merezhkovsky entourage, attacking their lack of true sexuality in their artificial and literary pursuit of a mystical eroticism that transcended the flesh. For Rozanov, there could be no access to the metaphysical without a true understanding and love for the physical. The prevailing intellectual demonism by which he believed that these writers were possessed could only be counteracted through a renewal of the nerve of life and the life of the word, in a true reading of Lermontov.[38]

Rozanov's writing about sex is impassioned, full of reverence for a religious sense surrounding all of its manifestations. The loss of this sense runs through the entire culture, and is at the root of contemporary unhappiness. The demonic emptiness and disconnection between people and between things was a consequence of not heeding Lermontov. Solov'ev had warned against the terrible immanent demonism contained in Lermontov's writing. He claimed that this demonism had already found its expression in Rozanov and his contemporaries. Rozanov claimed, on the contrary, that the debt that was owing to Lermontov was not, as Solov'ev wrote, to relieve him of the burden of his fatal error, but to recognize the freeing nature of his perceptions. The intensity with which these views are expressed can be seen also as a personal refutation of Solov'ev's attacks on Rozanov of 1899, in which he branded Rozanov in the very terms that Rozanov had celebrated Lermontov in an earlier article, as an orgiast and Pythian (pifist), accusing him of a demonic self-intoxication. The force of his inspiration is clearly emphasized as coming "from below" (snizu). He had also called Rozanov a Nietzschean "superman" (sverkhchelovek), an inheritor of the demonism that he claimed Lermontov had initiated.[39] In an article for *Novyi put'*, Rozanov took issue with such personal attacks on him from the religious "ascetics," including Solov'ev.[40] He claimed that Solov'ev had called him an "Antichrist," and mocked such abuse from one who has so neglected the need of the family in his theological pursuits.[41] He also turned the charge of demonic Nietzscheanism back against his accusers, condemning prevailing attitudes to sex, childbirth, and marriage laws as a demonic pride: "Nietzsche, Nietzscheanism! An evil and mocking principle in history! ... And if Nietzsche is an evil mocker and destroyer, then he is truly a mere inexperienced boy in comparison with the immense Nietzscheanism that gave man the tempting commandment: 'Don't be fruitful! Don't multiply! And you will be – as gods'."[42]

Vladimir Solov'ev and Merezhkovsky

In a letter written to the newspaper *Novoe vremia*, in response to Solov'ev's lectures on the Antichrist, Rozanov argued that Solov'ev's portrayal was of a figure so similar to Christ that his Antichrist would be "the most successful Christian." He protests his disappointment with the ultimate "revelation;" in Solov'ev's vision the new heaven and earth were literary, even journalistic. The Antichrist was no more than "our literary brother," someone not unlike Solov'ev himself.[43] Rozanov not only challenged Solov'ev's conception of the demonic, he saw in Solov'ev's writing, and in the man himself, a profoundly demonic presence. Rozanov repeatedly returned to the figure of Solov'ev, as to an unresolved riddle.[44] He points out the devilish traits, not only of Solov'ev's words, but in his way of life, physiognomy, habits, and even laughter.

Yet in a review of the first collection of Solov'ev's posthumously published letters, Rozanov described the frightening power of Solov'ev's evocation of the imminent Antichrist in his apocalyptic work, *Three Conversations* (*Tri razgovora, 1900*): "Here Solov'ev casts his spell, like a magician. ... This magical, seerlike (vedovskoe, veshun'e) element was clearly strong in Solov'ev, and possibly he bore it like a grief, a burden, unable to break free from it."[45] Rozanov describes Solov'ev as creating a verbal mask of buffoonery and wit by which he shielded himself from the world: "a mask, decorated with jokes, farce, grimaces and buffoonery, in which Solov'ev was so thickly swathed and which kept him so firmly hidden from the eye of the 'uninitiated.' Indeed, one had to be 'initiated' into Solov'ev ... And he would not take off the mask or his jesting, one could say his jester's cape for any 'stranger'."[46] Rozanov's evocations of Solov'ev's dance, his mask and cloak, have resonances of Russian folk traditions of devilry. His emphasis on ridicule, laughter, and the use of the word jester (shut) also has a longstanding association with the devil in Russia. Averintsev has written about the deep-rooted connection between jokes, laughter, and the devil in Russian culture, and notes the use of the word *shut* as a popular word for the devil.[47] Rozanov consciously exploited these devilish associations to conjure up an ominous portrait of the philosopher for his readers. He made repeated references to the sinister quality of Solov'ev's laughter, to "his icy, unpleasant laugh, loud and metallic."[48]

In a footnote in *Literary Exiles* (*Literaturnye izgnanniki,* 1913), Rozanov again refers to Solov'ev's laugh as demonic. Here he portrays Solov'ev explicitly as an Antichrist and false prophet: "He was entirely gleaming, cold. ... A splinter of the true 'Enemy of Christ' ... had fallen into Solov'ev. ... He ... was a man who had nothing to speak about with other men, who 'talked only with God.' Here he inadvertently stumbled, that is to say, nature knocked him into a sort of 'awareness of his prophetic calling,' which was neither artificial nor pretended. 'I have nothing to speak about with people,' but with God – 'I speak freely,' 'the speech flows.' ... In him there was truly a false prophet and a false Messiah (the essence of the Antichrist)."[49] Rozanov's description of Solov'ev's "prophetic" writing, "with God – 'I speak freely,' 'the speech flows'," closely echoes statements in *Solitaria (Uedinennoe,* 1912) and *Fallen Leaves* about his own writing as a form of prophecy; his sense of aloneness with God fuelling a steady flow of speech, for which he does not hold himself accountable to his readers. However Rozanov called his writing "a prophecy of the home" (domashnee prorochestvo); it was an intimate prophecy, that he spoke from his isolation with God, but which was concerned with the forgotten everyday needs of people. Solov'ev, Rozanov claimed, sought to put himself above the existences of others, he shunned domestic comfort and intimacy, yet in his contempt for the everyday he distanced himself from God.[50] Solov'ev's demonism is the result of an immense egotism that removes him even from a sense of God: "He was 'demonic,' I think, in the highest degree. In fact he was the only person that I have ever met in my entire life who had a clearly expressed 'demonic element'" (*Mim.*, 224). Rozanov's preoccupation with Solov'ev's "demonism" was an attempt to resolve not only the clear hypocrisy he felt in Solov'ev's charges of demonism against Rozanov, but to define for himself more subtle areas of demonic temptation involved in the act of being a writer and literary journalist. Both men were prolific writers, adept at literary polemic. Rozanov's attacks on Solov'ev were an attempt to dissociate himself from a fate he felt all too closely, the temptation of his own literary talent, and to align himself with the sacred strand of Russian writing, with intimate prophecy of the sacred everyday rather than with the false prophecy of Solov'ev's *publitsistika*. In his attacks, Rozanov focused increasingly on the words themselves. Solov'ev's words condemn him because, unlike Rozanov's, they bear no relation to the life of everyday things.

In his review of Solov'ev's published letters, Rozanov described Solov'ev as a master conjuror, who made words dance for him and then spirit him away: "And there is not a letter in which that verbal hysteria is not spinning in its frenzied dance (v sudorozhnoi pliaske). ... It's as though something is carrying him and he would like to hold on to objects, to ideas, with his delicate, translucent fingers, but it's as if an inner whirlwind tore him from them and he was carried off further, and further ..."[51] The use of the word *pliaska* suggests the frenzied dances of religious sects, an association that Rozanov repeated in his 1914 book on the sectarians, where he describes the uncanny physical resemblance between the "sectarian Christ," the leader of the *khlysty*, and Solov'ev.[52] Solov'ev's use of words distances him from the world of people and things. Words do not renew the connection with the world, as they did for Rozanov, but perform their own devilish dance. In *Fleeting*, Rozanov's characterization of Solov'ev focuses again on the demonism evident in Solov'ev's use of words. Solov'ev lacks any sense of the details of real life, the lives of others, and the persistence of things and so his writing cannot engage with the reality of life, that which makes words alive, powerful and moving:

> Solov'ev did not have that eternal human *essence*, our common, simple, earthly and 'flesh and blood' essence. A shadow. An outline. ... One ought to find out whether his writings contain 'exclamation marks' and 'dots' – symptoms of soul in handwriting and print. It would be extremely interesting. ... His writing is constant noise, phrases, the chatter of phrases, syllogisms. As though his *speech is not flowing* (= blood), but his speech *is put together from words*. He knew his 'words,' as an academic, who has been through University and Theological College. Solov'ev had mastered and remembered a great deal of words. ... But there was not a *word of his own* (rodnogo-to slova) among them, they were all alien ...
> And he kept writing and writing ...
> And he became more and more unhappy ... (*Mim.*, 226)

Solov'ev lacks the *rodnoe slovo* to connect him to Russia or to God. His words are watery, they lack full-blooded life. In *Fleeting* Rozanov's anxiety about Russia's future and the demonic potential of her writers in shaping it becomes increasingly intense. Solov'ev and Merezhkovsky are seen as prime exemplaries of the cold emptiness that blows through the immensity of their written output and by which they try to drown out the unhappiness caused by their isolation from life and God. Yet their words are impotent, not being written in blood but with ink and plasma.[53] Rozanov claimed that his own writing was mixed with human blood and seed. He defiantly asserted the physical nature of his writing, as if to draw closer to those cultures that had a direct *physical* communication with God. Rozanov does not make direct reference here to what was surely an underlying factor of his critique: both men's evasion of sexual relationships within a family. Their lack of an innate blood connection leaves their words hollow:

> It seems to me sometimes (often), that there is *no* Merezhkovsky ... That it's a *shadow* around another ... Or rather the shadow of another, thrown onto the reader. ... And amongst this ... in the *gaps* between things, someone, something, nothing, a hole: and in this hole are the *shadows of everything* ... But shadows are not the things themselves. ... This is why all sorts of thoughts, feelings, joys and hatreds are stuffed into this "emptiness" ... precisely because this place is *empty*.
> O how terrifying to love nothing, to hate nothing, to know everything, to read prodigiously, to read constantly and eventually, as the ultimate tragedy, to write endlessly, that is, to endlessly transcribe one's emptiness and make eternal what would be misery enough for any one, were he even to be aware of it.
> This is why Merezhkovsky is so endlessly sad. (*Mim.*, 133)

The terrifying aspect for Merezhkovsky is his lack of actuality. His unreality.

And yet he keeps trying to become incarnate. And this is why he keeps on talking. (*Mim.,* 48)

Solov'ev and Merezhkovsky are both characterized by their absence, both physically and in their use of words. They try to fill the gap between themselves and any living existence, this monstrous demonic absence, with words: "And generally there is this sort of strange (and for me, frightening) unreality about Solov'ev, just as there is about Merezhkovsky. 'It's as though they are *not here,*' 'just as though they *have not been born.*' Yet they go around amongst us like ghosts, under the pseudonym 'Solov'ev,' 'Merezhkovsky.' I can't express, nor 'prove,' something which I sense here with extraordinary clarity and stubbornness. Here lies the *essence of it all*' (*Mim.,* 225).

The devil of absence and non-being becomes increasingly prevalent in *Fallen Leaves* and *Fleeting* and is accompanied by Rozanov's growing preoccupation with death and his conviction of death as the ultimate end.[54] He repeatedly expresses his fear of Nothingness, non-existence, and of the fact that he would be unable even to sense his own non-existence: "No – is something I simply cannot bear. What is this 'no': HORRIBLE ..." (*Mim.,* 99). Rozanov refers to the insidious nihilism in Russian literary life as a presence: "NOBODY" (NIKTO).[55] These intimations take part in what seems to be a more general development in the literary perception and depiction of devils from a personified embodiment of spiritual malevolence to simply absence. Avril Pyman traces a transition from the presence of a devil or Antichrist, albeit ambiguous, in Solov'ev's poetry to a devil of absence, a personified nothingness in the writing of the symbolists.[56] This shift perhaps indicates the new character of spiritual and psychological unease and the way in which this unease was expressed.

Rozanov describes the spiritual absence of his contemporaries: "people 'who leave no trace behind them' ('the trace is removed,' magic). They are sort of intangible. Frightening. A particular category" (*Mim.,* 93). They lack a feeling for the aspects of Russian everyday life that Rozanov saw as sacred: "For some reason their tea is always cold and unpalatable. There are no buns. ... What they eat is generally dubious. But they smoke a lot and like wine" (*Mim.,* 93).[57] Having lost all sense of life, these people hardly notice the emptiness of their words: "intangible, fleshless, merely 'jabbering,' 'speaking,' and almost always very talented. People 'without any smell.' ... People who go across the ground without leaving any imprint in the ground. Not 'stinking' and 'not smelling'" (*Mim.,* 225–26). Smell was an important indicator of spiritual substance for Rozanov. In *Fleeting,* Merezhkovsky's state of fatal remoteness from Russia is symbolized by the artificial foreign perfumes by which he is surrounded: "Dostoevsky is all suffering for Russia, to which Merezhkovsky is so boundlessly indifferent. 'If anything stinks, then Russia does.' And Merezhkovsky and 'a bad smell' are incompatible. It seems to me that he was born in a phial of eau-de-cologne" (*Mim.*, 49). The reference to the eau-de-cologne has undertones of the preening Smerdiakov and Ivan's devil in *The Brothers Karamazov (Brat'ia Karamazovy)*, and their love of Western bourgeois refinements. The reference to Merezhkovsky's sterile birth in a phial like a microbe or small beast is also full of demonic sugggestion. Rozanov sees this lack of physical presence as particularly evident amongst writers, those who most of all should be renewing the connections to life, and between things. He condemns the artifice of the Merezhkovsky entourage, who are a part of the "particular category" of rootless, "intangible" people, conjuring their imaginary apocalypse in a haze of perfumed cigarette smoke. They are at once sinister and ridiculous. Rozanov mocks their childish naivety and the way that they interpret his own laughter (at them) as "Satanic."[58]

The charge of "un-Russianness" is central to Rozanov's demonization of Merezhkovsky and Solov'ev. He emphasizes Solov'ev's lack of attachment to place and people and to the corners of domestic life that were sacred to Rozanov, and to his use of the word.[59] For Rozanov, love for Russia was inextricable from a love of her most lowly details, everyday objects, food, and even smells. Without this one is adrift. Rozanov writes of Merezhkovsky, "it is as if he had never been in Russia" (*Mim.*, 49). The connection between "un-Russianness" and demonism in Dostoevsky's writing has been mentioned by W.J. Leatherbarrow in his discussion of the *obshchechelovek* (common man) in this volume. Dostoevsky's *obshchechelovek* is characterized by an emptiness and demonic non-being that was central to Rozanov's portrayal of contemporary writers in *Fleeting*. A prime incarnation of this phenomenon in Dostoevsky's writing was Stavrogin. In his 1900 article on Solov'ev's poetry Rozanov compares Solov'ev to Stavrogin.[60] The spiritual desolation that constitutes Stavrogin's demonism is very close to Rozanov's account of Solov'ev.

Gogol

Rozanov's insistence on the need for the restoration of a sacred, more prayer-like form of literature becomes more strident as he senses that "cold" satire and criticism are winning. "All (our) literature of the nineteenth century had no other aim than to eat out man's soul and replace it with EMPTY TALK (PUSTOSLOVIE)" (*Mim.*,

17). Into this void steps Gogol, who becomes, in *Fleeting*, the devil of absolute nothingness, the ultimate embodiment of the fatal satiric nihilism of Russia's literary impulse: "Then came Gogol and started to snigger. Thus came the devil" (*Mim.*, 17). Gogol is portrayed as a soulless laughing devil, laying waste anything of value in Russia. He is a magician (koldun) who waved his magic wand and turned Russia into a vast mediocrity: "Without ideas ... Without an ideal ... A great mediocrity (meshchanstvo). ... a self-satisfied mediocrity, with the telephone and the Eiffel tower" (*Mim.*, 113). This *meshchanstvo* has all the latest refinements of Western civilization. As in the depiction of Solov'ev and Merezhkovsky, the symbols of Western refinement are connected to a fatal and demonic indifference to Russia's fate. Rozanov associates Gogol with this Western demonic corruption, presenting him as idly enjoying foreign luxury while despising things Russian.[61] Foreign names are cited with an almost incantatory power, as representatives of evil. The civilization that they embody is *death*. Rozanov claims that Gogol's *Dead Souls* (*Mertvye dushi*) was a conscious destruction of the old Russia:

> Gogol knew very well that he was overcoming the imperial reign, and this was how he named his *Dead Souls*, calling it a "poem" (poema). Such pride and self-awareness are in this title (poem): "With this I will create everything anew." ...
> And he struck up his "funeral march." ...
> The devil smiled.
> – Well, sing then, sing your old songs ...
> Mouths were opened: no singing came. They hadn't the voice. A groan broke out and wolfish wails ...
> The devil laughed. (*Mim.*, 114)

Rozanov links Gogol with the godless, sneering crowd which flocks to laugh at his ridicule of Russian provincial life: "he *fell into, coincided with* the most crude and execrable aspect of the Russian national character – *with cynicism,* with the Russians' *talent for mockery,* with the power of the *laughing crowd,* which ... cuts down and tramples tears, idealism and suffering" (*Mim.*, 117).[62] Demonic laughter is rife in the passages on Gogol, like a warning of his presence. In an article of 1916 Rozanov emphasizes the destructive power of laughter: "Clearly there is 'creation' that is essentially unreligious. This is laughter. ... All of this is somehow 'without God' and 'apart from God.' ... It's a sort of fundamental evil in the world, and I can't [explain] it otherwise than that it comes from the devil. ... Laughter is not of the world, and so it diminishes creation, it steals something from God, precisely 'all the mocked things,' plunging them into nonexistence. Here is the beast and his horns. Enticing horns. Since laughter is often intoxicating."[63] Rozanov sought to reassert the per-

sistence of a sacred substance that would resist the destructive effects
of Gogol's laughter:

> From Chingis Khan to the Christian martyrs, from Nebuchadnezzar to
> Lermontov's poetry there was 'something,' which not one jester would
> laugh at, however much he was possessed with laughter. Anyone, even a
> jester, would bow, revere and embrace.[64]

> Petr and Ivan Kireevsky, Serafim Sarovsky – and all who came to them
> in pain, grieving and beseeching – these are the ESSENCE of Rus, and
> they *cannot come from Gogol* in any way. ... This is something new, differ-
> ent. (*Mim.*, 146)

Rozanov sought to associate his writing with this sacred tradition
against the pernicious influence of satirical writing by his sacralization of *melochi*, the details of everyday life, in his "fallen leaves"
genre. He argued that these everyday unspoken details contained
the sacred substance that could defy the emptiness of satire. He
fought his fear of an impending void by reasserting the tangible connections to the world of things, through writing.[65] His writing was an
attempt to reinforce the incomplete and forgotten existences of the
everyday; by transcribing their passing he claimed to confer a sort of
eternity on ordinariness. Literature had betrayed this primary duty.
Words no longer engaged with the life of things, thus words themselves had lost all tangible substance, spirit, and detail. "The human
soul has fallen apart over words. And thoughts? – 'We can't'" (*Mim.*,
152). Rozanov fought non-being with words that would reinvigorate
the surrounding world of things. This is what he saw as "sacred" in
his writing, and that he compared to religious texts: "Today this
flashed past on a carriage: THE SACRED IS. This is my slogan and
my greeting to the world. And I say to everything: 'Greetings, THE
SACRED IS.' Yes, that's my essence. It wouldn't be wrong to say
that in *Sol[itaria]* and *Fall[en] L[eaves]* I stood as though crucified."[66]
   This was not an isolated comparison of his role as a writer to a
Christ-like martyrdom; Rozanov's late writing was marked by an
increasingly strident assertion of his own "sacred" literary aims: to
defy the sterile satire and vanity of literature and assume the role of
a spiritual guide or prophet for Russia. Nor was this merely a literary
flourish. In *Fleeting*, he maintained that only the rich potential of his
writing could combat the emptiness brought by Gogol (*Mim.*,
116–17). In this late work, not intended for publication during his
lifetime, Rozanov juxtaposed his own task as a redeemer of the Russian word to the evil work of Gogol, who is a constant presence, alive
as a laughing devil, continuing his malevolent work after his death.
He declared that he would expose Gogol's emptiness through the
fecundity of his own words. He claims that his writing is as rich as
dung, but insists that Christ was born in a dung-filled stable (*Mim.*,

118). He repeatedly describes himself in Christ-like terms and portrays his writing as a sacred text or prophecy. Yet his increasingly hyperbolic assertion of his "sacred" mission was, characteristically, the time of his deepest anxiety about his own achievement and purpose as a writer. He feared that despite his defiant celebration of spontaneous life against literature he might himself prove to be the writer who had lived least of all, since every last flicker of thought was a potential literary product. At times he suspects a demonic possession in himself, he fears that his writing was not a sacred overcoming of the tyranny of literature but its opposite, an enslavement, a compulsion to write that cuts him off rather than connects him to the world. It is a demonic distancing.[67] He had hoped that the restoration of the sacred strand of Russian writing, rooted in prayer, prophecy, and human speech, could combat this blind faith in nihilist socially critical writing that could only incite revolution. Yet he too was seduced by his talent for literary polemics and failed to be the final writer, to write the ultimate sacred *slovo* (word) for Russia:

> When I thought: "I'll overcome the whole of literature," – I thought this precisely about *Sol*[*itaria*] and *Fall*[*en*] *L*[*eaves*]. And I could have overcome it all, if *Sol*[*itaria*] had remained ALONE. After all, I knew from letters – from Gor'ky's for example, that for some reason it had produced a permanent impression, that people "began to measure time" from it. This was the tip of the devil's tail: I had the idea of "helping him." This would be like "the apostles starting to write footnotes to their letters;" or Christ starting to "explain His parting with his disciples": and the illusion was dispersed. Everything turned into cardboard and cotton wool. ...
>
> The illusion dispersed. And *Solitaria* –
>   words, words, and words,
> but not one necessary
>   WORD.
>   But I was writing
>   the WORD.
> And it was written. Completed.
> No one could destroy it. ... And suddenly I started to break up the monument myself, piece by piece, and to hurl it at unpleasant literary and social personalities.
>
> I became petty, just like those rogues I was fighting against. That's all there is to it. ...
>
> Ha-ha-ha-ha ...
>
> Laugh – devil. But I am crying. And yet I am still a man and greater than you. No – stronger than you. Since I am with God – at His feet, and you are far in the distance "the Enemy of God."
>
> I am pathetic and ridiculous. But I am unhappy. You, devil, – you can never be unhappy – and that it is your limitation ... and your wretchedness. (*Mim.*, 329–30)

The devil laughs at the misery of his fate, but Rozanov's tears are more powerful than the devil's laughter. In the final instance, this "cry" is Rozanov's only certainty before the bedevilling ambiguities of his role as a writer. He calls his writing "a writer's lament at his writing" (plach pisatelia o svoem pisatel'stve).[68] It is a cry at not having enough faith to live without writing.

Rozanov's acute awareness of the conflicts in Russia's overwhelmingly literary existence and in his own role as a writer led him to externalize and personify these threats in his writing. Thus he created various devils: Gutenberg and his printing press, Solov'ev, Gogol, the Merezhkovsky entourage, and the radical journalists and satirists. Yet the ultimate, and far more insidious demon lay in his literary talent. This compulsion to write, and not always for reasons so sacred and honourable as those he proclaimed, meant that he remained deeply divided in the elucidation of his own literary role. He was unable to resolve these conflicts in any other way than by more writing and increasingly controversial journalism that isolated him from other writers and readers. He sought a temporary refuge in writing that was not for (immediate) publication, portraying himself as a prophet leading the downtrodden Russian people. But the image remained a literary one. The inescapable literariness of his existence could only be expiated by continuing to write.

Rozanov's attempt to counteract the demonism of contemporary life by immortalizing the everyday and inexpressible in writing came to mean that his life was lived increasingly through and for the literature that it became and this contradiction threatened his own, not literature's collapse. This opposition of life and the literary fuelled Rozanov's personal apocalypse in literature, yet he saw his own fate as embodying the entire fate of Russia. Russia too would be destroyed by its purely literary existence. This intertwining of personal and national apocalypse found its ultimate expression in his last major work, *Apocalypse of Our Time.* In 1918, Rozanov claimed that it was Russia's stubborn faith in the sacred status of all its texts that led to its destruction at the hands of its own literature.[69] He too was a victim of the national literary obsession.

Rozanov's preoccupation with the inner demons of his own literary talent, and the close connection of writing to the demonic in his portrayal of his contemporaries, indicates his sense of the moral precariousness of the writer's position at the beginning of the twentieth century. His uniqueness is shown by the acuity with which he opened up fundamental aspects of Russian literary life to question, challenging accepted hierarchies of value, both in individual reputation and literary style and form. Perhaps his most lasting achievement was this challenge to both the form and subject matter of what could be considered "literature." Rozanov had claimed to be battling against "literary" values and the predominance in Russia of literature over spontaneous life and thought, yet he expanded the possibilities for future writing vastly, reinvigorating, not diminishing, its hold over Russian consciousness. Although he did not suceed in "overcoming" literature, he did change for ever readers' perceptions of the literary. His onslaught on the demon of print anticipates the futurists' emphasis on unique and handwritten documents. His battle against all static, ossified and established canons of Russian literature was of great importance for both the futurists and the formalists, as was the fragmentary construction of his books, his insistence on their "manuscript" status and his inclusion of documents, letters, and notes from everyday life.[70] Conventions of literary language were subverted both by this smuggling of extra-literary writings into his books and in Rozanov's own range of "spoken" styles and voices, his defiance of grammatical and syntactical correctness. His battle for the restoration of the impassioned, tangible, spoken word to counteract the prevailing demonic cold in writing prefigures the futurist campaigns for the resurrection of the "word as such" (slovo kak takovoe).[71]

Rozanov's fight against the emptiness and cold of a culture which lacks binding, intimate words was of lasting importance. His battle against the pseudo-objectivity of "official" speech and against writers whose words lack an honest emotional charge had particular relevance in the years of Soviet literature that suppressed his writings. His emphasis on the physical presence and uniqueness of the word, the specific situatedness of an utterance, and the importance of intonation as an indicator of shared values, conveying vital warmth, influenced not only the futurists, but also writers such as Mandel'shtam and Mikhail Bakhtin; both men explored the life of words and contexts of speech in their articles of the 1920s.[72] Mandel'shtam emphasized that Rozanov's life was a furious battle for the word, for the life glowing in conversations, in familiar namings, in shared intonations and citations, within the private context of friendship or family, that was the kernel of the survival of language in any nation.[73] At the time when Mandel'shtam was writing this, these values were in peril. He claimed that Rozanov had understood this threat. This was the repeated terror of the death, emptiness, and cold that Rozanov claimed was penetrating printed words, the words of his writer contemporaries, and even the words spoken between people. Rozanov's warnings against the demonic depersonalization, the uprooting of words, and the loss of shared values that might ward off the imminent Satanic cold and distancing between people, were felt keenly by future generations. The demons of non-being and empty words, the sense of a life that had to be preserved in intimate words, as a focus of warmth in an immense cold, lasted far beyond the "apocalypse" of 1917.

Notes

1. See V.V. Rozanov, *Opavshie list'ia. Korob vtoroi i poslednii,* in his *O sebe i zhizni svoei,* ed. V.G. Sukach (Moscow: Moskovskii rabochii, 1990), 331–576(487): "despite my weaknesses and faults, I feel that there is no 'Cainism' (kainstva) in me, no 'demonism' (demonstva), I am the most ordinary of men, a simple man, I feel that I am a good man." All translations in this essay are mine.

2. D.S. Merezhkovskii, "Revoliutsiia i religiia," in his *Polnoe sobranie sochinenii,* 17 vols. (St. Petersburg and Moscow: Izdanie T-va M. O. Vol'f, 1911–13), 10:33–92(69).

3. On the central role of the word in Russian religious thought see V.F. Ern, *Bor'ba za Logos,* in his *Sochineniia,* comp. N.V. Kotrelev and E.V. Antonova (Moscow: Pravda, 1991), 9–294, and A.F. Losev, "Russkaia filosofiia," "Osnovnye osobennosti russkoi filosofii," in his *Filosofiia. Mifologiia. Kul'tura,* comp. Iu.A. Rostovtsev (Moscow: Politizdat, 1991), 209–36, 509–13. On the unique development and characteristics of the Russian verbal tradition, see Sergei Averintsev, "Grecheskaia 'literatura' i blizhnevostochnaia 'slovesnost'". Dva tvorcheskikh printsipa," in his *Religiia i literatura* (Ann Arbor: Hermitage, 1981), 5–33. I look in detail at Rozanov's relation to traditions of Russian religious thought in my PhD thesis "Rozanov and the Word" (School of Slavonic and East European Studies, University of London, 1996).

4. The genre of "fallen leaves" comprises: *Uedinennoe,* 1912; *Opavshie list'ia,* 1913; *Smertnoe,* 1913; *Pered Sakharnoi,* 1913; *V Sakharne,* 1913; *Posle Sakharny,* 1913; *Opavshie list'ia. Korob vtoroi i poslednii,* 1915; *Mimoletnoe,* 1914–16; *Poslednie list'ia,* 1918–22.

5. See the opening passage from V.V. Rozanov, *Uedinennoe,* in his *O sebe i zhizni svoei,* 35–132(36).

6. See "Poslednie mysli umiraiushchego V.V. Rozanova," in "Vospominaniia Tat'iany Vasil'evny Rozanovoi ob ottse, Vasilii Vasil'eviche Rozanove, i vsei sem'e s 1904–1969 gg.," ed. L.A. Il'iunina and M.M. Pavlova, *Russkaia literatura,* 1989, no.4:160–78(165–66).

7. See in this volume Pamela Davidson, "The Muse and the Demon in the Poetry of Pushkin, Lermontov, and Blok."

8. On Rozanov's use of literary device to evoke a sense of extra-literary language see V. Levin, "'Neklassicheskie' tipy povestvovaniia nachala veka v istorii russkogo literaturnogo iazyka," *Slavica Hierosolymitana* 5–6 (1981):245–75.

9. As Simon Franklin has suggested of Dostoevsky, the means of exorcizing the devil, in Dostoevsky's "literary demonism," could itself prove diabolical. See in this volume Simon Franklin, "Nostalgia for Hell: Russian Literary Demonism and Orthodox Tradition."

10. Richard Gustafson contrasts the interpretations of the fall in Western and Eastern Christianity. He writes that in the West, through the influence of Augustine, the fall is directly linked with sexual sin, guilt, and the need for redemption. In the East, the fall is seen less as an individual act but a general falling away from God, a transgression into coldness (a "cooling off"), seeking a reintegration; a salvation that can be a task in this world. Rozanov's writing claims to be undertaking this task, to restore a warmth and closeness to God. See Richard F. Gustafson, "Solov'ev's Doctrine of Original Sin," in *Freedom and Responsibility in Russian Literature. Essays in Honor of Robert Louis Jackson,* ed. Elizabeth Cheresh Allen and Gary Saul Morson (Evanston, Ill.: Northwestern University Press, 1995), 170–80(173).

11. V.V. Rozanov, *Mimoletnoe,* ed. A.N. Nikoliukin (Moscow: Respublika, 1994), 149. Hereafter cited in the text as *Mim.*

12. Rozanov, *Uedinennoe,* 39.

13. See Rozanov, *Opavshie list'ia. Korob vtoroi i poslednii*, 430.

14. V.V. Rozanov, *Posle Sakharny*, ed. Viktor Sukach, *Literaturnaia ucheba,* 1989, no. 2:89–122(97–98).

15. See for example, Rozanov, *Opavshie list'ia. Korob vtoroi i poslednii*, 367, 516–17; and *Mimoletnoe,* 263, 306.

16. See Rozanov's statement of intent in *Opavshie list'ia. Korob vtoroi i poslednii*, 332–33; see also *Posle Sakharny*, 109, 116, and *Mimoletnoe,* 294–95. The relationship between public and private discourse in Rozanov's writing is examined in Stephen C. Hutchings, "Breaking the Circle of the Self: Domestication, Alienation and the Question of Discourse Type in Rozanov's Late Writings," *Slavic Review* 52, no.1 (1993):67–86.

17. See, for example, Rozanov, *Mimoletnoe,* 27–28.

18. Ibid., 116, 303.

19. "'Don't act us a tragedy, but give us a vaudeville'," in V.V. Rozanov, *Apokalipsis nashego vremeni*, in his *O sebe i zhizni svoei,* 577–647(584); see also 581, 627. Rozanov had earlier contrasted the "censored" biblical tradition of Russian writing with the "kafe-shantan" of popular radical journalists; see V.V. Rozanov, "Istoriko-literaturnyi rod Kireevskikh," in his *O sebe i zhizni svoei,* 768–69(769 n.80). In his late writing, Rozanov repeatedly presents the Russian revolution as a cheap theatrical spectacle. Viktor Sukach has made the connection between Rozanov's emphasis on the revolution as theatre and his identification of the profoundly diabolic essence of acting and actors; see Rozanov, *O sebe i zhizni svoei,* 787 n.2, and V.V. Rozanov, "Akter," in his *Sredi khudozhnikov* (1913) (Moscow: Respublika, 1994), 311–16(314). See also V.V. Rozanov, "Rassypavshiesia Chichikovy," in his *Religiia. Filosofiia. Kul'tura,* comp. A.N. Nikoliukin (Moscow: Respublika, 1992), 367.

20. "At moments I have a strange feeling that I am *the last* writer, with whom literature in general will stop. ... Perhaps this is why I have the sense of some 'ultimate disaster,' which I feel to be united with 'my self.' 'My self' (ia) is terrible, repellent, immense and tragic as the ultimate tragedy: since in my self the colossal thousand year old 'self' of literature has somehow dialectically 'broken up and disappeared'." Rozanov, *Opavshie list'ia. Korob vtoroi i poslednii*, 333.

21. "I *wholeheartedly* consider myself ... as almost not a 'Russian writer,' but a genuine and ultimate Judaic prophet." V.V. Rozanov, Letter to A. Izmailov of 7 August 1918, in "Pis'ma V. Rozanova k A. Izmailovu," ed. D. Perchonko, *Novyi zhurnal* 136 (1979):121–26(126).

22. See V.V. Rozanov, "M.Iu. Lermontov (K 60–letiiu konchiny)" (1901), "Kontsy i nachala, 'bozhestvennoe' i 'demonicheskoe,' bogi i demony (Po povodu glavnogo siuzheta Lermontova)" (1902), "'Demon' Lermontova i ego drevnie rodichi" (1902), in his *O pisatel'stve i pisateliakh,* ed. A.N. Nikoliukin (Moscow: Respublika, 1995), 69–77, 78–95, 95–105, respectively.

23. Vladimir Solov'ev's public lecture on Lermontov, delivered in March 1899, was a warning against the demonic Nietzschean potential that Lermontov's poetry could have for the new generation of writers and God-seekers. The lecture was published posthumously in *Vestnik Evropy*, 1901, no.2. See V.S. Solov'ev, "Lermontov," in his *Filosofiia iskusstva i literaturnaia kritika,* ed. R. Gal'tseva and I. Rodnianskaia (Moscow: Iskusstvo, 1991), 379–98.

24. See Rozanov, "Kontsy i nachala," 78.

25. Rozanov, "'Demon' Lermontova," 98.

26. Rozanov contrasted the fate of ancient Judaic and non-Semitic nations. He repeatedly referred to the innate physical sense of connection to God that was was central to Judaism, expressed through blood ties and in the sexual act. Non-Semitic nations lacked this closeness to God and so were condemned to try to

make up the gap in words. The distinction between verbal and physical cultures is a constant in Rozanov's early collections of articles, *Religiia i kul'tura* (1899) and *V mire neiasnogo i nereshennogo* (1901). Lacking a blood tie to God, the approach to God and the culture of non-Semitic, in particular Christian, nations becomes "verbalized" and intellectual: "everywhere the order of words or if things, then things expressed through the word, connected through the word, transformed through the word and 'living in the word and about the word';" see V.V. Rozanov, "Nechto iz sedoi drevnosti," in his *Religiia i kul'tura*, comp. E.V. Barabanov (Moscow: Pravda, 1990), 246–86(258–59). See also "Iz zagadok chelovecheskoi prirody," in V.V. Rozanov, *V mire neiasnogo i nereshennogo*, ed. A.N. Nikoliukin (Moscow: Respublika, 1995), 21–39. Rozanov was familiar with Jewish culture and read the Talmud. Yet he chooses not to refer to the central role of the word in Judaic tradition, so as not to diminish the impact of his emphasis on the physical. This early distinction between two sources of culture foreshadows Rozanov's later, more strident opposition between Western and Eastern categories of thought and writing.

27. Rozanov, "'Demon' Lermontova," 104.

28. V.V. Rozanov, "Eshche o smerti Pushkina," in his *Mysli o literature*, ed. A.N. Nikoliukin (Moscow: Sovremennik, 1989), 247–62(248).

29. Rozanov, "Kontsy i nachala," 86.

30. Rozanov, "'Demon' Lermontova," 97. This assertion directly refuted Solov'ev's argument that Lermontov's prophetic intuition was fatally corrupted by his "pornographic muse" and that he was possessed by the "demon of impurity" (demon nechistoty); see Solov'ev, "Lermontov," 393–94. Rozanov repeatedly insisted that Lermontov's sexual focus was the source of his prophetic insight.

31. Rozanov, "Kontsy i nachala," 85. Rozanov frequently juxtaposed ancient religions with Dostoevsky's writing. He claimed that ancient Egyptian drawings could illustrate Dostoevsky's visions in the *Dream of a Ridiculous Man*, Versilov's dream of a Golden Age in *The Adolescent*, and many pages of Lermontov. See Rozanov, "Kontsy i nachala," 82, 92. Rozanov actually did this, illustrating the text of Dostoevsky's *Dream of a Ridiculous Man* with Egyptian drawings that he had traced in the St. Petersburg public library. See V.V. Rozanov, "Deti Solntsa … Kak oni byli prekrasny! …," in his *Semeinyi vopros v Rossii*, 2 vols. (St. Petersburg: Tipografiia M. Merkusheva, 1903), 484–516.

32. Rozanov claimed that the despondent mood in society was a mark of its separation from a sense of God. See Rozanov, "'Demon' Lermontova," 100. In articles and letters of this time Rozanov repeatedly evokes the all-pervasive "gloom" (unynie) and "boredom" (skuka) of modernity. See for example, V.V. Rozanov, "Vsemirnaia skuka," in his *Kogda nachal'stvo ushlo … (1905–1906 gg.)*, ed. A.N. Nikoliukin (Moscow: Respublika, 1997), 11–16, and his letter to Pertsov of September 1900, in V.V. Rozanov, *Sochineniia*, comp. A.L. Nalepin and T.V. Pomeranskaia (Moscow: Sovetskaia Rossiia, 1990), 510–12(510).

33 . "Everyone knows, and he himself relates how he wept and was covered in confusion from his visions of the 'demon;' but the public unaccountably senses a demon in the man himself." Rozanov, "M. Iu. Lermontov," 77.

34. Ibid., 75.

35. Ibid.

36. In his article on Solov'ev's lectures on the Antichrist, Rozanov holds up Lermontov as the representative of the "antichristian," but sacred, sense of the world. He claims that Christ's gospel teaching denied love and life. See V.V. Rozanov, "K lektsii g. Vl. Solov'eva," *Mir iskusstva*, 1900, no.9–10:192–95(192). Rozanov repeatedly attacked the refusal of Church and society to recognize the most essential secrets of life. He blamed this neglect on an intellectualized and

textually-based sense of religion, which he saw as a direct result of Christian teachings, together with the Gospels' urging of contempt for this world. He increasingly focused on the figure of Christ as a denier of this world. In later writings such as *Temnyi lik* (1911), he portrays Christ as almost his opposite, the Antichrist, the enemy of God. He suggested this more than once in private conversations (for example, his remark to Florensky, that it was Christ who was really "ot lukavogo").

37. Rozanov described the medieval demons of lust and sensual pleasure that visited hermits and saints: "everything that draws one to these origins of life was named in the Middle Ages 'demonic' and 'a demon'" (Rozanov, "'Demon' Lermontova," 97). The reference to sexual temptation as carried out by demons, and not as an original sin, is a crucial distinction between Eastern and Western Christianity. See Gustafson, "Solov'ev's Doctrine of Original Sin," 173.

38. In his late writings Rozanov repeatedly lamented the loss of Lermontov whom he held up as a sacred prophet, a lost spiritual leader for Russia. See, for example, V.V. Rozanov, "O Lermontove," in his *O pisatel'stve i pisateliakh*, 641–43.

39. V.S. Solov'ev, "Osoboe chestvovanie Pushkina," "Protiv ispolnitel'nogo lista," in his *Filosofiia iskusstva i literaturnaia kritika*, 300–310(307), 310–16, respectively. Solov'ev's attacks, in the form of letters to *Vestnik Evropy*, were written in reply to articles by Rozanov, Merezhkovsky, and Minsky for the Pushkin anniversary edition of *Mir iskusstva*, 1899, no.2. Rozanov's article was republished as V.V. Rozanov, "Zametka o Pushkine," in his *Mysli o literature*, 240–46.

40. See V.V. Rozanov, "Sredi obmanutykh i obmanuvshikhsia," *Novyi put'*, 1904, no.4:128–42, no.5:217–45, no.7:90–124, no.8:108–45.

41. Rozanov claimed that Solov'ev, while devoting his entire life to theology, had failed to write a page about the family. He also suggests that it would be different if Solov'ev had a child. Blok mocked this comment as typically Rozanovian in a letter to Chulkov; see his letter to G.I. Chulkov of 23 June 1905, in Aleksandr Blok, *Sobranie sochinenii*, ed. V.N. Orlov, A.A. Surkov, and K.I. Chukovskii, 8 vols. (Moscow and Leningrad: Gosudarstvennoe izdatel'stvo khudozhestvennoi literatury, 1960–63), 8:126–29(127). Yet this was an attack that Rozanov repeated against Solov'ev several times and that formed a part of his conviction about Solov'ev's inhuman, demonic character. See Rozanov, *O sebe i zhizni svoei*, 514–15.

42. Rozanov, "Sredi obmanutykh," *Novyi put'*, 1904, no.5:226–27. Charges of Nietzscheanism continued to be levelled at Rozanov, who claimed that he could not bear to read Nietzsche. Rozanov defended himself against Nietzscheanism as against demonism, in the pages of his "fallen leaves," by presenting himself as a small child in God's hands (see Rozanov, *O sebe i zhizni svoei*, 151, 378–79). It was this very position of innocence in God that gave Rozanov the freedom for his outspokenness and self-contradiction that was attacked as a demonic self-licence by contemporaries; see, for example, the attack of Gippius, writing as A. Krainii, "Literatury i literatura," *Russkaia mysl'*, 1912, no.5:26–31.

43. See V.V. Rozanov, "K lektsii g. Vl. Solov'eva OB ANTIKHRISTE," "Pis'mo v redaktsiiu gazety "NOVOE VREMIA," in *Kontekst-1992: Literaturno-teoreticheskie issledovaniia*, ed. A.V. Mikhailov (Moscow: Nasledie-Nauka, 1992), 81–88, 88–89, respectively. Solov'ev's journalistic ability is clearly connected to his demonism in Rozanov, *Mimoletnoe*, 223–26. In his biography of Solov'ev, Konstantin Mochul'sky sees Solov'ev's *Povest' ob Antikhriste*, the basis of his lecture, as a frightening personal confession of Solov'ev's own "lie;" a recognition that he himself might indeed be the talented literary Antichrist of his tale: "chitaia 'Povest',' nevozmozhno otognat' ot sebia strashnuiu mysl', chto avtor govorit o sebe, razoblachaet *svoiu lozh'*." K. Mochul'skii, *Vladimir Solov'ev. Zhizn' i uchenie*, 2d ed. (Paris: YMCA-Press, 1951), 259.

44. In articles, books, and footnotes, Rozanov paid more attention to the figure of Solov'ev than to almost any other writer; see V.G. Sukach, "K publikatsii stat'i V.V. Rozanova 'Avtoportret Vl.S. Solov'eva'," in _Obshchestvennaia mysl'. Issledovaniia i publikatsii_, ed. A.L. Andreev and K.Kh. Delokarov (Moscow: Nauka, 1989), 1:231–32(231).

45. V.V. Rozanov, "Avtoportret Vl.S. Solov'eva" (1908), ed. V.G. Sukach, in ibid., 1:232–46(244).

46. Ibid., 1:234.

47. S.S. Averintsev, "Bakhtin, smekh, khristianskaia kul'tura," in _M. M. Bakhtin kak filosof_, ed. L.A. Gogotishvili and P.S. Gurevich (Moscow: Nauka, 1992), 7–19, and "Bakhtin and the Russian Attitude to Laughter," in _Bakhtin: Carnival and Other Subjects_, ed. David Shepherd, Critical Studies, vol.3, no.2 and vol.4, no.1/2 (Amsterdam and Atlanta: Rodopi, 1993), 13–19(14–15). In his contribution to this volume W.J. Leatherbarrow also notes Lotman's and Uspensky's references to laughter and the demonic in the Russian Orthodox tradition: W.J. Leatherbarrow, "The Devils' Vaudeville: 'Decoding' the Demonic in Dostoevsky's _The Devils_."

48. Rozanov, "Sredi obmanutykh," _Novyi put'_, 1904, no.7:101. This laughter was noted by several contemporaries. Blok claimed that Solov'ev's laugh had a seemingly magical and self-protective force; see his letter to G.I. Chulkov of 23 June 1905, in Blok, _Sobranie sochinenii_, 8:126–27. Bely noted the misleadingly demonic quality of Solov'ev's laugh; see his letter to P.A. Florenskii of [12 August] 1904, in "Perepiska P. A. Florenskogo s Andreem Belym," ed. A.S. Trubachev and others, introduction and notes by E.V. Ivanova and L.A. Il'iunina, in _Kontekst-1991: Literaturno-teoreticheskie issledovaniia_, ed. A.V. Mikhailov (Moscow: Nauka, 1991), 23–61(35). However, in his description of Solov'ev's reading of _Povest' ob Antikhriste_, Bely is less inclined to deny the traces of demonic in the philosopher, "a cunning devil (lukavyi chert), disturbing the conversation with his deadly laughter;" see A. Belyi, "Vladimir Solov'ev. Iz vospominanii," in A. Belyi, _Arabeski. Kniga statei_ (reprint, Munich: Wilhelm Fink Verlag, 1969), 385–94(389).

49. V.V. Rozanov, _Literaturnye izgnanniki_ (London: Overseas Publications Interchange, 1992), 141–44 (note).

50. Rozanov's attack on Solov'ev's egoism echoes Solov'ev's own warnings about Lermontov in his 1899 speech. See Solov'ev, "Lermontov," 385–87. Solov'ev had warned that Lermontov was a dangerous prophet who lacked a sense of the world around him and was oblivious to anything but his own truth. Rozanov sees this as far truer of Solov'ev himself, as though in his article on Lermontov Solov'ev had been talking about himself.

51. Rozanov, "Avtoportret Vl.S. Solov'eva," 235.

52. See V.V. Rozanov, _Apokalipsicheskaia sekta (Khlysty i skoptsy)_ (St. Petersburg: Tipografiia F. Vaisberga i P. Gershunina, 1914), 89. Dostoevsky's implicit comparison of Stavrogin to a sectarian God as an aspect of his demonization is noted in this volume by Leatherbarrow, "The Devils' Vaudeville."

53. See Rozanov, _Mimoletnoe_, 225.

54. Ibid., 99, 221. See also V.V. Rozanov, "Smert' ... i chto za neiu," in _Al'manakh Smert'_ (St. Petersburg: Novyi zhurnal dlia vsekh, 1910), 243–63.

55. See Rozanov, _Mimoletnoe_, 17.

56. Pyman writes of Sologub's devil as the personification of emptiness (which she calls "a Russian devil if ever there was one"). She describes the devil as a fear of absence and nothingness in the writing of Briusov, Bely, and Blok; see Avril Pyman, _A History of Russian Symbolism_ (Cambridge: Cambridge University Press, 1994), 52–53, 232–33.

57. Traditional buns and pies were abundant at Rozanov's "Sundays." Descriptions by contemporaries evoke an atmosphere at these gatherings that was exemplary

of Rozanov and his combination of metaphysical speculation with the physical, homely details of Russian everyday life; see D. Lutokhin, "Vospominaniia o Rozanove," *Vestnik literatury,* 1921, no.4–5:5–7. In Merezhkovsky's account this was combined with apocalyptic discussions straight out of *The Devils* or *The Brothers Karamazov* (Merezhkovskii, "Revoliutsiia i religiia," 86).

58. See Rozanov, *V Sakharne,* in his *Religiia. Filosofiia. Kul'tura,* 343–56(352).

59. See Rozanov, *Mimoletnoe,* 225: "in this strange way he 'did not feel' the Russian soil, the fields, the woods. ... As though he had never eaten apples or cherries. Grapes were another matter: he ate them. And so on. Strange. Frightening. Inexplicable. In truth – Dark."

60. V.V. Rozanov, "Na granitsakh poezii i filosofii (Stikhotvoreniia Vladimira Solov'eva)," in his *O pisatel'stve i pisateliakh,* 48–56(50).

61. See Rozanov, *Mimoletnoe,* 113. According to Rozanov, Gogol's overcoat was made not in London or Paris but at "Rockefeller's" or "Edison's." The references to the telephone recall the passage in *Posle Sakharny,* where the telephone is seen as an extension of the work of the foreigner Gutenberg, in the apocalyptic distancing and freezing up of love; see Rozanov, *Posle Sakharny,* 97–98. The devil's foreign (European) origin is noted also by Simon Franklin who writes that Gogol's devil in "Noch pered rozhdestvom" is specifically a German. See in this volume Franklin, "Nostalgia for Hell."

62. See also Rozanov, *Mimoletnoe,* 17, 116–18, 319.

63. V.V. Rozanov, "'Sviatost'' i 'genii' v istoricheskom tvorchestve," in his *O pisatel'stve i pisateliakh,* 635–41(640).

64. V.V. Rozanov, "Pushkin i Lermontov," in his *O pisatel'stve i pisateliakh,* 602–4(603–4).

65. See Rozanov, *Opavshie list'ia* (1913), in his *O sebe i zhizni svoei,* 263–64.

66. Rozanov, *Posle Sakharny,* 109.

67. Rozanov wrote of his constant need to transcribe his experience: "It is so monstrous, that Nero would have envied me." Rozanov, *Opavshie list'ia. Korob vtoroi i poslednii,* 333.

68. V.V. Rozanov, "Mimoletnoe," ed. Iu.K. Terapiano, *Novyi zhurnal* 92 (1968):119–32(126).

69. See V.V. Rozanov, "Gogol' i Petrarka," "S vershiny tysiacheletnei piramidy (Razmyshlenie o khode russkoi literatury)," "Apokaliptika russkoi literatury," in his *O pisatel'stve i pisateliakh,* 658–59, 659–73, 673–76, respectively.

70. See in particular Viktor Shklovsky's writing on Rozanov in *Zoo, ili Pis'ma ne o liubvi* (1922), in Viktor Shklovskii, *Sobranie sochinenii,* introd. I. Andronikov, ed. L. Opul'skaia, 3 vols. (Moscow: Khudozhestvennaia literatura, 1973–74) 1:163–230(183); V.B. Shklovskii, *Rozanov. Iz knigi "Siuzhet kak iavlenie stilia"* (Petrograd: Izdatel'stvo "Opoiaz," 1921; reprint, Letchworth: Prideaux Press, 1974), and his "Literatura vne 'siuzheta'," in his *O teorii prozy* (Moscow: Federatsiia, 1929; reprint, Ann Arbor: Ardis, 1985), 226–45.

71. On the links between Rozanov's work and the aims of the futurists see V.N. Il'in, "Stilizatsiia i stil': 2 – Remizov i Rozanov," in *V.V. Rozanov: Pro et contra. Lichnost' i tvorchestvo Vasiliia Rozanova v otsenke russkikh myslitelei i issledovatelei. Antologiia,* ed. V.A. Fateev, 2 vols. (St. Petersburg: Izdatel'stvo Russkogo khristianskogo gumanitarnogo instituta, 1995), 2:406–30. Viktor Khovin compared the futurist achievements of Rozanov and Maiakovsky in his book *Na odnu temu,* and juxtaposed articles by Rozanov with the latest futurist publications in his journal *Knizhnyi ugol* in the 1920s; see Viktor Khovin, *Na odnu temu* (Petrograd: 2–ia Gosudarstvennaia tipografiia, 1921), 3–80, and "Rozanov umer," *Knizhnyi ugol* 6 (1919):3–6. See also *Knizhnyi ugol* 4 (1918):5–11, 5 (1918):6–11, 6 (1919):6–13, 7 (1921):3–8, and 8 (1922):9–12, and Viktor Khovin, *Ne ugodno-li-s?! Siluet V.V.*

Rozanova (Petrograd: Ocharovannyi strannik, 1916). Anna Lisa Crone compares Rozanov's writing with futurist manifestos and suggests this as a fertile area for research; Anna Lisa Crone, *Rozanov and the End of Literature. Polyphony and the Dissolution of Genre in Solitaria and Fallen Leaves* (Würzburg: jal-verlag, 1978), 122–26.

72. See in particular Osip Mandel'shtam, "Slovo i kul'tura," "O sobesednike," "O prirode slova," "Deviatnadtsatyi vek," in his *Sobranie sochinenii,* ed. G.P. Struve and B.A. Filippov, 2d ed., 3 vols. (New York: Inter-Language Literary Associates, 1967–71), 2:222–27, 233–40, 241–59, 276–83, respectively; M.M. Bakhtin, "Avtor i geroi v esteticheskoi deiatel'nosti," in his *Estetika slovesnogo tvorchestva,* comp. S.G. Bocharov (Moscow: Iskusstvo, 1979), 7–180(126). Bakhtin returned to certain themes of his early writing in his late writings, where he again focuses on the importance of intonation and spoken context in the life of words; see M.M. Bakhtin, "Problema rechevykh zhanrov," in his *Estetika slovesnogo tvorchestva,* 237–80(268).

73. See Mandel'shtam, "O prirode slova," 249.

Chapter 10

The Demon. The Mythopoetic World Model in the Art of Lermontov, Vrubel, Blok

Avril Pyman

"Vrubel's Demon and Blok's Demon are not twins. But they are like brothers, resembling one another more than their father. There is something about them that was not really known to Lermontov's time." So wrote V. Al'fonsov in a pioneering study of Blok and Vrubel written in 1961. He sees the evolution of the Demon's image from Lermontov's Romantic individualist, through Vrubel's more elemental, ambivalent creature, hardly a personality at all, who exists "almost in an historical vacuum," to Blok's Demon which, discouraged by a tragic awareness of the illusory nature of romantic freedom, "has merged with the persona of the Third Volume."[1]

As a socio-psychological analysis this has much to recommend it, although it fails to account for the basic paradox of Blok's Third Volume, in which the lyrical hero is not only a Demon, a lost or dead soul, but also a "sentry unrelieved," in Blok's parlance the guardian of a "religious" truth about "what is outside time."[2] Al'fonsov puts his finger on the nature of the link between Blok's and Vrubel's Demons when he notes that, "many symbolists swore by Vrubel, but only Blok truly understood that the 'eternal' values of his art were born of profoundly contemporary pathos." However, as a Soviet critic writing in 1961, he would not have been permitted to pursue the intuition even had he had the equipment to do so. Commenting on

Blok's "almost paradoxical remark" as to how Vrubel – struggling to depict the Demon – had once painted a head of unheard of beauty, perhaps the one which would not come right in Leonardo's *Last Supper*, Al'fonsov explains, a shade patronizingly: "But, you know, the critics of the time wrote that in *The Last Supper* it was the head of Christ that 'wouldn't come right' for the artist."[3]

Well, yes, we do know. So, undoubtedly, did Blok – and this paradox we shall look at more closely in the light of some comparatively recently published Russian works on the nature of Demons,[4] the nature of mythopoetic art[5] and of the symbolist triadic "salvation models," as discreetly spelt out for us as early as 1979 by Dmitrii Maksimov and Zara Mints.[6] In modern criticism, semiotics have preserved scholars from the embarrassment of interpreting literature theologically while allowing us free reign to explore (without commitment to or rejection of belief) the realm of ideas in the Platonic sense, the non-material sphere to which the Demon by definition belongs, and the possibility of a dialectical relationship between the spheres of reality and ideas not endemic to Plato's dualistic world-view. A kind of shorthand has developed, which I shall try to use and not abuse. If we set the term "demon" in the context of the mythopoetic world model, we may escape the equally misleading paths of altogether disassociating Lermontov's, Vrubel's, and Blok's "Demons" from the Christian context or, on the contrary, of completely identifying them with it.

Originally, according to Losev in the post-fetishistic, pre-animistic stage, the notion of the demon as the idea or energy which informs things, nature, and people erupted "in the human mind under the impression of an unforeseen event. This demon has as yet *neither form nor face nor any kind of outline* but is, for the time being, evaluated *as a force of unknown origin,* a sudden jet of power triggered by some kind of catastrophe."[7] It was the mythologizing process which sought to give this ambiguous force shape and form. Divine or demonic beings were (as in the imagination of a child) thought of as real and endowed with human attributes.

According to Toporov, it is possible, by reference to archaic structures, archetypes and rites which posit a constant interplay between past, present, and future, not as sequential but as parallel events which go to form a single synchronic/diachronic pattern, to reconstruct "a single overall universal system" which he calls the "mythopoetic model of the world."[8] This "world model" posits a direct link between microcosm and macrocosm, enabling the human mind to impose order and harmony on its own nature and on a universe seemingly beyond its scope and essentially chaotic, thus providing a secondary recodification of information about ourselves and our relationship to the world about us. The term "religion" being, for the purposes of such recodification, narrower than "myth," suggests one or other of various possible semantic systems which can co-exist within this all-embracing whole.[9]

To the arts, Toporov's "mythopoetic world model" stands in a twofold relationship: on the one hand "ritual, together with the myth of creation, was the origin of epos, drama, lyric poetry, choreography, the art of music ... which in their turn have come to serve as that material from which the archaic world is often reconstructed;" on the other, the world model is a reservoir "from which later epochs draw ... tropes and figures which form the basis of modern poetic imagery."[10]

It was, of course, the stimulus provided by scholarly discoveries in the field of linguistics, anthropology, archaeology, comparative religion, and psychology in the second half of the nineteenth and early twentieth century which opened up to Vrubel and Blok that "something not really known to Lermontov's time" and engendered the mythopoeic art of European (and Russian) modernism.[11] *Mifotvorchestvo* (mythopoeia) directed men's minds from individual to archetype, from personal psychology to the unconscious and collective unconscious which, in art, pre-empted the Jungian formulations, themselves often based on examples from world literature.[12]

Nevertheless, both Blok's and Vrubel's Demons are directly and explicitly descended from Lermontov's, and so cannot be understood outside the Christian and post-Renaissance, individualistic literary tradition. When Christianity brought the Bible and apocryphas to Europe, indistinct glimpses of "sons of God" who seduced "daughters of men" (Gen.6:2) and of Satan the deceiver, rather shakily identified with the fallen Lucifer,[13] were driven into unholy alliance with the "demonic or divine beings" of myth and the creatures of folklore.[14] During the Age of Faith demons were thought of as incorporeal and so protean, sexually and numerically ambivalent ("legion," as in the Gospel). Disruptive mischief-makers, they are eager to seduce and possess mere mortals. Yet they are essentially subordinated to an all-powerful God. Nevertheless, God having granted freedom to men and angels, the Devil (Satan, the mightiest of all demons) has a continued lease on this world, of which he is "Prince." As long as the world lasts he appears to have infinite powers of recuperation, taking form again and again after each defeat. In spite of this ability to "take form," because God is all, Satan is nothing: the essential minus, entropy, disintegration, and chaos, doomed to know in advance

> How all his malice served but to bring forth
> Infinite goodness, grace, and mercy, shown
> On Man by him seduced ...
> *(Paradise Lost,* 1:217–19)[15]

Yet still – a real threat: "le néant," the black hole. Such is the "theological" Devil, and he is basically the same in Greek Orthodox and Roman Catholic thinking, in Eastern and Western Europe, though, in his more bucolic, folkloric guises he may assume a local accent or manifest himself, like the demons of old, as the spirit of a country's flora, fauna, or weather.[16]

The re-evaluation of values culminating in the apotheosis of the Superman began with the Renaissance. The concept of an individual Rebel, bold enough to challenge the collective authority of State and Church and to upset the spiritual and ethical status quo, took on a new attraction. In *The Divine Comedy*, according to Peter Levi, Satan is grotesque "because Dante ... who mocks him and renders him monstrous with the terrifying trumpeting of the devil's fart, really believes in him, but Milton does not. Milton's Satan is a fiction and, to sustain an epic poem, must be heroic and terrible."[17] Goethe's Faust, no longer the trickster and necromancer of the ballads but a Seeker of the Enlightenment, plays out a complex time-travelling drama with his powerful *alter ego* Mephistopheles; the demonic hero is redeemed and the Devil vanquished not by the Passion of Christ but by the love of the Eternal Feminine. Romantic egotism leads to personal identification with the pride and sorrow of Lucifer, in Byron's case mitigated by a more human identification with the pride and sorrow of the disinherited Cain – the prototype of Camus's *L'homme révolté*.

This process of anthropomorphization did not get under way in Russia's history until the early eighteenth century, when Peter the Great, the "Antichrist" to the common people, appeared to embody some of the heroic and terrible features of Milton's Satan, or, in her literature, until the early nineteenth, when Romanticism invested the archetypal Demon with human (or angelic, humanoid) form. Levi, who in his book on Milton compares the state of revolutionary England to that of Russia in the Time of Troubles, notes that "the difference was huge, and rested on the Church, which in England had lost public confidence."[18] A seventeenth-century poem on a religious subject by a layman known to have publicly defended regicide would have been unthinkable, even had Russia, still totally reliant on Church Slavonic for lofty subjects, possessed a secular literary language rich and flexible enough to rival the instrument Milton had inherited from Spenser and Shakespeare and further ennobled from Latin and Italian sources.

Pushkin, who did dispose of such an instrument, gave a Russian rendering of the demonic theme in *The Bronze Horseman* (*Mednyi vsadnik*, 1833) but merely toyed with the European tradition in his "Scene from Faust" (*Stsena iz Fausta*, 1825) and related fragments, trying out different styles and abandoning the exercise unfinished.

"I'm bored, devil" (Mne skuchno, bes), begins the first "scene;" in another fragment, the devils in hell are playing cards, not for money "But just to pass eternity away!" (A tol'ko b vechnost' provodit'!).[19] Lermontov's Demon is bored too – by his too easy role as mischief-maker rather than at the thought of Eternity: "And evil had come to bore him" (I zlo naskuchilo emu).[20] In this, he resembles Vrubel's Demon as interpreted by Blok: "A sunset such as never was has touched the deep-blue-lilac clouds with gold. That is only our name for the three dominant colours which have as yet 'no name' and which serve only as a sign (a symbol) of the hidden essence of the Fallen One: 'And evil had come to bore him.' The immensity of Lermontov's thought is included in the immensity of Vrubel's three colours."[21] There is a feeling, right from the start, though Lermontov's *The Demon* (*Demon*) was written between 1829 and 1839 and thus undertaken a bare five years after the publication of Vigny's *Eloa* in 1824, that the Russians came late to the theme – not to the theme of the Demon as such, but specifically to the post-Renaissance Demon, capable of declaring with Milton's Satan: "Evil, be thou my Good" (*Paradise Lost*, 4:110).[22] Blok, in his speech at Vrubel's grave, does not defy but invokes Heaven, associating the "golden light of evening" with hope in the unconquered sun:

> And Vrubel's day still lights the mountain tops, but from below comes creeping the blue darkness of night. Of course, the night is victorious, of course, the dark-blue-lilac worlds are collapsing and flooding all about them. In this struggle between gold and dark-blue the normal thing is happening – the victory is going to the darker; so it was and is in art, so long as it is art *alone*. But in Vrubel something else gleams through, as with all geniuses, for they are not artists only, but also – already – prophets. Vrubel amazes us, for in his work we see how the dark-blue night hangs back and hesitates to press home its victory, perhaps with some presentiment of its future defeat. Not for nothing was Vrubel's master the golden Giovanni Bellini. Alone in all the universe, misunderstood and persecuted, he invokes the Demon himself to exorcize (zaklinat') the night by the light of his wondrous countenance, the peacock shimmer of his wings, his divine boredom with the dark-blue spells of nocturnal evil.[23]

This is the utmost step – according to Blok – that art, by nature demonic, could take towards religion.[24]

Yet Russia, however rich in hindsight and foresight thanks to its traumatically uneven development, has never, for all its best endeavours, found a "third way" or managed – in the long run – to skip a stage of European development. The Demon as hero, whose

> ... form has not yet lost
> All her original brightness, nor appeared
> Less than Archangel ruined ...
> (*Paradise Lost*, 1:591–93)

The Demon who is

> Beauteous, and yet not all as beautiful
> As he hath been, and might be ...
>   (*Cain*, 1.1.95–96)[25]

The Demon as "a shadowy angel ... young, sad and charming"
(Ange ténébreux ... jeune, triste et charmant" (Vigny, *Eloa*)[26] had to
be wholeheartedly celebrated. His celebrant in Russian literature
was Lermontov.

Lermontov: From Romantic Individualism towards Interiorization and Remythologization

Short-lived and deeply enamoured of European poetry, Lermontov
was haunted from childhood by thoughts of Paradise Lost which
stirred now angelic memories, now demonic frustration. In his lyric
poetry and at certain stages in the writing of his epic poem, the young
poet at first identified with his Demon.[27] Later, just as he came to distance himself from Byron and from his own "demonic" creation,
Pechorin, Lermontov shook off this "mad, passionate, childish delirium" (bezumnyi, strastnyi, detskii bred).[28] Blok pictures him as a seeing Demon, taking his stand, as an artist, firmly on the *brink* of the
abyss (5:76–77, 8:150). Indeed, over the years Lermontov gained control over his subject, transforming a series of profoundly-felt lyrical
fragments into a Romantic narrative poem (poema) with objectively
depicted characters acting in a recognizable geographical setting in –
more or less – historic time.[29] In 1830, Lermontov was still considering a Babylonian setting, possibly suggested by the biblical epigraphs
to Byron's *Heaven and Earth*.[30] The Caucasus and Tamara appear only
in the sixth (Lopukhina's) version of 1838, establishing a certain independence from the European models whose "chronotope" is largely
timeless and transcendental. The romance with a human girl is also
something of an innovation, though Lermontov occasionally borrows
shamelessly from Vigny's Satan's seduction of a fellow angel.[31] Milton's Satan, though lustful, is too much Devil to love. Byron's Lucifer,
as Lawrence Kelly points out, "does not fall in love with Eve or her
daughters; and generally is a heartless agent of temptation."[32]

Not surprisingly then, Lermontov's Demon, born of lyrical inspiration and in love with a human girl, is closer kin to Byron's Cain than
to his Lucifer; not so much fallen angel as disinherited human soul. He
has no cause to make (as Lucifer and Satan have) as to *why* he quit
heaven in the first place. He is simply unhappy and furiously resent-
ful at the *fait accompli* and, like Cain, too proud to seek reconciliation,
though at times, when his heart is touched, he wishes to try.[33]

Тоску любви, ее волненье
Постигнул Демон в первый раз;
Он хочет в страхе удалиться …
Его крыло не шевелится!
И, чудо! из померкших глаз
Слеза тяжелая катится …
Поныне возле кельи той
Насквозь прожженный виден камень
Слезою жаркою, как пламень,
Нечеловеческой слезой!..

(*The Demon*, 2:7.537–46)

[The longing and the thrill of love
Afflicted the Demon for the first time;
In fear he would have moved away…
His wing is paralysed!
And, oh wonder! From the clouded eyes
A heavy tear rolls…
To this day close to that cell
The stone can be seen, burnt through
By a tear, hot as flame,
No human tear!..]

"No human tear!" – not Cain, after all, but Lucifer. Yet Lucifer in love? Lucifer who leaves a trace in the rock? Who approaches his beloved's bed like a schoolboy his first tryst, "ready to love / With soul open to good" (liubit' gotovyi, / S dushoi, otkrytoi dlia dobra, 2:8.547–48)? In the poem, the duality is particularly in evidence in the Demon's attitude to Tamara (and hers to him) and in their feeling for "God's world" (Bozhii mir, 1:3.55),[34] and it is this duality which makes the poem so resistant to rational analysis. "In spite of the splendour of the poetry and the significance of the theme," wrote Vladimir Solov'ev, "to speak in all seriousness about the content of the poem *The Demon* is as impossible for me as to go back to fifth or sixth form at school" – a comment marked in Blok's copy of the article with an NB sign and an exclamation mark.[35]

Tamara, far from being the innocent victim fondly imagined by many critics, is a proud, passionate young woman who suffers a fate known in folklore to threaten all brides on the eve of their wedding: ready for love, in the midst of ritual preparation for a radical change of estate, she falls under the evil eye at her most vulnerable and, baulked of the consummation of her marriage, reacts eagerly and vigorously to the Demon's gentle wooing:

Все чувства в ней кипели вдруг;
Душа рвала свои оковы,
Огонь по жилам пробегал,

(*The Demon*, 1:16.369–71)

[Suddenly, all her senses seethed;
Her heart strained at its bonds,
Fire ran through her veins,]

The cloister is at once headlong retreat from temptation and defiant rejection of the world. Whether or not the Demon actually looms between her and the altar or only seems to do so in the "forbidden dream" (2:2.420) of the "young sinner" (2:3.438), he has already infected her with his despair. A breathtaking description of the mountainside monastery, drowning in almond blossom and bounded by sparkling waters, comes as a reprise of the magnificent aerial view of the Caucasus and "luxuriant Georgia" which, in the opening passages of the poem, awakes nothing but contempt and hatred in the heart of the Demon. Tamara's reaction echoes his:

> Но, полно думою преступной,
> Тамары сердце недоступно
> Восторгам чистым. Перед ней
> Весь мир одет угрюмой тенью;
> *(The Demon, 2:5.470–73)*

[But full of transgressive thought,
Tamara's heart is closed
To pure delights. In her eyes
The whole world is wreathed in dismal shade;]

Maksimov, unlike Rozanov, sees love of nature as an attitude *opposed* to the demonic.[36] Hatred of the world, he maintains, constitutes the Demon's tragic guilt, and he detects in the poem "a dialogical artistic system in which the chief protagonist and the world he has cursed, and this means also nature, are given equally great poetic power."[37] In this dialogue, Tamara is at one with the Demon *before* the seduction scene and it is her readiness to accept despair which gives him right of entry.[38]

Like Byron's Lucifer, who comes to seduce Cain in answer to his own rebellious self-questioning, the Demon knows "the thoughts of dust" (*Cain*, 1.1.101–2). He also knows angels are powerless against human freedom. Yet, according to the laws of God's providence and of his own nature, Lermontov's lovesick Demon, having assumed the trappings of Lucifer, is and remains the Enemy of mankind: Satan, who cannot win. All his mellifluous plaints and promises turn to unregenerate darkness, self-pity, and contempt. In one breath he declares his longing for reconciliation with heaven and promises to separate Tamara for ever from the Earth. It is not in his nature to repent:

> И он слегка
> Коснулся жаркими устами
> Ее трепещущим губам;
> Соблазна полными речами

Он отвечал ее мольбам.
Могучий взор смотрел ей в очи!
Он жег ее. Во мраке ночи
Над нею прямо он сверкал,
Неотразимый, как кинжал.
                                (*The Demon*, 2:11.872–80)

[And gently
He brushed his hot lips
Against her trembling mouth;
With seductive speeches
He answered her pleas.
The mighty gaze looked into her eyes!
He burnt her. In the darkness of night
He glittered directly above her,
Inevitable as a dagger.]

The Demon's triumph is Tamara's bane.

The dagger symbol inevitably suggests a Freudian interpretation, but here surely the Jungian explanation of the death of the earth-born partner of such miscegenation as the consequence of the transgression of natural boundaries is better suited to the subject matter.[39] In a recent reconsideration of our theme, Aleksandr Etkind, following Freud, sees Lermontov's Demon (to whom he refers somewhat misleadingly as "the original" of Vrubel's and Blok's) as "an embodiment of phallic power" who, in committing an act of rape against Tamara, kills her. Vrubel, Etkind suggests, endeavours to exorcize the guilt of the Demon's cruel sensuality by isolating, dematerializing, and emasculating him. According to Etkind, Blok (whose father, whom the critic describes as a "clinical sadist" whose most "secret" inclinations the poet admits he may have inherited, was known to have been obsessed by the Demon) welcomes the fading out of Tamara in Vrubel's paintings. In articles such as "Catiline" (Katilina, 1919), "The Confession of a Pagan" (Ispoved' iazychnika, 1918), and in the poem *The Twelve* (*Dvenadstat'*, 1918) (which Etkind sees as "rooted in Blok's personal mythology or, more precisely, demonology"), Blok constructs "a new monstrous ideal," a *ci-devant* Demon who has surgically cured himself of aggressive male sexuality.[40]

Such are the bare bones of Etkind's argument. To the fading out of Tamara we will return in due course. The Demon himself is a slippery subject for gender stereotyping, for his nature is such that he cannot be confined to the "aggressively male." Milton puts it simply and beautifully:

... For Spirits, when they please,
Can either sex assume, or both; so soft
And uncompounded is their essence pure,
                                (*Paradise Lost*, 1:423–25)

In Lermontov's poem, Tamara's physical death is not the end of the story, but a necessary transition to the spiritual dimension, for which, as we know, he composed two alternative endings. In the first (Lopukhina) version, Tamara joins the Demon in his defiant, desolate eternity and, presumably, becomes a Demon herself. Whether or not for the censor,[41] Lermontov wrote another version (the one we all know), more in line with "the rules," in which Tamara is reclaimed by her guardian angel:

> Она страдала и любила –
> И рай открылся для любви!
> (*The Demon*, 2:16.1049–50)
>
> [She suffered and loved –
> And Heaven opened to love.]

The Demon is left alone, as before, in a universe devoid of hope or love, no better and no worse off than Vigny's Satan who, though permitted to bear Eloa off to hell, is "plus triste que jamais."[42] Tamara's love, unlike Margarita's, is insufficient to redeem her lover; indeed, she shrinks from him. But then Goethe took the precaution of separating Faust from Mephistopheles, whereas in Lermontov's poem protagonist and author, Demon and poet, Lucifer and Cain are never disentangled.

The emotional, lyrical charge of the poetry is such that all our sympathies, as Tamara is wafted up to heaven by her severe but joyous guardian, are with the rejected lover. Lermontov was too great an artist not to be aware that the lines describing this scene are closer to the ridiculous than to the sublime.[43] Yet he neither vindicates the Demon, nor devalues his yearning for salvation. Precisely by stretching to the utmost the sympathy his predecessors had felt for the fallen angel, he brought his readers up short before the unsolved problem of evil.

Lermontov's *The Demon* was the culmination of an exhausted genre: "The age of Romantic poems is sped" (Umchalsia vek epicheskikh poem, 1.1) wrote Lermontov himself after he completed it, in *A Fairy-tale for Children* (*Skazka dlia detei*, 1840). Here his attempts to conjure a more diabolic demon foundered in formlessness and psychology:

> ... не раз
> Хотелось мне совет ей дать лукавый,
> Но ум ее, и сметливый и здравый,
> Отгадывал все мигом сам собой.
> (*A Fairy-tale for Children*, 24.5–8)
>
> [... More than once
> I felt like giving her some ill advice,
> But her quick mind and common sense
> Jumped to the same conclusions on their own.]

This, on the whole, was how the age of prose was to perceive the workings of a redundant or, at the very least, interiorized devil. It was many decades before the evil spirit began to adopt a new earthly form, precisely in the "petty" and "hideous" guise abortively attempted in *A Fairy-tale for Children* and triumphantly achieved in Briusov's "Demons of Dust" (Demony pyli, 1899) and in Sologub's *The Petty Demon (Melkii bes,* 1907).[44] Yet Lermontov, by bringing his tragic and beautiful Demon down from "beyond the stars" and endowing him with human feelings, had nevertheless already begun to turn up older seams of inspiration at the root of literary legend. It was not until after the passing of more than one generation that these seams were to be re-opened as *mifotvorchestvo* by the genius of Vrubel and Blok, not nostalgically but compulsively, as "symbols of our own time."[45]

Vrubel: Towards a Mythopoetic View of Man and Nature

The stepping stone which, in a prosaic, utilitarian age, provided a transition to Lermontov's outdated masterpiece,[46] was Rubinshtein's opera *The Demon.* Conceived in 1871, thirty years after the poet's death but only eleven after the first full publication of *The Demon* in Russia, the opera was staged at the Mariinsky theatre in Petersburg in 1875. Within the year, the young *dotsent* Aleksandr L'vovich Blok took a box for the performance, to which to invite – decorously chaperoned – his future wife the sixteen-year-old Aleksandra Beketova. He knew the whole opera by heart and played it obsessively in his own adaptation for piano,[47] so the Demon may be said to have presided over the poet Blok's conception, if not over his birth in the enlightened home of the Rector of St. Petersburg University. The future artist Mikhail Vrubel (1856–1910), in 1875 a first-year student of law at that same University, could not afford a ticket but, enchanted by Lermontov since childhood, approved the "profoundly tragic" subject.[48] In Kiev in 1886 he at last had the chance to see Rubinshtein's opera. Arguing with friends about the production, Vrubel stressed it was wrong to confuse the Demon with the devil. On the contrary, he personified "the rebellious human spirit in its eternal struggle to reconcile conflicting passions and in its search for knowledge (poznaniia zhizni), unable to find any answer to its doubts either on earth, or in heaven."[49] Fascinated and repelled, the artist saw the performance several times and found recollections of it hard to shake off when, in 1891, he was given a commission to illustrate the poem.[50] The illustrations (in spite of residual theatricality) became virtually *the* definitive visual interpretation and, in their turn, in the year 1904, inspired Korovin and Shaliapin to collaborate in an unforgettable visual realization of the opera which owed décor, costume, and the physical interpretation of the title role to Vrubel.[51] The artist, confined to a clinic, never saw the production, but, paradoxically, madness had brought him fame and the first-night public immediately recognized his spellbinding influence. Vrubel, to use his own word, had by then succeeded in "illusionizing" (illiuzionirovat')[52] spectators no longer capable of suspending disbelief in the splendid images of that phenomenon which Hansen-Löve, in his study of "diabolical symbolism," calls "black romanticism,"[53] and in obliterating the memory of the pantomime monster, encumbered by enormous wings and sporting an electric star flashing from his brow, who had affronted his gaze in the Kiev production in 1886.

Thus the artist's envisualization of the Demon altered his contemporaries' perception of both Rubinshtein's opera and Lermontov's poem. Such cross-fertilization between the arts is not uncommon, particularly in the theatre. The director Tovstonogov, writing of adapting the classics for the stage, begins with Vrubel: "Vrubel painted Lermontov's Demon. What did he embody – Lermontov or himself, Vrubel? Lermontov, without doubt. But tell me, looking at that picture, would you confuse Vrubel with any other artist? Never."[54]

Vrubel had, as we have seen, his own ideas about the true nature of the Demon which have survived in fragmentary remarks in his letters or recorded in the memoirs of his friends. On the whole, he preferred not to explain but to express concepts visually, through his work.[55] His achievement is to have elaborated a manner of handling space and colour to give form to Lermontov's "dumb and misty apparition" (prishlets tumannyi i nemoi, 1:16.378) in a manner which could not but express also his own ideas and intuitions.

How Vrubel acquired his technique is the story of his life in art. He entered the St. Petersburg Academy at the age of twenty-four in the autumn of 1880. Though he came late to his vocation, he was totally dedicated: "Art – this is our religion," he once said to his sister Aniuta, pointing at the picture he was absorbed in painting, "though maybe, who knows, one day we might yet be surprised by love" (eshche pridetsia umilit'sia).[56] As a young man he had insisted, to the same sister, that his work, like Raphael's, was neither pious nor sentimentally "Christian" in the accepted sense, but profoundly "realistic" and rooted "in technique."[57] If there is a paradox here, it is resolved *in* the art.

Vrubel's obsession with Lermontov's Demon is documented in detail in Suzdalev's study of the subject.[58] I have not space to elaborate, but one thing artist and poet had in common was a submerged memory that life should be joyful and inspired by a genuine sense of wonder, and a fierce contempt for what Vrubel called the "triviality of life" (poshlost' zhizni).[59]

It is the "divine discontent" of Lermontov's Demon, the sheer weight of alienation from the small doings of mankind which early captured Vrubel's imagination. The painter's Demon is not – like Lermontov's – disgusted with God's world but is rather allied with nature in opposition to all that is not sublime or elemental. Like Hamlet, whom Vrubel in 1883 tried to paint from his own face but who eventually, in 1888, emerged as a precursor of the Demon, the artist saw archetypal man as "like an angel! ... like a god! the beauty of the world! the paragon of animals!," yet, again like Hamlet, as despoiled of his heritage.[60] To envisage and depict such a figure through the medium of paint and clay in a society which tended to see human beings as "infusoria" and nature as "workshop rather than temple" was a titanic task.[61]

To return to the language of our preamble, Vrubel needed to "recodify" the world around him. In the art of his maturity, demonic presences emerge from natural phenomena closely studied and faithfully depicted: water-nymphs from study after study of a mother-of-pearl ashtray; Pan from a moonlit South Russian landscape; a satyr sitting shepherd-like watching over grazing horses at nightfall. The first step to the "demonic," however, was the Demon, who required personification: a face, a shape. It took the artist five years of conscious effort, from 1885 to 1890, to achieve this, and it is inconceivable he would have done it had it not been for his completely fortuitous introduction to Byzantine art and – literally – to imprints left in the wall by the age of faith.[62]

Professor A.V. Prakhov, having with difficulty persuaded the clergy in charge of the Church of the former Saint Cyril's Monastery near Kiev (at the time serving as a lunatic asylum) to entrust the restoration of its twelfth-century frescoes[63] to trained artists under his direction, engaged Vrubel to undertake vacation work at the end of the spring semester of 1884. At the Academy, Vrubel would have been well grounded in classic and Renaissance art, but Byzantine art was scarcely studied, the native Russian tradition virtually undiscovered, and the icon-painter (bogomaz) considered as craftsman rather than artist. Prakhov, however, was an enthusiast, and, seeing Vrubel's interest in the Kiev frescoes and mosaics, spent hours with him poring over chromo-lithographs and photographs and talking of his scholarly expeditions to Egypt, Asia Minor, Palestine, Italy, and Greece.

For Vrubel, this theoretical instruction was brought to life by the possibility of actually directing the restoration work.[64] He not only restored damaged frescoes, completely reconstituting the Archangel Gabriel "strictly in the Byzantine style" from what remained of the outline scratched in the stucco, but was allowed to add his own *Descent of the Holy Spirit* (*Soshestvie Sviatogo Dukha*, 1884) and *Lamentation* (*Nadgrobnyi plach*, 1884). From this he went on to the drum of the cupola of the Cathedral of Saint Sophia where one of four mosaic angels had been preserved. Vrubel recreated the three others *in situ*, "first painting their robes in smooth tones then, when this had dried, using a flat brush to mark out the small squares characteristic of mosaic in suitable colours. The modules were deliberately somewhat enlarged because pebbles painted on a flat surface in oils exactly to scale would not have had the iridescence of mosaic pebbles which, being faceted, reflect the light."[65]

This hands-on apprenticeship to forgotten proportions, perspective, form, and content was, for Vrubel, a revelation – one is tempted to say a conversion, though of a purely technical nature. First among his contemporaries, he understood that, in fresco painting, the realistic depiction of rounded figures against backgrounds drawn according to the rules of post-Renaissance perspective was self-defeating. Pattern, figures and, more difficult, landscape, had to be related to architectural space without breaking flat or convex surfaces, and drapery used in such a way as to suggest the mood and motion of incorporeal beings. Colours, too, even though the artist was using oils, not the materials of the old masters, could be coaxed to produce a mother-of-pearl iridescence or applied in daubs and flecks to imitate the sparkle of mosaic:[66] "I want all his body to be radiant," Vrubel was later to say of *The Demon Cast Down* (*Demon poverzhennyi*, preparatory sketches 1901, oil-painting 1902), "to sparkle like one huge, faceted diamond of life."[67] Whether or not, at the time, Vrubel believed in the Christ of the Roman Catholic Church in which he had been brought up or of the Orthodox Church in which he underwent his apprenticeship to ecclesiastical art, it was surely here that he conceived the ambition to create, if not for himself then "for the public I love … an illusion of Christ as beautiful as one could possibly conceive."[68]

At the end of the summer of 1884 Vrubel was given the opportunity – not to be missed by one who had hitherto studied the Renaissance masters through neo-classical engravings ("like reading Hamlet in an adaptation by Voltaire," as he once complained)[69] – to continue his study of Byzantine and Italian art in Venice. He never returned to the Academy. Venice, he informed his sister Aniuta, was for him infinitely more instructive: "a useful specialist book."[70] On his return to Russia, he tried briefly to set up independently with his friend Valentin Serov in Odessa. It was here, in the autumn of 1885, that he first conceived a grandiose project for a "tetralogy" (tetralogiia): "The subject is the Demon; Tamara; Tamara's death; Christ at Tamara's grave."[71] This plan was never realized. It is interesting, nevertheless, that he should from the outset have instinctively sought to restore the balance of the salvation model, replacing Lermontov's near-parodic angel, who, in the 1891 illustrations to the poem, he was to resolve as a bright double of the cloudy Demon, by Jesus Christ. He does not appear to have considered the alternative, truly demonic ending.

It was Evgenii Pavlovich Ivanov, brother of Vrubel's first biographer, who, in conversation with Aleksandr Blok, elaborated a whole new mythology, according to which contemporary man, having lost the grandeur and sorrow of the Demon together with the memory of Paradise, could only be restored to his true stature by a deliberate descent into hell, a downfall in which he had been preceded by both the Demon and Christ. The Son of God redeems by *sharing* the Demon's experience and, in a sense, the Demon is seen as man writ large, more particularly as cultured, agnostic, revolutionary man. Ivanov's interpretation is based on the visual symbiosis between Vrubel's depiction of the face of Christ in the grave and of the Demon's face, "seared," as though both had been through the "bloody flames of hell."[72] Whether Vrubel ever consciously thought anything of the kind is not known.

In the 1880s, the artist was more interested in the struggle to visualize his Demon and to devise a suitable background, using, according to Serov, the negative of a photograph which suggested "an extraordinarily complex pattern like an extinct crater or a lunar landscape."[73] Two circumstances troubled him: the lack of a model, which he tried to remedy by moulding and firing clay figures, none of which have been preserved, and the difficulty of blending figure and landscape. Of two reports of the Demon's face as it began to emerge in *grisaille*, the first, from the artist's father, a regular officer in Lermontov's Tengin regiment, shows precisely what Vrubel was up against. Misha, he informed their family in September 1886, was sure the Demon would make his name, but all he, his father, could see on the canvas was "an ill-tempered, sensual ... repulsive ... elderly woman. Misha ... says that the Demon is a spirit who combines male and female appearance. Not so much an evil spirit as suffering and sorrowful, but at the same time a spirit of power ... sublime ... That's as may be, but there's precious little of all that in his Demon at present."[74] The difficulty of showing the Demon at one with nature is suggested, somewhat incoherently, by another witness: "the background of the picture is a nocturnal landscape, it has to be the Demon too. How to do it ... he hadn't yet done it."[75]

How Vrubel eventually "did it" is again closely connected with his involvement with ecclesiastical art – this time with the internal decoration of the Cathedral of Saint Vladimir in Kiev from the beginning

of 1886 until autumn 1889.[76] Here Vrubel, suffering from excruciat-
ing migraine once or twice a month and from a chronic shortage of
cash, trying always for optimum results, gained a reputation for decadent experimentation and inability to meet deadlines. He became
increasingly frustrated and occasionally blamed this on the subject
matter, as in the letter to his sister, where he claims to feel "religious
ritual, even the Resurrection of Christ to be so alien as to be actually
irritating."[77] Yet, of his projects for *The Lamentation* (*Nadgrobnyi plach*,
1887), *The Resurrection* (*Voskresenie*, 1887), and *The Ascension* (*Voznesenie*,
1887), Vrubel wrote: "Never think that this is hack work and not pure
creativity," adding of his Demon that "although I'm not working on
him at the moment, I think that he's none the worse for that and that
when I finish the studies for the Cathedral I'll take him on with more
confidence and so am closer to my goal."[78] Clearest proof of the
cross-contamination between Vrubel's work for the Cathedral and on
the Demon are the sketches for *The Lamentation*.[79] The earlier versions
invoke the anguish of Nature herself and achieve the desired harmo-
nization of figure and subject. The second version for the 1887 *Lamentation*, a nocturnal scene in sub-aqueous blues, greens, and violets,
shows a huge-eyed Mary crouching over her exhausted Son, who
appears deep asleep. The first version (with a landscape background),
closest to the Demon, yet metaphysically and symbolically the most
optimistic, depicts a Christ whose face is seared from the Descent into
Hell, haloed only by the rising sun against which is outlined a fiery
but already distant Golgotha. His face and graveclothes, like Mary's
face, is still in deep green shade and she kneels above him, upright
and slender as the cypress behind her, the sorrowful inclination of the
head echoed by a trailing wisp of creeper. In the huge sky, a golden
light is just beginning to disperse the darkness of night and storm.

It was against such a sky that Vrubel at last succeeded in envisaging "something demonic": "a half-naked, winged, young, despondent thoughtful figure sits hugging his knees against a background of
sunset and gazes out over a flowering glade, from which branches
heavy with flowers stretch out towards him."[80] Although the thought
is of sunset rather than of sunrise, *The Seated Demon* (*Demon sidiashchii*,
1890) and the first version of *The Lamentation* (with a landscape background) are scenes from the same world model. In the picture, which
did not emerge in its final form until after Vrubel had left Kiev and
settled in Moscow, the seated youth is not winged and the luxurious
flowers (blue tulips in the watercolour sketch, according to Suzdalev)[81] have been transfigured into strange blossoms of rock crystal.

The same sky, though darker, the same lingering sunset, recurs in
the many preparatory versions of *The Demon Cast Down*. Between the
two pictures fall countless pen-and-ink, water-colour and brush

sketches, illustrations published and unpublished to the Lermontov jubilee edition of 1891 (see Illustrations 17 and 18), a ceramic head of the Demon (1894), and, beginning from 1898,[82] the unfinished but impressive picture of *The Demon in Flight* (*Letiashchii Demon*, 1899), a horizontal composition showing the Caucasian mountains and cities

17. M. Vrubel, *Head of the Demon*, 1890-91. Black watercolour and white on paper, 23 × 36 cm. The first illustration completed by Vrubel for the 1891 edition of Lermontov's works.

18. M. Vrubel, *Head of the Demon*, 1890-91. Watercolour and pressed charcoal on paper, 41 × 68 cm. This sketch, seldom reproduced, was not included in the 1891 edition of Lermontov's works.

through swirling cloud, as if glimpsed from an aeroplane. The Demon swims rather than glides or soars, his head cleaving the air like the bowsprit of some fantastic vessel. The face, though, is still the Demon we know, strong, huge-eyed, and despairing: the face of Lermontov's Demon before he set eyes on Tamara.

Indeed, Tamara, originally seen as the centre of the Tetralogy, is never shown in Vrubel's oil-paintings of the Demon; not, I think, for the reasons we have already examined advanced by Aleksandr Etkind, but because, with the insistence on the Demon as the "human soul" rather than the "evil one," she had lost her function. Also, her short-lived humanity is superfluous to his eternity. Vrubel had difficulty with this when envisaging his illustrations. In oil-painting, he could and did ignore the dichotomy so inescapable in the Demon's relationship with Tamara in the poem, a dichotomy later voiced by Blok:

> И в горном закатном пожаре,
> В разливах синеющих крыл,
> С тобою, с мечтой о Тамаре,
> Я, горний, навеки без сил…
>
> И снится – в далеком ауле,
> У склона бессмертной горы,
> Тоскливо к нам в небо плеснули
> Ненужные складки чадры…
>
> [And in the conflagration of the mountain sunset,
> In the shimmer of wings turning blue,
> With you, with the dream of Tamara,
> I, spirit of the mountains, am for ever powerless …
>
> And I dream – in the far village,
> By the slope of the immortal mountain,
> The unneeded folds of her *chadra*
> Flutter longingly towards us in the heavens…]

So Blok wrote in "The Demon" (Demon, 19 April 1910, 3:26), the first of two poems so titled. Speaking at Vrubel's funeral, he describes *The Demon Cast Down* in almost the same words: "The youth is in the grip of lethargic 'Boredom,' as if exhausted by some kind of cosmic embraces; broken arms, outspread wings; and the ancient evening keeps on pouring and pouring gold into the deep-blue clefts; that is all that remains; somewhere far below, visible to him alone, there is, perhaps, a glimpse of the unneeded *chadra* of the departed earthbound Tamara" (5:423).

"That is all that remains." *The Demon Cast Down* took Vrubel, for the first time, outside the context of Lermontov's text, though not, of course, outside the Lucifer myth.

Of the first sketches of a youthful, almost soldierly figure (see Illustration 19), reminiscent, were it not for the profoundly introspective

19. M. Vrubel, *The Demon Cast Down*, 1901. Sketch in watercolour and white over graphite on cardboard, 27,6 × 63,9 cm.

facial expression, of Prometheus bound, Vrubel's wife Nadezhda Zabela commented that this was a new Demon, "not Lermontov's at all but some kind of contemporary Nietzschean."[83] In 1901, Nietzsche was on the tip of everyone's tongue, but this one remark does not appear to me to justify Aline Isdebsky-Pritchard's conclusion that "had it not been for Nietzsche's concept of the overman," Vrubel might possibly never have returned to the subject of the Demon.[84] Suzdalev cites Kant, Schopenhauer, and Nietzsche as cardinal influences on Vrubel, but even this assertion – though probably true – remains unproven and unsourced.[85] The influence of Nietzsche is one of the many questions raised by the theme of this paper which requires a separate study based on further research. All I would say here is that I am satisfied in my own mind that the infiltration of Russian culture by Nietzsche in the last twenty years of the nineteenth century and beyond, to some extent mediated through Vladimir Solov'ev,[86] surely enriched rather than reversed Vrubel's attitude to Lermontov and his Demon.[87] The intense efforts the artist put into *The Demon Cast Down* in order to express something "strong and lofty,"[88] brought low yet defiant, appear, both from the evidence of successive sketches and of Van Mekh, who bought the picture, to be bound up with the desire to avoid a naturalistic or realist representation of a spirit.[89] Through rising madness, working directly on canvas, the artist obliterated image after image, often to the horror of friends and family. Nadezhda Zabela recalls a splendid, barbaric, bejewelled, almost naked figure lying on a loose-spread cloak in a rocky place, lizards darting about him in the light of the setting sun. Then, a month later, he changed it all: "Mikhail Aleksandrovich is driving me to despair with his Demon, he was already magnificent and then suddenly he changed everything and, to my mind, spoilt everything and wants to exhibit it like this, the critics will have a field-day (vot-to rugat' budut)."[90]

Sketches confirm a progressive attenuation of heroic masculinity until, at one stage, there appears a serpent-youth from an Eastern fairy-tale, not unlike Vigny's "Ange ténébreux," comfortably propped on one elbow and pensively waggling his sword, eyes lowered to gaze into the swift-moving waters of a mountain torrent.[91] "He's resting up, relaxing" (otdykhaet, nezhitsia), snapped Vrubel when asked about this particular transformation.

Vrubel continued to work on the picture during its first showing in Moscow and its second in St. Petersburg at the February-March 1902 *Mir iskusstva* exhibition. The result satisfied neither him nor his friends Serov and Ostroukhov, who refused to recommend it for purchase to the Tret'iakov Gallery, complaining of anatomical and technical faults. Indeed, the colours, dazzling and sparkling at the time of the exhibition, did subsequently fade, taking on a shadowy, subfusc glow perhaps better suited to the ambivalent subject, compared by Lermontov to a clear evening: "Neither day, nor night – neither darkness, nor light" (Ni den', ni noch', – ni mrak, ni svet, 1:16.390–91). The dislocated, misshapen figure, the tangled wings, the tormented head defiantly reared as though to halt the disastrous downward diagonal slide of the body, and the splendid background of Caucasian peaks (again, incongruously, executed from photographs) carry their own conviction.

The "huge faceted diamond of life" of which Vrubel had dreamt was achieved, beyond the bounds of clinical insanity, in the truly dematerialized, truly androgynous image of the *The Six-Winged Seraph (Azrael)* (*Shestikrylyi serafim [Azrail]*, 1904), and exhibited by Diaghilev in a special Vrubel room at his Paris exhibition of Russian Art in 1906. Critics are still arguing virulently as to whether the seraph is the Demon redeemed or his antithesis.[92] Angel, Demon, and muse are hard to disentangle in Lermontov's poetry and Vrubel's blue-eyed *Muse* (*Muza*, 1896; Illustration 13) relates artistic inspiration to both angelic and demonic images. Blok put the question "Evil or good?" (Zla, dobra li?) to his own muse, and could only answer "You are altogether not of this world" (Ty vsia – ne otsiuda, 3:7). Here there is a strong trend, formulated by Nietzsche if not introduced by him, towards an understanding of art as *beyond* good and evil.

Blok: The Reintegration of the Poet in History into the Mythopoetic World Model

"Vrubel lived simply, as we all live," said Aleksandr Blok at the artist's graveside. "Given all our passion for events, there were not enough events in the world for him, and events transferred themselves into his inner world – the fate of the contemporary artist; the more clearly the earth's surface is marked off for us into little squares, the deeper the gods of fire and light which move our being withdraw beneath the earth" (5:421).

With Blok, the restoration of the mythopoetic model becomes programmatic. Perceiving in the unconscious "the foundation of every artist's will and faith" (5:313), he set out quite deliberately to tap also the "collective unconscious" or, as the symbolists called it, "folk memory," to seek "along forgotten ways" "that well-spring of lyricism which invariably reflects the past as future, memory as promise" (5:10,12).

In this search, Blok's sources, as Maksimov points out in his seminal study "On the Mythopoetic Principle in Blok's Lyric Poetry,"[93] are comparable to multiple strata: the stratum of what he calls "the experiences of the lyrical 'I';" the stratum of literary and artistic images which have acquired the status of mythopoetic symbols; and, beneath all these but bubbling up through them like molten lava, the strata of the mythological, religious, and philosophical systems of the ancient world. From these, as Paperny argues, Blok conjures up "not his own ideas (as, for example, in Dostoevsky), and not abstract philosophegms, but products of the cultural tradition, culturegms."[94]

The Demon is present in every stratum. At the personal level, he materializes, for Blok as for Lermontov, with the awareness of Paradise Lost.[95] In the poems of the "Ante Lucem (1898–1900)" cycle the Demon is, as it were, in possession, not needing to "take form," speaking through the poet:

> Увижу я, как будет погибать
> Вселенная, моя отчизна.
> Я буду одиноко ликовать
> Над бытия ужасной тризной.[96]

> [I shall see the last end
> Of the Universe, my fatherland.
> I shall exult alone
> At the terrible funeral feast of Being.]

The first epigraph from Lermontov highlights Blok's feeling of having been, as Andrey Bely told him he had been in his first letter, "consecrated" by Lermontov:[97]

> К добру и злу постыдно равнодушны,
> В начале поприща мы вянем без борьбы.[98]

> [Shamelessly indifferent to good and evil,
> We wilt in the slips without resistance.]

But then, for Blok:

> Минувших дней младые были
> Пришли доверчиво из тьмы...[99]

[The young happenings of days gone by
Came trustfully out of the dark...]

And with this recollection of a prelapsarian world came the memory of a more comforting myth, the saving grace of the Eternal Feminine, the poet's "anamnesis."

The *Verses about the Beautiful Lady* (*Stikhi o Prekrasnoi Dame*) celebrate a sustained attempt to seek salvation in concentration and seclusion: mountain tops, the cloister, a fenced garden, the unspoilt countryside of Shakhmatovo. Blok retained faith in his salvation figure, but to his art she was "unanswering as a rose" (kak roza, bezotvetnoi, 1:197) and from the beginning he felt something new coming into being: "whether God or the Devil it doesn't matter" (7:28). Drawn, like the hero of Lermontov's *The Novice* (*Mtsyri*, 1833), to try his strength in the world outside his hallowed enclosure, the poet pictures himself as a dark monk, beset by temptation. The Demon, exorcized, seeks re-entry, bringing a swarm of his fellows:

Во сне и в яви – неразличимы
Заря и зарево – тишь и страх...
Мои безумья – мои херувимы...
Мой Страшный, мой Близкий – черный монах...
. . . .

Закрыт один или многие лики?
Ты знаешь? Ты видишь! Одежда пуста!..
До утра – без солнца – пущу мои крики,
Как черных птиц, на встречу Христа![100]

[In sleeping and in waking they are inseparable
Dawn and afterglow – calm and fear...
My deliriums – my cherubim...
My Terror, my Kin – the black monk...
. . . .

Behind the veil, is there one face, or many?
You know? You see! The garments are empty!..
Until the morning – without the sun – I shall let fly my cries,
Like black birds, to meet Christ!]

So Blok wrote on 9 January 1903 – as if from the depths of Vrubel's delirium,[101] and in a letter of the same year he acknowledged the influence of this artist "who draws me and frightens me in a very real way, especially if you remember what has become of him now."[102] "The most difficult thing of all these days," he advises Sergei Solov'ev in the same letter, "is to initiate others into your own fairest dream. ... To understand it they must first come to love it and, as everybody is busy with their own affairs, it is more effective (whether more eternal I do not know) to go to work with a dagger like Briusov, like Vrubel." So Blok was weaned from Pre-Raphaelite gold and azure and white lilies under the direct influence of Vrubel's demonic art.

Deliberately celebrating the Dormition and Ascension of his Most Beautiful Lady (1:323, 2:7), Blok opened his poetry to the demons she had briefly helped him to banish:

> Мы никогда не стучали при ней,
> Мы не шалили при ней.[103]
>
> [We never came knocking when she was there,
> We never played tricks in her company.]

The demons promised power as an artist: "The field with its flowers and the sky with its stars" (Lug s tsvetami i tverd' so zvezdami, 3:8). Encouraged by the keen interest of his fellow-symbolists (notably Viacheslav Ivanov and his circle) in folklore, myth, and magic, in 1906 Blok undertook an article on spells and incantation for Professor Anichkov's *Folk Literature* (*Narodnaia slovesnost'*, 1908), in which he compared the world of magic and ritual to a mine "where gleams the gold of true poetry; the gold which also supplies our bookish 'paper' poetry to this day. That is why incantations have taken on psychological, historical, and *aesthetic* interest."[104] Rituals were enacted and invocations pronounced as a form of contract between the speaker and the natural world in order to conjure divine or demonic beings, Blok explains in the article and, in his notebook that same year, writes that mysticism and the experience of ecstasy can be defined "as the conclusion of a contract with the world against people," whereas religion, which has nothing in common with mysticism, is "standing watch," "a contract with people against the world AS STASIS (KAK KOSNOSTI)." Religious art could, he thought, exist only as "a transient form," but "mysticism *can become one* of the ways to religion" and be sanctified by it.[105]

The *aesthetic* interest in the conclusion of contracts with elementals expressed in the article on incantations had already been demonstrated by Blok in his delightful "Bubbles of the Earth" (Puzyri zemli, 1904–1905, 2:8–25). The poems of this cycle serve as a living illustration to his comments in the article on incantations: "In the chaos of nature, among threads spun by the Fates and stretching out everywhere, it is essential to be constantly on guard; all elementals require a particular approach, one has to conclude some kind of contract with every one of them, because everything is in the image and likeness of man, lives side by side with him not only in the field, the wood and on the road, but also within the log walls of his home. Herbs, flowers, birds all require care and love" (5:38).

Formulae, substitutions, and repetitions are quoted at length in this article and it is possible to sense how Blok is using folk poetry as a technical laboratory, much as Vrubel used the art of Byzantium and Assyria, not imitating but learning techniques to be deployed unobtrusively, with the utmost discretion, in a twentieth-century context.

In his Second Volume, Blok not only opens his poetry to demons, he invokes them – most famously in the threefold "And every evening" (I kazhdyi vecher) which precedes the apparition of "The Stranger" (Neznakomka, 24 April 1906, 2:185–86). From the depth of "the police department" of his soul, from the association of sex with prostitution and of both with the glamour and terror of his native Petersburg, he conjured the "Antithesis," Ashtaroth as Milton named her, Astarte, the Stranger, the Snow Maiden. Associated with mist and falling stars, like Lermontov's Demon, and with the colour lilac and the dusk of evening like Vrubel's, she draws and seduces the poet to follow her into emptiness, apostasy, and "Liebestod." "Had I the means of a Vrubel, I would have created the Demon" (5:430).

In her religious, "eternal" aspect, Blok's Demonic Strangerwoman is the fallen World Soul, Sophia, who needs to be and *can only* be saved by Christ. This is a hypostasis of which he could not have been unaware, prompted by Vladimir Solov'ev and explicitly reminded by Viacheslav Ivanov,[106] but it is the Demon, not the eternal Sophia who is the "symbol of our time" (5:691); the task of the artist is to find the point of intersection. In her demonic aspect, the female persona of the Second Volume has many attributes of a folklore "demon."[107] She is associated with the serpent and the comet, ancient symbols, which carry a multiple semantic charge, phallic or erotic, suggesting rites of passage, forbidden knowledge, ultimate freedom, perdition.

Vrubel's lilac colour, which dominates in the Second Volume, fades from Blok's poetry after 1910,[108] reasserting itself powerfully in that year when the painter was most present to his mind in the "smoky-lilac mountains" (dymno-lilovye gory, 3:26) of the first Demon poem and, in a minor key, as in Vrubel's *The Demon Cast Down* (1902), in the dim, purple-grey aura once glimpsed by the poet, when – he does not recall, in the poem "To the Muse" (K Muze, 29 December 1912, 3:7–8).

As the poem I have described as the Ascension of the Most Beautiful Lady acts as an "Introduction" (Vstuplenie, 2:7) to the Second Volume, so "To the Muse" introduces the Third and has been used by Naum Korzhavin and others to emphasize the unregenerate demonism of Blok's poetry.[109] Yet, even as "Introduction" is about the First Volume, so "To the Muse" is essentially about the Second. Though both supernatural feminine beings have an eternal aspect in relation to the poetic persona, both are spoken of in the past. True, the muse lives on in the present, laughing, blazing up and tormenting the poet (as the tense of Blok's verbs shows) whereas the Lady, like religion, according to Blok, is "that (about that) which will be."[110] When he falls asleep She will pass by, but on a black day it is only to Her golden flute that he will set his lips (2:7).

The leitmotif of the Third Volume is the struggle back towards the "Synthesis": humanization, sobriety. Blok's feminine incarnation of the Demon fades with the colour lilac and, when she gleams through the poet's encounters with human women, it is in prosaic circumstances thanks to some glimpsed attribute: the heavy, snake-like train of a discarded dress; the silvery scales of a gypsy's rings. The increasing laconism of Blok's multi-dimensional later poetry is achieved by oblique reference to cultural signs and by rhythm. Often, as in "Dear friend, even in this quiet house ..." (Milyi drug, i v etom tikhom dome..., October 1913, 3:286), where the poet's domesticity is invaded by Vrubel's "angel of the storm – Azrael" (angel buri – Azrail), only a name and the thrill of beating wings recall the mythical subtext. Still more often, presences – malign and angelic – go unnamed:

> Там неба осветленный край
> Средь дымных пятен.[111]

> [There is the lighted rim of heaven
> Among smoky patches.]

The more control Blok gained over his poetry, the more glancing his references to the mythopoetic code became, for in a sense he had now written his whole life into the world model. A dead soul, the poetic persona, is still "standing watch," and the twentieth-century world in which he keeps vigil is animated (or demonized) through and through. Before the beginning of the First World War, the poet takes up the old, apocalyptic tale:

> Утром страшно мне раскрыть
> Лист газетный. Кто-то хочет
> Появиться, кто-то бродит.
> Иль – раздумал, может быть?[112]

> [In the morning I am afraid to open
> The newspaper. Someone wants
> To take shape, someone is on the prowl.
> Or has it changed its mind, perhaps?]

In 1910 as in 1901, when Blok felt "the approach of a being from another world," he preferred not to "uncover its face" (5:445). The second "Demon" poem (Demon, 9 June 1916, 3:60–61) is set between the confessional cycle "Black Blood" (Chernaia krov') and the despairing "Voice from the Chorus" (Golos iz khora). It is rung through with literary reminiscences, condensed, as always with Blok, intensified by incantatory rhythm. As Vigny's Satan addresses Eloa, so Blok's Demon addresses his victim as "my slave." He soars confidently with her to "a sparkling mountain range" and, like Lermontov's Demon, "burns" her, assuring her of the contemptibility of earthly passion. Even as Byron's Lucifer bears Cain at the speed of light beyond the earth to where

> ... As we move
> Like sunbeams onward, it grows small and smaller,
> And as it waxes little, and then less,
> Gathers a halo round it, like the light
> Which shone the roundest of the stars, when I
> Beheld them from the skirts of Paradise:
>
> (*Cain*, 2.1.39–43)

– so Blok's Demon bears the seduced soul

> ... туда,
> Где кажется земля звездою,
> Землею кажется звезда.
>
> [... there,
> To where earth seems a star,
> A star – an earth.]

The climax, though, is pure Blok: no tour of dead worlds, no excursion to the realms of death and beyond the gates of hell, just "a shining emptiness" through which the soul falls rippling like a stone, an image translated into sound in the next poem (3:62):

> И крик, когда ты начнешь кричать,
> Как камень, канет...
>
> [And your cry, when you begin to cry out,
> Will fall like stone...]

In 1916, Blok, for whom the persona of "the monk" no less than the persona of the Demon was more than a poetic conceit, recognized as his own the "demons" of the *Philokalia*.[113] As an artist, he had long since sought their help, putting himself in their power "by contract" – not necessarily with evil, but with chtonic forces. "All that is left is *ÉLAN. Only* flight and impulse. ... It is my lot to become a catacomb. A catacomb is a star flying through the empty, deep-blue ether, giving light" (7:326).

As a man, Blok had won through to a certain detached sobriety but, as a poet, he was beset by demons. Or, perhaps better, as he says in the article on spells and invocations, by elementals. Three times he "surrendered to the elements," lost his foothold up there with Lermontov on the *brink* of the abyss and flew headlong. The first two times were in January 1907 ("The Snow Mask") and in March 1914 ("Carmen"). The last, in January 1918, while writing *The*

Twelve: "That is why I do not disassociate myself from what I wrote then, because it was written in harmony with the element."[114]

As a man, Blok admired Lermontov's historical novel *Vadim* (1832–34), commenting that to be able to look the dark side of Revolution full in the face yet to see it as historically essential was a "sign of high culture."[115] As a poet, he felt the 1917 Revolution as a demonic event,[116] the eruption of subterranean forces, "a sudden jet of power triggered by some kind of catastrophe," as Losev puts it,[117] or, as Blok observed, the Russian people experienced it, "like a train-crash in the night, like a bridge crumbling beneath your feet, like a house falling down" (7:255). Here, only the a-logical "alternative codification" of the world model could restore some kind of harmony between man and his surroundings and the diachronic/synchronic bond. "In Blok's work," wrote Isupov in an article on the relationship of history to myth in the poet's work, "to the total mythologism of the symbolists there corresponds an emotional and willed hyperbolization of real events. Characteristic for Blok is the way from existence to essence, from appearance (oblik) to name, from "omen" to truth, from thing to idea."[118]

In *The Twelve*, Blok, in accordance with the symbolist "salvation model" which, as Zara Mints cautiously stated back in Soviet times, "is unthinkable without the line of New Testament images,"[119] did not "uncover the face" but he did name names: "If you look into the pillars raised by the blizzard along *that road*," he noted in one of his many hesitant attempts to explain the end of the poem, "you will see Jesus Christ" (7:330).

For Blok, the poet *was* the Demon and the Demon was the lyric poet:

> Among the mountain ridges, where the "solemn sunset" has mixed the blue of the shadows, the crimsons of the evening's sun and the gold of the dying day, mixed them and poured them together in one thick, gleaming lilac mass, a Human Being has lain down, hands twisted behind his head, experienced in sensual spleen, with all the riches of the world at his command, but – destitute, naked, having nowhere to lay his head. This Human Being – the fallen Angel-Demon – is the *first lyric poet*. The accursed poetic legend about him was sung by Lermontov, who flew into the abyss at the foot of Mashak, felled by a bullet. The accursed coloured legend about the Demon was painted by Vrubel, who must have penetrated more deeply than any of us into the secret of lyricism and because of that lost his way on the lonely paths of madness.[120]

This was the existential *condition humaine* of the artist. Beyond "the night of this present life,"[121] when art will no longer be needed, Blok had, from his very first demonic poems, looked for something else:

> Нет, светись,
> Светлячок, молчаливой понятный!

Кусочек света,
Клокочек рассвета...

Будет вам день беззакатный![122]

[No, shine,
Little glow-worm, companionably silent!
A morsel of light,
A tatter of dawn...

A day will come for you when the sun will never set!]

The great "fallen Angel-Demon" and the tiny glow-worm serve equally as figures for the artist; both are integral parts of the animated nature of the mythopoetic world model, first source of the arts constantly recalled and recreated by the artist. Bearers of light or the memory of light, they glow only through cloud and darkness. The light beyond is outside the scope of myth as of art.

Notes

1. V. Al'fonsov, "Blok i Vrubel'," in his *Slova i kraski. Ocherki iz istorii tvorcheskikh sviazei poetov i khudozhnikov* (Moscow and Leningrad: Sovetskii pisatel', 1966), 13–62(14, 33, 44). Translations are mine throughout this essay.
2. See Aleksandr Blok, *Sobranie sochinenii*, ed V.N. Orlov, A.A. Surkov, and K.I. Chukovskii, 8 vols. (Moscow and Leningrad: Gosudarstvennoe izdatel'stvo khudozhestvennoi literatury, 1960–63), 7:118. For the expression "standing watch" (stoiane na strazhe) used by Blok in the same context as "sentry unrelieved" (chasovoi nesmeniaemyi), see his letter to A. Belyi of 15–17 August 1907, in Blok, *Sobranie sochinenii*, 8:200. All further references to this edition will be given in the text and notes by volume and page number. One could, of course, cite many other paradoxical passages from Blok's prose and poetry which suggest light behind darkness, an exercise I undertook in "Alexander Blok: The Tragedy of the Two Truths," in *Aleksandr Blok Centennial Conference*, ed. Walter N. Vickery and Bogdan Saganov (Columbus: Slavica, 1984), 9–23. See also I.S. Prikhod'ko, "Obraz Khrista v poeme 'Dvenadtsat'," in her *Mifopoetika A. Bloka: Istoriko-kul'-turnyi i mifologicheskii kommentarii k dramam i poemam* (Vladimir: Vladimirskii gosudarstvennyi pedagogicheskii universitet, 1994), 10. Prikhod'ko's analysis of demonism, myth, and religion in Blok's poetry throughout her book is, in my opinion, virtually definitive, in that the author applies sophisticated techniques which the Tartu school was already using for the exploration of the mythopoetic subtext in the late 1970s, and is free to deploy knowledge of the essential New Testament references without disguise.
3. Al'fonsov, "Blok i Vrubel'," 19–20, 47.
4. A.F. Losev, *Mifologiia grekov i rimlian* (Moscow: Mysl', 1996). V.N. Toporov, "Model' mira (mifopoeticheskaia)," in *Mify narodov mira. Entsiklopediia v dvukh tomakh*, ed. S.A. Tokarev, 2d ed., 2 vols. (Moscow: Sovetskaia entsiklopediia, 1992), 2:161–64. V.N. Toporov, *Mif, ritual, simvol, obraz* (Moscow: Kul'tura, 1995).
5. Most important here are N.P. Krokhina, "Mifopoetizm A. Bloka v kontekste simvolistskogo mifomyshleniia," *Izvestiia Akademii nauk SSSR*, Seriia literatury i

iazyka, 49, no.6 (1990):515–26; D.E. Maksimov, "O mifopoeticheskom nachale v lirike Bloka (Predvaritel'nye zamechaniia)," and Z.G. Mints, "O nekotorykh 'neomifologicheskikh' tekstakh v tvorchestve russkikh simvolistov," both in *Uchenye zapiski Tartuskogo gosudarstvennogo universiteta* 49, *Tvorchestvo A.A. Bloka i russkaia kul'tura XX veka. Blokovskii sbornik III*, ed. Z.G. Mints (Tartu: Tartuskii gosudarstvennyi universitet, 1979), 3–33 and 76–120, respectively; I.S. Prikhod'ko, "Obraz Khrista v poeme 'Dvenadtsat'.'"

6. Maksimov speaks of the "Hegelian triad" of Paradise (thesis), the Fall (antithesis), and Redemption (synthesis); Maksimov, "O mifopoeticheskom nachale," 22. Mints suggests a Solov'evian triad in which the thesis is seen as All-Unity in God, the antithesis as the Creation of the material world and the "Fall" of the World Soul into multiplicity and chaos, and the synthesis as "the incarnation of the divine idea in the World;" Z.G. Mints, "Blok i russkii simvolizm," in *Literaturnoe nasledstvo*, vol.92, *Aleksandr Blok: Novye materialy i issledovaniia*, 5 vols. (Moscow: Nauka, 1980–93), 1:106–7. This Gnostic or neo-Platonic "triad" is perhaps more suited to the symbolists than Maksimov's more Orthodox salvation model.

7. Losev, *Mifologiia grekov i rimlian*, 60. Emphasis mine.

8. See Toporov, "Model' mira," 2:161–64.

9. See also Krokhina, "Mifopoetizm A. Bloka," 516, who refers to A.F. Losev, *Dialektika mifa* (Moscow: Izdanie avtora, 1930), 117, 124, 127. Losev, although much of his work remained unpublished or partially published at the time of writing, is rightly regarded as one of the founders of the "mythopoetical" approach to literature.

10. Toporov, "Model' mira," 2:163.

11. Particularly illuminating on this is Rachel Polonsky, *English Literature and the Russian Aesthetic Renaissance* (Cambridge: Cambridge University Press, 1998).

12. See particularly Krokhina, "Mifopoetizm A. Bloka," 515; Aleksandr Etkind, *Eros nevozmozhnogo: Istoriia psikhoanaliza v Rossii* (St. Petersburg: Meduza, 1993); Magnus Ljunggren, *The Russian Mephisto: A Study of the Life and Work of Emilii Medtner*, Stockholm Studies in Russian Literature, no.27 (Stockholm: Almqvist and Wiksell International, 1994), 7–8, 88, 156, 194.

13. The identification appears to rest on the loose linkage of Luke 10:18: "I beheld Satan falling as lightning from Heaven" (Christ to the seven disciples on their return from a missionary journey on which they cast out devils) and Isaiah 14:12: "O daystar, son of the morning," the prophet's superb diatribe against the king of Babylon. There is no mention of either Devil or Fallen Angel in the Creed, but the Lord's Prayer includes a petition for deliverance from "the Evil One": in Russian "ot Lukavogo." The Talmud, rather than the Bible, is the source for war in heaven and the casting down of Satan by the Archangel Michael.

14. See in this volume Simon Franklin, "Nostalgia for Hell: Russian Literary Demonism and Orthodox Tradition."

15. All references to *Paradise Lost* are from John Milton, *Paradise Lost* (London: J.G. and F. Rivington, 1833), and are given in the text by book and line number.

16. See in this volume Faith Wizgell, "The Russian Folk Devil and His Literary Reflections."

17. Peter Levi, *Eden Renewed. The Public and Private Life of John Milton* (London: Papermac, 1997), 208. Levi does, however, modify this opinion in the light of Milton's "On Christian Doctrine" (259).

18. Ibid., 131.

19. A.S. Pushkin, "Stsena iz 'Fausta'" and fragments, in his *Polnoe sobranie sochinenii v deviati tomakh*, ed. Iu.G. Oksman and M.A. Tsiavlovskii, 9 vols. (Moscow: Academia, 1935–37), 2:206–14(206, 213).

20. This line, from Lermontov's *Demon* (1:2.30), is quoted, as are all subsequent excerpts from Lermontov's verse, from M.Iu. Lermontov, *Polnoe sobranie stikhotvorenii,* introd. D.E. Maksimov, ed. E.E. Naidich, Biblioteka poeta, Bol'shaia seriia, 2 vols. (Leningrad: Sovetskii pisatel', 1989), 2:438. Further references to *Demon* are given in the text by part and stanza numbers, followed by the line number within the work as a whole.

21. "Pamiati Vrubelia," first published in *Iskusstvo i pechatnoe delo,* 1910, no.8–9, cited from Blok, *Sobranie sochinenii,* 5:423.

22. All the sources I have used, including Blok's note to Lermontov's *Demon* in M.Iu. Lermontov, *Izbrannye sochineniia v odnom tome* (Berlin and Petersburg: Izdatel'stvo Z.I. Grzhebina, [1920]), cited in Aleksandr Blok, *Sobranie sochinenii,* 12 vols. (Leningrad: Izdatel'stvo pisatelei v Leningrade, 1932–36), 11:414, give Lermontov's sources for *Demon* as Milton, Byron, Vigny, Thomas Moore, Goethe, and Klopstock (Blok adds Walter Scott). An excellently documented source for Milton in Russia is Valentin Boss, *Milton and the Rise of Russian Satanism* (Toronto: University of Toronto Press, 1991); for Lermontov and Milton, see particularly "Milton's Satan and Lermontov," 102–18. This chapter brings compelling evidence to suggest Lermontov was well acquainted with *Paradise Lost* as a schoolboy. One of his classmates actually gave an "English oration" on the subject and two of his tutors were engaged on new translations. Boss also recommends B.T. Udodov, *M.Iu. Lermontov. Khudozhestvennaia individual' nost' i tvorcheskie protsessy* (Voronezh: Izdanie Voronezhskogo universiteta, 1973), for "an informed discussion of the sources associated with *Demon;*" Boss, *Milton and the Rise of Russian Satanism,* 218 n.3.

23. A. Blok, "Pamiati Vrubelia (Pervaia redaktsiia)," in Blok, *Sobranie sochinenii,* 5:690–91. This quotation is taken from the speech Blok actually pronounced at the graveside, subsequently slightly revised for publication (see n.21 above). Andrei Bely uses *zaklinat'* in a similar context when he writes of discovering "znachenie novykh, magicheskikh slov, kotorymi vnov' i vnov' sumeem zakliast' [exorcize, conjure, or invoke; most probably, in context, the first] mrak nochi, navisaiushchii nad nami." Andrei Belyi, *Simvolizm: Kniga statei* (Moscow: Musaget, 1910), 448.

24. See in this volume Pamela Davidson, "The Muse and the Demon in the Poetry of Pushkin, Lermontov, and Blok."

25. *Cain: A Mystery,* in *The Poetical Works of Lord Byron,* introduced by Alexander Leighton (Edinburgh: W.P. Nimmo and Mitchell, 1889), 259. All references to *Cain* are given in the text from this edition by act, scene, and line number.

26. Alfred de Vigny, *Eloa,* in his *Oeuvres complètes,* ed. F. Baldensperger, Bibliothèque de la Pléiade, 2 vols. (Paris: Gallimard, 1948–50), 1:19. All further references to *Eloa* in the text and notes are to this edition.

27. See Lermontov, "Ia ne dlia angelov i raia ...," 1831), in which the poet declares "Kak demon moi, ia zla izbrannik" (first version: "s nebes izgnannik") and ends "Prochti, moiu s ego sud'boiu / Vospominaniem sravni / I ver' bezzhalostnoi dushoiu, / Chto my na svete s nim odni" (first version: "Chto my - s nim brat'ia, il' odni"). Lermontov, *Polnoe sobranie stikhotvorenii,* 1:227.

28. Lermontov, *Skazka dlia detei* (3.5), in Lermontov, *Polnoe sobranie stikhotvorenii,* 2:489–98(490). All references to this poem in the text and notes are given by stanza and line number.

29. D.E. Maksimov points out the ambivalence of the time factor in *Demon.* The Ossetians are armed with muskets, yet the poet writes of the buildings in which the events take place and the graves of the mortal characters as ruins of a far earlier age; see D.E. Maksimov, *Poeziia Lermontova* (Moscow and Leningrad: Nauka, 1964), 82 n.51.

30. See "[Zametki, plany i siuzhety]," in M.Iu. Lermontov, *Polnoe sobranie sochinenii*, ed. B.M. Eikhenbaum, 5 vols. (Moscow and Leningrad: Academia, 1935–37), 5:348, and the epigraph to *Heaven and Earth* in *The Poetical Works of Lord Byron*, 27: "And it came to pass ... that the sons of God saw the daughters of men that they were fair; and they took them wives of all which they chose" (Gen.6.1–2).

31. Vigny, *Eloa*, 1:20–29. The passage where, in answer to Tamara's timid enquiries about the torments of hell, the Demon replies that they are of no consequence since he will be with her there, is a brilliant adaptation of Vigny.

32. Lawrence Kelly, "Appendix 1: Byron and Lermontov," in his *Lermontov. Tragedy in the Caucasus* (London: Robin Clark, 1983), 191.

33. See also D.E. Maksimov who speaks of Cain *and* Lucifer as prototypes of Lermontov's Demon and writes: "V bibleiskom mife ob angele, kotoryi vosstal na Boga, – mife, legshem v osnovu proizvedenii Mil'tona, Bairona i Lermontova, – russkogo poeta interesuet ne samyi bunt angela, stavshego demonom, i ne ta kritika, kotoroi podvergaet Demon svoego nebesnogo vraga i ves' mir, a sud'ba Demona posle bunta." Maksimov, *Poeziia Lermontova*, 80.

34. In the edition I have used *bozhii* is spelt with a small "b," a Soviet practice which is particularly misleading in context. I have corrected on page.

35. See V. Solov'ev, "Lermontov" (1899), in his *Sobranie sochinenii*, ed. M.S. Solov'ev and G.A. Rachinskii, 8 vols. (St. Petersburg: Obshchestvennaia pol'za, 1901–1903), 7:387–404. For Blok's comments see D. Maksimov, "A. Blok i Vl. Solov'ev (Po materialam iz biblioteki Al. Bloka)," in *Tvorchestvo pisatelia i literaturnyi protsess: Mezhvuzovskii sbornik nauchnykh trudov*, ed. P.B. Kuprianovskii (Ivanovo: Ivanovskii gosudarstvennyi universitet, 1981), 180.

36. For Rozanov's thoughts on Lermontov's "antichristian" pantheism see V.V. Rozanov, "K lektsii g. Vl. Solov'eva," *Mir iskusstva*, 1900, no.9–10, 192–95(195). For his integration of Lermontov's Demon into the world of ancient myth, see his articles "Kontsy i nachala, 'bozhestvennoe' i 'demonicheskoe,' bogi i demony (Po povodu glavnogo siuzheta Lermontova" (1902), and "'Demon' Lermontova i ego drevnie rodichi" (1902), in V.V. Rozanov, *O pisatel'stve i pisateliakh*, ed. A.N. Nikoliukin (Moscow: Respublika, 1995), 78–95, 95–105, respectively. For further discussion of Rozanov's view of Lermontov, see in this volume Liza Dimbleby, "Rozanov and His Literary Demons."

37. Maksimov, *Poeziia Lermontova*, 82.

38. A. Camus, *Lettres à un ami allemand* (Paris: Gallimard, 1948), 72. The French writer disassociates his own metaphysical revolt from that of his Nazi friend as follows: "C'est que vous acceptiez légèrement de désespérer et que je n'y ai jamais consenti ... parce que vous avez fait de votre désespoir une ivresse, parce que vous vous en êtes delivrés en l'érigeant en principe, vous avez accepté de détruire les oeuvres de l'homme et de lutter contre lui pour achever sa misère essentielle."

39. See Karl Iung, *Libido, ego metamorfozy i simvoly*, ed. A.I. Belkin and M.M. Reshetnikov, Shedevry mirovoi nauki, no. 2 (St. Petersburg: Vostochno-evropeiskii institut psikhoanaliza, 1994), 114–15 (for a history of this Russian translation see the introduction by Boris Vysheslavtsev and Aleksandr Etkind). For the original, see Carl Jung, *Wandlungen und Symbole der Libido* (New York: Moffat and Yard, 1916); published in English as C.J. Jung, *Psychology of the Unconscious: A Study of the Transformations and Symbolisms of the Libido. A Contribution to the History of the Evolution of Thought*, trans. Beatrice M. Hinkle with an introduction by William McGuire (Princeton: Princeton University Press, 1991). Jung's point of departure is not Lermontov, but Byron's *Heaven and Earth*, one of the Russian poet's sources, and, of course, the biblical story of the sons of God and daughters of men.

40. Aleksandr Etkind, "Syn demona," in his *Sodom i Psikheia: Ocherki intellektual'noi istorii Serebrianogo veka* (Moscow: ITs-Garant, 1996), 72–75(72–73).

41. Maksimov, *Poeziia Lermontova*, 83–84, discusses this illuminatingly, pointing out that the Demon's isolation is of his own making, that the idea of just retribution is endemic to all variants of the poem, and that Tamara's reunion with the Demon on his terms would not have been a "happy ending," but perdition.

42. Vigny, *Eloa*, 1:31.

43. The absurdity stems from the similarity (accentuated by the repeated *abab* grammatical rhymes) of Lermontov's description of the guardian angel's retreat from Tamara's bedside when "grustnymi ochami / Na zhertvu bed^{} bedniuiu vzglianul / I medlenno, vzmakhnuv krylami, / V efire neba potonul" (2:9.585–88) and his triumphant ascension bearing her rescued soul when "strogimi ochami / Na iskusitelia vzglianul / I, radostno vzmakhnuv krylami, / V siian'e neba potonul" (2:16.1051–54).

44. The seminal influence of *Skazka dlia detei* in this direction has been followed up by Tomas Venclova, "K demonologii russkogo simvolizma," in *Christianity and the Eastern Slavs*, vol.3, *Russian Literature in Modern Times*, ed. Boris Gasparov and others, California Slavic Studies, no.18 (Berkeley: University of California Press, 1995), 134–60. This compelling study demonstrates symbolist interest in the dust-demons and the entropic Ahriman, a particularly virulent negative figure for the Devil, very present to the imagination of twentieth-century writers from the symbolists onward. For the text of Briusov's poem "Demony pyli" (1899), discussed by Venclova in detail, see Valerii Briusov, *Sobranie sochinenii v semi tomakh*, ed. P.G. Antokol'skii and others, 7 vols. (Moscow: Khudozhestvennaia literatura, 1973–75), 1:209.

45. Blok, *Sobranie sochinenii*, 5:691.

46. Blok, in his 1906 defence of Lermontov from the scholar N. Kotliarevsky, "Pedant o poete," writes: "Lermontov – pisatel', kotoromu ne poschastlivilos' ni v kolichestve monografii, ni v istinnoi liubvi potomstva. ... Tol'ko literatura poslednikh let mnogimi potokami svoimi stremitsia opiat' k Lermontovu kak k istochniku; ego chtut i poryvisto, i goriacho, i bezmolvno, i trepetno." Blok, *Sobranie sochinenii*, 5:25. D.S. Merezhkovsky, three years later, could still ask: "Pochemu priblizilsia k nam Lermontov? Pochemu vdrug zakhotelos' o nem govorit'?" D.S. Merezhkovskii, "M.Iu. Lermontov. Poet sverkhchelovechestva," in his *Izbrannoe* (Kishinev: Literatura Artistika, 1989), 474.

47. See M.A. Beketova, *Vospominaniia ob Aleksandre Bloke*, comp. V.P. Enisherlov and S.S. Lesnevskii (Moscow: Izdatel'stvo Pravda, 1990), 29–30. A. Blok, as a grown man, considered Rubinshtein's opera "smes' beskonechnoi glubiny s beskonechnoi poshlost'iu." See his note of 3 April 1919 in Aleksandr Blok, *Zapisnye knizhki*, ed. V.N. Orlov, A.A. Surkov, and K.I. Chukovskii (Moscow: Izdatel'stvo khudozhestvennaia literatura, 1965), 454–55.

48. See M.A. Vrubel', Letter to his sister Aniuta of 2 February 1875, in *Vrubel': Perepiska. Vospominaniia o khudozhnike*, comp. E.P. Gomberg-Verzhbinskaia, Iu.N. Podkopaeva, and Iu.V. Novikov, 2d ed. (Leningrad: Iskusstvo, 1976), 32.

49. N.A. Prakhov, "Mikhail Aleksandrovich Vrubel'," in *Vrubel'*, comp. Gomberg-Verzhbinskaia, 195. The words are Prakhov's paraphrase of the artist's views.

50. Vrubel illustrated not only *Demon* but also some lyric poems, short stories, and *Geroi nashego vremeni* for the half-centenary edition of Lermontov's works, M.Iu. Lermontov, *Sochineniia* (Moscow: Tovarishchestvo I.N. Kushnerova, 1891).

51. On Vrubel and Shaliapin see K.A. Korovin, "Shaliapin i Vrubel'," in *K.A. Korovin vspominaet*, comp. I.S. Zil'bershtein and V.A. Samkov (Moscow: Khudozhestvennaia literatura, 1971), reprinted under the general title "M.A. Vrubel'," in *Vrubel'*, comp. Gomberg-Verzhbinskaia, esp. 242–44. The story of

Shaliapin's performance in January 1904 is well retold in P.K. Suzdalev, *Vrubel' i Lermontov* (Moscow: Izobrazitel'noe iskusstvo, 1980), 196–200. For details of the opera and various stagings, see A. Gozenpud, *Kratkii opernyi slovar'*, 2d ed. (Kiev: Muzykal'naia Ukraina, 1989), 90.

52. See M.A. Vrubel', Letter to his sister-in-law Ekaterina Ivanovna Ge of [1902], in *Vrubel'*, comp. Gomberg-Verzhbinskaia, 95.

53. See Aage A. Hansen-Löve, *Der russische Symbolismus: System und Entfaltung der poetischen Motive*, vol.1, *Diabolischer Symbolismus* (Vienna: Verlag der Österreichischen Akademie der Wissenschaften, 1989), 71. Hansen-Löve posits three phases in the development of symbolism: the "diabolic," the "religious" or "theurgic," and the "grotesque" or "surreal." The "diabolic" 1890s are seen as so solipsistic and negative that it becomes a matter of self-preservation for the artist, no longer capable like "the Satanist of black romanticism" of communicating through images, to seek a more positive direction through "magic-mythical symbolism" (i.e. in the language of this article to recodify his/her ideas in accordance with the world model or, in Hansen-Löve's parlance, to reveal a mythical "Urtext"). Though I personally consider the attempt to establish a precise periodization of the "three phases" somewhat stultifying, since diabolical, mythopoetic, and grotesque often in fact coexist and jostle in the work of a single artist or group, there is a similar thought relating to myth as a way out of solipsism and towards the re-establishment of a common poetic language based on mutually acceptable images drawn from the "collective unconscious" elaborated, in more empirical language, in my *History of Russian Symbolism* (Cambridge: Cambridge University Press, 1994), 228–29, 241–42.

54. G. Tovstonogov, "Lermontovskii Demon kist'iu Vrubelia," *Literaturnaia gazeta*, 1 January 1985, no.1(5015), 7.

55. See for example E.I. Ge, "Poslednie gody zhizni Vrubelia," in *Vrubel'*, comp. Gomberg-Verzhbinskaia, 276. Writing of Vrubel's attempts to explain his *Demon Cast Down* in 1902, she comments: "Eto bylo novo, chto on ob"iasnial soderzhanie svoei kartiny, prezhde on nakhodil, chto, gonias' za soderzhaniem, khudozhnik portit svoe proizvedenie, tak kak forma – eto vse."

56. With these words (cited in *Vrubel'*, comp. Gomberg-Verzhbinskaia, 154) Anna Aleksandrovna (Aniuta) Vrubel ends her reminiscences of the brother she helped throughout his life and visited daily for long periods of his blindness in the years 1906–10.

57. M.A. Vrubel', Letter to A.A. Vrubel' of April 1883, in *Vrubel'*, comp. Gomberg-Verzhbinskaia, 38.

58. Suzdalev, *Vrubel' i Lermontov*.

59. See P.K. Suzdalev, *Vrubel'* (Moscow: Sovetskii khudozhnik, 1991), 146.

60. *Hamlet*, 2.2, in William Shakespeare, *The Complete Works*, ed. Peter Alexander (London and Glasgow: Collins, 1951), 1043.

61. For Lebiadkin's description of himself as an "infusoria," only distinguishable from the multitude of his fellows under a microscope, see F.M. Dostoevskii, *Besy* (part 1, chap.4:2), in his *Polnoe sobranie sochinenii v tridtsati tomakh*, ed. V.G. Bazanov and others, 30 vols. (Leningrad: Nauka, 1972–90), 10:106. For Bazarov's much quoted "Priroda ne khram, a masterskaia, i chelovek v nei rabotnik," see I.S. Turgenev, *Ottsy i deti* (chap.9), in his *Sobranie sochinenii v desiati tomakh*, 10 vols. (Moscow: Gosudarstvennoe izdatel'stvo khudozhestvennoi literatury, 1961–62), 3:154.

62. See Prakhov, "Mikhail Aleksandrovich Vrubel'," 173–75.

63. There is some dispute, not particularly relevant to this paper, as to whether the frescoes Vrubel worked on in the Kirillov Church were the work of itinerant Greek or local Russian masters. See V.N. Lazarev, *Drevnerusskie mozaiki i freski XI-XV vv.* (Moscow: Iskusstvo, 1973), 32.

64. The work was undertaken by N.I. Murashko and pupils from his art school in Kiev but, prompted by Prakhov, Murashko was only too glad to delegate to the young and energetic Vrubel.

65. Prakhov, "Mikhail Aleksandrovich Vrubel'," 178. The method of "restoration" may sound barbarous to the modern ear, but at the time it was usual to over-paint more or less in the style of the original. The work, originally delegated to A.V. Prakhov by the Dean of the Cathedral, was not considered prestigious for an academy-trained artist.

66. According to his first biographer A.P. Ivanov, Vrubel also found inspiration in the work of the Spanish artist Fortuni (1838–74) who used blobs and flecks of colour – before the elaboration of pointillisme; A.P. Ivanov, *Vrubel': Biograficheskii ocherk* (St. Petersburg, 1911), 12, cited in *Vrubel'*, comp. Gomberg-Verzhbinskaia, 310 n.6. Neither should it be forgotten that his "pre-cubist" technique of drawing a face as a series of planes which are gradually smoothed out (more or less as desired) by decreasing the module was acquired at the Academy from Professor Chistiakov. Church painting was, however, decisive. See also the description of Vrubel in his studio at the Vladimir Cathedral with what appeared to be a scattering of precious stones bordered by molten gold round his feet: "akvareli na obryvkakh bumagi, zapechatlennye khudozhestvennye zamysly chudesnoi ornamentiki," in G.G. Burdanov, "M.A. Vrubel'," in *Vrubel'*, comp. Gomberg-Verzhbinskaia, 169.

67. See Suzdalev, *Vrubel'*, 125.

68. M.A. Vrubel', Letter to his sister Aniuta of November 1887, in *Vrubel'*, comp. Gomberg-Verzhbinskaia, 50.

69. Gomberg-Verzhbinskaia, comp., *Vrubel'*, 38.

70. M.A. Vrubel', Letter to his sister Aniuta of 26 February/10 March 1885, in *Vrubel'*, comp. Gomberg-Verzhbinskaia, 46.

71. A.M. Vrubel', Letter to his daughter Aniuta of 22 October 1885, quoting a recent letter from his son in which the *Tetralogiia* is said to be already begun, in *Vrubel'*, comp. Gomberg-Verzhbinskaia, 116.

72. See E.P. Ivanov's note of 14 March 1905, in "Vospominaniia i zapisi Evgeniia Ivanova ob Aleksandre Bloke," ed. E.P. Gomberg and D.E. Maksimov, in *Blokovskii sbornik* (Tartu: Tartuskii gosudarstvennyi universitet, 1964), 392. For an English translation of this passage and illustrations, see Avril Pyman, *The Life of Aleksandr Blok*, vol.1, *The Distant Thunder 1880–1908* (Oxford: Oxford University Press, 1979), 193, and opposite 208 for the juxtaposition of a detail of a picture of Christ in the grave and a ceramic head of the Demon. Both were reproduced in the same issue of *Mir iskusstva* and could well have caught Ivanov's eye, although there are other examples of paintings and drawings of the Demon which he might have had in mind. In an unpublished article of 1906, "Demon i Tserkov'," quoted in L.A. Il'iunina, "A. Blok i E. Ivanov v gody pervoi russkoi revoliutsii (K voprosu o genezise obraza Khrista v poeme 'Dvenadtsat'")," *Uchenye zapiski Tartuskogo gosudarstvennogo universiteta* 881, *A. Blok i russkii simvolizm: Problemy teksta i zhanra. Blokovskii sbornik X* (Tartu: Tartuskii gosudarstvennyi universitet, 1990), 30–31 n.12, Ivanov pursues the idea that the intelligentsia, and more particularly the revolutionary intelligentsia, cannot renounce the Demon, whom they perceive as a spirit of knowledge and freedom who suffers from his separation from God. Only when the Church of the true Christ descends lovingly into hell will it reemerge with the Demon ("i iavitsia Tserkov' Khrista istinnogo[,] tserkov' vo ad soshedshaia i s Demonom iz ada isshedshaia," 31). We do not have Blok's reaction to these specific articles but he did write to Ivanov in 1910 that, although he was almost in agreement with his friend's articles of that time, there was something fundamentally unconvincing for him about them: "Vse blizko i pochti soglasen, no cho-to v korne dlia menia neubeditel'noe (tut chto-to obshchee s

Merezhkovskim)." A. Blok, Letter to E.P. Ivanov of 29 August 1910, in *Pis'ma Al. Bloka k E.P. Ivanovu*, ed. T.S. Vol'pe (Moscow and Leningrad: Izdatel'stvo Akademii nauk SSSR, 1936), 83.

73. S.P. Iaremich, *Mikhail Aleksandrovich Vrubel': Zhizn' i tvorchestvo* (Moscow: n.p., [1911]), 69–70, 181, cited in *Vrubel'*, comp. Gomberg-Verzhbinskaia, 312–13.

74. A.M. Vrubel', Letter to his daughter Aniuta of 11 September 1886, in *Vrubel'*, comp. Gomberg-Verzhbinskaia, 118.

75. V. Dedlov, "S vystavok," *Nedelia* 35 (1896), cited in *Vrubel'*, comp. Gomberg-Verzhbinskaia, 313.

76. For Vrubel's work in the Cathedral of Saint Vladimir see Burdanov, "M.A. Vrubel'," 169–70, and Prakhov, "Mikhail Aleksandrovich Vrubel'," 171–223.

77. M.A. Vrubel', Letter to his sister Aniuta of [December 1887], in *Vrubel'*, comp. Gomberg-Verzhbinskaia, 50.

78. M.A. Vrubel', Letter to his sister Aniuta of 7 June [1887], in *Vrubel'*, comp. Gomberg-Verzhbinskaia, 49.

79. Iaremich, *Mikhail Aleksandrovich Vrubel'*, 55, cited in Suzdalev, *Vrubel'*, 137.

80. M.A. Vrubel', Letter to his sister Aniuta of 22 May [1890], in *Vrubel'*, comp. Gomberg-Verzhbinskaia, 55–56.

81. See Suzdalev, *Vrubel'*, 72.

82. M.A. Vrubel', Letter to N.A. Rimskii-Korsakov of December 1898, cited in Suzdalev, *Vrubel' i Lermontov*, 169. Although Vrubel writes that he is "preparing the Demon," nothing much seems to have materialized for the next two years.

83. N.I. Zabela-Vrubel', Letter to Rimskii-Korsakov of 24 September 1901, cited in Suzdalev, *Vrubel' i Lermontov*, 172, from archive source (Otdel rukopisei GPB imeni M.E. Saltykova-Shchedrina).

84. See Aline Isdebsky-Pritchard, "Art for Philosophy's Sake: Vrubel against 'the Herd'," in *Nietzsche in Russia*, ed. Bernice Glatzer Rosenthal (Princeton: Princeton University Press, 1986), 219–48(233).

85. See Suzdalev, *Vrubel' i Lermontov*, 90. I do not wish to imply that either Suzdalev or Isdebsky-Pritchard are wrong on all points: there is plenty of evidence for Vrubel's interest in Kant and Schopenhauer elsewhere, and it is unthinkable he should not have read *some* Nietzsche. Neither Suzdalev, nor any other authority I have found, however, produces hard evidence of this, and we should not necessarily interpret Vrubel's ongoing anti-Tolstoi rather than antichristian polemic with the Ge family (his in-laws) in terms of a "Nietzsche-Tolstoi polarity" (Isdebsky-Pritchard, "Art for Philosophy's Sake," 233). The postscript to his letter to Ekaterina Ge of [1902], in *Vrubel'*, comp. Gomberg-Verzhbinskaia, 276, which is foregrounded in "Art for Philosophy's Sake," 228, is surely best understood in the context of this polemic and of the artist's increasingly melagomaniac resentment of his colleagues' failure to appreciate *The Demon Cast Down*. Moreover, the notes to the letter in *Vrubel'*, comp. Gomberg-Verzhbinskaia, 366, assume that the "German genius" to whom Vrubel refers in the same letter is not Nietzsche (as supposed in "Art for Philosophy's Sake," 224–25) but Kant, a likely assumption in view of Vrubel's use, here and elsewhere, of what may well be idiosyncratically translated Kantian terms such as *neobkhodimost'* (necessity) for "the imperative" and *vozmozhnost'* (possibility) for "the hypothetical."

86. All the artists of *Mir iskusstva*, according to A. Benois, considered themselves to some extent "supermen" and it was in this journal that Vladimir Solov'ev first published his "Ideia sverkhcheloveka" (*Mir iskusstva*, 1899, no.9, 87–91), suggesting that "the way of the superman" might help to rediscover the forgotten way of *imitatio Christi*.

87. V. Solov'ev, "Lermontov" (1899), 7:387, sees the poet as the "priamoi rodonachal'nik" of the mood called "nitssheanstvo." Merezhkovsky's essay

"M.Iu. Lermontov. Poet sverkhchelovechestva" (1909) would have come too late to affect Vrubel's Demon, and even A.P. Nalimov, "Lermontov i Nitche: 1841–1901," *Literaturnoe obozrenie*, 1902, no.1, 43–45, could be assumed to have influenced only the reception, not the conception of *The Demon Cast Down*. See also Blok's note to Lermontov's poem "K" ("My sluchaino svedeny sud'boiu ..."), in which he approves Solov'ev's identification of this poem as proof that Lermontov was a precursor of Nietzsche; Aleksandr Blok, *Sobranie sochinenii*, 12 vols. (Leningrad: Izdatel'stvo pisatelei v Leningrade, 1932–36), 11:407.

88. See E.I. Ge's record of Vrubel's words to her about his intent in *The Demon Cast Down*, in her "Poslednie gody zhizni Vrubelia," in *Vrubel'*, comp. Gomberg-Verzhbinskaia, 276.

89. Suzdalev, *Vrubel' i Lermontov*, 181–82.

90. Letter to B.K. Ianovskii of 22 November 1901, cited in Suzdalev, *Vrubel' i Lermontov*, 173–75, from archive source.

91. Whether this is a Dionysian figure or inspired by Vigny (for which I am aware of no evidence beyond the textual), I do not know. Lermontov provides no visual description of the Demon but the French poet's lounging young man, his black hair crowned or burdened by a golden crown blazing with mystic fires, clad in opalescent purple, his body bejeweled, wings folded, eyes cast down, and waving a golden sceptre bears a remarkable resemblance to versions of Vrubel's *The Demon Cast Down*, particularly the 1901 sketch described in the text (reproduced in Suzdalev, *Vrubel' i Lermontov*, 177, plate 62).

92. See Suzdalev, *Vrubel' i Lermontov*, 190–222, esp. 220, for an account of the polemics surrounding this picture (the exact title of which is also under dispute). For a possible source for Vrubel's *Shestikrylyi serafim (Azrail)* in Lermontov's poetry, see S. Durylin, "Vrubel' i Lermontov," in *Literaturnoe nasledstvo*, vol.45–46, *M.Iu. Lermontov II* (Moscow: Izdatel'stvo Akademii nauk SSSR, 1948), 541–622(597–98).

93. D.E. Maksimov, "O mifopoeticheskom nachale," 7.

94. See V.M. Papernyi, "Blok i Nitsshe," in *Uchenye zapiski Tartuskogo gosudarstvennogo universiteta* 491 (1979):88. Papernyi here rightly refers the reader to Z.G. Mints, "Funktsiia reministsentsii v poetike A. Bloka," in *Uchenye zapiski Tartuskogo gosudarstvennogo universiteta* 308, *Trudy po znakovym sistemam* 6 (1973):387–417.

95. See Pyman, *The Life of Aleksandr Blok*, 1:61–62 esp. and chap.3, "Paradise Lost."

96. Blok, "Uvizhu ia, kak budet pogibat' ..." (26 June 1900), 1:51; text revised in February 1914 for first publication in 1914.

97. See Andrei Belyi, Letter to A.A. Blok of 4 January 1903, in *Aleksandr Blok i Andrei Belyi. Perepiska*, ed. V.N. Orlov (Moscow: Izdanie Gosudarstvennogo literaturnogo muzeia, 1940), 7.

98. Epigraph from Lermontov's "Duma" (1838) to Blok's "Kogda tolpa vokrug kumiram rukopleshchet ...," 23 February 1899, 1:18, in which, unable to recapture the "holy fire" of youth, the (still extremely youthful) poet declares a hostile indifference to "the crowd."

99. Blok, "Ia vyshel. Medlenno skhodili ..." (25 January 1901), 1:75, the opening poem of the first section of *Stikhi o Prekrasnoi Dame*.

100. Blok, "Zdes' noch' mertva. Slova moi diki ..." (9 January 1903), 1:259, in the cycle "Rasput'ia." A few details of the punctuation and layout of this poem have been amended to match the text given in the recent edition: A.A. Blok, *Polnoe sobranie sochinenii i pisem v dvadtsati tomakh*, ed. A.L. Grishunin and others (Moscow: Nauka, 1997–), 1:144–45.

101. Sergei Solov'ev commented to Blok in an undated letter written after 10 November 1903: "Bugaev ochen' tonko zametil, chto v uzhasakh u tebia est' skhodstvo s Vrubelem." Blok, *Sobranie sochinenii*, 8:567 n.3 to letter 46.

102. See Blok, Letter to S.M. Solov'ev of 20 December 1903, 8:78–79. Further to the dagger symbol: among Vrubel's last pictures are the seraph Azrael (*Shestikrylyi serafim [Azrail]*, 1904) (incidentally the subject of an early dramatic version of *Demon* by Lermontov) and the angel of the vision of Ezekiel (*Videnie proroka Iezekiilia*, 1906) who hold sharp daggers or swords, as does the six-winged seraph in Pushkin's "Prorok." Briusov's "Kinzhal" (1903), a direct response to Lermontov's poem "Poet" (1838), bears the epigraph "Il' nikogda na golos mshchen'ia / Iz zolotykh nozhon ne vyrvesh' svoi klinok ...," and is a celebration of the poet's readiness to respond to outward events.

103. Blok, "Ty u kamina, skloniv sediny ..." (1 November 1903), 1:298, in the cycle "Rasput'ia."

104. Blok, "Poeziia zagovorov i zaklinanii" (October 1906), 5:36–65(37).

105. Note of 18 January 1906, in Blok, *Zapisnye knizhki*, 72–73.

106. See V. Ivanov, Letter to A. Blok of 12 November 1908, in N.V. Kotrelev, "Iz perepiski Aleksandra Bloka s Viach. Ivanovym," *Izvestiia Akademii nauk SSSR*, Seriia literatury i iazyka, 41, no.2 (1982):167–68.

107. Cf. N.Iu. Griakalova, "O fol'klornykh istokakh poeticheskoi obraznosti Bloka," in *Aleksandr Blok: Issledovaniia i materialy*, ed. Iu.K. Gerasimov, K.N. Grigor'ian, and F.Ia. Priima (Leningrad: Nauka, 1987), 58–68.

108. Two detailed studies of Blok's use of colour are L. Krasnova's chapter "Simvolika sveta," in her *Poetika Aleksandra Bloka: Ocherki* (L'vov: Izdatel'stvo L'vovskogo universiteta, 1973), 136–76, and Johanne Peters, *Farbe und Licht: Symbolik bei Aleksandr Blok*, Slavistische Beiträge, no.144 (Munich: Verlag Otto Sagner, 1981). It is interesting that, of all colours, lilac, most closely associated by Blok with Vrubel's Demon, appears exclusively in the period 1904–1910, the period of the Antithesis (Peters, *Farbe und Licht*, 195–205). "Lilac," writes Peters, "is the symbol-colour for a new kind of poetry that is no longer concentrated one way on the 'positive' values (the 'high' transcendence) but on 'evil' (the 'low' transcendence) in Baudelaire's sense ... at the same time, like all Blok's symbols, it is ambivalent" (205).

109. N. Korzhavin, "Igra s d'iavolom (Po povodu stikhotvoreniia Aleksandra Bloka 'K Muze')," *Grani* 95 (1975): 76–107; [Petrogradskii sviashchennik], "O Bloke," *Put'* 26 (1931):86–108; reprinted and attributed to P. Florenskii in *Vestnik russkogo khristianskogo dvizheniia* 114 (1974):169–92; see also A. Paiman, "Tvorchestvo Aleksandra Bloka v otsenke russkikh religioznykh myslitelei 20–30–kh godov," in *Blokovskii sbornik XII* (Tartu: Izdatel'stvo TOO "ITs-Garant," 1993), 54–70.

110. Blok, *Zapisnye knizhki*, 73.

111. Blok, "Tam neba osvetlennyi krai..." (September 1910), 3:264, in the cycle "Rodina."

112. Blok, "Kak rastet trevoga k nochi!..." (30 December 1913), 3:45, in the cycle "Strashnyi mir."

113. On Blok and the *Philokalia*, see Pyman, *The Life of Aleksandr Blok*, 2:233, and in this collection, Davidson, "The Muse and the Demon."

114. Blok, "Iz 'Zapiski o Dvenadtsati'" (1 April 1920), 3:474.

115. Aleksandr Blok, *Sobranie sochinenii*, 12 vols. (Leningrad: Izdatel'stvo pisatelei v Leningrade, 1932–36), 11:421.

116. D.M. Magomedova in "Blok i Voloshin (Dve interpretatsii mifa o besovstve)," in *Uchenye zapiski Tartuskogo universiteta* 917, *Blokovskii sbornik XI* (Tartu: Tartu Ülikool, 1990), 39–49, makes a vivid case for the "demonic" inspiration of *Dvenadtsat'*, to which in the context of this paper we might add that the poem begins with the same dichotomy we observed in Lermontov's *Demon*, a "Demon's eye view" of "God's earth," and also the clearly diabolical associations of the dog and of the refrain "blizok vrag."

117. Losev, *Mifologiia grekov i rimlian*, 60.
118. K.G. Isupov, "Istorizm Bloka i simvolistskaia mifologiia istorii (Vvedenie v problemu)," in *Aleksandr Blok: Issledovaniia i materialy*, ed. Iu.K. Gerasimov, N.Iu. Griakalova, and A.V. Lavrov (Leningrad: Nauka, 1991), 3–21(4).
119. See Mints, "O nekotorykh 'neomifologicheskikh' tekstakh," 118.
120. Blok, "O lirike" (June–July 1907), 5:131.
121. From the prayer of Saint Basil the Great, fifth in the order of Orthodox morning prayers. The context is as follows: "I darui nam bodrennym serdtsem i trezvennoiu mysliiu vsiu nastoiashchego zhitiia noch' proiti, ozhidaiushchym prishestviia svetlago i iavlennago dne Edinorodnogo Tvoego Syna, Gospoda i Boga i Spasa nashego Iisusa Khrista."
122. Blok, "Tvari vesennie" (19 February 1905), 2:13, in the cycle "Puzyri zemli."

Chapter 11

The Demonomania of Sorcerers: Satanism in the Russian Symbolist Novel

Adam Weiner

The Russian symbolists' fascination with the Devil, which is probably unsurpassed in the history of Russian literature, found expression in the visual arts as well as in belles-lettres, including literary criticism, poetry, drama, the short story, and the novel.[1] The last is of particular interest as it provided an ideal forum for extended debate on the religious and artistic dimensions of "the Devil's mysterious power," as the narrator of Briusov's *The Fiery Angel* (*Ognennyi angel*) puts it in the insinuatingly titled preface "Amico Lectori."[2] Dmitrii Merezhkovsky published his trilogy of novels *Christ and Antichrist* (*Khristos i antikhrist*) from 1895 to 1904.[3] Fedor Sologub's novel *The Petty Demon* (*Melkii bes*) came out in book form in 1907, Valerii Briusov's *The Fiery Angel* in 1908, Andrei Bely's novels *The Silver Dove* (*Serebrianyi golub'*) in 1910 and *Petersburg* (*Peterburg*) in 1916. Early on in the century, the Devil quickly became such a fashionable fixation with the intellectual and cultural élite that in May of 1906 the symbolist journal *Zolotoe runo* announced its intention of launching 1907 with an issue devoted to "artistic, poetic, and religious-philosophical conceptions" of the Devil; there was to be a contest for the best works on the demonic theme. As promised, the January 1907 issue contained drawings of the Devil by Mstislav Dobuzhinsky and others, several articles, including one by Sologub, some poetry, and two tales – one by Mikhail Kuzmin and Aleksei Remizov's "The Little Devil" (Chertik).[4]

It was a time when many artists, and novelists in particular, were testing what Briusov called "the terrible bond that exists between the life of humans and the life of demons."[5] Sologub's world in *The Petty Demon* is perforated with portholes leading to hell, so that the fiends can scurry through to invade the human sphere. The infernal and human worlds also interpenetrate in Bely's *Petersburg*, whose devil (named Shishnarfne) explains to the hero (Dudkin) that Petersburg "belongs to the country of the world beyond the grave": from there demons and shades assail and possess living Russia.[6] Like Peredonov, the haunted protagonist of *The Petty Demon*, the symbolist novelist has eyes that "wander, never resting on objects, as if he forever wanted to gaze past them, to the other side of the objective world, and he were looking for some kind of apertures."[7] This desire to peer into the fissures connecting the mortal world to the immortal, can become an irresistible temptation, fraught both with artistic promise and moral danger. And though the examples of Blake, Byron, and Baudelaire are sufficient to suggest that this temptation is nothing new with Russian symbolists, the works of the latter, appearing in the shadow of Nietzsche, also reflect a tumultuous redefinition of ethical norms that sets them apart from earlier forms of literary demonism. The Devil's mysterious power over Russian symbolism is such that the authorial personae, whether protagonist, narrator, or implied author,[8] are subject to the very demonism that is, by no simple coincidence, a central theme in three such exemplary symbolist novels as Merezhkovsky's *Christ and Antichrist*, Briusov's *The Fiery Angel*, and Sologub's *The Created Legend* (*Tvorimaia legenda*, 1914).[9]

I hope to demonstrate an increasingly disorientating use of narrative point of view on the demonic, from the authorial ambivalence of Merezhkovsky, to the narratorial connivance of Briusov, to the demonically compromised narrative structure of Sologub. The first of these works chronologically, *Christ and Antichrist*, is also the most congruous in its use of the traditional devices of narrative fiction. This trilogy of historical novels is consistently plotted in terms of setting and action, which are anchored in the biography of the three historical figures it interprets. It is also cogently narrated, the narrator being a usually silent reflector of the perceptions of the protagonists.[10] Merezhkovsky's novel only becomes disorientating in its ethically ambivalent characters and in its implied author, whose viewpoint is elusive and unsettled, despite his consistent use of symbolism.[11] Written a few years after the completion of *Christ and Antichrist*, Briusov's *The Fiery Angel* is already somewhat less stable in terms of plot, for, though it too is a kind of historical novel, its central characters are no longer historical figures with known biographies, but invented personae whose viewpoint is altogether preoccupied by what they perceive as their encounters with supernatural powers. The reader, moreover, cannot determine whether the fantastic events narrated belong to the realm of the real or imagined within the novel's world. If the former, then the narrator himself is a Satanist, relating his tale in a state of possession and is thus at best an unreliable source of information. The implied author manages the narrative's symbolism consistently, but, as I will argue, may implicate himself in the demonism of his plot and narration. *The Created Legend*, completed several years later, is remarkably unstable in almost all respects: its setting shifts in an unsettling manner from prosaic Russian provincial scenes of 1905, to the hero Trirodov's magical forest, to the heroine Ortruda's strange land, to the imaginary solar system of Mair; the action, too, bounces jarringly from the mundane to the marvellous; the characterization turns accepted morality on its head in its promotion of heroes who are egotistical, perverse, murderous, and diabolical. An inconsistent use of the novel's fundamental symbols destabilizes the implied author, who identifies capriciously with the gods and devils of the novel's cosmos.

Several factors help explain this chronological decay into narrative disorder: modernism's intensifying fragmentation of the more monolithic world-view of the realist novel; a certain interplay among the novels, whose authors were vying with one other for structural novelty; the progress of the revolutionary movement, which was undermining the institutions of Russian life. Nor should one discount the progressively corruptive influence of symbolism's twenty-year obsession with the demonic, with the way the Devil struggles against creation, chiefly by transforming order into chaos, unity into opposition. The old moral categories are no longer productive in the demonic novels considered here, so that traditional understandings of evil – as negation, deception, destruction, the absence of good – provide little illumination. If anything, evil here reveals itself to be the stagnation of received norms of behaviour, thought, and morality, while good is the destruction of that old world order. As the desire to find new values to live by grew ever more pervasive in Russian society, evil grew less relevant as an ethical condition, and demonism, understood as the destruction of order, and, alternatively, as the re-creation of a new order, became the productive term.[12] The hesitation over just how far either brand of demonism should be allowed to go helps to generate all of the ambivalence, duality, and dualism that compromise the narrative viewpoint in the novels I will discuss.[13]

Merezhkovsky: *The Gods Resurrected (Leonardo da Vinci)*

In *Christ and Antichrist* Merezhkovsky interprets his central idea of life's duality as a war between God and the Devil, Christianity and paganism, waged throughout the ages ensuing after the death of Christ. The three volumes of *Christ and Antichrist* detail three separate battles of this war, the arenas of which are alternately politics and art. The first and third volumes, *The Death of the Gods (Julian the Apostate)* and *Antichrist (Peter and Aleksei)*, describe the way the West's great emperors (the Roman emperor Julian and Russia's Peter the Great) have influenced Christianity during periods of history the author considers transitional – Julian's ill-starred attempt to halt Christianity's advance in a return to paganism, and Peter's efforts to reform the Russian Orthodox Church, which he would bring under the heel of the state. Following Dostoevsky's understanding of Antichrist as a military, secular, imperial power disguised as the Christian Church, Merezhkovsky suggests that Julian and Peter are manifestations or precursors of Antichrist. With characteristic caprice, however, he also presents plenty of evidence to the contrary, namely that they were essentially well-meaning rulers who were misunderstood by history. And, as if this framework were insufficiently nebulous, Merezhkovsky provides his readers with reason to believe that the great duality of Julian's paganism and the Christianity against which he fights might be synthesized into a new religion of flesh and spirit that would finally come to fruition in the mystical sectarianism and Old Belief of Merezhkovsky's day.[14] This is a form of second- or third-guessing on the author's part that constantly muddles the central idea and threatens to bring down the opposition on which the trilogy rests.

The middle volume, *The Gods Resurrected (Leonardo da Vinci)*, depicts an historical setting – the Italian Renaissance – where political powers are in relative decline, so that art ascends to take their place as the battleground in the continuing war of good and evil. Merezhkovsky's hero is the spokesman of this creative rebirth, where artists, through their awesome command of the beautiful, assume the power to sway the beholder towards Christ or Antichrist. Despite the trilogy's obvious interest in the past, it has a clear bearing on Merezhkovsky's own artistic age. The last volume, *Antichrist*, ends upon Aleksei's prophecy that the tsar, by daring to lay hands on his own son, has put a curse on future Russian tsars which will lead to their doom. It is appropriate, then, that in Merezhkovsky's day – the modern era of artistic efflorescence and political stagnation which produced the trilogy – art, not politics (the tsars really had fallen into fatal decline), is once again the battleground where Christ encounters

Antichrist. Therefore it is the middle volume of the trilogy, *The Gods Resurrected,* that most directly poses the question of art's role in the moral life of mankind – and particularly of the novel's role, since the work that raises this issue is itself a novel.[15] Let us consider, then, what *The Gods Resurrected* has to say about the ethics of art.

The novel's opening scene is the fifteenth-century excavation of an ancient Greek statue of Aphrodite (the "White She-Devil" – presumably the same idol Julian had worshipped in the previous volume).[16] Not only the unearthing of pagan idols, but the incipient Renaissance aesthetic, with its return to classical forms, has been stirring unrest in the simple folk of Milan. Even Leonardo's brother, Antonio da Vinci, grumbles against the new art: "Today's sculptors and painters serve Moloch, that is the Devil. They are making God's church into a temple for Satan. In their icons, in the guise of martyrs and saints, they depict unclean gods, before whom they bow down."[17] As to the rumours circulating about his brother Leonardo, Antonio confirms them with remarkable aplomb: "Leonardo is a heretic and a godless heathen. His mind is darkened by Satanic pride. By dint of mathematics and black magic he would penetrate nature's secrets" (1:315). The question of whether Leonardo's art and mechanics are indeed a form of black magic intended to serve the Devil is debated hotly throughout the novel, mostly by Leonardo's two apprentices, Cesari, who answers the question in a ringing affirmative, and the bewildered Giovanni, who feels he could not leave Leonardo's side, even if staying there "threatened him with eternal perdition, even if he became convinced that Leonardo really were the servant of Antichrist" (1:340). Cesari, who constantly tries to demonstrate the evil of Leonardo's art, exposes a frightening contradiction in his master's words about painting. When Leonardo expounds to his apprentices the (rather naive) notion that, in depicting God's beautiful truth and the Devil's ugly lie, the artist must observe "the same difference as between dark and light," Cesari reminds him of another of his recent aesthetic teachings, that "between dark and light there is something middling, equally belonging to the one and the other" (1:451). Cesari objects, "Really, master, your comparison spawns a great temptation in my mind, for the artist who seeks the secret of captivating beauty in the mixing of shade and light may well ask whether truth and lie combine in the same way" (1:452). At first taken aback and angered by Cesari's objection, Leonardo quickly overcomes his confusion and ends the dispute with a laugh, saying "Tempt me not. Get thee behind me, Satan," a response that satisfies neither his students nor, I suspect, most readers with regards to Leonardo's art ethics. In fact, we may well wonder at such moments whether the same "great temptation" occurred to Merezhkovsky, whether, in its chiaroscuro of dualities and second thoughts, a novel like *Christ and Antichrist* does not mix truth and lie for aesthetic effects.

Cesari soon finds an opportunity to develop his thoughts on the mixing of lie with truth (dark with light, evil with good), which he has identified as Leonardo's terrible genius. When Cesari and Giovanni break into Leonardo's study to rifle through his sketch-books, they are horror-struck by a design for a war machine: a cart on wheels with atrocious revolving iron razors meant to slice entire battalions into mincemeat at a run. Cesari marvels at this creation by a man who loves God's creatures so much that he refrains from eating meat: "A doubleheaded Janus: one face towards Christ, the other towards Antichrist. Go figure which is the true, which the false?! Or are they both true?" (1:464). Even in Leonardo's invocations of the sacred task of the artist one detects a "double," or secondary, sense, an impious challenge to God's creation: "Oh, artist, let your manifold forms be as unlimited as the phenomena of nature. Continuing what God began, attempt to multiply not the work of human hands, but the immortal creations of God. Never imitate anyone. Let each of your creations be as a new phenomenon of nature" (1:449).[18] Just as the *Mona Lisa*, in Merezhkovsky's interpretation, is, paradoxically, Leonardo's greatest *self*-portrait, Leonardo himself, I submit, is the self-portrait of the novel's implied author. In pondering the ethical sources of Leonardo's creativity, this author seems to be working out a matter of crucial import for his own art – whether it will be turned towards Christ or Antichrist, or both at once.[19] When Giovanni confesses in his diary to having become hopelessly confused in his thinking about Leonardo's motives as one "lost in the windings of a terrible labyrinth," the reader, too, will probably admit that he is lost in the maze of the novel's presentation of good and evil and their proper balance in art.[20] The labyrinthine imagery, by the way, fits into an important pattern of symbols involving Daedalus, author of the infamous Minoan labyrinth, and his son Icarus, both traditional icons for the dangerous or demonic artist, that is the mortal who dares, through human genius, to challenge the prerogative of the gods: to create, to fly, to achieve the impossible.[21] Presenting Leonardo, in his quest to fly, as one seduced by "the devil of Mechanics" (bes Mekhaniki, 2:29), Merezhkovsky artfully stitches biblical images into the pagan pattern. Leonardo is like Icarus and Daedalus in his challenge to the heavens; like Adam and Eve in being willing to eat the fruit of the tree of knowledge; like a seduced Christ (i.e. Antichrist) in yielding to the Devil's temptation to leap into the abyss from the pinnacle of the temple.[22] Moreover, Leonardo himself often plays the role of Satan in this conceit: "there will be wings! If not I, then another, it doesn't matter – man will fly. The Spirit lied not: those who have knowledge will be winged like gods. ... From the Mountain which takes its name from the conqueror – *Vinci-vincere* means *to conquer* – the Great Bird will make its first flight – man on the back of the great Swan, filling the world with wonder, filling all of the books with his immortal name" (2:76).

That these words of Satanic pride come from the mouth of such an attractive hero is characteristic of the ethical and aesthetic traps Merezhkovsky has set in the Daedalian labyrinth of his novel. In order that the reader bridge the gap between Leonardo's visual art and his own verbal art, Merezhkovsky includes such scenes as the argument, over which the villagers ask Leonardo to arbitrate, as to whether Dante's *Inferno* is the work of a pious Christian writer or a godless heretic. The narrator's comment that "the more they argued, the less fathomable the poet's secret became" (2:189) aptly characterizes the inferno of meanings Merezhkovsky's novel represents. In Leonardo's drawings Giovanni is troubled that "the sight of devils' mugs and monsters ... is a horror that attracts" (1:456). Merezhkovsky, like Leonardo, aestheticizes evil for the sake of the duality on which his trilogy stands. We find a good example of this in a passage like the following:

> Giovanni ... opened the book of Saint Paul's Epistles and, darkened by the insidious promptings of the Devil, that great logician, rearranged in his mind the words of Scriptures:
> "You cannot *but* drink from the cup of Lord and the cup of the Devil. You cannot *but* take part in the feast of the Lord and the feast of the Devil."
> Bitterly grinning, he raised his eyes to the sky, where he saw yesterday's star, like the luminary of the most beautiful of the angels of darkness, of Lucifer – the Lightbearer. (1:479)

In such scenes, *Christ and Antichrist* provides its reader with no narrative perspective – in the form, say, of irony directed at Giovanni – that would separate his viewpoint from that of his hero: the effect is that the implied author seems to admit in his hero's voice that the "doubling thought" which generates the entire trilogy of novels is the result of the Devil's "insidious promptings." The symbology of the passage binds light, beauty, and truth up in the notion that all men are doomed to live a life doubly inspired and nurtured by good and evil, Christ and Antichrist.

Even Leonardo seems at times to recognize the duality of his genius. As much becomes clear when Giovanni tells his teacher of a delirious (and Dostoevskian) episode in which Leonardo's "double," whom Giovanni eventually recognizes as "of the Devil," had paid him a visit. The Demon-Leonardo had informed Giovanni that "all is equal – truth or untruth, good or evil" and that "the serpent lied not: taste from the tree of knowledge, and you will be like gods." As Giovanni relates his terrible vision, "Leonardo listened with such curiosity, as though this were no longer the delirium of a sick man. He felt Giovanni's gaze, which was now almost calm, unmasking, penetrating into the most clandestine depth of his heart" (1:574). The narrator defines Leonardo's aesthetic as encompassing both a demonic and pious extreme, as in his first two artistic creations: "in *The Fall into Sin* – serpentine wisdom through reason's daring; in *The Adoration of the Magi* – dove-like simplicity through humbling faith" (2:70). This dualism, however, troubles Leonardo's viewers and students far more than it does Leonardo himself.

"I am perishing," despairs Giovanni, "going mad from these doubling thoughts, from the face of Antichrist showing through the face of Christ. Why have You abandoned me, oh Lord?" (1:469). The reader, who will probably not suffer to the extent Giovanni does, must nonetheless struggle to make sense of Merezhkovsky's puzzling double-exposure. No longer able to bear his master's moral ambivalence, Giovanni flees Leonardo to join up with Girolamo Savonarola, who is of a very different mind when it comes to art: "Brother Girolamo, speaking about art, demanded that every painting should be of use, should instruct and edify people with soul-saving meanings: demolishing, with an executioner's hand, seductive depictions, the Florentinians would be carrying out a cause pleasing to God" (1:478). This is just what Savonarola's holy army of children attempts to do, burning books, paintings, and sculptures of suspect moral content or form in a great *auto-da-fé*. When Giovanni, on whom years of apprenticeship under Leonardo have not been lost, questions one of Savonarola's priests as to the necessity of burning the *chefs-d'oeuvre* of artists and sages, the priest answers, "be comforted: what will be destroyed in this bonfire merits destruction, for what is evil and sinful cannot be beautiful, according to the testimony of the sages you so praise" (1:484–85). The priest's formulation is a parody of Leonardo's simplistic claim – that the godly is beautiful, the demonic ugly – a notion that flies in the face of Giovanni's and the reader's experience of Satanic beauty, of the horror that attracts. "Are you sure," Giovanni asks the priest not without irony, "that children can always faultlessly tell good from evil in works of art and science?" (1:485). Giovanni, after all, joined Savonarola for the reason that he, though no longer a child, found himself unable to make this very distinction. Again, readers should recognize the dilemma as their own in trying to grasp the ethical message of the novel: should such novels be shunned, burned for their snares, or read for their revelations?

The dispute of two Russian icon-painters and monks who are travelling in Leonardo's Italy answers this question unambiguously, while simultaneously developing the important notion of the time lapse between Western and Russian aesthetic thought. When one of the monks remarks that "all that is beautiful is holy," the other shuts him up with the angry retort that beauty and holiness are not the same thing, that "there is a beauty from the Devil" (2:275). By focusing his debate about the relationship between morality and art on a pivotal figure of the Western Renaissance, Leonardo, Merezhkovsky tries to fix the moment when Western artists ceased to be the obedient executors of a strict ecclesiastical aesthetic and began to serve other masters than the Church. As Merezhkovsky suggests, the analogous moment came considerably later in Russia, whose "Renaissance" at last occurred only in the nineteenth century. It is this delay in aesthetic thought that causes the Russian artists such horror at the audacity of Leonardo's art, which they mistrust and shun as inspired by the Devil. When the monks see Leonardo's *John the Baptist*, which contrasts so starkly with traditional, church-sanctioned representations of the saint, their reaction is to flee, as if from a Satanic temptation: "The Devil's filth! … Is this the Precursor, obscene, exposed like a whore, having neither a beard, nor mustache? If it is the Precursor, then not of Christ, but sooner of Antichrist… Let us go, Evtikhii, let us go as quickly as we may. My child, do not defame your eyes: it is unworthy for us Orthodox even to cast our gaze upon these icons of theirs, which are ferocious, Devil-pleasing – a curse upon them!" (2:309). Whether the implied author's seductive portrait of a religiously ambiguous Leonardo aims to please God or the Devil, or both at once, is, of course, one of the book's unfathomable ambiguities, or if one prefers, mysteries.

Whether it is a good or bad thing, both from a moral and artistic point of view, to have a moral haze at a novel's structural core, its narrative point of view, is a difficult question indeed. Zinaida Gippius, for one, was convinced that it was a mistake: "I think … that as early as *Julian* [*The Death of the Gods*], D.S. [Merezhkovsky] was experiencing a turn towards Christianity, the start of a deepening in him, even though in his next novel, *Leonardo* [*The Gods Resurrected*], the turn was not yet evident. For it was precisely there that the one could detect the 'duality' – Ormazd and Ahriman – with which he was reckoning."[23] This duality – Merezhkovsky's belief in the opposing ideals of light and darkness – was, as he wrote his trilogy, the cause of heated disputes between the two of them, for Gippius appears to have considered the notion a moral and artistic blunder, an imperfect cornerstone upon which to build so voluminous an artistic edifice as *Christ and Antichrist*.[24] She may well have been right.

Merezhkovsky made an important confession in 1911: "When I began the trilogy *Christ and Antichrist*, it seemed to me that two truths existed – Christianity, the truth of heaven, and paganism, the truth of the earth – and that the fullness of religious truth lay in the future union of these two truths. But as I was finishing it, I already knew that the union of Christ and Antichrist was a blasphemous lie; I knew that both truths – of heaven and earth – had already been united in Jesus Christ. ... But I now also know that I had to follow this lie through to its end, in order to see the truth."[25] This confession of an author's shifting intention for his novel, implies a certain irresponsibility from a moral point of view, for even if Merezhkovsky discovered a metaphysical truth for himself in the process of composition, he admits to having concealed it from readers, whom he tempts with the "blasphemous lie" of his duality. Still, this sort of shift is fairly typical of the symbolists' demonic art, of a literature lacking a unified, consistent ethical centre and whose moral sense and creative origin the author himself may, with luck, come to understand only through the creative act itself.

Briusov: *The Fiery Angel*

With Merezhkovsky a change in emphasis takes place, from the morally orientated nineteenth-century novel to the aesthetically charged symbolist novel. What unites Julian, Leonardo, and Peter more than anything else in Merezhkovsky's trilogy is that they are all three potential supermen, daring to live beyond good and evil.[26] Here good yields to beauty, which, as we have seen, may be Satanic in nature – a truth that Merezhkovsky sooner discovered in Dostoevsky than in Nietzsche. Merezhkovsky's move is, on the one hand, an impulse "to abandon Christianity completely" in the attempt "to escape from the tedium of life," and, on the other, a reflection of the author's obvious adoration of a pagan religion of fleshly beauty and self-love which he regarded as man's struggle against God.[27] With Briusov, the very urge to create a new aesthetic put some very unethical principles to work for his muse. Literature could be for Briusov, "a Moloch demanding human sacrifices."[28] As he reflected in his diaries as a young man, "it's decadence. Yes! Say what you like, it may be false, it may be ridiculous, but it points the way forward, and the future will belong to it, especially once it finds a worthy leader. And that leader will be me. Yes, me."[29] Decadent and symbolist art moves its stress from the object towards the subject, from the world towards the self. The Nietzschean speaker of Briusov's lyric "Temptation" (Iskushenie, 1903) urges himself to cast off the holies of the past in order to recreate himself in a form better equipped to master the exigencies of the new age:[30]

> О, сердце! в этих тенях века,
> Где истин нет, иному верь!
> В себе люби сверхчеловека …
> Явись, как бог и полузверь![31]

> [Oh, heart! in these, the century's shadows,
> Where there's no truth, believe in other things!
> Within you love the superman…
> Appear, as a god and half-beast!]

In a poem significantly dedicated to Zinaida Gippius, Briusov published his intention to glorify "both the Lord and the Devil" (I Gospoda i D'iavola) – a strident form of worship that is close to the Merezhkovsky of the *Christ and Antichrist* period.[32] Such metaphysical contradictions can make of a lyric a manifesto of perverse poetics, clouding such notions as divine inspiration to the point of obscurity. I would like to try to see how an analogous brand of ethical ambivalence may function in a novel.

The central uncertainty of Briusov's *The Fiery Angel* is the nature of the heroine Renate's first, fateful encounter with the supernatural.[33] When the narrator and hero, Ruprecht, first meets her, Renate claims to have been taken under the protection of an angel named Madiel in early childhood. All of her subsequent obsessions – from her fanatic Christian devotion to her erotic passions for Count Heinrich and Ruprecht to her Satan worship and demonomania – stem directly from her (suspiciously earthly) love for this fiery spirit. If Madiel is the servant of God he passes himself off for, then Renate is saved. Even Ruprecht might have some hope of forgiveness for the deviltry in which he entangles himself on her behalf, because it would then turn out that Ruprecht pledged his soul to the Devil in the name of good, namely the reunification of Renate and her angel through her moral rehabilitation. If Madiel's flames are of the infernal kind, however, then Renate, after her fatal rendezvous with the Inquisition, descends straight into hell, where she will doubtless await her partner in diablerie, Ruprecht.

To make the resolution of this, the novel's crucial uncertainty, less unlikely, Briusov nests Ruprecht's tale of eroto-demonic possession within a "Foreword to the Russian Edition" which is deceptively signed "Valerii Briusov." "Editor" Briusov's foreword, along with his abundant annotations, provides the modern reader with some perspective and makes Ruprecht's story seem like an historical document. The very language Ruprecht uses is so over-embellished with metaphors running away with themselves that it creates a sense of distance between the narrator and the editor. Ruprecht, left alone

with his grief upon his separation from Renate, likens himself to a
prisoner locked up with a wild ape who jumps up from time to time
and strangles him (4:194); in another absurdly contrived conceit,
Ruprecht declares that "my heart thumped in my breast like the
heart of a timid lizard seized by someone's coarse hand" (4:254). But
the editor, who takes an unseemly pleasure in undermining
Ruprecht's authority, is of course as much a "lizard" as Ruprecht,
both being Briusov's playthings. The editor's warning that Ruprecht
is full of prejudices and that his observations must not be mistaken
for fact anticipates Ruprecht's repeated avowals that Renate's words
cannot be trusted. To make matters worse, Mephistopheles reminds
us that "every man, according to Moses, is but a representation of
God," and then gives Moses' thought an appropriately devilish –
and modernist – twist: "And I should like to know, what you know
other than representations" (4:213). If all men are made in God's
image, then one wonders why it is the Devil's image that Briusov's
personages – Mephistopheles, Faust, Agrippa, Ruprecht, Renate – so
persistently evoke. Mephistopheles' second statement, which is
deceptively prefaced by a reference to Scripture, answers much better to Briusov's murky world of shifting representations. This notion
is illustrated by the narrative's cabbage-like structure of representation wrapped within representation wrapped within representation:
at the core of these concentric visions lies the tale Renate conveys to
Ruprecht of divine-demonic love. The same smudging of representation and reality is behind the depiction of Heinrich (is he an incarnation of Madiel or not?), Agrippa and Faustus (have they sold their
souls to the Devil?), and the explicitly infernal powers (do Ruprecht
and Renate in fact communicate with the "little demons" [malen'kie
demony, 4:58] whose pranks eventually condemn Renate, and the
demon Ruprecht summons forth, and the Devil himself, who puts in
an appearance at the Witches' Sabbath?). In the end readers must
ask themselves whether these evil spirits exist objectively or subjectively; what to make of all this rage and possession; what tale they
have read, one of salvation or damnation.

Such ponderous ambiguities seem a natural enough result of
Briusov's approach to literature. Bely described how Briusov, while
writing *The Fiery Angel,* would mix together life and art: "throwing an
overcoat on my shoulders, he would force me against my will to
pose for him, … asking questions from his novel and making me
answer them; meanwhile, I, not knowing his novel, did not understand why he was scrutinizing my dirty laundry, as if tracking me,
and testing me with his questions – about superstition, magic, the
hypnotism he was supposed to practise." The extratextual author's
active cultivation of a demonic persona must be at least partially

responsible for the demonism of the textual authorial agents, which is so disorientating for readers. The editor "Briusov" of Ruprecht's manuscript cites a sixteenth-century tract on witches and pacts with the Devil, the title of which could well stand as a personal motto for Briusov during the symbolist period: *La Démonomanie des sorciers*.[34] Bely believed, in fact, that even the great magician himself would sometimes lose control over his art: "Emptying out old Cologne into the daily life of Moscow, he himself would sometimes lose sight of the boundary between life and invention; so in his thoughts Muscovites would turn into the contemporaries of the Nettesheim magician, Erasmus and Doctor Faust."[35] Given the sort of "magic" interplay that Briusov established between his life and art, it is no wonder that the authorial personae of *The Fiery Angel* end up also looking like necromancers.[36]

The writer working in this sinister vein is like a sorcerer casting spells with his magic words, his writings – like the legendary "black book," thought to be the work of Satan and a guide for witches and warlocks. Works like Remizov's "The Little Devil," Sologub's *The Petty Demon*, and Briusov's *The Fiery Angel*, with varying degrees of self-consciousness, explore the fear of the black book. A character in Remizov's "The Little Devil" (appropriately called "Iaga") generalizes this fear when she shouts that "books are from the Devil, and keeping such filth at home will only please him."[37] Briusov's *The Fiery Angel* is most interesting in this respect since it looks back to the medieval roots of the black book, which it simultaneously holds up as its own generic prototype. Ruprecht's childhood friend Friedrich, who is branded as a "half-sane, or dangerous person" (4:18) thanks to his passion for books, becomes Ruprecht's first guide into the wonders, obsession, enlightenment, solitude – of books. The bookseller Gluck and witch Renate are his next teachers in the art of black magic. Agrippa of Nettesheim (1486–1535), whose *De Occulta Philosophia* Ruprecht extols as the bible of black magic, is his third mentor. It is this greatest teacher that Ruprecht accuses of irresponsible authorship (a charge one suspects that Briusov himself would have welcomed): "Why on earth, teacher, once you had attentively researched the realms of magic and found in them nothing but blunders, didn't you attempt to direct others away from the fruitless occupation with this science, but, to the contrary, were quick to print a work you yourself consider imperfect? … Do you not thereby lead your curious readers into great temptation, and wouldn't I be in the right if I recalled to you the words of the Gospels, that it would be better for a person who seduces one of small strength if a millstone were hung round his neck and he were drowned in the sea's abyss?" (4:130). The frank question Ruprecht puts to Agrippa – "as one of those seduced by your book, I only humbly ask you to tell me what magic is: truth or error?" (4:131) – is one that neither Agrippa nor Briusov will answer directly, though the evil signs accompanying Agrippa's death in the novel supply a kind of silent reply. Still, Satan, as *The Fiery Angel* everywhere shows, is an "artifex mirabilis" (4:78) or "marvellous artist," as well as an artful teacher, and he refuses to disclose his secrets except to those damned by them.

If Ruprecht's teachers artfully seduce him into moral error, and most of all by their books, then Ruprecht's tale leads the reader into a similar kind of temptation. The chain of unrequited love that forms the novel's erotic interest – Ruprecht loves Renate, and she loves Count Heinrich – gives rise to a chain of demonic seduction that proceeds in inverse order: Heinrich leads Renate into Devil-worship, and Renate leads Ruprecht.[38] Renate openly confesses this seduction to Ruprecht: "then a certain voice, belonging, naturally, to the enemy of mankind, whispered in her ear that the devils will give her back Heinrich if in exchange she helps them catch another soul in their nets. After this all of our life purportedly consisted only in Renate's attempts, by deception and hypocrisy, to draw me into mortal sins, stopping at no lies to do so" (4:179). If Satan made such a pact with Renate, who was to save Heinrich's soul by sacrificing her own and Ruprecht's, then Ruprecht may well have concluded a pact of his own in order to save Renate's soul at the expense of his own soul – and, with any luck, that of his manuscript's reader. Who, after all, is the beneficiary of Ruprecht's experiments in demonology and necromancy, if not the reader? Just as Renate deceives Ruprecht into witchcraft, so Ruprecht tempts the reader with his dubious claims and justifications: "I want to describe the very spell that we cast in all of its details in order that an experienced and knowledgeable person, if this Tale were to fall into his hands, could determine what we omitted and how to explain the pitiful and tragic failure of our enterprise" (4:101). There would, needless to say, be little sense in describing the deviltry in such depth as Ruprecht proceeds to do merely in order that an adept Satanist might have the satisfaction of knowing what blunders novices of his "science" have committed. Ruprecht recounts an attempt to master a devil that resulted in his being mastered, and the story of this possession, made so intriguing by its hypnotic accumulation of mysterious detail and by its ritualistic effects, is the reader's invitation to try his own hand at commanding the Devil. For as Ruprecht himself admits, in the presence, and under the impression, of deviltry, one's "soul, of its own accord, becomes enrapt in that which, according to Horace's expression, *scire nefas* [it is sinful to know], so that even the clear stigmata of hell no longer horrified me, nor confounded my will" (4:63). Readers, too, find themselves growing strangely accustomed to the invocation of devils, the witches' Sabbath, demonic possession, and so on. When, at the close, Ruprecht hypocritically expresses the hope that his story might be "a useful warning for weak souls who, like me, will want to bail certain powers from the black and dubious wells of magic and demonomania" (4:302), his dissembling is clear: if the reader is afflicted with anything like Ruprecht's own weak soul, then the story will serve not as a warning, but as a seduction, just as Heinrich's, Renate's, Agrippa's, and Faust's tragic stories proved fatefully seductive to Ruprecht.

Perhaps the primary lesson of Ruprecht's sad fate is that all human souls are hopelessly weak against the ubiquitous, inexorable, evil will that is the prime mover of Briusov's novel world. Mochul'sky observed that it was Briusov, first among the symbolists, who "established the persona of the artist-Demiurge, the grandeur of his creative will."[39] As his collection *Me eum esse* (1897) suggests, Briusov was not averse to playing at Demiurge-Creator in his art:

> Создал я в тайных мечтах
> Мир идеальной природы, –
> Что перед ним этот прах:
> Степи, и скалы, и воды![40]
>
> [I've created in secret dreams
> A world of ideal nature –
> What is this dust before it:
> The steppes, the cliffs, the waters!]

Ruprecht's chaotic world indeed resembles the creation of a Demiurge's malicious, dictatorial will. The Archbishop, attempting to exorcize Renate, cries out, "You – father of lie, and destroyer of truth, and inventor of untruth – ... Do you not, condemned spirit, submit to the will of our Creator?" (4:255). Given the bonds *The Fiery Angel* forges between its own fiction and the demonological tracts that seduce Ruprecht, it is conceivable that Satan's title of "the inventor of untruth" implicates the novel's implied author. As much is suggested by one of the novel's central metaphors, the "android" of Albert the Great, which the central heroes so often evoke. According to Ruprecht, Renate resembles this "miraculous automaton to the point of perfection" (4:42) after their first shared encounter with witchcraft, a visit to a witch which leaves Renate limp and as if without a will of her own. Ruprecht later likens himself to this automaton as well when he agrees to challenge Heinrich to a duel: "and now it was I who submitted with the obedience of Albert the Great's android" (4:142). Like the machine Albert the Great meticulously constructed over the course of thirty years, the heroes of the novel can move and perform certain actions, but they are ultimately deprived of free will and remain the slaves of their maker. And their creator, whether the implied author or some lesser local deity, wills them to evil with relentlessly malicious intent. When a fateful turn in the plot brings Ruprecht to Renate for the last time, he exclaims that such coincidences, "in their meaningful persistence, compel me to consider life not the plaything of blind elements, but the creation of a masterful artist" (4:214). The creator of the novel's world has ideally structured it to catch up its inhabitants in its evil and confound the reader, as to the point of view of the implied author towards this evil.

Sologub: *The Created Legend*

It was not Briusov, however, but Sologub who would take the symbolist vision of life as the creation of a masterful artist and make it the premise of a demonic novel. *The Created Legend* is based on the notion that the world is an ugly mistake that can only be remedied by the artistic genius with sufficient daring to alter, and even replace, life with a beautiful legend. The cult of the beautiful is taken so far in the novel that it often seems as if Sologub's literary agents will allow the most unspeakable (and bizarre) of crimes for its sake. The central hero Trirodov conducts a head-on assault against God and His world. He murders, shrinks his enemies and then preserves them in ghastly translucent cubes of his own alchemic invention. To assure the success of his brazen endeavours (which include a successful campaign to become the "king" of a legendary land), he enlists the help of zombies, which he resurrects from the grave. He propounds his Luciferian views in several key scenes throughout the novel. At a gathering of revolutionary-minded youth, Trirodov objects when Petr Matov, his rival in ideology and love, blames the evils of contemporary Russian life on Peter the Great. Mistakes were made, asserts Trirodov, considerably earlier in Russian history, and namely "during the creation of the world."[41] He goes on to explain the method by which he proposes to put right the blunders of the Creator: "And we, too – we love utopias. We read Wells. The very life which we are now creating combines elements of real life with fantastic, utopian elements" (74). Literature (Wells, Sologub, Trirodov – himself an author), then, is the inspiration and instrument by which man is to mend God's world.[42] When Trirodov leaves, Petr asks a timely question that has perhaps occurred to the reader, "And who the hell is he anyway? A charlatan? A dreamer? A sorcerer? Does he consort with the unclean spirit? What do you think? Or is this not really the Devil himself in human form?" (74). When Trirodov's lover Elisaveta defends Trirodov, accusing Petr of envy, he replies:

"Me – jealous? Of what? … You tell me where his talent lies. What he writes only seems to be poetry. But just make the sign of the cross, and you will see that all of it is bookish, artificial, dry. A giftless diabolical delusion" (d'iavol'skoe navazhdenie, 75).

Petr is doubtless partially correct in his evaluation of Trirodov's creativity; indeed the very name Trirodov, meaning something like "thrice born" or "of three races," suggests a hybrid of the divine, human, and demonic races. There is an undeniable Satanic pride in Trirodov's Sologubian cult of solitary invention: "There arose a joyful, proud dream about the transformation of life through the power of art that creates, about life created by a proud will" (158). But Sologub later has his revenge upon Petr for this rebellion of a creature against a Creator: "There was a small sort of daring in him – but no great audacity. He merely believed in Christ, in Antichrist, in his love, in her apathy – he merely believed! He was only seeking the truth and could not create – neither could he summon God from non-being, nor the Devil from dialectical schemes, nor victorious love from coincidental worries, nor victorious hate from stubborn 'no's.' And he loved Elisaveta!" (110). In short, there may be demonic audacity alongside godlike inventiveness in Trirodov's "created legend," but the laurels of victory – in this case the heroine Elisaveta, who, in the immortal words of Gor'ky, gives herself to Trirodov like a hunk of cold meat[43] – belong not to the one who merely lives life, but to the one who spirits it forth from "non-being."

As this hasty sketch of Trirodov's triple nature suggests, the world of *The Created Legend* is built upon some surprising values and deep contradictions, with the result that Sologub's use of narrative viewpoint is still more unsettling than Merezhkovsky's or Briusov's. To take one of the least easily resolved paradoxes of the novel, the narrator and positive heroes constantly extol and strive for harmony (achieved chiefly through nudity and sensual love) among people and between people and nature; yet violent conflict is the law of Sologub's land and determines the characters' intercourse, as well as their fate in a hostile world. To justify, as far as one may, this profound incongruity, one must attempt to shadow forth the cosmogony behind *The Created Legend* and determine the relation of the three chief authorial personae, Trirodov, the narrator, and the implied author, with respect to the three divinities of Sologub's universe, the Demiurge (Demiurg), Serpent (Zmii/Drakon), and Luminous Spirit (Svetozarnyi).[44]

According to the novel's pessimistic theodicy, the evil Demiurge who created this world – a demonized version of the God of Genesis – concealed a truth vital to all future living creatures in the process of Creation. Consequently Sologub's people live in a universe intrinsically hostile to them.[45] Queen Ortruda, who so often

speaks for the implied author, puts it like this: "The Demiurge concealed from us true knowledge. Enclosing all understanding and all
wisdom in his secret unity, he doomed us to ignorance, gave us over
to the torments of despair and of spiritual poverty, to unbearable languishing" (232). To account for the harmony, joy, and knowledge
that Sologub's creatures nevertheless possess, one must infer in his
novelistic world, as in some dualist religions and sects, a God more
original and powerful – though, to be sure, far less visible – than the
Demiurge. This implicit God was the original Creator of a universal
energy or substance which, while good in potential, was perverted
by the Demiurge when he created nature and people out of joint
with each other. If Sologub's people are to have any hope of redis-
covering that possible good, they must sunder the Demiurge's creation, replacing it with a "legend" of their own genius, crowned with
its subjective truth. It would seem, then, that the secret "true knowledge" that the Demiurge falsified in creating the world is nothing
more than pure creativity itself – each individual's freedom to create,
through the power of will and imagination, a world of his own. The
positive heroes attempt to escape "existence" (bytie), the evil creation of Genesis, in order to realize a higher "other existence"
(inobytie) of their own fancy through the transforming power of
love, dreams and, certainly, art. The novel allegorizes earthly existence as a dark tunnel from which one seeks an exit into another
world. One such subterranean passage connects Trirodov's mansion
to his greenhouse, actually a spaceship in disguise, poised to trans-
port Trirodov and his beneficiaries to a new life on the legendary
United Isles. Perhaps the most significant of these underground passages is the grave, which Trirodov shows to be just one more transition to another life when he brings people back from the dead into a
world of his own fashioning. When Ortruda opens the outer door of
the secret passageway leading from her castle to the sea, she momen-
tarily experiences "a joyful exodus from dark existence (bytie). The
sun of the day's expanses seemed another sun, and the sea shone
blue like a river washing the shores of an earthly paradise" (248–49).

   That people should yearn for the light of another sun than the customary diurnal luminary is entirely natural in Sologub's topsy-turvi-
cal world. The second divinity of his rather disorderly cosmic order
is the "Serpent," that is, the sun that eternally scorches the Demiurge's cruel world. For Sologub's deceived, God-fearing heroes, the
sun is emblematic of a Christian God's harmonious creation. The
Serpent deludes Petr, for instance, whom the narrator mocks for
thinking "that he loved freedom – Christ's freedom": "The reigning,
fiery Serpent (Zmii) seduced him ... with the temptations of triumphant harmony" (34). However, when the narrator announces

that "the ancient Serpent (Zmii) is not our sun" (96), he suggests that the sun represents no such harmony, but, to the contrary, a tragic rift between creature and Creator. This is consistent with the second role of the *Zmii* as the Serpent of Genesis: according to the novel's revision of the biblical creation myth, when the Serpent attempted to reveal to people the truth that the Demiurge hid from them, they, to their undoing, found this truth too bright to behold and fled from it into darkness, ignorance, and grief (Petr's predicament). Ortruda is once again the interpreter of the implied author's conception: "From the earth, from the red clay, like the first man, arose the consoling wise Serpent (Zmii). It wanted to reveal true knowledge to people, but they were afraid and did not retain their paradise, and ran cravenly into darkness" (232). Ortruda's vision of the Serpent as a power sympathetic to human misery seems to contradict the Serpent's deception of Petr, which shows its hostility to people. To preserve the coherence of the novel's symbology, one would have to argue that the Serpent is an ambivalent divinity who rewards the desperate, Promethean thirst for truth in such as Trirodov or Ortruda, while punishing the lack of that yearning in the likes of Petr, whom he deceives into a false knowledge of the world. Still, Sologub's conception remains inconsistent – or at least sufficiently protean to elude any stable meaning – for, as it turns out, the Serpent is in fact ignorant of any truth worth the knowing: "The celestial Dragon (Drakon) laughed in the crimson-blue heights, as if it knew what was to come. But it didn't know. Only the creative dream of the poet foresees, vaguely, the distances of the incomplete creation" (375–76).

The most one can say, it would seem, is that Sologub's more lucid – that is, Luciferian – heroes learn from the Serpent-Sun that the highest truth is in creating a new world with its own, better, sun. With Trirodov's help, Elisaveta replaces the ancient Serpent with the "new sun" of the legend she creates from love, drugs, and dreams (152). Under the influence of Trirodov's hallucinogens, the two of them travel to another planet where they instantaneously experience an entire lifetime, basking in the "sweet, blue light" of "miraculous Mair," "the good sun of a joyful earth" (459). Ortruda and her lover Afra come to the same revelation that "only the soul liberated from the power of any norms creates new worlds and exults in the bright triumph of transformation" (400). Christ's freedom is only meaningful so long as one lives within the Christian norms of goodness and meekness, but in the world of *The Created Legend* limiting oneself to any norms implies sacrificing one's freedom. By contrast, the Serpent's freedom, the fruit it offers to those heroes who dare to be like the gods, is the liberty to choose pride, knowledge – the will to use evil against the Demiurge's world of evil. Burned by the rays of the

Serpent, Sologub's positive heroes inflict the same seductive agony on others, multiplying cruelty along with freedom, stopping neither at bloodshed, nor murder. In the Demiurge's sadistic and masochistic world people bathe and luxuriate in the evil light of a sun that triumphs when "all of us, the people on this earth, are evil and cruel and love to torture and to see drops of blood and drops of tears" (95).[46]

If the Serpent inspires the strong-willed to unleash evil in the struggle against an evil world, then the third divinity of Sologub's heaven, the Luminous Spirit, urges them on to the final stage of Satanism: illicit Creation. The Serpent-Sun yields to the Luminous Spirit, a luminary of the dusk and dawn, as a sign of a positive transformation which Sologub's favourite heroes apprehend just beyond their horizon. Ortruda welcomes and worships this spirit – which, appropriately, recalls the Morning Star, or Lucifer – as the "beautiful, brilliant Spirit" which "ceaselessly summons mankind to freedom and knowledge," without terrifying him (like Sologub's Demiurge) "with the demonic voices of blindly raging storms and with incinerating anger." Her ecstatic hymn continues: "You boundlessly and constantly widen the horizons of thought; you do not establish dogmas and codices of rules; you destroy the ossified, eternally dead bonds of religious teachings; you free the conscience; you summon us to tireless religious creation (tvorchestvo). You illuminate all who come to you with the light of unheard-of joy and reveal to them ... the path to those heights where the gods are created" (262). The narrator affirms Ortruda's vision of "the great Spirit, in whose light the ferocious dragons of worldly suns melt like light, transparent smoke, the joyful Spirit whose name is Luminous" (Svetozarnyi, 261).

While benevolent to the intrepid, the Luminous Spirit, like the Serpent, is quite sinister to meeker worldlings. In an instance of the ambivalence that is so characteristic of the novel, Ortruda's page Astol'f – whose "horizons of thought" Ortruda is about to widen to include lust, murder, and suicide – apprehends the "enemy" of mankind in the spirit to whom Ortruda prays; he falls to the ground, gasping from horror as his mistress worships (262). The Luminous Spirit is a revisitation of the ideals and rhetoric of the Enlightenment, but with a modern twist: it is "human reason, eternally leading mankind forward through the gloom ... to the unsetting light of Truth" (379); yet it bases its hopes of building a better world not only upon the power of human reason (knowledge, science, technology) – but also upon utopian dreams and alchemistic nightmares.[47] It evokes, among other things, the Antichrist of the Book of Revelation, in the form of the Beasts of the abysses of the land and sea (Rev. 13): when Ortruda prays to it, "throwing her challenge to heaven," Afra comments that it is not from the heavens that the herald of their daring truth will descend, but, rather, from "the dark abyss the Luminous Spirit (Svetozarnyi) will arise" (232). Sologub transforms Revelation's Antichrist into mankind's Saviour, the one who will come finally to reveal the truth long ago hidden by the Demiurge. But this truth is subjective, and even solipsistic, so that each devotee of the Luminous Spirit must create a new universe within his own darkness: "In truth, here was a different world, and another life was being created. Only the joyful, dark sky of another existence (inobytie) looked over the fence of the high dark walls. Above them, who had descended into the mysterious depth, stretched another sky, and another sun shone upon them, the humble luminary of the Luminous Spirit" (Luchezarnyi, 397).

Certain clues in the text suggest that the Luminous Spirit, the future Saviour of Ortruda's enchanted land, is none other than Trirodov, who does, after all, ascend to Ortruda's throne when she dies. Like the Luminous Spirit, Trirodov rejects "Christ's freedom," opting instead for the demonic will to create the world anew. In his opposition to Christ, Trirodov, too, recalls Antichrist, as becomes evident when Christ himself pays Trirodov a visit in the person of Prince Emmanuil Osipovich Davidov.[48] As it turns out, Davidov-Christ has (understandably) been keeping his eye on Trirodov for some time. Trirodov, likewise, has heard much about his visitor from his acquaintances, the Pirozhkovskys, who "love and esteem" (191) Davidov. The Pirozhkovskys are a rather transparent parody of the Merezhkovskys, whose growing interest in Christianity during the 1900s finally brought Dmitrii Merezhkovsky around to rejecting as blasphemy the sort of Satanism that Sologub's novel flaunts. In Sologub's revision of Dostoevsky's (or rather Ivan Karamazov's) legend about the Grand Inquisitor, Trirodov presents his complaints to Davidov-Christ about the Christian faith, which Davidov recalls to Trirodov in a "fiery speech ... about faith, about miracle, about the hoped-for and inevitable transformation of the world through miracle, about the victory over the bonds of time and over death itself" (192). Not to be outdone, Trirodov responds with a fiery speech of his own: "Know that I will never be with you, won't accept your consoling theories. All of your literary and propagandistic activity is, in my eyes, a great mistake. A fateful mistake. ... There is no miracle. There was no resurrection. No one conquered death. To raise a single will over the inert, ugly world is a feat not yet accomplished. ... I know the true path. My path" (193). Both Christ and Trirodov are agreed about the need to defeat death and conquer nature's inertia, but their methods differ. Like Christ, Trirodov raises from the dead, but through dark charms of his own which, to put it mildly, lack divine authorization. When one of Trirodov's "quiet" (i.e. resurrected) children walks into the living room with a tray of tea in the middle of this debate, Davidov darts Trirodov a look full of rebuke and asks, "Why do you do it?" "You don't like it," responds Trirodov with "arrogant irony," "well, with your expansive ties you could easily hinder me." Christ is silent, but the narrator remarks, "Thus Satan would speak, tempting the one who fasted in the wilderness" (192). Later Trirodov talks of his occult powers to Elisaveta, revealing to her "the secret leading from the darkness of non-being (nebytie) to the quiet of the other existence (inobytie) of his quiet children" (455). Guiding people from being and non-being to "other existence" is precisely the promise of the Luminous Spirit.

Like Trirodov, the narrator and implied author resemble the three divinities of the novel's pantheon, though not altogether consistently. The narrator (along with the implied author) usually sides with Trirodov, Elisaveta, Ortruda, and Afra in upholding the outlook of the Luminous Spirit. But a few crucial passages identify the narrator and implied author with the evil Demiurge – a use of narrative viewpoint we saw Briusov employ in *The Fiery Angel.* I would note, however, that this identification is more organic to Sologub's novel than to Briusov's, thanks to Sologub's cosmogony, in which the Demiurge has central importance. Like Briusov's characters, Sologub's resemble puppets whose strings the implied author pulls to produce the action required of the plot: "Trirodov bore down on Petr, as if he didn't see him. He moved mechanically and quickly, like a doll driven by a precisely wound key" (110).[49] But Sologub bares the device of the implied author as Demiurge in a way foreign to the style of *The Fiery Angel* when Trirodov addresses the following startling speech to Elisaveta: "And we too imagine ourselves to be living people … yet perhaps we are not at all living people but merely the heroes of a novel, and the author of this novel is entirely unhindered by concerns of outward verisimilitude. He has transformed his fickle imagination into this dark earth and from this dark, sinful earth has grown these strange black maples … and us" (115). True, the implied author to whom Trirodov refers, unlike the Demiurge, shares his knowledge with his chosen ones, but that very knowledge, which often takes the form of witchcraft, bears the mark of the Demiurge: "Between him and the grave, where the youth who had departed from life was languishing in deathly sleep, ran a secret current, enchanting and awakening the one sleeping in the coffin" (155). The absolute command Trirodov exercises over his quiet, undead children, to say nothing of the servitude he exacts of them, suggests that Trirodov, made in the Demiurge's image, is himself a Demiurge to his creatures. To return to the puppet metaphor, Trirodov pulls his children's strings, just as the implied-author-as-Demiurge pulls Trirodov's: this is the evil chain of being under the Serpent-Sun, on the Demiurge's earth.

Despite this hierarchy, with its implicit strife between Creator and creature, *The Created Legend* is one of the uncanny novels where central hero, narrator, and implied author tend to telescope into one, as the book's very first lines make evident. "I take a chunk of life, coarse and meagre, and I create out of it a luscious legend, for I am a poet. Lie inert in the darkness, dull, prosaic, or rage in a furious conflagration – above you, life, I, the poet, will erect my created legend of enchantment and beauty" (16). One is at a loss as to which of the authorial personae makes this Luciferian claim. It seems, at first glance, to belong to the narrator, but Trirodov is in many senses the narrator's double and thinks in the same aesthetic categories.[50] The word "poet" in the cited passage invites us to reconsider the notion that "only the creative dream of the poet foresees, vaguely, the distances of the incomplete creation" (375–76). Again the same ambiguity arises: the poet who foresees the denouement of the novel's creative dream could equally be Trirodov, the narrator, or the implied author. The narrative hierarchy threatens to collapse in other passages as well, as when Trirodov reveals to Elisaveta, "you are my dream, my Elisaveta" (533), suggesting that he is but a mask for the one who truly dreamt up Elisaveta (along with the other dramatis personae) – the implied author. Elisaveta takes this communication in her stride, perhaps because, in her own dreams, she too has created a life – the life of Queen Ortruda. And so Ortruda is the creation (dream, legend) of Elisaveta, who is the creation of Trirodov, who is the creation of the implied author, their common point of view being the "legend of enchantment and beauty." Combined with the characteristic ambivalence of the demonic novel, such a lack of perspective works to mystify readers as to the author's perspective on the Satanism that motivates all of these personae.[51]

To recapitulate, the narrative point of view in Sologub's *The Created Legend* is subject to the sort of ambivalence I have indicated in both Merezhkovsky and Briusov, but Sologub's more straightforward and systematic use of the devices of the artist-Demiurge and novel-as-black-book produced – in a seeming paradox – a narrative structure considerably more entangled than in *Christ and Antichrist* or *The Fiery Angel*. An analysis of other symbolist novels on the demonic theme, say Sologub's *The Petty Demon*, Bely's *The Silver Dove*, or his *Petersburg* would, I believe, reveal a corresponding relation of chronology to narrative instability. *The Petty Demon* appeared roughly a year before *The Fiery Angel*, which it resembles in terms of the coherency of its narrative viewpoint. It is largely consistent in its use of setting, characterization, and symbolism; in terms of the demonic action, however, Sologub is every bit as ambiguous as Briusov, making it impossible, for instance, to decide whether the demon who haunts Peredonov exists in his world, or merely in his dementia. The narration slides disorientatingly between the increasingly mad perceptions of Peredonov and the highly ordered world-view of an omniscient narrator. Bely's *The Silver Dove*, which compares well with Sologub's roughly contemporaneous *The Created Legend*, makes use of a setting and characterization that are basically stable, but so resolutely symbolic that one can never be quite sure whether the action shifts back and forth between two provincial Russian towns (Tselebeevo and Likhov), between Eastern and Western civilization, or between heaven and hell. The narrator switches joltingly from the Gogolesque comic banter of a local bumpkin to a hypnotic weaving of words that connives in the heroes' devilish sorcery. Bely's prose is entrancingly wrought, and its ritualistic rhythms and patterns of images act to stun and entangle readers, as in the magical spider web the Satanic antagonist Kudeiarov uses to catch and doom the tragic protagonist Petr Dar'ialsky. The implied author seems torn between the opposing urges to abhor the Satanic ritual violence of the plot and to uphold it as preferable to spiritual stasis and religious orthodoxy: the reader who succumbs to the ritual appeal of Bely's prose may in fact prefer to burn in gory Satanic lust like Petr, rather than be free of this violent temptation.[52] *Petersburg*, the last great symbolist novel, was to take the idea of the author as Demiurge beyond even Sologub's conception, for Bely's narrator simply announces in the book's first chapter that he has created the novel's world and peopled it with shadowy beings (the characters) whom he has made in his own image to haunt the reader. Bely's narrative scheme – an explicitly presented chain of hateful, fearful creation in which the implied author creates the narrator, who creates a character, who creates another character, who, finally, creates a devil – confirms the relationship I have tried to demonstrate between the symbolist novel's evolving sense of the demonic and its chaotic structures by producing what is, doubtless, symbolism's most mind-bogglingly self-contradictory novel, a work that everywhere categorizes and orders only to obfuscate and fracture in the end.[53] And what could be more natural than the notion that a demonic narrative point of view should act to usher into the novel the equivocation and pandemonium that are so much the Devil's part?

Notes

1. Among works of non-fiction, M.A. Orlov's demonology *Istoriia snoshenii cheloveka s d'iavolom* (1904) and Dmitrii Merezhkovsky's *Gogol' i chert* (1906) were very influential.

2. Valerii Briusov, *Ognennyi angel,* in his *Sobranie sochinenii v semi tomakh,* ed. P.G. Antokol'skii and others (Moscow: Khudozhestvennaia literatura, 1973–75), 4:15. *Ognenennyi angel* was first published in instalments in the symbolist journal *Vesy,* 1907, nos.1–3, 5–12, 1908, nos.2, 3, 5–8. In 1908 the publishing house Skorpion published it in book form. All translations are mine unless otherwise stated.

3. The trilogy *Khristos i antikhrist* consists of the three volumes *Smert' bogov (Iulian Otstupnik), Voskresshie bogi (Leonardo da Vinchi)* and *Antikhrist (Petr i Aleksei).* What would later become *Smert' bogov* first appeared as *Otverzhennyi* in the journal *Severnyi vestnik,* 1895, nos.1–6; it was published under the same title as a separate volume, with substantial changes, in 1896; the final title appeared with the second edition in 1902. Parts of what was to become *Voskresshie bogi* appeared under the title *Vozrozhdenie* in the journal *Nachalo* in 1899, nos.1–2, 4. In 1900 the novel was printed complete in the journal *Mir Bozhii,* nos.1–12. It appeared as a separate volume in 1901, 1902, and 1906. *Antikhrist (Petr i Aleksei)* was first published in the journal *Novyi put'* in 1904, nos.1–5, 9–12. It appeared as a separate volume in 1905 and 1906.

4. See William Richardson, *"Zolotoe Runo" and Russian Modernism: 1905–1910* (Ann Arbor: Ardis, 1986), 133–34.

5. Valerii Briusov, *Sobranie sochinenii,* 4:60. Cited hereafter in the text by volume and page number.

6. Andrei Belyi, *Peterburg,* ed. L.K. Dolgopolov (Moscow: Nauka, 1981), 295.

7. Fedor Sologub, *Melkii bes,* in his *Svet i teni: Izbrannaia proza* (Minsk: Mastatskaia litaratura, 1988), 191.

8. My use of the term "implied author" in this chapter corresponds to Wayne Booth's definition of the author's "second self," his image – meaning his values, judgements, point of view – in a particular novel. See Wayne Booth, *The Rhetoric of Fiction* (Chicago: The University of Chicago Press, 1961), 151. I also have in mind Seymour Chatman's conception of the "trace," "residue," or "record" a novel leaves behind from its own creation. See Seymour Chatman, *Coming to Terms: The Rhetoric of Narrative in Fiction and Film* (Ithaca: Cornell University Press, 1990), 83, 86. I attribute a novel's use of symbols to its implied author as well. By "authorial personae" or "authorial agents" I mean the narrator, implied author, and any other textual representations – or misrepresentations – of the author.

9. *The Created Legend* was first published in four instalments. The first three instalments appeared in the almanac *Shipovnik:* with the title *Nav'i chary* (1907, no.3, *Chast' I. Tvorimaia legenda;* 1909, no.7, *Chast' II. Kapli krovi;* 1909, no.10, *Chast' III. Koreleva Ortruda.* The final instalment appeared in the almanac *Zemlia,* 1912, nos.10, 11, with the title *Dym i pepel.* In 1914 the work was published by Sirin in its entirety as the trilogy *Tvorimaia legenda: Roman,* in vols. 18–20 of Fedor Sologub, *Sobranie sochinenii* (St. Petersburg: Sirin, 1914; reprint, Munich: Wilhelm Fink, 1972). This second edition renamed the novel, reorganized the original four parts into three, and made some substantial changes, mainly the addition of certain episodes and the removal of others.

10. The chronicler-historian Ammian of the first volume of Merezhkovsky's trilogy evidently represents the narrator's impartiality in the trilogy. To the question of whether he intends to present Roman history from a Christian or pagan viewpoint or "leave [his] descendants in doubt about [his] beliefs," he responds, "I don't know. ... To be just to both – that is my goal. ... Let no one decide in the future who I was – as I myself have not decided." Dmitrii S. Merezhkovskii, *Sobranie sochinenii v chetyrekh tomakh,* ed. O.N. Mikhailov (Moscow: Pravda, 1990), 1:305. Cited hereafter in the text and notes by volume and page number.

11. Cf. Avril Pyman, *A History of Russian Symbolism* (Cambridge: Cambridge University Press, 1994), 126: "Artistically, the trilogy forms not so much a bridge as a series of stepping-stones from the realist novel of the nineteenth century, with its full-rounded characters and sequential plot, to the shifting, kaleidoscopic techniques of modernist prose."

12. See Tomas Venclova, "K demonologii russkogo simvolizma," in *Christianity and the Eastern Slavs*, vol. 3, *Russian Literature in Modern Times*, ed. Boris Gasparov and others (Berkeley: University of California Press, 1995), 134–60. As Venclova explains, Viacheslav Ivanov, in his influential writings, divided demonism into Luciferian and Ahrimanian, the first being the spirit of proud, rebellious, creative self-assertion and the second – of formless, despondent decay. The evidence of my analysis suggests an inverse relation between the content and form of symbolist novels in terms of Ivanov's two categories of the demonic. The more a novel's content valorizes creativity, the more it tends toward chaotic form: Luciferian content produces Ahrimanian form.

13. By "duality" I mean the conflict of two antithetical or opposing ideas. I use the term "dualism" in the theological sense of a religious outlook (e.g. Zoroastrianism, Manichaeism, Gnosticism, Bogomilism) that views life as a conflict between good (often understood as what is of spirit and light) and evil (of matter, darkness), attributing all manifestations of the first to a good deity (God) and all manifestations of the second to an evil deity (the Devil). There are, to be sure, coincidences of duality and dualism: dualism, for instance, is built upon such dualities as God and Devil, light and darkness, etc.

14. See Maria Carlson, "*The Silver Dove*," in *Andrey Bely: Spirit of Symbolism*, ed. John E. Malmstad (Ithaca and London: Cornell University Press, 1987), 67: "Merezhkovsky was fascinated by the possibility that the blend of revolutionary apocalypticism, millennialism, and pagan and Christian traditions characteristic of Russian mystical sectarianism might indeed offer the possibility of the synthesis of flesh and spirit that he envisioned." See also C. Harold Bedford, *The Seeker: D.S. Merezhkovskiy* (Lawrence, Manhattan, and Wichita: The University Press of Kansas, 1975), 60: "he revealed in his prose works the attraction that ancient paganism held for him, and he also exhibited the same inclination towards Christianity that appeared in his later poetic compositions."

15. For a different reading of *The Gods Resurrected*, see Pierre Hart, "Time Transmuted: Merezhkovsky and Briusov's Historical Novels," *Slavic and East European Journal* 31, no.2 (1987):187–201. Hart argues that Merezhkovsky is "only sporadically concerned with aesthetic issues" (190). But Pyman, who writes that "Merezhkovsky works and thinks through the medium of art alone," supports my view; Pyman, *A History of Russian Symbolism*, 126.

16. Cf. Pyman, *A History of Russian Symbolism*, 128.

17. Merezhkovskii, *Sobranie sochinenii*, 1:315.

18. Such statements as these anticipate Berdiaev's spirited defence of human creativity in *Smysl tvorchestva: Opyt opravdaniia cheloveka* (1916). On the relationship between Merezhkovsky's and Berdiaev's aesthetic thought see Peter G. Christensen, "Merezhkovsky and Berdyaev: Leonardo and the Meaning of the Creative Act," *Symposium: A Quarterly Journal in Modern Foreign Literatures* 45, no.3 (Fall 1991):172–82. Christensen argues that Leonardo, in Merezhkovsky's novel, while he "admittedly, pays little attention to traditional concepts of good and evil" (172), has nonetheless "taken the path to salvation through creativity rather than through obedience to traditional morality" (177). That Leonardo's way represents a detour around conventional morality is clear; whether he achieves good through his creative ethics is, however, a much more doubtful proposition.

19. Berdiaev criticized Merezhkovsky as someone "bent upon a synthesis of Christianity and paganism" who "mistakenly identifies it with a synthesis of spirit and flesh" and thus seems to want "to synthesize Christ and antichrist." Nicholas Berdyaev, *The Russian Idea*, trans. R.M. French (London: Geoffrey Bles, 1947), 225; cited in Christensen, "Merezhkovskii and Berdyaev," 175.

20. See Bedford, *The Seeker: D.S. Merezhkovskiy*, who intelligently argues that the impulse to balance good and evil comes to Merezhkovsky through his admiration of Greek paganism: "Above all, for Merezhkovskiy the ancients represented a synthesis. They united into one harmony all that contemporary mankind was separating: heaven and earth; nature and people; good and evil" (61). Bedford admits, however, that Leonardo usually resembles more a mass of moral contradictions than a balance or synthesis of them (76).

21. Ernst Kris and Otto Kurz, *Legend, Myth, and Magic in the Image of the Artist: A Historical Experiment* (New Haven: Yale University Press, 1979), esp. 84. For Merezhkovsky's further development of the Icarus and Daedalus motif see also Merezhkovskii, *Sobranie sochinenii*, 2:17, 28, 74–76, 307.

22. See, for example, Luke 4:9–13.

23. Zinaida Gippius, *Dmitrii Merezhkovskii* (Paris: YMCA-Press, 1951), 60. Ormazd and Ahriman, according to the dualistic theodicy of Zoroastrianism, are respectively the lords of light and darkness.

24. Cf. Gippius, *Dmitrii Merezhkovskii*, esp. 43.

25. D.S. Merezhkovskii, *Polnoe sobranie sochinenii*, 17 vols. (St. Petersburg and Moscow: Izdanie T-va M.O. Vol'f, 1911–13), 1:iii; cited in Bedford, *The Seeker: D.S. Merezhkovskiy*, 91.

26. Cf. Bedford, *The Seeker: D.S. Merezhkovskiy*, 66.

27. Ibid., 60, 64.

28. Konstantin Mochul'skii, *Valerii Briusov* (Paris: YMCA-Press, 1962), 22. Briusov's willingness to sacrifice life to art spawned confusion and grief, and not only for himself. As Khodasevich showed in his brilliant necrology, "Konets Renaty" (1928), this is exactly what happened in the real-life erotic triangles that are reflected in *Ognennyi angel*, a book whose making was, according to Khodasevich, the undoing of Renate's biographical counterpart Nina Petrovskaia. Vladislav Khodasevich, "Konets Renaty," in his *Nekropol'. Vospominaniia* (Moscow: Sovetskii pisatel', 1991), 7–19. See also Joan Delaney Grossman, "Valery Briusov and Nina Petrovskaia: Clashing Models of Life and Art," in *Creating Life: The Aesthetic Utopia of Russian Modernism*, ed. Irina Paperno and Joan Delaney Grossman (Stanford University Press, 1994), 122–50.

29. Briusov's notebooks for 1893; cited in Mochul'skii, *Valerii Briusov*, 24. As Mochul'sky shows, primary in Briusov's thoughts about the new art was vanity, which literature was merely a means of satisfying.

30. See Mochul'skii, *Valerii Briusov*, 40, who noted that Briusov's first independent book of poetry, *Chefs d'oeuvre* (1895), idealizes a world-view "beyond good and evil": "Praising passion, vice, perversion and transgression, Briusov annihilates the old morality, urges on the demise of the old world."

31. Briusov, *Sobranie sochinenii*, 1:297–98. Cf. the discussion of this poem in Mochul'skii, *Valerii Briusov*, 99.

32. "Z.N. Gippius" (December 1901), in Briusov, *Sobranie sochinenii*, 1:355.

33. See Julian W. Connolly, "Briusov's 'The Fiery Angel': By Love Possessed," *Selecta: Journal of the Pacific Northwest Council on Foreign Languages* 8 (1987):102,104. As Connolly points out, this hesitation between natural and supernatural explanations of human experience "touches upon one of the most important themes of Briusov's entire career – the indistinct boundary between the realms of the real and the illusory" (104).

34. Briusov, *Sobranie sochinenii*, 4:9. The work cited is Jean Bodin's *La Démonomanie des sorciers* (Paris: J. Du Puys, 1580). Briusov himself cultivated his persona as a "great sorcerer" (velikii mag), who was on personal terms with the Devil. Boris Sadovskoi, Briusov's colleague at the symbolist journal *Vesy*, recalled this aura surrounding Briusov's authorship. "Many poets of the *Vesy* circle confessed that in the presence of 'the master' they would become lost and instantaneously stupid. One poet-demonologist went so far as to insist that this phenomenon did not take place without a certain amount of deviltry, that Briusov possessed a diabolical power that subjugated people to him." Boris Sadovskoi, *Ozim': Stat'i o russkoi poezii* (Petrograd: Popov, 1915); cited in Mochul'skii, *Valerii Briusov*, 108.

35. Andrei Belyi, *Nachalo veka* (Moscow and Leningrad: Gosudarstvennoe izdatel'stvo khudozhestvennoi literatury, 1933), 283–84; cited in E.V. Chudetskaia, "'Ognennyi angel': Istoriia sozdaniia i pechati," in Briusov, *Sobranie sochinenii*, 4:346.

36. For a different reading, see Peter G. Christensen, "Psychology, History, and the Fantastic in Valery Bryusov's 'The Fiery Angel'," *Australian Slavonic and East European Studies* 3, no.2 (1989):1–16. Christensen claims that "to allegorize magic into Symbolist art only makes it harder to account for the power of the novel" (2), a statement with which I cannot agree.

37. A.M. Remizov, "Chertik," in his *Izbrannoe*, ed. Iu.A. Andreev (Moscow: Khudozhestvennaia literatura, 1978), 96.

38. On the linkage between erotic and demonic possession see Connolly, "Briusov's 'The Fiery Angel'."

39. Mochul'skii, *Valerii Briusov*, 47.

40. "Chetkie linii gor..." (12 June 1896), in Briusov, *Sobranie sochinenii*, 1:111.

41. Fedor Sologub, *Tvorimaia legenda* (Moscow: Sovremennik, 1991), 71. Cited hereafter in the text by page number.

42. George Kalbouss points out that Jesus pays a visit to Trirodov in the guise of the suggestively named Emmanuil Osipovich Davidov, and that Trirodov (in perfect Grand-Inquisitorial form) rejects the "way" of Christ as a mistake intended to seduce the weak, a mistake which Trirodov intends to correct with his own "bold and difficult design." George Kalbouss, "Russian Symbolism Breaking Away," *Perspectives on Contemporary Literature* 8 (1982):118.

43. Maksim Gor'kii, *Sobranie sochinenii v tridtsati tomakh* (Moscow: Gosudarstvennoe izdatel'stvo khudozhestvennoi literatury, 1949–55), 30:44.

44. Sologub's neologism *Svetozarnyi* (sometimes *Luchezarnyi*) is difficult to render in English. Its first root, *svet*, denotes "light" in this context. The second root, *zaria*, usually means "the dawn" or "sunrise," though it is infrequently also used to signify "twilight" or "sunset." Sologub seems to have both "twilight" and "dawn" in mind, as my subsequent discussion suggests.

45. See Irene Masing-Delic, "'Peredonov's Little Tear' – Why Is It Shed? (The Sufferings of a Tormentor)," in *The Petty Demon*, trans. S.D. Cioran, ed. Murl Barker (Ann Arbor: Ardis, 1983), 333–43. Masing-Delic's description of the Demiurge's role in Sologub's universe has bearing upon *The Created Legend*: "The 'Satanist' and 'Lucifer worshipper' Sologub created a poetic world which would seem to find its best explanation in Gnostic-Manichaean terms. The critique of the Demiurge's faulty creation – our imperfect world and those clay puppets called human beings – forms the all-dominating thematics of Sologub's works in any genre" (334).

46. On Sologub's relation to sadism, see Nadezhda Teffi, "Fedor Sologub" (1949), reprinted in *Vospominaniia o serebrianom veke*, ed. Vadim Kreid (Moscow: Respublika, 1993), 80-93, esp. 87. Teffi wrote that the cult of demonism and sadism that Sologub fostered in his writings reflected tragically on the artist himself: "Sologub

was considered a conjurer and a Sadist. In his poems he whipped, and he executed, and he conjured. A black power played in them" (87). See also Henryk Baran, "Fedor Sologub and the Critics: The Case of 'Nav'i Chary'," in *Studies in Twentieth-Century Russian Prose*, ed. Nils Åke Nilsson, Stockholm Studies in Russian Literature, no.14 (Stockholm: Almqvist and Wiksell International, 1982), 52. As Baran writes, in 1909 the students of the Circle of Literature and Art at St. Petersburg University held a mock trial where Sologub, along with Kuzmin and Artsybashev, was tried for pornography. The last two were acquitted, but Sologub, for *The Created Legend*, was found guilty of "seductive description of unnatural tendencies known as sadism." His sentence: the book was condemned to flames and Sologub was to be placed under arrest for one month.

47. See Kalbouss, "Russian Symbolism Breaking Away," who presents *The Created Legend* as a work of Wellsean science-fantasy.

48. Ibid., 118.

49. In her analysis of *The Petty Demon*, Masing-Delic shows how doll or puppet imagery is endemic to Sologub's conception of the Demiurge: "In their compact grossness, human bodies cannot but trap the spirit. The Demiurge's creative work was 'presumptuous and blundering' in its entirety but this characterization applies particularly to the creatures called human beings. To make them, the Demiurge chose coarse clay as raw material which he shaped into crude and graceless forms. ... His creatures ought not to be called men as they are but barely animated clay puppets. ... The 'spark of life,' without which these clay figures would 'crumble to dust,' is too feeble to move their heavy frame. They are therefore provided with a 'mechanism' which propels them forward. Consequently their movements are jerky. The puppets are run on 'electric batteries' and pulled by 'strings'" (Masing-Delic, "'Peredonov's Little Tear'," 334).

50. For example both Trirodov and the narrator think in terms of such dichotomies as the lyric impulse versus the ironic or Dulcinea versus Aldonsa. Compare 153 with 452–53, and 153 with 230.

51. As to Sologub's Satanism, Nadezhda Teffi wrote of it eloquently in her reminiscences (1949), where she cites Sologub's verses: "Kogda ia v burnom more plaval / I moi korabl' poshel ko dnu, / Ia tak vozzval: 'Otets moi, D'iavol, / Spasi, pomilui, – ia tonu'." "Having recognized the Devil as his father," Teffi comments, "he accepted from him all of his black inheritance as well: spiteful tedium, spiritual solitude, cold-heartedness, disgust at earthly joy and contempt for man." Teffi, "Fedor Sologub," 87. Teffi cites Sologub's "Kogda ia v burnom more plaval..." (23 July 1902) inexactly; I have reverted to Sologub's original, as given in Fedor Sologub, *Stikhotvoreniia*, ed. M.I. Dikman, Biblioteka poeta, Bol'shaia seriia (Leningrad: Sovetskii pisatel', 1975), 278. Because Sologub stands so close to his Satanic creations, it is difficult not to ascribe to him their views, whether on art, pedagogy, sexuality, religion, or whatever else. V. Kranikhfel'd, one of *The Created Legend*'s earliest critics, gloated that "those readers who ... decode ... the hieroglyphs of *Drops of Blood* [Part One of *The Created Legend*] will eventually realize that instead of the enigmatic Trirodov, Sologub stands before us, his identity guessed long ago, repeating for the tenth time the few tenets of his simplified solipsistic conception;" cited in Baran, "Fedor Sologub and the Critics," 42. Cf. also A.S. Dolinin: "Is it necessary to explain that Trirodov is Sologub himself and that his world is a realm of phantoms and visions, created by the unhealthy imagination of a man *organically* estranged from life?" A.S. Dolinin, "Estranged: Toward a Psychology of Sologub's Work," in *The Noise of Change: Russian Literature and the Critics (1891–1917)*, ed. and trans. Stanley Rabinowitz (Ann Arbor: Ardis, 1986), 134.

52. For the implication of the authorial personae in the novel's demonism, see Niko-
    lai Berdiaev, "Russia's Temptation – on Bely's *Silver Dove*," in *The Noise of Change*,
    ed. Rabinowitz, 188-90; K. Mochul'skii, *Andrei Bely: The Major Symbolist Fiction*
    (Cambridge, Mass.: Harvard University Press, 1985), 77, 93.
53. For an analysis of the relation between the demonic theme and narrative point
    of view in Bely's *Petersburg*, see the chapter on Bely in Adam Weiner, *By Authors
    Possessed: The Demonic Novel in Russia* (Evanston, Ill.: Northwestern University
    Press, 1998), 138-88.

Chapter 12

Symbolist Devils and Acmeist Transformation: Gumilev, Demonism, and the Absent Hero in Akhmatova's *Poem Without a Hero*

Michael Basker

In his acmeist manifesto of January 1913, Nikolai Gumilev complained that Russian symbolism had "directed its main endeavours to the realm of the unknown. It fraternized by turns with mysticism, theosophy, and occultism."[1] It will not surprise readers of other essays in the present volume that among the "imbalances" of the symbolist heritage which the new literary group therefore proposed to redress was an excessive preoccupation with the demonic. "As concerns angels, demons, elementals and other spirits," Gumilev wrote, "they are one component of an artist's material, and their specific gravity should no longer outweigh that of other images adopted by him" (3:19). Acmeism, in other words, would not entirely eschew the demonic; but, guided above all by aesthetic rather than metaphysical considerations, it would relegate demons and devilry to a position of lesser prominence than in the literature of its immediate predecessors. In the context of other acmeist pronouncements upon the "internal vices"[2] of symbolism, this may seem a remarkably mild dissociation from such quintessentially symbolist thematics. It will transpire that a degree of caution was entirely warranted.

The extensive subject of acmeist demonism has been little explored. This essay considers just two, quite separate but profoundly interrelated strands. It begins with a brief and necessarily schematic overview of the prominent place of demonism in the work of Nikolai Gumilev. The main part of the essay then concentrates on Anna Akhmatova's literary masterpiece, *Poem Without a Hero* (*Poema bez geroia*). Begun only in 1940, and not completed until the mid-1960s – half a century or more after the heyday of Russian modernist demonism – this "Petersburg Tale"[3] is unquestionably the most demonic of Akhmatova's works. After looking briefly at one of its possible "demonic" sources and its allegedly infernal origins, the essay examines in more detail the poem's setting in space and time, and its extensive use of "demonic prototypes" from the symbolist era. Unexpectedly, though consistently with his own writing, Gumilev proves to figure prominently among the latter. Yet Gumilev is also, and perhaps uniquely, associated with the path to transcendence of the demonic. Precisely on this basis, as Akhmatova's "Don Juan" theme finally corroborates, he can be considered the poem's "absent hero." Demonism – and Gumilev – thus prove fundamental to an interpretation of the whole; and this in turn should permit some fresh conclusions on the character of "acmeist demonism."

Gumilev was the first of the future acmeists to appear in print, and the most thoroughly immersed in symbolism. In a memorable formulation from Akhmatova's jottings "Towards the History of Acmeism" (K istorii akmeizma): "The most essential thing is to understand the character of G[umilev], and the main thing about his character: as a boy he put his faith in symbolism in the way people believe in God. It was an inviolable sanctum, but as he grew closer to the symbolists, and in particular to "The Tower" (V. Ivanov), his faith shook, and he began to feel that something within him had been defiled."[4] The implication of immature faith in a false God may seem suggestively redolent of demonic delusion; and certainly it might be deemed a consequence of Gumilev's early allegiance to symbolism that he was by far the most prolific and persistent acmeist demonologist. He was also the only one of the acmeists whose dealings in the demonic appear, however briefly, to have assumed a tangibly biographical, experimental dimension. If we are to believe what Gumilev told his Tsarskoe Selo neighbour, the painter Della-Vos-Kardovskaia, he and a more diffident group of fellow-students had endeavoured to "see the Devil" during his time at the Sorbonne (1906–1908): "To this end they had to undergo a series of trials – to read Cabalistic texts, to fast for several days, and on the appointed evening to drink some kind of potion. After this the Devil was to

have appeared, and it should have been possible to enter into conversation with him. His [Gumilev's] fellow-students very quickly
abandoned the project. Only N.S. persisted to the very end, and
indeed saw some vague figure in the semi-darkened room."[5] Della-
Vos-Kardovskaia found the episode comically schoolboyish (again
the implication of immaturity); and as early as October 1906,
Gumilev himself was protesting to Briusov that an original-looking
tie or a well-written poem were as exciting as conjuration of the
dead.[6] Yet his resolutely determined attempt to summon the Devil
was not inconsistent with his abiding interest in various forms of
occultism,[7] and implied at least some degree of openness at that
early stage to concretely literal belief in things demonic.

As for Gumilev's writings, his poetry and prose fiction were from
the outset heavily imbued with the demonic. It is indicative, for
instance, that of the three poems which marked his debut in 1906 in
the most prestigious symbolist journal, *Vesy*, two have demonic
themes. The poem afterwards entitled "The Cave of Dream"
(Peshchera sna, 1:63) has a probable Nietzschean subtext,[8] but nevertheless deals also with the occult phenomenon of "waking som-
nambulism" or "astral vision," whereby, in noteworthy accord with
Gumilev's student experiment, Lucifer is the object and possible
agent of "magnetic" conjuration.[9] And in "My old friend, my faithful Devil …" (Moi staryi drug, moi vernyi D'iavol …, 1:58), an "intelligent" Devil (the poem later acquired the title "Umnyi D'iavol")
assumes the unconventional role of truthful defender against metaphysical delusion, represented, with evident polemical intent, by the
siren call of a symbolistic lady in white. This sceptical guardian-
Devil is to all appearances indeed a "faithful friend" to the poet, and
perhaps the externalization of his rationalizing intellect.[10]

The most important precursor of these demonic poems in
Gumilev's published verse was the central, "ballad" section of his
"Fairy Tale of the Kings" (Skazka o koroliakh, 1903–1905):

> Пять могучих коней мне дарил Люцифер
> И одно золотое с рубином кольцо.
>
> $$(1:41)^{11}$$
>
> [Lucifer gave me five powerful steeds
> And one gold ring with a ruby.]

In this version of the Devil's intimate relationship with the lyric hero,
Lucifer's gifts might be interpreted as an allegory of the five senses
and the ardent heart; and for the first three of the poem's six stanzas,
they engender an exuberant, solipsistic pleasure in existence. But at
the "heights of consciousness" the hero meets a pallid, unresponsive
moon-maiden, to whom he surrenders his ruby ring. Lucifer retali-

ates contemptuously with a new "gift": not the traditional punishment of consignment to Hell, but, as one recent Russian scholar has noted,[12] the effective "demonization" of the lyric hero on an earth which, we might add, seems wholly in Lucifer's control:

> И смеясь надо мной, презирая меня,
> Мои взоры одел Люцифер в полутьму,
> Люцифер подарил мне шестого коня,
> И Отчаянье было названье ему.
>
> (1:41)

> [And mocking me, despising me,
> Lucifer clothed my sight in semi-darkness,
> Lucifer granted me a sixth steed,
> And Despair was its name.]

This twofold thematic development established the essential parameters of Gumilev's early demonism, elaborated in poem after poem of his collections *Romantic Flowers* (*Romanticheskie tsvety*, 1908) and *Pearls* (*Zhemchuga*, 1910).[13] One strand reflects a vigorous quest for hitherto inaccessible or forbidden knowledge, for the expansion of intellectual consciousness and spiritual experience into "spaces without limits."[14] The ultimate implication is doubtless a desire for transcendence of the mortal world's constraints; but immediately, as, for example, in "The Descendants of Cain" (Potomki Kaina, 1909), such explicitly "Luciferian" impulse can convey an exhilarating conviction of omnipotence:

> Он не солгал нам, дух печально-строгий,
> Принявший имя утренней звезды,
> Когда сказал: «Не бойтесь вышней мзды,
> Вкусите плод и будете, как боги».
>
> Для юношей открылись все дороги,
> Для старцев – все запретные труды,
>
> (1:83)

> [He did not lie to us, the sadly-severe spirit,
> Who took the name of the morning star,
> When he said: "Do not fear higher sanction,
> Taste the fruit and you shall be as gods."
>
> For young men all roads were opened,
> For elders – all forbidden works,]

More frequently, however, especially in Gumilev's prose fiction and poems of *Pearls*, the very acquisition of knowledge or experience may also be connected with bleak, quasi-suicidal despair: a sense, alternately rebellious or desolate, of divine abandonment, lapse of faith, entrapment, or defiant persistence in all-too-human self-reliance. Thus, for example, "mystery is ugly," the hero's home, lined with books from a hunched, sepulchral dealer in antiquities, is no place for things of beauty, and the malevolently proud spirit of "Portrait of a Man" (Portret muzhchiny, 1910), perpetrator of some unspecified, terrible crime, is unable either to speak of God or to mourn (plakat') over his misdemeanour.[15]

Perhaps inevitably for one nurtured on symbolism, the demonic also informed Gumilev's concept of art. This is forcefully elaborated in the opening poem of *Pearls*, "The Magic Violin" (Volshebnaia skripka, 1907), where artistic creation is both blessing and poison, a fatefully compelling path which might (demonically?) ennoble, but conceals a "dark terror," articulated through the imagery of rapacious wolves, fearful monsters, and the "spirits of hell" (dukhi ada). Art is destructive of innocence, and will ineluctably lead the happy, smiling, "dear boy" (milyi mal'chik) of the poem's opening line to a hideous, vainglorious death:

> На, владей волшебной скрипкой, посмотри в глаза чудовищ
> И погибни славной смертью, страшной смертью скрипача!
>
> (1:82)

> [Here, master the magic violin, look monsters in the eyes
> And die a glorious death, the terrible death of a violinist!]

As with so much "demonic" writing by Gumilev and his contemporaries, it is in this case virtually impossible to disentangle metaphysical substance from metaphorical representation of psychological disposition or predominantly literary exercise on well-tried themes. Gumilev's demonization of art and its origins was nevertheless persistent, and his story "The Stradivarius Violin" (Skripka Stradivariusa, 1908) – another musical connection – suggests that the very title of *Pearls*, and the subdivisions of the first edition into "Black," "Grey," and "Pink Pearl" (there is no mention of pure white), bore private connotations of Satanic inspiration.[16]

In the subsequent, acmeist period of Gumilev's career, demonic themes were less frequent, though his demonic repertoire paradoxically broadened into sometimes playful literary experimentation. So, for example, he found "Satanic malice," witchcraft, and a "welcoming Devil" of fiery destruction in the Africa of *The Tent* (*Shater*, 1918), saw Satan's "intolerable gleam" over the Tower of Pisa, and made Beelzebub and Astaroth the pivotal characters of his children's play *The Tree of Transformations* (*Derevo prevrashchenii*, 1918, 2:157–71).[17] The demonic element of the original was intensified in a fine translation of Southey's "The Surgeon's Warning;"[18] and to portray his young wife, Akhmatova, Gumilev turned to a folkloric demonology (serpent's lair, Bald Mountain, the curse of God) reminiscent of the work of his acmeist colleagues Sergei Gorodetsky and, in particular, the Ukrainian Vladimir Narbut:

Из логова змиева,
Из города Киева,
Я взял не жену, а колдунью.
                              (1912, 1:131)[19]

[From the serpent's lair,
From the city of Kiev,
I took not a wife but a sorceress.]

The programatically acmeist play, *Actaeon* (*Akteon*, 1913), on the other hand, contained the seeds of a radical departure from earlier demonism. With a notable switch from musical to architectural metaphor, Gumilev developed in the hero, Cadmus, an ideal image of the artist-craftsman, who labours piously at his creation, his pride subjugated to the higher authority of God, and attains what may be described as a majestic equilibrium and plenitude of being in confident possession of the highest wisdom that is legitimately accessible to mortal man.[20] By comparison with the boundless Luciferian quest (or the immoderate aspirations of the play's Dionysiac anti-hero, Actaeon), the way of Cadmus necessarily involves an austere element of determined self-limitation – the wilful control apparently intended by the term "chastity" (tselomudrie) in Gumilev's acmeist manifesto (3:19). It is thus an exacting goal, and often an elusive one; for the soul frequently remains open to dazzling spiritual temptation, potentially demonic (besnovataia) in its ill-suppressed, disequilibrating yearning for the distant stars.[21] Previous demonic themes accordingly re-emerge with disquieting force in such major poems of Gumilev's last years as "The Forest" (Les, 1919, 1:290) or "At the Gypsies" (U tsygan, 1920, 1:300–301). In the latter, for instance, music (again) in a gypsy tavern evokes a majestic vision-reminiscence of a fearsomely destructive Satan, barring the way to the true Creator: but this gives way to the banality of a female vampire and prosaic Asmodeus; and distant echoes of Blok and Baudelaire[22] seem to underscore the recurring theme of art's potential function as insidious metaphysical trap, as will-sapping, soul-engulfing damnation. Though we will return below to Akhmatova's particular assessment of Gumilev's (anti-)demonic development, the apparent evidence of such poems is that "victory over Beelzebub" (1:188) may be strongly desired, even confidently perceived, but less than securely effected.

Akhmatova's own earlier poetry (roughly up until the second edition of *Anno Domini* in 1923) is outwardly strikingly consistent with Gumilev's manifesto in its treatment of "demons, elementals and other spirits." Although diabolical material is not avoided, its role is invariably subordinated to the concretization of an emotional state or other elaboration of a poem's main theme, which it never itself constitutes. Moreover, overt demonic reference always entails a palpable irony or hyperbole which serves to intensify its psychological function, and seems incompatible with any metaphysical reality.[23] Yet a religious awareness of transgression and potential damnation also constitutes a frequent undercurrent of her early, "acmeistic" verse. This typically arises from a recognition of personal culpability or guilty complicity in the pain caused by love. In consequence, the persona may feel her home, social milieu, or "world" to be somehow blighted, abandoned by God if not necessarily possessed by the Devil.[24] In addition, specifically demonic implications characterize some of Akhmatova's many poems about art. Not only the erotic content of the poetry, but also the wilful estrangement from others and self that its creation demands can appear sinful, and the consequences of the irresistible creative impulse, for those close to the poet, seem profoundly malign.[25] Conversely, however, a formidable inner strength may be the poet's diabolic "recompense" for such transgression into the emotional no man's land of art:

> Дьявол не выдал. Мне всё удалось.
> Вот и могущества явные знаки.
>
> (1922, 1:143)

[The Devil did not betray. I succeeded in everything.
Here are the visible signs of power.]

A separate study might trace in detail the development from these beginnings both of what might be termed an uncanny or supernatural demonism,[26] and also of a "political demonization" of Stalin and the Soviet order,[27] the extra-textual roots of which can be traced back through the "hell" of Tsushima (1:329), to the "Dostoevskian and demonic" urban atmosphere of the late nineteenth century, and even to the influence of that traditional "demon" of Slavophiles and sectarians, Peter the Great.[28] For present purposes, however, it should simply be noted that both strands find much their fullest expression in the quasi-necromantic *Poem Without a Hero* (hereafter *Poem*), which also takes to its furthest extent the theme of demonic inspiration seemingly closer to the symbolist Gumilev of "The Magic Violin" than to the spirit of his acmeist manifesto. It is to this work – including its many variants, and the copious prose fragments Akhmatova devoted to it (hereafter "The Prose") – that we now turn.

Albeit with apparent irony, the attribution of *Poem* to an initial demonic incitement (or entrapment) is clearly stated within the text:

> Бес попутал в укладке рыться …
>
> (1:339)

[A demon beguiled me to ransack the casket …]

Poem "arrived" unbidden and unexpected (1:319), it employed the
"forbidden device" of the cryptogram and inverted (= demonic?)
"mirror writing" (1:339), and Akhmatova recalled the "demonic
ease" (demonskaia legkost') with which she wrote it (1:353). At the
same time, the urgency of the poetic material became an unremitting,
fiendish obsession, of which the poet was powerless to rid herself:

> Я пила ее в капле каждой
> И бесовскою черной жаждой
> Одержима, не знала, как
> Мне разделаться с бесноватой:
>
>   (1:340)
>
> [I drank it in every drop,
> And possessed by demonic black thirst
> I did not know how
> To shake myself free of the demonic one:]

Even the image of the boomerang, which Akhmatova used twice in
"The Prose" (1:359, 361) to describe *Poem's* persistent returns to her,
may have had private demonic significance She doubtless recalled
that for Gumilev, in his "musical" story "The Stradivarius Violin,"
the Devil himself had been the boomerang's proud inventor.[29]

   As Akhmatova made clear in "The Prose," the casket in which the
"demon" prompted her to rummage contained belongings abandoned by O.A. Glebova-Sudeikina: "letters and poems" (1:350),
relating to the suicide of Vsevolod Kniazev in 1913, which provided
the kernel of *Poem's* lyric "plot." Yet *Poem's* genesis was exceptionally
complex, and beyond the fiendishly insistent claim of "Ol'ga's
things" to their "place beneath the poetic sun" (1:355) – a "rebellion
of the inanimate," mockingly attributed to the folkloric demon,
Kashchei (1:360) – scholars have also traced the essential crystalliza-
tion of the compositional impetus both to public events (the occupation of Paris and bombing of London in 1940),[30] and to Akhmatova's
(re-)acquaintance with a series of cultural "texts." These have
included such disparate items as Mikhail Kuzmin's "The Trout
Breaks the Ice" (Forel' razbivaet led), Meierkhol'd's productions of
Lermontov's *Masquerade* (*Maskarad*) and Tchaikovsky's *The Queen of
Spades* (*Pikovaia dama*), Strauss's "Juristen Waltzer," or Mandel'shtam's oral recollections of Gumilev.[31] As far as I am aware, however,
there has been no discussion in this connection of another acmeistic
text with infernal as well as Gumilevian orientation – M.A. Zenkevich's "Fictionalized Memoirs" (Belletricheskie memuary) recently
published under the title *A Peasant Sphinx* (*Muzhitskii sfinks*, 1928).[32]

   Though there is scarcely a devil to be found in Zenkevich's verse
during more than fifty years,[33] the demonic cast of his memoirs is
established from the very first sentence: "What devil brought me to

this dead, terrifying Petersburg!"[34] Against a background of incessant references to "devilry" (chertovshchina) and tormenting "Petersburg mirage,"[35] immediately redolent of *Poem* (see below), Zenkevich seems particularly to anticipate Akhmatova in presenting his recollections as a "fevered amalgamation of events in distorted temporal perspective,"[36] inextricably mingling the living and the dead, the real, the literary and the chimerical, across bewildering shifts and contaminations of chronological boundaries. A central presence over the first half of these diabolically contorted memoirs is the executed Gumilev, who eerily rematerializes from the dead in his First World War uniform, and guides and beguiles his former acmeist colleague, Zenkevich, through a temporal (con)fusion of pre-War days (the "Wandering Dog" and *Apollon*) and post-Revolutionary "events" (Uritsky's murder and the Tagantsev conspiracy). Akhmatova, too, appears in person, "recollected" from November 1921 in a separate, brief chapter; but her presence can be detected also behind the main female character, Gumilev's chillingly "undead" companion, El'ga Gustavovna – a dangerous and imperiously seductive temptress, endlessly mutable in appearance, with devilish, miasmal fire in her eyes.[37] Like the dramatis personae of *Poem*, she is a composite image, drawn partly from literature, partly from a plurality of real-life prototypes.[38] Other identities, too, are fluid and spectral. Blok, for instance, is no longer himself but the photograph of his corpse, superimposed upon the (death-?)mask of Pushkin (the mask is another important motif of *Poem*) and the werewolf of Gogol's demonic tale, "A Terrible Vengeance" (Strashnaia mest').[39] The unremitting impact of many such feverishly diabolical encounters brings Zenkevich's Author-persona close to suicide or the "doubling" and irreversible fragmentation of his own personality: "But to the Devil with them, all these terrible thoughts! A little more, and you might put a bullet through your temple or see yourself split in two not only internally, but externally, see your double right here, alone with you in the room, as in a large mirror, only not imitating you, but performing its own independent movements."[40] Again the similarities to *Poem*, in which the mirror world (zazerkal'e) is prominent, and Author and all else are liable to "double and treble" (1:361), are readily apparent. Akhmatova's authorial experience is sufficiently "terrible" to prompt thoughts of evasion at any cost;[41] while the "bullet through the temple" is the method of her cornet of dragoons, Kniazev (1:328). Zenkevich, moreover, likewise portrays a young poet-soldier, prematurely deceased and improperly mourned: not, it is true, the suicide Kniazev on the eve of War, but second lieutenant A.A. Konge (whom Akhmatova would have known from the Poets' Guild), killed in action in 1915.[42] Further potential links between memoirs and poem can be discerned in, for instance, Zenkevich's consciousness of guilt for the crimes of others; his reflections on the poet trapped by his own verse; or his extended portrayal of Rasputin – the archetypal historical demon of the 1910s.[43]

According to Zenkevich, Akhmatova read and praised his unpublishable memoirs at some unspecified date after their completion.[44] Perhaps, then, her approving reference in "The Prose" (1:362) to Zenkevich's view that *Poem's* language is acmeistic, and its use of the fantastic close to Gumilev's "Lost Tram" (Zabludivshiisia tramvai, 1919, 1:297–99), is a characteristic piece of (demonic?) misdirection: an encrypted acknowledgement of the role of Zenkevich's diabolical phantasmagoria as one of *Poem's* points of departure.[45] Typically, though, Akhmatova's purpose was probably creative re-adujstment if not exactly polemical refutation: for as an intermediate, demonic link between Gumilev's famous, forbidden poem[46] and Akhmatova's own presentation of the historical era, Zenkevich's (artistically inferior) text contains no hint of that transformative element which, as we shall see, was essential to her thinking.

The demonic content of *Poem* itself is most intense in the first and longest part, "The Year 1913" (Deviat'sot trinadtsatyi god), while Part 2, "Tails" (Reshka), is essentially a semi-ironic commentary on the creative methods and sources of Part 1. In so far as Akhmatova's inspiration is explicitly attributed to the promptings of a "demon," this metapoetic discourse is inevitably a demonic tale. Part 3, "Epilogue," addressed in the aftermath of the purges to the ruined Leningrad of the blockade, belongs to an authorial voice already "on the far side of hell" (1:338), and will be of less relevance here.

The "devilry" of Part 1 is explicitly "Petersburgian" (1:326) and, as the subtitle "Petersburg Tale" implies, is as firmly grounded in Petersburg's demonic cultural tradition as in the reality of 1913. The setting is "that same / Old witch's City / Of the Queen of Spades" (tot samyi / Staroi ved'my Pikovoi Damy / Gorod).[47] Yet it is also "Dostoevskian and demonic" (1:332), and its spectral ambience and eerie events (carriages plunging into the Neva, portraits that come alive, the city's disappearance into its own spectral fog) resonate, too, with the demonic episodes of Gogol's "The Portrait" (Portret), "The Overcoat" (Shinel'), and "Nevsky Prospect" (Nevskii prospekt), Bely's *Petersburg* (*Peterburg*) and Stravinsky's *Petrushka.*[48] Akhmatova probably draws in addition on V.F. Odoevsky and other "Petersburg Hoffmannists" of the 1830s and 1840s,[49] and not surprisingly implies in her "Introduction" that her mental revisitation of this city from 1940 (or the besieged Leningrad on the twentieth anniversary of Gumilev's execution in August 1941)[50] is tantamount to a descent into the nether regions:

КАК БУДТО ПЕРЕКРЕСТИЛАСЬ
И ПОД ТЕМНЫЕ СВОДЫ СХОЖУ.
(1:322)

[AS IF I HAD CROSSED MYSELF
AND DESCEND BENEATH DARK VAULTS.]

Topographical implications further contribute to the demonic ambience in that these "vaults" might serve in part to identify the "Wandering Dog,"[51] the subterranean "cabaret artistique" whose leading
lights Akhmatova had associated with the inevitable road to hell as
early as December 1912.[52] The cabaret's fantastic decor merges in
Poem with that of its successor, the "Comedians' Halt" (another cel-
lar, which contained a chamber known to habitués as the "Devil's
Room");[53] but a blasphemous inversion of the motif of the "road to
Damascus" (1:334) serves to intimate that it remains unalterably a
place of licentious and adulterous rendezvous.[54] It is equally the
place of "accursed dance" (okaiannaia pliaska), such as that of the
"goat-legged woman" (kozlonogaia) with "evil horns in her pale
curls," whose "little boots" resound like (devil's?) "hooves"
(1:327–28),[55] and perhaps of such others of *Poem's* unholy performances as the dance of Salomé (1:323), the "Danse macabre"
(1:331), and even the "hellish Harlequinade of 1913" (1:335) which
forms the core of Part 1.[56] In all probability, the spectre of the cellar-
cabaret also informs the indeterminate location characterized in the
"Interlude" of Part 1 as "the depths of the hall, stage, hell" (and alternatively, with a shift to the heights which brings no contrasting relief
from the infernal, the classic locale of the witches' sabbath, "the summit of Goethe's Brocken" [1:328]).

The temporal setting of "1913" is no less rich in demonic implications. *Poem* depicts an "evil midnight" (1:341) in "a bleak December"
(the first redaction took the latter phrase, from Poe's "Raven," as an
introductory epigraph [1:304], presumably with the attendant, infernal connotation of a "thing of evil! – prophet still, if bird or devil!,"
knocking unbidden at the poet's chamber door).[57] The darkness is
punctuated by "terrifying sound – / Bubbling, groan and scream of
bird" (strashnyi zvuk – / Klokotan'e, ston i klekot, 1:335); and the
authorial persona, who expresses fear (1:325), horror (e.g. 1:324),
and "boundless anxiety" (1:334), experiences a "dank cold" which
seems truly hellish, causing her to "burn" as well as freeze:

И я чувствую холод влажный,
Каменею, стыну, горю …
(1:323)

[And I feel a dank cold,
Petrify, freeze and burn …]

Worse still, the night (or nights) appears fathomless, without the blessed relief of the cock-crow which traditionally drives away evil spirits – the "Petersburg devilry" so palpably abroad at this most appropriate time of year:[58]

> Крик петуший нам только снится,
>   За окошком Нева дымится,
>   Ночь бездонна – и длится, длится
>   Петербургская чертовня ...
>
>   (1:326)

[We only dream of the cock's crow,
    Outside the window the Neva smoulders,
        The night is bottomless – and lasts,
            The Petersburg devilry lasts ...]

In addition to pervasive fog, smoke, and gloom (mrak) – such as penetrates even the protagonist's love at the moment of suicide (1:328) – *Poem's* Goya-esque atmosphere (1:324) of nocturnal malice is further sustained by recurrent "blackness," so that the "goat-legged woman" seems to appear from a "black-figured vase" (1:328), and the portrait from which she (or another?) "comes alive" (1:328) should doubtless be associated with the "black picture-frame" before which the author is left alone in the gathering gloom (sumrak, 1:326; cf. 1:330). Most strikingly, "black" also qualifies "rose" (1:330) and "crime" (1:331), and its connotations become manifest in reference to the "*demonic* black thirst" (1:340; emphasis mine) by which *Poem* possesses Author. At the head of this associative chain, even the poet's famous declaration that she is writing on another's "draft" (chernovik, 1:320) implies the familiar notion of poetic creativity as an accursed, consciously diabolical act; and of course other textual details – the route of the Guest from the Future who turns "*left* from the bridge" (1:325; emphasis mine), the numerological implications of several dates, the tripartite combinations of rhythm, phrase, image, and plot with which Akhmatova's "Triptych" (1:319) is unremittingly laden – readily acquire "sinister," demonic overtones in the context of the whole.[59] It is, however, the individual participants in the "midnight Hoffmanianna" (1:325) who best exemplify and ultimately elucidate the poem's demonic content. To some of this "swarm of ghosts" (1:336) and their putative protoypes we must now turn.

Of evident importance here is Akhmatova's Demon (1:330,336) – who, she asserted in "The Prose," "was always Blok" (1:359). The intertextual basis of *Poem's* "Blok line" has probably been more thoroughly explored than any other, and his "presence" behind the passage from which the following lines are taken is not at issue.[60] The type of demonism portrayed nevertheless bears closer scrutiny:

На стене его твердый профиль.
Гавриил или Мефистофель
Твой, красавица, паладин?
Демон сам с улыбкой Тамары,
Но такие таятся чары
В этом страшном, дымном лице:
Плоть, почти что ставшая духом.
И античный локон над ухом –
Всё таинственно в пришлеце.

(1:330)

[His firm profile is on the wall.
My beauty, is your paladin
Gabriel or Mephistopheles?
The Demon himself with Tamara's smile,
But such charms are secreted
In this terrible, smoky face:
Flesh, almost become spirit.
And the classical curl above the ear –
Everything is mysterious in the newcomer.]

The antithetical mode of exposition frequently adopted by Akhmatova in *Poem* is here employed with an intensity that verges on self-parody. The lines present a startling accumulation of contrarieties, each encompassed within this single being: male and female, predator and victim, flesh and spirit, fearful aspect and concealed charms – and, of course, angel and devil, heaven and hell. Arguably, however, the seemingly pivotal question as to whether this "paladin" is "Gabriel" or "Mephistopheles" is fundamentally flawed (or demonically misleading). The truly angelic, as Blok himself undoubtedly accepted, cannot be ambivalent.[61] By contrast – as is confirmed by the example of Lermontov's Demon, so appositely invoked here by Akhmatova – doubt, ambiguity, indeterminacy of contour (and, in *Poem*, "confusion"), are of the devil.[62] The demonic quality of Akhmatova's Demon, in other words, lies precisely in his mystery (vse tainstvenno), his enticing uncertainty of identity, and – his "firm profile" notwithstanding – his beguiling, androgynous incorporeality.[63] This absence of definition (*nedovoploshchennost'* might be the best Russian equivalent) is further developed in the lines that follow. Was it he who sent the black rose, or was it a dream? Was it he who met the Commendatore? (1:330). But though allusion to Blok's work is here at its most transparent, the implication of a corresponding *moral* amorphousness – of moral indeterminacy and passive turpitude – should evidently be understood in the light of Akhmatova's broader, suprapersonal conception of Blok as "man-epoch": one who "occupied a special place in the life of the entire pre-Revolutionary generation."[64]

In keeping with his status as Demon among lesser spirits in the hellish Harlequinade, this figure plays the central, fateful role in

Poem's melodramatic love-triangle: he casually seduces the frivolous "Colombine of the 1910s" (1:330) during a night at the demonic cabaret, and thereby drives the cornet of dragoons to suicide. The emblematic resonance is the more unmistakable in that the episode is a fabrication. Empirically, Blok was innocent of any connection with Kniazev's death; and the culpability which Akhmatova's plot imputes to him should presumably be related to his crucial signifi-cance in forming a moral climate in which such erotic encounters and melodramatic responses were a behavioural norm. Logically enough, moreover, Akhmatova's seducer is destructive not only of others. The phrase "with dead heart and dead gaze" (s mertvym serdtsem i mertvym vzorom, 1:330), which occurs immediately after the passage quoted above, denotes a moribund sterility at the very core of her "Demon," and heralds both his own ineluctable demise, and that of the epoch he embodies. In the following, third chapter of "1913," the same lack – or deliberate evasion – of clear self-definition is accordingly identified once more with the demonic, but the overt referent is now the most broadly generic of human terms, man:

> Словно в зеркале страшной ночи
> И беснуется и не хочет
> Узнавать себя человек,
>
> (1:333)
>
> [As though in the mirror of frightening night
> Man in demonic frenzy does not
> Wish to recognize himself,]

Yet here, too, Blok's presence is strongly implied. He is both man and Demon, and it is precisely as representative man-Demon that he is Akhmatova's "tragic tenor of the epoch."[65]

The "demonic" principle of uncertainty extends further, however. Though Blok should certainly be identified with the Demon (or rather, Demon and Tamara, Gabriel and Mephistopheles ...), the presence of Akhmatova's "man-epoch" can also be discerned behind the "Don Juan line" of *Poem*, with its significant theme of retribution; and behind the images of Iron Mask, of Harlequin, and perhaps of Poet-mile-post.[66] Blok is seemingly intertwined, too, with the faceless devil of folk legend behind the sinister personage "without face or name"[67] who marks the logical apogee of *Poem's* demonic motif of evasive identity. And of course each of these images has one – or more likely, several – other sources or "prototypes;" for just as "one person can play several roles," so, as Wendy Rosslyn has stated of *Poem*, "a single role can be played in life by many people."[68] Despite Akhmatova's misleadingly categorical identification of Demon with Blok, in the "Ballet Libretto" to *Poem* she could therefore write instead (or as well, with an accuracy attested by other essays in this volume) of "the shade of Vrubel": "from him [came] all the demons of the twentieth century, he himself first" (1:365). Lermontovian precedent apart, other modern figures, too, evidently inform her image. The "firm profile on the wall," for instance, is itself enough to suggest Meierkhol'd as another of the Demon's prototypes[69] – and possibly even the Author herself.[70] Such fragmentation, doubling and redoubling may seem particularly apposite in relation to Blok, who, as Toporov reminds us, wrote of the transformation of his ideal into an infernal doll: "in the lilac twilight of the unencompassable world rocks an enormous white catafalque, on which is a dead doll with a face vaguely recalling that which could be glimpsed through the roses of heaven. ... He who experiences all this is no longer alone; he is full of many demons (otherwise known as doubles)."[71] And, as the Author's shadowy presence in the "Demon passage" implies, it is absolutely fundamental to the (demonic) poetics of *Poem*, in which significance and meanings are fluid, quotations and identities intersect, "everything doubles," and doubles engender in turn a potentially endless series of further doubles or mirror reflections. "Everything splits into two and into three, down to the very bottom of the casket" (1:361).

It is predictable, therefore, that alongside the Demon – and ultimately not entirely distinct from him – *Poem* presents another prominent diabolical figure, the "Lord of Darkness" (Vladyka Mraka). This "unclean spirit" is lame and urbane, with a tail hidden beneath the tails of his coat, and he is universally popular, despite his gruesomely indefinite "visage":

> Маска это, череп, лицо ли –
> Выражение злобной боли,
> Что лишь Гойя мог передать.
> Общий баловень и насмешник,
> Перед ним самый смрадный грешник –
> Воплощенная благодать ...
>
> (1:324)[72]

[Be this mask, skull, or face –
An expression of malicious pain,
Which only Goya could convey.
Everyone's favourite and mocker,
Next to him the most arrant sinner
Is grace incarnate ...]

Akhmatova explained in "The Prose" (1:357) that this same figure reappears in Part 2 as "Satan himself":

> Это старый чудит Калиостро –
> Сам изящнейший сатана,
> Кто над мертвым со мной не плачет,

Кто не знает, что совесть значит
И зачем существует она.

(1:337)

[This is old Cagliostro clowning –
The most elegant Satan himself,
Who does not mourn the dead with me,
Who does not know what conscience means
And for what purpose it exists.]

The main prototype in this case is Mikhail Kuzmin, whose failure to "mourn the dead" relates most specifically to his apparent behaviour after the suicide of Pierrot-Kniazev (whose funeral he did not attend), but is extrapolated into a contemptuous indictment of a being horrifyingly devoid of moral sense: "one of those," in Akhmatova's words, "for whom all is possible. I am not going to list what was possible for him, but if I did so, the modern reader's hair would stand on end" (1:357).[73] The cumulative charge against "Satan," then, is less amorphous indefiniteness than omnivorous indifference, an unrestrained and utterly unrepentant hedonism, rendered the more unpalatable by a graceful frivolity far removed from the romantic aloofness which dignifies the elusive Demon. It is precisely the failure to take anything seriously – a quality of mockery reminiscent of Pushkin's "Demon," rather than Lermontov's[74] – that makes this "general favourite" more Satanic than the most heinous sinner, and Akhmatova denigrates him with a contemptuous partiality that betokens a deep-seated personal resentment. As "Lord of Darkness," he is, like the Demon, both directly involved in her "dark" text's central plot, and implicitly emblematic of, or perniciously influential over, his entire, unthinking epoch-generation.[75] But for the deprecating author he is also "just a devil" (poprostu chert, 1:357), and her observation that to him "all is possible" (vse mozhno, 1:357) seems a derisively reductive echo of the Dostoevskian "all is permitted" (vse dozvoleno).[76] There is, moreover, a disparaging, diabolically paradoxical irony in Akhmatova's wilful (mis-)construction, on the basis of literature and rumour (or gossip), of the fictionalized version of the fateful events of 1913 through which her "most elegant" cultivator of gossip is indicted.[77] If gossip (engenderment of uncertainty, obfuscation of truth) and mockery are demonic, they are also integral components of *Poem's* poetics.

It could plausibly be argued that each of the other New Year's masked figures is also tinged with the infernal, not least in that their spectrally uncertain "ontological" status – "real" ghosts, actors, dolls? – inherently contributes to their demonic aura. Only two, however – "Faust" and "the demonic Doctor Dapertutto" (1:365) – require further consideration here. Faust is identified in the libretto as Viacheslav Ivanov,[78] and Roman Timenchik has indicated that Akhmatova felt her portrayal of Ivanov in *Poem* to have much in common with that by Berdiaev in *Self-Cognition* (*Sampoznanie*): of a pivotal figure in a "Russian renaissance" which lacked "moral character," aesthetic clarity, or conscious volition, a man glitteringly accomplished, charming and mercurially accommodating, but also, at root, a despotic, even "vampiric" "fisher of human souls" (lovets chelovekov).[79] In view of Akhmatova's quotation, in her notes towards the libretto, from Ivanov's poem "Dream" (Son) – the heroine of which regards Faust as the Devil's double – the Faustian-demonic impulse implicit in *Poem* nevertheless invites more pointed definition.[80] On a purely personal level, the libretto's necromantic image of an aged Faust dancing with the dead Gretchen[81] conceivably alludes not merely in a general sense to Ivanov's culpable irresponsibility in the ready manipulation of others' fates, but also, specifically and tastelessly, to his "scandalous" third marriage to his step-daughter, Vera Shvarsalon (a metaphorical-diabolical "reanimation" of the dead wife-mother? Kuzmin, moreover, had previously been asked to marry the pregnant Vera,[82] and *Poem's* "Satan" thus "doubled" with Ivanov in a shadowy, rumour-obfuscated triangle.) And it seems inconceivable that in portraying Ivanov (author of a 1912 article on Goethe)[83] as Faust, Akhmatova should not have had in mind his erudition as well as his passion, his quest for all-encompassing synthesis of experience and knowledge which may indeed seem quintessentially emblematic of the age.

Several commentators have written illuminatingly on the reflection in *Poem* of productions and performances by Dapertutto, the familiar pseudonym which Vsevolod Meierkhol'd adopted for his work outside the Imperial Theatres. These, too, are of specific significance to its demonic thematics. Most relevant to the central plot-triangle is Meierkhol'd's emphatic association with the *commedia dell'arte*, established primarily through his productions of Blok's *Puppet Booth* (*Balaganchik*) – apropos of which he later described the traditional Harlequin as "the emissary of infernal powers," alternately "the foolish buffoon from Bergamo or the Devil"[84] – and *Colombine's Scarf* (*Sharf Kolombiny*), the adaptation of Schnitzler's pantomime *Veil of Pierrette* into a "chilling grotesque," a "combination of the supernatural and the banal, the terrifying and the ridiculous."[85] Noteworthy, too, is Meierkhol'd's connection with the Don Juan theme of *Poem*, through the "blackamoors" (arapchata, 1:329) most famously associated with his production of Molière's *Don Juan*.[86] "The Stranger" from his production of Lermontov's *Masquerade* – "not so much a man as a devil in disguise," according to the actor Iakov Maliutin[87] – is one of the probable sources for Akhmatova's demonic fig-

ure "without face or name;"[88] and that production's monumental
masked ball and characteristically Meierkhol'dian "Venetian" decor,
"masks, candles, and tall mirrors," suggest further detailed parallels
to the eerie nocturnal ambience of Akhmatova's work.[89] Other
Meierkhol'd productions evoked by *Poem*, all with more than a hint
of the demonic, include Wilde's *Salomé* and Tchaikovsky's *The Queen
of Spades*, and his film scenario of *The Picture of Dorian Gray* (in which
Meierkhol'd himself played a "Satanic" Lord Henry).[90]

   Meierkhol'd's presence is further manifest through his extensive
personal connections with *Poem's* demonic prototypes and loci. His
renowned production of *Puppet Booth*, for instance, involved close collaboration with *Poem's* most prominent "Harlequins" – both "Demon"-
Blok, and "Satan"-Kuzmin (who composed the music). And the first
issue of his *Love of Three Oranges: The Journal of Doctor Dapertutto* (*Liubov'
k trem apel'sinam: Zhurnal Doktora Dapertutto*) brought Blok (whom he
had persuaded to edit the poetry section) together with his future
demonic double, Akhmatova, for the public inception of their poetic
dialogue.[91] As for Kuzmin – whose appellation of "Cagliostro" in *Poem*
(1:337) stems from the short novel he dedicated to Meierkho'ld[92] – the
association was more enduring. Indicatively, it could even be said that
"demonic Doctor Dapertutto" emanated directly from *Poem's* Satanic
"general favourite," for it was none other than Kuzmin who suggested
Meierkhol'd's pseudonym (taken, of course, from another profound
influence on his activity, E.T.A. Hoffmann). With almost uncannily
predictive relevance to the "midnight Hoffmaniana" of *Poem*, the precise source was "Adventure on New Year's Eve."[93] *Poem's* "black-
amoors" may also place Dapertutto at Ivanov's Tower, in his 1910
production of Calderon's *Adoration of the Cross* – designed by Sudeikin,
performed by a cast including Meierkhol'd himself, Vera Shvarsalon,
and (again!) Kuzmin, and celebrated, *arapchata* and all, in a poem
from *Tender Mystery* (*Nezhnaia taina*). Ivanov described Meierkhol'd
there as "ubiquitous, many-faced" (vezdesushchii, mnogolikii);[94] and
his "almost constant, if invisible presence" naturally shaped also the
"demonic" programme, atmosphere, and decor of the "Wandering
Dog" and "Comedians' Halt."[95]

   Such multiple associations richly confirm Dapertutto's demonic
credentials in *Poem*, and imply a figure as "ubiquitously" representative of "the epoch" as any of those demons already discussed. The
consequent inference is that "Demon Meierkhol'd," too, is in some
mysterious sense responsible, as generative and orchestrating presence, for both the central demonic plot-triangle, and the entire "hellish Harlequinade" of "1913." Evidently, the demonic is in this respect
a function of "theatricality," a blurring of boundaries between art(ifice)
and life in dedicated pretence, a spirit of unremitting masquerade

emblematically embodied in the director-performer, with his double identity, endless inventiveness, and many roles. Outwardly, this is perhaps a more consciously cultivated, less *angst*-laden variant of the demonic amorphousness described above; but the distinction is ultimately slender. At some deep level diabolical prototypes tend to coalesce indistinguishably (perhaps, one might hazard, into a devilish composite "without face or name"), and beneath the shifting, glitteringly eclectic surface, the infernal associations of *Poem's* "theatrical" settings intensify connotations of public and private doom.[96] The importance of the "Meierkhol'dian line" is emphasized, moreover, by Akhmatova's intimations in "The Prose" that the dress-rehearsal of *Masquerade* was one of *Poem's* inspirational sources (e.g. 1:359–60); while Rosslyn has argued that in *Poem*, Akhmatova herself "mentally becomes performer, dramatist, and director," much concerned, like Meierkhol'd, with "the opposition between reality and illusion," and "the divide between actors and audience."[97] These observations may be extended: for Meierkhol'd's well-developed theories of stylization, the mask, and the grotesque, each seem in strikingly detailed accord with the poetic procedures of Akhmatova's exceptionally theatrical poem.[98] The profile of Gorenko-Akhmatova is thus for good reason superimposed upon that of "demonic" Meierkhol'd-Dapertutto against the background of the Blok-like Demon. Once again the Author seems to merge into *Poem's* diabolical coalescence; and her art partakes deeply of the devilry she portrays.

It might naturally be supposed that a counterbalance to *Poem's* demonism is to be found in what Akhmatova termed the "Line of the Absent Hero." With a reticence which perhaps encourages greater trust than her more categorical statements, she cited from several poems she did not name, to identify this paradoxical figure with Gumilev.[99] Yet though Timenchik and his co-authors have suggested that Gumilev is indeed an "antipode" to Blok and an antithesis to Kuzmin,[100] it nevertheless transpires that the absent hero, too – whom "the Stalinist secret police" sought in *Poem* "avidly" but in vain, and on whose absence "much is based" (1:358) – is substantially contaminated by the demonic. This emerges in part through association with each of the figures so far discussed.

To begin with what is at first sight the least tangible of connections, Meierkhol'd – who is one of the Author's demonic doubles – conceivably doubles, too, for the absent hero. As Akhmatova well knew, in the early 1910s Meierkhol'd had played the role of "Gumilev" in an improvised pantomime entitled "Gumilev in Africa," the very possibility of which, incidentally, indicates that Gumilev's life to that date constituted a prime example of the "theatricality" described above.[101] Significantly, too, the performance took place at Ivanov's Tower – the milieu to which *Poem's* black-amoors may in part refer, and with which Gumilev himself had been intimately involved during 1909–1910 (when also Kuzmin happened to be a constant denizen!). And if Akhmatova invoked the "demonism" of the "Tower's" host, Ivanov, through his Faustian "Dream" – which V.K. Shileiko later quoted to characterize his marriage to Akhmatova[102] – Gumilev, too, was author of a Faustian dream-poem, based on a dream of Akhmatova's own. Its demonic motifs, including the already familiar ruby ring, conveyed a disturbing apprehension of *their* private relationship in the year of their marriage.[103] True, this "Faustian parallel" between Gumilev and Ivanov is complicated in that Gumilev's Faust (a foreshadowing of the mummers of *Poem*?) proves to be the imagined creation of his "Margarita," who is left with the "reality" only of her doomed brother, Valentin, and her "mocking" (curiously Kuzminian!) devil-*nasmeshnik*, Mephistopheles. Their doubling is underpinned, however, by Faustian motifs in other demonic poems of Gumilev's, precisely from the period of Ivanov's greatest (and, in Akhmatova's view, entirely pernicious) influence.[104]

A further devilish convergence, involving Gumilev (also!) with *Poem's* "Demon," was first noted by Tsiv'ian, who points out that the reference to the Demon's "dead heart and dead gaze" (1:330) is almost a verbatim quotation from Gumilev's "Life" (Zhizn', 1911, 1:130–31). Her observation has been expanded by Toporov, who adduces a network of texts linking Blok, Gumilev, and Akhmatova.[105] The demonic doubling of Gumilev with Blok is likewise indicated by the "lunar ring" which preceded the "dead heart" in a draft of the 1940s:

И обломок луны в кольце

[And a fragment of moon in a ring]

Timenchik has persuasively interpreted this line as "a 'stylistic portrait' of one of the persistent themes of Blok's lyric verse."[106] Akhmatova, however, must surely also have had in mind again the ring which the demonized hero of Gumilev's Luciferian "Ballad" gave to the moon-maiden who was one of her own earliest verse portraits:

И я отдал кольцо этой деве Луны
За неверный оттенок разбросанных кос.

(1:41)

[And I gave my ring to that Maiden of the Moon
For the uncertain shade of her ungathered plaits.]

She vividly recollected these lines as late as the 1960s, quoting the second to demonstrate her presence in Gumilev's "tragic" love poetry, from *Path of Conquistadors* (*Put' konkvistadorov*) to "Margarita" and other poems of *Alien Sky* (*Chuzhoe nebo*).[107]

It is predictable, then, that a series of textual echoes of Gumilev can be discerned also in the "Kuzmin" sections of *Poem*. Timenchik, Toporov, and Tsiv'ian have established, for instance, that an early variant of the "Cagliostro" passage (1:337), quoted above, clearly echoed Gumilev's "At the Gypsies." They have been curiously reluctant, however, to draw the obvious inference of "demonic contamination" from their acute perception.[108] Similarly, their relation of Akhmatova's 1960 description of her "general favourite's" eyes:

> Пусть глаза его, как озера
>
> [Though his eyes are like lakes]

to Gumilev's "Portrait of a Man":

> Его глаза – подземные озера
> (1:86)
>
> [His eyes are underground lakes]

surely invites a direct identification between Gumilev and the "Satanic" Kuzmin, all the more so in that the demonic hero of Gumilev's youth strikingly shares the heinous sin of Akhmatova's Satan in his inability to shed tears or to mourn (plakat').[109]

A final, more unexpected, instance of demonic association also links the "absent" Gumilev with the "Dragoon Pierrot" (1:331). The contrastive comparison between the latter's suicide and other premature deaths, suggested in *Poem* by means of the phrase "I am ready for death" (Ia k smerti gotov, 1:326), has frequently been taken to show that: "the cornet represents not only the naivety and immaturity of a Knyazev, but also commemorates the destruction by the Soviet regime of a Mandelstam or a Gumilev."[110] The attendant *similarity* between Gumilev and the "stupid boy" (1:334) appears, however, to have gone unremarked.

That the suicide motif in *Poem* is quasi-demonic is initially established by the uncertain figure "between stove and cupboard" (1:326): a disturbing image which seems at once to evoke Kirillov's suicide in Dostoevsky's *The Devils* (*Besy*),[111] perhaps also the emergence of Mephistopheles "hinter dem Ofen" in *Faust*,[112] – and Gumilev's expression of nocturnal terror in "Reader of Books" (Chitatel' knig, 1:108).[113] Suicide is also implicitly intertwined with the demonic through allusion to Gumilev's "Life" in the motif of the "dead heart and gaze;"[114] and the association with Gumilev intensifies in *Poem's* final "re-depiction" of the cornet's death (demonic "doubling and tripling" on the level of plot!). Akhmatova's description of his suicidal despair:

Кому жить осталось немого,
Кто лишь смерти просит у Бога
(1:334)

[Who had little time left to live,
Who asks only death from God]

in which Timenchik, Toporov, and Tsiv'ian discern a parallel to
Kniazev's verse,[115] is surely reminiscent also of Gumilev's overtly
autobiographical "Ezbekie":

О смерти я тогда молился Богу
И сам ее приблизить был готов.
(1:226)[116]

[At that time I prayed to God for death,
And was ready to hasten it myself.]

Similarly, the combination of sister and wife (widow) in the cornet's
dying words:

«Я оставлю тебя живою,
Но ты будешь моей вдовою,
Ты – Голубка, солнце, сестра!»
(1:326; repeated in altered sequence, 1:334)

[*"I will leave you alive,
But you will be my widow,
You – Dove, sun, sister!"*]

mirrors Lera's repeated appeal to her brother-bridegroom at the climax of *Gondla* (Gumilev's finest work, in Akhmatova's view),[117] resonates powerfully with the persistent brother/sister motifs in verse
portraits of each other by Akhmatova and her first husband (including "Margarita"),[118] and possibly echoes the haunting words to the
widow attributed to Gumilev in Akhmatova's "Another Voice" (Dru-
goi golos, 1921, 1:145). Perhaps, then, in inserting into the libretto an
episode in which the preoccupied cornet of dragoons fails to salute a
general, Akhmatova had in mind not only, as Zhirmunsky suggests,
the corresponding scene in Tchaikovsky's *The Queen of Spades* – presumably with the attendant implication of Hermann's operatic suicide – but also a real-life "double" in ensign Gumilev's arrest for the
same misdemeanour, in Petrograd in early 1917.[119]

Given Akhmatova's personal distance from Kniazev, it is natural
to suppose that *Poem's* depiction of the cornet's final act – in one
respect evidently emblematic of the many suicides symptomatic of a
demonic era[120] – also "carries a symbolic significance which can only
be unveiled when viewed against an autobiographical background."[121] Timenchik has identified the suicide of Mikhail Lindberg
in a military barracks in Vladikavkaz in December 1911 as one still
barely accessible part of this concealed, intimately autobiographical

layer.[122] The above suggests that Gumilev's several abortive suicide attempts in his early, "demonic" years were another. Akhmatova, of course, had no doubt that Gumilev's "tragic" love for her was their cause; and her potential complicity in "black crime" (1:331) makes more comprehensible both her retrospective acknowledgement of the insouciant, goat-legged Columbine of the 1910s as her demonic double, and the self-lacerating remorse (ne tebia, a sebia kazniu, 1:328) which permits identification of her past self, "the *mocker* / And *favourite* of all her friends, / Tsarskoe Selo *cheerful sinner*" (*nasmeshnitse* / I *liubimitse* vsekh druzei, / Tsarskosel'skoi *veseloi greshnitse*," 1:198; emphasis mine) with *Poem's* darkest demonic prototype, Kuzmin.

The "autobiographical background" extends further, for Gumilev's doubling with Kniazev as Pierrot (the latter, incidentally, also perhaps Meierkhol'd's most memorable acting role, and thus another link between Gumilev and the demon Dapertutto)[123] entails even a shared "demonic Harlequin" – the Kuzmin whom, it is now plain, *Poem* implicitly charges with mourning neither for Kniazev nor Gumilev. While nothing fresh can be said here on Kuzmin and Kniazev (who explicitly portrayed himself as Pierrot in several poems reflecting his relationship with Sudeikina and Kuzmin), it is significant that eventual full publication of Kuzmin's diaries will certainly reveal Kuzmin's discontent at Gumilev's marriage, which brought their closest friendship to an end. Indeed, Kuzmin subsequently endeavoured to effect a rift between Gumilev and Akhmatova. When living with the Gumilevs at Tsarskoe Selo for some weeks in February-March 1912, Kuzmin talked of his (unreciprocated!) feeling for Gumilev, and was eventually driven out by Akhmatova.[124] Such scandalously intemperate behaviour not only helps to explain the depth of Akhmatova's personal resentment towards *Poem's* "most elegant Satan," but suggests that beneath other variants of *commedia dell'arte* devilry, a shadowy demonic triangle involving "Author," "Absent Hero" and "Lord of Darkness" lies at the profoundly concealed core of *Poem*. Here too, moreover, demonic prototypes (and triangles!) possibly coalesce; for Akhmatova maintained that Viacheslav Ivanov, too, attempted early in her marriage to persuade her to abandon Gumilev for the latter's spiritual good.[125]

Although *Poem* readily combines contrasting (or apparently contrasting) significations within a single image, it was suggested above with reference to "Gabriel or Mephistopheles" that ambiguity is inherently diabolical. It should therefore follow that the demonic associations of the "absent" Gumilev (albeit as victim of contemporary "fishers of men," for diabolical predators and victims also merge) thoroughly undermine any claim he might have to heroic

status. The counter-argument, however – which must now be pursued in conclusion – is simply that *Poem's* "absent hero" is structured
along different principles from other personae, consistent instead
with Akhmatova's observation to Luknitsky: "Nikolai Stepanovich
was a profoundly tragic personality. Although he never wanted to
think so. *There are several Gumilevs. Other people do not alter...*"[126] To
elucidate further: several commentators have justifiably seen
Gondla's last speech as a subtext to *Poem's* necessarily oblique reflection of its author Gumilev's "profoundly tragic" death:[127]

> Я вином благодати
> Опьянился и к смерти готов,
> Я монета, которой Создатель
> Покупает спасенье волков.
>
> (2:90)

> [I am drunk
> On the wine of grace and am ready for death,
> I am the coin with which the Creator
> Procures the salvation of wolves.]

But the underlying dynamic of the "heroic line" of *Poem* is perhaps
better conveyed by another character's summation of Gondla's final,
radical transformation:

> Ты был мальчиком, ныне стал мужем,
> (2:86)

> [You were a boy, have now become man,]

It is precisely because Gondla has so "altered" that he can triumph,
albeit *in extremis,* over the accursed magic of the "frenzied wolves."
The mature "man-hero" is purified of their demonic influence; and he
gives up his life in charismatic gesture for the salvation of others. In
death he is likened to a majestic white swan, and attains "resounding
glory" in place of the "black perdition" which had previously threatened (2:90–91). As Akhmatova noted,[128] the negative imagery is that
by which Gumilev had ten years earlier described the "boy's" dilemma
in "The Magic Violin" (a poem, it may be added, which he almost certainly wrote in the aftermath of attempted suicide).[129] The "positive"
swan is another recurrent mythologeme of Gumilev's autobiographical
verse, used, in part, in implicit delineation of his own emergence from
symbolist apprenticeship to (acmeistic) poetic maturity: in Akhmatova's contemporary formulation, from "grey cygnet" to "haughty
swan."[130] In this light, Gumilev's demonic alignment with the various
characters and prototypes of *Poem* (NB "there are several Gumilevs")
can be seen to undergo a similarly radical, "heroic" transformation.

Unlike *Poem's* cornet of dragoons, Gumilev of course narrowly
avoided the ignominy of suicide. "Ezbekie," to which Akhmatova

apparently alludes, records that he consciously foreswore that demonic temptation, and instead vowed before God to accept the more difficult path of life (1:226). Thereafter, it could be said, he grew beyond the "stupid boy" (mal'chik) with whom he so nearly coincided – or transcended the theatricality of the *commedia dell'arte* Pierrot by which his death is represented in the image-system of *Poem*[131] – to attain the heroic stature of *muzh*: in one sense, self-possessed husband to the woman who had earlier driven him to the very threshold of death; more importantly – since Akhmatova herself insisted that "marriage" (brak) was a term inappropriate to Gumilev[132] – the leader of a literary movement which he defined, precisely, as a "*man*ly, firm and clear view of life" (*muzh*estvenno-tverdyi i iasnyi vzgliad na zhizn', 3:16; emphasis mine).

According to Gumilev, the acmeist, "manly" view of life demanded a conscious concern for exact contour and precise definition, including "a more accurate knowledge of the relationship between subject and object than was the case in symbolism" (3:16). This might reasonably be regarded as a direct antithesis not merely to the spectral vagueness of symbolism, but specifically to that fluid uncertainty of identity, lack of demarcation, and consequent moral amorphousness which, in Akhmatova's *Poem*, is symptomatic of its demonic essence. Given the strong ethical framework of Gumilev's formulations, this distinction alone may seem sufficiently fundamental to explain how Akhmatova could write of a temporal-generational "abyss" which, after Gumilev's youthful "period of symbolism," separated him as mature acmeist from Blok:[133] in truth, only six years his elder, the tenor of *his* generation, and prototype of *Poem's* foremost, androgynously "unmanly," "man-Demon."

Gumilev's manly break with the symbolism in which he had wholeheartedly "put his faith" as "a boy" was also pointedly determined by his opposition to another of *Poem's* demons, Viacheslav Ivanov. For Akhmatova, Gumilev's acmeist rebellion against Ivanov's redoubtable authority belonged squarely within the semantic complex of "heroic maturity," as an act of colossal "civic courage" (grazhdanskoe *muzhestvo*).[134] Moreover, Gumilev's Cadmus, the regal craftsman of *Actaeon*, whose "chaste" concentration in purpose perhaps most nearly embodies the ideal of acmeist "manliness," had been conceived in direct, polemical refutation of Ivanov's theories. By a reversal of the relative ages of the play's prototypes, these theories are primarily refracted in the "ill-balanced, ill-judging, ultimately sacrilegious" behaviour of Cadmus's youthful antagonist Actaeon.[135] However, intertextual echoes also reveal a connection between Actaeon and Gumilev's earlier, symbolist verse,[136] allowing Actaeon simultaneously to be considered a projection of the dark, romantic-demonic (Ivanov-inspired?) younger self which must be "heroically" overcome. Cadmus – whose maturity is emphasized from the outset, when he is contrasted, as *muzhchina*, to the misguided "boys," Actaeon and Pentheus (2:12) – demonstrates how this may be achieved, attaining a profundity and fullness of being through dedicated labour, in austere resistance to any temptation of physical or spiritual profligacy. The play's masonic imagery lends his constructive endeavour a strong moral and religious dimension, which is more fully developed in *Gondla*, and confirms Gumilev's acmeist "Man" as a true antithesis to the demonic. He courageously accepts life, death, and self, in "clear" awareness of the limits and limitations they are subject to.

Gumilev's acmeist manliness similarly divorces him from *Poem's* Satanic prototype, Kuzmin. Thus, Akhmatova sought to claim that the establishment of the "Poets' Guild" – arguably the first stage in Gumilev's development beyond the "Tower" which united Kuzmin with Ivanov, and which Akhmatova associated with Gumilev's boyish sense of spiritual defilement – brought an immediate end to his personal and literary association with Kuzmin. Furthermore, the serious-minded discipline of acmeism's normative poetics was so uncongenial to *Poem's* "favourite and mocker" that he continued to express unseemly opposition even after Gumilev's death.[137] And in the refraction of *Poem*, his Satanic combination of graceful, theatrical frivolity and profound immorality could scarcely be further from the sober responsibility of the outwardly unprepossessing acmeistic hero. Yet for all this, Gumilev as mature, heroic *muzh* (a conflation of literary image and living prototype comparable to the other *dramatis personae* of *Poem*) remains an essentially absent entity, significant primarily through implicit contrast. For final, textual confirmation that his "absent presence" in *Poem* extends beyond demonic negativity, we should therefore look briefly at Akhmatova's "Don Juan" theme, taken in the context of her personal interpretation of Pushkin's presentation thereof in *The Stone Guest* (*Kamennyi gost*).

Akhmatova begins her critical study of *The Stone Guest* by accounting for Pushkin's contemporary unpopularity after 1830 by reference to his inner transformation: "He altered" (2:111), or, quoting Pushkin himself: "With the years – the young poet matures" (iunyi poet muzhaet, 2:112). Although Akhmatova had privately emphasized the unusualness of Gumilev's maturation, it was thus not unique, but linked him to the most unimpeachable precedent. In *The Stone Guest*, she maintains, Pushkin's sharp inward change is reflected in his "division of himself" (2:132) between the two male characters of the spectral love-triangle. On the one hand, there is the immoral Don

Juan, who reflects Pushkin's sinful *youth*, and through whose depiction Pushkin "punishes himself" (2:125). Juan, who is "without conscience, without faith" (2:118), is characterized by his elegance (iziashchestvo) and "society manners" (2:115), and can "act through frivolous-mindedness (legkomyslie) as an evildoer" (2:117). In short (remarkably like Akhmatova's Kuzmin!) he is the "very demon" (sushchii demon), and a "rake, devil" (povesa, d'iavol, 2:115).[138] On the other hand, the second phase of the author's inner evolution is marked by the "absent," murdered, morally upright (2:124), posthumously slighted Commendatore, who by a notable departure from tradition is husband – *muzh* – not father to Donna Anna.

Akhmatova draws attention to two further significant departures from tradition in Pushkin's *The Stone Guest*. First, she claims to believe Pushkin unique in making his Don Juan a poet (2:114). In fact, Gumilev had followed suit in his play *Don Juan in Egypt* (*Don Zhuan v Egipte*, 1912, 1:159–70); and her misleading observation undoubtedly points to the "absent presence" of her dead husband.[139] Second, in Akhmatova's view, Pushkin's demonic anti-hero himself radically alters, finally becoming a "tragic" figure: through the agency of Donna Anna, he supposedly undergoes a genuine moral rebirth, declaring his love of virtue and yearning for heavenly bliss (2:119–21). Here again, textually as well as biographically, Pushkin's allegedly idiosyncratic approach finds substantive parallels in Gumilev, in the latter's other main approaches to the Don Juan theme. His young, proud Don Juan from the demonic period of *Pearls* is a reprobate, occasionally sufficiently lucid to recognize his moral redundancy, and (albeit with a certain perversity) he dreams of a contrasting later life of Christian repentance beneath "the redeeming burden / Of a heavy iron cross" (spasaiushchee bremia / Tiazhelogo zheleznogo kresta, 1:107). And in "Iambic Pentameters" (Piatistopnye iamby, 1912, revised 1915), the overtly autobiographical lyric hero identifies his younger self with a Don Juan who failed to find comfort in his aptly named Donna Anna (Akhmatova). He passes through infernal depths of solitary despair to indeed find, in the poem's first, "masonic" version, clarity, wisdom, and God in a dedication to pious, constructive labour thoroughly consonant with that of Cadmus. In notable anticipation of *Gondla*, the acmeist-Adamist imagery of "manly firmness" also incorporates "white swans" in a metaphor of universal, brotherly love:

> Нас много здесь собралось с молотками,
>
> . . . .
>
> Одна любовь сковала нас цепями,
> Что адаманта тверже и светлей,

И машет белоснежными крылами
Каких-то небывалых лебедей.

(1:515)

[Many of us are gathered here with hammers,

. . . .

Love alone has shackled us in chains
That are firmer and brighter than adamant,
And flaps the snow-white wings
Of imaginary swans.]

This spiritual ecumenism is predicated upon fundamental maturation
beyond the "first Adam" (or Juan!) within, involving determined
renunciation of the world's transient seductions, and the blandish-
ments of personal, potentially demonic (lukavyi) sexual love.[140] And in
an ending entirely rewritten during the experience of the First World
War (the post-"1913" beginning of Akhmatova's "True Twentieth Century"), the emphasis becomes more religious than ethical, in contemplation of a monastic retreat from the "demonic" world (the epithet
lukavyi is retained), to "chaste" contemplation of its natural splendour:

Туда б уйти, покинув мир лукавый,
Смотреть на ширь воды и неба ширь ...
В тот золотой и белый монастырь!

(1:180)

[To go, abandoning the insidious world,
To look upon the breadth of water and the breadth of sky ...
To that gold and white monastery!]

This reformulates, without irony, the conclusion to Gumilev's first
Don Juan poem, and it is scarcely surprising that the culmination of
his spiritual biography of a Don Juan transfigured has another subtext in the "mature," religiously inclined Pushkin.[141]

Poem's "Don Juan line" has previously been extensively examined in relation to Blok and – in an illuminating study which argues
that Juan's attributes are allotted to *Poem*'s women as well as men,
and hence that "the sins of Don Juan are the sins of a whole generation" – with reference to Akhmatova herself.[142] From the foregoing
discussion, there can be no doubt that the deeply concealed presence of the absent Gumilev – whose real-life "Don-Juanism" Akhmatova readily acknowledged, even constructing a "Don Juan's list" for
his biographer Luknitsky[143] – is of no lesser importance. In recapit-
ulation of the "unique" example of Pushkin and his creation, and in
sharp contradistinction to the composite Don Juan poet of the symbolist era, Gumilev indeed "alters." He passes from the limitless
questing, profligate selfhood, and morally indeterminate entangle-
ments of symbolist-demonic "boyhood," not to remorseful self-chas-

tisement or Blok-like, passive expectation of inevitable "retribution," but to the clear-sighted affirmation of a morally and religiously restructured individualism, that dovetails precisely with the acmeist notion of the mature, spiritually restrained, *muzh.* Literary concept and prototype thus merge in a single, absent-heroic mode. And it might finally be added that Gumilev's death, like his hero Gondla's, becomes in this light no pointless, boyish suicide, but a gesture that sacrificially validates the model. As such, it is arguably crucial to the tentative anticipation of regeneration in *Poem's* "Epilogue," beyond the demonism of "1913" and ensuing historical darkness.

That, however, is another story. To conclude where we began, it might now appear that Gumilev's manifesto was over-cautious in its attitude to the demonic heritage of symbolism: for Akhmatova in *Poem* draws a definitive distinction between symbolism and acmeism precisely in terms of acmeism's thoroughgoing transcendence of the demonic. It must equally be argued, however, that Akhmatova's treatment of Gumilev's departure from demonism is a somewhat schematic simplification, which neglects the lingering demons of his late verse. Plainly, too, there is a substantial (and demonic?!) blurring of contours in the very nature of Akhmatova's poetic masterpiece. Not only is the poet's "past self" clearly tainted by the demonism of the 1913 era; the artistry by which that era is reconstructed (a form of demonic-necromantic re-evocation?) partakes substantially of its supposedly demonic poetics (doubling and indeterminacy, Meierk-hol'dian stylization and the grotesque, gossip-mongering and mockery, et cetera). Not for nothing, then, is *Poem's* very inspiration portrayed as demonic (a quintessentially symbolist concept, such as found clear articulation in Gumilev's "The Magic Violin").

Moreover, as is clear from the analysis of the dynamics of demonism offered in the introduction to this volume, Akhmatova's notion of demonism both as dead stagnation (the "doomed generation" of 1913) and as a springboard to (post-symbolist) transformation (which Akhmatova associates, with curious partiality, only with the figure of Gumilev – though the relation between "absent hero" and "author" might form the subject of a separate study) is also scarcely a radical departure from her predecessors. Far from reducing the "specific gravity" of the demonic, as Gumilev's manifesto counselled, to that of any other image, *Poem* seems to place it (perhaps inevitably) at the very centre of its discourse. To intimate the heroic transcendence of demonism is of course to remain preoccupied with the topic, not to marginalize or ignore it. *Poem Without a Hero* is the last, glorious artistic testimony to the inexorable hold of demonism and the demonist cast of mind over the entire cultural consciousness of Russia's Silver Age.

Notes

1. Nikolai Gumilev, *Sochineniia v trekh tomakh*, ed. N.A. Bogomolov and others (Moscow: Khudozhestvennaia literatura, 1991), 3:18; hereafter cited in the text. All translations of Russian texts are mine, unless otherwise indicated.
2. S.M. Gorodetskii, "Nekotorye techeniia v sovremennoi russkoi poezii," *Apollon*, 1913, no. 1:46–50(46).
3. "Peterburgskaia povest'," an overt borrowing of the subtitle of Pushkin's *Mednyi vsadnik*, is the subtitle of Part 1 of *Poem Without a Hero*, "Deviat'sot trinadtsatyi god." Anna Akhmatova, *Sochineniia v dvukh tomakh*, ed. M.M. Kralin (Moscow: Pravda, 1990), 1:322; hereafter cited in the text.
4. A. Kheit, *Anna Akhmatova: Poeticheskoe stranstvie. Dnevniki, vospominaniia, pis'ma A. Akhmatovoi* (Moscow: Raduga, 1991), 230.
5. O.L. Della-Vos-Kardovskaia, "Vospominaniia o N.S. Gumileve," in *Zhizn' Nikolaia Gumileva: Vospominaniia sovremennikov*, ed. Iu.V. Zobnin, V.P. Petranovskii, and A.K. Staniukovich (Leningrad: Mezhdunarodnyi fond istorii nauki, 1991), 30–35(31–32).
6. Letter to V.Ia. Briusov of 11 November 1906, in N. Gumilev, *Neizdannoe i nesobrannoe*, ed. M. Basker and S. Duffin Graham (Paris: YMCA-Press, 1986), 99–100.
7. This interest is now widely recognized in the scholarly literature: see, for example, N.A. Bogomolov, "Okkul'tnye motivy v tvorchestve Gumileva," *De Visu*, 1992, no. 0:46–51(46).
8. See N.A. Bogomolov's commentary in Gumilev, *Sochineniia*, 1:489.
9. See Michael Basker, "'Stixi iz snov': Art, Magic and Dream in Gumilev's *Romantičeskie cvety*," in *Nikolaj Gumilev 1886–1986: Papers from the Gumilev Centenary Symposium Held at Ross Priory, University of Strathclyde 1986*, ed. Sheelagh Duffin Graham (Oakland, California: Berkeley Slavic Specialties, 1987), 27–68(36–38, 64 n.31).
10. *Vesy*, 1906, no. 6:6–9. On the symbolist sources of "Umnyi D'iavol," see the detailed commentary in N. Gumilev, *Polnoe sobranie sochinenii v desiati tomakh*, ed. Iu.V. Zobnin and others (Moscow: Voskresen'e, 1998–), 1:370–71.
11. The opening line was subsequently revised by Gumilev to read: "Piat' konei podaril mne *moi drug* Liutsifer" (1:51; emphasis mine).
12. S.L. Slobodniuk, *N.S. Gumilev: Problemy mirovozzreniia i poetiki* (Dushanbe: Sino, 1992), 51–52.
13. A substantial selection of these poems is grouped in the thematically organized anthology section of *Nikolai Gumilev: Pro et Contra. Lichnost' i tvorchestvo Nikolaia Gumileva v otsenke russkikh myslitelei i issledovatelei. Antologiia*, ed. Iu.V. Zobnin (St. Petersburg: Russkii Khristianskii gumanitarnyi institut, 1995), 101–21.
14. The quotation is from "Zaklinanie" (1907, 1:65). Compare such poems as "Rasskaz devushki" (1905, 1:28–29), "Karakalla" (1906, 1:77–79), "Segodnia u berega nashego brosil ..." (1906, 1:338–39), "Maskarad" (1907, 1:56–57), and "Vliublennaia v D'iavola" (1907, 1:63–64).
15. See "Popugai" (1909, 1:107), "U menia ne zhivut tsvety ..." (1910, 1:108), and "Portret muzhchiny" (1910, 1:86–87). On the likely sources of the latter poem's demonism in Poe, Bal'mont, and Baudelaire, see my note in Gumilev, *Polnoe sobranie sochinenii*, 1:465–66.
16. The "lord of darkness" (temnyi vladyka) and "father of sin," who appears in a dream to incite the story's violinist-hero to the sublime heights of composition and subsequent destructive frenzy, is adorned in pearls of these three colours (2:218–23[220]).

17. See "Sakhara" (1:265–68); "Galla" (1:274–75); "Sudan" (1:269–71); and "Piza" (1912, 1:181).

18. "Predosterezhenie khirurga," in Robert Sauti, *Ballady*, ed. N. Gumilev (Petersburg: Vsemirnaia literatura, 1922), 9–16.

19. On Gumilev's recourse to Ukrainian demonology in this poem, including the theme of *Vii* also exploited by Narbut and – less predictably – by Akhmatova in "Shiroko raspakhnuty vorota ..." (1915/1921, 1:170), see R.D. Timenchik, "Khram Premudrosti Boga: Stikhotvorenie Anny Akhmatovoi 'Shiroko raspakhnuty vorota'," *Slavica Hierosolymitana* 5–6 (1981):297–317(311).

20. See Michael Basker, "Gumilyov's *Akteon*: A Forgotten Manifesto of Acmeism," *Slavonic and East European Review* 63 (1985): 498–517(508–17).

21. See, e.g., "Paduanskii sobor" (1912, 1:188–89); "Razgovor" (1913, 1:176–77); and "Dusha i telo" (1919, 1:291–93).

22. See Bogomolov's commentary in Gumilev, *Sochineniia*, 1:546.

23. Thus, for example, the description of the loved one's eyes as "d'iavol'skie seti" in "'Goriat tvoi ladoni, ...'" (1915, 1:52), or the exclamation "O, kak ty krasiv, prokliatyi," in "Smiatenie" (1913, 1:45).

24. See, for example, "Za to, chto ia grekh proslavliala ..." (1914, 2:29); "V tot davnii god, kogda zazhglas' liubov' ..." (1921, 1:146); "Tam ten' moia ostalas' i toskuet ..." (1917, 1:112); "V tom dome bylo ochen' strashno zhit' ..." (1921, 1:261–62); "O Bozhe, za sebia ia vse mogu prostit' ..." (1916?, 2:32).

25. See, for example, the implication of prostitution in "Tvoi belyi dom i tikhii sad ostavliu ..." (1913, 1:73); and the expression of guilt in "Ia gibel' naklikala milym ..." (1921, 1:168–69).

26. Prominent examples include "Novogodniaia ballada" (1923, 1:242), "Podval pamiati" (1940, 1:190), the cycle "Novosel'e" (1943–44, 1:222–23), and "Kogda lezhit luna lomtem chardzhuiskoi dyni ..." (1944, 1:217).

27. Perhaps the clearest example occurs in the "Dedication" to *Requiem*: "Gde teper' nevol'nye podrugi / Dvukh moikh *osatanelykh* let" (1940, 1:197; emphasis mine).

28. For Akhmatova's pronouncements on the catastrophic significance of Tsushima, see V.N. Toporov, "Ob istorizme Akhmatovoi (dve glavy iz knigi)," in *Anna Akhmatova 1889–1989: Papers from the Akhmatova Centennial Conference, Bellagio Study and Conference Center, June 1989*, ed. Sonia I. Ketchian (Oakland, California: Berkeley Slavic Specialties, 1993), 194–237(198–99). The phrase "Dostoevskii i besnovatyi" is from *Poem Without a Hero* (1:332), but can be related to Akhmatova's evocation of the social and moral evils of the nineteenth century in her "Predystoriia" (1:259–60), usefully discussed in D.N. Wells, *Anna Akhmatova: Her Poetry* (Oxford: Berg, 1996), 87–90. On Akhmatova's politically charged, negative images of Peter I, see Michael Basker, "'Fear and the Muse': An Analysis and Contextual Interpretation of Anna Achmatova's 'Voronež'," *Russian Literature* 45–3 (1999):245–360(295–309).

29. Gumilev, *Sochineniia*, 2:221.

30. Wells, *Akhmatova*, 102.

31. On Kuzmin and Meierkhol'd, see below; on Strauss, see B. Kats and R. Timenchik, *Akhmatova i muzyka: Issledovatel'skie ocherki* (Leningrad: Sovetskii kompozitor, 1989), 55; on Mandel'shtam, see Inna Chechel'nitskaia, "Skrytoe prisutstvie N. Gumileva v *Poeme bez geroia* A. Akhmatovoi," in Graham, ed., *Nikolaj Gumilev*, 77–101(80–81).

32. Mikhail Zenkevich, *Skazochnaia era: Stikhotvoreniia. Povest'. Belletricheskie memuary*, ed. S.E. Zenkevich (Moscow: Shkola-Press, 1994), 412–624.

33. The somewhat oblique exceptions are the poems "Ty dlia menia davno mertva ..." (1917) and "Videl ia, kak ot napriagsheisia krovi ..." (1913). Zenkevich, *Skazochnaia era*, 113, 99.

34. Ibid., 413.
35. "Izmuchivshee menia galliutsinatsiiami mertvoe peterburgskoe marevo," ibid.,
    458. For occurrences of *chertovshchina*, see 427, 428, 430, 440, 479; and cf. 416,
    450.
36. Ibid., 412.
37. Ibid., 469, 473.
38. The most obvious literary source is Gumilev's 1920 poem "Ol'ga" ("El'ga, El'ga!
    – zvuchalo nad poliami," 1:299–300). Besides Akhmatova, whom Zenkevich's
    wife regarded as the "prototype of this demonic heroine" (Zenkevich, *Ska-
    zochnaia era*, 658), it seems possible to discern biographical features of at least
    two of Gumilev's female entourage during 1918–21: Irina Odoevtseva (pse-
    donym of Iraida *Gustavovna* Geinike); and the dedicatee of "Ol'ga," Ol'ga Niko-
    laevna Arbenina.
39. Ibid., 436.
40. Ibid., 442.
41. Hence, for example: "Za odnu minutu pokoia / Ia posmertnyi otdam pokoi"
    (1:327).
42. Zenkevich, *Skazochnaia era*, 439–40. Zenkevich mistakenly gives the year of
    Konge's death as 1916.
43. See, respectively, Zenkevich, *Skazochnaia era*, 450; 477–78; 492–501 and 509.
    Rasputin is mentioned by name in both "The Prose" (1:353) and the "Ballet
    libretto" of *Poem*: Anna Akhmatova, *Sochineniia*, vols. 1 and 2, ed. G.P. Struve
    and B.A. Filippov (Munich: Inter-Language Literature Associates, 1967–68),
    vol. 3, ed. G.P. Struve, N.A. Struve, and B.A. Filippov (Paris: YMCA-Press,
    1983), 3:162, 165. On his powerful, unnamed demonic presence behind *Poem*
    itself, see Aleksandr Etkind, *Sodom i Psikheia: Ocherki intellektual'noi istorii Sere-
    brianogo veka* (Moscow: ITs-Garant, 1996), 209–13.
44. Zenkevich, *Skazochnaia era*, 412–13.
45. It could also be shown that *A Peasant Sphinx* was one of the subtexts of her
    densely allusive "Podval pamiati" (1:190), a work of 1940 closely related to
    Poem. Compare, in particular, Akhmatova's description of solitary descent:
    "Kogda *spuskaius'*... v podval, / ... / A znaiu, chto idu *tuda*, k vragu. / ... / ...
    No tam / Temno i tikho. ... / ... / Skvoz' etu plesen', etot chad i tlen" with
    Zenkevich's: "mne vdrug zakhotelos' posmotret' 'Brodiachuiu sobaku.' ... Kak
    teper' bylo by zhutko *spustit'sia tuda*, v syrost' i temnotu, i postoiat' tam
    odnomu!.." (Zenkevich, *Skazochnaia era*, 421; emphasis mine).
46. Significantly, for example, Gumilev first emerges into Zenkevich's narrative
    from the end of a tram-queue (ibid., 422); and the author-narrator's fantastical
    night-time ride on a mysterious, empty, scaffold-like tramcar, in which the
    phrase "ia vskochil na ego podnozhku" clearly echoes Gumilev's "Kak ia
    vskochil na ego podnozhku, / Bylo zagadkoiu dlia menia," initiates the action of
    chap.10 (ibid., 444–45).
47. Amended to "Strashnyi gorod Pikovoi Damy," in a stanza finally excluded from
    "Tails." See Anna Akhmatova, *Poema bez geroia*, ed. R.D. Timenchik with V.Ia.
    Morderer (Moscow: MPI, 1989), 144.
48. For some "Petersburgian" parallels in Dostoevsky, see Boris Filippov, "Poema
    bez geroia," in Akhmatova, *Sochineniia*, 2:53–92(68, 87–88); L. Dolgopolov,
    "Dostoevskii i Blok v *Poeme bez geroia* Anny Akhmatovoi," in *V mire Bloka:
    Sbornik statei* (Moscow: Sovetskii pisatel', 1981), 454–80 (esp. 473–76). For reflec-
    tions of Gogol's "Portret" in *Poem*, see R.D. Timenchik, V.N. Toporov, and T.V.
    Tsiv'ian, "Akhmatova i Kuzmin," *Russian Literature* 6 (1978):213–305(250). On
    "Shinel'," see R.D. Timenchik, "Blok i ego sovremenniki v *Poeme bez geroia*:
    Zametki k teme," *Uchenye zapiski Tartuskogo gosudarstvennogo universiteta* 857,

Blokovskii sbornik IX (Tartu: Tartuskii gosudarstvennyi universitet, 1989):114–23(115); and on "Nevskii prospekt," see Lev Losev, "Geroi *Poemy bez geroia*," in *Akhmatovskii sbornik 1*, ed. S. Dediulin and G. Superfin (Paris: Institut d'Etudes slaves, 1989), 109–22(112). For numerous parallels to the themes and setting of Bely's *Peterburg*, see esp. S.P. Il'ev, "'Peterburgskie povesti' Andreia Belogo i Anny Akhmatovoi (*Peterburg – Poema bez geroia*)," in *Tsarstvennoe slovo: Akhmatovskie chteniia* (Moscow: Nasledie, 1992), 150–65. For parallels to the Devil's buffoonery in Stravinsky's "Petersburg ballet," see Kats and Timenchik, *Akhmatova i muzyka*, 203.

49. On Odoevsky's "Bal," see Timenchik, Toporov, and Tsiv'ian, "Akhmatova i Kuzmin," 294 n.140; on the nineteenth-century Hoffmannists, see V.N. Toporov "Akhmatova i Gofman: K postanovke voprosa," in his *Akhmatova i Blok (K probleme postroeniia poeticheskogo dialoga: "Blokovskii" tekst Akhmatovoi)* (Berkeley: Berkeley Slavic Specialties, 1981), 157–202(165 and passim).

50. Though the text refers to "the year 1940," the passage is dated "25 August 1941" (1:322). The Gumilevian connection is expounded in Chechel'nitskaia, "Skrytoe prisutstvie," 79, 91–93.

51. The "Wandering Dog" is explicitly invoked by Akhmatova in "1913" ("My otsiuda eshche v Sobaku," 1:327). Its distinctive vaulted ceiling has often been remarked upon: see the accounts cited in A.E. Parnis and R.D. Timenchik, "Programmy 'Brodiachei sobaki'," in *Pamiatniki kul'tury. Novye otkrytiia: Pis'mennost', iskusstvo, arkheologiia. Ezhegodnik 1983* (Leningrad: Nauka, 1985), 160–257(204, 248 n.111). The dateline "1941. Avgust (vozdushnaia trevoga). Osazhdennyi Leningrad" beneath the relevant lines in the first redaction of *Poem's* "Introduction" (1:306) seems to corroborate the identity: in a later prose fragment, Akhmatova related her unintended "last half hour in the Dog" precisely to an air raid warning at the start of the Blockade in 1941, when she and B.V. Tomashevsky were compelled to seek the nearest shelter (Akhmatova, *Poema bez geroia*, 81).

52. See "Vse my brazhniki zdes', bludnitsy ..." (1:48), originally entitled "Cabaret artistique."

53. See V. Vederina, "Iz 'Vospominanii o khudozhnike S.Iu. Sudeikine'," cited in Akhmatova, *Poema bez geroia*, 221. Veriginа's evocative description of Sudeikin's "startling" decor of "Prival komediantov," including his mural of "Olechka Glebova" as "woman-doll," further emphasizes the demonic aura of the milieu in terms strikingly consonant with the thematic core of Akhmatova's work.

54. For the contemporary sources of Akhmatova's "obratnyi put' iz Damaska" and some indication of their implications, see Timenchik, Toporov, and Tsiv'ian, "Akhmatova i Kuzmin," 225.

55. The probable reference is to Glebova-Sudeikina's leading role in I. Sats's ballet "The Fauns" (Plias kozlonogikh), at least four performances of which (partial or complete) she gave at the "Wandering Dog" during 1913 (see Parnis and Timenchik, "Programmy 'Brodiachei sobaki'," 211, 213, 214).

56. For the staging of these items at the "Wandering Dog" – the last a "Night of Masks," notable for its "mass of 'white Pierrots'" – see ibid., 214, 223, 208. Harlequin, Pierrot, and Pierrette, moreover, were among the paintings which adorned the Cabaret's walls (ibid., 173). This is not to deny that each item also has a multiplicity of purely literary sources.

57. Akhmatova's epigraph from Poe's "Raven" also merits attention with reference to Gumilev. Poe had been Gumilev's "favourite poet" at the outset of his career and relationship with Akhmatova (see Gumilev, *Neizdannoe i nesobrannoe*, 95). His "The Magic Violin" shares its relatively rare trochaic octameter with "The Raven," and he made detailed reference to "The Raven" in a late essay on

poetic translation (3:28–33[29]). Since, moreover, Gumilev's indebtedness to Poe had seriously occupied Akhmatova as early as the mid-1920s (I.G. Kravtsova, "N. Gumilev i Edgar Po: Sopostavitel'naia zametka Anny Akhmatovoi," in *N. Gumilev i Russkii Parnas* [St. Petersburg: Muzei Anny Akhmatovoi v Fontannom Dome, 1992], 51–57), it seems entirely conceivable that her epigraph constituted an initial signal of Gumilev's connection with the demonic line of *Poem*. Naturally, however, Akhmatova's epigraph prompted other associations, too – most obviously with Mandel'shtam (see Timenchik, Toporov, and Tsiv'ian, "Akhmatova i Kuzmin," 282–83 n.68).

58. The general association of Yuletide with the spirit world is well known. A folk tradition which regards New Year's Eve in particular as the time when a "throng of demons" emerges from the nether regions (preispodniaia) is described in Il'ev, "Peterburgskie povesti," 154.

59. For a discussion of "sinister" numbers and dates, see Jerzy Faryno, "Whose Messenger is Akhmatova's *Poema bez geroia*?," in *The Speech of Unknown Eyes: Akhmatova's Readers on her Poetry*, ed. Wendy Rosslyn, 2 vols. (Nottingham: Astra Press, 1990), 1:97–111(101–104); on her *troichatki*, see Losev, "Geroi *Poemy bez geroia*," 116–17, 119–20.

60. See, in particular, Toporov, *Akhmatova i Blok*, 7–147(15–30). This is the seminal contribution to the subject of Blok in Akhmatova's *Poem*, but provides little interpretative analysis to elucidate a staggering wealth of copiously annotated material. For more analytical approaches to particular aspects, see, for example, Sam Driver; "Axmatova's *Poema bez geroja* and Blok's *Vozmezdie*," in *Aleksandr Blok Centennial Conference*, ed. Walter N. Vickery with Bogdan B. Sagatov (Columbus: Slavica, 1984), 89–99; and Anna Lisa Crone, "Blok as Don Juan in Axmatova's *Poema bez geroja*," *Russian Language Journal* 35, nos.121–122 (1981):145–62.

61. See, for example, Blok's diary entry for 11 October 1912, quoted in this volume in the section on Blok in Pamela Davidson, "The Muse and the Demon in the Poetry of Pushkin, Lermontov, and Blok": "*what* in art is *infinity*, unclear 'about what,' beyond everything ..., perhaps *that same thing* in religion is the *end*, clear about what, ... salvation. ... I once knew something greater than art, i.e. not infinity, but the End."

62. Akhmatova's reference to Lermontov's poem in the passage under discussion evidently goes beyond the obvious allusion to "The Demon ... with Tamara's smile," and is justified not only in terms of the genealogy of Blok's Demon, analysed in detail in this volume by Pamela Davidson in "The Muse and the Demon" and by Avril Pyman in "The Demon: The Mythopoetic World Model in the Art of Lermontov, Vrubel, Blok," but also in terms of the paradoxical antitheses typical of the evil she portrays. Lermontov's most famous of Russian Demons is able to swear to *his* "krasavitsa" ("Zachem, *krasavitsa*? Uvy," 2:10.639; emphasis mine) by both heaven and hell ("Klianusia nebom ia i adom," 2:10.785), and finds both paradise (cf. Gabriel) and hell (cf. Mephistopheles) in her eyes ("Moi rai, moi ad v tvoikh ochakh." 2:10.644). And in the final stanza of Part 1, in which Lermontov's Demon, too, is "*prishlets* tumannyi i nemoi" (emphasis mine), his indeterminacy is emphatic: he is neither "angel-nebozhitel'" nor "ada dukh uzhasnyi;" "Ni den', ni noch, – ni mrak, ni svet!.." (1:16.378, 384, 388, 391; reference to part, stanza, and line number are from the text of *Demon* in M.Iu. Lermontov, *Polnoe sobranie stikhotvorenii*, introd. D.E. Maksimov, ed. E.E. Naidich, Biblioteka poeta, Bol'shaia seriia, 2 vols. [Leningrad: Sovetskii pisatel', 1989], 2:436–89). With regard to the demonic connotations of "confusion" in *Poem*, cf. the demon's "confusing incitement" (bes poputal, 1.339) of the Author, and the role of "Confusion" (Putanitsa) danced by the *goat-legged* Columbine-heroine (1:321, 328).

63. For reflections on the ambivalent sexuality of the Demon, see in this volume Pyman, "The Demon;" and with reference specifically to Akhmatova's Demon, as a perceptive metaphor for Blok's inner conflict, Davidson, "The Muse and the Demon."

64. Akhmatova, *Sochineniia*, 2:412.

65. Akhmatova described Blok as "tragicheskii tenor epokhi" in "I, v pamiati chernoi poshariv, naidesh' ...," the second of "Tri stikhotvoreniia" (1:290–91). The third of these poems, in its use of the generic "chelovek" ("Kak pamiatnik nachalu veka, / Tam etot chelovek stoit – "), can be coupled with her comment on Blok as "chelovek-epokha" as strong evidence for a "Blokian" reading of the lines quoted here.

66. On Don Juan, see below; on Blok's connection with the other images, see respectively, for example, Toporov, *Akhmatova i Blok*, 41, 19–20; Filippov, "Poema bez geroia," 57.

67. Toporov, *Akhmatova i Blok*, 14–21.

68. W. Rosslyn, "Theatre, Theatricality and Akhmatova's *Poema bez geroya*," *Essays in Poetics* 13, 1 (1988):90–104(94).

69. Timenchik, "Blok i ego sovremenniki," 117.

70. Cf., for instance, the profile, both "accursed" (prokliatyi) and androgynous ("Ne zhenskii, ne muzhskoi, no polnyi tainy"), which remains imprinted on the wall in "A v knigakh ia posledniuiu stranitsu ..." (1943, 1:223–24), and which can be identified with A.K. Kozlovsky's profile portrait of Akhmatova in Tashkent (see Kralin's note in 1:408).

71. "O sovremennom sostoianii russkogo simvolizma," cited in Toporov, *Akhmatova i Blok*, 18.

72. The phrase "nechistyi dukh" was used in the first redaction (1:307). Other variants include "Tot, kto khrom i liubezen" (Akhmatova, *Sochineniia*, 2:373), and "On liubimets obshchii, nasmeshnik" (cited in Timenchik, Toporov, and Tsiv'ian, "Akhmatova i Kuzmin," 248).

73. For the events passed over in silence here, see in particular R.D. Timenchik, "Rizhskii epizod v *Poeme bez geroia* Anny Akhmatovoi," *Daugava* 80 (1984):113–21. For the seminal study of their literary refraction, see Timenchik, Toporov, and Tsiv'ian, "Akhmatova i Kuzmin," 213–305.

74. Cf. the lines from Pushkin's "Demon" (1823): "Na zhizn' *nasmeshlivo* gliadel – / I nichego vo vsei prirode / Blagoslovit' on ne khotel." A.S. Pushkin, *Polnoe sobranie sochinenii*, 10 vols. (Moscow: Akademiia nauk SSSR, 1956–58), 2:159. Emphasis mine.

75. Cf. Akhmatova's insistence in.1940, that Kuzmin's entourage "*had the most harmful influence on young people*: they took it for the pinnacle of thought and art, but in fact it was the debauchery of thought, because everything was regarded as a toy, everything was ... mocked." Lidiia Chukovskaia, *Zapiski ob Anne Akhmatovoi*, vol. 1, 1938–41 (Paris: YMCA-Press, 1976), 150–51. Emphasis mine.

76. It is especially appropriate that a late, sardonic reiteration of this important concept in Dostoevsky's work belongs to Ivan Karamazov's Devil; F.M. Dostoevskii, *Polnoe sobranie sochinenii v tridtsati tomakh*, ed. V.G. Bazanov and others, 30 vols. (Leningrad: Nauka, 1972–90), 15:84. A connection between Akhmatova's Kuzmin-as-Devil and Ivan's nightmare Devil may be one line of association – hitherto, apparently, unexplored – behind *Poem's* explicit invocation of the "Dostoevskian and demonic" (1:332).

77. Compare Akhmatova's allegation that a "real cult of gossip" governed Kuzmin's "salon" (Chukovskaia, *Zapiski*, 1:150), with her admission in "The Prose" that she was remote from the events she depicts in *Poem*: Kniazev's "*real* biography was too unfamiliar to me and related entirely to his collection of verse (Mikhail

Kuzmin)" (1:358–59). Recent scholarship has suggested that even her version of Kuzmin's indifference to Kniazev's death may be distorted: for a subtle and vigorous biographical defence of Kuzmin the man (in contradistinction to the artistic image of *Poem*), see N.A. Bogomolov, *Mikhail Kuzmin: Stat'i i materialy* (Moscow: Novoe literaturnoe obozrenie, 1995), 36–38; and (along different lines) N.A. Bogomolov and Dzhon E. Malmstad, *Mikhail Kuzmin: Iskusstvo, zhizn', epokha* (Moscow: Novoe literaturnoe obozrenie, 1996), 116–19, 175–79.

78. Akhmatova, *Sochineniia*, 3:165.

79. "Ob odnom iz poslednikh sobesednikov Akhmatovoi: Iubileinye zametki," *Daugava*, 1989, no. 6:100–102(100–101).

80. The line quoted by Akhmatova (*Poema bez geroia*, 91) is "Est', Faust, kazn'." The heroine of Ivanov's poem subsequently addresses Faust, her "midnight executioner," with the words: "Ty, znaiu, d'iavol." Viacheslav Ivanov, *Stikhotvoreniia. Poemy. Tragedii*, ed. R.E. Pomirchii, 2 vols. (St. Petersburg: Gumanitarnoe agentstvo "Akademicheskii proekt," 1995), 1:438–39.

81. Akhmatova, *Sochineniia*, 3:162.

82. See N.A. Bogomolov, "K odnomu temnomu epizodu v biografii Kuzmina," in *Mikhail Kuzmin i russkaia kul'tura XX veka*, ed. G.A. Morev (Leningrad: Muzei Anny Akhmatovoi v Fontannom Dome, 1990), 166–69(166).

83. "Gete na rubezhe dvukh stoletii," in *Istoriia zapadnoi literatury 1800–1910 gg.*, ed. F.D. Batiushkov, vol. 1 (Moscow: Izdanie t-va "Mir," 1912), 113–56.

84. "Balagan" (1912), in *Meyerhold on Theatre*, trans. and ed. with critical commentary by Edward Braun (London: Methuen, 1969), 131.

85. Edward Braun, *Meyerhold: A Revolution in Theatre*, 2d ed. (London: Methuen, 1995), 97, 99. Meierkhol'd's *commedia dell'arte* stagings also included V.N. Solov'ev's *Harlequin, the Marriage Broker*. Detailed description of all Meierkhol'd productions mentioned here can be found in Braun's well-indexed monograph.

86. See Wendy Rosslyn, "Don Juan Feminised," in *Symbolism and After: Essays on Russian Poetry in Honour of Georgette Donchin*, ed. Arnold McMillin (London: Bristol Classical Press, 1992), 102–21(103).

87. *Aktery moego pokoleniia* (1959), cited in Braun, *Meyerhold*, 144. On the "Stranger" as an "emissary of the infernal powers," see also *Meyerhold on Theatre*, 79.

88. Wells, *Akhmatova*, 106.

89. The quotation is from a production note of Meierkhol'd's, cited in Braun, *Meyerhold*, 144. For details of the production's lavish design by Golovin, see ibid., 144–49; and for an indication of its relevance to *Poem*, see Timenchik, Toporov, and Tsiv'ian, "Akhmatova i Kuzmin," 255.

90. See Rosslyn, "Theatre, Theatricality," 99; and, on Lord Henry, Braun, *Meyerhold*, 145. For fuller analysis of the relevance of Meierkhol'd's *Queen of Spades*, see Kats and Timenchik, *Akhmatova i muzyka*, 218–32.

91. See Toporov, *Akhmatova i Blok*, 34.

92. *Chudesnaia zhizn' Iosifa Bal'zamo, grafa Kaliostro* (1919) – to which Akhmatova's "Eto staryi chudit Kaliostro" (1:337; emphasis mine) makes obvious punning reference.

93. I.e. "Die Abenteuer der Sylvester Nacht," in *Fantasiestücke in Callot's Manier*. See Braun, *Meyerhold*, 101, 320 n.51.

94. "Khoromnoe deistvo," in Ivanov, *Stikhotvoreniia. Poemy. Tragedii*, 1:460–61.

95. See Parnis and Timenchik, "Programmy 'Brodiachei sobaki'," 169–70.

96. Publicly, for instance, *Poem's* allusion to "Meierkhol'd's" *Masquerade* probably serves to signal the intertwining of historical tragedy with social frivolity; privately, his own gruesomely protracted end must have been fresh in Akhmatova's mind when she began *Poem*; see Wells, *Akhmatova*, 105–7.

97. Rosslyn, "Theatre, Theatricality," 103.

98. For Meierkhol'd's definition of stylization, "tied up with the idea of convention, generalization, and symbol" with the aim of revealing "the inner synthesis of a period or phenomenon," see Braun, ed., *Meyerhold on Theatre*, 43 (note), 62–64, and, with pertinent reference to adaptations of Hoffmann and *commedia dell'arte*, 140–44. On the mask (which permits the spectator to see, for example, "not only the actual Arlecchino before him but all the Arlecchinos who live in his memory," and thence "every person who bears the merest resemblance to the character"), see ibid., 131, 132–34, 60, 64. On the grotesque (which, for Meierkhol'd, is associated with Goya, Poe, and Hoffmann, and has its basis in "the artist's constant desire to switch the spectator from the plane he has just reached to another which is totally unforeseen"), see esp. ibid., 137–42.

99. See 1:357–58; and the continuation of the same passage in Timenchik, "Blok i ego sovremenniki," 118–19.

100. Ibid., 119; Timenchik, Toporov, and Tsiv'ian, "Akhmatova i Kuzmin," 253, 254.

101. R.D. Timenchik, "K semioticheskoi interpretatsii *Poemy bez geroia*," *Trudy po znakovym sistemam* 6 (1973):438–42(442). On the theatricality of Gumilev's biography, see M. Basker, "Lermontov and Gumilev: Some Biographical Parallels," in *Mikhail Lermontov: Commemorative Essays (1991)*, ed. A.D.P. Briggs (Birmingham: Birmingham Modern Languages Publications, 1992), 7–34.

102. See Akhmatova, *Poema bez geroia*, 156.

103. The poem in question is "Margarita" (1:140–41); its dream origins are indicated by Akhmatova in "'Samyi neprochitannyi poet': Zametki Anny Akhmatovoi o Nikolae Gumileve," ed. V.A. Chernykh, *Novyi mir*, 1990, no.5:222. "Margarita" was first published in 1910, and reprinted in the section of *Chuzhoe nebo* (1912) dedicated "To Anna Akhmatovu." Curiously, the unusual phrase *chuzhoe nebo* also occurs in Ivanov's "Son" ("V moi vzor gliadit / Chuzhogo neba biriuza …"); Ivanov, *Stikhotvoreniia. Poemy. Tragedii*, 1:439. It is not impossible to see a reflection of Ivanov's continuing, insidious influence in Gumilev's choice of title.

104. Examples are the stifling, book-lined alchemist's cell of "Popugai" (1:107), the reworking of a similar subject in "Chitatel' knig" (1:108), and the theme of the "forbidden works of the elders" in "Potomki Kaina" (1:83), the general conception of which might also derive from the elder poet. All three poems were written between August 1909 and April 1910.

105. T.V. Tsiv'ian, "Zametki k deshifrovke *Poemy bez geroia*," *Trudy po znakovym sistemam* 5 (1971):27; Toporov, *Akhmatova i Blok*, 28–29, 45.

106. Timenchik, "Blok i ego sovremenniki," 115. The phrase was replaced in later versions by "Vse tainstvenno v prishletse" (1:330).

107. See Chernykh, ed., "'Samyi neprochitannyi poet'," 220.

108. Timenchik, Toporov, and Tsiv'ian, "Akhmatova i Kuzmin," 246–47.

109. Ibid., 253–54. The variant of *Poem* is reproduced in Akhmatova, *Poema bez geroia*, 194.

110. Wells, *Akhmatova*, 104.

111. See, e.g., Filippov's lengthy note in Akhmatova, *Sochineniia*, 2:382.

112. In the section "Studierzimmer" of *Faust*, Part 1.

113. See Timenchik, Toporov, and Tsiv'ian, "Akhmatova i Kuzmin," 300 n.185.

114. "S tusklym vzorom, s mertvym serdtsem v more brosit'sia so skaly …" (1:130).

115. Timenchik, Toporov, and Tsiv'ian, "Akhmatova i Kuzmin," 279 n.52.

116. A complex echo of these same lines from Gumilev's "Ezbekie," in Akhmatova's "Bol'shaia ispoved'" (2:298) and another, untitled fragment of "Enuma Elish" (2:281), has recently been noted by P.E. Poberezkina, who comments astutely: "as a rule, one and the same work by Gumilev is cited several times by Akhmatova in different texts, while in those texts, echoes of several works of Gumilev

may be simultaneously present;" P.E. Poberezkina, "Anna Akhmatova i Nikolai Gumilev: K voprosu o gumilevskikh alliuziiakh v tvorchestve Akhmatovoi," in *Akhmatovskie chteniia: A. Akhmatova, N. Gumilev i russkaia poeziia nachala XX veka* (Tver': Tverskoi gosudarstvennyi universitet, 1995), 68–75(73–74). By the same token, the adjective "gotov," used with reference to "smert'" in Gumilev's lines, constitutes another possible context for Akhmatova's use of the phrase "Ia k smerti gotov."

117. Cf. Lera's: "Brat, zhenikh, ia tebia umoliaiu ..." (2:88); and: "On – zhenikh moi, i nezhnyi i strastnyi, / Brat, sklonivshii zadumchivo vzor." (2:91). Although the dove (golub'/golubka) does not appear in *Gondla*, the swan is a crucial leitmotif (see below); and Lera-Laik, the dualistic heroine, is strongly associated with the sun (solntse) in one of her two hypostases (e.g. 2:81). For Akhmatova's evaluation of *Gondla*, see V. Luknitskaia, *Pered toboi zemlia* (Leningrad: Lenizdat, 1988), 340.

118. See, most pertinently, Akhmatova's comments on her own verse in Luknitskaia, *Pered toboi zemlia*, 332–33; and on Gumilev's in Chernykh, ed., "'Samyi neprochitannyi poet'," 220, 222.

119. See Akhmatova, *Sochineniia*, 3:163–64; the editorial note in Anna Akhmatova, *Stikhotvoreniia i poemy*, ed. V.M. Zhirmunskii (Leningrad: Sovetskii pisatel', 1976), 521 (which confirms that the cornet's arrest is indeed to be understood from the somewhat elliptical libretto); and Gumilev, *Neizdannoe i nesobrannoe*, 180, 290.

120. Cf., e.g., V.Ia. Vilenkin, *V sto pervom zerkale* (Moscow: Sovetskii pisatel', 1987), 252; and the materials under the heading "Pokolenie samoubiits" in Akhmatova, *Poema bez geroia*, 140–44.

121. A.M. Van der Eng-Liedmeier, "Anna Axmatova's *Poèma bez geroja*," in *Dutch Contributions to the Sixth International Congress of Slavicists, Prague, 1968*, ed. A.G.F. van Holk (The Hague: Mouton, 1971), 67–97 (85–86).

122. Timenchik, "Rizhskii epizod," 121.

123. See the reactions of Valentina Verigina and Sergei Auslender, two contemporaries and close associates of Akhmatova and Gumilev respectively, cited in Braun, *Meyerhold*, 64–65.

124. I am indebted to Iu.V. Zobnin for this information. See also the commentary to Gumilev's poem "Liubov'" in Gumilev, *Polnoe sobranie sochinenii*, 2:269–70.

125. Kheit, *Akhmatova*, 224. Cf. also Chukovskaia, *Zapiski*, 1:120.

126. Luknitskaia, *Pered toboi zemlia*, 333. Emphasis mine.

127. See, for example, Timenchik, Toporov, and Tsiv'ian, "Akhmatova i Kuzmin," 300 n.185; Wells, *Akhmatova*, 104; and Kralin's note in Akhmatova, *Sochineniia*, 1:431.

128. Chernykh, ed., "'Samyi neprochitannyi poet'," 223.

129. According to P.N. Luknitsky's still unpublished papers, now in Pushkinskii Dom. I am grateful to Iurii Zobnin for this information.

130. See Michael Basker, "Gumilev, Annensky and Tsarskoe Selo: Gumilev's 'Tsarskosel'skii krug idei'," in *A Sense of Place: Tsarskoe Selo and its Poets*, ed. Lev Loseff and Barry Scherr (Columbus: Slavica, 1993), 215–41(esp. 227–29, 235). The quotations are from Akhmatova's "V remeshkakh penal i knigi byli ..." (1912, 1:65), which undoubtedly alludes to imagery used by Gumilev.

131. Cf. in this connection Mandel'shtam's description of Gumilev's maturation from young student to "Petersburgian acmeist": "No v Peterburge akmeist mne blizhe, / Chem *romanticheskii P'ero* v Parizhe" (emphasis mine). Significantly enough, the lines are known only through Akhmatova's memoirs (2:155).

132. P.N. Luknitskii, *Acumiana: Vstrechi s Annoi Akhmatovoi*, Vol. 1, 1924–25 (Paris: YMCA-Press, 1991), 180.

133. Cf. Kheit, *Akhmatova*, 235–36.

134. Vera Luknitskaia, *Nikolai Gumilev: Zhizn' poeta po materialam domashnego arkhiva sem'i Luknitskikh* (Leningrad: Lenizdat, 1990), 114. Emphasis mine.

135. Basker, "Gumilyov's *Akteon*," 516–17.

136. This is explored in a revised and updated version of "Gumilyov's *Akteon*," to be published as a chapter of my *Rannii Gumilev: Stanovlenie poeta-akmeista* (St. Petersburg: Russkii Khristianskii gumanitarnyi institut, [forthcoming]).

137. Luknitskii, *Acumiana*, 128; Timenchik, Toporov, and Tsiv'ian, "Akhmatova i Kuzmin," 222–23.

138. For the intertextual basis for inclusion of Kuzmin in *Poem*'s "Don Juan" orbit, see esp. his "Chuzhaia poema:" M.A. Kuzmin, *Stikhotvoreniia*, ed. N.A. Bogomolov (St. Petersburg: Gumanitarnoe agentstvo "Akademicheskii proekt," 1996), 395–98.

139. David Wells, *Akhmatova and Pushkin: The Pushkin Contexts of Akhmatova's Poetry* Birmingham Slavonic Monographs, no.25 (Birmingham: University of Birmingham, 1994), 51.

140. Thus: "Mgnovennyi mir menia *ne obol'stit*, / I zhenskii vzor, to nezhnyi, to *lukavyi*, / Lish' izredka, vo sne, menia tomit. // Lish' izredka nadmenno i upriamo / Vo mne krichit vetshaiushchii Adam" (1:515; emphasis mine).

141. Cf. the lines from "Monastyr' na Kazbeke" (1829): "Tuda b, skazav prosti ushchel'iu, / Podniat'sia k vol'noi vyshine! / Tuda b, v zaoblachnuiu kel'iu, / V sosedstvo Boga skryt'sia mne!..". Pushkin, *Polnoe sobranie sochinenii*, 3:141.

142. Rosslyn, "Don Juan Feminised," esp. 110. On Blok, see Toporov, *Akhmatova i Blok*, 36–45, 115–20; and Crone, "Blok as Don Juan," esp. 146–54.

143. Luknitskii, *Acumiana*, 146.

Chapter 13

Playing Devil's Advocate: Paradox and Parody in Zamiatin's "The Miracle of Ash Wednesday"

Philip Cavendish

To discuss demonism in the work of Evgenii Zamiatin might at first glance appear misguided. Despite an Orthodox background – his father was a priest and his mother the daughter of a priest – Zamiatin was either an agnostic or an atheist for whom the sacred truths of Christian belief were essentially fictions. For much of his career, both in terms of his fiction and his journalistic writing, he preached the values of heresy and intellectual rebellion, quoting approvingly in 1924 Anatole France's paradoxical statement that "it requires extraordinary strength of spirit to be a non-believer."[1] Like France, Zamiatin adhered in his fiction to the values of relativism, irony, and scepticism, preferring to believe in the virtue of revolt for its own sake, irrespective of the prevailing ideological system. As is well known, his persistent challenge to Bolshevik "orthodoxies" in the field of literature and the arts after the October Revolution led to his gradual exclusion from cultural life and subsequent exile abroad in 1931.

Unlike the symbolists, for whom the relationship between religion and art was a central element in their philosophical and aesthetic inquiry, Zamiatin would doubtless have denied the ontological status of the Devil. This did not mean, however, that he denied the Devil symbolic status, or status as a cultural, social, or psychological metaphor. Zamiatin's Romantic identification with Lucifer as the "spirit of doubt and eternal rebellion" is present both in his art and in his journalism.[2] Furthermore, he was perfectly capable of donning a Satanic mask when his narrative conceit required it, a prime example being the three "miracle tales" or *chudesa*: "The Saintly Sin of the Precious Virgin. A Eulogy" (O sviatom grekhe Zenitsy-devy. Slovo pokhval'noe, 1917), "The Healing of the Novice Erasmus" (O tom, kak istselen byl otrok Erazm, 1922), and "The Miracle of Ash Wednesday" (O chude, proisshedshem v Pepel'nuiu Sredu, 1926).[3] If, citing Erasmus, the work of the Devil consists of "anything that deters us from Christ and his teaching," then these tales are clearly demonically inspired.[4] Not only are they blasphemous attacks on the values promoted in the legends of the saints, but as parodies which assume the guises of sacred texts only to subvert their edificatory function, they can be read as literary forgeries whose *jouissance*, to borrow briefly from Barthes, consists of gradually stripping away the impression of authenticity to reveal the underlying burlesque and carnivalesque intent.[5] Indeed, in their use of the obscene, the bawdy, and the grotesque, and in their general formalistic playfulness, they have their roots in the sphere which Bakhtin has defined as carnival, laughter, or "anti-world" culture, a sphere in which official values, rituals, and modes of expression are mocked and subverted.[6] Thus the demon which haunts these narratives is not so much the defiant and gloomy rebel of Romantic poetry, but rather the scandal-mongering joker of the folk-religious imagination. He is the demon of vaudevillean laughter and street theatre, the mask-wearing charlatan, manipulator, and intriguer, the crude vulgarian who seeks to provoke, corrupt, and play tricks on the naive and gullible.[7]

In "The Miracle of Ash Wednesday" Zamiatin adopts "devil's advocacy" as a form of post-symbolist literary conceit. The fatal paradox, according to which art is viewed as a collaborative continuation with God of Creation, but a collaboration inevitably tainted with the Satanic because it rivals that Creation, is here radically transformed, even parodied, in a display of ludic provocation. The artist-demiurge of symbolist poetics is replaced by the artist-buffoon or *skomorokh*, the strolling minstrel whose bawdy laughter and song was associated in the medieval imagination with the work of the Devil.[8] The antics of the modern artist-*skomorokh*, insofar as they applied to literature and art, envisaged a wide range of transgressive behaviour: commitment to "low genres," such as *skaz*-style narration; interest in the apocryphal, marginal, and censored; subversion of religious and secular institutions; celebration of the erotic, the obscene, and the sexually taboo; promotion of the verbal prank and whimsical joke as legitimate literary subjects; and a penchant for the fanciful, absurd, and bizarre. In spirit, Zamiatin's hagiographical parodies are influenced greatly by the carnivalesque experiments of Gogol, in particular his vision of the Devil as the embodiment of the absurd and the deceptive.[9] "The Miracle of Ash Wednesday" features the Devil as a fictional character in his own right; furthermore, as an authorial alter ego, this Devil is a subversive and corrupting presence who threatens the coherence and logicality of the text. This text constitutes a surreal riddle which challenges not only the desired norms of serious and ideologically correct Soviet literature in the 1920s, but also the expectation of sense on the part of the reader. It is the challenge of unravelling this riddle, and drawing out the demonic strategy inherent in Zamiatin's tale, which provides the central focus of this essay.

In order to appreciate "The Miracle of Ash Wednesday" as an example of demonic mask-play, consideration needs to be given to a broad range of literary and aesthetic influences. The first part of this essay examines Zamiatin's interest in hagiography, an interest shared by many writers in the second half of the nineteenth century and after. The adaptations of *vitae* undertaken by Leo Tolstoi and Anatole France, for example, in Zamiatin's view the great religious heretics of his time, are important in this regard. I will be drawing attention to the stylized, parodic features of Zamiatin's earlier *chudesa*, their use of bawdy and obscene images, and the ways in which they constitute a transgression of ecclesiastical norms.

In this context, it is important to appreciate the influence of Aleksei Remizov, a writer with whom Zamiatin enjoyed a close personal and professional relationship at this time. The conceit of the modern artist as *skomorokh*, for example, derives primarily from Remizov, and I will be examining his pornographic aetiological tale "What Tobacco Is" (Chto est' tabak, 1908) as a prototypical example of carnivalesque playfulness. It is instructive that Zamiatin was coopted into Remizov's Great and Free Order of Apes (Obezvelvolpal), a mock-literary society devoted to anarchic and subversive laughter, in the immediate aftermath of the October Revolution.[10] The fate of the artists associated with this society is symptomatic of the continuation of various forms of censorship into the post-Revolutionary era and the appearance under a secular authority of new forms of political, social, and cultural taboo. While it was appropriate now to mock and ridicule the Orthodox Church as an institution (a fact which gave rise to numerous anti-ecclesiastical subjects), the Bolsheviks were puritan and conservative as far as sexual mores were concerned; indeed, they despised and sought to suppress all forms of carnivalesque activity, including the very carnival itself.[11] Literature devoted to parody, satire, and the subversion of secular norms was quickly relegated to the margins of cultural activity and officially disparaged, if not banned altogether.

As pseudo-hagiography, Zamiatin's *chudesa* belong to the wave of interest in hagiographic materials characteristic of a number of Russian writers, including such literary giants as Dostoevsky, Tolstoi, Leskov, and Merezhkovsky.[12] In the main these writers were concerned with the moral values promoted in the *Lives* and their relevance for modern-day humanity. It was common to borrow standard themes (*topoi*) from well-known *vitae*, to model fictional characters on celebrated saintly types, to adapt a particular *vita* for a modern, secular audience, and to rework entire narratives for polemical, sometimes anti-ecclesiastical purposes. If parody and stylization were not a primary concern of these writers, their approaches ranged from the reverent to the extremely irreverent (it was not uncommon, for example, to use the legends as a literary "Trojan horse" with which to disarm the Tsarist censors).[13] The attitudes of these writers towards the hagiographic sources themselves varied. Tolstoi, for example, considered the miracles in the legends of the saints to be "fairy tales" for the uninitiated; while Leskov considered the various tales in the Russian *Synaxary* (*Prolog*) to be "rubbish," but argued that they provided unusual and interesting raw material on which the artist could profitably draw.[14] In many cases, the adaptations of these writers constituted arguments about revealed religion, the value of certain forms of ritual and worship (kenotic versus ascetic), and the practices of the Russian Orthodox Church, in particular the clergy. If Tolstoi was excommunicated, for example, this was not because he rejected belief in a Supreme Being as such, but because he rejected certain important aspects of Orthodox doctrine and was vehemently critical of the hierarchy.[15]

For Zamiatin, Tolstoi was one of the great religious heretics of his time. Along with Anatole France, a writer well known for his scepticism, he was an important champion of free thinking in the modern era, the proof of his heresy reflected in the banning of his fiction by the Russian Orthodox Church. We may presume that the iconoclastic views of both writers were influential in shaping Zamiatin's attitude towards religion; moreover, it is interesting to note that both men adapted *vitae* as a means by which to polemicize with their opponents. Zamiatin, however, was careful to draw a distinction between the philosophical and moral outlooks of the two men.[16] France's adaptions of hagiographic legends were tainted by a neopaganist eroticism which would have been unacceptable to the puritan Tolstoi.[17] Indeed, his penchant for libertinage and gauloiserie, an aspect of his writing which derives primarily from the Enlightenment works of Voltaire and Diderot, in many respects prefigures Zamiatin's own amoral tendencies in his reworkings of similar types of material. Another influence was undoubtedly the fascination for the obscene and sexually perverse in the first decades of the twentieth century on the part of certain symbolist and decadent writers in Russia.[18] While it is true that this interest was explored within a specifically religious and mystical context, this made it no less acceptable to the Orthodox Church or to the Tsarist autocracy – hence the continuing problem with the censors during this period with regard to supposed depravity and the corruption of public morals.[19]

One of the figures from this milieu to whom Zamiatin owed a great debt was Remizov, a writer whose interest in the transgressional was well established by the time Zamiatin made his acquaintance in 1913 in the editorial offices of *Zavety*, the Socialist Revolutionaries' cultural almanac. In 1908 Remizov founded the society Obezvelvolpal, adopting as his pseudonym the name of the Vogul Prince who had allegedly murdered the Bishop of Perm in the fifteenth century.[20] His anti-ecclesiastical prejudices were particularly strident at this time, as can be witnessed by the pornographic tale "What Tobacco Is," which he published in the very same year. Printed privately in twenty-five copies, and allegedly the product of meetings between himself, Rozanov, Kuzmin, Bakst, Somov, and Nuvel in 1906 to explore the nature of the erotic, this is a scurrilous, bawdy, and seedy tale with few rivals in terms of its frivolous, anarchic, and nihilistic spirit.[21] Generically speaking, "What Tobacco Is" is a demonic aetiological tale with strong roots in Russia's folk tradition.[22] It is ostensibly written at Christmas, a time of licensed festivity on the part of the Church, and a key stylistic device involves the attribution of authorship to a fictitious narrator. This was a device typical of the purveyors of obscene material in Russia – see, for example, the false bibliographical details given in the first emigré edition of Afanas'ev's celebrated *Secret Tales of Russia (Russkie zavetnye skazki)*, which was actually published in Geneva in 1872.[23] Remizov introduces his tale as the account of Gonosius, an ancient sage concerned to correct various popular but misconceived notions about the origins of the evil weed (his story might be read as a malicious riposte to Tolstoi's public renunciation of tobacco in his article "Why Do Men Stupefy Themselves?").[24] Gonosius's account opens with a brief review of the more intriguing popular fables regarding the origins of tobacco; he then proceeds to expound his own version, according to which the tobacco plant is spawned from the gigantic loins of a monk calling himself Savrasius. The story takes place in a pious fraternity called the "Monastery of Miracles" (Chudov Monastyr'). The antics of Savrasius, who arrives mysteriously at the monastery and is suspected by many to be a *iurodivyi* (holy fool) possessed by the Devil, are obscene and loathsome; suffice to say, the climax of the tale involves a violent and bizarre confrontation between Savrasius and a monk called Niukh, the outcome of which leads to their mutual destruction and dissolution into a lake of tar, in the middle of which floats a large penis. The burial of their remains gives rise next spring to a flower, the aroma of which is so seductive that the monks use the leaves to make cigars and export them for recreational use. Hence the origin of the tobacco plant which, after a brief period of official approval, is then angrily condemned as the work of the Devil.

It has been argued that Remizov's entire career consists of a buffoon-like transgression of the official.[25] His position vis-à-vis ecclesiastical culture, however, is more ambiguous than such a statement would allow. If "What Tobacco Is" is the epitome of *skomorokh*-style obscenity, and plays mischievously with the ambiguous status of the *iurodivyi* in Russian culture, it is a rather extreme example of Remizov's "black art" and is not characteristic of his work as a whole. His attitude towards the spiritual and cultural heritage of Orthodox Christianity was celebratory, rather than subversive, as can be witnessed by the tales of *Leimonarium* (*Limonar'*, 1907), *Paraleipomenon* (*Paralipomenon*, 1912), and *The Golden Chain* (*Tsep' zlataia*, 1913), the last of which Zamiatin himself reviewed in 1914.[26] The apparent paradox which underlines Remizov's position is vividly illustrated in Zamiatin's own depiction of him in his short story "Alatyr" (Alatyr', 1914) as the character of the archpriest Father Peter, a man renowned locally for his interest in marsh-demons (bolotnye cherti) and for his learned treatise "On the Lives and Subsistence of Devils" (O zhitii i propitanii diavolov), but unmistakably a man of religion.[27] On the other hand, Remizov's private correspondence with such friends as Rozanov (chief "phallus-bearer" in the society Obezvelvolpal), and his interest in linguistic transgression (swear words) and newspaper stories about exotic sexual-religious practices (the Flagellants), stands somewhat at odds with his respectful attitude towards Orthodox religious culture in general. While moving in a milieu which was critical of the institutions of Orthodoxy, but sought nevertheless to renew contact with religion and mysticism through the exploration of Eros, there can be little doubt that Remizov's position was essentially ambiguous. However provocative and obscene, "What Tobacco Is" is not ultimately an erotic piece of work, or even a celebration of the carnival in the free-wheeling style of Rabelais, but rather a dark, sinister tale with disturbing imagery and a distaste for the physically sexual. Like a church gargoyle, it is a crude and vulgar grotesque which provokes revulsion on the part of the reader, as well as laughter at its more outrageous, fanciful episodes.[28]

Remizov's stylizations of folk-ecclesiastical genres, while not parodies, are important precursors for Zamiatin. He was certainly
acquainted with "What Tobacco Is," although it is not clear how early
in his career. In his mock epistle "The Turkish Drum" (Tulumbas,
1920), an open response to Remizov's Obezvelvolpal manifesto, he
manages to include a reference to the evil habit of smoking and
"Savrasius's gigantic, loathsome member" (Savrasieva merzkogo
udishcha).[29] On the whole, Zamiatin possesses a far less ambiguous
attitude towards the sacred traditions of the Orthodox Church. At the
same time, the main difference between his ecclesiastical parodies
and Remizov's aetiological tale lies not in the aesthetic impulse, but
rather in the sphere of literary strategy. While anti-ecclesiastical in
spirit, "What Tobacco Is" does not pretend to formal respectability.
By contrast, Zamiatin seeks to give the illusion of an official or semi-
official document, while at the same time undermining its piety
through thematic subversion and the incorporation of bawdy,
grotesque details. Remizov's tale is diabolical because it boasts a
demonic subject (the Devil as the originator of tobacco) and an
"author" who does not purport to belong to the Church (Gonosius's
status as "sage" suggests a pagan magus). Zamiatin's parodies are
demonic because the author adopts a saintly mask behind which he
conceals his diabolical intentions. Disguise, of course, is part of the
Devil's armoury of weapons; thus Zamiatin's fictions might be said to
constitute the fictional equivalents of the devils in hagiographic literature who assume disguises in order to corrupt the pure and innocent.

Although first published in 1917, we now know, thanks to the
release of archival materials, that "The Precious Virgin" was written
in 1915 and entrusted to Remizov for publication while Zamiatin
was working in Great Britain on a ship-building mission.[30] In his
own words, the tale was an attempt to give the "illusion" of an early
medieval narrative.[31] The title in Russian refers to a type of hagiographic sub-genre – the encomiastic sermon – with stylistic origins in
the sermons of the early Christian period.[32] As a stylization, the work
purports to be that of a medieval chronicler: draft versions reveal
that Zamiatin conceived the author of the tale either as an anonymous monk, or a monk calling himself Gleb, who had witnessed the
events of the narrative – in other words, the text was intended to be
read as a "found document," and thus essentially as apocryphal in
origin.[33] The narrative incorporates several themes from the virgin-
martyr *passiones* and subverts several *topoi* from the legends of female
and male saints. These include the expelling of serpents from the
womb;[34] the healing of mutilated breasts after torture;[35] and the
preservation of the body from mortal decay.[36] A similar exploitation
of hagiographic themes occurs in Zamiatin's second tale, "The Heal-

ing of the Novice Erasmus," which tells the story of a gifted and talented icon-painter whose erotic visions prove dangerous to the religious community in which he serves. The plot of this tale incorporates the menological account of the *Life of Saint Mary of Egypt*, the harlot whose conversion and many years of penitence spent in solitude in the Egyptian desert inspired such writers as Dostoevsky, Boris Almazov, and Elizaveta Shakhova, and was twice celebrated by Remizov in 1907 and 1915.[37] Like "The Precious Virgin," "The Healing of the Novice Erasmus" purports to be the work of a hagiographer, this time a scribe called Innokentii who has compiled his account for the "edification" and "instruction" of the elders in his monastery. The conceit of ecclesiastical authenticity extended even to the design of the original booklet in which the story was first published in Berlin; it carried a series of grotesque chimeras by Kustodiev very much in the style of medieval hagiographic collections (see Illustration 20).[38]

Gor'ky's complaint that "The Healing of the Novice Erasmus" was little more than a "vulgar joke" (grubaia shutka), and a failed reworking of the stories of Remizov and France, rather missed the point.[39] It is very much an element of the carnival text that the joke is a permitted literary form. This is not to ignore the polemical strategy which informs Zamiatin's writing in this vein. On the one hand, his parodies are allegorical vehicles with which to satirize contemporary events (I argue elsewhere that "The Precious Virgin" alludes to the rumours of a royally-negotiated "separate peace" circulating in Petersburg towards the end of 1915).[40] On the other hand, they also constitute an attempt to polemicize with certain doctrines of the Orthodox Church – in particular, the celebration of virginity as a spiritual ideal. In their reversal of the usual edificatory themes of hagiographic literature, and the incorporation of bawdy details into the fabric of what purports to be a pious text, the author's blasphemous strategy becomes transparent. The miracles of the saints, a feature of their *Lives* which served as important proof of their divine powers in the posthumous bid for canonization, are ironized; the laudatory function of the genre itself is subverted, if not reversed; and the Orthodox teaching on the insoluble link between bodily and spiritual purity is openly challenged. Common to both stories is the acceptance, rather than rejection of sexual sin as an act of virtue; furthermore, in both texts demons are figuratively present. In "The Precious Virgin," it is the barbarian warlord Erman, described as a "proud king and architect of evil" (3:65): he is the person to whom the Precious Virgin gives herself, thus sacrificing her vows of celibacy, but saving her compatriots from further invasion and brutal repression. In "The Healing of the Novice Erasmus," it is the

казанный инокъ Еразмъ еще во чревѣ матери посвященъ былъ Богу. Родители его долгіе годы ревностно, но тщетно любили другъ друга и, наконецъ, истощивъ всѣ суетныя средства, пришли въ обитель къ блаженному Памвѣ. Вступивъ въ келью старца, жена преклонила предъ нимъ колѣни, но стыдъ женскій запечаталъ ей уста, и такъ молча предстояла старцу. Блаженному же Памвѣ и не надо было

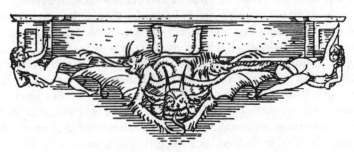

20. B. Kustodiev, Illustration to E. Zamiatin's short story, "The Healing of the Novice Erasmus," 1922.

laughing devils (besy) which besiege Erasmus's cell in true medieval style (in his drawings Kustodiev used the conventional images of ugly beasts with horns and tails) and are representative of the sexual licentiousness to which the entire monastery falls victim. The

demonic is synonymous in this story with the forces of erotic libera-
tion. As a result of the "divine" instruction given to Pamva, Erasmus's guardian – "Release the arrow, and the bowstring will lose its
tension, and the bow will no longer be deathly" (Spusti strelu, i
oslabnet tetiva, i uzhe ne budet bolee smertonosen luk, 1:474) – Erasmus is permitted knowledge of the forbidden secrets of the flesh in
order fully and accurately to depict the penitent whore as she stands
naked in the desert.

Although the miracle tales are not as vulgar as Remizov's "What
Tobacco Is," there can be little doubting their fundamental obscenity. The description of Erman licking the severed breasts of the Precious Virgin as they are brought to him on a plate after her torture
(3:67); the mention of Erasmus's erection as Saint Mary reveals her
naked body to him (1:469); the droplets of sperm which rain down
on the assembled monks during his reading of Solomon's "Song of
Songs" (1:466); and the curious aroma of the virginal Mary's "fourth
secret" (1:468) all belong to the realm of the "lower bodily world,"
and therefore to the carnivalesque in the Bakhtinian understanding.
Hand in hand with such transgression goes Zamiatin's authorial pact
with the Devil of lust and carnal desire. It is symptomatic that in a
later article on Kustodiev he mentioned the *topos* of temptation in the
menological collections, and wondered whether he himself, like the
demons who visited the saints of old in the wilderness, had not
tempted Kustodiev into impious transgression.[41] Unlike Remizov,
Zamiatin took great pleasure in the employment of sexually explicit
material. One thinks of his description of Nelson's column in terms
of a phallus in "Fisher of Men" (Lovets chelovekov, 1921), a story
which would not be published in Britain for several decades because
of its barely-concealed eroticism.[42] In "A Reliable Place" (Nadezh-
noe mesto, 1924), we read the story of a pious woman on a pilgrimage to Zadonsk who has her life's savings stolen after succumbing to
the devilish charms of a male travelling companion: he has the red
hair of a Russian folk devil (ryzhii chert), and the "reliable place" in
question turns out to be inside her knickers![43] These works are striking illustrations of Zamiatin's Boccaccio-like treatment of nominally
religious subjects. Indeed, as I hope to show, the bawdy Western
humour of *The Decameron*, as well as the Russian folk bawdy tradition
itself, is a shaping influence in "The Miracle of Ash Wednesday," and
constitutes a key element in Zamiatin's carnival-style humour.

Although first published in 1926 in the journal *Novaia Rossiia*, Zamiatin's "The Miracle of Ash Wednesday" was actually written in the
summer of 1923 at the same time as his article "About Literature,
Revolution and Entropy" (O literature, revoliutsii i entropii, 1924).[44]

In a letter to Lev Lunts, his erstwhile student at the House of Arts, Zamiatin characterized his tale as tiny and "indecorous" (*neprilichen*), and compared it to "The Healing of the Novice Erasmus," explaining that it was conceived during a heatwave, "when, as you know, the demon of carnal desire is powerful."[45] The view that these two stories should be read as companion pieces is supported by the fact that they were both parodied in a humorous account of the conception and staging of *The Flea* (*Blokha*, 1924) which Zamiatin himself composed in December 1926 for a special evening of parody at FIGA (Fizeo-geotsentricheskaia assotsiatsiia).[46] Furthermore, they were reprinted alongside each other in *Impious Tales* (*Nechestivye rasskazy*, 1927), a collection which included several examples of Zamiatin's anti-ecclesiastical whimsy.[47]

The uncanny quality of this text lies partly in the incongruity between the event described and the setting in which it takes place. Approaching "The Miracle of Ash Wednesday" from the parodies ostensibly set in Russia, the reader is initially unsettled by the unfamiliar surroundings. The location purports to be that of a Benedictine monastery somewhere in Central or Eastern Europe, and the story opens with a young canon and a doctor discussing a supposed miracle which neither is able to explain scientifically. The nature of this miracle is only gradually revealed during the course of the narrative. We learn that during mass to celebrate the Festival of the Apostle Peter-in-Chains (1 August), the young Simplicius begins to feel faint at the moment when he lifts the bread at Eucharist. After a few months of nervous fretting, during which his stomach has increased in size, he is examined by a friend, Dr Voichek, and allegedly found to be pregnant. The doctor decides to operate immediately. On Ash Wednesday, Simplicius is wheeled into surgery and made to wait briefly alongside a woman about to give birth for the third time; he is then given a general anaesthetic. After regaining consciousness the next morning, he is appalled to discover that he has apparently given birth to a baby boy; at the same time he learns that the woman awaiting surgery in the room alongside him has died. Dr Voichek advises Simplicius to pretend that the boy belonged to the dead woman, and that he has adopted him out of a sense of charity. This is the act of generosity, presumably, for which the young canon becomes venerated in later years, and which, according to the mock-hagiographical conceit of the narrative, provides the impulse for the account of the "miracle." On his deathbed, however, Simplicius admits to being his son's mother; more bizarrely, he claims that the father of the child is Archbishop Benedict, the head of the monastery who, we have been told, returned from a visit to Rome and entertained Simplicius with wine and crayfish only seven days before the mass took place. The story concludes with the image of Dr Voichek laughing through tears as his former patient drifts quietly off into eternal sleep.

Unsurprisingly, perhaps, contemporary readers were bewildered by this narrative, and slightly scornful. A correspondent for the Berlin emigré newspaper *Dni*, after attending a reading of the story in May 1924 along with Akhmatova, Chukovsky, Efros, and Pil'niak, dismissed the story as "rubbish" (vzdor) and "utter nonsense" (chepukha narochitaia).[48] Clearly there is a sense in which Zamiatin is trivializing the purpose and function of literature in an epic, revolutionary age. Chudakova observes that as literature in the 1920s became ever more serious, grandiose, and ideologically pretentious, so the conceit of the artist-*skomorokh* inspired Zamiatin to ever greater acts of "buffoonery" (shutovstvo).[49] Certainly, this is one method of approaching the story's undeniable surrealism. It can fruitfully be argued, for example, that the absurdity and frivolity of the story challenges epic expectation and seriousness of purpose in much the same way as Gogol's surreal fantasy "The Nose" (Nos, 1836) cocked a snook at the reactionary demand for morally edifying literature in the 1830s.[50] The meaning of the tale may thus be seen to lie in the deliberate discomfiting and unsettling of reader expectations as to what constitutes acceptable forms of literature. A microcosm of this problem is introduced into the very text itself in the form of Dr Voichek's remark to Simplicius regarding the postponement of deadlines: he suggests that travelling continuously westwards, and winding one's watch backwards as one does so, is a way of gaining crucial time (1:476). This is a riddle, rather than a scientific explanation of time-differences around the world; nevertheless, it torments Simplicius by means of its mathematical legerdemain in much the same way as the reader is baffled by the biological sleight of hand at the heart of the story's narrative.[51] This is literature as enigma or opaque joke, with the reader forced into the position of trying to restore logic to the text and make sense of the author's purpose. Not for nothing, perhaps, was Zamiatin's pseudonym in Obezvelvolpal "Zamutius, Bishop of the Apes," his name deriving from the Russian verb meaning "to muddy" or "to make obscure."[52]

The modern reader may well share the bafflement expressed by the early "victims" of "The Miracle of Ash Wednesday." Nevertheless, it is important to recognize that this is a conscious literary strategy, and that the confusion which arises is the product of Zamiatin's authorial pact with the Devil. This pact exists on various different levels. Another way of approaching this story, for example, would be as a carnivalized text which deliberately subverts Orthodox norms. While obviously not a counterfeit product in the anachronistic style of the two earlier *chudesa*, "The Miracle of Ash Wednesday" is nevertheless a parody of an ecclesiastical mode of writing. The title alludes specifically to the *chudo*, a short text of hagiographic provenance which forms a part of the individual *vita* or can sometimes appear as a self-contained fragment on its own. Examining the story in this light, we see that several of the defining features of hagiographic literature are present. The main protagonist is a saintly type, and the narrative, although set in modern times, and employing a transparently modern idiom, is also clearly intended as an "instructive" and "edificatory" account of the act of virtue with which his life is associated. Like the two earlier *chudesa*, Zamiatin's strategy lies in the subversion of these stock elements. The very idea of saintliness is ridiculed; moreover, in its deliberate playing with notions of credibility and credulity, "The Miracle of Ash Wednesday" questions the value of didactic literature generally and mocks the gullibility of those who are prepared to accept the fantastic nature of the miracles attributed to the saints. The central joke or absurdity in this tale is that the miracle in question defies medical science and the known facts of human biology. Indeed, as distinct from the medieval hagiographer, who warns readers in advance of the fantastic events to be described, but attributes them to the powers of divine intervention, Zamiatin's author is unable to explain the miracle at the heart of the narrative and seems not even to wish to do so.[53] Not only does he willingly repudiate authorial omnipotence, he seems to suggest that if there are divine mechanisms in operation in this world, they operate in a mystifying and bizarre fashion. As we will see, his subversion of fantastic *topoi* relate not only to the legends of the saints, but also to the *topos* of the miraculous birth in the Old and New Testaments.

A related approach to "The Miracle of Ash Wednesday" would be to view it as a post-symbolist demonological tale – in other words, as a tale which plays with the conceit of the artist-*skomorokh*. Alex Shane, for instance, considers Zamiatin's story "in all probability a parody of some ribald medieval Czech tale about the evil powers of the Devil."[54] Although this proposition is unconvincing as far as the literary origin of the parody is concerned, it is interesting to observe that he places Dr Voichek at the centre of the tale's labyrinth as a palpably demonic presence. Voichek, in fact, "corrupts" the text in two ways: firstly, as a fictional character, he may be responsible for playing some kind of joke on Simplicius, just as the joker of the bawdy tradition plays tricks on the gullible clergyman;[55] secondly, as the only person to have witnessed the events in question, he enjoys a status equal to the author. His laughter through tears at the end of the story suggests privileged information; and if readers are tempted to solve the riddle of the text and restore logic by trying to guess the

content of his knowledge, then this is very much part of the tantalizing game which Zamiatin is playing. This view of the Devil combines various traditions into one composite: the Devil as evil-doer
who seeks to tempt the innocent from the path of virtue (the expression "the Devil has led me astray" [chert menia poputal] is common
in Russian);[56] as magician who seeks to pull the wool over the eyes
of the public and overturn scientific logic; and as Satanic, post-symbolist *skomorokh* or clown who seeks to disrupt the normal procedures of literature in favour of surrealism. This Devil is a master of
parody; but he is also one who "tempts" the reader into fitting all the
pieces into a coherent whole. It is precisely this aspect of Zamiatin's
tale which is most intriguing, and what follows is an attempt to establish a rationale for the events which take place.

One explanation which restores logic to the text, but which still
relies on a degree of implausibility, is that Zamiatin's humble protagonist is not a young man at all, but a young woman – in other
words, like the main character in Johann Jacob Grimmelshausen's
celebrated seventeenth-century novel, with whom he shares a first
name, Simplicius might well be so perfectly ignorant of life generally
that he is unaware even of his own gender.[57] Although this stretches
the bounds of credibility, it is subtly implied at several intervals in
the course of the narrative. At no point is objective proof of the
young canon's masculinity furnished by the author; indeed, a number of remarks are made in relation to Simplicius which stress his
fresh-faced youthfulness and effeminate qualities. He is wide-eyed
and innocent, we are told, his eyes described as "two little babes with
thumbs in their mouths" (1:476); he has fetching dimples, which
make him endearing to those around him (1:476); and he has a
plumpish body, which is compared to a chair in a woman's bed-
room, "upholstered in pink satin, full of warm creases and folds, and
alive – almost ready to replace the mistresses who normally occupy
them" (1:477). From this, more logical point of view, only Dr
Voichek and Archbishop Benedict need be aware of Simplicius's
true gender; moreover, an early indication that the doctor might in
fact be colluding in the young canon's ignorance is given when he
first asks Simplicius to undress for a physical examination. This is followed by a smile and the characteristic twisting of his curly "horns"
(1:477), an indication either of his surprise in relation to the size of
Simplicius's swollen stomach (he is at least seven months pregnant),
or a hint perhaps that something more fundamental is amiss. Could
it be knowledge of Simplicius's bizarre secret that causes the doctor's
mirth at the end of the story?

The plausibility of this interpretation is certainly strengthened by
the fact that concealed sexual identity and illegitimate birth are *topoi*

in a number of female saints' *Lives*. These are young women, many of them virgins converted to Christianity, who are forced to marry pagans against their will by their parents. Invariably, they escape from home disguised in male clothing and later serve with model humility in monasteries until revealed to be female on their deathbeds; quite frequently, they find themselves accused of seducing women from secular society or nuns from neighbouring convents. Saint Margaret (feast day, 8 October), for example, enters a monastery disguised as a man, is rewarded for her uncommon devotion by being placed in charge of a neighbouring convent, and is later accused of seducing a nun under her care.[58] A similar circumstance, although differing in certain details (the heroine is happily married, but betrays her husband and joins a monastery so that he will not be able to find her), arises in the *Life* of Saint Theodora (feast day, 11 September), a text reworked by the radical thinker and writer Aleksandr Herzen in 1836.[59] A stock theme in this kind of narrative involves the (female) monk being amorously pursued by a woman from outside the monastery who labours under a comic and almost grotesque misapprehension with regard to her love object's true identity. In the case of Theodora, it is the daughter of a local hotel owner in Alexandria who solicits her attentions and, her attempted seduction rebuffed, later accuses her of fathering her baby. Theodora's protestations of innocence are not believed by the authorities; she is banished beyond the monastery walls as punishment and forced to bring up the illegitimate child on her own; and it is only after her death, when burial preparations reveal that she is a woman after all, that she receives proper vindication. Another variation on the disguise theme occurs in the *Life* of Saint Euphrosine, which Anatole France adapted in 1891, although in her case the *topos* of the failed seduction and accusation of fatherhood is absent.[60]

It is not suggested here that Simplicius is synonymous with these errant female "monks" – these virgins were obviously aware of their own gender, but sought to conceal it from outsiders – merely that there is an established tradition in certain *vitae* of male impersonation and falsely attributed pregnancy which Zamiatin sought consciously to parody. There are certain important similarities, for example, between his treatment of this subject and Herzen's secular adaptation of Theodora's legend. Like Zamiatin, Herzen exploits ignorance of Theodora's gender as a device with which to increase dramatic tension; by entitling his tale simply "The Legend," and giving his heroine the name Theodor, Herzen endeavoured to disguise his literary source and thus hopefully to prevent his readers from guessing the curious denouement. Indeed, in terms very similar to the description of Simplicius in Zamiatin, the true nature of her secret is implied discreetly early on in the tale (Herzen focuses on the youthful innocence and "girl-like" locks of the young boy's hair).[61] Ultimately, however, the two authors have a different strategic purpose. Herzen was interested in the legend as a proto-feminist document, as a refutation of the widespread prejudice among certain religious circles that women were incapable of serious feats of ascetic discipline – thus by disguising the gender of his protoganist, he causes the reader to consider carefully, or reconsider, his or her preconceived ideas of male and female behaviour (a key *topos*, for example, is the scene in which the misogynistic abbot or Father Superior, without realizing the virgin's true identity, warns her on entering the monastery about the evil, fickle, and corrupting nature of women). Zamiatin's project is imbued with a more anarchic and nihilistic spirit. The revelation at the end of "The Miracle of Ash Wednesday" is essentially a mock revelation. If true, it confirms only that Simplicius, admittedly innocent and gullible, is far from the pure or virtuous model of the legends, a fact which somewhat compromises his "saintly" act of adoption. Zamiatin's narrative thus takes its place among a number of tales in the Eastern and Western bawdy tradition which tell of sexual malpractice at the very heart of religious worship. An interesting precedent, since it demonstrates that the *topoi* of sexual indeterminacy and monastic effeminacy may have crossed from hagiography into oral literature, is the bawdy Russian folktale entitled "The Monk and the Mother Superior" (Monakh i igumen'ia), which Afanas'ev recorded in the nineteenth century.[62] There is no evidence that Zamiatin actually knew this tale directly. It is intriguing, nonetheless, that the denouement involves the mysterious impregnation of a young nun by a male monk dressed in female garb, and that the story culminates with a joke about sexually indeterminate babies.[63]

If we accept this suspicion about Simplicius's true gender, but approach the text from a different angle, an obviously blasphemous, rather than merely anti-clerical dimension emerges. There are several hints in "The Miracle of Ash Wednesday" that Simplicius's inexplicable pregnancy may have a precedent in the story of the Virgin Birth.[64] On two occasions, both of them significant junctures in the text, Simplicius raises an exclamation in the name of the Blessed Virgin. The first occurs when Dr Voichek examines his belly for the first time and announces that he will operate: "But why? What do I have? In the name of the Holy Mary?" (1:478); while the second takes place as he is presented in hospital with the child to which he has ostensibly given birth: "But I ... Holy Virgin! But I'm, after all, a man!" (No ved' ia zhe ... Presviataia Deva! – ved' ia zhe vse-taki muzhchina!, 1:480). The syntactical ambiguity here, lost in English translation, does more than hint at Simplicius's sexual androgyny. Moreover, the day on which we are led to believe that the conception of his child takes place – the Archbishop's party is given seven days prior to 1 August on 25 July – happens to coincide with the feast of Saint Anne, the mother of the Virgin Mary. Simplicius is thus linked with two women celebrated by the Church for miraculous births which take place thanks to divine intervention. In the case of Anne, of course, the surrealism is somewhat spectacular, since she is barren for much of her life and conceives after lengthy supplication only at the age of seventy (!); whereas for Mary, the birth of Jesus occurs after the annunciation by the Archangel Gabriel through the power of the Holy Spirit. The joke at the heart of "The Miracle of Ash Wednesday" derives from the fact that no one would possibly believe such miraculous conceptions if they were to occur in modern, scientific times.[65] Indeed, much humour is derived from the comic reversal, according to which the young canon, a religious believer brought up strictly on the articles of the Catholic faith, and one who readily accepts the resurrection of the dead, nevertheless finds the miracle of Felix's conception incredible, while his friend, a doctor and a man of science, has no such rational qualms: "Nevertheless ... You understand, I am a doctor, it's much more difficult for me to believe in a miracle than it is for you – a priest. And yet, it can't be helped! I must believe" (1:480).

The irony is doubly felicitous here. It is absurd that a young canon should forget the celebrated legend of the Virgin Birth as a historical precedent for his own pregnancy. Further humour is derived retrospectively from the inquiry to his friend regarding the historical precedents for such an event at the very beginning of the tale: "But still ... still, have you found nothing, nothing at all in your books, perhaps another case – perhaps in antiquity?" (1:475). Simplicius is referring to medical books here, but the reader will undoubtedly be reminded of that most ancient of texts – the New Testament. When the reader learns that Archbishop Benedict is the father, along with various hints that something sinful happened on the night when he returned from Rome, the biblical myth is ridiculed and the supposedly inexplicable and fantastic miracle revealed to have a normal biological explanation after all.

This approach to Zamiatin's tale depends on Simplicius's ignorance of his own gender and the assumption that he was named by his parents without his gender being taken into consideration. Such a reading is thus undeniably absurd. Nevertheless, the committing of sin and the acceptance of guilt are clearly two of the story's themes. This holds true even if we construct a reading of the text on the basis that Simplicius is a young man, albeit a rather effeminate one.

According to this reading, the birth of Felix, his son, is a miraculous event indeed, so miraculous that no logical or biological explanation can be offered at all, and the tale acquires the hallmarks of a grotesque parody of the Virgin Birth, one in which the sex of the Mother of God has been obscenely reversed. It remains for the reader to speculate on the possibility that Simplicius has been in some way punished for an illicit homosexual encounter, the true nature of which remains something of a mystery to him. The title of the story hints that the punishment of sins and the acceptance of guilt is a central theme. According to the calendar, Ash Wednesday is the first day of the Lenten Fast, an occasion on which Christians cele- brate the start of Jesus' forty days in the wilderness by marking their foreheads with a cross made of ash in symbolic recognition of their sins. Dr Voichek himself speculates on the possibility that the child has been conceived as a punishment and should best be viewed as a "test" (ispytanie, 1:480) of the canon's faith. This seems to be recog- nized even by Simplicius himself. It is with a sense of guilt – likened to the admission of sins at confession (na ispovedi, 1:476) – that Sim- plicius first tells Dr Voichek of the events preceding his sudden ill- ness; indeed later, after the birth of Felix, we are informed that Simplicius bears his burden humbly precisely because he under- stands why God might have chosen him for such punishment: "The canon submitted to it and bore it as meekly as the Apostle Peter bore his iron chains. It even seemed to him that he knew why heaven had so punished and rewarded him" (1:480).

The literary precedents for Simplicius's "sin" in anti-clerical litera- ture are extensive. For Boccaccio, the practice of sodomy on the part of monks and friars was traditional, and several of his stories in *The Decameron* employ deliberate homosexual innuendo;[66] moreover, as Adam Olearius records, the depiction of "vile sodomies" by street entertainers was apparently an integral part of Russian folk culture in the seventeenth century.[67] In this context, it is interesting to note the images of phallic penetration which punctuate Zamiatin's story, often in the vicinity of anus-like orifices. A particularly important sequence occurs at the very beginning of the tale. When Dr Voichek inquires after the health of the Archbishop, for example, he is smoking a ciga- rette (1:475). Simplicius's embarrassment in relation to this question is described in terms of being roasted alive like a woodcock on a spit (1:475). A few sentences later, the young canon's eyes are compared to two babies sucking their thumbs (1:476), an image of fellatio and/or anal penetration made even more suggestive perhaps by the mention immediately afterwards of the "dimples" (literally, "little trenches" [iamochki]) on his "cheeks" (1:476). These images hint at a counter- narrative of homoerotic impropriety. Naturally, for a successful reading of this kind, it must be assumed that the canon's confession to Felix at the end of the story reflects not so much the truth of his feminine gender, but rather his confused conviction that since he gave birth to a baby, he must therefore, technically, be his "mother." Even the admission of motherhood does not de facto rule out masculinity, since it could simply be recognition of his nurturing role.

The precedents for bizarre pregnancies of this kind, especially where it is a man who is thought to be giving birth, are well established in the folk tradition. The subject draws on the medical and cultural phenomenon of couvade, and is essentially Western and medieval in origin, although it is clear that certain versions migrated into Russian folk culture at some point later. In Boccaccio's *The Decameron*, for instance, the painter Calandrino is persuaded by his friends and a doctor called Master Simone that he is pregnant.[68] It turns out that the painter is the naive victim of a ruse to extract money from him by means of a miraculous cure which results a few days later in a "miscarriage;" hilariously, he has earlier concluded that the pregnancy must have been the result of unconventional sexual practices with this wife (she prefers to straddle him during lovemaking, rather than assume the missionary position). A similarly absurd situation arises in the bawdy Russian folktale about the priest who gives birth mysteriously to a calf, one version of which can be found in the emigré editions of Afanas'ev's *Secret Tales of Russia*, and another of which was published legally by Onchukov in his 1908 collection of Northern Russian folktales.[69] Initially, according to the latter version, there is evidence that the priest has something medically wrong with him: his stomach is said to have increased in size over several months "until it has grown quite large."[70] Worried by this development, he sends a sample of urine in an earthenware pot to the local doctor for diagnosis via one of his servant-girls. Unfortunately, the young girl trips over en route, spills the contents of the pot all over the road, but instead substitutes a sample taken from a cow in a nearby field which later turns out to be pregnant. The doctor informs the priest that he is due to give birth to a bullock, the priest spends the night in a local cowshed to avoid the embarrassment of giving birth in front of his wife, and this turns out to be the very same shed in which the pregnant cow is about to give birth herself. The priest wakes up the next morning to find that the diagnosis has proved accurate. He gives his thanks to the Lord for having avoided the humiliation of a home birth, and rushes home to tell his wife the good news.

If these tales are based on unlikely coincidences, and involve a certain degree of stupidity on the part of their victims, they do at least conform to the known facts of biology. Boccaccio makes no attempt to disguise the fact that Calandrino is not really pregnant; indeed, none of the physical symptoms usually associated with the condition are betrayed. Likewise, although the priest in the Russian folktale might initially exhibit similar symptoms (we never discover the true cause of his swollen belly), it is quite clear that he is not pregnant either. If these bizarre stories have a rationale, therefore, it would appear to lie in the mocking of ignorance and gullibility. Like Simplicius, whose name derives from the Latin for "simplicity" (simplicitas), Calandrino is renowned for his naivety, so much so that his name has become coterminous in the Italian language with a simpleton.[71] By the same token, priests in the Russian bawdy tradition are frequently mocked and ridiculed for their naivety or wilful blindness in sexual matters, so regularly are they cuckolded by labourers, jokers (shuty), and other representatives of secular society. One *topos* of the bawdy tale involves a member of the clergy as the victim of a prank or joke, the result of which is the sexual abuse of his kith and kin (usually his wife or daughter).[72] One might speculate that the pregnancy *topos* derives from the popular analogy in anti-clerical literature between the fat-bellied priest (puzatyi pop) and the pregnant woman. Avvakum, for instance, denounced the representatives of the Nikonian hierarchy in precisely such terms.[73] He also mocked the effeminacy of the clergy and their penchant for luxurious, silk-lined clothing.[74] Zamiatin might well have been aware of this kind of popular analogy. He uses the expression "fat-bellied priest" in his discussion of religious entropy in "Scythians?" (Skify li?), an essay written in 1918.[75] Moreover, it is intriguing that he employs a vulgar turn of phrase ("to sit on your backside"), attributed to Avvakum, in the very same letter to Lunts in which he describes the writing of "The Miracle of Ash Wednesday."[76] The fact that Simplicius is also described in terms of a silky obesity might lead us to speculate that he is not pregnant at all, merely overweight; this possibility is surely strengthened when he remarks that his friends think he has "put on weight" (1:477). The time-symbolism of the story – Ash Wednesday follows Shrovetide (Maslenitsa), and thus marks the launch of the Lenten Fast after a period of dietary self-indulgence – is also suggestive in this regard.[77]

Since the joke at the expense of the innocent victim is a commonplace in the bawdy tradition, we should perhaps also consider the possibility that Simplicius is the victim of a sleight of hand, this time at the hands of his friend, the sinister Dr Voichek; indeed, the latter might be considered akin to the joker or *shut* in the bawdy tradition who plays a carnivalesque trick on the hapless and gullible representative of the church.

We need not doubt the doctor's essentially devilish provenance, even if Zamiatin has taken care to disguise him thinly in the form of a doctor. His goat-like eyes and russet-red "horns," and the description of him as a "demon" (1:479) in the scene immediately after the operation is testament to the Devil's power to assume any disguise in order to further his aims.[78] Without a doubt, the doctor is an unnerving and paradoxical presence in the story. It is ironic that he should represent the medical profession, one dedicated to restoring the health of its patients, rather than inflicting harm. This is reflected in his symbolic association with the colour white – the colour of clinical efficiency, health, and purity – rather than the traditional black, as witnessed in the description of his "other-worldly" surgery.[79] The doctor's love of dominoes, however, should make us wary of this façade. The domino, as well as being a black piece of ivory on which numbers of white dots appear, also functions in Italian as a word for the black cloak and half-mask worn at masquerades; in other words, it is a garment used to conceal one's true identity.[80] The fact that Dr Voichek is fond of games – in the Russian folk-religious imagination, devils have a passion for cards, dice, and chess (like Dr Voichek, they are also associated with the smoking of cigarettes)[81] – should also alert us to the possibility that his friendship with Simplicius is not disinterested. As I have already pointed out, one "game" he plays with Simplicius, a game which parallels his interest in dominoes, and thus in numbers generally (the Devil's association with numbers – three sixes being the "number of the beast" in the Book of Revelation [13:18] – is traditional), involves the idea that by travelling continuously in a westward direction one can halt time and postpone the future (on two occasions, intriguingly, this deadline is couched explicitly in terms of the Last Judgement).[82] This is unscientific, of course, and hints at Dr Voichek's disruptive potential and his power to torment his victims by means of mental trickery. Like Goethe's Mephistopheles, who appears before Faust in the guise of a travelling scholar, the doctor is also said to possess an "extraordinary mind" (1:476).

Voichek's diabolic role in "The Miracle of Ash Wednesday" operates on two levels. As a symbolic presence in the narrative, his association with temptation provides an ironic commentary on the events connected with the Archbishop's party: the image of the goat – an image associated in the folk imagination with the carnival and the cuckold – links neatly with the idea that Simplicius's downfall has been caused by over-indulgence in food and drink, both of them symbolic of the carnival.[83] Simultaneously, Voichek's propensity for jokes and pranks – the traditional role of demons in the folk-religious imagination – provides a second explanation for the curious events which occur. It is not inconceivable, for example, that Simplicius is not really pregnant at all, and that his alleged sinning is the product of slanderous insinuation on the part of the doctor. There is no evidence of the pregnancy as such. We are treated only to the testimony of others that he has put on weight; to the information that he feels dizzy during the celebration of Mass; and to the sensation of heaviness in his stomach, all of which may have an ordinary explanation.[84] Secondly, the doctor's diagnosis that a Caesarian section should be undertaken immediately seems premature from the medical point of view; indeed, the subsequent assertion that the baby belongs to Simplicius need not be taken at face value (in the Russian folk-religious imagination, for example, the Devil's penchant for abducting small babies is well known).[85] Since the operation takes place while Simplicius is unconscious – the second occasion when a crucial event takes place while the canon is under the influence of a drug (the first, we are led to suspect, being the alcohol consumed at the Archbishop's party) – we cannot exclude the possibility that the doctor has taken the baby from the dead peasant woman and passed it off as belonging to Simplicius. While it is obvious that the boy is sired by the Archbishop – the twofold mention of his huge forehead (1:480, 481) is explicit – the identity of the mother is open to question if we suspect that the doctor's word cannot be trusted (the Devil, after all, is the father of all lies).[86] It is interesting to note that the woman's boots are the same colour as the doctor's hair (1:479), a sinister detail which establishes a partial, if essentially unfathomable connection between the two. It is insinuated, furthermore, that she is the very same woman who is taken ill at the same time as Simplicius during the Festival of Apostle Peter-in-Chains – thus she is a person with a connection to the same religious institution, and thus, potentially, to Archbishop Benedict. The possibility of Voichek's direct involvement in the train of events, like the reading of Simplicius as a woman, also reduces the miraculous to the level of the banal, although it establishes a clear kinship between fictional character and ostensible author, both of whom are indulging in deceptions.

"The Miracle of Ash Wednesday" is a story which plays subtly with the idea of confusion and clarity. If, as Simon Franklin maintains in his contribution to this volume, hagiographers employed dramatic irony in their works so that the participants remained ignorant or temporarily deceived, while the implied author and reader saw with knowledge and clarity, then Zamiatin has pushed the device beyond the realms of the plausible. Not only does the participant remain ignorant of the edificatory message which the narrative contains, but the reader is denied access to crucial facts which make comprehension of this message possible. The text is full of innuendo and insinuation, rather than unambiguous information; furthermore, it unfolds in an atmosphere of the uncanny which encourages the reader to view the events described as the product of dream or nightmare. The final line, which expresses the canon's vision of the laughing Dr Voichek in terms of a dream (kak skvoz' son, 1:481), is suggestive. We are reminded of Gogol's warning not to trust the streetlamps on Nevsky Prospect because they have been lit by the "demon himself" (sam demon) and present things "in an unreal light" (ne v nastoiashchem vide);[87] we should recall also Dostoevsky's warning in *The Brothers Karamazov* (*Brat'ia Karamazovy*, 1880) that Ivan Karamazov's encounter with the devil (chert) may be the product of a feverish hallucination.[88] The disorientating power of Zamiatin's tale owes much to the fact that crucial events occur "offstage" while the leading protagonist is unconscious or semi-conscious. It is significant that his death is described in terms of falling asleep.[89] We might add to this sensation the indeterminate location of the narrative (Poland, Germany, the Ukraine, or Czechoslovakia are all possibilities) and the strange tricks played with time. I am referring here to the repeated use of the word *mladenets* in relation to Simplicius both at the beginning and end of the story; the fact that he gives birth and dies in February; and the fact that Dr Voichek discovers about the pregnancy after seven months, yet we are told that Simplicius sought his advice when it "first started" (kak s kanonikom eto nachalos', 1:476). This suggests that time has not elapsed according to the normal laws of nature. Further uncanny details emerge as a result of Zamiatin's use of colour imagery. The dying peasant woman's boots, as we have already noted, are the same colour as the doctor's hair; the crayfish eaten at the Archbishop's party are as "rosy as a new-born baby" (1:476); Simplicius's flesh is compared to "rosy silk" (1:477); and Felix, the new-born baby, is described as a "red baby" (1:479). This establishes the doctor at the centre of a sinister nexus based around the colour red, although it is not clear whether these links should be considered significant or not.

As a dream or nonsense text, "The Miracle of Ash Wednesday" clearly owes much to Gogol, in particular his vision of the "demon of disorder and stupidity" (demon putanitsy i gluposti) which Shevyrev observed stalking the pages of *Dead Souls* (*Mertvye dushi*, 1842).[90] It is a world, to paraphrase Gogol himself, which has been crumbled into idiotic fragments by some demon and presented in an unreal light, a world of absurdity and illogicality, of incredible events which border on the nonsensical. Shevyrev pinpoints this world as the fixed axis of Gogol's comic genius. However, we must draw a distinction between the early and late works of Gogol's fiction, and the fact that while Zamiatin clearly sought to embrace this absurd world, it was, for Gogol, the embodiment of moral bankruptcy and dehumanized existence. He drew a sharp distinction between the humour of his later works and the kind of humour encountered at the vaudeville or carnival. In one statement, for example, he juxtaposed the "elevated, triumphant" laughter of *Dead Souls* with the tomfoolery (krivlian'e) of the fairground *skomorokh*.[91] In his view, the laughter which functioned purely as festive entertainment was light-hearted, licentious, and spiritually empty, whereas his own brand of humour grew out of a love of humanity and exhibited a serious moral concern.[92] He also drew a distinction between his early works of fiction, which were full of "pure, unalloyed humour," and the later works, for example after *The Inspector General* (*Revizor*, 1836), which sought to communicate sad truths beyond their surface gaiety.[93] If "The Miracle of Ash Wednesday" bears a Gogolian imprint, therefore, it does so without the later moral and philosophical concerns, owing more to the free-wheeling, carnivalesque tradition of the Dikanka stories and the bawdy innuendo of "The Nose." It is significant that the Ukraine is one of the locations in which Zamiatin's tale could take place, since this is a key space in Gogol's folk-religious fantasy world.

In "I Am Afraid" (Ia boius', 1921), an essay on the dangers of the new culture of conformity, Zamiatin declared that true literature existed only where it was produced by "madmen, hermits, visionaries, rebels and sceptics."[94] He should, perhaps, have included buffoons and clowns on his list. "The Miracle of Ash Wednesday" shows his penchant for the absurd, the bizarre, and the farcical, and his fascination for the anecdotal, whimsical, and vaudevillean. More importantly, it illustrates his interest in art as pure play. This aspect of his artistic temperament is also revealed in *The Flea*, the adaptation for stage of Leskov's "A Tale About the Cross-Eyed Left-Hander of Tula and the Steel Flea" (Skaz o tul'skom kosom Levshe i o stal'noi blokhe, 1881) which drew its stylistic inspiration from the carnival tradition of Russian street theatre and the Italian *commedia dell'arte*. The central conceit of this play is the buffonade (skomorosh'ia igra), with the buffoons in question – the Chaldeans (Khaldei) – modelled on the participants of the medieval Russian Furnace Play (Peshchnoe deistvo). This was a sacred ritual which took place in churches in the days between Christmas and Epiphany. The Chaldeans themselves, however, were demonic figures who belonged to the sphere of carnival culture. Like the devils who took part in the medieval French *diablerie*, and roamed the streets in special costumes prior to their performance in the mystery plays of the time, these entertainers were given licence to play fun and games in the days before Epiphany as a concession to the festive spirit of Yuletide.[95] Zamiatin's identification with them as author was later made explicit in his essay "Popular Theatre" (Narodnyi teatr, 1927): just as the Chaldeans were reported to have run amok gaily setting fire to the beards of peasant onlookers, so his modern mummers would aim, through their merry escapades, to "inflame" (podzhigat') their audience.[96] It is symptomatic that in an earlier letter to the producer Aleksei Diky, written during the preparations for the play's production in Moscow, he signed himself "Your Buffoon" (Vash khaldei).[97]

"The Miracle of Ash Wednesday" demonstrates how demonism could make the transition from the mystical inquiries of the symbolists into the age of secular art. This is the age in which the demons of the medieval imagination have been banished through the study of medicine and psychology, the age in which, as illustrated by Sigmund Freud's 1923 study of seventeenth-century demonization in Germany, the Devil is now understood as a neurotic symptom, a symbol of all that men and women sexually desire in secret, but cannot admit openly for fear of social and moral retribution.[98] Freud's analysis neatly anticipates the hysteria of modern ideological politics, according to which secular authority taps into deep-seated anxieties and neuroses in order to blacken the reputation of political opponents. Zamiatin found himself at the receiving end of such a campaign of political persecution in 1929, and it is interesting to note that in his letter to Stalin he borrows the language of medieval demonization in order to describe it: "Just as the Christians created the devil (chert) as a convenient personification of all evil, so the critics have transformed me into the devil of Soviet literature. Spitting at the devil is regarded as a good deed, and everyone spat to the best of his ability. In each of my published works, these critics have inevitably discovered some diabolical intent."[99]

"Diabolical," here, means "anti-Soviet" and "criminal," not "anti-Christian," and is an indication of the degree to which the word "devil" was a free-floating signifier in Zamiatin's lexicon, one which could take on a variety of meanings, depending on the context. The devilish mask of his fiction, and the diabolical provocation of some of his public antics – most famously, his adoption of aristocratic English dress-codes and pipe-smoking at a time of spartan commissarial, military fashion – were self-conscious reflections of this fact. Indeed, it might be argued, paraphrasing Voltaire, that if the Devil did not exist, Zamiatin would have had to invent him.

Notes

1. See "Anatol' Frans (Nekrolog)" (1924), in Evgenii Zamiatin, *Sochineniia*, 4 vols. (Munich: Neimanis, 1970–88), 4:196. Henceforth, unless otherwise stated, all citations of Zamiatin will be from this edition and will be given in the text and notes by volume and page number. Unless otherwise indicated, all translations are my own.
2. As an example, see his allusion to the myth of Lucifer as rebel angel in the essay "Rai" (1921), 4:524–31. The theme of Satanic rebellion has also been identified

in the dystopian novel *We* (*My*, 1927). See Richard A. Gregg, "Two Adams and Eve in the Crystal Palace: Dostoevsky, the Bible, and 'We'," *Slavic Review* 24 (1965):680–87.

3. The dates given refer to the date of publication, rather than to the time of writing. "O sviatom grekhe Zenitsy-devy. Slovo pokhval'noe" (3:64–67) first appeared in the SR newspaper *Delo naroda* on 15 October (Old Style) 1917. "O tom, kak istselen byl otrok Erazm" (1:463–74) was first published as a booklet with illustrations by the artist Boris Kustodiev – see *O blazhennom startse Pamve Nereste, o narochitoi premudrosti ego, o mnogikh proisshedshikh chudesnykh znameniiakh i o tom, kak istselen byl inok Erazm* (Berlin: Petropolis, 1922). "O chude, proisshedshem v Pepel'nuiu Sredu" (1:475–81) was first published in the journal *Novaia Rossiia*, 1926, no. 1:57–62. Translations of "O tom, kak byl istselen otrok Erazm" and "O chude, proisshedshem v Pepel'nuiu Sredu" are taken from Yevgeny Zamyatin, *The Dragon and Other Stories*, trans. and ed. Mirra Ginsburg (London: Penguin, 1975), 150–63 and 208–15, respectively. Henceforth, for the sake of simplicity, the first miracle tale will be called "The Precious Virgin."

4. Cited in Peter Stanford, *The Devil. A Biography* (London: Heinemann, 1996), 181.

5. "Text of sexual enjoyment (texte de jouissance): one that brings about a state of loss, one that causes discomfort (even a certain annoyance), shakes the historical, cultural, psychological bases of the reader, the consistency of his tastes, his values, his memories, causes a crisis in his relationship with language." See Roland Barthes, *Le Plaisir du texte* (Paris: Les Editions du Seuil, 1973), 26. For a detailed examination of Zamiatin's miracle stories as hagiographic parodies, see the fifth chapter of my doctoral dissertation, "Evgenii Zamiatin and the Literary Stylization of Rus'" (Ph.D. diss., School of Slavonic and East European Studies, University of London, 1997), 257–350.

6. Bakhtin discusses hagiographic parodies as carnivalized texts in Mikhail Bakhtin, *Rabelais and His World*, trans. Hélène Iswolsky (Bloomington: Indiana University Press, 1984), 1–58, esp. 13–15. For a discussion of Bakhtin's conception of carnival laughter as it relates to medieval Russian culture, see D.S. Likhachev, A.M. Panchenko, and N.V. Ponyrko, eds., *Smekh v drevnei rusi* (Leningrad: Nauka, 1984), 3–25.

7. For the folk-religious view of the devil in terms of a clown (shut), one whose evil machinations include various types of prank (koznia), intrigue (prokaza), and joke (shutka), see Sergei Maksimov, *Nechistaia, nevedomaia i krestnaia sila* [1903], 2 vols. (reprint, Moscow: Kniga, 1989), 1:6–22.

8. The Orthodox Church condemned all forms of laughter and secular music and entertainment as the work of the Devil. See Ju.M. Lotman and B.A. Uspenskij, "New Aspects in the Study of Early Russian Culture," in their *The Semiotics of Russian Culture*, ed. Ann Shukman, Michigan Slavic Contributions, no.11 (Ann Arbor: Department of Slavic Languages and Literatures, University of Michigan, 1984), 36–52. For a history of the *skomorokhi* and their formal proscription by the Church, see Russell Zguta, *Russian Minstrels. A History of the "Skomorokhi"* (Oxford: Clarendon Press, 1978).

9. For an examination of this tendency in Gogol's work, see "Komicheskii alogizm," in Aleksandr L. Slonimskii, *Tekhnika komicheskogo u Gogolia* [1923] (reprint, Providence, R.I.: Brown University Press, 1963), 33–65.

10. Remizov's Great and Free Order of Apes (Obez'ian'ia Velikaia i Vol'naia Palata [Obezvelvolpal]) was founded in 1908, but proclaimed officially only in 1917, after the February Revolution – for details regarding the Order's establishment, membership, and activities during this period, see S.S. Grechishkin, "Arkhiv Remizova," in *Ezhegodnik rukopisnogo otdela Pushkinskogo Doma na 1975 god*, ed. M.P. Alekseev and others (Leningrad: Nauka, 1977), 20–44. It is not known when

exactly Zamiatin was coopted into the Order. Remizov first mentions his pseudonym (Bishop Zamutius) in connection with the series of arrests made by the
Cheka in February 1919 of artistic figures believed to be sympathetic to the Left
Socialist Revolutionaries – see the relevant sections of the diary he was keeping
at the time, reprinted in A. Remizov, *Vzvikhrennaia Rus'* (Moscow: Sovetskii pisatel', 1991), 377. These arrests gave rise to Remizov's "Manifest," issued in the
name of his pseudonym, Asyka the First, in which the anarchic principles of the
Order were enunciated. The text of this document, his *skomorokh* manifesto
("Tulumbas"), and other texts relating to the establishment of the Order were first
published together in *AKHRU. Povest' Peterburgskaia* (Berlin and St. Petersburg,
Moscow: Izdatel'stvo Z.I. Grzhebina, 1922), 47–51.

11. For a discussion of official attitudes towards street culture in the immediate
aftermath of the Revolution, see Catriona Kelly, *Petrushka. The Russian Carnival
Puppet Theatre* (Cambridge: Cambridge University Press, 1990), 179–211.

12. For a detailed discussion of this literary phenomenon, see Margaret Ziolkowski,
Hagiography and Modern Russian Literature (Princeton: Princeton University Press,
1988), 3–33.

13. Ibid., 83.

14. Ibid.

15. For a discussion of Tolstoi's attitude towards religion and the doctrines of the
Russian Orthodox Church, see Ernest J. Simmons, *Introduction to Tolstoy's Writings*
(Chicago and London: University of Chicago Press, 1968), 94–117.

16. "From Tolstoi – the absolute, pathos, faith (although this is compromised by
virtue of his faith in reason). From France – relativism, irony, scepticism (...):
both are great heretics; and many of their works belong to that most prestigious
category for writers: the banned book." See "Anatol' Frans (Nekrolog)," 4:195.

17. See, for example, "Scholastica" (1889), *Légende de Thaïs, comédienne* (1889), "Sainte
Euphrosine" (1891), "La Légende des saintes Oliverie et Liberette" (1891), and "Le
Miracle du grand saint Nicolas" (1909). For a more detailed discussion of this sub-
ject in France's work, see the chapter entitled "Eroticism and *Gauloiserie*," in Dushan
Bresky, *The Art of Anatole France* (The Hague and Paris: Mouton, 1969), 159–78.

18. For a more detailed discussion of Tsarist censorship as it related to taboo subjects,
see N. Bogomolov, "'My – dva grozoi zazhzhennye stvola',," in *Anti-mir russkoi
kul'tury. Iazyk. Fol'klor. Literatura*, ed. N. Bogomolov (Moscow: Ladomir, 1996),
297–327.

19. Ibid.

20. For the origins of this sobriquet, and its connection with hagiographic sources,
see the footnote in Grechishkin, "Arkhiv Remizova," 32.

21. Slobin reports that after the abolition of censorship in 1905 these artists were
allegedly collaborating on an encyclopaedia of erotica, to be entitled "On Love" (O
liubvi), which would comprise folk notions and advice on sex. See Greta N. Slobin,
Remizov's Fictions. 1900–1921 (DeKalb: Northern Illinois University Press, 1991), 66.

22. In the folk-religious imagination, the production of both spirits and tobacco is
attributed to the devil: "In stories about the origins of tobacco there is even more
difference of opinion: either it sprouted from the grave of a brother and sister
who had been involved in an incestuous relationship, or from the head of a Biblical whore (Viatka province), or from the body of a nun who had strayed from
the path of piety and been struck down by lightning (Penza province), or, finally,
from the grave of some unknown person (Simbirsk province)." See Maksimov,
Nechistaia, nevedomaia i krestnaia sila, 1:10.

23. Bizarrely, in view of the contents, the editors of Afanas'ev's *Secret Tales of Russia*
tried to conceal the true identity of the author-collector by pretending that the
book had been published by the Valaam Monastery, universally recognized as

one of the most pious in Russia. Presumably, this was to protect Afanas'ev from potential legal action. See *Secret Tales of Russia*, with an introduction by G. Legman (New York: Brussel and Brussel, 1966), v.

24. The name of Remizov's sage, rather amusingly in light of his account, derives from the Greek word *gnosos*, meaning someone who possesses a special knowledge of spiritual mysteries. The name also alludes to the Gnostics, a heretical Christian sect in the first to the third centuries, the members of which claimed to possess such knowledge.

25. "In medieval life, Remizov would have been one of the *skomorokhi* (merry folk), the entertainers forbidden by the Orthodox church. In his own versions of the established literary tradition, he rejected all authority, whether religious or secular." See Slobin, *Remizov's Fictions*, 34–35.

26. See "Sirin. Sbornik pervyi i vtoroi" (1914), 4:497–99.

27. Zamiatin revealed Remizov as the model for this character in "Zakulisy" (1930), 4:304. It is worth noting that the information given in "Alatyr'" (1:158) about marsh-demons, including the use of the word *khokhlik* to indicate their hirsute qualities, echoes extremely closely the discussion of this phenomenon in Maksimov, *Nechistaia, nevedomaia i krestnaia sila*, 1:8.

28. An important part of Remizov's grotesque strategy involves the use of chimeras – for example, the demonic Sea-Monster (Chudo morskoe) which makes an appearance early in the tale. This is presumably based on a *lubok* picture described in the celebrated collection of Dmitrii Rovinsky. See the version of this picture reprinted in T.A. Novichkova, *Russkii demonologicheskii slovar'* (St. Petersburg: Peterburgskii pisatel', 1995), 97.

29. "Tulumbas," 3:72–73. The archaic term employed here to mean "private part" (ud, udishche) was used earlier in Remizov's tale and, interestingly, can also be found with the same meaning in "The Precious Virgin": "udy zhe nezhnyia ikh opaliaemy byli povsiudu lampadami ognennymi," 3:65.

30. In a letter written to Remizov while in Great Britain, Zamiatin inquired after the progress of his short story "Africa" (Afrika, 1916) and "The Precious Virgin," which suggests that they were both written prior to his departure in March 1916. See Zamiatin's letter to Remizov dated 22 April (Old Style) 1916, in "Pis'ma E.I. Zamiatina A.M. Remizovu," ed. V.V. Buznik, *Russkaia literatura* 1 (1992):177–78.

31. "'The Precious Virgin' – a difficult, but successful experiment in the stylization of language: a work which is not written in medieval Russian, but one which gives the illusion of having been so." See "O iazyke," the title of Zamiatin's lecture given at the Petrograd House of Arts in 1920–21, and published for the first time in "Evg. Zamiatin. Tekhnika khudozhestvennoi prozy," ed. A. Strizhev, *Literaturnaia ucheba* 6 (1988):81.

32. For further discussion of this genre in the early Christian and medieval periods, see Julia Alissandratos, *Medieval Slavic and Patristic Eulogies* (Florence: Sansoni, 1982).

33. See Zamiatin's archive in the Institute of World Literature of the Academy of Sciences in Moscow (IMLI), fond 47, opis' 1, ed. khr. 58–61.

34. The healing of a woman who has swallowed a snake while drinking a cup of water occurs, for example, in the *Life* of Simeon the Stylite. See the modern Russian version, "Zhizn' i deianiia blazhennogo Simeona Stolpnika," in *Vizantiiskie legendy*, ed. S.V. Poliakova (Moscow: Ladomir, 1994), 29.

35. Breast mutilation as a *topos* in the legends of the virgin-martyrs is discussed in Thomas J. Heffernan, *Sacred Biography. Saints and Their Biographers in the Middle Ages* (New York and Oxford: Oxford University Press, 1988), 282–83.

36. For the stock theme of the fragrant body, see Al'bert Opulskii, *Zhitiia sviatykh v tvorchestve russkikh pisatelei XIX veka* (East Lansing, Mich.: Russian Language Journal, 1986), 21.

37. For further discussion of Saint Mary's popularity in nineteenth-century Russia, see Ziolkowski, *Hagiography and Modern Russian Literature*, 73–78.

38. See n.3. Interestingly, Bakhtin draws attention to the paradox that hagiographic texts in the Middle Ages were often accompanied by illustrations of a grotesque nature. See Bakhtin, *Rabelais and His World*, 96.

39. See Gor'ky's letter to Nikolai Tikhonov dated 23 October 1924, cited in N. Primochkina, "M. Gor'kii i E. Zamiatin (K istorii literaturnykh vzaimootnoshenii)," *Russkaia literatura* 4 (1987):151.

40. See Cavendish, "Evgenii Zamiatin and the Literary Stylisation of Rus'," 279–85.

41. See "Vstrechi s B.M. Kustodievym" (1927), 4:169.

42. See 1:347.

43. See 4:48–50.

44. See Zamiatin's letter to Lunts dated 13 November 1923, in "L. Lunts i Serapionovy brat'ia," *Novyi zhurnal* 82 (1966):185.

45. Ibid.

46. See "Shutochnaia miniatiura 'Zhitie Blokhi'" (1929), 2:507–18.

47. See Zamiatin, *Nechestivye rasskazy* (Moscow: Artel' pisatelei "Krug," 1927), 129–52, 153–66.

48. Cited in M. Chudakova, "Eretik, ili matros na machte," in *Evgenii Zamiatin, Sochineniia* (Moscow: Kniga, 1988), 504. It is interesting to note that these words echo Gogol's narrator in "Nos." At one point he exclaims: "All sorts of nonsense (chepukha) takes place in the world." Later, he dismisses one possible interpretation of the story (offered by himself!) as "rubbish" (vzdor). See "Nos," in N.V. Gogol', *Sobranie sochinenii*, 6 vols. (Moscow: Khudozhestvennaia literatura, 1976–79), 3:61, 63.

49. See Chudakova, "Eretik, ili matros na machte," 504.

50. See Ann Shukman, "Gogol's *The Nose* or the Devil in the Works," in *Nikolay Gogol. Text and Context*, ed. Jane Grayson and Faith Wigzell (Basingstoke and London: Macmillan, 1989), 64–82.

51. "Every evening, at departure, Doctor Voichek left some such thorny point stuck in the canon's head. Afterwards the canon twisted and tossed in bed, thinking and thinking, turning the matter this way and that" (1:476).

52. The verb *zamutit'* in modern Russian means simply "to make cloudy or turgid." However, its archaic sense means "to create disorder" and "to sow discord" (privesti v bespokoistvo, smiatenie). See *Slovar' russkogo iazyka*, 4 vols. (Moscow: Izdatel'stvo "Russkii iazyk," 1981–84), 1:547.

53. Bishop Sophronius, by comparison, introduces the extraordinary events in his *Life of Saint Mary of Egypt* as follows: "No one should have any doubts about believing me, for I am writing about what I have heard, and no one should think in astonishment over the magnitude of the miracles that I am inventing fables. God deliver me from inventing and falsifying an account in which his name comes … If, however, such readers of this narrative are found, who are so overcome by the miraculous nature of this account that they will not want to believe it, may the Lord be merciful to them! For they consider the infirmity of human nature and think that miracles related about people are impossible." See Sophronius, *Life of Saint Mary of Egypt*, in *Harlots of the Desert*, trans. and ed. Benedicta Ward (London and Oxford: Mowbray, 1987), 36.

54. See Shane, *The Life and Works of Evgenij Zamjatin*, 178.

55. This *topos* in the bawdy tale will be examined in detail below.

56. See Maksimov, *Nechistaia, nevedomaia i krestnaia sila*, 1:6–22.

57. "But as to knowledge of things divine, none shall ever persuade me that any lad of my age in all Christendom could there beat me, for I knew nought of god or man, of heaven or hell, of angel or devil, nor could discern between good and

evil. So may it be easily understood that I, with such knowledge of theology, lived like our first parents in Paradise, which in their innocence knew nought of sickness or death or dying, and still less of the Resurrection ... Yes, I was so perfected in ignorance that I knew not that I knew nothing." See Johann Jacob Grimmelshausen, *Simplicissimus*, trans. S. Goodrich (Sawtry, Cambridgeshire: Dedalus/ Hippocrene, 1989), 3.

58. See the abridged version of Saint Margaret's legend in *The Golden Legend of Jacobus de Voragine*, trans. from the Latin by William Granger Ryan and Helmut Ripperger (New York, London and Toronto: Longmans, Green & Co., 1948), 613–14.

59. See "Legenda," in A.I. Gertsen, *Sobranie sochinenii*, 30 vols. (Moscow: Izdatel'stvo Akademii nauk SSSR, 1954–66), 1:81–106.

60. See "Saint Euphrosine," in Anatole France, *Oeuvres*, 4 vols. (Paris: Gallimard, 1964–91), 1:903–13.

61. "His white face was extraordinarily tender, and every time he flicked away the curly locks which fell across his eyes with his hand, he might have been mistaken for a young girl." See Gertsen, "Legenda," 84–85.

62. See *Narodnye russkie skazki A.N. Afanas'eva*, 3 vols. (Moscow: Nauka, 1986), 3:318.

63. "Time passed – and the nun gave birth. I was at the christening, only I couldn't make out the sex of the child: a boy or a girl?" Ibid., 3:319.

64. It is worth noting, perhaps, that this was the subject of Pushkin's *Gavriiliada* (1821), which had been published legally for the first time in Russia only in 1918. See M.P. Alekseev, "Zametki o Gavriiliade," in his *Pushkin: Sravnitel'no-istoricheskie issledovaniia* (Leningrad: Nauka, 1962), 281–325, esp. 283–84.

65. This is reflected in the author's opening address to the reader: "If you take a miracle that happened long ago, to someone else – that's somehow easier to accept. I could believe in it, and so could you. But just imagine – if it should happen now, if it happened yesterday, to you – yes, precisely, to you!" (1:475).

66. See, for example, the homosexual innuendo in Fr. Cipolla's sermon (tenth story of the sixth day), in Giovanni Boccaccio, *The Decameron*, trans. with an introduction and notes by G.H. McWilliam, 2d ed. (Harmondsworth: Penguin, 1995), 469–77.

67. "But as [the Muscovites] are given up to all licentiousness, even to sins against Nature, not only with Men, but also with Beasts, he who can tell most stories of that kind, and set them out in most gestures, is accompted the bravest Man." Cited in Kelly, *Petrushka. The Russian Carnival Puppet Theatre*, 50.

68. See Boccaccio, *The Decameron* (third story of the ninth day), 658–63.

69. The Afanas'ev version, "Skazka o tom, kak pop rodil telenka" [1872], is reprinted in *Russkie zavetnye skazki* (St. Petersburg: Biblioteca Erotica, 1994), 136–39. The Onchukov version, "Pop telenka rodil," is reprinted in *Zavetnye skazki iz sobranii N.E. Onchukova* (Moscow: Ladomir, 1996), 226–27.

70. Ibid., 226.

71. See Boccaccio, *The Decameron*, cxl.

72. See, in particular, the following tales from Onchukov's collection: "Shut," "Pop ispovednik," "Pop i rabotnik," "Na glazakh u popa," "Pro popa," "Popad'ia ponemetski zagovorila," "Ispoved'," "Smekh i slezy," "Chudov monastyr'," and "Popovna i monakhi."

73. "You, you pregnant woman, careful not to damage the baby in your stomach by placing a belt around your breasts!" (Ty, chto chrevataia zhenka, ne izvredit' by v briukhe robenka, podpoiasyvaesse po titkam!). Cited in V.P. Adrianova-Peretts, *Russkaia demokraticheskaia satira XVII veka* (Moscow and Leningrad: Izdatel'stvo Akademii nauk SSSR, 1954), 158.

74. Ibid., 157.

75. "And worse – Christ victorious in practice is the fat-bellied priest (puzatyi pop) in a silk-lined, purple cassock giving his blessing with his right hand and collecting alms with his left." See "Skify li?," 4:504.

76. "The censors, to coin a phrase from Archpriest Avvakum, have 'sat their backside' on my novel" (Na roman moi zdes' tsenzura "gubkom sela" – protopopoavvakumovski govoria) – see Zamiatin's letter to Lunts, 185. Unfortunately, the misprint in *Novyi zhurnal* distorts Zamiatin's allusion. *Gubkom*, the meaning of which is unclear, should read *guznom*, a vulgar expression for the backside – see *Slovar' russkogo iazyka*, 1:356. This can be seen from a letter written by Zamiatin a month earlier, this time to Maksimilian Voloshin, in which exactly the same expression is used: "I arrived – and was greeted straightaway with the news that the Katkovs have, to coin a phrase from Avvakum, 'sat their backside' on my novel" (Priekhal – pervoe, s chem pozdravili: Katkovy na moi roman "guznom seli" – po avvakumovski govoria). See "'Pishu vam iz Rossii …' (Pis'ma E.I. Zamiatina M.A. Voloshinu)," ed. V. Kupchenko, *Pod"em* 5 (1988):121.

77. It is also mentioned in the story itself: "And it was on Wednesday, Ash Wednesday, the first day of Lent (postom na pervoi nedele) that it all happened" (1:478).

78. See Maksimov, *Nechistaia, nevedomaia i krestnaia sila*, 1:10.

79. "The room was quiet, with eerily white walls, doors, and benches, as if it were no longer here, on earth, where everything is varicoloured, noisy, where black and white are always intermingled" (1:478).

80. See *Entsiklopedicheskii slovar' Brokgauza i Efrona*, 42 vols. and 4 suppl. vols. (St. Petersburg: Tipografiia I.A. Efrona, 1890–1907), 10a:959.

81. See Maksimov, *Nechistaia, nevedomaia i krestnaia sila*, 1:9.

82. "My dear friend, if you are troubled by the thought of the next world, of retribution and all that – which is understandable – I can put your mind at ease" (1:476).

83. The idea that food, wine, "the genital force" and the organs of the body are the driving forces of the carnival experience is mentioned in Bakhtin, *Rabelais and his World*, 62.

84. Couvade is a custom in some cultures whereby a man takes to his bed and enacts certain rituals when his wife bears a child. It is now used more as a medical term which refers to men who experience phantom pregnancies or illnesses akin to those of their wives during pregnancy. It is discussed as a source for the story of Calandrino's pregnancy in A.C. Lee, *The Decameron. Its Sources and Analogues* (London: David Nutt, 1909), 277–81.

85. Maksimov, *Nechistaia, nevedomaia i krestnaia sila*, 1:17.

86. See John 8:44.

87. "Nevskii prospekt" (1835), in Gogol', *Sobranie sochinenii*, 3:39.

88. See F.M. Dostoevskii, *Polnoe sobranie sochinenii v tridtsati tomakh*, ed. V.G. Bazanov and others, 30 vols. (Leningrad: Nauka, 1972–90), 15:69–70.

89. "However, all this came to him mistily, from far away, as in a dream: the babe was already going off to sleep" (1:481).

90. Cited in Slonimskii, *Tekhnika komicheskogo u Gogolia*, 33.

91. Ibid., 9.

92. Ibid., 10.

93. Ibid.

94. See 4:255.

95. For a discussion of carnival rituals in medieval Russia, in particular the Furnace Play and its relation to the French *diablerie*, see Likhachev, Panchenko, and Ponyrko, eds., *Smekh v drevnei rusi*, 158–75.

96. See "Narodnyi teatr" (1927), 4:429.

97. See Zamiatin's letter to Diky dated 12 November 1924, in "Perepiska s E.I. Zamiatinym i B.M. Kustodievym po povodu spektaklia 'Blokha'," in *A. Dikii. Stat'i. Perepiska. Vospominaniia* (Moscow: Iskusstvo, 1967), 302.

98. See Freud, "A Seventeenth-Century Demonological Neurosis" (Eine Teufelsneurose im siebzehnten Jahrhundert, 1923), in *Sigmund Freud. Standard Edition*, trans. and under the General Editorship of James Strachey, 24 vols (London: The Hogarth Press, 1953–74), 19:72–105.

99. "Pis'mo Stalinu" (1931), 4:310–11.

Chapter 14

Literary Representations of Stalin and Stalinism as Demonic

Rosalind Marsh

Satan has besought God for radiant Russia, so that he might turn her crimson with the blood of martyrs.

Archpriest Avvakum[1]

The Stalinist epoch has receded into the past, already judged, ridiculed, despised, caricatured, but not yet understood.

Aleksandr Zinov'ev[2]

Rulers and historical figures have frequently been portrayed in Russian literature, since there has been a longstanding tradition among Russian writers of depicting and analysing the history of their country in their literary works.[3] Writers in Russia have never espoused the Western European concept of the necessary segregation between history and imaginative literature, which has only recently been challenged in post-structuralist theory and post-modernist literary texts.[4] The aim of this chapter is to demonstrate how the Russian tradition of mythologizing historical figures, particularly autocratic rulers, came to be extended into the twentieth century. The literary representation of Iosif Stalin, the uncontested ruler of the USSR from 1929 until his death in 1953, can be regarded as a case study illustrating general principles related to the demonization of the ruler in Russian literature as a whole.[5]

Concepts of the Demonic

It will be helpful initially to provide a brief discussion of those interpretations of the terms "devil," "demon," and "demonization," and their associated concepts and imagery which are most relevant to the representation of Stalin and Stalinism in Russian literature. To "demonize" a historical figure means "to turn into, or represent as, a demon."[6] The terms "devil" and "demon," however, are more difficult concepts to interpret, possessing multiple possible resonances which find reflection in literary portraits of Stalin.

The Russian word *d'iavol* in its singular form can be used to mean the Devil, "the head of the evil spirits, of the 'unclean force,' opposing God, pushing man to sin," and is often identified as a ruler, the Prince of Darkness, or "the ruler of hell."[7] The New Testament tradition that the Devil (variously personified as Satan, Lucifer, or Beelzebub) was a fallen angel who set himself up as "the prince of this world" (John 12:31; 14:30), a rival to God, is drawn upon by some Russian Christian writers who demonstrate that Stalin originally studied in a theological seminary, but rejected God to become a powerful earthly ruler. The main characteristics associated with the New Testament Satan – pride, despotism, murder, lying, cruelty and destructiveness, melancholy and isolation – also find reflection in literary representations of Stalin. Since Satanic rituals frequently involve a reversal of religious observances, Russian writers, particularly Christian believers, sometimes present the cult of Stalin as a distorted parody of true religion.

In another common interpretation which has applied throughout the Christian era and is still in general current use, the words "devil" and "demon" denote an evil spirit, one of many, a supernatural being of malignant nature who is not necessarily omnipotent, omniscient, or in total control of his subjects. In Russia, the word *d'iavol* (frequently in its plural form) has often been used interchangeably with *zloi dukh* (evil spirit), *bes, chert,* or *demon,* all varieties of lesser devils (for example, the malignant spirits which, in pagan Russia before the conversion, were believed to inhabit woods, fields, and houses). Following this tradition, Stalin is frequently depicted in literature as an evil spirit, a petty demon, or as the leader of a host of lesser demons which tempt or destroy human beings.

Evil spirits in both pre-Christian and Christian times have often been associated with the false gods or idols of the heathen. In Judaeo-Christian history, an explicit parallel has sometimes been drawn between evil spirits and false objects of worship: for example, the name of the Canaanite god Baal, whose power over the Israelites was contested by Elijah (1 Kings 18:17–40), means "lord" or "master." Idol worship is an analogy frequently used by writers hostile to the cult of Stalin.

Demons or "unclean spirits" dwelling inside human beings were formerly held to be the cause of some species of "possession" (insanity, *delirium tremens*, or epilepsy), and were sometimes represented as baleful, melancholy spirits haunting the human personality. A number of Russian writers either depict Stalin himself as an evil spirit, or imply that his abnormal psychology – paranoia, megalomania, cruelty, or depression – indicated possession by demonic forces.

Two other widespread, interrelated interpretations of the word "devil" are "the personification of evil,"[8] or a person of diabolical character or qualities, a malignantly wicked or cruel man. The majority of Russian texts demonizing Stalin adopt one, or a combination, of these two approaches, since, as the writer Vladimir Voinovich said to the present author in April 1998, Stalin was not actually Satan, or a supernatural spirit of evil, but simply a very evil human being. The term "devil" used in a generic sense is related to the Greek word *diavolos* meaning "accuser," "calumniator," or "slanderer" (the equivalent of the Russian term *klevetnik*). As many writers demonstrate, Stalin was an arch calumniator who had numerous innocent people imprisoned or executed.

The term "fiend in human form" is sometimes used to describe a man of hideous appearance, or of gigantic stature or strength, such as Peter the Great.[9] Some Russian writers draw on this tradition, dwelling on Stalin's physical imperfections, deformities, or ugliness (in particular his pock-marked face, withered arm, deformed foot, or small stature) in order to contrast the reality of Stalin's appearance with the falsified image of a tall, handsome Stalin prevalent in the "cult" period.

Russian authors also draw on multiple associations surrounding the devil or demons in Russian Orthodoxy and folk culture. One set of images particularly emphasized by Russian writers representing Stalin and Stalinism as demonic is the devil's association with horned beasts, dragons, and animals of all kinds. Other recurrent themes are the Russian devil's association with an evil foreigner, his mastery of disguise, and his predilection for gluttony, drunkenness, and debauchery.

Another tradition which has exerted an equal, if not more important, influence on Russian writers portraying Stalin than images of the Devil or demons has been the legend of the Antichrist, which, according to Bernard McGinn, "has probably been more powerful in Russia than in any other Christian land in the past three centuries."[10] Some Russian writers also draw upon the origins of this legend in apocalyptic Judaic texts (200 B.C.–A.D. 100), written during the centuries when the Jews were suffering from Syrian and Roman oppression, and full of predictions that the end of the world would be preceded by the reign of a tyrannical ruler, the last Emperor or

False Messiah, who would attempt to rival the power of God. Visions of the end of the world are most prevalent in apocryphal texts such as *The Book of Enoch* (second century B.C.), but the Old Testament also contains apocalyptic attacks on powerful kings who claimed divine status for themselves. These include Antiochus IV, the Seleucid emperor from 175 to 164 B.C, demonized as the "little horn" (Dan.7–12); Pharaoh, King of Egypt, who was punished by God for his treachery to Israel (Ezek.29); a King of Babylon (probably Nebuchadnezzar or Nabonidas) who attempts to ascend to the throne of God, depicted as Lucifer (Day-Star), later associated with the New Testament Satan, who falls down to hell when his rays are eclipsed by the rising of the sun (Isa.14:12–15); and the evil Assyrian ruler Sennacherib (Isa.37). The main vices of these rulers were blasphemy against God, persecution of God's faithful, and false religious leadership – all features emphasized in portraits of Stalin.

In subsequent Christian apocalyptic texts evil rulers were often identified as the Antichrist, traditionally regarded as the son of the Devil and a human woman, the great enemy of Christ, who was expected to dominate the world in its last days. This trend has always been accentuated at times of political and cultural crisis, when rulers and political leaders could easily be made to fit the part. Nero was the first ruler identified as the Antichrist, and subsequently this term has been applied to many other major figures in Russian and world history.

Russians were very familiar with the legend of the Antichrist, which they had inherited from Byzantium through works on the second coming of Christ. Apart from the Revelation of Saint John, the most popular texts in Russia were the revelations of Saint Ephraem the Syrian (known in Russia since the eleventh century), the Tracts of Hippolytus of Rome on the Antichrist and the end of the world (known in Church Slavonic from the end of the twelfth century), and the *Revelations of the Pseudo-Methodius of Patara* (A.D. 691), which stated that a Last World Emperor would appear, whose role was to defeat the Ishmaelites (Islam) and then to journey to Jerusalem to hand over his crown to God, at which moment the time of the Antichrist would begin. In Russia, the references of the Pseudo-Methodius to the evil rulers Gog and Magog were rapidly identified with the Tatars.[11]

In fifteenth- and sixteenth-century Russia, these eschatological traditions became readily associated with the notion of "Moscow the third Rome": the utopian conception of a succession of sacred kingdoms representing unsullied Orthodox Christianity which were destined to lead a degenerate world to the culmination of history in the Second Coming. After the fall of Rome and Constantinople, the fate of Christianity and the salvation of the world were regarded as inextricably linked with the destiny of Russia, and the Pope was often stigmatized as the Antichrist. Subsequently, after Patriarch Nikon's church reforms of 1652–55 were perceived by Old Believers as a blasphemy against the true Orthodox Church, the concept of the Russian ruler as Antichrist became particularly common, especially among Old Believers such as Archpriest Avvakum, burnt at the stake in 1682. Some Old Believers considered that "each successive Russian ruler was the physical Antichrist while he ruled."[12]

In addition to the Bible and apocalyptic texts, twentieth-century Russian writers depicting Stalin also draw on a multitude of literary allusions and precedents. Perhaps because, as Simon Franklin demonstrates in this volume, there is little tradition of a single devil enthroned in majesty in Russian culture, writers who wish to portray Stalin as the supreme spirit of evil tend to draw more upon the Western European cultural tradition, notably the representations of the Devil by Dante, Milton, and Goethe.

The most significant Russian literary influence is Dostoevsky, whose novels draw on elements of the Christian apocalyptic tradition, particularly the Revelation of Saint John. Literary depictions of Stalin and Stalinism are frequently associated with Dostoevsky's Satanic revolutionaries in *The Devils (Besy)*, or with Ivan Karamazov's devil or the Grand Inquisitor in *The Brothers Karamazov (Brat'ia Karamazovy)*. The protagonist of Ivan Karamazov's fable "The Legend of the Grand Inquisitor," who sets himself up as a rival to Christ, advocates the domination of the majority of the population by a self-selected élite. He promises the people happiness – at the expense of freedom, the gift which Christ offers – and rules the world through "mystery, miracle and authority," the temptations of the Devil which Christ rejected in the wilderness. Dostoevsky's Grand Inquisitor, who admits that he is in league with the Devil, is related to the Antichrist, but cannot be totally identified with him, since he is a more tragic figure who does not deceive himself as well as others. As the Antichrist and Grand Inquisitor are earthly rulers, they are often considered by Russian writers to be more appropriate images to evoke the evil of Stalin and Stalinism than the Devil himself.

The modern usage of the word "demonization" also possesses multiple resonances. Often used simply to refer to the representation of a historical character as a very evil human being, it may sometimes allude to the unjust denigration of a historical figure, or to the persecution of a group of political or religious opponents imagined as incarnations of evil.[13] As will be demonstrated below, some neo-Stalinist critics in post-Stalin Russia have taken a similar view of texts demonizing Stalin.

The concept of "political demonology" has recently been used by Michael Paul Rogin to refer to "the creation of monsters by the inflation, stigmatization and dehumanization of political foes."[14] Rogin argues that the demonologist or "countersubversive" (a term he uses to denote such political figures as Ronald Reagan) splits the world into two, attributing a magical, pervasive power to a conspiratorial centre of evil – as Stalin did when accusing his enemies of such ill-defined crimes as being "enemies of the people," members of the so-called "Trotskyite-Zinov'evite bloc," or "rootless cosmopolitans." As Rogin suggests, "Demonization allows the countersubversive, in the name of battling the subversive, to imitate his enemy."[15] This insight can be usefully adapted to characterize Russian writers' techniques of demonizing Stalin. Writers struggling with the devil (Stalin) frequently use arms traditionally associated with the devil (mockery, carnality, or cruel satire), thus succeeding in demonizing the demonizer.

The Historical Tradition

Russian writers approaching the figure of Stalin were heirs to what Kevin Platt in this volume calls the "dual tradition of interpretation" regarding tyrannical rule which either elevated the ruler as divine, or stigmatized him as a personification of evil, as Satan or the Antichrist. On the one hand, Russia inherited the Byzantine concept of *basileus*, the emperor who is simultaneously the spiritual and secular leader of his Christian realm, an idea dating back to Emperor Constantine (288?-337), who united Christianity and imperial Rome.[16] Ivan the Terrible, who was crowned with great ceremony in 1547, subsequently consolidated the notion of Russia as holy empire and himself as *basileus*; in his reign the emphasis shifted from saintly prince to pious tsar, with his paternal, godlike role. On the other hand, from the seventeenth century onwards the Russian ruler was frequently anathematized as the Antichrist, particularly by Old Believers. Tsar Aleksei Mikhailovich (ruled 1645-76), for example, was dubbed "not tsar but a horn of the Antichrist" by a follower of the monk Kapiton;[17] and Peter the Great, the revolutionary Westernizer, was frequently denounced as the Antichrist incarnate.[18]

This ambivalent cultural heritage helps to explain why many powerful rulers of the past have been depicted by Russian writers with a mixture of fascination and repugnance: we need only recall the portraits of Peter the Great in Pushkin's *The Bronze Horseman* (*Mednyi vsadnik*, 1833), Nicholas I in Tolstoi's *Hadji Murat* (*Khadzhi Murat*, written in 1904, first published in 1912), or Napoleon in Tolstoi's *War and Peace* (*Voina i mir*, 1869). Just as Satan in Milton's *Paradise Lost* (first translated into Russian in 1745 by Baron Aleksandr

Stroganov)[19] was devilishly attractive, tyrannical rulers, including Stalin, have often held a diabolical fascination for Russian writers. The character and historical legacy of Iosif Stalin have also made him an eminently suitable subject for either deification or demonization in literature. On the one hand, he presided over the transformation of the USSR into a powerful state capable of defeating Nazi Germany and ultimately of rivalling the U.S.A. in industrial and military might. Even some Western historians, such as Isaac Deutscher and Ian Grey, have argued that Stalin was not a purely destructive tyrant like Hitler.[20] On the other hand, many other historians have emphasized that for more than two decades Stalin arbitrarily controlled the life of his nation and people with an authoritarian cruelty which has few equals in history.

Although there have been many disagreements among commentators in Russia and the West about the interpretation of Stalin and Stalinism,[21] they nevertheless tend to agree that Stalin was a great, larger-than-life figure: a ruler of great power, or of great evil. Not surprisingly, then, his image has lent itself to representation in superhuman terms, as either a god or a devil. Just as the identification of the Russian tsar with divinity in folklore and dogmatic texts established a semiotic precedent for the representation of the tyrannical ruler as an anti-divine figure, so the depiction of Stalin as a god in literature published in the USSR during his lifetime paved the way for his portrayal as a demonic figure in the underground and after his death.

This chapter aims to demonstrate that Russian writers depicting Stalin draw upon many diverse, albeit sometimes interrelated, traditions about the concepts of "demon," "devil," and "demonization," reconfiguring Stalin's image in a variety of ways, often mediating their portraits through earlier Russian and foreign literary texts. Allusions to the devil or devils in critical portraits of Stalin are designed to highlight the nature and origins of his evil and to evoke the enormous suffering he caused.

Early Demonizing Texts

In Stalin's lifetime, few writers dared to demonize Stalin overtly, since derogatory references to him could mean persecution, imprisonment, or death. However, in the 1920s, a period of relative literary freedom before Stalin established uncontested power over the party, some writers provided a general representation of despotic rule, drawing on the tradition of the demonic in Russian culture. Such works were often read retrospectively as portraits of Stalin, helping to build up the tradition of depicting Stalin and Stalinism in literature.

One of the first works which was subsequently interpreted as referring to Stalin was Kornei Chukovsky's narrative poem for children, "Tarakanishche" (The Big Bad Cockroach, 1923). Chukovsky paints an allegorical picture of an idyllic animal kingdom terrorized by "A dreadful giant / … The Big Bad Cockroach!" (Strashnyi velikan / … Tarakanishche!) which rages and twitches its moustache, snarling "I'll devour you, I'll devour you, I won't show any mercy" (Proglochu, proglochu, ne pomiluiu).[22] Chukovsky's cockroach could be related to the image of the devil, with his giant stature, evil and "bestial" nature, and power of metamorphosis into an animal or insect shape. It is also associated with the image of the tyrant-cockroach, a figure common in Russian folklore.[23]

As Lev Losev has argued, since the Russian cockroach has whiskers, *Tarakan* (the Cockroach) is often used as a nickname for any man possessing a thick, bristly moustache. Because Chukovsky composed his poem before Stalin became dominant, at a time when several of the contenders for power in the party had moustaches, his satire was not explicitly aimed at any specific ruler, but at any dictatorship imposed by a small political faction against the will of the majority of the population. It was only with hindsight that Chukovsky's vision could be regarded as prophetic, and was interpreted in this way in the USSR.[24] Stalin's nickname "the Cockroach" (Tarakan), which was in use from the beginning of the 1930s, was derived from Chukovsky's poem. One particularly vivid use of this image can be seen in Mandel'shtam's famous epigram on Stalin (1933), which contains the line "His great cockroach moustache laughs" (Tarakan'i smeiutsia usishcha).[25]

As W.J. Leatherbarrow and Philip Cavendish suggest in this volume, one strategy adopted by some Russian writers was to take on the devil with what are perceived in Russian folklore as his own instruments: laughter, offensiveness, and the desecration of the sacred.[26] Comedy possesses a "demonic" power, proving to be an excellent means of deflating pomposity and debunking the myth of the dictator's genius and infallibility. One of the first Russian prose writers to attempt a comic portrayal of a character bearing some resemblance to Stalin was Evgenii Zamiatin, in his story "X" (Iks, 1926).[27] Zamiatin depicts Comrade Papalagi, a member of the Cheka (Secret Police) whose foreign-sounding name and "terrible black moustache" are reminiscent of Stalin (whose real name was Dzhugashvili). Papalagi's pointed moustache is described as a pair of "horns"[28] ready to gore his hapless victims – an image recalling the traditional image of the devil. Papalagi, like Stalin himself, does not speak Russian well, perhaps suggesting the frequent identification of the Russian devil with a foreigner.[29] Zamiatin parodies religious imagery in order to evoke the quasi-religious nature of the Bolshevik dictatorship. Papalagi shines a light into his victims' eyes, forcing them to confess to absurd crimes (a practice which suggests the image of the devil as false accuser, or *klevetnik*). In particular, Papalagi shouts "Confess!"[30] at a deacon, Indikoplev, who admits to making the sign of the cross in public – a traditional means of warding off the devil. In Zamiatin's story, however, the deacon fails to drive the devil away.

Some writers of the 1920s draw on Dostoevskian themes to warn of the dangers of a dictatorship of the future, or of a materialist utopia. The all-powerful Benefactor (Blagodetel') in Zamiatin's *We* (*My*, written in 1920–21, but not published in Russia until 1988),[31] like Dostoevsky's Grand Inquisitor, is a man-god opposed to Christ and human freedom, a "sufferer for humanity" who surrenders personal happiness in order to create the happiness of his enslaved people. Another character reminiscent of the Grand Inquisitor is the self-confident village activist in Andrei Platonov's novella *The Foundation Pit* (*Kotlovan*, written at the height of the collectivization drive in 1929–30, but not published in Russia until 1987),[32] whose exhortations to the peasantry to dig a foundation pit in order to build a many-storeyed building called socialism evokes Stalinist plans and slogans. The implication is that the Soviet people were promised an earthly paradise, but instead all they do is dig a pit, which, like hell in popular tradition, is imagined as an "abyss," an expanse below the earth.

The first character in Russian literature obviously recognizable as Stalin was depicted in Boris Pil'niak's *Tale of the Unextinguished Moon* (*Povest' nepogashennoi luny*, 1926).[33] Pil'niak suggests that a prominent military man, Commander Gavrilov, was killed on the orders of his superior, the shadowy "Number One" (Pervyi) or "the Unbending Man" (negorbiashchiisia chelovek) – just as, according to rumour, Stalin had ordered the murder of M.V. Frunze, People's Commissar for Military and Naval Affairs, who died in October 1925 during an operation for a stomach ulcer undertaken at the behest of the party. It is said that Stalin recognized himself in the image of this powerful bureaucrat, and that this was probably one of the main reasons why Pil'niak was shot in 1938.[34] The "Unbending Man," an appellation related to the Soviet phrase "inflexible Bolshevik" (nesgibaemyi bol'-shevik), is never named, just as in folklore Russian peasants tried to avoid naming the devil. He is compared with the moon, with its demonic associations of night, darkness, immobility, loneliness, silence, and death – traits similar to those of Lermontov's Demon and Dostoevsky's Stavrogin. When the dictator rushes out of the city in his car, he is depicted as a master of the universe who can change the direction of the moon, recalling the Devil, who, as the "prince of this world," was assumed to have power over both human society and the natural world; the crescent moon has often been associated with the Devil through images of snakes and horns.[35]

In early texts of the 1920s alluding indirectly to Stalin or to the growing despotism of the Soviet system, various traditions of demonization were already established: carnivalizing elements of humour, profanity, and blasphemy; the Aesopian depiction of Stalin in various forms of disguise; and the metaphysical identification of a dictator with Satan, or with devils in Russian literature. None of these traditions of depicting a tyrannical ruler was new; rather, they had been extended into the twentieth century from earlier periods of Russian culture.

The Cult of Stalin

Throughout most of his rule, from 1929 to 1953, Stalin was portrayed as a god. He was eulogized in quasi-religious terms in countless songs, poems, and novels with a hagiographical extravagance which has surrounded few rulers in modern history.[36] The religious overtones of the cult of the leader, which clashed with the professed secularism of the Soviet state, sprang from Russia's deep-rooted autocratic traditions: age-old peasant respect for personal authority, and Russian Orthodox veneration for the tsar as a divinely appointed ruler.[37] Many epithets and images in literature of the "cult" period are those associated with God or gods in religious literature: Stalin is constantly addressed as "father," described as a "sun," "star," or source of light, and presented as "immortal," "eternal," or the master of nature. Some eulogistic images, notably the sun, had previously been prevalent in hagiographical portraits of autocratic tsars.[38] Just as tsars of the past gained legitimacy from their rightful succession, Stalin is frequently depicted in apostolic succession to Lenin.

Certain unique new literary genres were specifically engendered by the cult of Stalin's personality: the "song about Stalin" and "folk-tale about Stalin," which, like saints' lives, were highly stylized in language and imagery. Most imagery in songs and tales about Stalin is drawn from archaic rural folklore rather than from modern urban life: Stalin is often portrayed as a "mountain eagle" (an image earlier used to refer to Lenin), or as a folk hero (bogatyr') riding a great horse, as in Aleksandr Tvardovsky's poem *The Land of Muraviia* (*Strana Muraviia*, 1936).[39] Stalin is, however, sometimes depicted in Moscow, where, like the tsars of the past, he is seen as the embodiment of Russia's capital city and of the Kremlin, the symbol of imperial power. The light in the Kremlin window at night symbolizes his fatherly concern for his people.

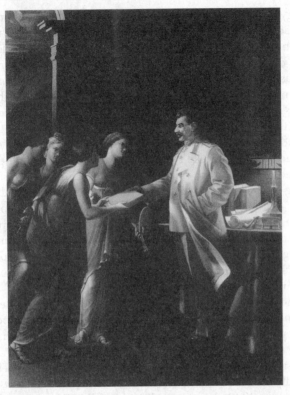

21. V. Komar and A. Melamid, *Stalin and the Muses*, 1981-82. Oil on canvas, 173 × 132 cm. A satirical retrospective view of Stalin's role as the author of a Soviet cultural project and protector of the arts, from the painters' *Nostalgic Socialist Realism* series.

Other more traditional genres skilfully exploited by Russian writers to eulogize Stalin were novels and films on historical topics. Historical works were particularly effective in inculcating Stalinist values, especially pride in Holy Mother Russia, glorification of autocracy, and an apologia for Stalin's tyranny. Stalin's imperial legitimacy was established by such writers and film directors as Aleksei Tolstoi and Sergei Eizenshtein through implicit comparisons with earlier ruthless tsars, such as Peter the Great or Ivan the Terrible.[40]

Texts Demonizing Stalin in His Lifetime

After Stalin's rise to power in 1929, it was only in underground, unpublished, and unpublishable works that writers implied, sometimes with great subtlety, that Stalin was a demonic figure, or that an ideology designed to lead the Russian people to the communist paradise had actually created hell on earth. Many of the images, themes, and genres used by writers to eulogize Stalin and Stalinism were turned on their head in demonizing texts. Instead of portraying Stalin as a god, some writers depict him as a diabolic character, whose main characteristic, as in Russian folklore, is total hostility towards man; he exists for the sole purpose of inflicting harm and prompting evil deeds.[41]

Mandel'shtam's 1933 epigram on Stalin contains several oblique demonic allusions. Stalin's cronies are depicted as "half-people" (poluliudei): subhuman creatures who fawn around their master mewing and whining,[42] suggesting the power over animals traditionally attributed to the devil or *leshii* (wood demon). Stalin is portrayed as a murderer and peasant-slayer who forges iron decrees like horseshoes which are flung at vulnerable parts of the human body, recalling the depictions of the devil in Russian folklore stopping at the blacksmith's to get his horses shod.[43] The images of stone and mountain implied in the epithet "Kremlin mountaineer" (kremlevskogo gortsa)[44] which suggest Stalin's hard-heartedness and remoteness, were later echoed in another Mandel'shtam poem of 1936 depicting an inhuman idol in the middle of a mountain[45] – an oblique allusion to the worship of Stalin as a false god.

Allusions to stone, a recurrent image in Mandel'stam's poetry, are frequently used in Akhmatova's poetic cycle *Requiem* (*Rekviem,* mostly written in the 1930s, but not published in full in Russia until 1987).[46] In an earlier poem of 1924, Akhmatova had compared her Muse with that of Dante,[47] implying that her task in describing contemporary Russia was similar to Dante's in the *Inferno.* Subsequently, in the "Dedication" (Posviashchenie, 1940) of *Requiem,* Akhmatova drew a subtle parallel between Stalin's Terror and Dante's *Inferno* when she asked, referring to the women waiting in prison queues with her:

> Где теперь невольные подруги
> Двух моих осатанелых лет?[48]

> [Where are they now, the involuntary friends
> Of my two diabolical years?]

The word *osatanelykh* ("diabolical" in the sense of "demented," "possessed") introduces the additional letter "l" into the name *Satana* from which it is formed. This strengthens the euphonic link which already exists between the names of Satan and Stalin (s-t-n), perhaps hinting that the city of Leningrad was under Satan's dominion during the Stalin period. In the "Epilogue" (Epilog) of *Requiem,* Akhmatova makes it clear that her aim is to preserve for posterity the memory of those who suffered and perished in the inferno of the Ezhov terror.

Very occasionally, during Stalin's lifetime, the literary genres officially devoted to adulation of Stalin were subverted by writers hostile to Stalin as a means of demonizing him. An ironic song which affords a striking contrast to the artificially sponsored adulatory songs and folk tales about Stalin is "Comrade Stalin, You're a Real Big Scholar" (Tovarishch Stalin, vy bol'shoi uchenyi) by a former convict, Iuz Aleshkovsky, which circulated in the prison camps and became a genuine folk song of the late Stalin era.[49] The song parodies various divine qualities attributed to Stalin during the period of the "cult of personality," such as wisdom and immortality, juxtaposing Stalin's privileged life with the hard lot of the prisoners in Stalin's camps.

If historical works could be used to extol Stalin, they could also be subverted to express criticism of him through Aesopian devices. Mikhail Bulgakov's play *Batumi* (*Batum*, completed in 1939 but banned by Stalin) and the final part of Sergei Eizenshtein's film *Ivan the Terrible* (*Ivan Groznyi*, part 2, 1946), which was also censored, are ambiguous texts which exploit the equivocal nature of the tyrannical ruler in Russian culture. The young Stalin in Bulgakov's play and Eizenshtein's Ivan emerge as overtly praiseworthy figures, but both can be interpreted on a deeper level of Aesopian parody.[50] In Bulgakov's play, when the rector of the Georgian seminary expels the young Stalin, he uses phrases which could be construed as a veiled allusion to Satan's sin of apostasy, such as "human society proclaims an anathema on the noxious tempter." The reference to the "black dragon" which "stole the sun from humanity," a possible allusion to Stalin's terror of the 1930s,[51] evokes the Book of Revelation, in which Satan takes on the form of a "great red dragon" (Rev.12:3).[52] In Eizenshtein's film, the play in the cathedral in which Shadrach, Medrach, and Abednego are symbolically cast into the fiery furnace draws a parallel between the cruelty of Ivan (or Stalin) and the evil Babylonian ruler Nebuchadnezzar. In the banquet scene, with its wild dance of the *oprichniki* (Ivan's secret police) and its vivid use of black and red, the representation of Ivan evokes Satan presiding over some demonic orgy.

The most famous work written in Russia in Stalin's lifetime which drew an implicit parallel between Stalinism and devilry was Bulgakov's *The Master and Margarita* (*Master i Margarita*, written in 1928–40). Bulgakov chose to approach the figure of Stalin obliquely, through allegory and fantasy. Although Bulgakov's novel cannot be reduced to a mere "cryptotext" for Stalin's Russia, it has been plausibly argued by Donald Piper that many aspects of Bulgakov's portrait of the Devil, Woland, suggest Stalin,[53] who was also mysterious, aloof, and rarely seen in the 1930s, a foreigner who had difficulty with the Russian language, destructive when attacked, demanding subservience from his followers, impressive in his self-control, establishing a strange and ambiguous relationship with certain great writers, such as Mandel'shtam, Bulgakov, and Pasternak. It could, however, be argued that there is a closer general parallel between the Rome of Tiberius Caesar and the Moscow of the 1930s: both societies are permeated by a cult of the ruler based on philistine values, spying, denunciations, and secret police terror. Bulgakov's reference to ancient Rome also has apocalyptic connotations: it is generally accepted that the Antichrist in the Book of Revelation was an oblique reference to the Emperor Nero.[54]

Many of Woland's characteristics are typical of the devil in Russian culture (as well as demonstrating the influence of Goethe's Mephistopheles and, perhaps, of Milton's Satan).[55] As Simon Franklin suggests in this volume, the Devil himself does not often appear to man in Russian Orthodox tradition; instead, a host of lesser demons tempt and play pranks on mankind, as Woland's retinue does in *The Master and Margarita*. At the end of the novel, however, Woland and his followers Korov'ev, Begemot, and Azazello appear in their true demonic guise as "dark silhouettes" on "black horses,"[56] recalling the four horsemen of the Apocalypse (thus subverting the popular eulogistic image of Stalin as the benign *bogatyr'* on horseback), a particularly suitable image to suggest the apocalyptic nature of Stalinism.[57] Bulgakov's final vision parodies the utopian pretensions of Stalinist culture, which, as Boris Groys has observed, "looks upon itself as postapocalyptic culture – the final verdict on all human culture has already been passed, and all that was once temporally distinct has become forever simultaneous in the blinding light of the Final Judgement and the ultimate truth revealed in Stalin's *Short Course* of party history."[58]

Whether or not Bulgakov intended to draw a parallel between Stalin and Woland or Stalin and Tiberius (or both, as seems most plausible), it is indisputable that the Soviet censorship in the 1960s read the novel in this way. This is demonstrated by the fact that in the version published in the journal *Moskva* in 1966–67, several passages were deleted which can be interpreted as ironic references to the cult of Stalin's personality. In one such passage, the cat Begemot speaks of the grandeur of Satan's ball, but, after being contradicted by Woland, immediately hastens to agree obsequiously with his master: "Of course, messire. … If you think it wasn't very grand, I immediately find myself agreeing with you."[59] The censor also heavily cut passages in chapter 26 in which Pilate holds an ambiguous conversation with his secret police chief Afranii about the murder of Judas, which would have suggested to Soviet readers Stalin's alleged dealings with the secret police over the assassination of Kirov in 1934.[60] One prominent Russian intellectual to support the association between Woland and Stalin was Andrei Siniavsky; in an article of 1974 published after his emigration, he directly compared Woland's relationship with the Master to Stalin's eccentric patronage of Bulgakov.[61]

Texts Published in the USSR after Stalin's Death

In view of the hagiography with which Stalin had previously been surrounded, it might have been expected, after Stalin's death and subsequent dethronement by Khrushchev in 1956, that Russian writers would immediately have turned the former religious imagery on its head, and presented Stalin as a demonic figure, or as Satan himself. Instead, the 1950s and 1960s, especially under Khrushchev, witnessed a certain resurgence of communist utopianism.[62] The repudiation of the Russians' former idol and their traditional need for worship of their leader left an enormous vacuum in Russian psychology and culture which could only be filled by another object of worship.[63] In literature, the former cult of Stalin was replaced by a renewed cult of Lenin (as well as lesser, temporary cults of Khrushchev and Brezhnev), which only began to be undermined under *glasnost'*, in the years 1989–90.

Demonization of Stalin through Realism

The demonization of Stalin in post-Stalin literature has taken a variety of forms. The simplest method, practised in the majority of works published in the USSR from Stalin's death to the end of Soviet rule, when it was possible to tell at least some of the truth about Stalin, has been a realistic depiction of Stalin as a despotic ruler responsible for heinous crimes. Writers tried to come to terms with the historical Stalin by portraying him in a style similar to the "critical realism" of nineteenth-century Russian literature. Their justification for this approach was that, since Russian historians were backward in analysing Stalin and Stalinism, they had a duty to establish historical truth in their literary work. Realism was the only strategy available to the writer who wished to make a serious contribution to the biographical and historical analysis of Stalin.

Although literature depicting Stalin and Stalinism published in the USSR from the 1950s until the end of Soviet rule was truer to life than before, it was still only partial and ambiguous, since Stalin's image was subject to all the political reevaluations imposed by Khrushchev and his successors.[64] The most truthful depictions of

Stalin's life and character are to be found in realistic works by dissident writers which remained unpublished in Russia until the Gorbachev era, such as Aleksandr Bek's *New Appointment* (*Novoe naznachenie*, published in the West in 1971, in Russia in 1986), the novels of Anatolii Rybakov, and the plays of Mikhail Shatrov,[65] as well as in the realistic sections of novels by Vladimir Maksimov and Aleksandr Solzhenitsyn which attempt to provide an extended analysis of Stalin's personality and actions. The representation of Stalin in such works partakes of the demonic only in so far as he is portrayed as a very evil man, a calumniator falsely accusing his enemies Bukharin, Zinov'ev, and Kamenev of odious crimes, as in Rybakov's *1935 and Other Years* (*Tridtsat' piatyi i drugie gody*, 1989), or as the instigator of the suicide of his former friend Ordzhonikidze, as in Bek's *New Appointment* (in the Russian Orthodox Church and Russian folklore the devil was frequently held responsible for suicide, which was considered a mortal sin by the Orthodox Church).[66]

Parody of the Cult

Another important method of demonizing Stalin in post-Stalin texts is the deliberate subversion of ideas and imagery used to eulogize him during the period of the "cult of personality." Demonization is achieved primarily by a simple reversal of deification.

Since *glasnost'*, Russian critics have distinguished five virtually permanent characteristics from which Stalin's godlike image was created during the period of the "personality cult": 1) Stalin as a great revolutionary; 2) Stalin as the Lenin of today; 3) Stalin as a great statesman, leader, and teacher; 4) Stalin as a great military leader; 5) Stalin as the wise master of the country, the father of his people.[67] These were the main points which demonizing texts were concerned to repudiate. The refutation of the lies propagated during the period of the Stalin cult has been a more common feature of "liberal" and "dissident" works, even those published in the Gorbachev era, than the explicit portrayal of Stalin as a demonic figure.[68] However, some neo-Stalinists expressed a desire for the return of their god,[69] and in the Brezhnev era a partial rehabilitation of Stalin took place.[70]

During the "cult," numerous portraits, novels, and films had presented a gigantic Stalin as the central focus of attention, often standing upright above the masses to demonstrate his absolute control and inspired leadership.[71] By contrast, writers hostile to Stalin were intent to draw a distinction between Stalin, the hero of the cult, and Stalin the man, with his small stature, pock-marked face,[72] withered arm,[73] and deformed left foot on which the second and third toes had grown together (regarded as the "sign of the Antichrist").[74] Writers often chose to depict Stalin at the end of his life, as a small, sick, wrinkled, frightened old man.[75]

Another common epithet used to describe Stalin in novels of the 1930s, such as Petr Pavlenko's *In the East* (*Na vostoke*, 1936) and Aleksei Tolstoi's *Bread* (*Khleb*, 1937), was *spokoinyi* (calm, confident): references to his "calm countenance" are reminiscent of the representation of Christ or the saints in icons. Stalin's "calmness" was designed to be interpreted as a sign of complete self-control and firmness in the revolutionary faith. In demonizing texts, by contrast, emphasis is constantly placed on Stalin's yellow, suspicious eyes (a feature mentioned in many memoirs, notably those of Djilas and Trotsky),[76] which reflect his potential for violence.

Some writers of the post-Stalin period subverted the former god-like image of Stalin, depicting him in bestial terms. Bulat Okudzhava's song "The Black Tomcat" (Chernyi kot, 1960) portrays a violent, despotic cat with yellow eyes and was widely interpreted as referring to Stalin. The black cat is also common in Russian folklore as a witch's familiar and as one of the common metamorphoses of the devil.[77] Similarly, Vasilii Aksenov's despotic "steel bird" with its yellow eyes which express "the ancient dream and longing of Tamerlane,"[78] and its revolting smell (another trait commonly attributed to the devil),[79] can be seen as a parody of the former eulogy of Stalin as a "mountain eagle."

The Demonic Power of Comedy

Comic portraits of Stalin can be seen as belonging to the sphere of "carnival," as defined by the critic Mikhail Bakhtin in *Rabelais and His World* (*Tvorchestvo Fransua Rable i narodnaia kul'tura srednevekov'ia i Renessansa*, written in 1940, first published in Russia in 1965).[80] For Bakhtin, carnival represented a form of medieval popular culture in which masked surrogates for kings, high officials, and church dignitaries were degraded and deprived of their official identities. Carnival is associated with the demonic in that it involves the periodic debunking of all that a particular society holds dear – or, in particular, everything it fears – thus subverting authoritarian rule and conquering religious fear, while affirming the material life of the body and the earthly world. Mocking carnival laughter and the sexual and scatological humiliations inflicted on masked rulers are a means of defying the pretensions of state and religious officialdom to personal power.

One of the first writers to make deliberate use of subversive laughter to undermine Stalin's tyranny was the émigré writer Vladimir

Nabokov, in his story "Tyrants Destroyed" (Istreblenie tiranov, 1938). His villain is a composite character, but the allusions to Stalin are more numerous and explicit than the passing references to Lenin and Hitler.[81] Nabokov believes in the artist's power to destroy tyranny by making it appear ridiculous: "I see that, in my efforts to make him terrifying, I have only made him ridiculous, thereby destroying him."[82] In later years he commented that "tyrants and torturers will never manage to hide their comic stumbles behind their cosmic acrobatics," and described tyrants as "the clowns of history."[83]

In the post-Stalin period, many underground or émigré writers had come to regard simple realism as an inadequate, limited means of portraying the larger-than-life figure of Stalin. Just as Stalin had been elevated into a fantasy figure through the "personality cult," so authors hostile to Stalin felt the need to approach his hyperbolic figure through comedy, fantasy, and the grotesque. Since, for many writers, Soviet reality under Stalin, and the idealization of the dictator himself, appeared absurd and fantastic, they regarded comedy and fantasy as the most appropriate means of conveying a faithful picture of Stalinism.[84]

Two works written in Russia during the post-Stalin period which display the technique of carnivalization in a highly developed manner are Vladimir Voinovich's story "A Circle of Friends" (V krugu druzei, written in 1967) and Fazil Iskander's *Sandro of Chegem* (*Sandro iz Chegema*, published in the West in 1979). Both use elements of humour and scandal to illuminate Stalin's character[85] and choose to depict a well-known aspect of his life: his long drunken banquets with other members of the Politburo, at which he often tempted his colleagues and tested their loyalty. The treatment of this theme reflects Bakhtin's concept of the "carnival" element of the feast, when kings were uncrowned.[86]

Following the tradition established by Nabokov, Voinovich's Stalin (who appears under his revolutionary name, Koba), is portrayed as a clown who gladly discards his props – his moustache and pipe – when alone. When he is not in his room he places a dummy in his own likeness at his lighted window in the Kremlin to make people think that he never sleeps, but is always working on their behalf (a parody of the familiar "cult" image). As Platt and Leatherbarrow note in this volume, the concept of imposture (particularly of the "false tsar," or *samozvanets*) carries a demonic charge in the Russian tradition. The carnival element of scandal is accentuated when Stalin forces Khrushchev to dance the Ukrainian *gopak* – a real incident graphically described in Khrushchev's memoirs.[87]

At the end of the story Stalin speaks frankly to his parodic double, his own reflection in a mirror, confessing that he killed millions of people, ruined Soviet agriculture, and created a reign of terror to enhance his own personal power. Because of this the people hate him; and since he has always demanded lies, there is now no one to tell him the truth. Stalin, who comes to realize that his morbid suspicion of enemies is futile, eventually shoots at his own reflection, saying "You are the number-one enemy of the people, the number-one counter-Kobaist."[88]

Some authors develop the concept of carnivalization even further, using a more profane, erotic form of humour to satirize the Stalin cult and expose the widespread nature of Stalin's crimes. In Aleksandr Zinov'ev's *The Yawning Heights* (*Ziiaiushchie vysoty*, 1976), a powerful satire on the Soviet system, Stalin appears as "the Boss," who inflicted a "general thrashing" on his subjects, and after his death was denounced by Hog (Khrushchev). Zinov'ev satirizes the Stalin cult, presenting it as the glorification of the leader's penis, with which, according to legend, he strikes all his enemies: "Songs were written in honour of the Boss's prick, towns were named after it, processions were held to glorify it. At the corner where Boss Street (now Leader Street) met Boss Avenue (now Leader Avenue), a public urinal was erected in honour of the Boss's prick. On its walls Artis, winner of all the prizes and bearer of all titles, drew a large image of the Boss's prick in full working order, with all the leading statesmen of Europe and America sitting astride it."[89]

Portrayal of Stalin as a Diabolic Figure

Only relatively few writers published in Russia after Stalin's death attempted to introduce a supernatural element into their portrayal of Stalin, or to depict him as an explicitly diabolic figure, alluding particularly to Dante and Dostoevsky.

Leonid Leonov's novel *The Russian Forest* (*Russkii les*, written in 1950–53, first published in 1953, shortly after Stalin's death),[90] is an exceptional case in which, in a work censored by Stalin himself,[91] a liberal author managed to use symbolism and Aesopian imagery to imply that Stalin and Stalinist values had demonic associations. The villain of Leonov's novel, the unscrupulous professor of forestry Gratsiansky, who denounces his ideological opponent for the political crime of attempting to "limit socialist construction,"[92] can only be obliquely identified with Stalin. However, certain features of his life – his theological background, activities as a tsarist police spy, persecution of opponents and isolation from ordinary people – suggest known or alleged facets of Stalin's own biography. Moreover, his insistence that the Russian forests are inexhaustible and can be felled ruthlessly in the interests of socialist construction can be interpreted as an allegory of the destruction of millions of people in Stalin's purges.

There are scattered references to Dante throughout the novel, and the recurrent images of ice, which in the later book version of the novel (1956) culminate in Gratsiansky's apparent suicide in a hole in the ice,[93] are reminiscent of the fate of Dante's Satan, lying eternally paralysed in a lake of ice in the deepest circle of the *Inferno*. Through this oblique parallel between Gratsiansky, Stalin, and Satan, Leonov suggests that Stalin is the source of evil in Soviet society. Leonov's anti-Stalinist and demonic allusions in this novel are so subtle that at the time of its publication only one Western critic, Max Hayward, recognized Leonov's clever use of "devious symbolism" to "suggest that human affairs and the fate of Russia are much more complex than the crude oversimplifications of official thought would ever allow."[94] The validity of Hayward's interpretation has recently been borne out by the publication of Leonov's last work which he worked on for about forty-five years and published when he was in his nineties, the apocalyptic anti-Stalinist novel *Pyramid* (*Piramida*, 1994), some pencil drafts of which predated the publication of *The Russian Forest.*[95]

During the Khrushchev and Brezhnev periods, some liberal and dissident writers explicitly portrayed Stalin as an evil spirit in order to suggest that unless de-Stalinization were fully carried through in Russia, Stalin would continue to exert a malign influence on his successors from beyond the grave. Evgenii Evtushenko's poem "Stalin's Heirs" (Nasledniki Stalina, 1962) and Anatolii Gladilin's novella *Rehearsal on Friday* (*Repetitsiia v piatnitsu*, 1978), for example, use this image to suggest that Stalin may come to life again if the evil he represented is not confronted and put finally to rest.[96] Stalin is also portrayed as an evil spirit in Andrei Siniavsky's *Good Night* (*Spokoinoi nochi*, 1984), a semi-autobiographical novel written after his emigration, in which he follows his own earlier injunction to Soviet writers to create a "phantasmagorical art with hypotheses instead of an aim, and with the grotesque instead of realistic description."[97] Stalin is presented as an "indignant spirit" who comes to visit the telepathic Alla, a former prisoner, in the free settlement at Vorkuta two or three days after his death, but before the Politburo has officially announced the news. Like the sinners in the Apocalypse, or the tyrannical Russian ruler on whom justified retribution is visited after death,[98] Stalin's ghost is faced with a second, final death unless his sins can be redeemed.

One demonic aspect of Stalin's ghost is that he is never referred to by name, but simply called *on* (he) or *tot* (that one), as the devil was in folklore, or "the moustachio'd one." He appears not in human form, but as a transparent column of gaseous cold, recalling the coldness and loneliness of Dante's Satan: it is as if "he had shut himself up in his frozen solitude." Stalin's ghost angrily demands that Alla "pay his debts," but she replies that God has not given her the power to forgive on behalf of all Stalin's prisoners. Although she is prepared to forgive him on her own account, she tells him to visit all his victims in turn, both living and dead, in order to ask each one for personal forgiveness. The narrator comments that such a task will last for the whole of eternity, and parodies the Soviet concept of rehabilitation: "Where, to what wild regions did he go, he who had emerged from the darkness, to attain rehabilitation?"[99]

Some dissident writers associate Stalin with the Devil or devils in the Russian literary tradition, or portray Stalin in conversation with, or in league with, the Devil. The suggestion that Stalin was possessed by demonic forces is designed to accentuate his cruelty and destructiveness. In Iurii Dombrovsky's *The Faculty of Useless Knowledge* (*Fakul'tet nenuzhnykh veshchei*, 1978), Stalin appears to the protagonist, the archaeologist Zybin, in a dream, speaking to him in a matter-of-fact tone which recalls the "banality of evil" of Ivan Karamazov's shabby devil in Dostoevsky's *The Brothers Karamazov*.[100] Stalin's demonic essence, opposed to Christ, is also implied by Zybin's (mis)quotation of two lines from Pushkin's "Message to the Censor" (Poslanie tsenzoru, 1822):

> Для узкого ума придворного льстеца
> Кутейкин и Христос – два равные лица.[101]

> [The flattering toady courtier's narrow mind
> Sees Jesus and Kuteikin as one kind.]

Dombrovsky's Stalin identifies with Kuteikin, a seminarist from Fonvizin's comedy *The Minor* (*Nedorosl'*, 1782), who represents cunning and petty wheeling and dealing: "The Christs pronounce and pass through, it's us Kuteikins who have to do the building." He explains the philosophy behind his mass terror, which Zybin likens to the ideas of Saint-Just during the French Revolution: "To build a bridge requires years of work and thousands of people; to blow it up needs only an hour and a handful of men. Those are the handful we're getting after now." Zybin, speaking for the author, suggests that Stalin's incomprehension of the difference between good and evil has, like Satan, "brought the world to the edge of the pit." Dombrovsky also draws an implicit parallel between Stalin and Antichrist through his use of religious imagery, and his reference to the dangers ahead if Stalin is successful in the "final conflict": "We must fall down before the arms and military boots by which we are crushed, as before an icon. That is what I will say if you are right and victorious in the final conflict. ... Then the world is lost. Then man is condemned. For all eternity ..."

Iuz Aleshkovsky's novel *The Hand* (*Ruka*, 1980), written in the form of a monologue by one of Stalin's executioners, implies a direct relationship between Stalin and the Devil, thus countering the myth of Stalin's divinity propagated during the "cult" period. Aleshkovsky's Stalin, whose main characteristics are hatred and fear, is portrayed descending into Lenin's mausoleum, not to pray to his mentor, as people imagine, but to gloat over his dead enemy. Like Voinovich in "A Circle of Friends," Aleshkovsky emphasizes the anti-Soviet nature of Stalinism: Stalin tells the executioner that he (the executioner) is "even more anti-Soviet than ..." (the sentence is left unfinished, but the implication is that Stalin himself is anti-Soviet).[102]

Aleshkovsky also demonizes Stalin through ideas inspired by Dostoevsky's *The Devils*, which he manipulates for his own purposes. He suggests that Stalin's Russia is in the grip of the Satanic power of reason, which, as Dostoevsky demonstrated, distances the soul from God and leads it towards death. Drawing on dualist concepts of the equal power of good and evil, Aleshkovsky claims that Stalin's terror can only be explained by the fact that the Devil is in control of the world and has made a pact with the party: the party acquires unlimited power, while the Devil gains "slogans, ideology, aims."[103] This arrangement suits Stalin, who cannot abandon the "party religion" for fear that he himself might be toppled. Aleshkovsky suggests that Stalin's victims are themselves agents of the Devil, since they believe in Lenin and socialism. Moreover, these "living corpses" are inculcated with love of their murderer Stalin – a sentiment which goes against logic and must, therefore, be inspired by the Devil. His victims' love of death takes the cunning form of the ideals of socialism and communism, which lead to a conflict with God and hence to the ultimate destruction of the world. Eventually, like Dostoevsky's Ivan Karamazov, Aleshkovsky's Stalin finds that he is unable to escape from the power of the Devil, as the Devil is within him.

A metaphysical interpretation of Stalin's evil is sometimes conveyed through a parody of biblical texts, or by an emphasis on Stalin's profanation of true religion. Aleksandr Galich's *Poem about Stalin* (*Poema o Staline*, 1972), for example, presents Stalin as a demonic figure in direct competition with Jesus, suggesting the quasi-religious nature of Stalin's "personality cult" and the pretensions of both Stalinism and Christianity to be total world systems. Galich draws an ironic parallel between biblical figures and historical events, depicting a grotesque version of the Nativity in which Stalin, with his "evil smile" (nedobraia usmeshka), leans over the crib of the baby Jesus and addresses him as his rival and tormentor. The second part of the poem consists entirely of a monologue by Stalin, one of the most powerful evocations in Russian literature of the unmitigated evil of Stalin's personality. Stalin mocks Christ as "not the son of God, but of man, / If you could exclaim: 'Do not kill!'" (ne Bozhii syn, a chelovechii, / Esli smog voskliknut': "Ne ubii!"), who "believed ... in God and the tsar" (veril ... i Bogu, i tsariu), but was abandoned by his disciples in his hour of need. He ridicules the pitiful results of Christ's teaching after two thousand years, claiming that he will not repeat his predecessor's mistakes, but will create an "eternal" kingdom.[104]

The rest of Galich's poem, however, demonstrates that Stalin's pretensions to "man-godhood" are doomed to failure. When he grows old, he appeals vainly for help from the ghost of his former friend, Sergo Ordzhonikidze, whom he drove to suicide,[105] but ultimately God's power proves to be greater than the demonic Stalin's: a church bell rings and Stalin tries to pray, but cannot remember the Lord's Prayer; finally he dies, begging for forgiveness and salvation.

A number of Christian writers dwell on Stalin's youth as a student in an Orthodox seminary, in order to suggest that, as in the case of Satan or the Grand Inquisitor, his evil originated from his proud rejection of God. Vladimir Maksimov's *Quarantine* (*Karantin*, 1973) depicts the young Stalin as a "quiet seminarist" who becomes the "leading atheist" in his seminary.[106] Initially portrayed as a shy, hardworking scholar, he becomes possessed by an overweening ambition to save humanity. Maksimov draws on the tradition that demons can disguise themselves as monks or angels,[107] depicting a "holy man" at Mount Athos, Father Ignatii, who advises Stalin to join those who, "trampling God's commandments under foot, would turn Christ's children into a herd of obedient slaves, whose life and death shall depend on their will alone." The young seminarist fulfils Ignatii's injunction to "practise betrayal and sacrilege, theft and murder, hypocrisy and lies. ... Above all, forget God and conscience."[108] It is only when he has become "ruler of almost half the world," ostensibly in the name of God, that Stalin belatedly realizes that he has been deceived by the demonic monk, but by this time "there is no room in his heart for light or repentance."[109]

A similar image of Stalin as the personification of evil emerges from Maksimov's later novel *The Ark for the Uncalled* (*Kovcheg dlia nezvanykh*, 1979), which presents a realistic and metaphysical portrait of Stalin in 1945. Maksimov suggests that Stalin's soul is already lost, since he made the choice between Good and Evil long ago. He adds a new dimension to the theme of Stalin's profanation of true religion, depicting the dictator's condescending attitude to the Russian Orthodox Patriarch, whom Stalin deceived into making a pact with the state in 1941. Drawing on the tradition of "Moscow the third Rome," Maksimov portrays the Old Believer Matvei Zagladin, a survivor of the camps, who refers to Stalin as "lame Satan"[110] (Satan was often depicted as lame because of his fall from heaven) and complains that the official Orthodox Church has sold out to the Antichrist by making an accommodation with Stalin.

The most extended depiction of Stalin as a diabolical figure is Solzhenitsyn's portrait in the revised, ninety-six chapter version of *The First Circle* (*V kruge pervom*, published in the West in 1978 and in Russia in 1990), which suggests that it was Stalin's original betrayal of God and attempt to usurp his throne that turned him into a living Satan, or Antichrist.[111] If the image of Stalin in the original eighty-seven chapter version of *The First Circle* (1968) bore a resemblance to the portrait of Satan in canto thirty-four of Dante's *Inferno* (and to Dostoevsky's devils and man-gods),[112] the longer, revised version of 1978 (now accepted as the authorized text) demonstrates that Solzhenitsyn was fully conscious of the symbolic identification of Stalin with Satan, and sought to reinforce this parallel.

The title of Solzhenitsyn's novel, and the whole conception behind it, are based on Dante's *Inferno*. The first circle of hell, which the scientists in the special prison inhabit, recalls Dante's conception of limbo, the resting place of the sages of antiquity who were born before the Christian era. Stalin appears to be at the summit of the Soviet hierarchy but, as in Dante's *Inferno*, where Satan is imprisoned in the deepest circle of hell, the eternal ice of the lake Cocytus, the tyrant is actually incarcerated in the hell of his windowless underground bunker, an immobile prisoner of night, time, space, mortality and the MVD troops who surround him. One clear example of Solzhenitsyn's stylistic retouching in the revised version is the more detailed physical description of Stalin which he provides, laying emphasis on the colour of his features: "a yellow-eyed old man with reddish hair (which was portrayed as pitch-black [smolianymi] in paintings) … with dark uneven teeth."[113] Such details are based on real descriptions of Stalin, but also possess a symbolic significance: the colours of the three faces of Dante's Satan are yellowish-white, black, and red. Other characteristics of Dante's Satan accentuated in Solzhenitsyn's new portrait of Stalin are his immobility and imprisonment, the unreality of his existence, and his hatred of the sun, the light of life and the symbol of God.[114]

The clearest parallel with Dante in the revised version is the new emphasis which Solzhenitsyn lays on the sin of treachery. Dante reserves the bottom circle of hell for treachery, and its last subdivision, Judecca, for the great traitors of the world – Judas, Brutus, and Cassius – and the greatest traitor of them all, Satan himself, who was guilty of the ultimate sin of treachery against the authority and grace which form the divine order of the world.[115] Similarly, in his novel

Solzhenitsyn places great stress on Stalin's successive treachery to God and to the revolutionary movement. He suggests that Stalin's ultimate treachery was to resurrect a crude parody of the nineteenth-century Russian values of Orthodoxy and Nationality, pretending to the Russian people that the Soviet Union he has created was identical with traditional "Holy Russia." Solzhenitsyn's extended parallel between Stalin and Dante's Satan is designed to illustrate "the drama of the soul's choice"[116] – the process by which a human being freely chooses great evil.

Stalin's proud rejection of God is presented as the original sin from which his Satanic pride and tyrannical man-godhood stem. Like Maksimov, Solzhenitsyn emphasizes Stalin's distortion of true religion through his rejection of the seminary, his pact with the Orthodox Church, and his misuse of biblical terminology. Stalin, like evil rulers in the Old Testament,[117] has attempted to replace God; he feels himself to be a lonely being of great power soaring in a realm far above the earth, with only God, if He exists, as his rival.

Solzhenitsyn's image of Stalin draws on certain traditional features associated with the devil in Russian folklore and Christian tradition: a foreign accent, mistrust, lies, and deception. Solzhenitsyn has admitted that he feels "spiritually close" to Dostoevsky;[118] and there are also many echoes of Dostoevskian themes in *The First Circle*.[119] Stalin's "mediocrity" and poverty of thought, for example, are reminiscent of the ordinariness and vulgarity of Ivan Karamazov's devil. Solzhenitsyn's Stalin is both an epigone of the Grand Inquisitor in *The Brothers Karamazov*, who proved to be in league with Satan, the "spirit of destruction and non-being," and a historical product of his spiritual cross-breeding with other Dostoevskian "man-gods" and "devils."

Like the Grand Inquisitor, who believes the people need to be ruled by "miracle, mystery and authority," and like Petr Verkhovensky from *The Devils*, who wishes to present Stavrogin to the people as a god, Stalin, conditioned by his religious upbringing, feels that the "orphaned … godless" Russian people need a god to believe in, and constant "correct explanations" to set them on the right course.[120] Like Stavrogin, Stalin is "neither cold nor hot," but indifferent to everything. Although he sets himself up as a rival to God – a point emphasized by Solzhenitsyn's use of the godlike attribute "Almighty" – he lives in a metaphysical void, and like all Dostoevsky's atheists, is suffused by a cosmic boredom.

The whole of *The First Circle*, with its extended image of hell, is an ironic comment on the Soviet dream of the "earthly paradise." In Solzhenitsyn's opinion, the reality of Stalin's communist empire is worse even than the Inquisitor's fantasy of a human "anthill;" it is closer to the view of Shigalev, the gloomy theorist in Dostoevsky's

The Devils, that "all shall be equal and all shall be slaves." Solzhenit-syn suggests that Stalin, by rejecting the divine order of the universe and setting himself up as a rival to God, has become the personifi-cation of Satan on earth, a Dostoevskian man-god who rejects the existence of God and the "God-man" Christ.

The *Perestroika* and Post-*Perestroika* Periods

During *perestroika*, the repudiation of socialist realism and the rise of post-modernist experimentation allowed writers greater freedom than before to draw on the non-realistic, metaphysical tradition to present new demonic portrayals of Stalin and Stalinism.[121] The con-tinuing need for the Soviet people to repent their Stalinist past was vividly dramatized in Tengiz Abuladze's influential film *Repentance* (*Pokaianie*, 1986) through the image of Varlam Aravidze, a compos-ite, demonic dictator-figure based on Hitler, Beria, Mussolini, and Stalin, a man who wants to create heaven on earth. After his death, his body is repeatedly dug up by the daughter of one of his victims, who states: "As long as I live, Varlam Aravidze will not lie in the earth. I will dig him up not three but three hundred times."[122]

Dostoevsky's devils have also enjoyed an enduring vitality in lit-erature of the *perestroika* and post-*perestroika* periods. In Vladimir Makanin's story "Baize-Covered Table With Decanter" (Stol, pokry-tyi suknom i s grafinom poseredine, 1993), the ideas of the revolu-tionary Sergei Nechaev and his circle, on which Dostoevsky's *The Devils* is based, are presented as the possible source of Russians' obsession with utopian schemes based on violence.[123] However, they are invoked most frequently in works by Russian Orthodox, nation-alist writers to suggest that the espousal of Western European values, notably the search for a materialist utopia under Lenin and Stalin, was a betrayal of Russian national traditions. In the second part of Boris Mozhaev's novel *Peasant Men and Women* (*Muzhiki i baby*, 1987), for example, the hero Dmitrii Uspensky, a priest's son, interprets col-lectivization as the culmination of the aberrant tradition of Russian radical and atheistic thought which he traces back to the French Revolution, particularly to the ideas of Babeuf.[124] The third part of Vasilii Belov's novel *Eves* (*Kanuny*, 1987) is permeated by an apoca-lyptic sense of foreboding. The old peasant Nikita, who is besieged by a flock of devils, asks for a reading of the Book of Revelation which relates how after the Day of Judgement, "the third part of trees was burnt up, and all green grass was burnt up" (Rev.8:7), "the third part of the creatures ... died" (Rev.8:9), and "two prophets tor-mented them that dwelt on the earth" (Rev.11:10.)[125] The old people see this as a prophecy of what will happen in Russia; and one listener identifies the two false prophets as Lenin and Stalin. Such conservative, nationalist thinkers as Mozhaev and Belov do not single out Stalin for specific criticism, but rather demonize the Communist party in general (predominantly composed of Jews and non-Russians) for the persecution of the Russian Orthodox Church in the 1920s and the ravages of collectivization.

Although by the late Gorbachev period the theme of Stalin and Stalinism had lost much of its novelty and fascination for Russian readers, in 1990 the critic Andrei Vasilevsky maintained that "Stalin as a constantly renewable myth has now become eternal."[126] This view is borne out by the fact that in the 1990s some authors and film directors were still attempting to come to terms with Stalin and his legacy.

Chingiz Aitmatov, in his story "The White Cloud of Genghiz Khan" (Beloe oblako Chingiskhana, 1990), a text which could not be published in the original version of his novel *The Day Lasts Longer than a Hundred Years* (*I dol'she veka dlitsia den'*, 1980), uses a legend about Genghiz Khan to refer to the despotism and false idolatry of the Stalin era.[127] Anatolii Korolev's innovative story "Gogol's Head" (Golova Gogolia, 1992) deals with the transfer, on Stalin's demand, of Hitler's jaw from Berlin to Moscow. Drawing on the works of Gogol and Dostoevsky, Korolev uses the recurrent image of a severed head, referring particularly to the victims guillotined during the French Revolution, to evoke the senseless nature of revolutionary violence. Stalin and the Devil are explicitly juxtaposed and appear to share similar views, blaming God for the evil in the world.[128]

Leonid Leonov's last major work, *Pyramid*, published in 1994, the year of his death, is a metaphysical novel about Stalin's Russia influenced by Dostoevsky, Dante, Goethe, and apocalyptic texts such as *The Book of Enoch* and the *Revelations of the Pseudo-Methodius.* In one key scene, Leonov depicts a meeting between Stalin and Dymkov, an envoy from another galaxy who is regarded as an angel by people on earth. Stalin attempts to enlist Dymkov's supernatural powers to help him build a new society based, like that of Dostoevsky's Shigalev, on the principle of total equality; the first stage in his programme will be to crush the physical and mental differences which lead to human inequality. Leonov does not portray Stalin as a demon, but as the personification of evil, an "indomitable tyrant" and "absolute ruler" who regards himself as more ruthless than the harsh tsars of the past. At night he converses with the spirit of Ivan the Terrible, berating him for his weakness in repenting his sins, and for his failure to kill enough of his opponents. He also sees himself as a descendant of oriental tyrants, particularly the Egyptian Pharaohs, who built the Pyramids using "significantly more human bones than stones." Leonov does, however, suggest that Stalin's plan partakes of the demonic, in that it is presented as "suicidal," involving the "damnation of the next generation" and their "consignment to the fire." There are also apocalyptic echoes in the references to the "current, last and decisive battle of the worlds" in which it will be necessary to destroy all spiritual values accumulated throughout the centuries, "once called the national Russian God."[129] Eventually Dymkov chooses to leaves the earth, since he proves incapable of defeating the forces of evil currently in control of Russia.

With a few exceptions, most writers and film directors of the 1990s were less interested in presenting Stalin as a demonic figure than in deconstructing certain key concepts in Russian history which had formerly been exalted: the value of revolution; the dream of the materialist utopia; and the image of the wise, authoritarian ruler.[130] In the post-communist period, less attention has been paid to Stalin's actual crimes, but the cult of Stalin still continues to be satirized, as in Nikita Mikhalkov's Oscar-winning film *Burnt by the Sun* (*Utomlennye solntsem,* 1994).

Conclusion

Literary texts demonizing Stalin have inherited the equivocal Russian conception of the ruler, and been deeply influenced by the anti-utopian and apocalyptic traditions in Russian culture. The demonization of Stalin in literature has taken a variety of forms. Many writers have simply presented Stalin realistically, alluding frankly to his crimes, which in literature published in Russia from Stalin's death until the late 1980s has often been considered sufficient to demonize him, in the loose general meaning of the term. Truth has been many Russian writers' chief weapon against Stalin; they have only "demonized" him in the sense that Stalin, like Satan, has been exposed as a calumniator, or "a murderer," "a liar, and the father of it" (John 8:44).

Many literary works suggest that Stalin was a demonic figure in the sense that he was the personification of evil passions such as cruelty, suspiciousness, menace, or destructiveness. This view has been accentuated by writers' repeated emphasis on Stalin's malignant physical features, such as his yellow tiger-like eyes, and his military boots, evocative of sadism and violence.

Another widespread method of demonizing Stalin in post-Stalin literature has been a repudiation or parody of the former worship of him as a god or genius during the "cult" period. Although, as we have seen, many Russian writers have attempted to come to terms with the former deification of Stalin, this is still a very controversial subject in literary history which has not yet been fully investigated in Russia itself (although it still has important implications for the way in which rulers are portrayed today).[131]

A number of writers also demonize Stalin by analogy, suggesting parallels between Stalin and harsh rulers of other countries and periods (Tiberius or Caligula, the Pharaohs, Sennacherib, Nebuchadnezzar, Tamerlane, Genghiz Khan, Ivan the Terrible, Peter the Great, Robespierre, or Hitler). Some prominent writers use the "demonic" force of laughter to undermine Stalin's power, while others use allegory and fantasy to present a deeper, metaphysical portrait of Stalin as a demonic ruler. Russian writers draw on a multitude of traditions and discourses in presenting Stalin as a diabolic figure, including Russian folklore, theological, historical, and philosophical texts, and literary models, especially the demonic figures of Lermontov, Gogol, and Dostoevsky, as well as the conceptions of Western European writers, notably Dante, Milton, and Goethe. While the majority of depictions of Stalin in Russian literature include only a few demonic images and associations, Solzhenitsyn's *The First Circle* provides a more extended portrayal of Stalin as a Satanic figure.

In some works on the theme of Stalin's terror which have appeared in Russia since *glasnost'*, writers or film directors have seen their role as the provision of a simple documentary account of the hell of Stalinism. Varlam Shalamov, for example, who was imprisoned for seventeen years, described himself as "not an Orpheus who has descended into the underworld, but a Pluto who has clambered up from hell."[132] Other authors, however, have a clear moral purpose: to suggest to the people of the former Soviet Union that they should repent the crimes of Stalinism in order that they should never be repeated.

The majority of literary representations of Stalin as demonic take the orthodox New Testament view that God triumphed over Satan, suggesting that Stalin ultimately failed in his attempt to rival God's power. Recurrent references to Stalin's old age, illness, and death are designed to demonstrate that he was neither omnipotent nor immortal, and that he and the evil he caused were ultimately defeated by God. Only a few writers, such as Aleshkovsky, Leonov, and Korolev, invoke dualistic heresies such as those of the Manicheans and Cathars to suggest that in Stalin's time Satan's power was equal to God's.

For many Russian writers, Stalin's evil is linked with hell, and his own fate is seen as eternal damnation with no escape or possibility of redemption. Solzhenitsyn and Siniavsky, for example, suggest that Stalin is still suffering the torments of hell or wandering the earth as an unquiet spirit, while Maksimov's *Quarantine* implies that Stalin ultimately rejected the forgiveness and grace offered by the crucified Christ. Very few writers imply that Stalin himself may find some kind of redemption. One exception is Anatolii Korolev, whose "Gogol's Head" concludes with an idyllic vision of Christ in the Holy Land, suggesting (somewhat unconvincingly, and against the logic of the work as a whole) that redemption may be possible even for Stalin and his henchmen.

Other writers place greater emphasis on the purgatorial value of the evil inflicted by Stalin on Russian society. For many, the best that can be hoped for, as at the end of Akhmatova's *Requiem*, is that Russia may experience a cathartic sense of peace and resignation after the "diabolical years" (osatanelykh let) of Stalinism. The view of Stalinism as purgatory is also implicitly espoused by many writers of the post-Stalin era who present realistic or comic portraits of Stalin: the very fact that writers are now able to denounce Stalin's crimes or mock his physical and psychological characteristics proves that Russia has managed to survive this traumatic historical period.

Another aspect of the purgatorial approach to evil, suggested through some of the more metaphysical portraits of Stalin, is that epitomized by Archpriest Avvakum: that God sends demons to bring about a form of spiritual redemption, and that evil can therefore be seen as a "scourge of God" (Bozhii bich), cleansing and purifying the Russian people. In Maksimov's *The Ark for the Uncalled*, for example, Stalinism is explicitly depicted as the Flood sent by God as an ordeal to try the Russian people. The conclusion of this work suggests that those who have survived the prison camps offer some hope for the collective redemption of Russian society. Although Maksimov's view of Stalin as the instrument of God's judgement on the Russian people does not – from a Christian theological point of view – lead to the exoneration of Stalin or the Russian nation for their own guilt or complicity, such a view can nevertheless lend itself to disturbing distortions. A more extreme example of this approach is evident in works published since *glasnost'* by Russian nationalist writers, which by "demonizing" Stalin and his henchmen manage to absolve the Russian people as a whole for their complicity in their own fate. In this way, some Russian writers, while appearing to recognize the evil of Stalinism, in fact contribute to yet another myth of Russia's positive historical development.[133] While such an approach is most evident in recently published novels by Belov and Mozhaev, a similar view is also implicit in the writings of many Russian writers who lay special emphasis on Stalin's Georgian or Asiatic origins, drawing on the traditional association of the devil with a foreigner.[134]

Margaret Ziolkowski has commented on the narrow range of themes and images in Russian texts depicting Stalin, claiming that the literary demonology of Stalin is little more than a simplistic reversal of the hagiography of the "cult" period.[135] While Ziolkowski is undoubtedly correct in emphasizing Russian writers' deliberate subversion of the former cult of Stalin (a powerful imperative felt by many authors which may be difficult for Western critics to understand) and their use of recurrent images and characteristics, such as Stalin's yellow eyes, pock-marked face, or intellectual mediocrity, she nevertheless overstates her case.

In the first place, Russian literature contains a greater variety of portraits of Stalin, or of some composite dictator-figure partially reminiscent of Stalin, than Ziolkowski gives credit for. Secondly, since Stalin was a real historical figure it is hardly surprising that writers use some of the same details in their physical descriptions or psychological characterizations of the dictator (especially since authors writing in the USSR before *glasnost'* only had access to a limited number of memoirs and historical texts about Stalin). Thirdly, the stylization prevalent in portraits of Stalin could be seen as a strength rather than a weakness: many Russian writers have deliberately selected demonic images and parallels in order to build up a tradition of representing Stalin as a personification of evil, as the Devil, the Grand Inquisitor, or the Antichrist.

Rather than criticizing Russian writers' use of recurrent motifs in portraits of Stalin, it is more useful to emphasize the positive aspects of the interpretive paradigm established in Russian literature. Similar themes and images are passed on from writer to writer and work to work, establishing a rich network of intertextuality, and of what Andrew Wachtel has called a complex "intergeneric dialogue" on the theme of Stalin's evil.[136] As Caryl Emerson has argued in relation to the theme of Boris Godunov in Russian culture, the various treatments of Stalin and Stalinism can be seen as a form of "transposition": "one category of 'translation' where coauthorship is not hidden but rather celebrated, where the independence of the second voice is guaranteed by the new genre or medium, and where dialogue among versions is inevitably explicit. A good part of the audience's interest lies precisely in watching a multiple *co*authorship at work."[137] The demonization of Stalin in literature provides a graphic illustration of the persistent attempts by Russian writers to seize control of, and attempt to subvert the authoritarian script formerly imposed by the Soviet regime, as they struggle to come to terms with the past and present of their country.

Notes

1. Archpriest Avvakum, *The Life Written by Himself with the Study of V.V. Vinogradov*, trans., annotations, commentary, and a historical introduction by Kenneth N. Brostrom, Michigan Slavic Translations, no.41 (Ann Arbor: Michigan Slavic Publications, 1979), 87.

2. Aleksandr Zinov'ev, *Nashei iunosti polet: Literaturnyi-sotsiologicheskii ocherk stalin-izma* (Lausanne: L'Age d'homme, 1983), 110. Translations are my own through-out this essay unless otherwise indicated.

3. Gary Saul Morson, ed., *Literature and History: Theoretical Problems and Russian Case Studies* (Stanford: Stanford University Press, 1986).

4. Andrew Wachtel, *An Obsession with History: Russian Writers Confront the Past* (Stanford: Stanford University Press, 1994), 16–17.

5. This chapter reworks some material contained in the author's book, Rosalind Marsh, *Images of Dictatorship: Portraits of Stalin in Literature* (London and New York: Routledge, 1989).

6. *Oxford English Dictionary*, ed. J.A. Simpson and E.S.C. Weiner, 2d ed., 20 vols. (Oxford: Clarendon Press, 1989), 4:568.

7. "D'iavol," in *Bol'shaia Sovetskaia Entsiklopediia*, 3d ed., 30 vols. (Moscow: Izdatel'stvo "Sovetskaia Entsiklopediia," 1970–78), 8:566, col. 1685.

8. Ibid.

9. See Xenia Gasiorowska, *The Image of Peter the Great in Russian Fiction* (Madison: The University of Wisconsin Press, 1979), 76, 109.

10. Bernard McGinn, *Antichrist: Two Thousand Years of the Human Fascination with Evil* (San Francisco: Harper, 1996), 263.

11. For further discussion, see Will Ryan, "The Great Beast in Russia: Aleister Crowley's Theatrical Tour in 1913 and his Beastly Writings on Russia," in Arnold McMillin, ed., *Symbolism and After: Essays on Russian Poetry in Honour of Georgette Donchin* (London: Bristol Classical Press, 1992), 137–61.

12. Robert O. Crumney, *The Old Believers and the World of Antichrist: The Vyg Community and the Russian State. 1694–1855* (Madison: The University of Wisconsin Press, 1970), 16.

13. See, for example, Jacob Lassner, *Demonizing the Queen of Sheba: Boundaries of Gender and Culture in Postbiblical Judaism and Medieval Islam* (Chicago: University of Chicago Press, 1993); Norman Cohn, *Europe's Inner Demons: The Demonization of Christians in Medieval Christendom*, rev. ed. (London: Pimlico, 1993).

14. Michael Paul Rogin, *Ronald Reagan, the Movie, and Other Episodes in Political Demonology* (Berkeley: University of California Press, 1987), xiii.

15. Ibid.

16. Michael Cherniavsky, "Khan or Basileus: An Aspect of Russian Mediaeval Political Theory;" Dimitri Obolensky, "Russia's Byzantine Heritage;" both in Michael Cherniavsky, ed., *The Structure of Russian History: Interpretive Essays* (New York: Random House, 1970), 65–79 and 3–28, respectively; David M. Bethea, *The Shape of Apocalypse in Modern Russian Fiction* (Princeton: Princeton University Press, 1989), 16.

17. Ia.L. Barskov, *Pamiatniki pervykh let russkogo staroobriadchestva* (St. Petersburg: Tip. Aleksandrova, 1912), 333.

18. See in this volume Kevin Platt, "Antichrist Enthroned: Demonic Visions of Russian Rulers;" Bethea, *The Shape of Apocalypse*, 21; Gasiorowska, *The Image of Peter the Great*, esp. 19, 23, 52, 168. Although the *basileus* is primarily a "messianic" concept, it does have links with the apocalyptic tradition through the image of the Last Emperor in the *Revelations of the Pseudo-Methodius*.

19. Valentin Boss, *Milton and the Rise of Russian Satanism* (Toronto: University of Toronto Press, 1991), 17.

20. I. Deutscher, *Stalin: A Political Biography* (London: Oxford University Press, 1949); Ian Grey, *Stalin: Man of History* (London: Weidenfeld and Nicholson, 1979).

21. For an assessment of Stalin in biography and historiography, see Marsh, *Images of Dictatorship*, 11–16; J. Arch Getty, "Bibliographic Essay," in his *Origins of the Great Purges: The Soviet Communist Party Reconsidered, 1933–1938* (Cambridge: Cambridge University Press, 1985), 211–20.

22. Kornei Chukovskii, "Tarakanishche," in his *Sobranie sochinenii v shesti tomakh,* 6 vols. (Moscow: Khudozhestvennaia literatura, 1965–69), 1:173–80(174).

23. For an elaboration of this idea, see Lev Loseff, *On the Beneficence of Censorship: Aesopian Language in Modern Russian Literature* (Munich: Otto Sagner in Kommission, 1984), 201–2. Chukovsky's work was also significant in that it helped to establish a whole genre of successful anti-Stalinist Aesopian satire in the guise of children's literature.

24. According to Loseff, *On the Beneficence of Censorship,* 199, in the 1950s, in a performance in Leningrad based on Chukovsky's *The Big Bad Cockroach,* "the title character was played as an undisguised caricature of Stalin."

25. "My zhivem, pod soboiu ne chuia strany ..." (November 1933), in Osip Mandel'shtam, *Sobranie sochinenii,* ed. G.P. Struve and B.A. Filippov, 2d ed., 3 vols. (Washington: Inter-Language Literary Associates, 1967–71), 1:202.

26. From the 1920s onwards, following another longstanding Russian tradition of depicting rulers, a rich oral folklore of rumours, stories, and jokes about Stalin also began to circulate in Russia, subsequently constituting an important source for many Russian writers: see Iurii Borev, *Staliniada* (Moscow: Sovetskii pisatel', 1990). In contrast to the "cult" texts, which could include no humour or references to Stalin's personal life, many light-hearted anecdotes were disseminated about his genealogy, alleged sexual conquests, and the circumstances of his birth and death. For irreverent or negative perceptions of Stalin among the working class, see Sarah Davies, *Popular Opinion in Stalin's Russia: Terror, Propaganda and Dissent, 1934–1941* (Cambridge: Cambridge University Press, 1997), 168–82; and among the peasantry, see Sheila Fitzpatrick, *Stalin's Peasants: Resistance and Survival in the Russian Village after Collectivization* (Oxford and New York: Oxford University Press, 1994), 286–312.

27. Evgenii Zamiatin, "Iks," *Novaia Rossiia,* 1926, no.2:49–62. Reprinted in Evgenii Zamiatin, *Izbrannye proizvedeniia* (Moscow: Sovetskaia Rossiia, 1990), 216–31.

28. Ibid., 230.

29. See in this volume W.J. Leatherbarrow, "The Devils' Vaudeville: 'Decoding' the Demonic in Dostoevsky's *The Devils,*" on Petrushka puppet plays performed by foreigners; and the reference to Stalin as an "Ossete" in Mandel'shtam's 1933 epigram on Stalin (see n.25 above).

30. Zamiatin, *Izbrannye proizvedeniia,* 230.

31. Evgenii Zamiatin, *My: Roman, Znamia,* 1988, no.4:126–77; no.5:104–54.

32. Andrei Platonov, *Kotlovan,* first published in *Grani* no.70 (1969):3–107; reprinted in Andrei Platonov, *Kotlovan* (Ann Arbor: Ardis, 1973); first Russian publication, *Novyi mir,* 1987, no.6:50–123.

33. Boris Pil'niak, "Povest' nepogashennoi luny," *Novyi mir,* 1926, no.5:5–33; republished in *Znamia,* 1987, no.12:105–28.

34. Vitaly Shentalinsky, *The KGB's Literary Archive,* trans., abridged, and ed. John Crowfoot (London: The Harvill Press, 1995), 140, 144, 149, 157.

35. On the moon's demonic associations, see Jeffrey Burton Russell, *Prince of Darkness: Radical Evil and the Power of Good in History* (London: Thames and Hudson, 1989), 11–12. In Pil'niak's story the moon is an ambiguous symbol which sometimes also suggests the eternal, inextinguishable spirit of life and nature. Satan's shield is compared to the moon in Milton's *Paradise Lost,* 1:284–87.

36. For further elaboration, see Hans Günther, ed., *The Culture of the Stalin Period* (Basingstoke: Macmillan, 1990); Marsh, *Images of Dictatorship,* 24–44; Feliks J. Oinas, *Essays on Russian Folklore and Mythology* (Columbus: Slavica, 1985), 143, 148, 152–53.

37. On the origins of the cult, see Nina Tumarkin, *Lenin Lives! The Lenin Cult in Soviet Russia* (Cambridge, Mass.: Harvard University Press, 1983); Robert C.

Tucker, "The Rise of Stalin's Personality Cult," *American Historical Review* 84 (April 1979):347–48.

38. See in this volume Leatherbarrow, "The Devils' Vaudeville."

39. Aleksandr Tvardovskii, *Strana Muraviia*, in his *Sobranie sochinenii*, 5 vols. (Moscow: Khudozhestvennaia literatura, 1966–71), 7–118 (esp. 37–41).

40. See, in particular, Aleksei Tolstoi's novel *Peter the First* (1929–45); and Eizenshtein's film *Ivan the Terrible* (part 1), which, according to Herbert Marshall, *Masters of Soviet Cinema: Crippled Creative Biographies* (London: Routledge and Kegan Paul, 1983), 174, attempted to fulfil Stalin's behest that Ivan should be depicted as a "great and wise ruler." For further discussion of these two works in this volume see Platt, "Antichrist Enthroned."

41. Linda J. Ivanits, *Russian Folk Belief* (Armonk, N.Y., and London: M.E. Sharpe, 1989), 38.

42. Mandel'shtam, *Sobranie sochinenii*, 1:202.

43. Oinas, "The Devil in Russian Folklore," in his *Essays on Russian Folklore and Mythology*, 97–103 (esp. 99).

44. Nadezhda Mandelstam, *Hope against Hope* (London: Collins and Harvill Press, 1971), 199, explains that Mandel'shtam had in mind the phonetic associations in Russian between the words *kreml'* (Kremlin), *kremen'* (flint), and *kamen'* (stone).

45. "Vnutri gory bezdeistvuet kumir …" (December 1936), in Mandel'shtam, *Sobranie sochinenii*, 1:227. Nadezhda Mandel'shtam, commenting on this poem, has drawn an analogy between Stalin and the "Assyrian" (presumably a reference to the evil Assyrian king Sennacherib). Mandelstam, *Hope against Hope*, 199.

46. Anna Akhmatova, *Rekviem*, *Oktiabr'*, 1987, no.3:103–5.

47. Anna Akhmatova, "Muza" (1924), in her *Izbrannoe* (Moscow: Khudozhestvennaia literatura, 1974), 277.

48. Anna Akhmatova, *Rekviem*, in her *Ia – golos vash …* (Moscow: Knizhnaia palata, 1989), 156–61(157).

49. Iuz Aleshkovskii, "Tovarishch Stalin, vy bol'shoi uchenyi," in "Narodnye sovetskie pesni," *Student*, 1964, no.2–3:81–84.

50. On Eizenshtein, see in this volume Platt, "Antichrist Enthroned."

51. M. Bulgakov, *Batum*, in *Neizdannyi Bulgakov: Teksty i materialy*, ed. Ellendea Proffer (Ann Arbor: Ardis, 1977), 141, 156.

52. On the image of the beast, see also Rev.4:6–11; 13; Dan.7–8; Peter Stanford, *The Devil: A Biography* (London: Arrow Books, 1998), 66–68. Another powerful use of the image of the dragon is Evgenii Shvarts's "fairytale for adults" *The Dragon* (*Drakon*, 1940), which makes a subtle equation between Hitler and Stalin. Shvarts's work formed the basis of a popular anti-Stalin film directed by Mark Zakharov, *Ubit' drakona*, issued in 1988.

53. D.G.B. Piper, "An Approach to Bulgakov's *The Master and Margarita*," *Forum for Modern Language Studies* 7, no.2 (1971):134–57(146–47).

54. Stanford, *The Devil*, 67. A similar comparison between Stalinism and the despotism of ancient Rome is implied in Pasternak's *Doctor Zhivago*, which refers to "the bloody beastliness of cruel pock-marked Caligulas:" Stalin himself was pock-marked. See Boris Pasternak, *Doktor Zhivago* (Moscow: "Zemlia i fabrika" [Frankfurt am Main: Posev], n.d.), 19.

55. Elisabeth Stenbock-Fermor, "Bulgakov's *The Master and Margarita* and Goethe's *Faust*," *The Slavic and East European Journal* 13, no.3 (1969):309–25; Boss, *Milton*, 237.

56. M. Bulgakov, *Master i Margarita* (Frankfurt am Main: Posev, 1969), 472.

57. On Bulgakov's image of the horseman, see Bethea, *The Shape of Apocalypse*, 186–229.

58. Boris Groys, *The Total Art of Stalinism: Avant-garde, Aesthetic Dictatorship, and Beyond*, trans. Charles Rougle (Princeton: Princeton University Press, 1992), 48.

59. Compare the version of Bulgakov's novel published in *Moskva*, 1966, no.11:6–130; 1967, no.1:56–144, with Bulgakov, *Master i Margarita*, 351. The Posev edition renders the censored passages in italics. See also Pilate's fulsome toast to Tiberius Caesar as "the best and dearest of men," ibid., 383, which was cut in the journal version.

60. Ibid., 351.

61. Andrei Siniavskii, "Literaturnyi protsess v Rossii," *Kontinent*, 1974, no.1:158–61.

62. Edith W. Clowes, *Russian Experimental Fiction: Resisting Ideology after Utopia* (Princeton: Princeton University Press, 1993), 208.

63. Abram Terts [Andrei Siniavskii], "Chto takoe sotsialisticheskii realism," in his *Fantasticheskie povesti* (New York: Inter-Language Literary Associates, 1967), 444–45.

64. See Marsh, *Images of Dictatorship*, 54–102.

65. Aleksandr Bek, *Novoe naznachenie*; first published in Russia in *Znamia*, 1986, no.10:3–72, no.11:3–66; original publication A. Bek, *Novoe naznachenie* (Frankfurt am Main: Posev, 1971). Anatolii Rybakov, *Deti Arbata: Roman* (Moscow: Sovetskii pisatel', 1988); Anatolii Rybakov, *Tridtsat' piatyi i drugie gody* (Moscow: Sovetskii pisatel', 1989). Mikhail Shatrov, *Dal'she ... dal'she ... dal'she!*, *Znamia*, 1988, no.1:3–39.

66. Oinas, "The Devil in Russian Folklore," 99; see also in this volume Leatherbarrow, "The Devils' Vaudeville."

67. M. Chegodaeva, "Osleplenie," *Sovetskaia kul'tura*, 24 June 1989; E. Dobrenko, "Sdelat' by zhizn' s kogo? (Obraz vozhdia v sovetskoi literature)," *Voprosy literatury*, 1990, no.9:3–34.

68. For attacks on the "cult," see, among numerous examples, Aleksandr Tvardovskii, "Za daliu – dal'," *Novyi mir*, 1960, no.5:10; Aleksandr Tvardovskii, "Po pravu pamiati," *Novyi mir*, 1987, no.3:198; A. Solzhenitsyn, *V kruge pervom* (New York and Evanston: Harper and Row, 1968), 80; Vladimir Voinovich, *Zhizn' i neobychainye prikliucheniia soldata Ivana Chonkina: Roman-anekdot* (Paris: YMCA-Press, 1981), 29, 51–52; Bek, *Novoe naznachenie*, 102.

69. See, for example, Feliks Chuev's poem of 1968 demanding "Put Stalin back on his pedestal," cited in Stephen F. Cohen, ed., *An End to Silence: Uncensored Opinion in the Soviet Union. From Roy Medvedev's Underground Magazine "Political Diary"* (New York: Norton, 1982), 174.

70. Marsh, *Images of Dictatorship*, 68–70.

71. Helena Goscilo, *Dehexing Sex: Russian Womanhood During and After Glasnost* (Ann Arbor: University of Michigan Press, 1996), 160–62, likens such portraits to pornography.

72. See, for example, Bek, *Novoe naznachenie*, 34; Rybakov, *Deti Arbata*, 143; A. Galich, *Poema o Staline*, in his *Pokolenie obrechennykh* (Frankfurt am Main: Posev, [1972]), 275–87(276); V. Maksimov, *Kovcheg dlia nezvanykh*, in his *Sobranie sochinenii*, 6 vols. (Frankfurt am Main: Posev, 1979), 6:36; Maksimov, *Karantin* (Frankfurt am Main: Posev, 1973), 83.

73. Fazil Iskander, *Sandro iz Chegema* (Ann Arbor: Ardis, 1979), 206.

74. Iu. Dombrovskii, *Fakul'tet nenuzhnykh veshchei* (Paris: YMCA-Press, 1978), 411.

75. See, for example, Solzhenitsyn, *V kruge pervom* (1968), 80; Maksimov, *Kovcheg dlia nezvanykh*, 57–58.

76. Milovan Djilas, *Conversations with Stalin*, trans. Michael B. Petrovich (Harmondsworth: Penguin Books, 1963), 52; Leon Trotsky, *Stalin: An Appraisal of the Man and His Influence*, ed. and trans. Charles Malamuth, 2d ed. (New York: Harper, 1941), 244.

77. Bulat Okudzhava, "Chernyi kot," *Sel'skaia molodezh'*, 1966, no.1:33. Okudzhava's tomcat is also reminiscent of the petty demon Begemot in Bulgakov's *The Master and Margarita*.

78. Vasilii Aksenov, "Stal'naia ptitsa," *Glagol*, 1977, no.1:71.

79. On the Devil's association with bad smells and the scatological, see, for example, Jeffrey Burton Russell, *Lucifer: The Devil in the Middle Ages* (Ithaca and London: Cornell University Press, 1984), 243; Stanford, *The Devil*, 155. In Milton, *Paradise Lost*, 1:236–37, Satan lands on Etna, "all involved / With stench and smoke;" in 4:839–40, the angel Zephon tells Satan: "thou resemblest now / Thy sin and place of doom obscure and foul;" and in 9:164–65, the Devil is described as "constrained / Into a beast, and, mixed with bestial slime."

80. Mikhail Bakhtin, *Rabelais and his World*, trans. Hélène Iswolsky (Bloomington: Indiana University Press, 1984). For further discussion, see Ken Hirschkop and David Shepherd, eds., *Bakhtin and Cultural Theory* (Manchester and New York: Manchester University Press, 1985), esp. 110–13, 194–211, 226–27, 238–39. It should, however, be noted that Bakhtin, writing in the Stalin era, possibly overstated the case for the subversive power of medieval carnival in order to launch his own Aesopian critique of Stalinism.

81. Vladimir Nabokov, *Tyrants Destroyed and Other Stories*, trans. Dmitri Nabokov in collaboration with the author (London: Weidenfeld and Nicolson, 1975), 36. See also the portrayal of the dictator Paduk as a dummy in Vladimir Nabokov, *Bend Sinister* (Harmondsworth: Penguin Books, 1974), 127–28.

82. Nabokov, *Tyrants Destroyed*, 36.

83. Vladimir Nabokov, *Strong Opinions* (London: Weidenfeld and Nicolson, 1974), 58; Pierre Dommergues, "Entretien avec Vladimir Nabokov," *Langues Modernes* 62, no.1 (January-February 1968):102.

84. This view is expressed, for example, in "An Interview with Vladimir Voinovich. The newly-exiled Russian novelist is interviewed in Paris by Richard Boston," *Quarto* (April 1981):7; and Abram Terts [Andrei Siniavskii], *Spokoinoi nochi: Roman* (Paris: Syntaxis, 1984), 273–77.

85. Vladimir Voinovich, "V krugu druzei," in his *Putem vzaimnoi perepiski* (Paris: YMCA-Press, 1979); Iskander, "Piry Valtasara," in his *Sandro iz Chegema*, 187–229. The title of Voinovich's story suggests either a parallel with, or a parody of Solzhenitsyn's *V kruge pervom*; the image of the circle has demonic associations in folklore and in Dante's *Inferno*. In this volume Faith Wigzell, "The Russian Folk Devil and His Literary Reflections," connects *chert* with *chertit'* (to draw) and the idea of drawing a magic circle as protection from evil spirits.

86. Bakhtin, *Rabelais and his World*, 198.

87. N.S. Khrushchev, *Khrushchev Remembers*, with an Introduction, Commentary, and Notes by Edward Crankshaw, trans. Strobe Talbott (London: Sphere Books, 1971), 267.

88. Voinovich, "V krugu druzei," 188. The concept of *vrag* (enemy), frequently used to denounce people in Stalin's time, was also a name used to refer to the devil.

89. Aleksandr Zinov'ev, *Ziiaiushchie vysoty* (Lausanne: L'Age d'homme, 1976), 291; cited from Alexander Zinoviev, *The Yawning Heights*, trans. Gordon Clough (Harmondsworth: Penguin Books, 1981), 426. For other examples of profane humour in the representation of Stalin, see Iuz Aleshkovskii, *Ruka (Povestvovanie palacha)* (New York: Russica Publishers, 1980), 137; Iuz Aleshkovskii, *Kenguru: Roman* (Ann Arbor: Ardis, 1981), 114.

90. Leonid Leonov, "Russkii les," *Znamia*, 1953, no.10:3–134; no.11:3–142; no.12, 9–156.

91. Max Hayward, quoted in Martin Dewhirst and Robert Farrell, eds, *The Soviet Censorship* (Metuchen, N.J.: Scarecrow Press, 1973), 13.

92. Leonid Leonov, *Russkii les*, in the sixth supplementary volume (1956) to his *Sobranie sochinenii v piati tomakh* (Moscow: Gosudarstvennoe izdatel'stvo khudozhestvennoi literatury, 1953–54), 6:53.

93. On Dante, see ibid., 6:110, 499, 701; for references to ice, see 6:271, 505, 536, 755.

94. Max Hayward, *Writers in Russia, 1917–1978*, ed. and with an introduction by Patricia Blake (London: The Harvill Press, 1983), 100.

95. Leonid Leonov, *Piramida* (Moscow: Golos, 1994). On the composition and editing of the manuscript, and the influence of Dante on Leonov, see O. Ovcharenko, "O romane Leonida Leonova 'Piramida'," in ibid., 3–5. For further discussion of the novel, see below in this essay.

96. Evgenii Evtushenko, "Nasledniki Stalina," *Pravda*, 21 October 1962, 4; Anatolii Gladilin, *Repetitsiia v piatnitsu* (Paris: YMCA-Press, 1978).

97. Terts [Siniavskii], *Fantasticheskie povesti*, 446.

98. See in this volume the section on "The Medieval Inheritance" in Platt, "Antichrist Enthroned."

99. Terts [Siniavskii], *Spokoinoi nochi*, 277–78, 285.

100. Dombrovskii, *Fakul'tet nenuzhnykh veshchei*, 94. On Ivan Karamazov's devil, see above in this essay. The phrase "banality of evil" is attributed to Hannah Arendt.

101. These lines are cited as (mis)quoted in the Russian text of the novel; in Pushkin's poem the first line reads "Khot' v uzkoi golove pridvornogo gluptsa." All quotations from the novel (here and below) are taken from Yury Dombrovsky, *The Faculty of Useless Knowledge*, trans. Alan Myers (London: The Harvill Press, 1996), 94–97.

102. Aleshkovskii, *Ruka*, 216; on Voinovich, see above in this essay. This suggestion by Aleshkovsky and Voinovich was subsequently taken up by the historian Iurii Borisov, who maintained that after 1956 Stalin "remained as before a symbol, however no longer of the victories of socialism, but of deviations from it. This is a kind of Dorian Gray phenomenon." Iurii Borisov, "Chelovek i simvol," *Nauka i zhizn'*, 1987, no.9:63.

103. Aleshkovskii, *Ruka*, 226.

104. Galich, *Poema o Staline*, in his *Pokolenie obrechennykh*, 276, 278.

105. On the devil's responsibility for suicide, see n.66 above.

106. "Preobrazhenie tikhogo seminarista," chap.12 of Maksimov, *Karantin*, 83–90.

107. See in this volume Franklin, "Nostalgia for Hell."

108. Maksimov, *Karantin*, 86.

109. Ibid., 88.

110. Maksimov, *Kovcheg dlia nezvanykh*, 267.

111. Aleksandr Solzhenitsyn, *V kruge pervom: Roman*, in his *Sobranie sochinenii*, 18 vols. (Vermont and Paris: YMCA-Press, 1978–88), vols. 1–2; for its first publication in Russia, see A. Solzhenitsyn, *V kruge pervom*, *Novyi mir*, 1990, no.1:5–94; no.2:6–88; no.3:31–118; no.4:23–120; no.5:6–108. In his short introduction (*Novyi mir*, 1990, no.1:5), Solzhenitsyn describes his novel as "written – 1955–58; distorted – 1964; resurrected – 1968." For a more detailed discussion of Solzhenitsyn's portrait of Stalin in *The First Circle*, see Marsh, *Images of Dictatorship*, 135–97.

112. For further discussion, see Gary Kern, "Solzhenitsyn's Portrait of Stalin," *Slavic Review* 33, no.1 (1974):16–17; Vladimir Grebenschikov, "Les cercles infernaux chez Soljénitsyne et Dante," *Canadian Slavonic Papers* 13 (1971):147–63(154–58). On the link between *V kruge pervom* and Goethe's *Faust*, see Kern, "Solzhenitsyn's Portrait," 17.

113. Solzhenitsyn, *Sobranie sochinenii*, 1:116.

114. On Satan's hatred of the sun, see Milton, *Paradise Lost*, 4:37–41.

115. See Dante, *Inferno*, 34:39, 43, 45.

116. Dorothy Sayers, "Introduction," in *The Comedy of Dante Alighieri, the Florentine: Cantica I: Hell (L'Inferno)*, trans. Dorothy L. Sayers (Harmondsworth: Penguin Books, 1949), 11.

117. On the evil rulers in the Old Testament, see above in this essay. See particularly the reference to the King of Babylon: "Thou hast said in thy heart ... I will exalt my throne above the stars of God ... . Yet thou shalt be brought down to hell, to the sides of the pit" (Isa.14:13, 15).

118. A. Solzhenitsyn, "Interv'iu na literaturnye temy s N.A. Struve, mart 1976," *Vestnik russkogo khristianskogo dvizheniia*, no.120 (1977):130–58(155–56).

119. On the parallels with Dostoevsky in the original, eighty-seven chapter version of *V kruge pervom* (1968), see Vladislav Krasnov, *Solzhenitsyn and Dostoevsky: A Study in the Polyphonic Novel* (London: Prior, 1980), 24–34; Sviatoslav Ruslanov, "Epigon velikogo Inkvizitora: K portretu Stalina v romane A.I. Solzhenitsyna 'V kruge pervom'," *Grani*, no.92–93 (1974):279–94.

120. Solzhenitsyn, *Sobranie sochinenii*, 1:118.

121. See Mikhail Shatrov's play *Diktatura sovesti*, *Teatr*, 1986, no.6:4–37, in which Dostoevsky's Petr Verkhovensky recites his sinister speech on socialism (9–11); and the discussion of Viktor Korkia's play *Chernyi chelovek ili ia, bednyi Soso Dzhugashvili* (1987) in Boss, *Milton*, 163–64, 231 n.18, 237.

122. For the quotation and discussion of the film, see Ninel' Izmailova, "The Life and Death of Varlam Aravidze – the Moscow Premiere of *Repentance*, a Film by the Well-Known Film Director Tengiz Abuladze," *Nedelia*, 2–8 February 1987, 19; translation cited from *Current Digest of the Post-Soviet Press*, 39, no.5 (4 March 1987), 1–4(1). For further discussion of *Repentance*, see Rosalind Marsh, *History and Literature in Contemporary Russia* (Basingstoke: Macmillan, 1995), 34–37.

123. Vladimir Makanin, "Stol, pokrytyi suknom i s grafinom poseredine: Povest'," *Znamia*, 1993, no.1:9–53. According to rumour, Stalin himself was fascinated by Nechaev, the prototype of Dostoevsky's "devil" Petr Verkhovensky; see Borev, *Staliniada*, 33. Apart from Makanin and the authors mentioned here, many other former underground and émigré writers, as well as new writers whose works were first published in the *glasnost'* era, also engage in a rich intertextual dialogue with Dostoevsky on the nature and origin of evil in Russian society. These include Petr Aleshkovsky, Iurii Mamleev, Viktor Erofeev, Liudmila Petrushevskaia, Viacheslav P'etsukh, and Aleksei Slapovsky, to name but a few. This is a vast and fascinating subject which falls outside the scope of the present essay.

124. Boris Mozhaev, *Muzhiki i baby: Roman. Kniga vtoraia*, in his *Sobranie sochinenii v chetyrekh tomakh*, 4 vols. (Moscow: Khudozhestvennaia literatura, 1990), 4. On the links with the French Revolution, see esp. 300–15; for references to Dostoevsky's devils, see esp. 301–2, 305.

125. Vasilii Belov, *Kanuny: Khronika kontsa 20-kh godov* (Moscow: Molodaia gvardiia, 1988), esp. 346–47, 440–42.

126. Andrei Vasilevskii, "Stalin (li) s nami," *Literaturnaia gazeta*, 2 May 1990, 5, a review of Borev's *Staliniada* which suggest that folklore about Stalin has entered the Russian "collective consciousness."

127. Chingiz Aitmatov, "Beloe oblako Chingizkhana: Povest' k romanu," *Znamia*, 1990, no.8:7–57.

128. Anatolii Korolev, "Golova Gogolia," *Znamia*, 1992, no.7:7–66. See also Mikhail Kuraev's "Zerkalo Montachki: Roman v stile kriminal'noi siuity, v 22-kh chastiakh, s introduktsiei i teoremoi o prizrakakh," *Novyi mir*, 1993, no.5:3–68; no.6:67–131, which refers to demonology in order to investigate the sources of evil in Russian society; and Vasilii Aksenov, *Moskovskaia saga*, 3 vols. (Moscow: Tekst, 1993–94), which specifically refers to Stalin in demonic terms: the poet

Nina Gradova thinks to herself "The big devil leads his round dance and we shuffle after him like little devils" (1:198).

129. For the scene as a whole and the individual phrases quoted, see Leonid Leonov, *Piramida*, 566–626 (573, 608, 594, 598, 613, 606).

130. See Sergei Selianov's film *The Russian Idea* (*Russkaia ideia*, 1993) which quotes extensively from Eizenshtein's *Ivan the Terrible*.

131. See Dobrenko, "Sdelat' by zhizn' s kogo?" The continuing preoccupation with the portrayal of rulers can be seen in recent Russian performances of Pushkin's *Boris Godunov* (such as that of the Pushkin State Theatre Centre from St. Petersburg, brought to Bristol in March 1997), which might be interpreted, particularly by a Russian audience, as suggesting an implicit comparison between Boris Godunov and Boris El'tsin.

132. "Varlam Shalamov: Proza, stikhi," *Novyi mir*, 1988, no.6:106–7. Cf. Akhmatova's "Muza," discussed above in this essay, in which the poet's role is more reminiscent of an "Orpheus descending to the underworld."

133. This view is explicitly warned against in Solzhenitsyn's essay "Repentance and Self-Limitation in the Life of Nations," in Alexander Solzhenitsyn and others, *From Under the Rubble*, trans. A.M. Brock and others under the direction of Michael Scammell (London: Fontana/Collins, 1976), 105–43.

134. One recent example is Georgii Vladimirov, *General i ego armiia* (Moscow: Knizhnaia palata, 1997), in which Stalin, who chooses to speak to Beria in Georgian in front of the army, is presented as a foreigner who has "humiliated, violated a foreign country." The narrator comments: "The Leader was now with his army which was prepared to die for him, and he hated it, was suspicious of it, and did not wish to speak to it in a language it could understand" (282). Earlier, the "literary scholar V," whom the general met in prison, told him: "The Lord God is no longer on your side, Satan is ruling everything now" (263).

135. Margaret Ziolkowski, "A Modern Demonology: Some Literary Stalins," *Slavic Review* 50, no.1 (1990):59–69, esp. 68–69. For further elaboration, see Margaret Ziolkowski, *Literary Exorcisms of Stalinism: Russian Writers and the Soviet Past* (Columbia, S.C.: Camden House, 1998).

136. Wachtel, *Obsession with History*, 10–11.

137. Caryl Emerson, *Boris Godunov: Transpositions of a Russian Theme* (Bloomington: Indiana University Press, 1986), 8.

INDEX

Titles of individual works are listed under the author's name. As a general rule, authors and works cited in the notes are not included in the index.